THE CRICKETERS'
WHO'S WHO

COMPETITION

Collect five players' signatures from each first-class county first XI to win two Test match tickets and meet David Gower.

Prizes: 1st: 2 tickets to a Test match and the chance to meet David Gower after the day's play
2nd: A cricket bat signed by England cricketers

How to enter: Collect the signatures of five players from the first XI of each of the 17 first-class counties. Ask the players to sign their names across their entry in *Cricketers' Who's Who*. Send your *Cricketers' Who's Who*, complete, to The Editor, Cricketers' Who's Who Competition, Queen Anne Press, Macdonald & Co (Publishers) Ltd, Greater London House, Hampstead Road, London NW1 7QX by 30 June 1986. Please ensure that your name and address is written inside your book; all books will be returned after the competition result is announced.

Rules: The prizes will be awarded to the first and second correct entries opened on 1 July. The decision of the judges is final and binding; no correspondence will be entered into. Employees of Macdonald & Co (Publishers) Ltd and their families are not eligible to compete.

Proof of entry: Only complete books will be eligible for the competition. Proof of posting is not proof of entry.

THE
1986 CRICKETERS' WHO'S WHO

compiled and edited by
IAIN SPROAT

associate editor
RALPH DELLOR

Macdonald
Queen Anne Press

A **Queen Anne Press** Book published in association with The Cricketers' Who's Who Limited

© Iain Sproat, 1986
First published in Great Britain in 1986 by
Queen Anne Press, Macdonald & Co (Publishers) Ltd
Greater London House, Hampstead Road, London NW1 7QX

A BPCC plc Company

British Library Cataloguing in Publication Data
The Cricketer's who's who.—7th ed.
  1. Cricket players—Biography
  I. Sproat, Iain
  796.35'8'0922   GV915.A1
  ISBN 0-356-12306-5
  ISBN 0-356-12307-3 Pbk

Cover design *Clare Forte*
Cover photographs, left to right: Graham Gooch *Patrick Eagar*
                                David Lawrence *Adrian Murrell/All-sport*
                                Steve O'Shaughnessy *Jan Traylen*
                                for Patrick Eagar
Portraits: *Bill Smith*

Typeset by Margaret Spooner Typesetting,
Bridport, Dorset
Printed in Great Britain by Hazell, Watson & Viney Ltd,
Member of the BPCC Group, Aylesbury, Bucks.

PREFACE

AS THE volume which you hold in your hands is the seventh
successive edition of *The Cricketers' Who's Who*, the central
formula of this book clearly and increasingly appeals to
followers of the game. That central formula, of course, is to
provide all the latest statistical and biographical information
about those cricketers playing in the current English season.
This book covers not only cricketers eligible to play for
England, but also those eligible to play for other countries —
so long as they also play for a first-class English county. The
statistics cover not only all first-class matches (with the
exception of those relating to players who turn out only for
Oxford or Cambridge Universities), but cover also the one-
day competitions as played by the first-class counties.

No other book, to the best of my knowledge, provides this
width and depth of fact, plus individual photographs, about
today's players.

Of course, other books do other things: the incomparable
Wisden, for example, encompasses fascinating tracts of the
history of the game, as well as covering a mass of last season's
statistics from cricket around the world. *Wisden* is a great
institution, and I buy it avidly every year — just as I do
Playfair. But, for all that, neither of those two books attempts
to do what *The Cricketers' Who's Who* does, namely, tell you in
depth everything you need to know about the cricketers you
will be watching this season in England. I therefore see *The
Cricketers' Who's Who* as being very much complementary to
the information which *Wisden*, and the others, provide.

Each season I look to see if there is any way, within the

pressures of size and price, to improve *The Cricketers' Who's Who*. Last year, I thought I had discovered such a major improvement, namely, to list the counties in alphabetical order, and then the players, within the counties, also in alphabetical order. The point being, that if you are watching, say, Derbyshire v Somerset, and you have the book in your hand, making reference to various cricketers from the two sides, as play proceeds, it is handier to have all eleven from each side close to each other: fewer pages to flick through each time you check up something about an individual player. At least, that was my theory when I made the change. And that is how the book appeared. Now, this change was greatly liked by some people — particularly by those professionally involved in the game; but equally disliked by others. Among the latter I quickly came, on balance, to number myself. Somehow, in practice, I found that the new method was just not so handy. So, this year, I have returned to the original formula of straight alphabetical listing of all players, regardless of county.

One other minor point: one eminent reviewer of last year's edition said, in an otherwise kindly review, that he could not see why I gave so much space to a player who had retired at the end of the previous season. The example he gave was that of Roger Knight, who had retired at the end of the 1984 season. Well, it is a fair query. But my reason for putting in those who have retired at the end of the previous season, is that I think there should be, somewhere in the long line (hopefully) of *The Cricketers' Who's Who* upon your shelves, one volume which contains the final career figures and facts and opinions of any individual cricketer. If I did not include a cricketer in the *Who's Who*, the season after he retired, then there would, by definition, be one season's achievements of his, as well as his career summary, missing from any *Who's Who*.

As in last year's edition, I am making use of some of the spaces that inevitably occur on certain pages to include cricket quiz questions — some easy, some not — to help while away those rain-spoilt hours of an English summer. Answers are at the back of the book.

If you have any ideas for information to be added to next year's edition, please write and tell me.

The cricketers listed in this volume include all those who played for their county at least once last season, either in the county championship, John Player Special League, Benson & Hedges or NatWest matches. The statistics are accurate up to the end of the last English season — with one exception: it has proved impossible to guarantee the accuracy of the statistics of certain matches, classified as first class, in India and Pakistan. However, Test match figures in those countries have been included. Figures about 50 wickets and 1000 runs, etc. in a season refer to matches in England only.

The following abbreviations apply: * means not out; JPL means John Player Special League and B&H means Benson & Hedges. Where there are two lines of bowling figures, the top line refers to eight ball overs, the bottom line to six. Normally there is only one line, referring to six ball overs. The figures for batting and bowling averages refer to 1985, followed in brackets by the 1984 figures. Inclusion in the first-class batting averages depends on a minimum of eight innings, and an average of at least 10 runs; a bowler has had to have taken at least 10 wickets in at least 10 innings.

Readers will notice certain occasional differences in the way the same kind of information about cricketers is presented. This is because I have usually tried to follow the way in which the cricketers themselves have provided the relevant information.

I should like to acknowledge with particular gratitude the very wide-ranging help I have had from Mr Ralph Dellor, the cricket broadcaster, journalist and N.C.A. staff coach. Once again I am indebted to Mr Robert Brooke for his splendidly professional work in the collection of the statistics, and to Mr Bill Smith, F.R.P.S. who personally took most of the photographs. I should also like to thank Master Edward Lewis of Cumbria for contributing Question 198. Above all I am grateful to the cricketers themselves without whose generous support this book could not have been compiled.

Iain Sproat

ABRAHAMS, J.   Lancashire

Full Name: John Abrahams.
Role: Left-hand bat, off-break bowler.
Born: 21 July 1952, Cape Town,
South Africa.
Height: 5′ 7″ **Weight:** 10st. 4lbs.
Nickname: Abey.
County debut: 1973.
County cap: 1982.
1000 runs in a season: 3.
1st-Class 50s scored: 44.
1st-Class 100s scored: 9.
1st-Class 200s scored: 1.
One-day 50s: 14.
Place in batting averages: 134
average: 26.63; (1984: 67
average: 36.84).
1st-Class catches 1985: 14
(career: 141).
Parents: Cecil John and
Cynthia Jean Abrahams.
Marital status: Single.
Education: Heywood Grammar School (later became Heywood Senior High
School).
Qualifications: 9 O-levels, A-level Biology, N.C.A. Preliminary Coaching
Certificate.
Jobs outside cricket: Shop manager and representative, Beaverwise Plant Hire,
Oldham.
Family links with cricket: Father was professional with Milnrow and Radcliffe
in Central Lancashire League. Brother Basil professional at Castleton Moor.

LAST SEASON: BATTING

	I.	N.O.	R.	H.S.	AV.
TEST					
OTHER FIRST CLASS	39	4	932	101*	26.63
INT					
JPL	10	1	234	66	26.00
NAT.W	2	0	30	15	15.00
B & H	4	0	114	57	28.50

CAREER: BATTING

	I.	N.O.	R.	H.S.	AV.
TEST					
OTHER FIRST CLASS	333	44	8225	201*	28.46
INT					
JPL	103	21	2041	79*	24.89
NAT.W	19	2	303	51*	17.76
B & H	23	5	483	66*	26.83

LAST SEASON: BOWLING

	O.	M.	R.	W.	AV.
TEST					
OTHER FIRST CLASS	31.2	10	99	4	24.75
INT					
JPL					
NAT.W	11	2	36	2	18.00
B & H	2	0	11	0	–

CAREER: BOWLING

	O.	M.	R.	W.	AV.
TEST					
OTHER FIRST CLASS	880.2	190	2571	51	50.41
INT					
JPL	57.2	3	317	6	52.83
NAT.W	25	3	112	3	37.33
B & H	5	0	25	0	–

Brother Peter at Milnrow in Central Lancashire League. Basil professional for Heyside in Saddleworth League in 1980.

Overseas teams played for: Player-coach for Mowbray C.C., Tasmania, 1980-81; Western Creek C.C., Canberra, 1983–84, 1984–85.

Cricketers particularly learnt from: Jack Bond and Peter Lever.

Cricketers particularly admired: Clive Lloyd and Mike Brearley.

Other sports: Badminton, golf, watching rugby union on T.V.

Relaxation: "Listening to pop music: Rod Stewart, Fleetwood Mac, for example."

Extras: Has lived in UK since 1962. Substitute for England in place of Brian Rose in Fifth Test against West Indies at Headingley in August 1980. "Would very much like to be a physiotherapist when I retire." Gold award winner in 1984 B&H final. Captain 1984 and 1985.

Best batting performance: 201* Lancashire v Warwickshire, Nuneaton 1984.

Best bowling performance: 3-27 Lancashire v Worcestershire, Old Trafford 1981.

ACFIELD, D.L. Essex

Full Name: David Laurence Acfield.
Role: Right-hand bat, off-break bowler.
Born: 24 July 1947, Chelmsford, Essex.
Height: 5' 9" **Weight:** 11st. 2lbs.
Nickname: Ackers.
County debut: 1966.
County cap: 1970.
50 wickets in a season: 7.
1st-Class 5 w. in innings: 33.
1st-Class 10 w. in match: 4.
Place in bowling averages: 106 average: 40.83; (1984: 63 average: 29.74).
1st-Class catches 1985: 6 (career: 132).
Benefit: 1981 (£42,788).
Parents: Robert and Ena Acfield.

Wife and date of marriage: Helen, 27 October 1973.
Children: Clare Louise, 10 December 1977; Rosemary Helen, 16 March 1982.
Education: Brentwood School; Christ's College, Cambridge.
Qualifications: M.A. (Cantab) History.

Jobs outside cricket: Schoolmaster.
Off-season 1985–86: Teaching/working for Barwell & Jones, Wine Merchants.
Family links with cricket: Late elder brother, Ian 1944–68, member of M.C.C., Incogniti, Cambridge University Crusaders, etc.
Overseas tours: With M.C.C. to East Africa 1973–74.
Other sports: Fencing (sabre), British Olympic team 1968 and 1972. Commonwealth Games Gold Medal (team event) 1970, British champion 1969–70–71–72, now retired. Cambridge Blue for fencing.
Relaxations: Bird-watching; films, especially Westerns; wine.
Extras: Cambridge cricket Blue 1967, 1968.
Best batting performance: 42 Cambridge University v Leicestershire, Leicester 1967.
Best bowling performance: 8-55 Essex v Kent, Canterbury 1981.

LAST SEASON: BATTING

	I.	N.O.	R.	H.S.	AV.
TEST					
OTHER FIRST CLASS	21	11	80	14	8.00
INT					
JPL	2	2	1	1*	–
NAT.W	–	–	–	–	–
B & H	–	–	–	–	–

CAREER: BATTING

	I.	N.O.	R.	H.S.	AV.
TEST					
OTHER FIRST CLASS	398	202	1625	42	8.29
INT					
JPL	47	32	79	9*	5.26
NAT.W	7	6	4	2*	–
B & H	4	3	15	8*	–

LAST SEASON: BOWLING

	O.	M.	R.	W.	AV.
TEST					
OTHER FIRST CLASS	588.4	130	1674	41	40.83
INT					
JPL	29	3	134	4	33.50
NAT.W	2	0	3	2	1.50
B & H	11	2	33	0	–

CAREER: BOWLING

	O.	M.	R.	W.	AV.
TEST					
OTHER FIRST CLASS	10865.5	3113	25888	917	28.23
INT					
JPL	744.2	71	2928	117	25.02
NAT.W	95.3	21	284	10	28.40
B & H	142	18	502	14	35.86

1. When was the first match at the current Lord's, and which sides played?
2. In what year did W.G. Grace play his last cricket match?
3. In what year did the B.B.C. broadcast its first cricket commentary, and what was the match?

ADDISON, J.P.   Leicestershire

Full Name: Jonathan Paul Addison.
Role: Right-hand bat, slow left-arm bowler.
Born: 14 November 1965, Leek, Staffordshire.
Height: 6′ 0″ **Weight:** 13st.
County debut: 1983.
1st-Class 50s scored: 1.
1st-Class catches 1985: — (career: 1).
Parents: Paul Anthony and Beryl Addison.
Marital status: Single.
Family links with cricket: Father still plays in the North Stafford-shire and District League.
Education: Beeches Junior School; Blythe Bridge High School.
Qualifications: GCE O-levels.
Jobs outside cricket: Working in the pottery industry.
Cricketing superstitions: "Too numerous to mention."

Cricketers particularly learnt from: Ken Higgs, Mike Haysman and father.
Cricketers particularly admired: Brian Davison, Garfield Sobers.
Overseas tours: With Young England to West Indies 1984–85.
Other sports: Football, tennis, squash, golf.
Relaxations: "I find that listening to music is the best way to unwind."
Extras: Made debut in Leicester 2nd XI in 1981. Best bowling 7-24 and 8-80 v Derbyshire 2nd XI, 1983. Best batting 68 v Lancashire 2nd XI, 1983. Signed as professional for Caverswall who play in the North Staffordshire and South

LAST SEASON: BATTING

	I.	N.O.	R.	H.S.	AV.
TEST					
OTHER FIRST CLASS					
INT					
JPL	–	–	–	–	–
NAT.W					
B & H					

CAREER: BATTING

	I.	N.O.	R.	H.S.	AV.
TEST					
OTHER FIRST CLASS	2	0	67	51	33.50
INT					
JPL	1	0	10	10	–
NAT.W					
B & H					

LAST SEASON: BOWLING

	O.	M.	R.	W.	AV.
TEST					
OTHER FIRST CLASS					
INT					
JPL					
NAT.W					
B & H					

CAREER: BOWLING

	O.	M.	R.	W.	AV.
TEST					
OTHER FIRST CLASS					
INT					
JPL	1	0	16	0	–
NAT.W					
B & H					

Cheshire League. They were champions in season 1983. Youngest professional in League. Left staff after 1985 season.
Best batting performance: 51 Leicester v New Zealanders, Leicester 1983.

AFFORD, J.A. Nottinghamshire

Full Name: John Andrew Afford.
Role: Right-hand bat, slow left-arm bowler.
Born: 12 May 1964, Crowland, Nr. Peterborough.
Height: 6′ 1″ **Weight:** 13 st.
Nickname: Aff, Bert.
County debut: 1984.
1st-Class catches 1985: 2 (career: 3).
Parents: Jill Afford.
Marital Status: Single.
Education: Spalding Grammar School; Stamford College for Further Education.
Qualifications: 5 O-levels, N.C.A. Coaching Certificate.
Off-season 1985-86: Playing and coaching in Hutt Valley, New Zealand.

Cricketing superstitions: Wear the same shirt and trousers if successful previous day.
Cricketers particularly learnt from: David Johnson at Bourne C.C. and everyone at Nottinghamshire.

LAST SEASON: BATTING

	I.	N.O.	R.	H.S.	AV.
TEST					
OTHER FIRST CLASS	1	0	2	2	–
INT					
JPL					
NAT.W					
B & H					

CAREER: BATTING

	I.	N.O.	R.	H.S.	AV.
TEST					
OTHER FIRST CLASS	1	0	2	2	–
INT					
JPL					
NAT.W					
B & H					

LAST SEASON: BOWLING

	O.	M.	R.	W.	AV.
TEST					
OTHER FIRST CLASS	25	5	77	2	38.50
INT					
JPL					
NAT.W					
B & H					

CAREER: BOWLING

	O.	M.	R.	W.	AV.
TEST					
OTHER FIRST CLASS	113.3	37	333	9	37.00
INT					
JPL					
NAT.W					
B & H					

Cricketers particularly admired: Richard Hadlee, Bishen Bedi, Derek Underwood.

Other sports: "Play any sport within reason — possibly one of the worst golfers in the world!! Enjoy watching most sports as long as horses aren't involved."

Relaxations: Enjoys listening to music.

Opinions on cricket: "2nd XI pitches have not been of a very high standard this year, thus making the gulf between 2nd and 1st XI cricket that much more difficult to bridge."

Best batting performance: 2 Nottinghamshire v Lancashire, Trent Bridge 1985.

Best bowling performance: 2-49 Nottinghamshire v Lancashire, Old Trafford 1984.

AGNEW, J.P.   Leicestershire

Full Name: Jonathan Philip Agnew.

Role: Right-hand bat, right-arm fast bowler, outfielder.

Born: 4 April 1960, Macclesfield, Cheshire.

Height: 6' 4" **Weight:** 12st. 7lbs.

Nickname: Spiro (after former US Vice-President Spiro Agnew).

County debut: 1978.

County cap: 1984.

Test debut: 1984.

No. of Tests: 3.

No. of One-Day Internationals: 3.

50 wickets in a season: 2.

1st-Class 50s scored: 1.

1st-Class 5 w. in innings: 11.

1st-Class 10 w. in match: 2.

Place in batting averages: 253 average: 10.08.

Place in bowling averages: 35 average: 27.49; (1984: 54 average: 28.72).

1st-Class catches 1985: 3 (career: 26).

Parents: Philip and Margaret Agnew.

Wife and date of marriage: Beverley, 8 October 1983.

Children: Jennifer, 31 October 1985.

Education: Uppingham School.

Qualifications: 9 O-levels, 2 A-levels.

Jobs outside cricket: Cricket Coach. Spent 1981-82 off-season coaching at Sindia High School, Zimbabwe. Production control at T.L. Bennett's Windows Ltd.

Off-season 1985-86: England B Tour.

Cricketing superstitions: "I never use a bowling marker so am never popular with groundsmen!"

Cricketers particularly learnt from: Ken Higgs, Andy Roberts, Frank Tyson, Peter Willey.

Cricketers particularly admired: Imran Khan.

Family links with cricket: First cousin, Mary Duggan, Captain of England's Women's XI in 1960s.

Overseas tours: Young England tour of Australia, 1978–79; Leicestershire C.C.C. to Zimbabwe, 1981; England to India and Australia, 1984–85.

Overseas teams played for: Whitbread scholarship, 1978, playing for Essendon C.C., Melbourne, and in 1980; Alexandra C.C., Salisbury, Zimbabwe, 1981-82; Central Cumberland District Cricket Club, Sydney, 1982-83.

Other sports: Hockey, badminton, squash, table-tennis.

Injuries 1985: Sprained both ankles within a fortnight.

Relaxations: Music (all kinds). Playing piano and tuba. Coaching cricket. "I became very interested in game viewing in Zimbabwe. I spent days driving around to study and photograph — particularly elephants."

Extras: Played for Surrey 2nd XI 1976–77. Back trouble in 1979 season.

Opinions on cricket: "Over-rate required is still far too high and the rate stipulated must come down to encourage a decent standard of cricket."

Best batting performance: 56 Leicestershire v Worcestershire, Worcester 1982.

Best bowling performance: 9-70 Leicestershire v Kent, Leicester 1985.

LAST SEASON: BATTING

	I.	N.O.	R.	H.S.	AV.
TEST	1	1	2	2*	–
OTHER FIRST CLASS	14	2	119	36	9.92
INT					
JPL	3	3	21	13*	–
NAT.W	1	0	5	5	–
B & H	1	0	1	1	–

CAREER: BATTING

	I.	N.O.	R.	H.S.	AV.
TEST	4	3	10	5	–
OTHER FIRST CLASS	91	15	723	56	9.51
INT	1	1	2	2*	–
JPL	8	5	29	13*	9.66
NAT.W	2	1	9	5	–
B & H	6	2	29	23*	7.25

LAST SEASON: BOWLING

	O.	M.	R.	W.	AV.
TEST	23	2	99	0	–
OTHER FIRST CLASS	417.4	88	1413	55	25.69
INT					
JPL	61	3	290	9	32.22
NAT.W	19	5	55	2	27.50
B & H	59.5	6	242	8	30.25

CAREER: BOWLING

	O.	M.	R.	W.	AV.
TEST	92	22	373	4	93.25
OTHER FIRST CLASS	2187.2	404	7790	267	29.18
INT	21	0	120	3	40.00
JPL	173.3	10	906	24	37.75
NAT.W	50	5	163	7	23.29
B & H	153.2	23	571	23	24.83

ALLOTT, P.J.W.　　　　　　　Lancashire

Full Name: Paul John Walter Allott.
Role: Right-hand bat, right-arm
fast-medium bowler.
Born: 14 September 1956,
Altrincham, Cheshire.
Height: 6' 4" **Weight:** 14st.
County debut: 1978.
County cap: 1981.
Test debut: 1981.
No. of Tests: 13.
No. of One-Day Internationals: 13.
50 wickets in a season: 3.
1st-Class 50s scored: 3.
1st-Class 5 w. in innings: 18.
Place in batting averages: 205
average: 17.43; (1984: 237
average: 15.52).
Place in bowling averages: 10
average: 22.89; (1984: 5
average: 18.93).
1st-Class catches 1985: 6
(career: 40).
Parents: John Norman and Lillian Patricia Allott.
Wife and date of marriage: Helen, 27 October 1979.
Education: Altrincham Grammar School; Bede College, Durham.
Qualifications: Qualified teacher. Cricket coach.
Jobs outside cricket: Teacher. Cricket coach for Manchester Education
Committee. Coach in Tasmania for Tasmanian Cricket Association.
Overseas tours: With England to India 1981–82, India and Australia 1984–85;
to Jamaica with International XI 1982–83.
Family links with cricket: Father was dedicated club cricketer for 20 years with
Ashley C.C. and is now active with Bowdon C.C. (Cheshire County League) as
a selector, administrator and junior organiser.
Cricketers particularly learnt from: Dennis Lillee, Steve Murrills.
Other sports: Golf, football, squash, rugby, tennis.
Relaxations: Playing golf, watching all sports, listening to music, eating out,
photography.
Extras: Played as goal-keeper for Cheshire schoolboys. Took part in 10th
wicket record partnership for England with Bob Willis, 70, v India, at Lord's,
June 1982. Wears contact lenses. Forced by injury to return early from Indian
tour in 1984–85.
Best batting performance: 78 Lancashire v Gloucestershire, Bristol 1985.
Best bowling performance: 8-48 Lancashire v Northamptonshire, North-
ampton 1981.

LAST SEASON: BATTING

	I.	N.O.	R.	H.S.	AV.
TEST	5	1	27	12	6.75
OTHER FIRST CLASS	16	5	245	78	22.27
INT	1	0	2	2	–
JPL	3	1	11	7*	5.50
NAT.W	–	–	–	–	–
B & H	3	0	7	4	2.33

CAREER: BATTING

	I.	N.O.	R.	H.S.	AV.
TEST	18	3	213	52*	14.20
OTHER FIRST CLASS	117	33	1223	78	14.56
INT	6	1	15	8	3.00
JPL	32	18	215	32*	15.35
NAT.W	6	3	36	19*	12.00
B & H	11	3	48	15*	6.00

LAST SEASON: BOWLING

	O.	M.	R.	W.	AV.
TEST	113	22	297	5	59.40
OTHER FIRST CLASS	447.2	145	1031	53	19.45
INT	28	2	132	2	66.00
JPL	53	2	243	10	24.30
NAT.W	7	3	8	2	4.00
B & H	38.2	5	132	1	–

CAREER: BOWLING

	O.	M.	R.	W.	AV.
TEST	370.5	75	1084	26	41.69
OTHER FIRST CLASS	3182	853	8471	337	25.14
INT	136.3	19	552	15	36.80
JPL	501.5	47	2015	84	23.98
NAT.W	119.4	24	354	24	14.75
B & H	253.1	41	806	29	27.79

AMISS, D.L.   Warwickshire

Full Name: Dennis Leslie Amiss.
Role: Right-hand bat, slow left-arm chinaman bowler, slip fielder.
Born: 7 April 1943, Harborne, Birmingham.
Height: 5' 11'' **Weight:** 13st.
Nickname: Sacker.
County debut: 1960.
County cap: 1965.
Test debut: 1966.
No. of Tests: 50.
No. of One-Day Internationals: 18.
1000 runs in a season: 21.
1st-Class 50s scored: 200.
1st-Class 100s scored: 93.
1st-Class 200s scored: 3.
One-day 50s: 68.
One-day 100s: 13.
Place in batting averages: 47
average: 39.87; (1984: 11 average: 55.97).
1st-Class catches 1985: 24 (career: 398).
Benefit: 1975 (£34,947).
Testimonial: 1985 (when part of proceeds went to schools' cricket in Warwickshire).
Wife: Jill.
Children: Paul, Becca.
Family links with cricket: Father, A.F. Amiss, played good club cricket.
Jobs outside cricket: Sales executive for Officescape Midlands Ltd. (Interior design and construction group).

Overseas tours: Pakistan 1966–67; India, Pakistan and Sri Lanka 1972–73; West Indies 1973–74; Australia, New Zealand 1974–75; India, Sri Lanka and Australia 1976–77.

Overseas teams played for: World Series Cricket 1978–79.

Other sports: Golf, tennis, squash.

Relaxations: Bridge, gardening.

Extras: Scored two centuries in one match, 155 n.o. and 112 v Worcestershire at Birmingham 1978. Slipped a disc at 17 playing football and the injury means he still has to take precautionary exercise every day. "There is still a stiffness in the back which takes three or four minutes loosening-up work to get rid of." Banned from Test cricket for three years for playing for England rebels in South Africa, 1982.

Best batting performance: 262* England v West Indies, Kingston 1973–74.

Best bowling performance: 3-21 Warwickshire v Middlesex, Lord's 1970.

LAST SEASON: BATTING

	I.	N.O.	R.	H.S.	AV.
TEST					
OTHER FIRST CLASS	44	5	1555	140	39.87
INT					
JPL	14	1	388	78*	29.84
NAT.W	2	0	69	64	34.50
B & H	4	0	116	53	29.00

CAREER: BATTING

	I.	N.O.	R.	H.S.	AV.
TEST	88	10	3612	262*	46.31
OTHER FIRST CLASS	960	107	37061	232*	43.45
INT	18	0	859	137	47.72
JPL	216	18	6486	117*	32.75
NAT.W	49	5	1774	135	40.32
B & H	60	6	1861	115	34.46

LAST SEASON: BOWLING

	O.	M.	R.	W.	AV.
TEST					
OTHER FIRST CLASS					
INT					
JPL					
NAT.W					
B & H					

CAREER: BOWLING

	O.	M.	R.	W.	AV.
TEST					
OTHER FIRST CLASS	213.1	32	718	18	39.89
INT					
JPL	3	0	23	1	–
NAT.W	12.1	0	67	0	–
B & H	0.2	0	4	0	–

4. Which Australian cricket association celebrated which anniversary with a World Cup tournament in 1985?

5. What are three nicknames given to C.A. Connor of Hampshire, and what are his real first two names?

6. What have Wayne Daniel, Geoff Miller, Phil Carrick and Graham Gooch got in common?

ANDERSON, I.S.   Derbyshire

Full Name: Iain Stuart Anderson.
Role: Right-hand opening bat, off-break bowler.
Born: 24 April 1960, Derby.
Height: 6′ 0″ **Weight:** 11st. 2lbs.
Nickname: Tommy, Tom.
County debut: 1978.
County cap: 1985.
1000 runs in a season: 1.
1st-Class 50s scored: 22.
1st-Class 100s scored: 2.
One-day 50s: 3.
Place in batting averages: 128
average: 27.37; (1984: 198
average: 29.64).
1st-Class catches 1985: 16
(career: 94).
Parents: May and Norman
Anderson.

Wife and date of marriage: Linda,
28 September 1985.
Education: Dovecliff Grammar School; Wulfric School, Burton.
Qualifications: 8 O-levels, 3 A-levels, Preliminary Coaching Certificate.
Family links with cricket: Father and brother (Kenny) played club cricket.
Overseas tours: England Young Cricketers Tour Australia 1979.
Overseas teams played for: Bergvliet, Cape Town, 1979–80 and 1980–81;
Kew, Melbourne, 1982; Ellerslie, Auckland, 1982; Boland, South Africa,
1983–84.
Other sports: Soccer, squash.

LAST SEASON: BATTING

	I.	N.O.	R.	H.S.	AV.
TEST					
OTHER FIRST CLASS	35	3	876	95	27.37
INT					
JPL	10	2	287	64	35.87
NAT.W	1	0	4	4	–
B & H					

CAREER: BATTING

	I.	N.O.	R.	H.S.	AV.
TEST					
OTHER FIRST CLASS	181	24	3870	112	24.65
INT					
JPL	34	3	706	64	22.77
NAT.W	4	0	85	47	21.25
B & H	1	0	32	32	–

LAST SEASON: BOWLING

	O.	M.	R.	W.	AV.
TEST					
OTHER FIRST CLASS	3	1	9	0	–
INT					
JPL					
NAT.W					
B & H					

CAREER: BOWLING

	O.	M.	R.	W.	AV.
TEST					
OTHER FIRST CLASS	355.5	67	1290	20	64.50
INT					
JPL	7.1	2	28	2	14.00
NAT.W					
B & H					

Off-season 1985–86: Working (hopefully!).
Relaxations: Eating, listening to music, sleeping.
Best batting performance: 112 Derbyshire v Kent, Chesterfield 1983.
Best bowling performance: 4-35 Derbyshire v Australia, Derby 1981.

ANDREW, S.J.W. Hampshire

Full Name: Stephen Jon Walter
Andrew.
Role: Right-hand bat, right-arm
medium bowler.
Born: 27 January 1966, London.
Height: 6′ 3″ **Weight:** 13st.
Nickname: Rip.
County debut: 1984.
1st-Class 5 w. in innings: 1.
Place in bowling averages: 68
average: 33.06; (1984: 131
average: 48.18).
1st-Class catches 1985: 5 (career: 6).
Parents: Jon Trevor and
Victoria Julia Maud Andrew.
Marital status: Single.
Education: Hordle House Prep.
School; Milton Abbey Public School.
Qualifications: 3 O-levels.
Off-season 1985–86: Coaching in
Durban, South Africa.
Overseas teams played for: Pirates C.C., Durban, South Africa, 1983–84; South
African Police C.C., 1984.

LAST SEASON: BATTING

	I.	N.O.	R.	H.S.	AV.
TEST					
OTHER FIRST CLASS	5	4	9	6	–
INT					
JPL	–	–	–	–	–
NAT.W					
B & H					

CAREER: BATTING

	I.	N.O.	R.	H.S.	AV.
TEST					
OTHER FIRST CLASS	11	8	21	6*	7.00
INT					
JPL					
NAT.W	–	–	–	–	–
B & H	1	1	1	1*	–

LAST SEASON: BOWLING

	O.	M.	R.	W.	AV.
TEST					
OTHER FIRST CLASS	284	53	992	30	33.06
INT					
JPL					
NAT.W	10	1	28	1	–
B & H					

CAREER: BOWLING

	O.	M.	R.	W.	AV.
TEST					
OTHER FIRST CLASS	446.2	96	1522	41	37.12
INT					
JPL					
NAT.W	10	1	28	1	–
B & H	18	1	60	6	10.00

Overseas tours: Young England to West Indies 1985.
Cricketers particularly learnt from: Peter Sainsbury, Malcolm Marshall.
Cricketers particularly admired: D.K. Lillee, Malcolm Marshall.
Other sports played: Squash, golf. Interested in most sports.
Relaxations: Listening to music.
Extras: Youngest bowler to have opened bowling for Hampshire.
Opinions on cricket: "Politics should not interfere with any sport. I feel very strongly about the isolation of South Africa as a sporting nation."
Best batting performance: 6* Hampshire v Middlesex, Bournemouth 1984.
Best bowling performance: 6-43 Hampshire v Gloucestershire, Bournemouth 1985.

ASIF DIN, M.   Warwickshire

Full Name: Mohamed Asif Din.
Role: Right-hand bat, leg-break bowler.
Born: 21 September 1960, Kampala, Uganda.
Height: 5′ 9″ **Weight:** 9st. 8lbs.
Nickname: Gunga.
County debut: 1981.
1st-Class 50s scored: 10.
1st-Class 100s scored: 1.
1st-Class 5 w. in innings: 1.
One-day 50s: 6.
Place in batting averages: 68 average: 36.11; (1984: 252 average: 14.14).
1st-Class catches 1985: 2 (career: 40).
Marital status: Single.
Family links with cricket: Brother, Abid, plays for Smethwick 1 XI in Birmingham League.
Education: Ladywood Comprehensive, Birmingham.
Overseas tours: With M.C.C. to Bangladesh, 1980–81 and East and Central Africa, 1981.
Other sports: Hockey, squash, badminton.
Extras: Plays in spectacles. Trained on M.C.C. groundstaff at Lord's.
Best batting performance: 102 Warwickshire v Middlesex, Coventry 1982.
Best bowling performance: 5-100 Warwickshire v Glamorgan, Edgbaston 1982.

LAST SEASON: BATTING

	I.	N.O.	R.	H.S.	AV.
TEST					
OTHER FIRST CLASS	11	2	325	89	36.11
INT					
JPL	9	1	150	44	18.75
NAT.W	1	0	25	25	–
B & H					

CAREER: BATTING

	I.	N.O.	R.	H.S.	AV.
TEST					
OTHER FIRST CLASS	112	13	2568	102	25.94
INT					
JPL	51	8	1060	56*	24.65
NAT.W	7	2	127	45	25.40
B & H	13	2	271	16	24.64

LAST SEASON: BOWLING

	O.	M.	R.	W.	AV.
TEST					
OTHER FIRST CLASS	5.2	2	7	1	–
INT					
JPL	5	0	23	1	–
NAT.W					
B & H					

CAREER: BOWLING

	O.	M.	R.	W.	AV.
TEST					
OTHER FIRST CLASS	455.1	86	1852	34	54.47
INT					
JPL	11	1	60	2	30.00
NAT.W					
B & H	2	0	20	0	–

ASLETT, D.G.   Kent

Full Name: Derek George Aslett.
Role: Right-hand bat, leg-break bowler.
Born: 12 February 1958, Dover.
Height: 6' **Weight:** 12st.
Nickname: Spacko and variations.
County debut: 1981.
County cap: 1983.
1000 runs in a season: 2.
1st-Class 50s scored: 19.
1st-Class 100s scored: 10.
1st-Class 200s scored: 1.
One-day 50s: 7.
One-day 100s: 1.
Place in batting averages: 82 average: 33.27; (1984: 76 average: 35.50).
1st-Class catches 1985: 5 (career: 51).
Parents: George and Jean Aslett.
Wife and date of marriage: Bernadine, 17 November 1984.
Education: Dover Grammar School; Leicester University.
Qualifications: B.A. (Hons) History.
Family links with cricket: Father played club cricket for Dover.
Jobs outside cricket: Postman, orderly, window cleaner for Jim Day International.
Overseas teams played for: West Perth C.C. 1981 and 1982, Bayswater C.C. 1983–84 on Whitbread Scholarship.

Cricketers particularly learnt from: Father, Nigel Sutton, Andy Froude, Graham Mart, and senior Kent players.
Cricketers particularly admired: Mark Benson, Bob Woolmer, C.B. Fry.
Other sports: Rugby, hurling, tennis and diving.
Relaxations: Reading, yoga, music.
Extras: Scored 146 in debut v Hants, 168 and 119 v Derbyshire, 1983. Wears spectacles.
Best batting performance: 221* Kent v Sri Lanka, Canterbury 1984.
Best bowling performance: 4-119 Kent v Sussex, Hove 1982.

LAST SEASON: BATTING

	I.	N.O.	R.	H.S.	AV.
TEST					
OTHER FIRST CLASS	23	1	732	174	33.27
INT					
JPL	8	0	144	44	18.00
NAT.W	2	0	49	25	24.50
B & H	5	1	91	49	23.75

CAREER: BATTING

	I.	N.O.	R.	H.S.	AV.
TEST					
OTHER FIRST CLASS	136	12	4642	221*	37.44
INT					
JPL	39	1	1015	100	26.71
NAT.W	12	0	274	67	22.83
B & H	11	1	262	49	26.20

LAST SEASON: BOWLING

	O.	M.	R.	W.	AV.
TEST					
OTHER FIRST CLASS	17.1	1	78	1	–
INT					
JPL					
NAT.W					
B & H					

CAREER: BOWLING

	O.	M.	R.	W.	AV.
TEST					
OTHER FIRST CLASS	157	17	731	11	66.45
INT					
JPL					
NAT.W	0.5	0	0	1	–
B & H					

ATHEY, C.W.J.   Gloucestershire

Full Name: Charles William Jeffrey Athey.
Role: Right-hand bat, occasional seamer.
Born: 27 September 1957, Middlesbrough, Yorkshire.
Height: 5' 10" **Weight:** 12st.
Nickname: Bumper, Wingnut.
County debut: 1976 (Yorkshire), 1984 (Gloucestershire).
County cap: 1985.
Test debut: 1980.
No. of Tests: 3.
No. of One-Day Internationals: 2.
1000 runs in a season: 4.
1st-Class 50s scored: 49.
1st-Class 100s scored: 19.
One-day 50s: 35.

One-day 100s: 4.

Place in batting averages: 27 average: 46.52; (1984: 63 average: 37.75).

1st-Class catches 1985: 26 (career: 202).

Parents: Peter and Maree Athey.

Wife and date of marriage: Janet Linda, 9 October 1982.

Education: Linthorpe Junior School; Stainsby Secondary School; Acklam Hall High School.

Qualifications: 4 0-levels, some C.S.E.s. National Cricket Association Coaching Certificate, New South Wales, Australia.

Family links with cricket: "Father played league cricket in North Yorkshire and South Durham League for 29 years, 25 of them with Middlesbrough. President of Middlesbrough C.C. since 1975. Brother-in-law Colin Cook played for Middlesex, other brother-in-law (Martin) plays in Thames Valley League. Father-in-law deeply involved in Middlesex Youth cricket."

Jobs outside cricket: Barman, building labourer, sports shop assistant.

Overseas tours: D.H. Robins XI to Canada in 1976; South America 1979; Australasia 1980; England U-19 to West Indies in 1976 and with England to West Indies in 1981; Barbican XI to Gulf States.

Overseas teams played for: Manly Warringah, Sydney, Australia, 1977–78, 1978–79, 1979–80; Balmain, Sydney, Australia, 1980–81; Schoeman Park, Bloemfontein, South Africa, 1981–82; Papatoetoe, Auckland, New Zealand, 1983–84.

Cricketers particularly learnt from: D. Padgett.

Cricketers particularly admired: G. Greenidge, M. Marshall.

Off-season 1985–86: Hopefully working in Bristol.

Other sports: Squash, tennis, soccer. Follows most sports.

Relaxations: Music, good films, good food!

Extras: Played for Teeside County Schools U-16s at age 12, also 1971–72–73, and approached by Northamptonshire County Cricket Club. Made debut in 1972 North Yorkshire and South Durham League. Played for Yorkshire Colts 1974; played for North of England Young Cricketers XI v West Indies Young Cricketers at Old Trafford in 1974. Played football for Middlesbrough Schools

LAST SEASON: BATTING

	I.	N.O.	R.	H.S.	AV.
TEST					
OTHER FIRST CLASS	38	7	1442	170	46.52
INT					
JPL	15	4	663	131*	60.27
NAT.W	3	0	128	72	42.67
B & H	4	1	109	77	36.33

CAREER: BATTING

	I.	N.O.	R.	H.S.	AV.
TEST	6	0	17	9	2.83
OTHER FIRST CLASS	352	32	10040	170	31.38
INT	2	0	83	51	41.50
JPL	115	12	3658	121*	35.51
NAT.W	20	3	690	115	40.59
B & H	34	6	768	94*	27.43

LAST SEASON: BOWLING

	O.	M.	R.	W.	AV.
TEST					
OTHER FIRST CLASS	41.1	6	189	8	23.63
INT					
JPL	6	0	21	2	10.50
NAT.W					
B & H					

CAREER: BOWLING

	O.	M.	R.	W.	AV.
TEST					
OTHER FIRST CLASS	394.2	76	1303	29	44.93
INT					
JPL	90.4	1	510	20	25.50
NAT.W	18	1	92	1	–
B & H	52.4	4	218	13	16.77

U-16 XI 1972–73, 1973–74. Played for Middlesbrough Juniors 1974–75. Offered but declined apprenticeship terms with Middlesbrough F.C. Captained North Riding U-19 XI 1975–76. Yorkshire debut 1976; cap 1980.
Injuries 1985: Bad right shoulder.
Best batting performance: 170 Yorkshire v Derbyshire, Derby 1985.
Best bowling performance: 3-3 Yorkshire v Hampshire, Bristol 1985.

ATKINSON, J.C.M.   Somerset

Full Name: Jonathon Colin Mark Atkinson.
Role: Right-hand bat, right-arm medium bowler.
Born: 10 July 1968, Glastonbury.
Height: 6′ 3″ **Weight:** 13st. 7lbs.
Nickname: Atko, Sprog.
County debut: 1985.
1st-Class 50s scored: 1.
Parents: Colin R.M. and Shirley Atkinson.
Marital status: Single.
Education: Millfield School.
Qualifications: 11 O-levels.
Family links with cricket: Father Captain of Somerset C.C.C. 1965–67; President of Somerset C.C.C.
Off-season 1985–86: At school, taking A-levels.
Cricketers particularly learnt from: Father, Gerry Wilson (Millfield pro.), Martin Crowe.

LAST SEASON: BATTING

	I.	N.O.	R.	H.S.	AV.
TEST					
OTHER FIRST CLASS	5	1	167	79	41.75
INT					
JPL	–	–	–	–	–
NAT.W					
B & H					

CAREER: BATTING

	I.	N.O.	R.	H.S.	AV.
TEST					
OTHER FIRST CLASS	5	1	167	79	41.75
INT					
JPL	–	–	–	–	–
NAT.W					
B & H					

LAST SEASON: BOWLING

	O.	M.	R.	W.	AV.
TEST					
OTHER FIRST CLASS	65	9	250	2	125.0
INT					
JPL					
NAT.W					
B & H					

CAREER: BOWLING

	O.	M.	R.	W.	AV.
TEST					
OTHER FIRST CLASS	65	9	250	2	125.0
INT					
JPL					
NAT.W					
B & H					

Cricketers particularly admired: I.V.A. Richards, I.T. Botham (admire their competitive natures).
Other sports: Rugby, hockey and basketball.
Relaxations: Music tapes (Bob Dylan, Dire Straits).
Injuries 1985: Ankle ligaments strain.
Best batting performance: 79 Somerset v Northamptonshire, Weston 1985.

BAIL, P.A.C. Somerset

Full Name: Paul Andrew Clayden Bail.
Role: Right-hand bat.
Born: 23 June 1965, Burnham-on-Sea.
Height: 5' 11" **Weight:** 11st. 12lbs.
Nickname: Pac-man, Smilts, Fish, The Wanderer.
County debut: 1985.
1st-Class 50s scored: 1
Parents: John Clayden and Erica.
Marital status: Single.
Education: Berrow Primary; King Alfred's Highbridge; Blue School, Wells; Millfield School, Street; Cambridge University from Oct. 1985.
Qualifications: 10 O-levels, 3 A-levels.
Family links with cricket: Father captained local cricket side, President of Somerset League.
Overseas tours: Barbados, March 1985.
Off-season 1985–86: Cambridge University.
Cricketing superstitions: Always puts left pad on first.
Cricketers particularly learnt from: Coached by Tom Cartwright, Ken Palmer and Peter Robinson; learnt mainly from them.
Cricketers particularly admired: "There are many but most of all Geoff Boycott and Viv Richards."
Other sports: Soccer, hockey.
Relaxations: Rock music, preferably heavy; concerts, videos, TV, reading.
Extras: 200 v Lancashire IIs in 1984; 2nd in minor county averages 1984; represented England Schools U-19s in 1984; English Public Schools soccer team in 1983 and 1984.
Opinions on cricket: "I would advocate 4-day cricket provided the wickets are good enough."
Best batting performance: 78* Somerset v Kent, Canterbury 1985.

LAST SEASON: BATTING

	I.	N.O.	R.	H.S.	AV.
TEST					
OTHER FIRST CLASS	9	2	127	78*	18.14
INT					
JPL					
NAT.W					
B & H					

CAREER: BATTING

	I.	N.O.	R.	H.S.	AV.
TEST					
OTHER FIRST CLASS	9	2	127	78*	18.14
INT					
JPL					
NAT.W					
B & H					

LAST SEASON: BOWLING

	O.	M.	R.	W.	AV.
TEST					
OTHER FIRST CLASS	4	2	4	0	–
INT					
JPL					
NAT.W					
B & H					

CAREER: BOWLING

	O.	M.	R.	W.	AV.
TEST					
OTHER FIRST CLASS	4	2	4	0	–
INT					
JPL					
NAT.W					
B & H					

BAILEY, R.J.   Northamptonshire

Full Name: Robert John Bailey.
Role: Right-hand bat, off-break bowler.
Born: 28 October 1963, Biddulph, Stoke-on-Trent.
Height: 6′ 3″ **Weight:** 14st.
Nickname: Bailers or Blaster.
County debut: 1982.
County cap: 1985.
No. of One-Day Internationals: 1.
1000 runs in a season: 2.
1st-Class 50s scored: 15.
1st-Class 100s scored: 5.
One-day 50s: 8.
One-day 100s: 1.
Place in batting averages: 52 average: 38.52; (1984: 67 average: 37.97).
1st-Class catches 1985: 6 (career: 26).
Parents: John and Marie Bailey.
Marital status: Single.
Education: Biddulph High School.
Qualifications: 6 C.S.E.s, 1 O-level.
Jobs outside cricket: "Worked for three winters in electrical trade."
Off-season 1985–86: Coaching in South Africa.
Family links with cricket: Father played in North Staffordshire League for 30 years, for Knypersley and Minor Counties cricket for Staffordshire as wicket-keeper.
Overseas tours: England to Sharjah 1985 for Rothmans 1-day International tournament.

Overseas teams played for: Rhodes University, Grahamstown, 1982–83; Witenhage C.C., South Africa, 1983–84, 1984–85.
Cricketers particularly learnt from: My father, Stan Crump.
Other sports: Badminton, football, golf.
Relaxations: Listening to music.
Extras: Played for Young England v Young Australia, 1983. Scored 2 hundreds in match v Middlesex II 1984.
Best batting performance: 114 Northamptonshire v Somerset, Northampton 1984.
Best bowling performance: 3-33 Northamptonshire v Cambridge University, Cambridge 1984.

LAST SEASON: BATTING

	I.	N.O.	R.	H.S.	AV.
TEST					
OTHER FIRST CLASS	38	7	1194	107*	38.52
INT					
JPL	12	3	348	103*	38.66
NAT.W	2	1	26	18*	–
B & H	3	1	97	52	48.50

CAREER: BATTING

	I.	N.O.	R.	H.S.	AV.
TEST					
OTHER FIRST CLASS	91	16	2709	114	36.12
INT	1	1	41	41*	–
JPL	32	7	819	103*	32.76
NAT.W	7	3	152	56*	38.00
B & H	7	1	332	77	55.33

LAST SEASON: BOWLING

	O.	M.	R.	W.	AV.
TEST					
OTHER FIRST CLASS	3	0	16	0	–
INT					
JPL					
NAT.W	1	0	2	1	–
B & H	4	0	22	1	–

CAREER: BOWLING

	O.	M.	R.	W.	AV.
TEST					
OTHER FIRST CLASS	39	11	96	4	24.00
INT	6	0	25	0	–
JPL	5	0	49	0	–
NAT.W	2	0	16	1	–
B & H	4	0	22	1	–

BAINBRIDGE, P.   Gloucestershire

Full Name: Philip Bainbridge.
Role: Right-hand bat, right-arm medium bowler, cover fielder.
Born: 16 April 1958, Stoke-on-Trent.
Height: 5′ 10″ **Weight:** 11st. 13lbs.
Nickname: Bains, Robbo.
County debut: 1977.
County cap: 1981.
1000 runs in a season: 5.
1st-Class 50s scored: 43.
1st-Class 100s scored: 11.
1st-Class 5 w. in innings: 2.
One-day 50s: 9.
Place in batting averages: 12 average: 56.69; (1984: 104 average: 32.38).

Place in bowling averages: 51 average: 30.00; (1984: 135 average: 53.28).
1st-Class catches 1985: 10 (career: 72).
Parents: Leonard George and Lilian Rose Bainbridge.
Wife and date of marriage: Barbara, 22 September 1979.
Children: Neil, 11 January 1984; Laura, 14 January 1985.
Education: Hanley High School; Stoke-on-Trent Sixth Form College; Borough Road College of Education.
Qualifications: 9 O-levels, 2 A-levels, B.Ed., M.C.C. Coaching Certificate.
Jobs outside cricket: P.E. Lecturer, Marketing Executive Gloucs. C.C.C.
Family links with cricket: Cousin, Stephen Wilkinson, played for Somerset 1969–72.
Overseas tours: Holland with N.C.A. North of England Youth team 1976; Barbados, Trinidad and Tobago with British Colleges 1978; Barbados 1980 with Gloucestershire C.C.C.; Pakistan 1983 for two Zaheer Abbas benefit matches; Zimbabwe 1985 with English Counties XI.
Cricketers particularly learnt from: All senior players at Gloucestershire — and county coach.
Cricketers particularly admired: Mike Procter.
Off-season 1985–86: Lecturing at Brunel Technical College.
Other sports: All sports — football, rugby, squash, horse-riding.
Relaxations: Photography, wine-making, beer-making, listening to music, "walking in the country with my Golden Retriever dog and my wife. Entertaining my children."
Injuries 1985: Broken index finger and cracked cheekbone.
Extras: Enjoys coaching. Played for four 2nd XIs in 1976: Gloucestershire, Derbyshire, Northamptonshire and Warwickshire. Played for Young England v Australia 1977. Won Commercial Union U-23 Batsman of the Year 1981. Scored first century for Stoke-on-Trent aged 14. Played scrum-half for Clifton Rugby Football Club 4th XV. Runs a part-time mail order business with Chris Broad marketing gold and silver cricket bat pendants (Rosga Sporting Jewellery). Runs Gloucestershire Cricketers' Charity football team, helping to raise about £1500 for various charities in a season.

LAST SEASON: BATTING

	I.	N.O.	R.	H.S.	AV.
TEST					
OTHER FIRST CLASS	38	9	1644	151*	56.69
INT					
JPL	12	2	115	41	11.50
NAT.W	3	0	73	55	24.33
B & H	4	1	100	53	33.33

CAREER: BATTING

	I.	N.O.	R.	H.S.	AV.
TEST					
OTHER FIRST CLASS	255	43	7169	151*	33.82
INT					
JPL	79	13	1070	55	16.21
NAT.W	11	2	365	75	40.55
B & H	20	5	406	80	27.07

LAST SEASON: BOWLING

	O.	M.	R.	W.	AV.
TEST					
OTHER FIRST CLASS	200	46	570	19	30.00
INT					
JPL	54	4	330	12	27.50
NAT.W	32	2	109	6	18.17
B & H	25	0	104	1	–

CAREER: BOWLING

	O.	M.	R.	W.	AV.
TEST					
OTHER FIRST CLASS	1822.5	436	5486	141	38.91
INT					
JPL	518.1	16	2640	86	30.69
NAT.W	128	15	408	16	25.50
B & H	173.2	19	615	20	30.75

Best batting performance: 151* Gloucestershire v Derbyshire, Derby 1985.
Best bowling performance: 6-59 Gloucestershire v Glamorgan, Swansea 1982.

BAIRSTOW, D.L. Yorkshire

Full Name: David Leslie Bairstow.
Role: Right-hand bat, wicket-keeper, occasional medium pacer.
Born: 1 September 1951, Bradford.
Height: 5′ 10″ **Weight:** 14st. 7lbs.
Nickname: Bluey.
County debut: 1970.
County cap: 1973.
Benefit: 1982 (£56,913).
Test debut: 1979.
No. of Tests: 4.
No. of One-Day Internationals: 21.
1000 runs in a season: 3.
1st-Class 50s scored: 64.
1st-Class 100s scored: 7.
One-day 50s: 12.
One-day 100s: 1.
Place in batting averages: 24
average: 47.24; (1984: 64
average: 37.48).
Wife: Gail Lesley.
Children: Andrew David, Claire Louise.
Education: Hanson Grammar School, Bradford.
Qualifications: O and A-levels.
Jobs outside cricket: Sales representative.
Family links with cricket: Father, Lesley, played cricket for Laisterdyke.
Overseas tours: Australia 1978–79 and 1979–80; West Indies 1981.
Overseas teams played for: Griqualand West in 1966–67 and 1977–78 as Captain.
Cricketers particularly learnt from: Laurie Bennett, maths and sports master at school; Mike Fearnley.
Cricket superstitions: "I will pat the ground three times or fiddle with my gloves three times. It is ridiculous but I do not want to stop it. I was in a pub a couple of days before the Leeds Test, and a lad I had never seen before gave me a medallion, and told me to keep it in my pocket for luck. Many people would have forgotten completely, but that medallion went into the pocket of my flannels, and stayed there for the whole match."
Relaxations: Gardening.
Other sports: Turned down an offer to play for Bradford City F.C., plays golf.

Extras: Played for M.C.C. Schools at Lord's in 1970. First Yorkshire wicket-keeper to get 1000 runs in a season (1982) since Arthur Wood in 1935. Set Yorkshire record of seven catches v Derbyshire at Scarborough, 1982. 133 consecutive John Player League matches. His 145 for Yorkshire v Middlesex is the highest score by a Yorkshire wicket-keeper. Allowed to take an A-level at 6 am at school in order to make Yorkshire debut. Published *A Yorkshire Diary – a year of crisis* 1984. Captain 1984–.

Best batting performance: 145 Yorkshire v Middlesex, Scarborough 1980.

Best bowling performance: 3-82 Griqualand West v Transvaal B, Johannesburg 1976-77.

LAST SEASON: BATTING

	I.	N.O.	R.	H.S.	AV.
TEST					
OTHER FIRST CLASS	35	10	1181	122*	47.24
INT					
JPL	12	0	255	40	21.25
NAT.W	1	0	13	13	–
B & H	3	1	56	31*	28.00

CAREER: BATTING

	I.	N.O.	R.	H.S.	AV.
TEST	7	1	125	59	20.83
OTHER FIRST CLASS	536	106	11341	145	26.37
INT	20	6	206	23*	14.71
JPL	179	42	2806	78	20.48
NAT.W	22	5	413	92	24.29
B & H	44	9	618	103*	17.66

LAST SEASON: BOWLING

	O.	M.	R.	W.	AV.
TEST					
OTHER FIRST CLASS					
INT					
JPL					
NAT.W					
B & H					

CAREER: BOWLING

	O.	M.	R.	W.	AV.
TEST					
OTHER FIRST CLASS	79	15	247	6	41.17
INT					
JPL					
NAT.W					
B & H	3	0	17	0	–

LAST SEASON: WICKET KEEPING

	C.	ST.			
TEST					
OTHER FIRST CLASS	45	13			
INT					
JPL	9	2			
NAT.W	1	–			
B & H	13	1			

CAREER: WICKET KEEPING

	C.	ST.			
TEST	12	1			
OTHER FIRST CLASS	803	128			
INT	17	4			
JPL	187	19			
NAT.W	28	2			
B & H	92	4			

7. Which England Test cricketer was born in Durham and played for both Yorkshire and Lancashire and was described by Neville Cardus as "one of the greatest right-handed off-breakers I have seen anywhere"?

8. Which bowler took 3278 first-class wickets, third only to Rhodes and Freeman in English cricket history and yet was chosen to play for England only once?

BALDERSTONE, J.C.   Leicestershire

Full Name: John Christopher Balderstone.
Role: Right-hand bat, slow left-arm bowler, slip fielder.
Born: 16 November 1940, Huddersfield, Yorkshire.
Height: 6' 2" **Weight:** 12st. 7lbs.
Nickname: Baldy, Chris, Dad.
County debut: 1971.
County cap: 1973.
Testimonial: 1984 (£64,470).
Test debut: 1976.
No. of Tests: 2.
1000 runs in a season: 11.
1st-Class 50s scored: 101.
1st-Class 100s scored: 31.
1st-Class 5 w. in innings: 5.
One-day 50s: 31.
One-day 100s: 5.
Place in batting averages: 63 average: 36.31; (1984: 65 average: 37.06).
1st-Class catches 1985: 10 (career: 207).
Parents: Frank and Jenny Balderstone.
Wife and date of marriage: Madeline, April 1962.
Children: Sally Victoria, 15 September 1970; Michael James, 3 January 1973.
Education: Paddock County School, Huddersfield.
Qualifications: Advanced cricket coach, soccer coach.
Jobs outside cricket: Professional footballer with Huddersfield Town, Carlisle United, Doncaster Rovers, Queen of the South, Enderby Town. Representative for a sports shop.
Overseas tours: With Leicester to Zimbabwe, March 1981 and to Oman, 1984.
Cricketers particularly learnt from: "Everyone."
Injuries 1985: Bruised hand.
Other sports: Golf, professional football.
Relaxations: Do-it-yourself, golf, reading and all sports.
Extras: Played for Yorkshire 1961–70. Once played first-class cricket match and a league football match on the same day, 15 September 1975 (Leicestershire v Derbyshire at Chesterfield 11.30 am to 6.30 pm and Doncaster Rovers v Brentford at Doncaster 7.30 pm to 9.10 pm). Former Chairman of Cricketers' Association.
Best batting performance: 181* Leicestershire v Gloucestershire, Leicester 1984.
Best bowling performance: 6-25 Leicestershire v Hampshire, Southampton 1978.

LAST SEASON: BATTING

	I.	N.O.	R.	H.S.	AV.
TEST					
OTHER FIRST CLASS	40	5	1271	134	36.31
INT					
JPL	4	0	27	19	6.75
NAT.W	2	0	50	35	25.00
B & H	7	1	272	77	45.33

CAREER: BATTING

	I.	N.O.	R.	H.S.	AV.
TEST	4	0	39	35	9.75
OTHER FIRST CLASS	592	60	18585	181*	34.93
INT					
JPL	122	23	2583	96	26.09
NAT.W	30	2	780	119*	27.86
B & H	57	12	2059	113*	45.76

LAST SEASON: BOWLING

	O.	M.	R.	W.	AV.
TEST					
OTHER FIRST CLASS	15	3	68	1	–
INT					
JPL					
NAT.W					
B & H					

CAREER: BOWLING

	O.	M.	R.	W.	AV.
TEST	16	0	80	1	–
OTHER FIRST CLASS	3142	948	7937	307	25.85
INT					
JPL	58.3	2	296	12	24.66
NAT.W	48	12	176	11	16.00
B & H	30	4	103	5	20.60

BANKS, D.A.   Worcestershire

Full Name: David Andrew Banks.
Role: Right-hand bat, right-arm medium bowler.
Born: 11 January 1961, Pensnett.
Height: 6′ 3″ **Weight:** 14st. 7lbs.
Nickname: Banksy, D.B.
County debut: 1983.
1st-Class 50s scored: 3.
1st-Class 100s scored: 1.
Place in batting averages: —
average: —; (1984: 243
average: 14.67).
1st-Class catches 1985: 2 (career: 8).
Parents: William and Betty Banks.
Marital status: Single.
Education: St. Mark's Primary School; Pensnett Secondary Modern; Dudley Technical College.
Qualifications: 3 O-levels; 5 C.S.E.s; Certificate of Engineering Craftsmanship City and Guilds; Mechanical and Fabricational Engineering. N.C.A. Coach.
Jobs outside cricket: Craft Apprentice, Gibbons Bros. Ltd. 1977–81; coached school and club cricket, winter 1981–82.
Off-season 1985–86: Playing in Perth, Western Australia.
Family links with cricket: "Father and brother and myself all played club cricket for Brierley Hill Athletic Club; father has retired, but brother still plays."

Cricketing superstitions: Left pad on first.

Overseas tours: Landlsey Green Youth Cricket Club tour to Barbados, October 1981.

Overseas teams played for: Leprechauns Cricket Club (of Dublin) on their annual tour of England, 1982; North Perth C.C. 1983–84; Melville, Western Australia, 1984–85.

Cricketers particularly admired: Gordon Greenidge, Les Varis (Captain of North Perth).

Other sports: Football, tennis, table-tennis, darts, golf, "horse-racing as the girlfriend's family has racehorse."

Relaxations: "Women, movies, listening to music."

Injuries 1985: Thigh strain (four weeks).

Extras: Century on first-class debut (v Oxford University) — first Worcestershire player to do so for 55 years. Also, highest aggregate in a match on Worcestershire debut, with 53 in the 2nd innings. Plays for same side in Australia as Dennis Lillee and Graeme Wood. Left staff after 1985 season.

Best batting performance: 100 Worcestershire v Oxford University, Oxford 1983.

LAST SEASON: BATTING

	I.	N.O.	R.	H.S.	AV.
TEST					
OTHER FIRST CLASS	7	2	196	76	39.20
INT					
JPL	2	0	13	13	6.50
NAT.W					
B & H					

CAREER: BATTING

	I.	N.O.	R.	H.S.	AV.
TEST					
OTHER FIRST CLASS	29	3	691	100	26.58
INT					
JPL	11	1	91	23	9.10
NAT.W					
B & H					

LAST SEASON: BOWLING

	O.	M.	R.	W.	AV.
TEST					
OTHER FIRST CLASS					
INT					
JPL					
NAT.W					
B & H					

CAREER: BOWLING

	O.	M.	R.	W.	AV.
TEST					
OTHER FIRST CLASS	4	0	17	0	–
INT					
JPL					
NAT.W					
B & H					

9. Which county captain has the nickname "Wristy"?

10. Which county has playing for it regularly in its first choice XI, two West Indian Test cricketers, two would-have-been South African Test cricketers, two sons of former England Test cricketers and two brothers? And who are they?

BAPTISTE, E.A.E.   Kent

Full Name: Eldine Ashworth Elderfield Baptiste.
Role: Right-hand bat, right-arm fast-medium bowler.
Born: 12 March 1960, Liberta, Antigua.
Height: 6' 1" **Weight:** 12st.
Nickname: Soca or Bapo.
County debut: 1981.
County cap: 1983.
Test debut: 1983–84.
No. of Tests: 9.
No. of One-Day Internationals: 29.
50 wickets in a season: 2.
1st-Class 50s scored: 14.
1st-Class 5 w. in innings: 7.
One-day 50s: 3.
Place in batting averages: 99 average: 31.36; (1984: 163 average: 24.50).
Place in bowling averages: 44 average: 28.64; (1984: 42 average: 27.21).
1st-Class catches 1985: 12 (career: 52).
Parents: Gertrude and Samuel Baptiste.
Children: Forbes, 29 December 1981; Daved, 24 June 1982.
Family links with cricket: Father played for Liberta 1940–48. Brother, Rowan, played for Liberta at School level.
Education: Liberta Primary; All Saints Secondary School.
Jobs outside cricket: Sports officer in the Sports Department of the Ministry of Education.
Off-season 1985–86: Playing and coaching with Geelong C.C. in Australia.
Cricketing superstitions: The numbers 49 and 13.
Overseas tours: With Leeward Youths to Barbados 1978; to Australia, St Lucia, St Kitts, St Thomas and Montserrat with Antigua National team in 1979; to England with Antigua Youth in 1979; with West Indies to India 1983, England 1984, Australia 1984–85.
Cricketers particularly learnt from: Guy Yearwood, Viv Richards, Andy Roberts, Malcolm Marshall.
Other sports: Playing football, tennis, volleyball. Follows boxing.
Relaxations: Watching movies, music — especially calypso — and meeting people.
Extras: Awarded Viv Richards Schools Cricket Trophy for the Most Outstanding Cricketer 1979, Sportsman of the Year in Antigua 1979. Hat-trick twice for Liberta School v Cobbs Cross School. Scored 201 for Kent 2nd XI v Surrey at The Oval, 1982.
Best batting performance: 136* Kent v Yorkshire, Sheffield 1983.
Best bowling performance: 6-42 Kent v Northamptonshire, Northampton 1985.

LAST SEASON: BATTING

	I.	N.O.	R.	H.S.	AV.
TEST					
OTHER FIRST CLASS	36	5	972	82	31.36
INT					
JPL	13	1	264	60	22.00
NAT.W	3	1	3	3	1.50
B & H	5	1	73	43*	18.25

CAREER: BATTING

	I.	N.O.	R.	H.S.	AV.
TEST	10	1	224	87*	24.89
OTHER FIRST CLASS	134	22	3157	136*	28.19
INT	10	2	119	28*	14.88
JPL	32	4	528	60	18.85
NAT.W	8	1	60	22	8.57
B & H	6	1	74	43*	14.80

LAST SEASON: BOWLING

	O.	M.	R.	W.	AV.
TEST					
OTHER FIRST CLASS	562	116	1661	58	28.64
INT					
JPL	83	4	384	12	32.00
NAT.W	24	3	55	1	–
B & H	48	7	172	8	21.50

CAREER: BOWLING

	O.	M.	R.	W.	AV.
TEST	204	55	485	15	32.33
OTHER FIRST CLASS	2092.5	458	6452	239	27.00
INT	246	17	989	27	36.63
JPL	249	12	1074	40	26.85
NAT.W	85	15	264	11	24.00
B & H	59	9	200	8	25.00

BARCLAY, J.R.T.   Sussex

Full Name: John Robert Troutbeck Barclay.
Role: Right-hand bat, off-break bowler, slip fielder.
Born: 22 January 1954, Bonn, West Germany.
Height: 5′ 10″ **Weight:** 12st.
Nickname: Trout.
County debut: 1970, aged 16 yrs 6 mths, while still at school.
County cap: 1976.
Benefit: 1986.
1000 runs in a season: 4.
50 wickets in a season: 1.
1st-Class 50s scored: 46.
1st-Class 100s scored: 9.
1st-Class 5 w. in innings: 7.
1st-Class 10 w. in match: 1.
One-day 50s: 6.
Place in batting averages: 163 average: 23.36; (1984: 72 average: 23.78).
Place in bowling averages: 48 average: 29.45; (1984: 51 average: 28.42).
1st-Class catches 1985: 12 (career: 215).
Parents: C.F.R. Barclay, Mrs J.B. Denman.
Wife and date of marriage: Mary Louise, 16 September 1978.
Children: Georgina Clare, 9 January 1981.
Education: Summerfields School, Oxford; Eton College.
Jobs outside cricket: Marketing Executive with International Factors Ltd.
Family links with cricket: Great uncle, F.J.J. Ford, played for Middlesex.
Cricketers particularly learnt from: Vic Cannings.

Cricketers particularly admired: David Steele.

Overseas tours: India 1970–71 with England Schools' Cricket Association (Vice-Captain); England Young Cricketers to West Indies 1972 as Captain.

Overseas teams played for: Orange Free State, 1978–79; Waverley C.C., Sydney, 1981.

Off-season 1985–86: Working for International Factors Ltd. as public relations executive.

Other sports: Golf.

Relaxations: Fishing.

Extras: Sussex Captain since 1981.

Best batting performance: 119 Sussex v Leicestershire, Hove 1980.

Best bowling performance: 6-61 Sussex v Sri Lankans, Hove 1979.

LAST SEASON: BATTING

	I.	N.O.	R.	H.S.	AV.
TEST					
OTHER FIRST CLASS	17	6	257	37*	23.36
INT					
JPL	2	2	11	7*	–
NAT.W	1	0	0	0	–
B & H	3	2	49	29*	

CAREER: BATTING

	I.	N.O.	R.	H.S.	AV.
TEST					
OTHER FIRST CLASS	431	44	9641	119	24.91
INT					
JPL	101	34	1240	48	18.50
NAT.W	22	2	340	48	17.00
B & H	42	4	1083	93*	28.50

LAST SEASON: BOWLING

	O.	M.	R.	W.	AV.
TEST					
OTHER FIRST CLASS	300.4	55	913	31	29.45
INT					
JPL	21	1	162	6	27.00
NAT.W					
B & H	16	1	46	1	–

CAREER: BOWLING

	O.	M.	R.	W.	AV.
TEST					
OTHER FIRST CLASS	3484.2	843	9871	324	30.27
INT					
JPL	585	27	2701	105	25.73
NAT.W	128.3	17	425	23	18.48
B & H	274.5	33	1010	36	28.06

11. What has Paul Terry of Hampshire got in common with John Barclay of Sussex?

12. Which England Test cricketer has fox-hunting as one of his relaxations?

13. Who is the only county captain to have won all four major county competitions?

BARLOW, G.D.   Middlesex

Full Name: Graham Derek
Barlow.
Role: Left-hand bat, right-arm
medium bowler.
Born: 26 March 1950, Folkestone,
Kent.
Height: 5' 10" **Weight:** 12st. 12lbs.
Nickname: Ed.
County debut: 1969.
County cap: 1976.
Benefit: 1984.
Test debut: 1976–77.
No. of Tests: 3.
No. of One-Day Internationals: 6.
1000 runs in a season: 7.
1st-Class 50s scored: 57.
1st-Class 100s scored: 25.
One-day 50s: 32.

One-day 100s: 5.
Place in batting averages: 22 average: 47.96; (1984: 149 average: 26.56).
1st-Class catches 1985: 6 (career: 134).
Parents: Derek Albert and Millicent Louise (Betty) Barlow.
Education: Woolverstone Hall; Ealing Grammar School; Loughborough
College of Education.
Qualifications: Certificate of Education for Physical Education and English,
N.C.A. Coach.
Jobs outside cricket: P.E. teacher, Brentside School, Greenford 1973–74.
Coach to Wynberg Boys' School, Cape Town 1975–76. Printing representative
for Hildesley Ltd. 1974–75. Abbey Life Assurance Co. Ltd.
Off-season 1985–86: Playing abroad having had two enforced winters at home
due to benefit.
Family links with cricket: "Negligible. Distant great-uncle played good club
cricket, but that's it."
Overseas tours: India, Sri Lanka and Australia 1976–77.
Overseas teams played for: Greenpoint C.C., Cape Town, 1977–78, 1979–80; St.
Kilda, Melbourne, 1978–79; Subiaco Floreat C.C., Perth, 1982–83.
Other sports: General fitness and particularly squash and running, especially
when away in the winter. Played rugby for Loughborough.
Cricketers particularly learnt from: Peter Parfitt.
Relaxations: "Music — cross-section of taste from Beethoven and particularly
Sibelius to 'Yes' on the 'heavier' side. Reading when time permits, likewise
cinema and, to a lesser extent, theatre."
Injuries 1985: "Back problem in August caused me to miss the last three
championship matches."
Extras: Played rugby union for Loughborough Colleges, Leicestershire,

England U-23 and, briefly, Rosslyn Park. Played in M.C.C. Schools matches in 1968. Runs pre-season training for Middlesex.
Best batting performance: 177 Middlesex v Lancashire, Southport 1981.

LAST SEASON: BATTING

	I.	N.O.	R.	H.S.	AV.
TEST					
OTHER FIRST CLASS	32	4	1343	141	47.96
INT					
JPL	12	1	303	72	27.54
NAT.W	2	0	43	35	21.50
B & H	6	0	110	44	18.33

CAREER: BATTING

	I.	N.O.	R.	H.S.	AV.
TEST	5	1	17	7*	4.25
OTHER FIRST CLASS	393	57	12176	177	36.24
INT	6	1	149	80*	29.80
JPL	147	14	3762	114	28.28
NAT.W	29	3	884	158	34.00
B & H	46	4	983	129	23.41

LAST SEASON: BOWLING

	O.	M.	R.	W.	AV.
TEST					
OTHER FIRST CLASS	3	0	14	0	–
INT					
JPL					
NAT.W					
B & H					

CAREER: BOWLING

	O.	M.	R.	W.	AV.
TEST					
OTHER FIRST CLASS	19.1	2	68	3	22.67
INT					
JPL	15.3	0	91	4	22.75
NAT.W					
B & H	4	0	18	1	–

BARNETT, K.J. Derbyshire

Full Name: Kim John Barnett.
Role: Right-hand bat, leg-break or seam bowler.
Born: 17 July 1960, Stoke-on-Trent.
Height: 6′ **Weight:** 13st.
Nickname: Wristy.
County debut: 1979.
County cap: 1982.
1000 runs in a season: 3.
1st-Class 50s scored: 41.
1st-Class 100s scored: 15.
1st-Class 5 w. in innings: 1.
One-day 50s: 9.
One-day 100s: 3.
Place in batting averages: 46 average: 40.21; (1984: 30 average: 45.63).
Place in bowling averages: 53 average: 30.24; (1984: — average: —).

1st-Class catches 1985: 13 (career: 96).
Parents: Derek and Doreen Barnett.
Wife and date of marriage: Nancy, 31 September 1984.
Education: Leek High School, Staffs.
Qualifications: 7 0-levels.

Jobs outside cricket: Bank clerk, National Westminster Bank 1978.
Overseas tours: With England Schools to India 1977; Young England to Australia 1978–79; Derrick Robins XI to New Zealand and Australia 1979–80.
Overseas teams played for: Boland, South Africa, 1982–83, 1984–85.
Other sports: Football. Has played soccer semi-professionally for Cheshire League side, Leek Town F.C. Tennis. Follows horse-racing.
Extras: Played for Northants. 2nd XI when aged 15. Played one Minor County match for Staffordshire; also for Warwickshire 2nd XI. Became youngest captain of a first-class county when appointed in 1983.
Opinions on cricket: "Would like to see the introduction of 4-day cricket to the County Championship to make the difference between Test match cricket and the County Championship smaller and hopefully promote more attacking cricket."
Best batting performance: 144 Derbyshire v Middlesex, Derby 1984.
Best bowling performance: 6-115 Derbyshire v Yorkshire, Bradford 1985.

LAST SEASON: BATTING

	I.	N.O.	R.	H.S.	AV.
TEST					
OTHER FIRST CLASS	41	2	1568	134*	40.21
INT.					
JPL	14	2	419	82*	34.91
NAT.W	1	0	53	53	–
B & H	4	0	96	86	24.00

CAREER: BATTING

	I.	N.O.	R.	H.S.	AV.
TEST					
OTHER FIRST CLASS	252	24	7759	144	34.03
INT.					
JPL	91	17	2199	131*	29.71
NAT.W	13	2	402	88	36.55
B & H	23	1	394	86	17.91

LAST SEASON: BOWLING

	O.	M.	R.	W.	AV.
TEST					
OTHER FIRST CLASS	173.4	33	514	17	30.24
INT.					
JPL	4	0	22	0	–
NAT.W					
B & H					

CAREER: BOWLING

	O.	M.	R.	W.	AV.
TEST					
OTHER FIRST CLASS	617.5	111	2132	38	56.11
INT.					
JPL	42.3	2	278	7	39.71
NAT.W					
B & H	9	2	33	2	16.50

14. To whom has Test commentator Brian Johnston given the nickname "The Alderman"?

15. To whom has Brian Johnston given the nickname "Sir Frederick"?

16. To whom has Brian Johnston given the nickname "The Boil"?

BARRETT, B.J.   Worcestershire

Full Name: Brian Joseph Barrett.
Role: Right-hand bat, right-arm
seam bowler.
Born: 16 November 1966, Auckland,
New Zealand.
Height: 6' 3" **Weight:** 12st. 7lbs.
Nickname: Burglar, Kiwi.
County debut: 1985.
Parents: Patrick Joseph and
June Florence Barrett.
Marital status: Single.
Education: Anchorage Park Primary;
Pakuranga Intermediate and Edgewater
College.
Qualifications: 4 School Certificate
subjects.
Jobs outside cricket: Work for New
Zealand Telecoms.
Off-season 1985–86: Playing club and
hopefully first-class cricket in New Zealand.
Overseas teams played for: Auckland Youth 1980–83; Howick/Pakuranga
1973–1985; North Island Select side 1981, 1983.
Cricketing superstitions: "Right boot always goes on first. Have to be the last
person out of the dressing room and of course bowl with the wind!"
Cricketers particularly learnt from: Paul Pridgeon of Worcester, Basil
D'Oliveira, Dennis Lillee.
Cricketers particularly admired: Richard Hadlee, Dennis Lillee.
Other sports: Soccer, basketball, squash and fitness work. Had to choose one
so cricket came first.

LAST SEASON: BATTING

	I.	N.O.	R.	H.S.	AV.
TEST					
OTHER FIRST CLASS	–	–	–	–	–
INT					
JPL	1	1	5	5*	–
NAT.W					
B & H					

CAREER: BATTING

	I.	N.O.	R.	H.S.	AV.
TEST					
OTHER FIRST CLASS	–	–	–	–	–
INT					
JPL	1	1	5	5*	–
NAT.W					
B & H					

LAST SEASON: BOWLING

	O.	M.	R.	W.	AV.
TEST					
OTHER FIRST CLASS	18	7	40	1	–
INT					
JPL	8	0	43	0	–
NAT.W					
B & H					

CAREER: BOWLING

	O.	M.	R.	W.	AV.
TEST					
OTHER FIRST CLASS	18	7	40	1	–
INT					
JPL	8	0	43	0	–
NAT.W					
B & H					

Relaxations: "Getting my feet up and watching a good movie. Writing home to family and friends."
Injuries 1985: Niggling trouble with left knee.

BARWICK, S.R. Glamorgan

Full Name: Stephen Royston Barwick.
Role: Right-hand bat, right-arm medium bowler.
Born: 6 September 1960, Neath.
Height: 6′ 2″ **Weight:** 13st. 7lbs.
Nickname: Baz.
County debut: 1981.
50 wickets in a season: 1.
1st-Class 5 w. in innings: 5.
Place in batting averages: —
average: —; (1984: 267
average: 10.50).
Place in bowling averages: 94
average: 38.22; (1984: 37
average: 26.28).
1st-Class catches 1985: 4
(career: 18).
Parents: Margaret and Roy Barwick.
Marital status: Single.
Family links with cricket: "My uncle David played for Glamorgan 2nd XI."
Education: Cwrt Sart Comprehensive School; Dwr-y-Felin Comprehensive School.

LAST SEASON: BATTING

	I.	N.O.	R.	H.S.	AV.
TEST					
OTHER FIRST CLASS	15	5	57	29	5.70
INT					
JPL	6	3	3	1*	1.00
NAT.W	1	0	4	4	–
B & H	3	1	10	6*	5.00

CAREER: BATTING

	I.	N.O.	R.	H.S.	AV.
TEST					
OTHER FIRST CLASS	63	28	339	29	9.69
INT					
JPL	10	6	23	12*	5.75
NAT.W	4	2	13	6	6.50
B & H	10	6	40	18	10.00

LAST SEASON: BOWLING

	O.	M.	R.	W.	AV.
TEST					
OTHER FIRST CLASS	473.4	94	1376	36	38.22
INT					
JPL	73	5	273	13	21.00
NAT.W	23	5	69	5	13.80
B & H	31.1	6	100	6	16.67

CAREER: BOWLING

	O.	M.	R.	W.	AV.
TEST					
OTHER FIRST CLASS	1476.1	351	4321	136	31.77
INT					
JPL	240.5	15	1104	30	36.80
NAT.W	46.2	9	131	10	13.10
B & H	106.1	16	366	19	19.26

Qualifications: "Commerce, human biology, mathematics, English."
Jobs outside cricket: Ex-steel worker.
Other sports: Badminton, squash, table-tennis, football (watching Swansea City).
Extras: Made debut on 25 April 1981 v Oxford University, and took 4 wickets in 1st innings.
Best batting performance: 29 Glamorgan v Somerset, Cardiff 1985.
Best bowling performance: 8-42 Glamorgan v Worcestershire, Worcester 1983.

BENSON, M.R. Kent

Full Name: Mark Richard Benson.
Role: Left-hand bat.
Born: 6 July 1958, Shoreham, Sussex.
Height: 5' 10'' **Weight:** 12st. 7lbs.
Nickname: Benny.
County debut: 1980.
County cap: 1981.
1000 runs in a season: 4.
1st-Class 50s scored: 40.
1st-Class 100s scored: 15.
One-day 50s: 17.
One-day 100s: 1.
Place in batting averages: 59 average: 37.53; (1984: 61 average: 38.08).
1st-Class catches 1985: 15 (career: 55).

Parents: Frank and Judy Benson.
Marital status: Single.
Education: Sutton Valence School.
Qualifications: O- and A-levels and 1 S-level.
Jobs outside cricket: Marketing assistant with Shell U.K. Oil.
Off-season 1985–86: Trying to build up career outside cricket.
Family links with cricket: Father played for Ghana.
Overseas teams played for: Balfour Guild C.C., 1979–80; Johannesburg Municipals, 1980–81; Port Adelaide C.C., 1981–82.
Cricketers particularly learned from: Eldine Baptiste.
Cricketers particularly admired: Derek Aslett.
Other sports: Golf, hockey. Follows horse-racing.
Extras: Scored 1000 runs in first full season; record for most runs in career and season at Sutton Valence School.
Opinions on cricket: "Believe 4-day County Championship matches should

operate. Each county plays each other once during the season."
Best batting performance: 162 Kent v Hampshire, Southampton 1985.

LAST SEASON: BATTING

	I.	N.O.	R.	H.S.	AV.
TEST					
OTHER FIRST CLASS	43	3	1501	162	37.53
INT.					
JPL	12	1	316	93	28.72
NAT.W	3	0	178	78	59.33
B & H	5	0	94	34	18.80

CAREER: BATTING

	I.	N.O.	R.	H.S.	AV.
TEST					
OTHER FIRST CLASS	185	18	6341	162	37.97
INT.					
JPL	58	1	1737	97	30.47
NAT.W	15	1	649	113*	46.36
B & H	19	4	369	65	24.60

LAST SEASON: BOWLING

	O.	M.	R.	W.	AV.
TEST					
OTHER FIRST CLASS	20.2	0	138	1	–
INT.					
JPL					
NAT.W					
B & H					

CAREER: BOWLING

	O.	M.	R.	W.	AV.
TEST					
OTHER FIRST CLASS	33.2	1	210	1	–
INT.					
JPL					
NAT.W					
B & H					

BENT, P. Worcestershire

Full Name: Paul Bent.
Role: Right-hand bat, off-break bowler.
Born: 1 May 1965, Worcester.
Height: 6′ 1″.
Education: Worcester Royal Grammar School.
Extras: Made debut for 2nd XI in 1984.

	I.	N.O.	R.	H.S.	AV.
TEST					
OTHER FIRST CLASS	1	0	14	14	–
INT					
JPL					
NAT.W					
B & H					

CAREER: BATTING

	I.	N.O.	R.	H.S.	AV.
TEST					
OTHER FIRST CLASS	1	0	14	14	–
INT					
JPL					
NAT.W					
B & H					

BILLINGTON, D.J   Leicestershire

Full Name: David James Billington.
Role: Right-hand bat, slip fielder.
Born: 6 December 1965, Leyland (nr. Preston).
Height: 5' 7'' **Weight:** 12 st.
Nickname: Billi.
County debut: 1985.
1st-Class catches 1985: 1 (career: 1).
Parents: David and Kathy Billington.
Marital status: Single.
Education: Kirkbie Kendal School, Kendal; Leeds University; going to Loughborough University in 1986.
Qualifications: 9 O-levels, 4 A-levels.
Cricketing superstitions: Always puts left pad on first but otherwise not really superstitious.
Cricketers particularly learnt from: K. Higgs and Tim Boon. Learns by watching most players.
Cricketers particularly admired: D.I. Gower, S. Gavaskar.
Other sports: Rugby union. Played for Kendal R.U.F.C. last season and the U.A.U. Eastern Division.
Injuries 1985: Injured left shoulder in August which kept him out of the game for the rest of the season and resulted in an operation in September.

LAST SEASON: BATTING

	I.	N.O.	R.	H.S.	AV.
TEST					
OTHER FIRST CLASS	1	0	19	19	–
INT					
JPL					
NAT.W					
B & H					

CAREER: BATTING

	I.	N.O.	R.	H.S.	AV.
TEST					
OTHER FIRST CLASS	1	0	19	19	–
INT					
JPL					
NAT.W					
B & H					

Opinions on cricket: "The qualification period for overseas players becoming 'English' ought to be longer."
Best batting performance: 19 Leicestershire v Warwickshire, Hinckley 1985.

BIRCH, J.D.　　　　　　Nottinghamshire

Full Name: John Dennis Birch.
Role: Right-hand bat, slip fielder.
Born: 18 June 1955, Nottingham.
Height: 6' 1" Weight: 13st.
Nickname: Bonk.
County debut: 1973.
County cap: 1981.
1000 runs in a season: 2.
1st-Class 50s scored: 37.
1st-Class 100s scored: 5.
1st-Class 5 w. in innings: 1.
One-day 50s: 12.
Place in batting averages: 140
average: 25.56; (1984: 105
average: 32.32).
1st-Class catches 1985: 5
(career: 134).
Parents: Bill and Mavis Birch.
Wife and date of marriage: Linda,
23 May 1980.
Children: Nathalie and Daniel (twins), 21 January 1981.
Education: William Crane Bilateral School.
Qualifications: O-levels.
Family links with cricket: Father was a local cricketer.
Jobs outside cricket: Runs a small building firm with a friend and brothers.
Cricketers particularly learnt from: Clive Rice.
Cricketers particularly admired: Clive Rice, Richard Hadlee, Geoffrey Boycott.
Other sports: Playing soccer (player/manager of local team), golf, snooker, and watching any other sports.
Relaxations: "Gardening and fishing."
Extras: "Would like to thank Frank Woodhead for giving me the chance to play for Notts. and all who have helped me at the club."
Best batting performance: 125 Nottinghamshire v Leicestershire, Trent Bridge 1982.
Best bowling performance: 6-64 Nottinghamshire v Hampshire, Bournemouth 1975.

BLACKETT, M.   Leicestershire

Full Name: Mark Blackett.
Role: Right-hand bat, short-leg fielder.
Born: 3 February 1964, Edmonton, Middlesex.
Height: 5' 7" **Weight:** 12st. 7lbs.
Nickname: Little Gatt, Dumpy, Blackers.
County debut: 1985.
Parents: Frederick Albert and Audrey Betty Blackett.
Marital status: Single.
Education: Edmonton County School.
Qualifications: Senior Coaching Award.
Family links with cricket: Father played club cricket.
Jobs outside cricket: Working in sports shop.
Off-season 1985–86: Playing cricket in Sydney, Australia.
Cricketing superstitions: Always put right pad on first.
Cricketers particularly learnt from: Don Wilson, Ken Higgs, Brian Taylor.
Cricketers particularly admired: David Gower, Viv Richards, Chris Balderstone for his professional attitude and approach to the game.
Other sports: Snooker.
Relaxations: Listening to music, playing snooker.

Extras: Spent two years on the M.C.C. ground staff at Lord's (1983–84 seasons) and three years playing for Middlesex 2nds and U-25s (1982–84).
Opinions on cricket: "I feel that politics should in no way interfere with sport."
Best batting performance: 28* Leicestershire v Worcestershire, Leicester 1985.

LAST SEASON: BATTING

	I.	N.O.	R.	H.S.	AV.
TEST					
OTHER FIRST CLASS	4	2	41	28*	20.50
INT					
JPL	3	2	33	21*	–
NAT.W					
B & H					

CAREER: BATTING

	I.	N.O.	R.	H.S.	AV.
TEST					
OTHER FIRST CLASS	4	2	41	28*	20.50
INT					
JPL	3	2	33	21*	–
NAT.W					
B & H					

BLAKEY, R.J.   Yorkshire

Full Name: Richard John Blakey.
Role: Right-hand bat, occasional wicket-keeper.
Born: 15 January 1967, Huddersfield.
Height: 5' 8" **Weight:** 11st.
Nickname: Dick, Mutley.
County debut: 1985.
1st-Class 50s scored: 2.
Place in batting averages: 136 average: 25.90; (1984: — average: —).
1st-Class catches 1985: 12 (career: 12).
Parents: Brian and Pauline.
Marital status: Single.
Education: Rastrick Grammar School.
Qualifications: 4 O-levels.
Off-season 1985–86: In Melbourne, Australia.
Overseas tours: Young England to West Indies 1985.
Cricketers particularly learnt from: My father Brian, Doug Padgett, Steve Oldham.
Other sports: Golf, squash, snooker. Follows Leeds United football.
Relaxations: Music.
Best batting performance: 90 Yorkshire v Somerset, Headingley 1985.

	I.	N.O.	R.	H.S.	AV.
TEST					
OTHER FIRST CLASS	22	2	518	90	25.90
INT					
JPL					
NAT.W					
B & H					

	I.	N.O.	R.	H.S.	AV.
TEST					
OTHER FIRST CLASS	22	2	518	90	25.90
INT					
JPL					
NAT.W					
B & H					

BOON, T.J.   Leicestershire

Full Name: Timothy James Boon.
Role: Right-hand bat.
Born: 1 November 1961, Doncaster, South Yorkshire.
Height: 6' 0" **Weight:** 12st.
Nickname: "Ted Moon, Cod, amongst others."
County debut: 1980.
1000 runs in a season: 1.
1st-Class 50s scored: 9.
1st-Class 100s scored: 4.
Place in batting averages: — average: —; (1984: 52 average: 39.73).
1st-Class catches 1985: 0 (career: 19).
Parents: Jeffrey and Elizabeth.
Marital status: Single.
Education: Mill Lane Primary; Edlington Comprehensive. Three months at Doncaster Art School.
Qualifications: 1 A-level, 6 O-levels. Coaching qualifications.
Family links with cricket: Father played club cricket.
Overseas tours: Toured the Caribbean with England Young Cricketers 1980, as captain; Leicestershire C.C.C. tour of Zimbabwe, March 1981.
Overseas teams played for: Old Hararians, Zimbabwe, 1980–81; Ceylon C.C., Colombo, 1981–82; Pirates C.C., Durban, 1982–83, 1984–85.
Cricketing superstitions: "Constantly changing."
Cricketers particularly learnt from: The late Mike Fearnley, Ken Higgs, Chris Balderstone, Peter Willey.
Other sports: "Enjoy playing and watching all sports."
Relaxations: Sleeping.
Injuries 1985: Missed 1985 season recovering from broken leg sustained in car crash in South Africa in the winter.
Extras: Captain England Young Cricketers Tour West Indies 1980; Captain

England Young Cricketers v Indian Young Cricketers 1981; Most Promising Schoolboy Cricketer 1979.
Best batting performance: 144 Leicestershire v Gloucestershire, Leicester 1984.

LAST SEASON: BATTING

	I.	N.O.	R.	H.S.	AV.
TEST					
OTHER FIRST CLASS					
INT					
JPL					
NAT.W					
B & H					

CAREER: BATTING

	I.	N.O.	R.	H.S.	AV.
TEST					
OTHER FIRST CLASS	100	12	2383	144	27.08
INT					
JPL	30	7	410	48	17.82
NAT.W	3	2	26	22*	–
B & H	3	2	42	36*	–

LAST SEASON: BOWLING

	O.	M.	R.	W.	AV.
TEST					
OTHER FIRST CLASS					
INT					
JPL					
NAT.W					
B & H					

CAREER: BOWLING

	O.	M.	R.	W.	AV.
TEST					
OTHER FIRST CLASS	16	5	57	0	–
INT					
JPL	2	0	14	0	–
NAT.W					
B & H					

BOOTH, P.A. Yorkshire

Full Name: Paul Anthony Booth.
Role: Left-hand bat, slow left-arm bowler.
Born: 5 September 1965, Huddersfield.
Height: 6′ **Weight:** 11st. 4lbs.
Nickname: Boot, Boothy.
County debut: 1982.
Place in bowling averages: — average —; (1984: 126 average 44.06).
1st-Class catches 1985: 2 (career 4).
Parents: Colin and Margaret Booth.
Marital status: Single.
Education: Honley High School.
Qualifications: 2 O-levels.
Family links with cricket: Father has played local cricket at Meltham for more than 30 years and is still playing.
Jobs outside cricket: Carpenter and joiner.
Overseas tours: Young England to West Indies 1985.

Cricketers particularly learnt from: Doug Padgett (county coach).
Other sports: Football and golf.
Extras: Made county debut at 17 years and 3 days, and first championship wicket was that of Allan Lamb. Played for Yorkshire Schools U-15s. Represented County U-19 side which won Oxford and Cambridge Festival 1983.
Opinions on cricket: "(1) Should revert back to uncovered pitches to give more help to the spinners. (2) Would like to see South Africa back in Test cricket. (3) Bring overs down to 105 per day."
Best batting performance: 26 Yorkshire v Worcestershire, Scarborough 1984.
Best bowling performance: 3-22 Yorkshire v Northamptonshire, Northampton 1984.

LAST SEASON: BATTING

	I.	N.O.	R.	H.S.	AV.
TEST					
OTHER FIRST CLASS	2	0	4	4	2.00
INT					
JPL	–	–	–	–	–
NAT.W					
B & H	1	0	1	1	–

CAREER: BATTING

	I.	N.O.	R.	H.S.	AV.
TEST					
OTHER FIRST CLASS	18	4	82	26	5.86
INT					
JPL	–	–	–	–	–
NAT.W	1	1	6	6*	–
B & H	1	0	1	1	–

LAST SEASON: BOWLING

	O.	M.	R.	W.	AV.
TEST					
OTHER FIRST CLASS	117.1	4	288	6	48.00
INT					
JPL	8	0	57	1	–
NAT.W					
B & H	8	0	28	2	14.00

CAREER: BOWLING

	O.	M.	R.	W.	AV.
TEST					
OTHER FIRST CLASS	491.1	134	1109	23	48.22
INT					
JPL	8	0	57	1	–
NAT.W	11	2	33	2	16.50
B & H	8	0	28	2	14.00

17. To whom has Brian Johnston given the nickname "Arl"?

18. Which Australian Test cricketer who played in the Bodyline series said, "Bodyline apart, I consider Jardine the most efficient, scientific and shrewdest Test captain I played with or against."?

BOOTH, S.C. Somerset

Full Name: Stephen Charles Booth.
Role: Right-hand bat, slow left-arm bowler.
Born: 30 October 1963, Leeds.
Height: 5' 9" **Weight:** 10st. 7lbs.
Nickname: Boothby, Heathcliffe, Eh-up.
County debut: 1983.
Place in batting averages: 116 average: 15.60; (1984: 249 average: 14.29).
Place in bowling averages: 104 average: 40.64; (1984: 69 average: 30.84).
1st-Class catches 1985: 13 (career: 33).
Parents: Eric and Kathleen Booth.
Wife and date of marriage: Jane, 20 October 1984.

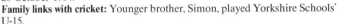

Family links with cricket: Younger brother, Simon, played Yorkshire Schools' U-15.
Education: Boston Spa Comprehensive.
Qualifications: 6 O-levels.
Off-season 1985–86: Working in Taunton.
Cricketing superstitions: Always puts left pad on first (more through habit).
Cricketers particularly learnt from: Don Wilson, Andy Wagner.
Cricketers particularly admired: "Admire anyone who's played first-class cricket."
Other sports: Football (tries any sport).

LAST SEASON: BATTING

	I.	N.O.	R.	H.S.	AV.
TEST					
OTHER FIRST CLASS	8	3	78	28	15.60
INT					
JPL					
NAT.W					
B & H					

CAREER: BATTING

	I.	N.O.	R.	H.S.	AV.
TEST					
OTHER FIRST CLASS	34	15	202	42	10.63
INT					
JPL					
NAT.W					
B & H					

LAST SEASON: BOWLING

	O.	M.	R.	W.	AV.
TEST					
OTHER FIRST CLASS	390.2	112	1138	28	40.64
INT					
JPL					
NAT.W					
B & H					

CAREER: BOWLING

	O.	M.	R.	W.	AV.
TEST					
OTHER FIRST CLASS	1085.2	314	3159	87	36.31
INT					
JPL					
NAT.W					
B & H					

Extras: Had spleen removed after a football accident in 1982. Released by Yorkshire to take up contract with Somerset.
Opinions on cricket: "Championship should be made into 16 4-day games."
Best batting performance: 42 Somerset v Derbyshire, Taunton 1984.
Best bowling performance: 4-26 Somerset v Middlesex, Lord's 1983.

BOTHAM, I.T. Somerset

Full Name: Ian Terrence Botham.
Role: Right-hand bat, right-arm fast-medium bowler, slip fielder.
Born: 24 November 1955, Heswall, Cheshire.
Height: 6' 1" **Weight:** 14st. 7lbs.
Nickname: Guy the Gorilla, Both.
County debut: 1974.
County cap: 1976.
Benefit: 1984 (£90,822).
Test debut: 1977.
No. of Tests: 79.
No. of One-Day Internationals: 75.
1000 runs in a season: 4.
50 wickets in a season: 7.
1st-Class 50s scored: 64.
1st-Class 100s scored: 27.
1st-Class 200s scored: 2.
1st-Class 5 w. in innings: 50.
1st-Class 10 w. in match: 7.
One-day 50s: 23.

One-day 100s: 2.
Place in batting averages: 4 average: 69.54; (1984: 109 average: 31.88).
Place in bowling averages: 58 average: 31.27; (1984: 38 average: 26.47).
1st-Class catches 1985: 17 (career 246).
Parents: Les and Marie Botham.
Wife and date of marriage: Kathryn, 31 January 1976.
Children: Liam James, 26 August 1977; Sarah Lianne, 3 February 1979; Rebecca Kate, 13 November 1985.
Education: Millford Junior School, Yeovil; Buckler's Mead Secondary School, Yeovil.
Jobs outside cricket: Representative for father-in-law's company, Promuco.
Family links with cricket: Father played for Navy and Fleet Air Arm; mother played for V.A.D. nursing staff.
Overseas tours: Pakistan and New Zealand 1977–78; Australia 1978–79;

Australia and India 1979–80: West Indies 1981, as Captain; India 1981–82; Australia and New Zealand 1982–83.

Cricketers particularly learnt from: "Admired Gary Sobers."

Off season 1985–86: Walking from John O'Groats to Land's End to raise money for Leukaemia Research and on tour to West Indies with England.

Cricket records: Holds record for having scored 1000 runs and taken 100 wickets in fewest Test matches. First player to score a century and take 8 wickets in an innings in a Test Match, v Pakistan at Lord's in 1978. Most sixes in a first-class season and most instances of 5 wickets in a Test innings (both 1985). Leading wicket-taker for England in Tests.

Other sports: Captained school soccer team, and has played for Scunthorpe United, making debut as striker v Bournemouth in March 1980. Offered terms by Crystal Palace. Now plays for Yeovil Town. U-16 Somerset champion, badminton doubles.

Relaxations: "Time with my family"; golf (handicap 11), shooting, fishing (salmon and trout). First president of Clubworld Angling. Musical taste includes Rolling Stones and Rod Stewart. Has learned to fly. Racing, owns his own horses.

Extras: Captain of England 1980–81. Took five Australian wickets in his first day of Test Match cricket aged 21. Played for County 2nd XI 1971. On M.C.C. staff 1972–73. Played for county in last two John Player League matches 1973. Honorary townsman of Epworth, South Humberside, where he lives, and Freeman of Yeovil, Somerset. Subject of "This is Your Life" television programme in November 1981. Was Best Man at Viv Richards' wedding in March 1981 in Antigua. Published *The Incredible Tests 1981.* Voted BBC TV Sportsview Sporting Personality of 1981. Having a go at baseball in Los Angeles in September 1981 easily exceeded the striking rate of established American baseball stars: he complained that Americans could not pitch the ball fast enough. Scored fastest 100 of 1982 and 1985 seasons. Scored 200 in 272 minutes for England v India at The Oval, 9 July 1982, third fastest Test century

LAST SEASON: BATTING

	I.	N.O.	R.	H.S.	AV.
TEST	8	0	250	85	31.25
OTHER FIRST CLASS	19	5	1280	152	91.43
INT	2	0	101	72	50.50
JPL	8	2	238	58	39.66
NAT.W	2	0	101	64	50.50
B & H	3	0	116	48	38.67

CAREER: BATTING

	I.	N.O.	R.	H.S.	AV.
TEST	125	3	4409	208	36.14
OTHER FIRST CLASS	289	28	9028	228	34.59
INT	66	8	1248	72	21.52
JPL	117	18	2854	106	28.83
NAT.W	28	6	825	96*	37.50
B & H	44	6	842	57*	22.16

LAST SEASON: BOWLING

	O.	M.	R.	W.	AV.
TEST	251.4	36	855	31	27.58
OTHER FIRST CLASS	154.4	28	521	13	40.08
INT	29	5	106	4	26.50
JPL	46.5	1	215	12	17.91
NAT.W	31	2	120	1	–
B & H	41.5	9	147	5	29.40

CAREER: BOWLING

	O.	M.	R.	W.	AV.
TEST	259.4 2719.1	42 631	9046	343	26.37
OTHER FIRST CLASS	190.3 6837.4	43 1584	13911	553	25.16
INT	38.7 604.1	2 77	2639	100	26.39
JPL	859.1	53	3729	164	22.73
NAT.W	341.3	56	1162	41	28.34
B & H	526	102	1783	81	22.01

by an Englishman, after Walter Hammond (240 mins, v New Zealand in 1932) and Denis Compton (245 mins. v Pakistan in 1954). Crashed two £12,000 sports cars at 100 m.p.h. in same afternoon in May 1982. Among the books he chose to take to a desert island was Jack Fingleton's book on the great Australian cricketer *The Immortal Victor Trumper*. First cricketer since W.G. Grace to have painting commissioned by National Portrait Gallery.

Best batting performance: 228 Somerset v Gloucestershire, Taunton 1980.
Best bowling performance: 8-34 England v Pakistan, Lord's 1978.

BOYCOTT, G. Yorkshire

Full Name: Geoffrey Boycott.
Role: Right-hand opening bat, right-arm medium bowler.
Born: 21 October 1940, Fitzwilliam, Yorkshire.
Height: 5′ 10″ **Weight:** 11st. 7lbs.
Nickname: Fiery or Boycs (or Thatch, "but only from Ian Botham").
County debut: 1962.
County cap: 1963.
Benefit: 1974 (£20,639).
Test debut: 1964.
No. of Tests: 108 (Captain in 4).
No. of One-Day Internationals: 36.
1000 runs in a season: 23.
1st-Class 50s scored: 230.
1st-Class 100s scored: 139.
1st-Class 200s scored: 10.

One-day 50s: 70.
One-day 100s: 7.
Place in batting averages: 2 average: 75.32; (1984: 8 average: 62.68).
1st-Class catches 1985: 10 (career: 260).
Marital status: Single.
Education: Hemsworth Grammar School
Qualifications: 7 O-levels.
Jobs outside cricket: Was civil servant, worked for Yorkshire Electricity Board.
Family links with cricket: Brothers Peter and Tony both play cricket, but father did not play at all.
Overseas tours: South Africa 1964–65; Australia, New Zealand 1965–66 and 1970–71, returning home early with broken arm; West Indies 1967–68 and 1973–74; Pakistan and New Zealand 1977–78 as Vice-Captain; Australia 1978–79 and 1979–80, West Indies 1981, India 1981–82.

Overseas teams played for: Northern Transvaal 1971–72.

Players particularly learnt from: "At the start of every season and before I go on tour I visit Johnny Lawrence who has coached me since I was nine years old."

Other sports: Golf, tennis.

Relaxations: Reading, theatre, cinema. Watching television programmes (thrillers). Enjoys classical ballet — "I don't understand modern ballet". Favourite reading includes World Wildlife Fund magazines. "I am a member of the Fund because I believe strongly that we should conserve nature. To me, life, whether human or animal is precious. I've been to most of the major game parks in Africa. They are marvellous places to visit."

Extras: Finished top of the batting averages 1971 with an average of 100.12, the only English batsman ever to have an average of over 100 for a season. Repeated 1979 with average of 102.53. Captained Hemsworth Grammar School and the local Schools XI; at 13, played for Ackworth in Yorkshire Council League; at 15, played for Yorkshire Schoolboys' and Barnsley. Before playing for Yorkshire for first time at age 21, he was top of batting averages for Leeds, Yorkshire Colts and Yorkshire 2nd XI. Plays in contact lenses. Wears cap when bowling. Scored two centuries in a match (103 and 105) v Notts. at Sheffield in 1966, and 160 n. o. and 116 for England v the Rest at Worcester in 1974. On exhibition at Madame Tussaud's. Bowled in the Lord's Test v West Indies 1980 wearing his cap back to front. Awarded O.B.E. in 1980. Rarely drinks alcohol. Published *Put to the Test*, 1979; *Opening Up*, 1980; *In the Fast Lane*, 1981 and *Master Class*, 1982. Also *Geoffrey Boycott's Book for Young Cricketers*. Banned from Test cricket for three years in 1982 for playing for an England XI in South Africa. Elected to Yorkshire committee in 1984, the sixth man to serve with the club as player and committee member.

Best batting performance: 261* M.C.C. v Presidents XI, Bridgetown 1973–74.

Best bowling performance: 4–14 Yorkshire v Lancashire, Leeds 1979.

LAST SEASON: BATTING

	I.	N.O.	R.	H.S.	AV.
TEST					
OTHER FIRST CLASS	34	12	1657	184	75.32
INT					
JPL	2	0	45	38	22.50
NAT.W	2	1	94	70*	–
B & H					

CAREER: BATTING

	I.	N.O.	R.	H.S.	AV.
TEST	193	23	8114	246*	47.73
OTHER FIRST CLASS	801	138	39320	261*	59.31
INT	34	4	1082	105	36.06
JPL	157	24	5051	108*	37.97
NAT.W	38	4	1347	146	39.62
B & H	53	8	1970	142	43.78

LAST SEASON: BOWLING

	O.	M.	R.	W.	AV.
TEST					
OTHER FIRST CLASS	10	2	29	0	–
INT					
JPL	3	0	12	0	–
NAT.W					
B & H					

CAREER: BOWLING

	O.	M.	R.	W.	AV.
TEST	28 120.3	4 41	382	7	54.57
OTHER FIRST CLASS	28.4 434.2	2 134	1067	38	28.08
INT	28	1	105	5	21.00
JPL	151.5	11	611	14	43.64
NAT.W	78	15	238	8	29.75
B & H	63	4	227	2	113.5

BOYD-MOSS, R.J. Northamptonshire

Full Name: Robin James Boyd-Moss.
Role: Right-hand bat, slow left-arm bowler.
Born: 16 December 1959, Hatton, Sri Lanka.
Height: 5' 10" **Weight:** 12st. 9lbs.
Nickname: Mossy, Mouse.
County debut: 1980.
1000 runs in a season: 2.
1st-Class 50s scored: 32.
1st-Class 100s scored: 11.
1st-Class 5 w. in innings: 1.
One-day 50s: 6.
Place in batting averages: 129 average: 27.36; (1984: 121 average: 30.17).
Place in bowling averages: 92 average: 38.00; (1984: — average: —).
1st-Class catches 1985: 6 (career: 51).
Parents: Michael and Shelagh Boyd-Moss.
Marital status: Married December 1985.
Education: Bedford School; Cambridge University.
Qualifications: 3 A-levels. B.A. in Land Economy.
Off-season 1985–86: Coaching/teaching in Kenya.
Other sports: Rugby football. Played centre for Cambridge v Oxford in 100th Varsity Match. Double Blue. Golf, squash.
Relaxations: Wildlife, photography.
Injuries 1985: Back injury.

LAST SEASON: BATTING

	I.	N.O.	R.	H.S.	AV.
TEST					
OTHER FIRST CLASS	31	3	766	121	27.36
INT					
JPL	6	0	98	51	16.33
NAT.W	2	0	62	51	31.00
B & H					

CAREER: BATTING

	I.	N.O.	R.	H.S.	AV.
TEST					
OTHER FIRST CLASS	202	16	5658	139	30.62
INT					
JPL	38	4	766	99	22.52
NAT.W	7	2	207	88*	41.40
B & H	15	0	215	58	14.33

LAST SEASON: BOWLING

	O.	M.	R.	W.	AV.
TEST					
OTHER FIRST CLASS	125.4	30	380	10	38.00
INT					
JPL					
NAT.W	12	1	47	3	15.67
B & H					

CAREER: BOWLING

	O.	M.	R.	W.	AV.
TEST					
OTHER FIRST CLASS	537.4	124	1879	43	43.70
INT					
JPL					
NAT.W	12	1	47	3	15.67
B & H	12	1	49	0	–

Best batting performance: 139 Cambridge University v Oxford University, Lord's 1983.
Best bowling performance: 5-27 Cambridge University v Oxford University, Lord's 1983.

BRASSINGTON, A.J.   Gloucestershire

Full Name: Andrew James Brassington.
Role: Right-hand bat, wicket-keeper.
Born: 9 August 1954, Bagnall, Stoke-on-Trent.
Height: 6' **Weight:** 11st. 9lbs.
Nickname: Imma.
County debut: 1974.
County cap: 1978.
Parents: Joan Ursula and John Reginald.
Wife and date of marriage: Rosalyn, 26 February 1977.
Children: Emma Louisa.
Education: Endon Secondary Modern.
Qualifications: 6 C.S.E.s.
Jobs outside cricket: Salesman and promotional work.
Overseas tours: To Malawi with Gloucestershire, 1978.
Cricketers particularly learnt from: Bob Taylor.

LAST SEASON: BATTING

	I.	N.O.	R.	H.S.	AV.
TEST					
OTHER FIRST CLASS	2	2	3	3*	–
INT					
JPL	–	–	–	–	–
NAT.W					
B & H					

CAREER: BATTING

	I.	N.O.	R.	H.S.	AV.
TEST					
OTHER FIRST CLASS	155	46	881	35	8.08
INT					
JPL	21	12	93	14*	10.33
NAT.W	1	0	20	20	–
B & H	7	2	21	9	4.20

LAST SEASON: WICKET KEEPING

	C.	ST.			
TEST					
OTHER FIRST CLASS	6	–			
INT					
JPL	–	1			
NAT.W					
B & H					

CAREER: WICKET KEEPING

	C.	ST.			
TEST					
OTHER FIRST CLASS	215	48			
INT					
JPL	33	9			
NAT.W	3	–			
B & H	8	2			

Cricketers particularly admired: Alan Knott, Bob Taylor, Greg Chappell, Rod Marsh, Viv Richards, Mike Procter.
Other sports: Football (goalkeeper) and follows football and rugby.
Relaxations: Watching TV, playing Scrabble and music.
Best batting performance: 35 Gloucestershire v Sussex, Hastings 1982.

BRIERS, N.E. — Leicestershire

Full Name: Nigel Edwin Briers.
Role: Right-hand bat, right-arm medium bowler, cover fielder.
Born: 15 January 1955, Leicester.
Height: 6′ 0″ **Weight:** 12st. 5lbs.
Nickname: Kudu.
County debut: 1971, aged 16 yrs 104 days.
County cap: 1981.
1000 runs in a season: 3.
1st-Class 50s scored: 31.
1st-Class 100s scored: 9.
1st-Class 200s scored: 1.
One-day 50s: 23.
One-day 100s: 3.
Place in batting averages: 166 average: 23.04; (1984: 215 average: 18.12).
Place in bowling averages: — average: —; (1984: 13 average: 22.00).
1st-Class catches 1985: 7 (career: 75).
Parents: Leonard Arthur Roger and Eveline Briers.
Wife and date of marriage: Suzanne Mary Tudor, 3 September 1977.
Children: Michael Edward Tudor, 25 March 1983.
Education: Lutterworth Grammar School; Borough Road College.
Qualifications: B.Ed. Hons., M.C.C. Advanced Coach.
Jobs outside cricket: Lecturer in Physical Education at Leicester Polytechnic.
Off-season 1985–86: Teaching P.E. at Ludgrove School.
Family links with cricket: Father was captain and wicket-keeper of Narborough and Littlethorpe Cricket Club, first division of Leicestershire League, for 15 years. Mother was scorer for team. Father was Captain of South Leicestershire Representative XI and played for the Royal Marines in the same team as Trevor Bailey. Cousin, Norman Briers, played for Leicestershire in 1967.
Overseas tours: Toured South America with Derrick Robins XI in 1978–79; M.C.C. tour to the Far East 1981; toured Zimbabwe with Leicestershire 1981.

Cricketers particularly learnt from: Maurice Hallam, Jack Birkenshaw and Ray Illingworth. Admires Barry Richards.
Other sports: Rugby, basketball, squash, hockey.
Extras: Former Captain of England Young Cricketers, England Schoolboys and British Colleges XI. Record 5th wicket partnership for Leicestershire of 233 with R.W. Tolchard v Somerset at Leicester in 1979. Youngest player to appear for Leicestershire at 16 years, 104 days. Captain 1985 when Gower and Willey on Test duty.
Best batting performance: 201* Leicestershire v Warwickshire, Edgbaston 1983.
Best bowling performance: 4–29 Leicestershire v Derbyshire, Leicester 1985.

LAST SEASON: BATTING

	I.	N.O.	R.	H.S.	AV.
TEST					
OTHER FIRST CLASS	29	4	576	129	23.04
INT					
JPL	14	4	359	77	35.90
NAT.W	2	1	58	31*	–
B & H	4	0	32	19	8.00

CAREER: BATTING

	I.	N.O.	R.	H.S.	AV.
TEST					
OTHER FIRST CLASS	294	30	7248	201*	27.46
INT					
JPL	107	16	3137	119*	34.47
NAT.W	17	2	291	59	19.40
B & H	26	2	384	71*	16.00

LAST SEASON: BOWLING

	O.	M.	R.	W.	AV.
TEST					
OTHER FIRST CLASS	85.4	18	303	8	37.88
INT					
JPL	3	0	20	0	–
NAT.W	2	0	8	1	–
B & H					

CAREER: BOWLING

	O.	M.	R.	W.	AV.
TEST					
OTHER FIRST CLASS	318.5	69	910	30	30.33
INT					
JPL	59.2	5	268	9	29.77
NAT.W	14	0	75	6	12.50
B & H	38	3	183	2	91.50

BROAD, B.C.   Nottinghamshire

Full Name: Brian Christopher Broad.
Role: Left-hand bat, right-arm medium bowler, outfielder.
Born: 29 September 1957, Bristol.
Height: 6′ 4″ **Weight:** 14st. 7lbs.
Nickname: Norfolk, Wally, Beena, Jessie.
County debut: 1979 (Gloucester-shire), 1984 (Nottinghamshire).
County cap: 1981 (Gloucester-shire), 1984 (Nottinghamshire).
Test debut: 1984.
No. of Tests: 5.
1000 runs in a season: 5.
1st-Class 50s scored: 50.
1st-Class 100s scored: 11.
One-day 50s: 20.

One-day 100s: 1.
Place in batting averages: 45 average; 40.59: (1984: 32 average: 44.50).
1st-Class catches 1985: 15 (career: 60).
Parents: Nancy and Kenneth Broad.
Wife and date of marriage: Carole Ann, 14 July 1979.
Education: Colston's School, Bristol; St Paul's College, Cheltenham.
Qualifications: 5 O-levels. N.C.A. advanced coach.
Jobs outside cricket: Floor laying, lorry loading.
Family links with cricket: Father and grandfather both played local cricket. Father member of Gloucestershire Committee until retired; father on T.C.C.B. development sub-committee.
Overseas tours: Gloucestershire C.C.C. tour of Malawi 1978 and Barbados 1980; British Colleges to Trinidad and Barbados 1979.
Other sports: Played rugby for English Colleges, Bristol United, St Paul's College, and now plays for Clifton.
Relaxations: "Playing any sport, watching TV with my wife. Running a mail order jewellery business."
Extras: Ended 1979 with a century (129) in last match for Gloucs. v Northants., and hit a century (120) for Gloucs. v Oxford University in first match of 1980. With Gloucestershire 1979–83 (cap 1981).
Best batting performance: 171 Nottinghamshire v Derbyshire, Derby 1985.
Best bowling performance: 2-14 Gloucestershire v West Indies, Bristol 1980.

LAST SEASON: BATTING

	I.	N.O.	R.	H.S.	AV.
TEST					
OTHER FIRST CLASS	47	3	1786	171	40.59
INT					
JPL	15	1	417	69	29.78
NAT.W	5	0	142	64	28.40
B & H	4	0	88	70	22.00

CAREER: BATTING

	I.	N.O.	R.	H.S.	AV.
TEST	9	0	281	86	31.22
OTHER FIRST CLASS	241	18	8607	171	38.60
INT					
JPL	77	1	2069	96	27.22
NAT.W	13	0	416	98	32.00
B & H	25	0	605	122	24.20

LAST SEASON: BOWLING

	O.	M.	R.	W.	AV.
TEST					
OTHER FIRST CLASS	15.3	3	58	3	19.33
INT					
JPL					
NAT.W					
B & H					

CAREER: BOWLING

	O.	M.	R.	W.	AV.
TEST					
OTHER FIRST CLASS	233.5	56	845	16	52.81
INT					
JPL	111.3	4	602	19	31.68
NAT.W					
B & H	50.4	2	282	5	56.40

19. For whom did Test umpire H.D. Bird play first-class cricket?

20. Who wrote the school cricket novel *Mike*?

BROWN, A.M.   Derbyshire

Full Name: Andrew Mark Brown.
Role: Left-hand opening bat, off-break bowler ("very occasionally"), cover fielder.
Born: 6 November 1964, Heanor, Derbyshire.
Height: 5′ 9″ **Weight:** 10st.
Nickname: Brownie.
County debut: 1985.
1st-Class 50s scored: 1.
1st-Class catches 1985: 3 (career: 3).
Parents: John Derek and Marion Brown.
Marital status: Single.
Education: Aldercar Comprehensive, South-East Derbyshire College of F.E.
Qualifications: 8 O-levels, 1 A-level, N.C.A. Coaching Certificate.
Off-season 1985–86: Coaching and playing in Hawkes Bay, New Zealand.
Overseas teams played for: Pukekohe C.C. and Counties Association 1983–84, New Zealand; Old Boys Hastings and Hawkes Bay Association 1984–85, New Zealand.
Family links with cricket: Father is County Coaching Organiser for Derbyshire and was also a good league player. Brother Stephen played for Derbyshire U-13 – U-19. Sister Helen played for club junior boys' sides.
Cricketers particularly learnt from: My father John, John Wright, John Wiltshire.
Cricketers particularly admired: John Wright, Geoff Boycott, Dennis Lillee.
Other sports: "Football, tennis (very badly). Follow football and most other sports but I don't like wrestling."
Relaxations: Enjoys watching Nottingham Forest play, listening to music, playing computer games.
Extras: Made senior debut in J.P.L. game against Nottinghamshire at Heanor only about 200 yards from where he was born.
Opinions on cricket: "A championship of 16 4-day games might be a good idea. Playing one-day games at the weekend, this would take a lot of the strain off

LAST SEASON: BATTING	I.	N.O.	R.	H.S.	AV.
TEST					
OTHER FIRST CLASS	3	0	93	74	31.00
INT					
JPL	1	1	2	2*	–
NAT.W					
B & H					

CAREER: BATTING	I.	N.O.	R.	H.S.	AV.
TEST					
OTHER FIRST CLASS	3	0	93	74	31.00
INT					
JPL	1	1	2	2*	–
NAT.W					
B & H					

quick bowlers and then we might produce a few more home-grown quick bowlers, if we only play a maximum of six days a week."
Best batting performance: 74 Derbyshire v Warwickshire, Chesterfield 1985.

BROWN, K.R. Middlesex

Full Name: Keith Robert Brown.
Role: Right-hand bat, wicket-keeper.
Born: 18 March 1963, Edmonton.
Height: 5′ 11″ **Weight:** 13st.
Nickname: Browny, Gloves.
County debut: 1984.
1st-Class 50s scored: 1.
1st-Class 100s scored: 1.
Place in batting averages: 84
average: 33.11; (1984: —
average: —).
1st-Class catches 1985: 8 (career: 9).
Parents: Kenneth William and
Margaret Sonia.
Wife and date of marriage: Marie,
3 November 1984.
Family links with cricket: Brother
Gary is on Middlesex staff as well.
Education: Chace Boys' School.
Jobs outside cricket: Plasterer, light engineering.
Cricketing superstitions: "None, but it's nice to get off the mark. I bite my gloves when keeping."

LAST SEASON: BATTING

	I.	N.O.	R.	H.S.	AV.
TEST					
OTHER FIRST CLASS	11	2	298	102	33.11
INT					
JPL	3	0	58	33	19.33
NAT.W					
B & H					

CAREER: BATTING

	I.	N.O.	R.	H.S.	AV.
TEST					
OTHER FIRST CLASS	12	2	304	102	30.40
INT					
JPL	3	0	58	33	19.33
NAT.W					
B & H					

LAST SEASON: BOWLING

	O.	M.	R.	W.	AV.
TEST					
OTHER FIRST CLASS					
INT					
JPL					
NAT.W					
B & H					

CAREER: BOWLING

	O.	M.	R.	W.	AV.
TEST					
OTHER FIRST CLASS	1	1	0	0	–
INT					
JPL					
NAT.W					
B & H					

Overseas tours: N.C.A. tour to Denmark in 1981. Played for South of England.

Cricketers particularly learnt from: Father and Don Bennett (county coach).

Cricketers particularly admired: Clive Radley — admires his approach to the game and never say die attitude.

Other sports: Rugby, golf, tennis, snooker, but follows all of them.

Relaxations: Playing snooker and drinking a pint of best bitter.

Extras: Had promising boxing career but gave it up in order to concentrate on cricket.

Best batting performance: 102 Middlesex v Australia, Lord's 1985.

BULLEN, C.K.   Surrey

Full Name: Christopher Keith Bullen.

Role: Right-hand bat, off-break bowler, slip fielder.

Born: 5 November 1962, Clapham, London.

Height: 6' 5" **Weight:** 14st.

Nickname: CB, Jasper, Bullo.

County debut: 1985.

1st-Class catches 1985: 2 (career: 2).

Parents: Keith Thomas and Joan Bullen.

Marital status: Single.

Education: Glenbrook Primary; Chaucer Middle; Rutlish School.

Qualifications: 6 O-levels.

Family links with cricket: Parents are enthusiastic cricket watchers.

Jobs outside cricket: Worked on a building site — winter.

Off-season 1985–86: Playing in Perth, Australia, for Claremont Cottesloe.

Overseas tours: Surrey Schools U-19 tour to Australia winter 1980–81.

Overseas teams played for: Claremont Cottesloe, Perth, 1984–85.

Cricketing superstitions: Always puts left things on first, i.e. socks, shoes, batting gloves.

Cricketers particularly learnt from: Micky Stewart, Geoff Arnold.

Cricketers particularly admired: Pat Pocock, Jim Laker.

Other sports: Golf, soccer. Watches rugby.

Injuries 1985: Torn ankle ligaments.

Relaxations: Listening to music, leisurely walk after a golf ball.

Extras: Spends free time playing cricket for club Wimbledon who won the league and cup for the second successive year.

Opinions on cricket matters: "County games should be played over four days; limit of one overseas player only per county."
Best batting performance: 19 Surrey v Gloucestershire, The Oval 1985.
Best bowling performance: 2-36 Surrey v Cambridge University, Cambridge 1985.

LAST SEASON: BATTING

	I.	N.O.	R.	H.S.	AV.
TEST					
OTHER FIRST CLASS	4	0	53	19	13.25
INT					
JPL	2	0	19	10	9.50
NAT.W					
B & H					

CAREER: BATTING

	I.	N.O.	R.	H.S.	AV.
TEST					
OTHER FIRST CLASS	4	0	53	19	13.25
INT					
JPL	2	0	19	10	9.50
NAT.W					
B & H					

LAST SEASON: BOWLING

	O.	M.	R.	W.	AV.
TEST					
OTHER FIRST CLASS	28	11	75	2	37.50
INT					
JPL	6	0	35	0	–
NAT.W					
B & H					

CAREER: BOWLING

	O.	M.	R.	W.	AV.
TEST					
OTHER FIRST CLASS	37	11	104	2	52.00
INT					
JPL	6	0	35	0	–
NAT.W					
B & H					

BUTCHER, A.R. Surrey

Full Name: Alan Raymond Butcher.
Role: Left-hand bat, slow left-arm and medium bowler.
Born: 7 January 1954, Croydon, Surrey.
Height: 5' 8" **Weight:** 11st. 7lbs.
Nickname: Butch, Budgie.
County debut: 1972.
County cap: 1975.
Test debut: 1979.
No. of Tests: 1.
No. of One-Day Internationals: 1.
1000 runs in a season: 7.
1st-Class 50s scored: 66.
1st-Class 100s scored: 27.
1st-Class 200s scored: 1.
1st-Class 5 w. in innings: 1.
One-day 50s: 36.
One-day 100s: 4.

Place in batting averages: 87 average: 32.72; (1984: 59 average: 38.24).
Place in bowling averages: 122 average: 44.90; (1984: — average: —).

1st-Class catches 1985: 12 (career: 126).
Parents: Raymond and Jackie Butcher.
Wife and date of marriage: Elaine, 27 September 1972.
Children: Mark, Gary, Lisa.
Education: Heath Clark Grammar School.
Qualifications: 5 O-levels, 1 A-level.
Jobs outside cricket: Football coach, physical education master, Cumnor House School, South Croydon, Surrey.
Family links with cricket: Brother, Martin, M.C.C. Young Professionals. Brother, Ian, joined Leicestershire, 1979, debut v Surrey in John Player League.
Other sports: Football.
Relaxations: Most sport, rock music, reading.
Extras: Scored a century before lunch v Glamorgan at The Oval, 1980.
Best batting performance: 216 Surrey v Cambridge University, Cambridge 1980.
Best bowling performance: 6-48 Surrey v Hampshire, Guildford 1972.

LAST SEASON: BATTING

	I.	N.O.	R.	H.S.	AV.
TEST					
OTHER FIRST CLASS	46	3	1407	126	32.72
INT					
JPL	12	2	383	81*	38.30
NAT.W	1	0	18	18	–
B & H	4	0	94	56	23.50

CAREER: BATTING

	I.	N.O.	R.	H.S.	AV.
TEST	2	0	34	20	17.00
OTHER FIRST CLASS	463	43	14066	216*	33.49
INT	1	0	14	14	–
JPL	153	17	3950	113*	29.04
NAT.W	22	3	550	86*	28.95
B & H	47	4	1077	80	25.05

LAST SEASON: BOWLING

	O.	M.	R.	W.	AV.
TEST					
OTHER FIRST CLASS	156	35	449	10	44.90
INT					
JPL	37	1	181	7	25.85
NAT.W	4	0	26	0	–
B & H	13	2	38	4	9.50

CAREER: BOWLING

	O.	M.	R.	W.	AV.
TEST	2	0	9	0	–
OTHER FIRST CLASS	1404.2	288	4494	113	39.77
INT					
JPL	303	22	1349	32	42.15
NAT.W	48.2	7	192	3	64.00
B & H	161.3	28	484	22	22.00

21. Which great fast bowler had the nickname "Fot"?

22. For which Australian state does Alan Border play?

23. For which English county did Greg Chappell play?

24. Which is the oldest of the Chappell brothers, Greg, Trevor or Ian?

BUTCHER, I.P. — Leicestershire

Full Name: Ian Paul Butcher.
Role: Right-hand bat, slip fielder.
Born: 1 July 1962, Farnborough, Kent.
Height: 6' 0" **Weight:** 13st. 7lbs.
Nickname: Butch, Dog.
County debut: 1980.
County cap: 1984.
1000 runs in a season: 2.
1st-Class 50s scored: 15.
1st-Class 100s scored: 9.
One-day 50s: 5.
One-day 100s: 1.
Place in batting averages: 83
average: 33.11; (1984: 97
average: 32.90).
1st-Class catches 1985: 20
(career: 61).

Parents: Ray and Jackie Butcher.
Wife and date of marriage: Marie, 12 March 1983.
Education: John Ruskin High School.
Jobs outside cricket: Football coach, Cumnor House School, South Croydon.
Family links with cricket: Brother, Alan, Surrey C.C.C. and England. Brother, Martin, M.C.C. Young Pros.
Overseas tours: England Young Cricketers tour of West Indies 1980.
Cricket superstitions: " I have many! . . . If I score runs I like to do everything (if possible) the same, the following day. I always wear a sweatband on left wrist while batting."

LAST SEASON: BATTING

	I.	N.O.	R.	H.S.	AV.
TEST					
OTHER FIRST CLASS	39	3	1192	120	33.11
INT					
JPL	11	0	152	48	13.81
NAT.W	2	0	43	31	21.50
B & H	7	0	313	101	44.72

CAREER: BATTING

	I.	N.O.	R.	H.S.	AV.
TEST					
OTHER FIRST CLASS	122	8	3752	139	32.91
INT					
JPL	42	2	743	71	18.57
NAT.W	6	0	170	81	28.33
B & H	11	0	439	101	39.91

LAST SEASON: BOWLING

	O.	M.	R.	W.	AV.
TEST					
OTHER FIRST CLASS	2	1	5	0	–
INT					
JPL	1	0	4	0	–
NAT.W	0.3	0	6	1	–
B & H					

CAREER: BOWLING

	O.	M.	R.	W.	AV.
TEST					
OTHER FIRST CLASS	6	2	20	1	–
INT					
JPL	1	0	4	0	–
NAT.W	0.3	0	6	1	–
B & H					

Off-season 1985–86: Playing football, and Asst. Sports Director, Leicester University.
Cricketers particularly learnt from: Brian Davison, Graham Gooch and Chris Balderstone.
Other sports: Football, golf. "Try my hand at anything!"
Relaxations: Sleeping, good beer, good food.
Extras: Made his debut for Leicestershire C.C.C. in the John Player League 1979 v Surrey, the team for which his brother, Alan Butcher, plays. Made his county debut 1980 v Oxford University. Scored century on championship debut at Grace Road.
Best batting performance: 139 Leicestershire v Nottinghamshire, Leicester 1983.

BUTCHER, R.O. Middlesex

Full Name: Roland Orlando Butcher.
Role: Right-hand bat, right-arm medium bowler.
Born: 14 October 1953, East Point, St Philip, Barbados.
Height: 5′ 7″ **Weight:** 12st.
Nickname: Butch.
County debut: 1974.
County cap: 1979.
Test debut: 1980–81.
No. of Tests: 3.
No. of One-Day Internationals: 3.
1000 runs in a season: 3.
1st-Class 50s scored: 51.
1st-Class 100s scored: 13.
One-day 50s: 19.
One-day 100s: 1.
Place in batting averages: 56

average: 37.81; (1984: 50 average: 40.18).
1st-Class catches 1985: 24 (career: 229).
Parents: Robert and Doreen Butcher.
Wife: Cheryl Denise Butcher.
Children: Paul Nicholas Roland, 2 January 1979; Michelle Denise, 11 November 1982.
Education: Secondary.
Qualifications: Advanced Cricket Coaching Certificate, Football Association Preliminary Coaching Certificate.
Jobs outside cricket: Coaching. Played semi-professional soccer for Biggleswade and Stevenage. Football coach. Insurance salesman.

Family links with cricket: Cousin is Basil Butcher, of Guyana and West Indies.

Overseas teams played for: Played for Barbados 1974–75 Shell Shield Competition. Spent 1979-80 off season playing cricket in Barbados.

Other sports: Football.

Relaxations: Television, horse-racing, cinema.

Extras: Arrived in England aged 13. Does work for Inter-Action Group in deprived areas of London. A devout member of the Anglican church.

Best batting performance: 197 Middlesex v Yorkshire, Lord's 1982.

LAST SEASON: BATTING

	I.	N.O.	R.	H.S.	AV.
TEST					
OTHER FIRST CLASS	38	6	1210	120	37.81
INT					
JPL	12	1	213	49	19.36
NAT.W	2	0	61	59	30.50
B & H	4	0	60	29	15.00

CAREER: BATTING

	I.	N.O.	R.	H.S.	AV.
TEST	5	0	71	32	14.20
OTHER FIRST CLASS	311	31	8956	197	31.99
INT	3	0	58	52	19.33
JPL	114	10	2363	109	22.72
NAT.W	19	2	284	59	16.72
B & H	16	2	327	85	23.37

LAST SEASON: BOWLING

	O.	M.	R.	W.	AV.
TEST					
OTHER FIRST CLASS	18	4	46	2	23.00
INT					
JPL					
NAT.W					
B & H					

CAREER: BOWLING

	O.	M.	R.	W.	AV.
TEST					
OTHER FIRST CLASS	32	7	122	2	61.00
INT					
JPL	0.4	0	4	0	–
NAT.W	2	0	18	1	–
B & H					

25. Who was the original "Demon Bowler"?

26. For which Lancashire League club did Dennis Lillee play, and when?

27. Of which Australian Test cricketer did Australian fans chant, "He's fat, he's round, he bounces off the ground!"?

BYAS, D.   Yorkshire

Full Name: David Byas.
Role: Left-hand bat, right-arm
medium bowler, slip or cover fielder.
Born: 28 August 1964, Kilham,
Driffield.
Height: 6′ 4″ **Weight:** 13st. 7lbs.
Nickname: Billy.
County debut: 1985.
Parents: Richard and Anne Byas.
Education: Scarborough College.
Qualifications: 1 O-level (Engineering).
Jobs outside cricket: Farmer.
Cricketers particularly learnt from:
Coached by F.S. Trueman, Don Wilson.
Cricketers particularly admired:
D. Gower, I. Botham.
Other sports: Hockey.
Relaxations: Game shooting,
watching rallies.

Extras: Scarborough Cricket Club captain. Only player to score 200 (n.o.) in Yorkshire league, most runs in Yorkshire league (broke M. Crowe's record).

LAST SEASON: BATTING

	I.	N.O.	R.	H.S.	AV.
TEST					
OTHER FIRST CLASS					
INT					
JPL	1	0	15	15	–
NAT.W					
B & H	1	0	2	2	–

CAREER: BATTING

	I.	N.O.	R.	H.S.	AV.
TEST					
OTHER FIRST CLASS					
INT					
JPL	1	0	15	15	–
NAT.W					
B & H	1	0	2	2	–

28. Who said, "I won my first Test as captain so I suppose I can't complain about losing my last."?

29. What current Test cricketer's nickname is "Smokey"?

CAPEL, D.J.　　　　Northamptonshire

Full Name: David John Capel.
Role: Right-hand bat, right-arm
medium bowler, outfielder.
Born: 6 February 1963, Northampton.
Height: 6′ **Weight:** 12st. 4lbs.
Nickname: Capes.
County debut: 1981.
1st-Class 50s scored: 15.
1st-Class 100s scored: 1.
1st-Class 5 w. in innings: 2.
One-day 50s: 2.
Place in batting averages: 147
average: 24.96; (1984: 84
average: 34.30).
Place in bowling averages: 64
average: 31.68; (1984: 125
average: 42.44).
1st-Class catches 1985: 5
(career: 33).

Parents: John and Angela Janet Capel.
Marital status: Single (engaged to Debbie).
Education: Roade Primary and Roade Comprehensive School.
Family links with cricket: Father and brother Andrew played in county
league.
Qualifications: 3 O-levels, 5 C.S.E.s., N.C.A. Coaching Certificate.
Jobs outside cricket: Surgical shoemaker, including hand-made cricket
boots.
Overseas teams played for: Played and coached in South Africa 1981–82;
Latrobe, Tasmania, 1982–83, on Whitbread Scholarship; Westview C.C., Port
Elizabeth, 1983–84.
Overseas tours: Dubai with *The Cricketer*, March 1983.
Cricketing superstitions: "I never eat duck the night before a game. Did once
and recorded only pair of noughts in career."
Cricketers particularly learnt from: Brian Reynolds, Peter Willey, Geoff Cook,
Wayne Larkins. "Admire Barry Richards, Imran Khan, Richard Hadlee."
Other sports: Occasionally golf and pool. Follows most sports.
Relaxations: Enjoys swimming, most types of music, loves Indian food and
barbecues.
Extras: Played for Young England v Young West Indies, August 1982, scoring
117 in 2nd "Test".
Opinions on cricket: "(1) Overseas players: One per county to make
championship and one-day games equal and fair competition between sides.
Counties may sign as many as they wish but should only be allowed to play
one at any time. I also think that English registration is given far too freely to

overseas-born players. Some county sides contain overseas-born players who have represented their nation at international level, e.g. Zimbabwe, and yet can play for their county sides as 'English' players. I feel that this is unfair to young English-born pros breaking through into the same side and opportunities go missing. I think that this is one way that is preventing young English talent progressing to the highest level in cricket and in a lot of instances even getting first-class championship games. Then people ask why no young talent emerges from England youth. The overseas 'English' signings also demand a lot of the game and dominate prime positions which I feel detracts in many ways from England producing the best national side possible with English players playing with all their heart and pride for their country. (2) Uncovered wickets I think is a good idea in theory, however I hope that next season, i.e. 1986, is a lot drier summer than 1985 otherwise I dread to think how much time we will spend in the changing room. Personally I also would welcome a change in the points system in championship games. Something along the lines of a points system for a first innings win."

Best batting performance: 109* Northamptonshire v Somerset, Northampton 1983.

Best bowling performance: 7-62 Northamptonshire v Lancashire, Weston 1985.

LAST SEASON: BATTING

	I.	N.O.	R.	H.S.	AV.
TEST					
OTHER FIRST CLASS	30	6	599	81	24.96
INT					
JPL	8	2	141	44	23.50
NAT.W	2	1	4	3	–
B & H	3	1	29	11*	14.50

CAREER: BATTING

	I.	N.O.	R.	H.S.	AV.
TEST					
OTHER FIRST CLASS	106	21	2419	109*	28.46
INT					
JPL	39	13	571	79	21.96
NAT.W	7	3	93	27	23.25
B & H	8	2	110	28	18.33

LAST SEASON: BOWLING

	O.	M.	R.	W.	AV.
TEST					
OTHER FIRST CLASS	384.3	63	1299	41	31.68
INT					
JPL	50	2	247	9	27.44
NAT.W	19	1	93	2	46.50
B & H	12	1	50	1	–

CAREER: BOWLING

	O.	M.	R.	W.	AV.
TEST					
OTHER FIRST CLASS	707.1	107	2642	66	40.03
INT					
JPL	140	4	794	32	24.81
NAT.W	22	1	109	3	36.33
B & H	44	5	169	7	24.14

30. Of which cricket ground did Sir Donald Bradman write: "This is without doubt the most beautiful ground in the world."?

CARR, J.D.　　　　　　　　　　　Middlesex

Full Name: John Donald Carr.
Role: Right-hand bat, off-break bowler.
Born: 15 June 1963, St. John's Wood, London N.W.8.
Nickname: Carsi.
County debut: 1983.
1st-Class 50s scored: 4.
1st-Class 100s scored: 4.
1st-Class 5 w. in innings: 3.
One-day 50s: 3.
Place in batting averages: 94 average: 31.60; (1984: 92 average: 33.43).
Place in bowling averages: 84 average: 36.24; (1984: 115 average: 40.23).
1st-Class catches 1985: 6 (career: 20).
Education: Repton School and Oxford University.
Family links with cricket: Father, D.B. Carr, is secretary of T.C.C.B. and played for Oxford University, Derbyshire and England, captaining all three at some stage.
Extras: Played for Oxford in Varsity Match 1984. Secretary of University in 1984. Came on as substitute fielder for Middlesex in the 1983 Benson and Hedges Cup Final, holding a vital catch to help his side defeat Essex. Received special clearance to play in the match having previously appeared for Combined Universities in the same competition.
Best batting performance: 123 Oxford University v Lancashire, Oxford 1984.
Best bowling performance: 6–61 Middlesex v Gloucestershire, Lord's 1985.

LAST SEASON: BATTING

	I.	N.O.	R.	H.S.	AV.
TEST					
OTHER FIRST CLASS	16	1	474	115	31.60
INT					
JPL	1	0	4	4	–
NAT.W					
B & H	4	0	93	67	23.25

CAREER: BATTING

	I.	N.O.	R.	H.S.	AV.
TEST					
OTHER FIRST CLASS	40	5	1009	123	28.83
INT					
JPL	2	1	4	4	–
NAT.W					
B & H	9	1	269	67	33.63

LAST SEASON: BOWLING

	O.	M.	R.	W.	AV.
TEST					
OTHER FIRST CLASS	249.1	65	616	17	36.24
INT					
JPL					
NAT.W					
B & H	35	3	156	1	–

CAREER: BOWLING

	O.	M.	R.	W.	AV.
TEST					
OTHER FIRST CLASS	762.1	208	1977	48	41.19
INT					
JPL					
NAT.W					
B & H	75.2	8	301	6	50.17

CARRICK, P.   Yorkshire

Full Name: Phillip Carrick.
Role: Right-hand bat, slow left-arm bowler, slip fielder.
Born: 16 July 1952, Leeds.
Height: 6′ 0″ **Weight:** 13st. 7lbs.
Nickname: Fergie.
County debut: 1970.
County cap: 1976.
Benefit: 1985.
50 wickets in a season: 7.
1st-Class 50s scored: 25.
1st-Class 100s scored: 3.
1st-Class 5 w. in innings: 35.
1st-Class 10 w. in match: 5.
Place in batting averages: 162 average: 23.48; (1984: 224 average: 17.39).
Place in bowling averages: 49 average: 29.59; (1984: 103 average: 36.50).

1st-Class catches 1985: 16 (career: 148).
Parents: Arthur (deceased) and Ivy Carrick.
Wife and date of marriage: Elspeth, 2 April 1977.
Children: Emma Elizabeth, 6 May 1980; Phillipa, 11 January 1982.
Education: Bramley C.S., Intake C.S., Park Lane College of Physical Education.
Qualifications: 2 O-levels, 8 C.S.E.s, N.C.A. coaching certificate.
Jobs outside cricket: Company Director, coach.
Family links with cricket: "Father and brother useful league players."

LAST SEASON: BATTING

	I.	N.O.	R.	H.S.	AV.
TEST					
OTHER FIRST CLASS	25	2	540	92	23.48
INT					
JPL	11	3	64	18	8.00
NAT.W	1	0	16	16	–
B & H	3	1	74	53	37.00

CAREER: BATTING

	I.	N.O.	R.	H.S.	AV.
TEST					
OTHER FIRST CLASS	358	66	6366	131*	21.80
INT					
JPL	77	24	722	43*	13.62
NAT.W	13	2	152	37	13.82
B & H	20	4	206	53	12.88

LAST SEASON: BOWLING

	O.	M.	R.	W.	AV.
TEST					
OTHER FIRST CLASS	712.3	185	1923	65	29.59
INT					
JPL	62	2	312	9	34.66
NAT.W	16	5	36	0	–
B & H	39	1	130	3	43.33

CAREER: BOWLING

	O.	M.	R.	W.	AV.
TEST					
OTHER FIRST CLASS	8472.5	2730	21230	721	29.45
INT					
JPL	514.5	24	2269	67	33.86
NAT.W	1105	13	320	9	35.55
B & H	235.5	36	793	22	36.05

Overseas tours: Toured with Derrick Robins XI to South Africa 1975–76; Far East 1977.
Overseas teams played for: Eastern Province in 1976–77 Currie Cup Competition, and Northern Transvaal 1982–83.
Cricketers particularly learnt from: Geoff Boycott, Ray Illingworth.
Cricketers particularly admired: D. Underwood, B. Bedi, G. Pollock.
Cricket superstitions: Left pad on first.
Other sports: Golf, follows most.
Opinions on cricket: "Let's go back to uncovered wickets!"
Best batting performance: 131* Yorkshire v Northamptonshire, Northampton 1980.
Best bowling performance: 8-33 Yorkshire v Cambridge University, Cambridge 1973.

CHADWICK, M.R. Lancashire

Full Name: Mark Robert Chadwick.
Role: Right-hand bat, off-break bowler.
Born: 9 February 1963, Rochdale, Lancashire.
Height: 6′ 1″ **Weight:** 13st.
Nickname: Chad.
County debut: 1983.
1st-Class 50s scored: 3.
1st-Class 100s scored: 1.
One-day 50s: 1.
Place in batting averages: 137 average: 25.63; (1984: 193 average: 20.93).
1st-Class catches 1985: 5 (career: 8).
Parents: Robert and Kathleen Chadwick.
Family links with cricket: "Father club cricketer and now umpires in C. Lancashire League. Mother washes all my kit and is very good critic but knows nothing about the game."
Education: Moorhouse County Primary School, Milnrow, Roch Valley High School, Milnrow.
Qualifications: 2 O-levels.
Jobs outside cricket: 1979–83 storeman for diesel engine firm: 1984 window cleaner.
Off-season 1985–86: Playing and coaching in Queensland.
Overseas tours: Barbados 1984 with Lancashire.
Cricketing superstitions: "Trying not to make a habit of fielding at short leg."

Cricketers particularly learnt from: Picked up lots of helpful tips from all the staff at Lancashire.

Cricketers particularly admired: Geoffrey Boycott – powers of concentration while at the crease, Viv Richards – domination of bowlers.

Other sports: Football, table-tennis, badminton, golf. Very keen rugby league fan.

Relaxations: Listening to music.

Extras: Central Lancashire League record run scorer for amateur. 1267 runs for Milnrow C.C. in 1983, beating the previous record of 1205 from 1915. Won gold award in first B&H match (1984 semi-final).

Opinions on cricket: "Counties should try harder to find winter employment for players. 20 minutes not long enough for tea."

Best batting performance: 132 Lancashire v Somerset, Old Trafford 1985.

LAST SEASON: BATTING

	I.	N.O.	R.	H.S.	AV.
TEST					
OTHER FIRST CLASS	17	1	410	132	25.63
INT					
JPL	2	0	6	6	3.00
NAT.W	1	0	43	43	–
B & H					

CAREER: BATTING

	I.	N.O.	R.	H.S.	AV.
TEST					
OTHER FIRST CLASS	33	1	705	132	22.03
INT					
JPL	3	0	16	10	5.33
NAT.W	1	0	43	43	–
B & H	1	0	87	87	–

LAST SEASON: BOWLING

	O.	M.	R.	W.	AV.
TEST					
OTHER FIRST CLASS	5	0	20	0	–
INT					
JPL					
NAT.W					
B & H					

CAREER: BOWLING

	O.	M.	R.	W.	AV.
TEST					
OTHER FIRST CLASS	5	0	20	0	–
INT					
JPL					
NAT.W					
B & H					

31. Which legendary cricketer wrote: "I cannot remember when I began to play cricket. Respect for the truth prevents me from saying I played the first year of my existence, but I have little hesitation in declaring that I handled a bat and ball before the end of my second."?

CHILDS, J.H.　　　　　　　　　Essex

Full Name: John Henry Childs.
Role: Left-hand bat, slow left-arm
orthodox bowler.
Born: 15 August 1951, Plymouth.
Height: 6′ 0″ **Weight:** 12st. 6lbs.
Nickname: Charlie.
County debut: 1975 (Gloucester-
shire), 1985 (Essex).
County cap: 1977 (Gloucestershire).
Testimonial match: 1985.
50 wickets in a season: 2.
1st-Class 5 w. in innings: 21.
1st-Class 10 w. in match: 2.
Place in bowling averages: —
average: —; (1984: 132
average: 49.07).

1st-Class catches 1985: 1 (career: 64).
Parents: Sydney and
Barbara Childs (both deceased).
Wife and date of marriage: Jane Anne, 11 November 1978.
Children: Lee Robert, 28 November 1980; Scott Alexander, 21 August 1984.
Education: Audley Park Secondary Modern, Torquay.
Qualifications: Advanced Cricket Coach.
Jobs outside cricket: Signwriter.
Cricketing superstitions: Dressing in white.
Overseas tours: Zambia, 1977; Barbados, 1983.
Overseas teams played for: Spent winter 1979–80 coaching in Gisborne, New
Zealand and 1982–83 in Auckland for Howice-Pakuranga.
Cricketers particularly admired: G. Sobers and M. Procter.

LAST SEASON: BATTING

	I.	N.O.	R.	H.S.	AV.
TEST					
OTHER FIRST CLASS	4	1	17	6	5.67
INT					
JPL					
NAT.W					
B & H					

LAST SEASON: BOWLING

	O.	M.	R.	W.	AV.
TEST					
OTHER FIRST CLASS	197	59	528	5	105.6
INT					
JPL					
NAT.W					
B & H					

CAREER: BATTING

	I.	N.O.	R.	H.S.	AV.
TEST					
OTHER FIRST CLASS	155	73	552	34*	6.73
INT					
JPL	17	9	74	16*	9.25
NAT.W	4	3	22	14*	–
B & H	7	5	25	10	12.50

CAREER: BOWLING

	O.	M.	R.	W.	AV.
TEST					
OTHER FIRST CLASS	5171.4	1500	13992	426	32.85
INT					
JPL	318.1	17	1444	39	37.02
NAT.W	60	12	180	7	25.72
B & H	156	35	466	14	33.29

Other sports: Most ball games.
Injuries 1985: Dislocated left thumb.
Relaxations: Watching rugby, decorating at home, "walking on moors and beaches. My family."
Extras: Played for Devon 1973–74. Released by Gloucestershire at end of 1984. Granted Testimonial Match by Gloucestershire v Essex in 1985.
Best batting performance: 34* Gloucestershire v Nottinghamshire, Cheltenham 1982.
Best bowling performance: 9-56 Gloucestershire v Somerset, Bristol 1981.

CHIVERS, I.J. Hampshire

Full Name: Ian James Chivers.
Role: Right-hand bat, off-break bowler.
Born: 5 November 1964, Southampton.
Height: 5′ 9″ **Weight:** 11st. 8lbs.
Nickname: Sheila, Chivs, Radar.
County debut: 1985.
Parents: Robert Edward and Barbra Chivers.
Marital status: Single.
Education: Hampton Park Comprehensive; Richard Tauntons VI Form College.
Qualifications: 7 O-levels.
Off season 1985–86: Hopefully in South Africa.
Overseas tours: N.C.A. tour to The Hague in Holland in 1983.

LAST SEASON: BATTING

	I.	N.O.	R.	H.S.	AV.
TEST					
OTHER FIRST CLASS	–	–	–	–	–
INT					
JPL					
NAT.W					
B & H					

CAREER: BATTING

	I.	N.O.	R.	H.S.	AV.
TEST					
OTHER FIRST CLASS	–	–	–	–	–
INT					
JPL					
NAT.W					
B & H					

LAST SEASON: BOWLING

	O.	M.	R.	W.	AV.
TEST					
OTHER FIRST CLASS	22	5	72	1	–
INT					
JPL					
NAT.W					
B & H					

CAREER: BOWLING

	O.	M.	R.	W.	AV.
TEST					
OTHER FIRST CLASS	22	5	72	1	–
INT					
JPL					
NAT.W					
B & H					

Overseas teams played for: Pinetown, Durban, South Africa 1984–85.
Cricketers particularly learnt from: Peter Sainsbury, Arthur Holt.
Cricketers particularly admired: Barry Richards, Malcolm Marshall, Gordon Greenidge.
Other sports: Soccer, golf. Follows most sports except motor-racing.
Injuries 1985: Ankle ligament trouble in June (but not serious).
Relaxations: Playing golf, occasionally watching TV, the odd social drink.

CLIFT, P.B. Leicestershire

Full Name: Patrick Bernard Clift.
Role: Right-hand bat, right-arm medium bowler.
Born: 14 July 1953, Salisbury, Zimbabwe.
Height: 6′ 1″ **Weight:** 14st.
Nickname: Paddy, Paddles.
County debut: 1975.
County cap: 1976.
50 wickets in a season: 6.
1st-Class 50s scored: 27.
1st-Class 100s scored: 2.
1st-Class 5 w. in innings: 23.
1st-Class 10 w. in match: 2.
One-day 50s: 4.
Place in batting averages: 161 average: 23.57; (1984: 179 average: 23.00).
Place in bowling averages: 55 average: 30.76; (1984: 31 average: 25.52).
1st-Class catches 1985: 10 (career: 136).
Parents: George Neville and Ivy Susan Clift.
Wife and date of marriage: Penelope Anne, 18 May 1978.
Children: Robert William Patrick, 16 September 1982; Josephine Anne, 10 May 1984.
Education: St. Michael's; Hartmann House, St George's College.
Qualifications: O-level.
Jobs outside cricket: Accounting, insurance.
Overseas tours: Rhodesia Ridgebacks 1974 U.K. tour.
Overseas teams played for: Rhodesia. Natal.
Cricketers particularly learnt from: Robin Jackman, Mike Procter, Duncan Fletcher, Jack Birkenshaw, Roger Tolchard, Ken Higgs, Jim Cornford, school coach at St. George's College.
Other sports: Squash, golf, tennis, jogging.
Relaxations: Stamp collecting, reading, listening to records.

Extras: Debut for Rhodesia 1971–72. Took 8 wickets for 17 in opening match in 1976 season v M.C.C. Performed hat-trick in 1976 at Grace Road v Yorkshire. Suffered from injury in 1981 and 1982 season. Rhodesian 7th wicket partnership record of 174 with Howie Gardiner v Western Province, and Rhodesian 9th wicket partnership of 154 with Robin Jackman v Eastern Province, both in Currie Cup Competition, South Africa.

Opinions on cricket: "We are forever discussing changes to over-rates, 3- or 4-days etc, to see if they improve attendances at county games. Surely the time has come when we need to closely examine the 'draw' result? The problem appears to lie in the third day's play. One-day cricket is based on a winning and losing system. More emphasis should be placed on captains setting 'match winning' targets thereby allowing spectators to savour exciting cricket."

Best batting performance: 106 Essex v Leicestershire, Chelmsford 1985.

Best bowling performance: 8-17 Leicestershire v M.C.C., Lord's 1976.

LAST SEASON: BATTING

	I.	N.O.	R.	H.S.	AV.
TEST					
OTHER FIRST CLASS	26	5	495	106	23.57
INT					
JPL	8	1	80	27*	11.42
NAT.W	2	0	10	7	5.00
B & H	4	2	35	11*	17.50

CAREER: BATTING

	I.	N.O.	R.	H.S.	AV.
TEST					
OTHER FIRST CLASS	398	86	7301	106	23.40
INT					
JPL	80	26	1120	51*	20.34
NAT.W	16	5	244	48*	22.18
B & H	22	4	357	91	19.83

LAST SEASON: BOWLING

	O.	M.	R.	W.	AV.
TEST					
OTHER FIRST CLASS	595.3	169	1446	47	30.76
INT					
JPL	72	9	299	14	21.35
NAT.W	21	4	51	3	17.00
B & H	74	14	232	10	23.20

CAREER: BOWLING

	O.	M.	R.	W.	AV.
TEST					
OTHER FIRST CLASS	7605	1995	19234	771	24.95
INT					
JPL	804.3	60	3310	150	22.06
NAT.W	159.3	19	574	17	33.76
B & H	330.4	46	1108	42	26.38

32. Mike Gatting scored his first Test 100 in England after 21, 33 or 40 innings?

33. Who was the Australian vice-captain on their England tour of 1985?

34. Who was the youngest player ever to play for England, at what age and when?

CLINTON, G.S.   Surrey

Full Name: Graham Selvey Clinton.
Role: Left-hand bat, right-arm
medium bowler.
Born: 5 May 1953, Sidcup.
Nickname: Clint.
County debut: 1974 (Kent),
1979 (Surrey).
County cap: 1980 (Surrey).
1000 runs in a season: 4.
1st-Class 50s scored: 43.
1st-Class 100s scored: 14.
One-day 50s: 12.
One-day 100s: 3.
Place in batting averages: 25
average: 47.11; (1984: 37
average: 43.09).
1st-Class catches 1985: 13
(career: 58).
Education: Chislehurst and Sidcup Grammar School.
Family links with cricket: Younger brothers Neil and Tony are regular
members of the Blackheath team.
Overseas tours: West Indies with England Young Cricketers 1972.
Extras: Formerly played for Kent, where he made his debut 1974. Left after
1978 season to join Surrey. Renowned as a dressing-room wit. At age 11, he
played for Kemnal Manor, Kent. Later played club cricket for Sidcup and for
Blackheath.
Best batting performance: 192 Surrey v Yorkshire, The Oval 1984.
Best bowling performance: 2-8 Kent v Pakistan, Canterbury 1978.

LAST SEASON: BATTING

	I.	N.O.	R.	H.S.	AV.
TEST					
OTHER FIRST CLASS	32	6	1225	123	47.11
INT					
JPL	12	3	342	72	38.00
NAT.W	1	0	146	146	–
B & H	4	1	178	106*	59.33

CAREER: BATTING

	I.	N.O.	R.	H.S.	AV.
TEST					
OTHER FIRST CLASS	284	35	8027	192	32.24
INT					
JPL	46	7	1103	105*	28.28
NAT.W	13	1	438	146	36.50
B & H	30	1	894	106*	30.83

LAST SEASON: BOWLING

	O.	M.	R.	W.	AV.
TEST					
OTHER FIRST CLASS	6	0	46	0	–
INT					
JPL					
NAT.W					
B & H					

CAREER: BOWLING

	O.	M.	R.	W.	AV.
TEST					
OTHER FIRST CLASS	23	1	173	4	43.25
INT					
JPL					
NAT.W	4	2	2	0	–
B & H	1.2	0	10	0	–

COBB, R.A. Leicestershire

Full Name: Russell Alan Cobb.
Role: Right-hand bat, slow
left-arm bowler, short-leg
fielder – "great!".
Born: 18 May 1961, Leicester.
Height: 5′ 11″ **Weight:** 11st. 5lbs.
Nickname: Cobby.
County debut: 1980.
1st-Class 50s scored: 5.
Place in batting averages: 92
average: 31.65; (1984: —
average: —).
1st-Class catches 1985: 11
(career: 37).
Parents: Alan and Betty Cobb.
Wife and date of marriage: Sharon,
30 March 1985.
Education: Woodbank School,
Leicester; Trent College,
Nottingham.

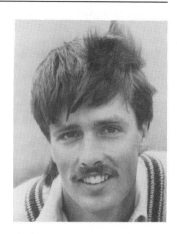

Qualifications: 7 O-levels, N.C.A. Advanced coaching certificate.
Family links with cricket: Father a club cricketer. Godfather, Maurice Hallam,
former Leicestershire captain.
Jobs outside cricket: Clerk for British Shoe Corporation, Leicester. Worked on
promotion for Leicestershire.
Off season 1985–86: Playing and coaching abroad.
Cricketing superstitions: "Always put my left pad on first. Must wear some sort
of headgear."
Overseas tours: Australia with Young England in 1979; West Indies with
Young England in 1980; Zimbabwe with Leicestershire in 1981.

LAST SEASON: BATTING

	I.	N.O.	R.	H.S.	AV.
TEST					
OTHER FIRST CLASS	23	4	601	78	31.63
INT					
JPL	1	1	0	0*	–
NAT.W					
B & H					

CAREER: BATTING

	I.	N.O.	R.	H.S.	AV.
TEST					
OTHER FIRST CLASS	91	5	1936	78	22.51
INT					
JPL	4	2	49	24	24.50
NAT.W					
B & H					

LAST SEASON: BOWLING

	O.	M.	R.	W.	AV.
TEST					
OTHER FIRST CLASS					
INT					
JPL					
NAT.W					
B & H					

CAREER: BOWLING

	O.	M.	R.	W.	AV.
TEST					
OTHER FIRST CLASS	4	2	5	0	–
INT					
JPL					
NAT.W					
B & H					

Overseas teams played for: Glenelg in Adelaide, South Australia, in 1980–81; Teachers Training College, Pretoria, 1983–84, 1984–85.
Cricketers particularly learnt from: Jack Birkenshaw and Chris Balderstone.
Cricketers particularly admired: "All who have played top class cricket for a number of years."
Other sports: Squash, badminton, watching rugby and football.
Relaxations: "A little gardening, walking, eating out."
Significant injuries in 1985: Fracture in left foot.
Best batting performance: 78 Leicestershire v Surrey, Leicester 1985.

CONNOR, C.A. Hampshire

Full Name: Cardigan Adolphus Connor.
Role: Right-hand bat, right-arm fast-medium bowler.
Born: 24 March 1961, West End, Anguilla.
Height: 5' 10'' **Weight:** 11st. 6lbs.
Nickname: "Christy, Cardy and many more."
County debut: 1984.
50 wickets in a season: 1.
1st-Class 5 w. in innings: 1.
Place in batting averages: 231 average: 13.00; (1984: — average: —).
Place in bowling averages: 110 average: 41.91; (1984: 76 average: 31.43).
1st-Class catches 1985: 9 (career: 16).
Parents: Ethleen Snagg.
Marital status: Single.
Education: Valley Secondary School, Anguilla; Langley College.
Qualifications: Engineer.
Jobs outside cricket: Timko Engineering, Slough Trading Estate.
Cricketing superstitions: Never changes before the end of the day's play.
Overseas tours: C.C.C. tour of Hong Kong, Singapore, New Zealand and Australia in 1983.
Overseas teams played for: Merriweather C.C., Newcastle, Australia, 1983–84 and 1984–85; West End C.C., Anguilla, 1973–76.
Cricketers particularly learnt from: Tim Tremlett. "He helped me a great deal in my first season."
Cricketers particularly admired: Viv Richards, Andy Roberts, Richard Hadlee.

Other sports: Most other sports: follows football, boxing, tennis, etc.
Relaxations: Music, wine bars, meeting people.
Extras: Played for Buckinghamshire in Minor Counties before joining Hampshire. First Anguillan-born player to appear in the County Championship.
Best batting performance: 36 Hampshire v Northamptonshire, Northampton 1985.
Best bowling performance: 7-37 Hampshire v Kent, Bournemouth 1984.

LAST SEASON: BATTING

	I.	N.O.	R.	H.S.	AV.
TEST					
OTHER FIRST CLASS	9	4	65	36	13.00
INT					
JPL	1	1	2	2*	–
NAT.W	–	–	–	–	–
B & H	1	0	0	0	–

CAREER: BATTING

	I.	N.O.	R.	H.S.	AV.
TEST					
OTHER FIRST CLASS	32	13	130	36	6.84
INT					
JPL	3	3	2	2*	–
NAT.W	1	1	3	3*	–
B & H	1	0	0	0	–

LAST SEASON: BOWLING

	O.	M.	R.	W.	AV.
TEST					
OTHER FIRST CLASS	467.5	91	1467	35	41.91
INT					
JPL	104.1	4	464	20	23.20
NAT.W	30.2	2	115	3	38.33
B & H	46.2	6	159	9	17.67

CAREER: BOWLING

	O.	M.	R.	W.	AV.
TEST					
OTHER FIRST CLASS	1110.4	246	3416	97	35.22
INT					
JPL	201.3	10	903	40	22.57
NAT.W	48.2	6	178	4	44.50
B & H	46.2	6	159	9	17.67

COOK, G.   Northamptonshire

Full Name: Geoffrey Cook.
Role: Right-hand bat, slow left-arm bowler.
Born: 9 October 1951, Middlesbrough, Yorkshire.
Height: 6' 0'' **Weight:** 12st. 10lbs.
Nickname: Geoff.
County debut: 1971.
County cap: 1975.
Benefit: 1985.
Test debut: 1981–82.
No. of Tests: 7.
No. of One-Day Internationals: 6.
1000 runs in a season: 10.
1st-Class 50s scored: 95.
1st-Class 100s scored: 27.
One-day 50s: 41.
One-day 100s: 3.
Place in batting averages: 56

average: 38.09; (1984: 53 average: 39.46).
1st-Class catches 1985: 19 (career: 367).
Parents: Harry and Helen Cook.
Wife and date of marriage: Judith, 22 November 1975.
Children: Anna, 21 May 1980.
Education: Middlesbrough High School.
Qualifications: 6 O-levels, 1 A-level.
Jobs outside cricket: Has taught at Spratton Hall Prep. School.
Family links with cricket: Father and brother, David, very keen club cricketers. "Father was virtually 'Mr Cricket' in Middlesbrough cricket in the 1960s. (President, Secretary, Chairman, of various leagues)."
Overseas teams played for: Eastern Province, 1978–81.
Overseas tours: With England to India 1981–82 and Australia 1982–83.
Cricketers particularly learnt from: Wayne Larkins.
Cricketers particularly admired: Clive Rice.
Other sports: "All sports when given opportunity." Football with Wellingborough in the Southern League.
Relaxations: Walking, reading, crosswords.
Extras: "Great believer in organised recreation for young people. Would enjoy time and scope to carry my beliefs through." Captain since 1981. Chairman of the Cricketers' Association.
Best batting performance: 172 Eastern Province v Northern Transvaal, Port Elizabeth 1979–80.
Best bowling performance: 3-47 England XI v South Australia, Adelaide 1983–84.

LAST SEASON: BATTING

	I.	N.O.	R.	H.S.	AV.
TEST					
OTHER FIRST CLASS	38	4	1295	126	38.09
INT					
JPL	11	0	386	98	35.09
NAT.W	2	0	184	130	92.00
B & H	5	1	107	78	26.75

CAREER: BATTING

	I.	N.O.	R.	H.S.	AV.
TEST	13	0	203	66	15.61
OTHER FIRST CLASS	631	47	18710	172	32.04
INT	6	0	106	32	17.67
JPL	183	13	4188	98	24.63
NAT.W	32	1	1215	130	39.19
B & H	53	4	1342	96	27.39

LAST SEASON: BOWLING

	O.	M.	R.	W.	AV.
TEST					
OTHER FIRST CLASS	1	0	6	0	–
INT					
JPL					
NAT.W					
B & H					

CAREER: BOWLING

	O.	M.	R.	W.	AV.
TEST	7	3	27	0	–
OTHER FIRST CLASS	164.1	32	658	14	47.00
INT					
JPL	1	0	6	0	–
NAT.W					
B & H					

COOK, N.G.B.　　　Northamptonshire

Full Name: Nicholas Grant
Billson Cook.
Role: Right-hand bat, slow left-
arm bowler, backward short-leg
fielder.
Born: 17 June 1956, Leicester.
Height: 6′ 0″ **Weight:** 12st.
Nickname: Beast.
County debut: 1978 (Leicestershire).
County cap: 1982 (Leicestershire).
Test debut: 1983.
No. of Tests: 9.
No. of One-Day Internationals: 1.
50 wickets in a season: 4.
1st-Class 50s scored: 2.
1st-Class 5 w. in innings: 19.
1st-Class 10 w. in match: 2.
Place in batting averages: 235

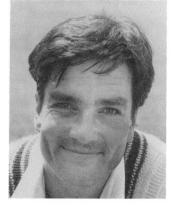

average: 12.67; (1984: 257 average: 12.19).
Place in bowling averages: 121 average: 44.40; (1984: 119 average: 41.89).
1st-Class catches 1985: 8 (career: 99).
Parents: Peter and Cynthia Cook.
Wife and date of marriage: Janet Elizabeth, 3 November 1979.
Education: Stokes Croft Junior; Lutterworth High; Lutterworth Upper.
Qualifications: 7 O-levels, 1 A-level, advanced cricket coach.
Jobs outside cricket: Has worked for Leicestershire C.C.C. on promotions,
organising lotteries, sponsored walks, general fund-raising projects. Also
coaching.
Family links with cricket: Father played club cricket.
Overseas tours: Whitbread Scholarship to Perth, Australia, 1980–81; Far East
tour with M.C.C. to Bangkok, Singapore, Hong Kong, 1981; Australia and
New Zealand with Derrick Robins XI, 1980; Zimbabwe with Leicestershire
C.C.C., 1981; Dubai, 1982, with Barbican XI; with M.C.C. to America, 1982–83,
and Kuwait 1983; New Zealand and Pakistan with England 1983–84.
Overseas teams played for: Claremont-Cottesloe C.C., Perth, 1980–81.
Cricketers particularly learnt from: Jack Birkenshaw and Roger Tolchard.
Other sports followed: Soccer, rugby, horse-riding.
Off-season 1985–86: Touring Bangladesh, Sri Lanka and Zimbabwe with
England B.
Relaxations: Crosswords; watching horse-racing and football, especially
Leicester City, and most sporting events; reading, especially Wilbur Smith;
good comedy programmes and good food.
Extras: Played for E.S.C.A. 1975. Played for Young England v Young West
Indies 1975. Played for M.C.C. v Middlesex at start of 1981 season. Played for
England B Team v Pakistan, August 1982. Left Leicestershire to join
Nottinghamshire for 1986 season.

Opinions on cricket: "Would like to see 16 4-day county cricket matches . . . Basically O.K.!"
Best batting performance: 75 Leicestershire v Somerset, Taunton 1980.
Best bowling performance: 7-63 Leicester v Somerset, Taunton 1982.

LAST SEASON: BATTING

	I.	N.O.	R.	H.S.	AV.
TEST					
OTHER FIRST CLASS	16	4	152	45	12.67
INT					
JPL	2	0	1	1	0.50
NAT.W					
B & H					

CAREER: BATTING

	I.	N.O.	R.	H.S.	AV.
TEST	15	1	101	26	7.21
OTHER FIRST CLASS	159	50	1354	75	12.42
INT	–	–	–	–	–
JPL	11	4	53	13*	7.57
NAT.W	–	–	–	–	–
B & H	3	1	29	23	14.50

LAST SEASON: BOWLING

	O.	M.	R.	W.	AV.
TEST					
OTHER FIRST CLASS	558.1	186	1332	30	44.40
INT					
JPL	8	0	26	3	8.67
NAT.W					
B & H					

CAREER: BOWLING

	O.	M.	R.	W.	AV.
TEST	498.2	162	1212	40	30.30
OTHER FIRST CLASS	5182.1	1668	12428	427	29.11
INT	8	0	34	1	–
JPL	172.2	17	761	21	36.23
NAT.W	36	8	131	4	32.75
B & H	67	11	224	4	56.00

COOMBS, R.V.J.   Somerset

Full Name: Robert Vincent Jerome Coombs.
Role: Right-hand bat, slow left-arm bowler.
Born: 20 July 1959, Barnet, Herts.
Height: 6′ 4″ **Weight:** 13st. 12lbs.
Nickname: Coombsee.
County debut: 1985.
1st-Class 5 w. in innings: 1.
Parents: John Michael, Dena Marjorie Coombs.
Marital status: Single.
Education: King's College Taunton; St. Luke's College, University of Exeter.
Qualifications: 10 O-levels, 2 A-levels.
Jobs outside cricket: Motor claims negotiator, Norman Frizzell.
Off-season 1985–86: Final year at university: degree course B.Ed. in Education, Chemistry and Science.
Family links with cricket: Brother a devoted club cricketer.
Cricketers particularly learnt from: Many school, club and county colleagues.

Cricketers particularly admired: Derek Underwood.
Other sports: Hockey (U-21). Enjoys watching most sports.
Relaxations: Watching television, meeting friends, cricket coaching.
Extras: N.C.A. coaching award. First-class debut v Middlesex returned figures 5-58. 1985 held dual registration with Dorset for whom he debuted in 1979. Plays club cricket for Bournemouth C.C. Played with Hampshire II 1982.
Opinions on cricket: "It is time for Oxford and Cambridge to lose their first-class status. The Benson and Hedges Combined Universities side should be selected from all British Universities."
Best batting performance: 1 Somerset v Kent, Canterbury 1985.
Best bowling performance: 5-58 Somerset v Middlesex, Weston 1985.

LAST SEASON: BATTING

	I.	N.O.	R.	H.S.	AV.
TEST					
OTHER FIRST CLASS	3	0	1	1	0.33
INT					
JPL					
NAT.W					
B & H					

CAREER: BATTING

	I.	N.O.	R.	H.S.	AV.
TEST					
OTHER FIRST CLASS	3	0	1	1	0.33
INT					
JPL					
NAT.W					·
B & H					

LAST SEASON: BOWLING

	O.	M.	R.	W.	AV.
TEST					
OTHER FIRST CLASS	93	17	268	16	16.75
INT					
JPL					
NAT.W					
B & H					

CAREER: BOWLING

	O.	M.	R.	W.	AV.
TEST					
OTHER FIRST CLASS	93	17	268	16	16.75
INT					
JPL					
NAT.W					
B & H					

35. True or false? Brian Close captained England seven times and never lost a Test.

36. True or false? Brian Close was capped for England before he was capped for Yorkshire.

COOPER, K.E.   Nottinghamshire

Full Name: Kevin Edwin Cooper.
Role: Left-hand bat, right-arm
fast- medium bowler.
Born: 27 December 1957, Sutton-
in-Ashfield.
Height: 6' 1" **Weight:** 12st 4lbs.
Nickname: Henry.
County debut: 1976.
County cap: 1980.
50 wickets in a season: 5.
1st-Class 5 w. in innings: 14.
Place in batting averages: 245
average: 11.58; (1984: —
average: —).
Place in bowling averages: 22
average: 25.67; (1984: 39
average: 26.75).
1st-Class catches 1985: 4
(career: 58).

Parents: Gerald Edwin and Margaret Cooper.
Wife: Linda Carol, 14 February 1981.
Children: Kelly Louise, 8 April 1982; Tara Amy, 22 November 1984.
Education: Secondary modern.
Jobs outside cricket: Has been warehouseman and maintenance man, also
P.R. in free trade department of local brewery.
Family links with cricket: Father played local cricket.
Overseas tours: Toured Australasia with Derrick Robins U-23 XI in 1979–80
off-season.
Other sports: Football, golf.

LAST SEASON: BATTING

	I.	N.O.	R.	H.S.	AV.
TEST					
OTHER FIRST CLASS	16	4	139	46	11.58
INT					
JPL	4	1	12	8	4.00
NAT.W	–	–	–	–	–
–					

CAREER: BATTING

	I.	N.O.	R.	H.S.	AV.
TEST					
OTHER FIRST CLASS	173	40	1252	46	9.41
INT					
JPL	32	10	110	31	5.00
NAT.W	4	1	29	11	9.66
B & H	13	8	62	25*	12.40

LAST SEASON: BOWLING

	O.	M.	R.	W.	AV.
TEST					
OTHER FIRST CLASS	604.3	187	1566	61	25.67
INT					
JPL	80.5	2	434	8	54.25
NAT.W	55.2	11	183	7	26.14
B & H	23	7	61	6	10.17

CAREER: BOWLING

	O.	M.	R.	W.	AV.
TEST					
OTHER FIRST CLASS	4412.4	1223	11867	432	27.47
INT					
JPL	650	38	3068	88	34.86
NAT.W	171.2	40	466	22	21.18
B & H	334.4	60	1193	38	31.40

Relaxations: Darts, dominoes, snooker, pool.
Extras: On 23 June 1974, playing for Hucknall Ramblers C.C., took 10 wickets for 6 runs in one innings against Sutton Coll. in the Mansfield and District League.
Best batting performance: 46 Nottinghamshire v Middlesex, Trent Bridge 1985.
Best bowling performance: 8-44 Nottinghamshire v Middlesex, Lord's 1985.

COWANS, N.G.   Middlesex

Full Name: Norman George Cowans.
Role: Right-hand bat, right-arm fast-medium bowler.
Born: 17 April 1961, Enfield St Mary, Jamaica.
Height: 6′ 3″ **Weight:** 14st.
Nickname: The Flash, Diamond Two, Persil, Cool Breeze.
County debut: 1980.
County cap: 1984.
Test debut: 1982–83.
No. of Tests: 19.
No. of One-Day Internationals: 23.
50 wickets in a season: 2.
1st-Class 50s scored: 1.
1st-Class 5 w. in innings: 13.
Place in batting averages: 254

average: 10.00; (1984: 263 average: 11.20).
Place in bowling averages: 12 average: 22.95; (1984: 11 average: 21.82).
1st-Class catches 1985: 5 (career: 36).
Parents: Gloria and Ivan Cowans.
Marital status: Single.
Education: Park High Secondary, Stanmore, Middlesex.
Qualifications: Qualified coach.
Jobs outside cricket: Squash and real tennis professional. Glassblower with Whitefriars hand-made glass.
Overseas tours: Young England tour to Australia 1979; Middlesex tour to Zimbabwe 1980; *Cricketer* tour to Dubai 1981; England to Australia and New Zealand 1982–83 and New Zealand and Pakistan 1983–84; International tour to Jamaica 1983; India and Australia with England 1984–85.
Overseas teams played for: Claremont-Cottesloe C.C., Perth, Australia.
Cricketers particularly learnt from: Dennis Lillee, Michael Holding, Wayne Daniel. "The aggression of Lillee, the power of Daniel, and the smoothness of Holding."

Other sports: Basketball, squash, table-tennis, swimming, tennis, real tennis.
Relaxations: Dancing, reading, being with friends, listening to music. Reggae. Arsenal F.C.
Extras: Two Young England Tests, one One-Day Youth International. Has won athletics championship in sprinting and javelin throwing.
Best batting performance: 66 Middlesex v Surrey, Lord's 1984.
Best bowling performance: 6-31 Middlesex v Leicestershire, Leicester 1985.

LAST SEASON: BATTING

	I.	N.O.	R.	H.S.	AV.
TEST	1	1	22	22*	–
OTHER FIRST CLASS	16	3	108	15*	8.31
INT	1	0	1	1	–
JPL	1	0	20	20	–
NAT.W	2	0	4	4	2.00
B & H	1	0	0	0	–

CAREER: BATTING

	I.	N.O.	R.	H.S.	AV.
TEST	29	7	175	36	7.96
OTHER FIRST CLASS	69	9	485	66	8.83
INT	8	3	13	4	2.60
JPL	9	4	61	20	12.20
NAT.W	9	2	32	12*	4.57
B & H	4	1	16	6	5.33

LAST SEASON: BOWLING

	O.	M.	R.	W.	AV.
TEST	33	6	128	2	64.00
OTHER FIRST CLASS	441.2	79	1548	71	21.80
INT	29.1	5	108	4	27.00
JPL	25	3	91	1	–
NAT.W	19	1	52	2	26.00
B & H	22	1	95	3	31.67

CAREER: BOWLING

	O.	M.	R.	W.	AV.
TEST	575.2	113	2003	51	39.27
OTHER FIRST CLASS	1638.4	314	5304	237	22.38
INT	213.4	17	913	23	39.70
JPL	176.2	8	794	27	29.40
NAT.W	129	19	438	18	24.33
B & H	94.2	10	345	18	19.17

COWDREY, C.S.   Kent

Full Name: Christopher Stuart Cowdrey.
Role: Right-hand bat, right-arm medium bowler.
Born: 20 October 1957, Farnborough, Kent.
Height: 6' 0" **Weight:** 13st.
Nickname: Cow.
County debut: 1977.
County cap: 1979.
Test debut: 1984–85.
No. of Tests: 5.
No. of One-Day Internationals: 3.
1000 runs in a season: 3.
1st-Class 50s scored: 35.
1st-Class 100s scored: 10.
1st-Class 5 w. in innings: 1.
One-day 50s: 19.
One-day 100s: 2.

Place in batting averages: 88 average: 32.70; (1984: 117 average: 30.56).
Place in bowling averages: 129 average: 50.40; (1984: 62 average: 29.71).
1st-Class catches 1985: 20 (career: 165).
Parents: Michael Colin and Penelope Susan Cowdrey.
Education: Wellesley House, Broadstairs; Tonbridge School.
Jobs outside cricket: Director, Personality Sports Promotions. Representative for Stuart Canvas Products, Warrington, Cheshire.
Family links with cricket: Grandfather, Stuart Chiesman, on Kent Committee, 12 years as Chairman. Pavilion on Kent's ground at Canterbury named after him. Father played for Kent and England, brother made Kent debut 1984.
Overseas tours: Captained Young England to West Indies, 1976; with Derrick Robins XI to Far East, South America and Australasia, 1979–80; India and Australia with England, 1984–85.
Overseas teams played for: Avondale C.C., Cape Town, 1983–84; Cumberland C.C., Sydney, 1978–79 and 1982–83.
Cricketers particularly learnt from: Asif Iqbal, Ray Dovey, Alan Dixon.
Other sports: "Any sport (get particular pleasure from beating Ellison at snooker)."
Relaxations: Watching Chelsea F.C., golf, writing, best bitter and fruit machines.
Extras: Played for Kent 2nd XI at age 15. Best man at Kim Barnett's wedding. 4th wicket partnership record for Kent in Benson & Hedges with Alan Ealham. Vice-captain 1984, Captain 1985.
Opinions on cricket: "We should play two one-day matches at weekends — a 40-over match on Saturday and a 2 innings per side match of 20 overs on Sunday."
Best batting performance: 159 Kent v Surrey, Canterbury 1985.
Best bowling performance: 3-17 Kent v Hampshire, Bournemouth 1980.

LAST SEASON: BATTING

	I.	N.O.	R.	H.S.	AV.
TEST					
OTHER FIRST CLASS	36	3	1079	159	32.70
INT					
JPL	14	2	202	38	16.83
NAT.W	3	0	38	19	12.67
B & H	5	0	158	54	31.60

LAST SEASON: BOWLING

	O.	M.	R.	W.	AV.
TEST					
OTHER FIRST CLASS	210.1	29	756	15	50.40
INT					
JPL	73	1	337	13	25.92
NAT.W	19	1	90	4	22.50
B & H	34	1	162	6	27.00

CAREER: BATTING

	I.	N.O.	R.	H.S.	AV.
TEST	6	1	96	38	19.20
OTHER FIRST CLASS	275	40	7357	159	31.31
INT	3	1	51	46*	25.50
JPL	109	15	2178	95	23.17
NAT.W	21	3	554	122*	30.78
B & H	32	4	758	114	27.07

CAREER: BOWLING

	O.	M.	R.	W.	AV.
TEST	61	2	288	4	72.00
OTHER FIRST CLASS	1108.3	202	3685	93	39.62
INT	8.4	0	55	2	27.50
JPL	310.3	4	1463	46	31.80
NAT.W	117	13	427	20	21.35
B & H	105	2	464	12	38.67

COWDREY, G.R.   Kent

Full Name: Graham Robert
Cowdrey
Role: Right-hand bat, right-arm
medium bowler, cover or short-
leg fielder.
Born: 27 June 1964,
Farnborough, Kent.
Height: 5' 11'' **Weight:** 13st.
Nickname: Cow, Van.
County debut: 1984.
1st-Class 50s scored: 2.
Place in batting averages: 74
average: 34.57; (1984: —
average: —).
1st-Class catches 1985: 5 (career: 6).
Parents: Michael Colin and
Penelope Susan Cowdrey.
Marital status: Single.
Family links with cricket: Father and
brother Chris played for England and Kent.
Education: Wellesley House, Broadstairs; Tonbridge School; Durham
University.
Qualifications: 8 O-levels, 3 A-levels, University entrance.
Off-season 1985–86: In Australia.
Overseas tours: Australia with Tonbridge School in 1980; "Christians in
Sport" India tour, 1985–86.
Overseas teams played for: Avendale C.C., Cape Town, 1983–84.
Cricketers particularly learnt from: Colin and Chris Cowdrey, Bob Woolmer,
Mark Benson.
Cricketers particularly admired: Graham Gooch, Paul Downton, Derek
Underwood.
Other sports: Most sports, particularly golf and squash.
Relaxations: Reading, theatre, music—"world authority on Van Morrison
(Irish musician), seen him 25 times in concert in three years. Ambition to see
him 100 times in concert. Love Bob Dylan, Paul Brady and Dire Straits."
Extras: Played for Young England and Australia. 1000 runs for Kent II first

LAST SEASON: BATTING

	I.	N.O.	R.	H.S.	AV.
TEST					
OTHER FIRST CLASS	9	2	242	53	34.57
INT					
JPL	2	0	41	21	20.50
NAT.W					
B & H					

CAREER: BATTING

	I.	N.O.	R.	H.S.	AV.
TEST					
OTHER FIRST CLASS	10	2	249	53	31.13
INT					
JPL	2	0	41	21	20.50
NAT.W					
B & H					

season on staff, captain of Kent II in 1984. Very interested in psychology of cricket. Broke 2nd XI record with 1300 runs in 26 innings in 1985.
Best batting performance: 53 Kent v Worcestershire, Worcester 1985.

COWLEY, N.G. Hampshire

Full Name: Nigel Geoffrey Cowley.
Role: Right-hand bat, off-break bowler.
Born: 1 March 1953, Shaftesbury, Dorset.
Height: 5' 7'' **Weight:** 11st. 7lbs.
Nickname: Dougall.
County debut: 1974.
County cap: 1978.
1000 runs in a season: 1.
50 wickets in a season: 5.
1st-Class 50s scored: 26.
1st-Class 100s scored: 3.
1st-Class 5 w. in innings: 4.
One-day 50s: 4.
Place in batting averages: 178 average: 21.30; (1984: 116 average: 30.65).
Place in bowling averages: 39 average: 27.95; (1984: 79 average: 31.77).
1st-Class catches 1985: 4 (career: 85).
Parents: Geoffrey and Betty Cowley.
Wife: Susan.

LAST SEASON: BATTING

	I.	N.O.	R.	H.S.	AV.
TEST					
OTHER FIRST CLASS	14	4	213	51	21.30
INT					
JPL	6	2	71	25	17.75
NAT.W	2	1	40	20*	–
B & H	4	0	25	11	6.25

CAREER: BATTING

	I.	N.O.	R.	H.S.	AV.
TEST					
OTHER FIRST CLASS	316	46	5980	109*	22.15
INT					
JPL	115	23	1794	74	19.50
NAT.W	4	1	70	30	23.33
B & H	7	1	60	23*	10.00

LAST SEASON: BOWLING

	O.	M.	R.	W.	AV.
TEST					
OTHER FIRST CLASS	247.5	60	699	25	27.95
INT					
JPL	86	5	417	13	32.07
NAT.W	29	1	114	5	22.80
B & H	45	4	144	5	28.80

CAREER: BOWLING

	O.	M.	R.	W.	AV.
TEST					
OTHER FIRST CLASS	4305.3	1155	11791	352	33.50
INT					
JPL	717.1	42	3375	112	30.13
NAT.W	52.2	2	181	10	18.10
B & H	85	16	247	6	41.17

Children: Mark and Darren.
Family links with cricket: Father played good club cricket.
Education: Mere Dutchy Manor, Mere, Wilts.
Overseas tours: Sri Lanka 1977, West Indies 1980.
Cricketers particularly learnt from: Peter Sainsbury.
Other sports: Football, badminton, golf — 10 handicap.
Extras: In charge of pre-season and match day training.
Best batting performance: 109* Hampshire v Somerset, Taunton 1977.
Best bowling performance: 6-48 Hampshire v Leicestershire, Southampton 1982.

CURRAN, K.M. Gloucestershire

Full Name: Kevin Malcolm Curran.
Role: Right-hand bat, right-arm fast-medium bowler.
Born: 7 September 1959, Rusape, Rhodesia.
Height: 6′ 2″ **Weight:** 13st. 3lbs.
Nickname: KC.
County debut: 1985.
County cap: 1985.
No. of One-Day Internationals: 6.
50 wickets in a season: 1.
1st-Class 50s scored: 8.
1st-Class 5 w. in innings: 2.
One-day 50s: 4.
Place in batting averages: 152 average: 24.58; (1984: — average: —).
Place in bowling averages: 14 average: 23.26; (1984: — average: —).
1st-Class catches 1985: 6 (career: 14).
Parents: Kevin Patrick Curran.
Marital status: Single.
Family links with cricket: Father played for Rhodesia 1949–53.
Education: Marandelias High School.
Qualifications: 6 O-levels, 2 M-levels.
Jobs outside cricket: Tobacco buyer/farmer.
Overseas tours: Sri Lanka 1982; World Cup 1983 with Zimbabwe.
Overseas teams played for: Zimbabwe 1981–85.
Cricketers particularly learnt from: Brian Davison, Duncan Fletcher.
Cricketers particularly admired: Brian Davison, Mike Procter, Graeme Pollock, Barry Richards.

Other sports: Rugby, squash and tennis.
Relaxations: Tiger fishing on the Zambezi and big game hunting.
Extras: Qualified to play in England by virtue of an Irish passport. Appeared for Zimbabwe in the 1982 I.C.C. Trophy, and then took part in the 1983 Prudential Cup. Had appeared in League cricket in Lancashire as professional for Rawtenstall before joining Gloucestershire.
Best batting performance: 96 Zimbabwe v Sri Lanka, Bulawayo 1982–83.
Best bowling performance: 5-35 Gloucestershire v Australia, Bristol 1985.

LAST SEASON: BATTING

	I.	N.O.	R.	H.S.	AV.
TEST					
OTHER FIRST CLASS	34	3	762	83	24.58
INT					
JPL	16	4	369	50	30.75
NAT.W	3	0	81	36	27.00
B & H	3	2	84	53*	

CAREER: BATTING

	I.	N.O.	R.	H.S.	AV.
TEST					
OTHER FIRST CLASS	64	8	1363	96	24.34
INT	6	0	212	73	35.33
JPL	16	4	369	50	30.75
NAT.W	3	0	81	36	27.00
B & H	3	2	84	53*	–

LAST SEASON: BOWLING

	O.	M.	R.	W.	AV.
TEST					
OTHER FIRST CLASS	471.5	103	1419	61	23.26
INT					
JPL	90.5	6	455	26	17.50
NAT.W	34	10	77	6	12.83
B & H	43.5	4	169	8	21.12

CAREER: BOWLING

	O.	M.	R.	W.	AV.
TEST					
OTHER FIRST CLASS	780.5	163	2474	106	23.34
INT	58.2	3	274	5	54.80
JPL	90.5	6	455	26	17.50
NAT.W	34	10	77	6	12.83
B & H	43.5	4	169	8	21.12

CURTIS, T.S. Worcestershire

Full Name: Timothy Stephen Curtis.
Role: Right-hand bat, leg-break bowler.
Born: 15 January 1960, Chislehurst, Kent.
Height: 5′ 11″ **Weight:** 12st. 5lbs.
Nickname: Tony, T.C.
County debut: 1979.
County cap: 1984.
1000 runs in a season: 2.
1st-Class 50s scored: 28.
1st-Class 100s scored: 4.
One-day 50s: 10.
Place in batting averages: 91 average: 31.75; (1984: 41 average: 42.57).
1st-Class catches 1985: 12 (career: 44).
Parents: Bruce and Betty Curtis.

Wife and date of marriage: Philippa, 21 September 1985.
Education: The Royal Grammar School, Worcester, Durham University, Cambridge University.
Qualifications: 12 O-levels, 4 A-levels, B.A. (Hons.) English, and postgraduate certificate in Education in English and Games.
Family links with cricket: Father played good club cricket in Bristol and Stafford.
Off-season 1985–86: Teaching in Worcester.
Overseas tours: N.C.A. U-19 tour of Canada 1979.
Cricketers particularly learnt from: Glenn Turner.
Other sports: Rugby, tennis, squash, golf.
Extras: Captained Durham University at cricket.
Opinions on cricket: "I am not convinced that 4-day county matches are a good idea because of reduced batting opportunities and the tendency of the increase in time to slow the game down even more. I think the reduction in overseas players was necessary and hope that the consequent reduction in crowd-pulling potential will be made up for by a greater sense of county identity, loyalty and support."
Best batting performance: 129 Worcestershire v Cambridge University, Worcester 1984.

LAST SEASON: BATTING

	I.	N.O.	R.	H.S.	AV.
TEST					
OTHER FIRST CLASS	45	2	1365	126*	31.75
INT					
JPL	13	2	304	76	27.63
NAT.W	4	0	187	92	31.17
B & H	5	0	204	75	40.80

CAREER: BATTING

	I.	N.O.	R.	H.S.	AV.
TEST					
OTHER FIRST CLASS	149	16	4174	129	31.38
INT					
JPL	33	9	755	76	31.45
NAT.W	7	1	292	92	48.67
B & H	12	0	313	75	26.17

LAST SEASON: BOWLING

	O.	M.	R.	W.	AV.
TEST					
OTHER FIRST CLASS					
INT					
JPL					
NAT.W					
B & H					

CAREER: BOWLING

	O.	M.	R.	W.	AV.
TEST					
OTHER FIRST CLASS	13.3	3	50	1	–
INT					
JPL					
NAT.W					
B & H	0.2	0	4	0	–

37. True or false? Brian Close plays golf to a single figure handicap, both right-handed and left-handed.

38. Who is the current editor of Wisden's Cricketers Almanack?

DANIEL, W.W.   Middlesex

Full Name: Wayne Wendell Daniel.
Role: Right-hand bat, right-arm
fast bowler.
Born: 16 January 1956, St Philip,
Barbados.
Nickname: Diamond.
County debut: 1977.
County cap: 1977.
Benefit: 1985.
Test debut: 1975–76.
No. of Tests: 5.
No. of One-Day Internationals: 18.
50 wickets in a season: 9.
1st-Class 50s scored: 2.
1st-Class 5 w. in innings: 31.
1st-Class 10 w. in innings: 7.
Place in bowling averages: 30
average: 26.72; (1984: 41
average: 27.09).
1st-Class catches 1985: 7 (career: 55).
Marital status: Single.
Relaxations: Enjoys listening to soul music.
Extras: Toured England with West Indies Schoolboys team 1974. Played for
Middlesex 2nd XI 1975. Debut for Barbados 1975–76. Toured with West Indies
to England 1976. Spent 1979–80 off-season in Barbados playing island cricket.
Best bowling record for Benson & Hedges Competition 1978 with 7 for 12 v
Minor Counties East at Ipswich.
Best batting performance: 53* Barbados v Jamaica, Bridgetown 1979–80; 53*
Middlesex v Yorkshire, Lord's 1981.
Best bowling performance: 9-61 Middlesex v Glamorgan, Swansea 1982.

LAST SEASON: BATTING

	I.	N.O.	R.	H.S.	AV.
TEST					
OTHER FIRST CLASS	15	5	48	19*	4.80
INT					
JPL	2	2	9	7*	–
NAT.W	2	1	9	7*	–
B & H	3	0	10	8	3.33

CAREER: BATTING

	I.	N.O.	R.	H.S.	AV.
TEST	11	4	46	11	6.57
OTHER FIRST CLASS	200	88	1335	53*	11.92
INT	5	4	49	16*	–
JPL	36	14	88	14	4.00
NAT.W	16	8	38	14	4.75
B & H	17	5	56	20*	4.67

LAST SEASON: BOWLING

	O.	M.	R.	W.	AV.
TEST					
OTHER FIRST CLASS	575.1	90	2111	79	26.72
INT					
JPL	73	6	296	15	19.73
NAT.W	21	2	71	2	35.50
B & H	60.4	10	236	11	21.45

CAREER: BOWLING

	O.	M.	R.	W.	AV.
TEST	292	61	910	36	25.28
OTHER FIRST CLASS	5619	1132	15881	735	21.61
INT	152				

DAVIDSON, I.C.   Lancashire

Full Name: Ian Charles Davidson.
Role: Right-hand bat, off-break bowler.
Born: 21 December 1964, Worsley, Lancashire.
Height: 5′ 8″ **Weight:** 10st. 10lbs.
Nickname: Davo, Lippy.
County debut: 1985.
1st-Class Catches 1985: 2 (career: 2).
Parents: James and Dorean Davidson.
Marital status: Single.
Education: Ellesmere Park High School, Eccles; Eccles VI Form College.
Qualifications: 9 O-levels, 1 A-level.
Off-season 1985–86: Playing for South Hobart in Tasmania.
Overseas tours: N.C.A. Young Cricketers, Holland, 1983.

Overseas teams played for: South Hobart C.C., Tasmania, 1983–84 and 1984–85.
Cricketers particularly learnt from: Jack Simmons, David Hughes, John Savage, teacher — Tony Potter.
Cricketers particularly admired: Clive Lloyd, Alan Border, John Emburey.
Other sports: Soccer, rugby league, lacrosse, squash.
Relaxations: Drink with friends, listening to tapes.
Best batting performance: 13 Lancashire v Warwickshire, Edgbaston 1985.
Best bowling performance: 2-24 Lancashire v Warwickshire, Edgbaston 1985.

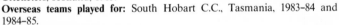

LAST SEASON: BATTING

	I.	N.O.	R.	H.S.	AV.
TEST					
OTHER FIRST CLASS	2	0	13	13	6.50
INT					
JPL					
NAT.W					
B & H					

CAREER: BATTING

	I.	N.O.	R.	H.S.	AV.
TEST					
OTHER FIRST CLASS	2	0	13	13	6.50
INT					
JPL					
NAT.W					
B & H					

LAST SEASON: BOWLING

	O.	M.	R.	W.	AV.
TEST					
OTHER FIRST CLASS	10	3	24	2	12.00
INT					
JPL					
NAT.W					
B & H					

CAREER: BOWLING

	O.	M.	R.	W.	AV.
TEST					
OTHER FIRST CLASS	10	3	24	2	12.00
INT					
JPL					
NAT.W					
B & H					

DAVIES, A.G. Surrey

Full Name: Alec G. Davies.
Role: Right-hand bat, wicket-keeper.
Born: 14 August 1962, Rawalpindi, Pakistan.
County debut: 1985.
1st-Class catches 1985: 3 (career: 3).
Education: Monmouth School; Bulmershe College, Reading.
Overseas teams played for: Adelaide Grade Cricket 1984–85.
Extras: Played for Gloucestershire 2nd XI and U-25s. Represented Middlesex County League and Middlesex Cricket Union.
Best batting performance: 26* Surrey v Zimbabwe, The Oval 1985.

LAST SEASON: BATTING

	I.	N.O.	R.	H.S.	AV.
TEST					
OTHER FIRST CLASS	1	1	26	26*	–
INT					
JPL					
NAT.W					
B & H					

CAREER: BATTING

	I.	N.O.	R.	H.S.	AV.
TEST					
OTHER FIRST CLASS	1	1	26	26*	–
INT					
JPL					
NAT.W					
B & H					

LAST SEASON: WICKET KEEPING

	C.	ST.			
TEST					
OTHER FIRST CLASS	3	–			
INT					
JPL					
NAT.W					
B & H					

CAREER: WICKET KEEPING

	C.	ST.			
TEST					
OTHER FIRST CLASS	3	–			
INT					
JPL					
NAT.W					
B & H					

39. For whom did the Bishop of Liverpool play first-class cricket?

40. For which county did Test Match umpire D.R. Shepherd play?

DAVIES, T.   Glamorgan

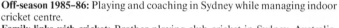

Full Name: Terry Davies.
Role: Right-hand bat, wicket-keeper.
Born: 25 October 1960, St Albans, Hertfordshire.
Height: 5' 6'' **Weight:** 10st. 4lbs.
Nickname: Sid.
County debut: 1979.
County cap: 1985.
1st-Class 50s scored: 6.
Place in batting averages: 115
average: 29.59; (1984: 250
average: 14.21).
Parents: Harry and Peggy Davies.
Wife and date of marriage: Noelle, 26 November 1983.
Education: Townsend Secondary School, St. Albans.
Jobs outside cricket: Carpet-fitter; worked in a sports shop.
Off-season 1985–86: Playing and coaching in Sydney while managing indoor cricket centre.
Family links with cricket: Brother playing club cricket in Sydney, Australia. "Father a fantastic back-garden bowler!"
Overseas teams played for: Bankstown Canterbury 1980–81, Bathurst 1981–82, Canberra 1982–83, Mosman 1983–86.
Cricketers particularly learnt from: Bob Taylor and Alan Knott.
Other sports: Squash, tennis, golf. Follows football.
Relaxations: Music, movies, good food.
Extras: Played soccer for Hertfordshire U-16 and for Watford and West Ham

LAST SEASON: BATTING

	I.	N.O.	R.	H.S.	AV.
TEST					
OTHER FIRST CLASS	25	8	503	75	29.59
INT					
JPL	7	2	54	20	10.80
NAT.W	2	0	19	12	9.50
B & H	3	1	16	7	8.00

CAREER: BATTING

	I.	N.O.	R.	H.S.	AV.
TEST					
OTHER FIRST CLASS	93	23	1459	75	20.84
INT					
JPL	23	13	239	46*	23.90
NAT.W	3	0	20	12	6.67
B & H	7	1	70	23	11.67

LAST SEASON: WICKET KEEPING

	C.	ST.			
TEST					
OTHER FIRST CLASS	44	5			
INT					
JPL	11	6			
NAT.W	6	–			
B & H	3	1			

CAREER: WICKET KEEPING

	C.	ST.			
TEST					
OTHER FIRST CLASS	133	19			
INT					
JPL	32	17			
NAT.W	6	–			
B & H	12	4			

Youths in the South-East Counties League. Had trials with West Ham F.C.,
Tottenham Hotspur and Luton. Trained with Watford for a season. On Lord's
ground staff 1977–78.
Best batting performance: 75 Glamorgan v Middlesex, Cardiff 1985.

DAVIS, M.R. Somerset

Full Name: Mark Richard Davis.
Role: Left-hand bat, left-arm fast-
medium bowler.
Born: 26 February 1962, Kilve,
Somerset.
Height: 6' 6'' **Weight:** 12st. 7lbs.
Nickname: Pooch.
County debut: 1982.
50 wickets in a season: 1.
1st-Class 50s scored: 1.
1st-Class 5 w. in innings: 4.
1st-Class 10 w. in match: 1.
Place in batting averages: 171
average: 22.50; (1984: 183
average: 22.25).
Place in bowling averages: 52
average: 52.04; (1984: 24
average: 23.77).
1st-Class catches 1985: 8 (career: 23).
Parents: Penelope and Robert Ernest Charles Davis.
Marital status: Single.
Education: Kilve Primary School; Williton First and Middle School; West
Somerset School; Bridgwater College.

LAST SEASON: BATTING

	I.	N.O.	R.	H.S.	AV.
TEST					
OTHER FIRST CLASS	20	6	315	40*	22.50
INT					
JPL	5	0	32	11	6.40
NAT.W	1	0	6	6	–
B & H	3	0	48	28	16.00

CAREER: BATTING

	I.	N.O.	R.	H.S.	AV.
TEST					
OTHER FIRST CLASS	63	19	683	60*	15.52
INT					
JPL	10	4	47	11	7.83
NAT.W	2	1	6	6	–
B & H	6	0	60	28	10.00

LAST SEASON: BOWLING

	O.	M.	R.	W.	AV.
TEST					
OTHER FIRST CLASS	366	61	1249	24	52.04
INT					
JPL	72	1	329	7	47.00
NAT.W	26	3	112	2	56.00
B & H	42	5	183	8	22.88

CAREER: BOWLING

	O.	M.	R.	W.	AV.
TEST					
OTHER FIRST CLASS	1252.1	231	4172	127	32.50
INT					
JPL	191.5	10	793	31	37.76
NAT.W	34	6	132	2	66.00
B & H	106	19	349	13	26.85

Qualifications: 7 O-levels.
Jobs outside cricket: Learning the building trade in father's firm.
Family links with cricket: "Father and relatives all play for my local club side, Kilve."
Cricketers particularly learnt from: P.J. Robinson (Somerset coach), M. Crowe, I. Botham, C. Dredge.
Cricketers particularly admired: I. Botham, M. Crowe.
Other sports: Squash and follows football.
Relaxations: "Music, skittles, my local pub."
Best batting performance: 60* Somerset v Glamorgan, Taunton 1984.
Best bowling performance: 7-55 Somerset v Northants, Northampton 1984.

DAVISON, B.F.   Gloucestershire

Full Name: Brian Fettes Davison.
Role: Right-hand bat, right-arm medium bowler.
Born: 21 December, Bulawayo, Rhodesia.
Height: 6' **Weight:** 13st.
Nickname: Davo, Shitzu.
County debut: 1970 (Leicestershire), 1985 (Gloucestershire).
County cap: 1971 (Leicestershire), 1985 (Gloucestershire)
Benefit: 1982 (with Leicestershire).
1000 runs in a season: 13.
1st-Class 50s scored: 150.
1st-Class 100s scored: 53.
1st-Class 5 w in innings: 1.
One-day 50s: 43.
One-day 100s: 2.
Place in batting averages: 72 average 35.14; (1984: — average: —).
1st-Class catches 1985: 9 (career: 330).
Parents: Jack and Vera Davison.
Wife and date of marriage: Caroline Ann, October 1971.
Children: Scott Fettes, 18 October 1973; Toni Jane, 18 September 1975.
Education: Gifford High School, Rhodesia.
Qualifications: National coach, 8 O-levels, 1 M-level.
Jobs outside cricket: Representative for Dunlop Ltd. and for finance company.
Family links with cricket: Father played for Combined Services team in Rhodesia during Second World War.

Overseas teams played for: Made debut for Rhodesia in 1967–68 Currie Cup Competition. Played cricket for Tasmania 1979–80, 1980–81, 1981–82.
Cricketers particularly learnt from: A.J. Pithey.
Other sports: Hockey international.
Relaxations: Golf, fishing and antiques.
Extras: Played 12 hockey Tests for Rhodesia. Now eligible to play cricket for England. Scored five consecutive centuries for Tasmania during 1980–81, equalling record of Don Bradman and David Hooks. Rejected invitation to play for Zimbabwe in I.C.C. Trophy in 1982 as he still hoped to play for England. Leicestershire 1970–83 (cap 1971). Returned to play for Gloucestershire in 1985.
Best batting performance: 189 Leicestershire v Australia, Leicester 1975.
Best bowling performance: 5-52 Rhodesia v Griqualand West, Bulawayo 1967-68.

LAST SEASON: BATTING

	I.	N.O.	R.	H.S.	AV.
TEST					
OTHER FIRST CLASS	35	7	984	111	35.14
INT					
JPL	13	2	410	103	37.27
NAT.W	3	0	136	81	45.33
B & H	3	0	85	41	28.33

CAREER: BATTING

	I.	N.O.	R.	H.S.	AV.
TEST					
OTHER FIRST CLASS	745	78	26923	189	40.36
INT					
JPL	185	28	4317	103	27.49
NAT.W	29	3	1100	99	42.31
B & H	60	5	1700	158*	30.91

LAST SEASON: BOWLING

	O.	M.	R.	W.	AV.
TEST					
OTHER FIRST CLASS					
INT					
JPL					
NAT.W					
B & H					

CAREER: BOWLING

	O.	M.	R.	W.	AV.
TEST					
OTHER FIRST CLASS	956.5	246	2660	82	32.43
INT					
JPL	220.2	10	1069	44	24.29
NAT.W	19	3	76	3	25.33
B & H	52	5	173	5	34.60

41. Which current first-class cricketer's nickname is "Arkle"?

42. Which fielding position is nicknamed "Suicide Corner" or "Boot Hill"?

DE FREITAS, P.A.J.   Leicestershire

Full Name: Phillip Anthony Jason De Freitas.
Role: Right-hand bat, right-arm medium bowler.
Born: 18 February 1966, Dominica.
Height: 6′ **Weight:** 12st.
Nickname: Arthur, Daffy, Half Chocolate.
County debut: 1985.
1st-Class 5 w. in innings: 1
Place in batting averages: 232
average: 13.00; (1984: —
average: —).
Place in bowling averages: 24
average: 26.04; (1984: —;
average: —).
1st-Class catches 1985: 2 (career: 2).
Parents: Sybil and Martin De Freitas.

Education: Willesden High School.
Qualifications: 2 C.S.E.s.
Off-season 1985–86: In Australia.
Family links with cricket: Father played in the Windward Is.
Overseas tours: Young England to West Indies 1985.
Cricketers particularly learnt from: Don Wilson, Ken Higgs, Paddy Clift.
Cricketers particularly admired: Paddy Clift.
Other sports: Football.
Relaxations: Music.
Best batting performance: 30* Leicestershire v Lancashire, Leicester 1985.
Best bowling performance: 5-39 Leicestershire v Lancashire, Leicester 1985.

LAST SEASON: BATTING

	I.	N.O.	R.	H.S.	AV.
TEST					
OTHER FIRST CLASS	12	3	117	30*	13.00
INT					
JPL	7	2	43	27	8.60
NAT.W					
B & H	–	–	–	–	–

CAREER: BATTING

	I.	N.O.	R.	H.S.	AV.
TEST					
OTHER FIRST CLASS	12	3	117	30*	13.00
INT					
JPL	7	2	43	27	8.60
NAT.W					
B & H	–	–	–	–	–

LAST SEASON: BOWLING

	O.	M.	R.	W.	AV.
TEST					
OTHER FIRST CLASS	234.2	43	703	27	26.04
INT					
JPL	57	1	315	13	24.23
NAT.W					
B & H	11	3	25	0	–

CAREER: BOWLING

	O.	M.	R.	W.	AV.
TEST					
OTHER FIRST CLASS	234.2	43	703	27	26.04
INT					
JPL	57	1	315	13	24.23
NAT.W					
B & H	11	3	25	0	–

DENNIS, S.J.   Yorkshire

Full Name: Simon John Dennis.
Role: Right-hand bat, left-arm
fast-medium bowler.
Born: 18 October 1960,
Scarborough, Yorkshire.
Height: 6′ 1″ **Weight:** 13st.
Nickname: Donkey.
County debut: 1980.
County cap: 1983.
50 wickets in a season: 1
1st-Class 50s scored: 1.
1st-Class 5 w. in innings: 4.
Place in batting averages: —
average: —; (1984: 194
average: 20.80).
Place in bowling averages: —
average: —; (1984: 109
average: 38.12).
1st-Class catches 1985: 1 (career: 13).
Parents: Margaret and Geoff.
Marital status: Single.
Education: Northstead County Primary School; Scarborough College.
Qualifications: 7 O-levels, 1 A-level, City and Guilds Computer Literacy.
Jobs outside cricket: Assistant groundsman at Scarborough C.C. Furniture
salesman.
Off-season 1985–86: Coaching and playing in South Africa.
Family links with cricket: Father captained Scarborough for many years.
Uncle, Frank Dennis, played for Yorkshire 1928–33. Uncle, Sir Leonard
Hutton, Yorkshire and England.
Overseas tours: India 1978–79 with E.S.C.A.; Australia 1980 with Young
England; with M.C.C. to East and Central Africa, 1981 and to America, 1982;
Gibraltar with Sheffield Cricket Lovers, 1983.
Overseas teams played for: Orange Free State 1982–83 and Durban
Collegians.
Cricketers particularly learnt from: Doug Padgett, Don Wilson, Ray
Illingworth.
Cricketers particularly admired: Dennis Lillee, John Lever.
Cricketing superstitions: "I fasten my pads on the inside instead of outside (not
that it does any good!)."
Injuries 1985: Played only three games due to an allergic reaction to an iodine
injection which resulted in three weeks in hospital.
Other sports: Rugby, hockey, squash, golf, American football, soccer.
Relaxations: Car maintenance, wine- and beer-making. Photography and real
ale. Home computer, video games. "Also terrible snooker player."
Extras: On debut for Yorkshire v Somerset, at Weston, 6 August 1980, got

Gavaskar as his first wicket. Cap awarded 6 August 1983.

Best batting performance: 53* Yorkshire v Nottinghamshire, Trent Bridge 1984.

Best bowling performance: 5-35 Yorkshire v Somerset, Sheffield 1981.

LAST SEASON: BATTING

	I.	N.O.	R.	H.S.	AV.
TEST					
OTHER FIRST CLASS	–	–	–	–	–
INT					
JPL	–	–	–	–	–
NAT.W					
B & H					

CAREER: BATTING

	I.	N.O.	R.	H.S.	AV.
TEST					
OTHER FIRST CLASS	51	20	313	53*	10.09
INT					
JPL	13	6	70	16*	10.00
NAT.W	2	0	14	14	7.00
B & H	2	0	10	10	5.00

LAST SEASON: BOWLING

	O.	M.	R.	W.	AV.
TEST					
OTHER FIRST CLASS	33.2	4	86	3	28.67
INT					
JPL	8	0	32	1	–
NAT.W					
B & H					

CAREER: BOWLING

	O.	M.	R.	W.	AV.
TEST					
OTHER FIRST CLASS	1333.3	266	4238	139	30.49
INT					
JPL	206.5	13	948	23	41.21
NAT.W	40.2	5	163	6	27.17
B & H	76	13	291	7	41.57

DERRICK, J. Glamorgan

Full name: John Derrick.
Role: Right-hand bat, right-arm medium bowler.
Born: 15 January 1963, Aberdare, South Wales.
Height: 6′ 2″ **Weight:** 13st. 11lbs.
Nickname: J.D., Bo.
County debut: 1983.
1st-Class 50s scored: 4.
Place in batting averages: 238 average: 12.31; (1984: 34 average: 43.88).
Place in bowling averages: 130 average: 50.43.
1st-Class catches 1985: 2 (career: 13).
Parents: John Raymond and Megan Irene Derrick.
Wife and date of marriage: Anne Irene, 20 April 1985.

Family links with cricket: Father and brother, Anthony, play club cricket for Aberdare.
Education: Glynhafod and Blaengwawr Primary Schools; Blaengwawr Comprehensive School.

Qualifications: School Certificate.
Jobs outside cricket: Coaching cricket.
Off-season 1985–86: Coaching cricket in New Zealand (Te Puke C.C.).
Overseas teams played for: Toombul C.C., Brisbane.
Cricketers particularly learnt from: Tom Cartwright, Don Wilson, Andy Wagner and senior Glamorgan players.
Cricketers particularly admired: Geoff Boycott, John Snow, Dennis Lillee.
Other sports: Soccer, squash, and golf; follows rugby and racing.
Relaxations: Listening to Lionel Richie, swimming, T.V.
Injuries 1985: Shoulder injury for one month.
Extras: Spent three years on M.C.C. groundstaff 1980–82. Coached at Lord's in winter of 1981.
Best batting performance: 69* Glamorgan v Surrey, Swansea 1984.
Best bowling performance: 4-60 Glamorgan v Northamptonshire, Northampton 1985.

LAST SEASON: BATTING

	I.	N.O.	R.	H.S.	AV.
TEST					
OTHER FIRST CLASS	15	2	160	52	12.31
INT					
JPL	6	1	39	10	7.80
NAT.W	1	0	4	4	–
B & H	3	1	60	42	30.00

CAREER: BATTING

	I.	N.O.	R.	H.S.	AV.
TEST					
OTHER FIRST CLASS	35	12	563	69*	24.48
INT					
JPL	16	5	112	18*	10.18
NAT.W	1	0	4	4	–
B & H	3	1	60	42	30.00

LAST SEASON: BOWLING

	O.	M.	R.	W.	AV.
TEST					
OTHER FIRST CLASS	226.1	39	706	14	50.43
INT					
JPL	46	2	221	2	110.5
NAT.W	23	6	41	4	10.25
B & H	28	4	108	2	54.00

CAREER: BOWLING

	O.	M.	R.	W.	AV.
TEST					
OTHER FIRST CLASS	368	71	1178	22	53.55
INT					
JPL	125.3	3	639	15	42.60
NAT.W	23	6	41	4	10.25
B & H	28	4	108	2	54.00

43. In how many Tests did D.R. Jardine captain England and what were the results?

44. Who is the Chairman of the Test and County Cricket Board?

DILLEY, G.R.   Kent

Full Name: Graham Roy Dilley.
Role: Left-hand bat, right-arm fast bowler.
Born: 18 May 1959, Dartford.
Height: 6' 4'' **Weight:** 15st.
Nickname: Picca.
County debut: 1977.
County cap: 1980.
Test debut: 1979–80.
No. of Tests: 18.
No. of One-Day Internationals: 18.
50 wickets in a season: 1.
1st-Class 50s scored: 4.
1st-Class 5 w. in innings: 11.
1st-Class 10 w. in match: 1.
Place in batting averages: 250
average: 10.93; (1984: —
average: —).
Place in bowling averages: 72
average: 33.59; (1984: — average: —).
1st-Class catches 1985: 1 (career: 54).
Parents: Geoff and Jean Dilley.
Wife and date of marriage: Helen, 6 November 1980.
Education: Dartford West Secondary School.
Qualifications: 3 O-levels.
Jobs outside cricket: Diamond setter.
Family links with cricket: Father and grandfather both played local cricket. His wife is his Kent colleague Graham Johnson's sister.
Overseas tours: With England to Australia 1979–80, West Indies 1981, India 1981–82, New Zealand and Pakistan 1983–84.

LAST SEASON: BATTING

	I.	N.O.	R.	H.S.	AV.
TEST					
OTHER FIRST CLASS	19	5	153	31	10.93
INT					
JPL	4	1	35	12	11.67
NAT.W	2	1	20	19	–
B & H	2	1	10	10*	–

CAREER: BATTING

	I.	N.O.	R.	H.S.	AV.
TEST	28	8	330	56	16.50
OTHER FIRST CLASS	110	39	1028	81	14.48
INT	11	3	96	31*	12.00
JPL	23	7	248	33	15.50
NAT.W	9	2	63	19	9.00
B & H	21	6	121	37*	8.07

LAST SEASON: BOWLING

	O.	M.	R.	W.	AV.
TEST					
OTHER FIRST CLASS	350.2	71	1075	32	33.59
INT					
JPL	37	0	166	4	41.50
NAT.W	21.5	4	53	1	–
B & H	31	4	86	5	17.20

CAREER: BOWLING

	O.	M.	R.	W.	AV.
TEST	521.4	103	1595	50	31.90
OTHER FIRST CLASS	2376.4	531	7202	252	28.58
INT	162	14	595	18	33.06
JPL	327.3	27	1306	56	23.32
NAT.W	114.5	21	349	16	21.81
B & H	239.5	30	818	40	20.45

Cricketers particularly learnt from: Dennis Lillee, John Snow.
Other sports: Golf, squash, badminton.
Relaxations: Music.
Extras: Got sacked from his first job with a Hatton Garden diamond firm after taking time off to play for Kent 2nd XI. Suffered from glandular fever at end of 1980 season, causing him to miss Centenary Test. Voted Young Cricketer of the Year 1980 by Cricket Writers' Club. Missed 1984 season after suffering back injury on 1983–84 tour.
Best batting performance: 81 Kent v Northamptonshire, Northampton 1979.
Best bowling performance: 6-66 Kent v Middlesex, Lord's 1979.

D'OLIVEIRA, D.B.   Worcestershire

Full Name: Damian Basil D'Oliveira.
Role: Right-hand bat, slow right-arm bowler.
Born: 19 October 1960, Cape Town, South Africa.
Height: 5′ 8″ **Weight:** 11st.
Nickname: Dolly.
County debut: 1982.
County cap: 1985.
1000 runs in a season: 1.
1st-Class 50s scored: 17.
1st-Class 100s scored: 3.
One-day 50s: 2.
One-day 100s: 1.
Place in batting averages: 114 average: 29.62; (1984: 155 average: 25.67).
Place in bowling averages: —
average: —; (1984: 94 average: 34.10).
1st-Class catches 1985: 21 (career: 53).
Parents: Basil and Naomi D'Oliveira.
Wife and date of marriage: Tracey, 26 September 1983.
Education: St. George's R.C. Primary School; Blessed Edward Oldcorne Secondary School.
Qualifications: 3 O-levels.
Off-season 1985–86: Working for Duncan Fearnley Cricket Sales.
Family links with cricket: Father played for Worcestershire and England.
Overseas tours: English Counties XI to Zimbabwe 1985.
Overseas teams played for: West Perth C.C., Western Australia, 1979–80; Christchurch Shirley 1982–83, 1983–84 on a Whitbread scholarship.

Cricketers particularly admired: Greg Chappell, Viv Richards.
Injuries 1985: Cartilege operation in January 1985.
Other sports: Football and most others.
Relaxations: Watching films, and eating out with friends.
Best batting performance: 139 Worcestershire v Sussex, Eastbourne 1985.
Best bowling performance: 2-50 Worcestershire v Lancashire, Old Trafford 1984.

LAST SEASON: BATTING

	I.	N.O.	R.	H.S.	AV.
TEST					
OTHER FIRST CLASS	44	2	1244	139	29.62
INT					
JPL	14	0	290	103	20.71
NAT.W	4	0	50	31	12.50
B & H	5	1	82	47*	20.50

CAREER: BATTING

	I.	N.O.	R.	H.S.	AV.
TEST					
OTHER FIRST CLASS	126	8	3105	139	26.31
INT					
JPL	44	2	753	103	17.92
NAT.W	7	1	117	48	19.50
B & H	11	2	171	57	19.00

LAST SEASON: BOWLING

	O.	M.	R.	W.	AV.
TEST					
OTHER FIRST CLASS	16	0	55	1	–
INT					
JPL					
NAT.W	8	0	37	2	18.50
B & H	2	0	22	0	–

CAREER: BOWLING

	O.	M.	R.	W.	AV.
TEST					
OTHER FIRST CLASS	198	38	658	15	43.86
INT					
JPL	39	2	232	7	33.14
NAT.W	20	4	65	4	16.25
B & H	30	2	136	2	68.00

DOUGHTY, R.J   Surrey

Full Name: Richard John Doughty.
Role: Right-hand bat, right-arm fast-medium bowler.
Born: 17 November 1960, Bridlington, Yorkshire.
Height: 6′ ½″ **Weight:** 13st.
Nickname: Dicky Doubts, Dangerous Dick.
County debut: 1981 (Gloucestershire), 1985 (Surrey).
1st-Class 50s scored: 1.
1st-Class 5 w. in innings: 2.
One-day 50s: 1.
Place in batting averages: 159 average: 23.90; (1984: — average: —).
Place in bowling averages: 19 average: 25.50; (1984: — average: —).
1st-Class catches 1985: 8 (career: 10).

Parents: Mary and Trevor Doughty.
Wife and date of marriage: Elizabeth, 2 April 1982.
Education: Scarborough College, N. Yorkshire.
Qualifications: 3 0-levels, 3 C.S.E.s.
Jobs outside cricket: "Anything I can get!"
Cricketers particularly learnt from: Don Wilson, Imran Khan, D.K. Lillee, Richard Edwards.
Other sports: Golf, rugby, skiing, surfing, squash. Watching motor-racing, high diving.
Relaxations: Music, eating, watching T.V., drawing, photography.
Extras: Released by Gloucestershire end of 1984 (debut 1981) and joined Surrey.
Best batting performance: 65 Surrey v Derbyshire, Derby 1985.
Best bowling performance: 6-33 Surrey v Warwickshire, The Oval 1985.

LAST SEASON: BATTING

	I.	N.O.	R.	H.S.	AV.
TEST					
OTHER FIRST CLASS	12	2	239	65	23.90
INT					
JPL	2	0	10	10	5.00
NAT.W					
B & H					

CAREER: BATTING

	I.	N.O.	R.	H.S.	AV.
TEST					
OTHER FIRST CLASS	31	9	453	65	20.59
INT					
JPL	16	6	156	50*	15.60
NAT.W	1	1	5	5*	–
B & H	4	0	69	31	17.25

LAST SEASON: BOWLING

	O.	M.	R.	W.	AV.
TEST					
OTHER FIRST CLASS	223.5	36	867	34	25.50
INT					
JPL	26	0	157	1	–
NAT.W					
B & H					

CAREER: BOWLING

	O.	M.	R.	W.	AV.
TEST					
OTHER FIRST CLASS	489.5	76	1806	57	31.68
INT					
JPL	128.3	0	804	14	57.42
NAT.W	15	2	60	2	30.00
B & H	44	4	193	3	64.33

45. What have Iain Anderson of Derby, Alan Green of Sussex and Robin Smith of Hampshire got in common?

46. Who is Chairman of the Pakistan selectors?

47. Who was the first recorded user of the reverse sweep in a Test match? (It was not Ian Botham.)

DOWNTON, P.R.   Middlesex

Full Name: Paul Rupert Downton.
Role: Right-hand bat, wicket-keeper.
Born: 4 April 1957, Farnborough, Kent.
Height: 5′ 10″ **Weight:** 11st. 9lbs.
Nickname: Nobby.
County debut: 1977 (Kent), 1980 (Middlesex).
County cap: 1979 (Kent), 1981 (Middlesex).
Test debut: 1980–81.
No. of Tests: 21.
No. of One-Day Internationals: 11.
1st-Class 50s scored: 22.
1st-Class 100s scored: 1.
One-day 50s: 3.
Place in batting averages: 51 average: 38.90; (1984: 153 average: 25.75).
Parents: George Charles and Jill Elizabeth Downton.
Wife and date of marriage: Alison, 19 October 1985.
Education: Sevenoaks School; Exeter University.
Qualifications: 9 O-levels, 3 A-levels, Law degree (LLB); N.C.A. coaching course.
Family links with cricket: Father kept wicket for Kent 1948–49.
Overseas tours: England tour of Pakistan and New Zealand 1977, West Indies 1980–81, India and Australia 1984–85, England Young Cricketers tour of West Indies (Vice-captain) 1976.
Overseas teams played for: Sandgate, Redcliffe 1981–82; Stellenbosch University 1983–4.

LAST SEASON: BATTING

	I.	N.O.	R.	H.S.	AV.
TEST	7	1	114	54	19.00
OTHER FIRST CLASS	22	6	742	104	46.38
INT	2	1	27	16*	–
JPL	7	2	163	70	32.60
NAT.W	2	0	24	15	12.00
B & H	4	0	32	24	8.00

CAREER: BATTING

	I.	N.O.	R.	H.S.	AV.
TEST	31	6	576	74	23.04
OTHER FIRST CLASS	202	41	3573	104	22.19
INT	9	3	165	44*	27.50
JPL	60	22	772	70	20.31
NAT.W	17	2	267	62	17.80
B & H	18	6	177	28	14.75

LAST SEASON: WICKET KEEPING

	C.	ST.			
TEST	19	1			
OTHER FIRST CLASS	38	4			
INT	1	–			
JPL	7	4			
NAT.W	2	–			
B & H	5	5			

CAREER: WICKET KEEPING

	C.	ST.			
TEST	54	3			
OTHER FIRST CLASS	370	53			
INT	7	1			
JPL	90	27			
NAT.W	29	4			
B & H	27	9			

112

Cricketers particularly learnt from: Father, Alan Knott, Clive Radley.
Cricketers particularly admired: Alan Knott, Rod Marsh.
Off-season 1985–86: On England tour of West Indies.
Other sports: Rugby (played in England U-19 squad 1975, Exeter University 1st XV), golf, tennis.
Relaxations: Reading.
Extras: Made debut for Kent C.C.C. in 1977, gaining cap in 1979. Played for Kent 2nd XI at age 16.
Best batting performance: 104 Middlesex v Northamptonshire, Lord's 1985.

DREDGE, C.H.   Somerset

Full Name: Colin Herbert Dredge.
Role: Left-hand bat, right-arm medium bowler.
Born: 4 August 1954, Frome, Somerset.
Height: 6' 5" **Weight:** 14st. 7lbs.
Nickname: Herbie, Bert.
County debut: 1976.
County cap: 1978.
50 wickets in a season: 4.
1st-Class 50s scored: 4.
1st-Class 5 w. in innings: 11.
Place in batting averages: 182 average: 20.67; (1984: 260 average: 11.89).
Place in bowling averages: 90 average: 37.16; (1984: 55 average: 28.94).
1st-Class catches 1985: 7 (career: 77).
Parents: Frederick and Kathleen Dredge.
Wife and date of marriage: Mandy, 9 December 1978.
Children: David, 13 November 1979; Mark, 6 July 1981; Neil, 27 June 1983.
Education: Wesley Methodist School; Milk Street School; Oakfield School.
Qualifications: Qualified toolmaker. Served apprenticeship Rolls Royce Ltd., Patchway, Bristol.
Jobs outside cricket: Toolmaker.
Family links with cricket: One of ten children, eight boys and two girls; all the brothers have played cricket for Frome C.C.
Cricketers particularly learnt from: Peter White, Peter Robinson.
Relaxations: "Football, watching TV, playing with my children."
Other sports: Played Western League football for Welton Rovers. Played for Bristol City Reserves 1974–76 and now for Frome Town A.F.C.

Best batting performance: 56* Somerset v Yorkshire, Harrogate 1977.
Best bowling performance: 6-37 Somerset v Gloucestershire, Bristol 1981.

LAST SEASON: BATTING

	I.	N.O.	R.	H.S.	AV.
TEST					
OTHER FIRST CLASS	13	7	124	31	20.67
INT					
JPL	3	3	17	13*	–
NAT.W	1	1	0	0*	–
B & H					

CAREER: BATTING

	I.	N.O.	R.	H.S.	AV.
TEST					
OTHER FIRST CLASS	197	65	1873	56*	14.19
INT					
JPL	47	26	240	25*	11.42
NAT.W	8	4	20	9	5.00
B & H	17	10	65	17*	9.29

LAST SEASON: BOWLING

	O.	M.	R.	W.	AV.
TEST					
OTHER FIRST CLASS	317.4	73	929	25	37.16
INT					
JPL	30	1	136	4	36.00
NAT.W	28	4	102	7	14.57
B & H					

CAREER: BOWLING

	O.	M.	R.	W.	AV.
TEST					
OTHER FIRST CLASS	4277.5	1017	11962	405	29.54
INT					
JPL	815.1	40	3612	140	25.80
NAT.W	236.3	32	806	36	22.39
B & H	355.2	41	1236	52	23.78

DYER, R.I.H.B. Warwickshire

Full Name: Robin Ian Henry Benbow Dyer.
Role: Right-hand bat.
Born: 22 December 1958, Hertford.
Height: 6′ 4″ **Weight:** 13st.
Nickname: "Dobbin, Donkey, Tuft — generally more nicknames than Christian names!"
County debut: 1981.
1000 runs in a season: 2.
1st-Class 50s scored: 18.
1st-Class 100s scored: 3.
One-day 50s: 2.
One-day 100s: 1.
Place in batting averages: 119 average: 28.88; (1984: 79 average: 34.91).
1st-Class catches 1985: 19 (career: 34).
Parents: Ian and Dee Dyer.
Marital status: Single.

Family links with cricket: "Father and mother gave me a lot of encouragement. Also my sister bowls in-swingers although she's not as 'big at the crease' as Sarfraz!"

Education: Wellington College, Berkshire; Durham University.
Qualifications: B.A. Hons in Politics; 3 A-levels.
Jobs outside cricket: Hamper-packer.
Cricketing superstitions: "I don't like changing my kit after scoring runs."
Overseas tours: With English Schools to India 1977–78.
Cricketers particularly learnt from: "Learnt a lot from Fred Berry, the former Surrey player, who was coach at Wellington. Specially admired M.J.K. Smith and Dennis Amiss."
Other sports: Golf and squash and watches Rugby Union regularly.
Relaxations: Listening to music (particularly Peter Gabriel), reading good books, watching films, theatre, eating and drinking in sociable situations, travelling.
Extras: Captained Durham University. Wears spectacles.
Best batting performance: 109* Warwickshire v Zimbabwe, Edgbaston 1985.

LAST SEASON: BATTING

	I.	N.O.	R.	H.S.	AV.
TEST					
OTHER FIRST CLASS	46	3	1242	109*	28.88
INT					
JPL	7	0	87	50	12.42
NAT.W	2	0	33	18	16.50
B & H	4	0	63	40	15.75

CAREER: BATTING

	I.	N.O.	R.	H.S.	AV.
TEST					
OTHER FIRST CLASS	106	9	2752	109*	28.37
INT					
JPL	22	2	357	50	17.85
NAT.W	7	0	205	119	29.29
B & H	6	0	128	54	21.33

LAST SEASON: BOWLING

	O.	M.	R.	W.	AV.
TEST					
OTHER FIRST CLASS					
INT					
JPL					
NAT.W					
B & H					

CAREER: BOWLING

	O.	M.	R.	W.	AV.
TEST					
OTHER FIRST CLASS	1	0	2	0	–
INT					
JPL	2	0	18	0	–
NAT.W					
B & H					

48. Who wrote *The Young Cricketer's Tutor*, published in 1833 and described by John Arlott as an "unassailable classic" of cricket?

49. What was the multi-coloured cricket club cap which Douglas Jardine sometimes wore when captaining England (M.C.C.) in Australia in 1933-34 which so infuriated some Australians?

EAST, D.E.   Essex

Full Name: David Edward East.
Role: Right-hand bat, wicket-keeper.
Born: 27 July 1959, Clapton.
Height: 5' 10" **Weight:** 12st. 7lbs.
Nickname: "Various insults, but Ethel seems popular."
County debut: 1981.
County cap: 1982.
1st-Class 50s scored: 11.
1st-Class 100s scored: 2.
Place in batting averages: 75 average: 34.19; (1984: 245 average: 14.57).
Parents: Edward William and Joan Lillian East.
Wife and date of marriage: Jeanette Anne, 14 September 1984.
Family links with cricket: Father played club cricket for Hadley C.C., an Essex touring side.
Education: Millfields Primary; Hackney Downs School; University of East Anglia.
Qualifications: B.Sc. Hons in Biological Sciences. Advanced cricket coach.
Jobs outside cricket: Shipping clerk, Byron Shipping, 1979; Field sales manager, M.C. Kirby Ltd., Norwich; insurance clerk, Flett Sinclair Ltd., Ilford, Essex.
Overseas teams played for: Avondale C.C., Cape Town, 1984–85.
Cricketing superstitions: The number 111.
Cricketers particularly learnt from: Bill Morris, Ilford Cricket School, Alan Knott.

LAST SEASON: BATTING

	I.	N.O.	R.	H.S.	AV.
TEST					
OTHER FIRST CLASS	32	6	889	131	34.19
INT					
JPL	6	1	28	14*	5.60
NAT.W	2	0	9	8	4.50
B & H	3	3	19	12*	–

CAREER: BATTING

	I.	N.O.	R.	H.S.	AV.
TEST					
OTHER FIRST CLASS	150	23	2703	131	21.28
INT					
JPL	31	11	234	43	11.70
NAT.W	11	4	81	25*	11.57
B & H	12	3	148	33	16.44

LAST SEASON: WICKET KEEPING

	C.	ST.
TEST		
OTHER FIRST CLASS	72	4
INT		
JPL	12	–
NAT.W	7	–
B & H	7	–

CAREER: WICKET KEEPING

	C.	ST.
TEST		
OTHER FIRST CLASS	297	24
INT		
JPL	58	10
NAT.W	18	2
B & H	30	–

Other sports: Hockey, squash, interested in most but loathes horse-racing.
Relaxations: Playing the piano, listening to various types of music, video.
Extras: Spent 1980 season with Northants. 2nd XI. Played for Essex 2nd XI at 16. Gordon's Gin Wicket-keeper of the Year 1983.
Best batting performance: 131 Essex v Gloucestershire, Southend 1985.

EDMONDS, P.H.   Middlesex

Full Name: Phillippe Henri
Edmonds.
Role: Right-hand bat, slow left-arm bowler.
Born: 8 March 1951, Lusaka,
Zambia.
Height: 6' 2''.
Nickname: Goat, Henry, Rommel,
Duke.
County debut: 1971.
County cap: 1974.
Benefit: 1983 (£80,000).
Test debut: 1975.
No. of Tests: 33.
No. of One-Day Internationals: 23.
50 wickets in a season: 11.
1st-Class 50s scored: 22.
1st-Class 100s scored: 3.
1st-Class 5 w. in innings: 47.
1st-Class 10 w. in match: 9.
One-day 50s: 2.
Place in batting averages: 229 average: 13.22; (1984: 197 average: 20.69).
Place in bowling averages: 20 average: 25.55; (1984: 43 average: 27.22).
1st-Class catches 1985: 23 (career: 314).
Wife: Frances.
Education: Gilbert Rennie High School, Lusaka; Skinner's School, Tunbridge Wells; Cranbrook School; Cambridge University.
Jobs outside cricket: Has worked for sports promotion and finance company.
Overseas tours: Pakistan and New Zealand 1977–78; Australia 1978–79; India and Australia 1984–85.
Overseas teams played for: Eastern Province in 1975–76 Currie Cup Competition.
Off-season 1985–86: With England in West Indies.
Other sports: Played rugby for Cambridge but missed blue. Squash.
Relaxations: "Read *Financial Times* avidly at breakfast," crosswords.

Extras: Cambridge cricket blue 1971-72-73, Captain 1973. Vice-captain of Middlesex, 1980.
Best batting performance: 142 Middlesex v Glamorgan, Swansea 1984.
Best bowling performance: 8-53 Middlesex v Hampshire, Bournemouth 1984.

LAST SEASON: BATTING

	I.	N.O.	R.	H.S.	AV.
TEST	5	0	47	21	9.40
OTHER FIRST CLASS	18	6	174	29*	14.50
INT	2	1	6	6*	–
JPL	4	0	13	7	3.25
NAT.W	2	1	1	1*	–
B & H	3	0	2	2	0.67

LAST SEASON: BOWLING

	O.	M.	R.	W.	AV.
TEST	225.5	59	549	15	36.60
OTHER FIRST CLASS	626.2	184	1393	61	22.84
INT	21	2	81	1	–
JPL	53.2	4	220	9	24.44
NAT.W	24	2	88	6	14.67
B & H	55	3	199	13	15.31

CAREER: BATTING

	I.	N.O.	R.	H.S.	AV.
TEST	39	6	652	64	19.76
OTHER FIRST CLASS	397	67	6393	142	19.37
INT	16	6	100	20	10.00
JPL	112	27	1259	52	14.81
NAT.W	30	9	368	63*	17.52
B & H	37	8	482	44*	16.62

CAREER: BOWLING

	O.	M.	R.	W.	AV.
TEST	199 1106.4	48 376	2866	88	32.57
OTHER FIRST CLASS	287 10873.5	72 3390	25343	1041	24.35
INT	28 157.2	1 14	687	20	34.35
JPL	924	72	3866	169	22.87
NAT.W	362.2	62	1071	43	24.91
B & H	612.3	77	1209	58	20.85

ELLCOCK, R.M.   Worcestershire

Full Name: Ricardo McDonald Ellcock.
Role: Right-hand bat, right-arm fast bowler.
Born: 17 June 1965, Barbados.
Height: 5' 11" **Weight:** 13st.
Nickname: Ricky.
County debut: 1982.
Place in batting averages: —
average: —; (1984: 147
average: 26.80).
Place in bowling averages: —
average: —; (1984: 26 average: 24.62).
1st-Class catches 1985: 5 (career: 3).
Parents: Everson McDonald (deceased) and Ione Marian Ellcock.
Marital status: Single.
Education: Welches Mixed School, Combermere, Barbados; Malvern College, England.
Qualifications: 6 0-levels.

Off season 1985–86: Playing cricket in Barbados.
Overseas teams played for: Combined Schools, Barbados, 1980; Carlton and Barbados.
Overseas tours: Around West Indies with Barbados.
Cricketers particularly learnt from: Malcolm Marshall. Admires Alvin Kallicharran and Michael Holding.
Cricketing superstitions: "Prayers."
Other sports: Table-tennis and basketball; watches soccer and motor-racing.
Relaxations: Movies, music, T.V. "Planning to learn to fly."
Best batting performance: 45* Worcestershire v Essex, Worcester 1984.
Best bowling performance: 4-34 Worcestershire v Glamorgan, Worcester 1984.

LAST SEASON: BATTING

	I.	N.O.	R.	H.S.	AV.
TEST					
OTHER FIRST CLASS	1	0	3	3	–
INT					
JPL					
NAT.W					
B & H					

CAREER: BATTING

	I.	N.O.	R.	H.S.	AV.
TEST					
OTHER FIRST CLASS	34	8	340	45*	13.08
INT					
JPL	5	2	6	5*	2.00
NAT.W	1	0	6	6	–
B & H	2	1	16	12	–

LAST SEASON: BOWLING

	O.	M.	R.	W.	AV.
TEST					
OTHER FIRST CLASS	28	0	91	0	–
INT					
JPL					
NAT.W					
B & H					

CAREER: BOWLING

	O.	M.	R.	W.	AV.
TEST					
OTHER FIRST CLASS	561.4	80	2011	63	31.92
INT					
JPL	61.3	4	235	13	18.08
NAT.W	10	2	49	3	16.33
B & H	25	4	98	3	32.67

50. What was the colour of the original M.C.C. "uniform"?

51. How did you hit a six before 1910?

52. When did batsmen start regularly wearing protective helmets?

ELLIS, R.G.P.　　　　　　　　Gloucestershire

Full Name: Richard Gary Peter Ellis.
Role: Right-hand bat.
Born: 20 December 1960, Paddington.
Height: 6′ 1″ **Weight:** 12st.
Nickname: Hermie.
County debut: 1982 (Middlesex), 1985 (Gloucestershire).
1st-Class 50s scored: 11.
1st-Class 100s scored: 2.
One-day 50s: 1.
1st-Class catches 1985: 2 (career: 20).
Parents: Peter and Lilian Ellis.
Family links with cricket: Father on Lord's ground staff; played one first-class game v Cambridge and was a pro. in Scotland.
Education: Oxford University; Haileybury College.
Qualifications: 9 O-levels, 4 A-levels, B.A. in History.
Jobs outside cricket: Squash professional, labourer, teacher.
Cricketing superstitions: The number 111.
Cricketers particularly admired: Tony Greig.
Other sports: Squash, rackets, real tennis, golf.
Relaxations: Reading, watching television, music.
Extras: Captain, Oxford University C.C. 1982. Also won blues in squash and rackets. Captain of Middlesex 2nd XI on return from university, 2nd XI cap in 1980. Played for England U-15 as an off-break bowler but no longer bowls. Released at end of 1984 season and joined Gloucestershire.
Best batting performance: 105* Oxford University v Surrey, Oxford 1982.
Best bowling performance: 2-40 Oxford University v Surrey, Oxford 1982.

LAST SEASON: BATTING

	I.	N.O.	R.	H.S.	AV.
TEST					
OTHER FIRST CLASS	2	0	23	20	11.50
INT					
JPL	2	0	28	21	14.00
NAT.W					
B & H					

CAREER: BATTING

	I.	N.O.	R.	H.S.	AV.
TEST					
OTHER FIRST CLASS	73	3	2020	105*	28.86
INT					
JPL	13	0	219	52	16.84
NAT.W	1	1	15	15*	-
B & H	8	0	54	16	6.75

LAST SEASON: BOWLING

	O.	M.	R.	W.	AV.
TEST					
OTHER FIRST CLASS	3	1	7	0	-
INT					
JPL					
NAT.W					
B & H					

CAREER: BOWLING

	O.	M.	R.	W.	AV.
TEST					
OTHER FIRST CLASS	86	21	271	4	67.75
INT					
JPL					
NAT.W					
B & H					

ELLISON, R.M.   Kent

Full Name: Richard Mark Ellison.
Role: Left-hand bat, right-arm
medium bowler, outfielder.
Born: 21 September 1959,
Ashford, Kent.
Height: 6′ 3″ **Weight:** 14st. 7lbs.
Nickname: Plank, Snooker,
Bungalow, Elly ("changing all
the time").
County debut: 1981.
County cap: 1983.
Test debut: 1984.
No. of Tests: 7.
No. of One-Day Internationals: 9.
50 wickets in a season: 3.
1st-Class 50s scored: 9.
1st-Class 100s scored: 1.
1st-Class 5 w. in innings: 7.
1st-Class 10 w. in match: 2.

One-day 50s: 4.
Place in batting averages: 131 average: 26.98; (1984: 159 average: 24.80).
Place in bowling averages: 1 average: 17.20; (1984: 16 average: 22.42).
1st-Class catches 1985: 4 (career: 35).
Parents: Peter Ellison (deceased) and Bridget Ellison.
Wife and date of marriage: Fiona, 28 September 1985.
Family links with cricket: Grandfather played with the Grace brothers.
Brother, Charles Christopher, played for Cambridge University in 1982.
Education: Friars Prep. School; Tonbridge School; St Luke's College, Exeter
University.
Qualifications: 8 O-levels, 2 A-levels, various teaching awards. B.Ed.
(teacher).
Overseas tours: With England to India and Australia 1984–85; England to
Sharjah 1985.
Overseas teams played for: University of Witwatersrand 1983–84, 1984–85.
Off-season 1985-86: England tour of West Indies.
Cricketers particularly learnt from: Derek Underwood, Bob Woolmer, Ray
Dovey.
Cricketers particularly admired: "Too many to mention."
Other sports: "Hockey (U.A.U. trial), snooker. Anything apart from horse-
racing and show-jumping."
Relaxations: "Music; T.V., golf, real ale."
Extras: Public Schools Cricketer of the Year 1978. Invited to tour with
M.C.C. to Bangladesh (1980) and East and Central Africa (1981) but unable
to go due to studies. Scored 55 n.o. on debut. "Overweight, so Chris Cowdrey
and Mark Benson keep telling me — but who are they to know?"
Injuries 1985: Ankle ligament strain (out for eight weeks).

Opinions on cricket: "Still too many overs leading to too late finishes. Fines for over-rates should be abolished."
Best batting performance: 108 Kent v Oxford University, Oxford 1984.
Best bowling performance: 7-87 Kent v Northamptonshire, Maidstone 1985.

LAST SEASON: BATTING

	I.	N.O.	R.	H.S.	AV.
TEST	1	0	3	3	–
OTHER FIRST CLASS	25	6	536	98	28.21
INT					
JPL	10	3	109	30	15.57
NAT.W	2	1	47	39*	–
B & H	2	0	15	15	7.50

CAREER: BATTING

	I.	N.O.	R.	H.S.	AV.
TEST	8	1	89	44	12.72
OTHER FIRST CLASS	103	29	1981	108	26.77
INT	9	4	59	24	11.80
JPL	39	16	635	84	27.60
NAT.W	12	6	231	49*	38.50
B & H	11	1	205	74	20.50

LAST SEASON: BOWLING

	O.	M.	R.	W.	AV.
TEST	75.5	20	185	17	10.88
OTHER FIRST CLASS	356.2	93	933	48	19.44
INT					
JPL	72	6	324	14	23.14
NAT.W	30	5	93	7	13.29
B & H	24.5	2	114	2	57.00

CAREER: BOWLING

	O.	M.	R.	W.	AV.
TEST	259.5	60	674	27	24.96
OTHER FIRST CLASS	1740.1	472	4385	179	24.50
INT	69	7	289	8	36.12
JPL	305.4	16	1342	57	23.54
NAT.W	135	26	410	22	18.64
B & H	120.5	22	370	16	23.13

EMBUREY, J.E.   Middlesex

Full Name: John Ernest Emburey.
Role: Right-arm bat, off-break bowler, slip or gully fielder.
Born: 20 August 1952, Peckham, London.
Height: 6' 2" **Weight:** 14st.
Nickname: Embers, Ernie.
County debut: 1973.
County cap: 1977.
Benefit: 1986.
Test debut: 1978.
No. of Tests: 28.
No. of One-Day Internationals: 8.
50 wickets in a season: 9.
1st-Class 50s scored: 19.
1st-Class 100s scored: 2.
1st-Class 5 w. in innings: 45.
1st-Class 10 w. in match: 8.
One-day 50s: 1.
Place in batting averages: 126
average: 27.66; (1984: 223 average: 17.54).
Place in bowling averages: 47 average: 29.44; (1984: 45 average: 27.47).
1st-Class catches 1985: 22 (career: 242).

122

Parents: John and Rose Emburey.
Wife and date of marriage: Susie, 20 September 1980.
Children: Clare, 1 March 1983 (Cape Town).
Education: Peckham Manor Secondary School.
Qualifications: O-levels, Advanced Cricket Coaching Certificate.
Jobs outside cricket: "No other jobs. Have been abroad coaching most years."
Family links with cricket: "An uncle, Charles Roff, was a very good cricketer. His father made him take an apprenticeship which stopped him going any further with cricket." Brother, Stephen, represented London Schools Colts in 1977.
Overseas tours: With England to Australia 1979-80 (following injury to Geoff Miller), West Indies 1981, India 1981–82.
Overseas teams played for: St Kilda C.C., Melbourne, 1979-80, 1984-85; Prahran, Melbourne, 1977-78; Western Province 1982-83, 1983-84.
Off-season 1985-86: Organising benefit and touring West Indies with England.
Cricketers particularly learnt from: "Many."
Other sports: Golf, squash.
Relaxations: Reading.
Extras: Played for Surrey Young Cricketers 1969-70. Middlesex Vice-captain since 1983. Banned from Test cricket for three years after playing for England rebels in South Africa. Hit 6 sixes in 7 balls for Western Province v Eastern Province 1983-84 (52 n.o. in 22 balls).
Best batting performance: 133 Middlesex v Essex, Chelmsford 1983.
Best bowling performance: 7-6 Middlesex v Cambridge University, Cambridge 1977.

LAST SEASON: BATTING

	I.	N.O.	R.	H.S.	AV.
TEST	6	2	130	33	32.50
OTHER FIRST CLASS	19	2	451	68	26.53
INT					
JPL	6	2	38	11*	9.50
NAT.W	2	0	12	10	6.00
B & H	4	3	64	38*	–

LAST SEASON: BOWLING

	O.	M.	R.	W.	AV.
TEST	248.4	75	544	19	28.63
OTHER FIRST CLASS	548.3	155	1193	40	29.83
INT					
JPL	64	5	257	13	19.76
NAT.W	24	2	69	5	13.80
B & H	54	11	165	9	18.33

CAREER: BATTING

	I.	N.O.	R.	H.S.	AV.
TEST	39	8	456	57	14.71
OTHER FIRST CLASS	282	62	4828	133	21.95
INT	7	1	31	18	5.17
JPL	94	33	943	40*	15.46
NAT.W	18	6	274	36*	22.83
B & H	26	9	363	50	21.35

CAREER: BOWLING

	O.	M.	R.	W.	AV.
TEST	144.4 886.1	49 278	2240	75	29.87
OTHER FIRST CLASS	155.1 8389.1	39 2512	19131	818	23.39
INT	72.3	9	262	5	52.40
JPL	936.5	84	3874	179	21.64
NAT.W	314	56	789	28	28.18
B & H	324.5	60	872	29	30.07

EVANS, K.P.   Nottinghamshire

Full Name: Kevin Paul Evans.
Role: Right-hand bat, right-arm medium bowler.
Born: 10 September 1963, Calverton, Nottingham.
Height: 6' 2" **Weight:** 12st. 8lbs.
Nickname: Kevans, Ghost.
County debut: 1984.
1st-Class catches 1985: 1 (career: 4).
Parents: Eric and Eileen Evans.
Marital status: Single.
Family links with cricket: Brother taken onto Nottinghamshire staff in 1985.
Education: William Lee Primary; Colonel Frank Seely Comprehensive School, Calverton.
Qualifications: 9 O-levels, 3 A-levels.
Jobs outside cricket: Bank work.
Cricketing superstitions: Putting left pad on first.
Cricketers particularly learnt from: Mike Hendrick, Mike Bore, Bob White.
Cricketers particularly admired: Richard Hadlee.
Other sports: Football, tennis, badminton, squash.
Relaxations: Listening to music, reading.
Opinions on cricket: Review of the points system on the B.A.C. Maybe give points to the team with a first innings lead so that the championship is not decided totally on declarations and weather.
Best batting performance: 42 Nottinghamshire v Cambridge University, Trent Bridge 1984.

LAST SEASON: BATTING

	I.	N.O.	R.	H.S.	AV.
TEST					
OTHER FIRST CLASS	3	0	24	13	8.00
INT.					
JPL	6	1	91	28	18.20
NAT.W	1	0	8	8	–
B & H	2	1	22	20	–

CAREER: BATTING

	I.	N.O.	R.	H.S.	AV.
TEST					
OTHER FIRST CLASS	7	0	72	42	10.29
INT.					
JPL	7	2	118	28	23.60
NAT.W	1	0	8	8	–
B & H	2	1	22	20	–

LAST SEASON: BOWLING

	O.	M.	R.	W.	AV.
TEST					
OTHER FIRST CLASS	30	8	69	1	–
INT.					
JPL	33	1	238	8	29.75
NAT.W	13	4	30	1	–
B & H	11	0	47	1	–

CAREER: BOWLING

	O.	M.	R.	W.	AV.
TEST					
OTHER FIRST CLASS	78	16	242	3	80.67
INT.					
JPL	45	1	312	9	34.66
NAT.W	13	4	30	1	–
B & H	11	0	47	1	–

FAIRBROTHER, N.H. Lancashire

Full Name: Neil Harvey
Fairbrother.
Role: Left-hand bat, left-hand
medium bowler.
Born: 9 September 1963,
Warrington, Cheshire.
Height: 5′ 8″ **Weight:** 11st.
Nicknames: Harvey, Farnsbarns,
Little Ted.
County debut: 1982.
County cap: 1984.
1000 runs in a season: 2.
1st-Class 50s scored: 25.
1st-Class 100s scored: 3.
One-day 50s: 2.
Place in batting averages: 48
average: 39.86; (1984: 112
average 31.61).
1st-Class catches 1985: 12
(career: 39).
Parents: Leslie Robert and Barbara Fairbrother.
Marital status: Single.
Education: St Margaret's Church of England School, Oxford; Lymn
Grammar School.
Qualifications: 5 O-levels.
Overseas tours: Denmark 1980 with North of England U-19.
Off-season 1985–86: Playing in Canberra.
Family links with cricket: Father and two uncles played local league
cricket.

LAST SEASON: BATTING

	I.	N.O.	R.	H.S.	AV.
TEST					
OTHER FIRST CLASS	39	4	1395	164*	39.86
INT					
JPL	11	3	240	49*	30.00
NAT.W	2	1	67	52*	–
B & H	3	0	26	16	8.67

CAREER: BATTING

	I.	N.O.	R.	H.S.	AV.
TEST					
OTHER FIRST CLASS	104	10	3355	164*	35.69
INT					
JPL	29	6	558	54*	24.26
NAT.W	5	1	151	52*	37.75
B & H	9	4	167	45*	33.40

LAST SEASON: BOWLING

	O.	M.	R.	W.	AV.
TEST					
OTHER FIRST CLASS	26	7	75	1	–
INT					
JPL	2	0	15	0	–
NAT.W					
B & H					

CAREER: BOWLING

	O.	M.	R.	W.	AV.
TEST					
OTHER FIRST CLASS	33.1	10	96	2	48.00
INT					
JPL	2	0	15	0	–
NAT.W					
B & H					

Other sports: Rugby, squash. Watches football, rugby union and rugby league.

Cricketers particularly learnt from: "All the senior players at Old Trafford have been a great help. Admire Clive Lloyd."

Relaxations: Music and playing sport.

Extras: "I was named after the Australian cricketer Neil Harvey, who was my mum's favourite cricketer." Three Tests and two U-19 one-day internationals v Young Australians 1983.

Opinions on cricket: "County championships should be 4-day games."

Best batting performance: 164* Lancashire v Hampshire, Liverpool 1985.

FELL, M.A. Derbyshire

Full Name: Mark Andrew Fell.

Role: Right-hand bat, slow left-arm bowler.

Born: 17 November 1960.

Height: 5′ 11″ **Weight:** 10st. 12lbs.

Nickname: Biggles, Felly, Steely.

County debut: 1982 (Nottinghamshire), 1985 (Derbyshire).

1st-Class 100s scored: 1.

Place in batting averages: 239 average: 12.25; (1984: — average: —).

1st-Class catches 1985: 0 (career: 13).

Parents: Gerald and Pat Fell.

Wife and date of marriage: Paula, 19 March 1983.

Education: Grove Comprehensive School.

Jobs outside cricket: Has helped in father's business.

Cricketer's particularly learnt from: Bob White.

Other sports: "Football mainly but will play any sport."

Relaxations: Golf, squash, football and any sports.

Extras: Nottinghamshire 1981–83.

Best batting performance: 108 Nottinghamshire v Essex, Trent Bridge 1982.

LAST SEASON: BATTING

	I.	N.O.	R.	H.S.	AV.
TEST					
OTHER FIRST CLASS	8	0	98	27	12.25
INT					
JPL	3	0	31	21	10.33
NAT.W					
B & H					

CAREER: BATTING

	I.	N.O.	R.	H.S.	AV.
TEST					
OTHER FIRST CLASS	35	0	506	108	14.46
INT					
JPL	15	2	109	28	8.38
NAT.W	1	0	6	6	–
B & H	2	0	30	26	15.00

LAST SEASON: BOWLING

	O.	M.	R.	W.	AV.
TEST					
OTHER FIRST CLASS					
INT					
JPL					
NAT.W					
B & H					

CAREER: BOWLING

	O.	M.	R.	W.	AV.
TEST					
OTHER FIRST CLASS	48	7	157	1	–
INT					
JPL	26	1	131	4	32.75
NAT.W	11	0	36	0	–
B & H	11	0	38	2	19.00

FELTHAM, M.A.   Surrey

Full Name: Mark Andrew Feltham.
Role: Right-hand bat, right-arm fast-medium bowler.
Born: 26 June 1963, London.
Height: 6' 2" **Weight:** 13st. 2lbs.
Nickname: Felts, Felpsi, Boff or Douglas.
County debut: 1983.
1st-Class 5 w. in innings: 1.
Place in batting averages: —
average: —; (1984: 199
average: 20.60).
Place in bowling averages: —
average: —; (1984: 71
average: 31.63).
1st-Class catches 1985: 0 (career: 5).
Parents: Leonard William and Patricia Louise Feltham.
Marital status: Single.
Family links with cricket: Mother involved in Ken Barrington Cricket Centre Appeal, brother plays for Surrey Young Cricketers.
Education: Roehampton Church School; Tiffin Boys' School.
Qualifications: 7 O-levels; advanced cricket coach.
Off-season 1985–86: Either playing and coaching in Durban or staying at home to get fit for next season.
Cricketing superstitions: Left pad on before right.
Overseas tours: Australia, 1980, with Surrey Cricket Association U-19s; Barbados, 1981, with M.C.C. Young Professionals.

Overseas teams played for: Glenwood High School Old Boys, Durban, 1984–85.

Cricketers particularly learnt from: Sylvester Clarke, Pat Pocock, Micky Stewart, Geoff Arnold.

Cricketers particularly admired: Ian Botham, David Gower, Graham Gooch.

Other sports: Football, snooker.

Injuries 1985: Car crash in South Africa in March — broke left arm and left leg.

Relaxations: Listening to music.

Extras: Played for England Schools at U-15 and U-19 levels. On the M.C.C. Young Professionals Staff 1981–82 seasons.

Opinions on cricket: "16 x 4-day matches. More encouragement for spinners in preparation of wickets. Speed up over rate. One overseas player per county."

Best batting performance: 44 Surrey v Derbyshire, The Oval 1984.

Best bowling performance: 5-62 Surrey v Warwickshire, Edgbaston 1984.

LAST SEASON: BATTING

	I.	N.O.	R.	H.S.	AV.
TEST					
OTHER FIRST CLASS	2	0	35	27	18.50
INT					
JPL	2	0	54	31	27.00
NAT.W					
B & H					

CAREER: BATTING

	I.	N.O.	R.	H.S.	AV.
TEST					
OTHER FIRST CLASS	17	5	241	44	20.08
INT					
JPL	11	6	77	31	15.40
NAT.W	1	0	4	4	–
B & H	4	1	45	22*	15.00

LAST SEASON: BOWLING

	O.	M.	R.	W.	AV.
TEST					
OTHER FIRST CLASS	11	1	74	0	–
INT					
JPL	30	2	170	4	42.50
NAT.W					
B & H					

CAREER: BOWLING

	O.	M.	R.	W.	AV.
TEST					
OTHER FIRST CLASS	320.2	59	1130	34	33.24
INT					
JPL	94.2	5	533	12	44.41
NAT.W	13	4	40	1	–
B & H	38.3	6	142	6	23.67

53. When was the length of a cricket pitch first decided in the laws? And what was it?

54. Name the teams that compete for the Sheffield Shield.

FELTON, N.A.   Somerset

Full Name: Nigel Alfred Felton.
Role: Left-hand bat.
Born: 24 October 1960,
Guildford, Surrey.
Height: 5' 7'' **Weight:** 10st. 7lbs.
Nickname: Will, Twiglets.
County debut: 1982.
1st-Class 50s scored: 14.
1st-Class 100s scored: 3.
One-day 50s: 4.
Place in batting averages: 76
average: 34.15; (1984:188
average: 21.69).
1st-Class catches 1985: 3 (career: 14).
Parents: Ralph and Enid Felton.
Marital status: Single ("tied down").
Education: Hawes Down Secondary
School, West Wickham, Kent;
Millfield School, Street, Somerset;
Loughborough University.
Qualifications: 6 O-levels, 2 A-levels, B.Sc.(Hons), Cert. of Education P.E./
Sports Sciences.
Cricketing superstitions: Always puts right pad on first.
Off-season 1985–86: Waneroro C.C., Perth, Western Australia.
Overseas tours: English Schools Tour of India, 1976–77; Young England in
Australia, 1978.
Cricketers particularly learnt from: Peter Denning.
Cricketers particularly admired: Alan Knott, Ian Botham and Viv
Richards.
Other sports: Most ball games.

LAST SEASON: BATTING

	I.	N.O.	R.	H.S.	AV.
TEST					
OTHER FIRST CLASS	27	0	922	112	34.15
INT					
JPL	10	0	180	52	18.00
NAT.W	3	1	106	72*	53.00
B & H					

CAREER: BATTING

	I.	N.O.	R.	H.S.	AV.
TEST					
OTHER FIRST CLASS	75	2	2143	173*	29.36
INT					
JPL	18	2	356	84*	22.25
NAT.W	5	1	222	87	55.50
B & H					

LAST SEASON: BOWLING

	O.	M.	R.	W.	AV.
TEST					
OTHER FIRST CLASS					
INT					
JPL	1	0	7	0	–
NAT.W					
B & H					

CAREER: BOWLING

	O.	M.	R.	W.	AV.
TEST					
OTHER FIRST CLASS	0.1	0	4	0	–
INT					
JPL	1	0	7	0	–
NAT.W					
B & H					

Relaxations: Music, reading, relaxing at home.

Extras: Joined Somerset in July 1981. Played a season for Kent in 1980 after leaving Millfield and before going to Loughborough. Left Kent at pre-season training 1981, due to the size of the staff. Joined Somerset at end of first year at Loughborough.

Injuries 1985: Broken third finger right hand (fielding), broken index finger on left hand (batting).

Opinions on cricket: "Despite the financial gains of the one-day game and our dependency on it, the 3-day game must be retained and not undervalued either by the media or the players."

Best batting performance: 173* Somerset v Kent, Taunton 1983.

FERGUSON, S.A.R.   Somerset

Full Name: Simon Alexander Ross. Ferguson.

Role: Right-hand bat, right-arm medium bowler.

Born: 13 May 1961, Lagos, Nigeria.

Height: 6' 2" **Weight:** 13st. 8lbs.

Nickname: Fergy, Ned and other assorted.

County debut: 1985.

Parents: Iain and Marjorie Ferguson.

Marital status: Single.

Education: Brandeston Hall; Framlingham College, Suffolk; Lancaster University.

Qualifications: Various O-levels, A-levels, degree from Lancaster.

Jobs outside cricket: Various jobs, worked for two years in fashion industry in 1983–84 off-season.

Off-season 1985–86: Sydney, Australia.

Cricketing superstitions: Always put buckles of left pad in before right pad.

Cricketers particularly learnt from: "Viv Richards, particularly his attitude to batting. My coach at school, Stuart Wesley."

Cricketers particularly admired: Viv Richards, Ian Botham.

Other sports: "Golf, tennis, hockey, rugby, but I enjoy all sports — currently tinkering with watersports."

Injuries 1985: "Back injury during August and September hampered me but not to the extent where I had to stop playing."

Relaxations: Watching T.V. , music, reading, good beer in country pubs.

Extras: Captained British Universities 1983. Topped Essex 2nd XI averages in 1983. Broke school record batting previously unbroken for 80 years.

Opinions on cricket: "I would like to see a British Universities side combining with Oxbridge to form the side that plays B/H rather than just Oxbridge."
Best batting performance: 8 Somerset v Middlesex, Weston 1985.

LAST SEASON: BATTING

	I.	N.O.	R.	H.S.	AV.
TEST					
OTHER FIRST CLASS	1	0	8	8	–
INT					
JPL					
NAT.W					
B & H					

CAREER: BATTING

	I.	N.O.	R.	H.S.	AV.
TEST					
OTHER FIRST CLASS	1	0	8	8	–
INT					
JPL					
NAT.W					
B & H					

FERREIRA, A.M. Warwickshire

Full Name: Anthonie Michal Ferreira.
Role: Right-hand bat, right-arm medium bowler, slip or gully fielder.
Born: 13 April 1955, Pretoria, South Africa.
Height: 6′ 3″ **Weight:** 15st. 5lbs.
Nickname: Yogi—"known as Anton".
County debut: 1979.
County cap: 1983.
50 wickets in a season: 3.
1st-Class 50s scored: 28.
1st-Class 100s scored: 3.
1st-Class 5 w. in innings: 18.
1st-Class 10 w. in match: 2.
One-day 50s: 2.
Place in batting averages: 122 average: 28.75; (1984: 122 average: 29.88).
Place in bowling averages: 40 average: 28.14; (1984: 49 average: 27.94).
1st-Class catches 1985: 14 (career: 92).
Parents: Anthonie and Eileen Ferreira.
Wife and date of marriage: Daléne, 28 March 1981.
Education: Hillview High School, Pretoria; Pretoria University.
Qualifications: B.A.(Ed.) Psychology and geography.
Jobs outside cricket: Employed by University of Pretoria as a full-time cricket coach and organiser.
Off-season 1985–86: University work and playing for Northern Transvaal.
Overseas tours: Toured U.K. with Pretoria University in 1975 and in 1978 with a group of young South African players sponsored by Barclays Bank. During tour played twice for Derrick Robins XI.

Cricket superstitions: "When the score is on 111, 222 or 333, hoping either for a wicket when fielding or a run when batting."

Cricketers particularly admired: "Tried to pick out sound advice from all team-mates and opponents throughout career and apply in own specific style."

Cricketers particularly admired: Mike Procter, Clive Rice.

Other sports: "I play golf, squash and tennis—provincial colours in boxing and soccer while still at school. I watch all sports whenever possible (T.V. or live)." Once fought Gerry Coetzee — since professional heavyweight champion.

Relaxations: Music, movies, videos and good restaurants.

Best batting performance: 112* Warwickshire v Indians, Edgbaston 1982.

Best bowling performance: 8-38 Northern Transvaal v Transvaal B, Pretoria 1977–78.

LAST SEASON: BATTING

	I.	N.O.	R.	H.S.	AV.
TEST					
OTHER FIRST CLASS	38	10	805	101*	28.75
INT					
JPL	11	2	200	38	22.22
NAT.W	1	0	18	18	–
B & H	3	1	74	42*	37.00

CAREER: BATTING

	I.	N.O.	R.	H.S.	AV.
TEST					
OTHER FIRST CLASS	287	56	6202	112*	26.85
INT					
JPL	64	16	1082	52	22.54
NAT.W	11	4	107	21	15.29
B & H	24	8	393	71	24.56

LAST SEASON: BOWLING

	O.	M.	R.	W.	AV.
TEST					
OTHER FIRST CLASS	673.3	129	2167	77	28.14
INT					
JPL	90.1	1	571	14	40.78
NAT.W	12	2	55	0	–
B & H	38.5	2	201	8	25.12

CAREER: BOWLING

	O.	M.	R.	W.	AV.
TEST					
OTHER FIRST CLASS	5261.4	1218	15346	520	29.51
INT					
JPL	606.4	25	3124	118	26.47
NAT.W	149	24	513	24	21.38
B & H	298.4	29	1318	47	28.04

55. For which state does Geoff Lawson play in Australia?

56. For which state does Wayne Phillips play in Australia?

57. When Ian Botham was of doubtful fitness for the Sixth Test v Australia last season, who was called up as an extra 12th man?

FERRIS, G.J.F.   Leicestershire

Full Name: George John Fitzgerald Ferris.
Role: Right-hand bat, right-arm fast bowler.
Born: 18 October 1964, Urlings Village, Antigua.
Height: 6' 3'' **Weight:** 13st. 7lbs.
Nickname: Ferro.
County debut: 1983.
50 wickets in a season: 1.
1st-Class 5 w. in innings: 3.
1st-Class 10 w. in match: 1.
Place in bowling averages: 134 average: 55.07; (1984: — average: —).
1st-Class catches 1985: 0 (career: 3).
Children: Imran J. Ferris.
Education: Jenning's Secondary.
Cricketers particularly learnt from: Andy Roberts (neighbour in Antigua).
Overseas tours: With Young West Indies to Zimbabwe 1983.

Overseas teams played for: Leeward Islands, Matabeleland.
Off-season 1985–86: Playing Shell Shield for Leeward Islands.
Other sports: Soccer and tennis.
Relaxations: Listening to music.
Opinions on cricket: Cricketers should be allowed to wear any advertising logos on their clothes like other sportsmen.
Best batting performance: 26 Leewards v Guyana, Nevis 1982–83.
Best bowling performance: 7-42 Leicestershire v Glamorgan, Hinckley 1983.

LAST SEASON: BATTING

	I.	N.O.	R.	H.S.	AV.
TEST					
OTHER FIRST CLASS	9	6	29	22*	9.67
INT					
JPL	2	1	13	9*	–
NAT.W	–	–	–	–	–
B & H	1	1	0	0*	–

CAREER: BATTING

	I.	N.O.	R.	H.S.	AV.
TEST					
OTHER FIRST CLASS	31	16	113	26	7.53
INT					
JPL	2	1	13	9*	–
NAT.W	–	–	–	–	–
B & H	1	1	0	0*	–

LAST SEASON: BOWLING

	O.	M.	R.	W.	AV.
TEST					
OTHER FIRST CLASS	231.3	32	826	15	55.07
INT					
JPL	30.5	3	133	6	22.17
NAT.W	6	1	9	0	–
B & H	40	3	209	6	34.83

CAREER: BOWLING

	O.	M.	R.	W.	AV.
TEST					
OTHER FIRST CLASS	712.1	126	2483	82	30.28
INT					
JPL	54.5	3	240	9	26.66
NAT.W	6	1	9	0	–
B & H	40	3	209	6	34.83

FINNEY, R.J. Derbyshire

Full Name: Roger John Finney.
Role: Right-hand bat, left-arm medium bowler.
Born: 2 August 1960, Darley Dale, Derbyshire.
Height: 6' 1" **Weight:** 12st. 10lbs.
Nickname: Albert.
County debut: 1982.
County cap: 1985.
50 wickets in a season: 2.
1st-Class 50s scored: 8.
1st-Class 5 w. in innings: 7.
One-day 50s: 1.
Place in batting averages: 222 average: 14.11; (1984: 192 average: 21.22).
Place in bowling averages: 34 average: 27.42; (1984: 53 average: 26.55).
1st-Class catches 1985: 3 (career: 13).
Parents: Roy and Janet Finney.
Marital status: Single.
Family links with cricket: Father played and captained local side for many years.
Education: Lady Manners School, Bakewell.
Qualifications: O-Levels.
Jobs outside cricket: Production clerk and sports salesman.
Cricket superstitions: "Always put left pad on first."
Overseas teams played for: Alexandrians, Pietermaritzburg, South Africa, 1980–82, 1984–85.

LAST SEASON: BATTING

	I.	N.O.	R.	H.S.	AV.
TEST					
OTHER FIRST CLASS	37	10	381	82	14.11
INT					
JPL	8	1	34	14	4.85
NAT.W					
B & H	2	0	23	14	11.50

CAREER: BATTING

	I.	N.O.	R.	H.S.	AV.
TEST					
OTHER FIRST CLASS	110	17	1677	82	18.03
INT					
JPL	30	7	397	50*	17.26
NAT.W	2	1	19	14*	–
B & H	7	0	133	46	19.00

LAST SEASON: BOWLING

	O.	M.	R.	W.	AV.
TEST					
OTHER FIRST CLASS	449.3	81	1453	53	27.42
INT					
JPL	75	2	370	10	37.00
NAT.W					
B & H	19.5	1	99	7	14.14

CAREER: BOWLING

	O.	M.	R.	W.	AV.
TEST					
OTHER FIRST CLASS	1329.2	256	4233	146	28.99
INT					
JPL	233.5	13	1185	35	33.85
NAT.W	32	7	86	3	28.67
B & H	65.5	6	286	11	26.00

Cricketers particularly learnt from: "Phil Russell (Derbyshire coach), Don Wilson (Head coach at Lord's)."
Other sports: Rugby, football, golf.
Relaxations: "Music, movies, good beer, eating at a good restaurant."
Extras: Before joining Derbyshire, spent two years with the M.C.C. Young Professionals.
Best batting performance: 82 Derbyshire v Gloucestershire, Derby 1985.
Best bowling performance: 7-61 Derbyshire v Lancashire, Old Trafford 1985.

FLETCHER, K.W.R. Essex

Full Name: Keith William Robert Fletcher.
Role: Right-hand bat, leg-break bowler.
Born: 20 May 1944, Worcester.
Height: 5' 10" **Weight:** 10st. 7lbs.
Nickname: Gnome, Fletch.
County debut: 1962.
County cap: 1963.
Test debut: 1968.
No. of Tests: 59.
No. of One-Day Internationals: 24.
1000 runs in a season: 20.
1st-Class 50s scored: 194.
1st-Class 100s scored: 60.
1st-Class 200s scored: 2.
1st-Class 5 w. in innings: 1.
One-day 50s: 59.
One-day 100s: 2.
Place in batting averages: 89 average: 32.38; (1984: 95 average: 33.00).
1st-Class catches 1985: 11 (career: 597).
Parents: Joseph and Doris Fletcher.
Wife and date of marriage: Susan Elizabeth, 22 March 1969.
Children: Tamara Jane, 2 August 1970; Sara Jane, 19 December 1972.
Jobs outside cricket: Has worked as oil representative.
Overseas tours: Pakistan 1966-67; Ceylon and Pakistan 1968-69; Australia and New Zealand 1970-71 and 1974-75; India, Sri Lanka and Pakistan 1972-73; West Indies 1973-74; India, Sri Lanka and Australia 1976-77; India and Sri Lanka 1981-82, as Captain.
Other sports: Golf, fishing, "shooting partridge — my second favourite sport after cricket."
Relaxations: Gardening.
Extras: Played for Essex at age of 17. Led Essex to first county

championship in 1979, second in 1983 and third in 1984. Also Benson & Hedges Cup in 1979 and John Player Special League in 1981, 1984 and 1985. NatWest Trophy 1985 to become first captain to win all four domestic competitions. Scored two centuries in a match, 111 and 102 n. o., v Notts., at Nottingham in 1976. Captain since 1974. Awarded O.B.E. in 1985 New Year's honours list. Gave up captaincy at end of 1985 season.
Best batting performance: 228* Essex v Sussex, Hastings 1968.
Best bowling performance: 5-41 Essex v Middlesex, Colchester 1979.

LAST SEASON: BATTING

	I.	N.O.	R.	H.S.	AV.
TEST					
OTHER FIRST CLASS	27	6	680	78*	32.38
INT					
JPL	11	7	146	37*	36.50
NAT.W	3	1	73	39*	36.50
B & H	5	3	60	24	30.00

CAREER: BATTING

	I.	N.O.	R.	H.S.	AV.
TEST	96	14	3272	216	39.90
OTHER FIRST CLASS	993	143	32421	228*	38.14
INT	22	3	757	131	39.84
JPL	209	35	5348	99*	30.73
NAT.W	41	4	957	97	25.86
B & H	65	13	1810	101*	34.81

LAST SEASON: BOWLING

	O.	M.	R.	W.	AV.
TEST					
OTHER FIRST CLASS	4	0	35	1	–
INT					
JPL					
NAT.W					
B & H					

CAREER: BOWLING

	O.	M.	R.	W.	AV.
TEST	20 20.5	1 5	193	2	96.50
OTHER FIRST CLASS	64.3 365.3	6 52	2094	48	43.63
INT					
JPL	2.5	0	37	1	–
NAT.W	10.3	1	43	2	21.50
B & H	4.4	0	30	1	–

FLETCHER, S.D. Yorkshire

Full Name: Stuart David Fletcher.
Role: Right-hand bat, right-arm medium bowler.
Born: 8 June 1964, Keighley.
Height: 5′ 10″ **Weight:** 12st.
Nickname: Fletch, Godber, Norman Stanley, Dr. Death, Ghostie.
County debut: 1983.
Place in batting averages: 242 average: 12.00; (1984: — average: —).
Place in bowling averages: 125 average: 48.19; (1984: 90 average: 33.64).
1st-Class catches 1985: 3 (career: 3).
Parents: Brough and Norma Hilda Fletcher.
Marital status: Engaged.
Family links with cricket: Father played in league cricket.

Education: Woodhouse Primary; Reins Wood Secondary.
Qualifications: O-level English and Woodwork. City and Guilds in Coach- building.
Jobs outside cricket: Coachbuilder at Reliance Commercial Vehicles Ltd.
Off-season 1985–86: Working at Ben Shaw's Pop Merchants.
Overseas tours: Holland 1983 with National Cricket Association U-19s.
Cricketers particularly learnt from: "My father, Phil Carrick, Steve Oldham."
Cricketers particularly admired: Ian Botham, Arnie Sidebottom.
Other sports: Snooker, golf, football. Watches Leeds United.
Relaxations: Watching T.V., snooker and golf.
Injuries 1985: Pulled rib muscle.
Extras: Played in the Yorkshire U-19s who were the first Yorkshire side to win the Cambridge and Oxford Festival, 1983.
Best batting performance: 28* Yorkshire v Kent, Tunbridge Wells 1984.
Best bowling performance: 4-24 Yorkshire v Somerset, Middlesbrough 1984.

LAST SEASON: BATTING

	I.	N.O.	R.	H.S.	AV.
TEST					
OTHER FIRST CLASS	10	7	36	15*	12.00
INT					
JPL	2	2	0	0*	–
NAT.W	–	–	–	–	–
B & H	1	1	0	0*	–

CAREER: BATTING

	I.	N.O.	R.	H.S.	AV.
TEST					
OTHER FIRST CLASS	19	10	85	28*	9.44
INT					
JPL	4	3	12	8	–
NAT.W	–	–	–	–	–
B & H	1	1	0	0*	–

LAST SEASON: BOWLING

	O.	M.	R.	W.	AV.
TEST					
OTHER FIRST CLASS	345.5	48	1253	26	48.19
INT					
JPL	63	0	419	12	34.91
NAT.W	24	5	69	3	23.00
B & H	28	0	116	1	–

CAREER: BOWLING

	O.	M.	R.	W.	AV.
TEST					
OTHER FIRST CLASS	563.3	90	1910	48	39.79
INT					
JPL	115	0	706	18	39.22
NAT.W	24	5	69	3	23.00
B & H	63.3	1	291	4	72.75

58. Name the teams that compete in the South African Currie Cup.

59. What is the highest team score by either side in an England v Australia Test, where and when?

FOLLEY, I.   Lancashire

Full Name: Ian Folley.
Role: Right-hand bat, slow left-arm bowler.
Born: 9 January 1963.
Height: 5' 10'' **Weight:** 12st.
Nickname: Thatch.
County debut: 1982.
1st-Class 50s scored: 1.
1st Class 5 w. in innings: 3.
Place in batting averages: 225 average: 13.79; (1984: 270 average: 10.21).
Place in bowling averages: 61 average: 31.37; (1984: 44 average: 29.85).
1st-Class catches 1985: 9 (career: 21).
Parents: James and Constance Folley.
Marital status: Single.
Education: Mansfield High School, Briersfield, Nelson and Colne College.
Qualifications: Business Studies.
Cricketers particularly learnt from: "County team-mates. D. Bloodworth as coach. Viv Richards, Ian Botham, Alvin Kallicharran and Derek Underwood."
Overseas tours: Barbados 1982 with Lancashire; Denmark 1981 with N.C.A.
Other sports: "All, except anything to do with horses. I'm a bad watcher."
Extras: Represented Lancashire Schools U-15s, and U-19s as captain. Represented Lancashire Federation 1979, 1980, 1981. England U-19 v India

LAST SEASON: BATTING

	I.	N.O.	R.	H.S.	AV.
TEST					
OTHER FIRST CLASS	27	8	262	69	13.79
INT					
JPL	–	–	–	–	–
NAT.W					
B & H					

CAREER: BATTING

	I.	N.O.	R.	H.S.	AV.
TEST					
OTHER FIRST CLASS	79	25	712	69	13.19
INT					
JPL	7	5	33	11*	16.50
NAT.W	1	1	3	3*	–
B & H	5	5	21	11*	–

LAST SEASON: BOWLING

	O.	M.	R.	W.	AV.
TEST					
OTHER FIRST CLASS	456.3	110	1286	41	31.37
INT					
JPL	8	0	41	0	–
NAT.W					
B & H					

CAREER: BOWLING

	O.	M.	R.	W.	AV.
TEST					
OTHER FIRST CLASS	1330.3	335	3581	109	32.85
INT					
JPL	114	4	518	8	64.75
NAT.W	15.3	2	48	4	12.00
B & H	84	17	215	14	15.36

U-19, three "Tests" in 1981. Young England v West Indies, three "Tests" and two 1-day "Internationals". Debut for Lancs. v Cambridge University at Fenners. In 1984 changed from left-arm medium pace to slow left-arm bowler.
Relaxations: Listening to Caribbean music, driving, golf.
Best batting performance: 69 Lancashire v Yorkshire, Old Trafford 1985.
Best bowling performance: 6-8 Lancashire v Oxford University, Oxford 1985.

FOSTER, N.A. Essex

Full Name: Neil Alan Foster.
Role: Right-hand bat, right-arm fast-medium bowler, outfielder.
Born: 6 May 1962, Colchester.
Height: 6' 4'' **Weight:** 12st. 7lbs.
Nickname: Fozzy.
County debut: 1980.
County cap: 1983.
Test debut: 1983.
No. of Tests: 6.
No. of One-Day Internationals: 8.
50 wickets in a season: 3.
1st-Class 50s scored: 2.
1st-Class 5 w. in innings: 13.
1st-Class 10 w. in match: 1.
Place in batting averages: 208 average: 17.00; (1984: 206 average: 18.73).
Place in bowling averages: 56 average: 27.57; (1984: 25 average: 24.11).
1st-Class catches 1985: 9 (career: 27).
Parents: Jean and Alan Foster.
Marital status: Engaged.
Family links with cricket: Father and brother both play local cricket.
Education: Broomgrove Infant & Junior Schools; Philip Morant Secondary Comprehensive, Colchester.
Qualifications: 9 O-levels, 1 A-level.
Overseas tours: N.C.A. tour of Canada 1978; Young England XI tour of West Indies 1980; Whitbread Scholarship 1981–82 in Tasmania (Glencory and District); England tour of New Zealand and Pakistan 1983–84, India and Australia 1984–85.
Off-season 1985–86: England tour to West Indies.
Jobs outside cricket: Played semi-pro. football some years.
Cricketers particularly learnt from: Essex players and Graham Saville.

Cricketers particularly admired: Dennis Lillee and Imran Khan.

Other sports: Plays nearly any sport and has had football trials with Colchester and Ipswich. Golf.

Extras: Was summoned from school at short notice to play for Essex v Kent at Ilford to open bowling. First ball went for 4 wides, but he went on to dismiss Woolmer, Tavaré and Ealham for 51 runs in 15 overs. Played for Young England v Young India 1981.

Opinions on cricket: "117 overs in a day too many. As the public leave at 6.30 p.m. for dinner there seems little point in trying to entertain empty stands. The principle is fine but the number of overs too many."

Best batting performance: 63 Essex v Lancashire, Ilford 1985.

Best bowling performance: 6–30 England v Northern Districts, Hamilton, 1983–84.

LAST SEASON: BATTING

	I.	N.O.	R.	H.S.	AV.
TEST	2	0	3	3	1.50
OTHER FIRST CLASS	13	3	201	63	20.10
INT	–	–	–	–	–
JPL	2	1	3	2*	–
NAT.W	1	0	0	0	–
B & H	2	2	29	23*	–

CAREER: BATTING

	I.	N.O.	R.	H.S.	AV.
TEST	12	2	78	18*	7.80
OTHER FIRST CLASS	66	21	979	63	21.76
INT	8	3	42	24	8.40
JPL	7	1	38	10	6.33
NAT.W	2	0	3	3	1.50
B & H	5	2	38	23*	12.67

LAST SEASON: BOWLING

	O.	M.	R.	W.	AV.
TEST	23	1	83	1	–
OTHER FIRST CLASS	413.5	87	1351	51	26.49
INT	11	0	55	1	–
JPL	33	1	165	4	41.25
NAT.W	45.2	8	150	7	21.43
B & H	60.1	5	215	17	12.65

CAREER: BOWLING

	O.	M.	R.	W.	AV.
TEST	329	72	985	27	36.48
OTHER FIRST CLASS	1644.5	396	5627	229	24.57
INT	139.4	9	600	14	42.86
JPL	103.4	4	484	13	37.23
NAT.W	88.2	17	256	15	17.07
B & H	151.1	13	546	29	18.83

---

60. True or false? Test umpire Ken Palmer was also an England player.

61. Which English Test umpire never played first-class cricket but played professional soccer and ice hockey?

62. Who was Jeff Thomson's first England victim in Test cricket: Geoffrey Boycott, Dennis Amiss or Mike Brearley?

FOWLER, G.   Lancashire

Full Name: Graeme Fowler.
Role: Left-hand opening bat,
cover fielder, occasional wicket-
keeper.
Born: 20 April 1957, Accrington.
Height: 5′ 9″ **Weight:** "Near 11st."
Nickname: Fow, Fox, Foxy.
County debut: 1979.
County cap: 1981.
Test debut: 1982.
No. of Tests: 21.
No. of One-Day Internationals: 24.
1000 runs in a season: 4.
1st-Class 50s scored: 34.
1st-Class 100s scored: 19.
1st-Class 200s scored: 2.
One-day 50s: 20.
One-day 100s: 2.
Place in batting averages: 207
average: 17.12; (1984: 81 average: 34.72).
1st-Class catches 1985: 4 (career: 60).
Education: Accrington Grammar School; Bede College, Durham University.
Wife: Stephanie.
Jobs outside cricket: Qualified teacher, swimming teacher. Advanced cricket
coach.
Overseas tours: England tour of Australia and New Zealand 1982-83, New
Zealand and Pakistan 1983-84, India and Australia 1984-85.
Overseas teams played for: Scarborough, Perth, Western Australia; Tasmania,
1981-82.
Injuries 1985: Badly torn neck muscles.

LAST SEASON: BATTING

	I.	N.O.	R.	H.S.	AV.
TEST					
OTHER FIRST CLASS	25	0	428	88	17.12
INT	1	0	10	10	–
JPL	11	1	328	98*	32.60
NAT.W	1	0	41	41	–
B & H	4	0	58	29	14.50

CAREER: BATTING

	I.	N.O.	R.	H.S.	AV.
TEST	37	0	1307	201	35.32
OTHER FIRST CLASS	186	9	6396	226	36.14
INT	24	2	714	81*	32.46
JPL	68	5	1640	98*	26.03
NAT.W	11	0	460	122	41.82
B & H	27	1	704	97	27.08

LAST SEASON: BOWLING

	O.	M.	R.	W.	AV.
TEST					
OTHER FIRST CLASS					
INT					
JPL					
NAT.W					
B & H					

CAREER: BOWLING

	O.	M.	R.	W.	AV.
TEST	3	1	11	0	–
OTHER FIRST CLASS	19.2	2	83	2	41.50
INT					
JPL	1	0	1	0	–
NAT.W					
B & H					

Extras: Has played for 2nd XI since 1973. Played in one John Player League match v Derbyshire at Chesterfield in 1978. At 15 he was the youngest opener in the Lancashire League. Scored two consecutive centuries v Warwickshire in July 1982 with aid of a runner. Never played cricket until he was 12. Played for Accrington and Rawtenstall in Lancashire League. In 1975 and 1976 played for E.S.C.A., N.A.Y.C., and M.C.C. Schools and Young England.
Best batting performance: 226 Lancashire v Kent, Maidstone 1984.

FOWLER, W.P. Derbyshire

Full Name: William Peter Fowler.
Role: Right-hand bat, slow left-arm bowler, bat/pad fielder.
Born: 13 March 1959, St. Helens, Lancs.
Height: 5' 10" **Weight:** 13st.
Nickname: Twister, Chook.
County debut: 1982.
1st-Class 50s scored: 15.
1st-Class 100s scored: 2.
One-day 50s: 2.
Place in batting averages: 185 average: 20.46; (1984: 113 average: 30.58).
1st-Class catches 1985: 3 (career: 37).
Parents: Robert Alan and Mary Catherine Fowler.
Marital status: Single.
Education: Tawa College; Kamo High School; Otago University and Auckland University.
Jobs outside cricket: Builder's labourer, and works in sports shop in New Zealand.
Family links with cricket: "Father once captained his House 2nd XI!"
Cricketing superstitions: "Never have lunch on a Sunday."
Overseas tours: Toured Australia with New Zealand Secondary Schools, 1975-76.
Overseas teams played for: Northern Districts, 1979-80, 1980-81; Auckland 1981-82, 1982-83.
Cricketers particularly learnt from: "I admire Richard Hadlee, and have learnt from most of the senior players at the club, especially John Wright."
Other sports: Squash. Watching anything sporting at all.
Relaxations: Reading, listening to music, and lazing about the house.
Extras: Left staff after 1985 season.

Best batting performance: 116 Derbyshire v Glamorgan, Derby 1984.
Best bowling performance: 2-44 Northern Districts v Central Districts, Gisborne, 1979-80.

LAST SEASON: BATTING

	I.	N.O.	R.	H.S.	AV.
TEST					
OTHER FIRST CLASS	14	1	266	79	20.46
INT					
JPL	4	0	60	22	15.00
NAT.W					
B & H	4	1	50	28	16.67

CAREER: BATTING

	I.	N.O.	R.	H.S.	AV.
TEST					
OTHER FIRST CLASS	107	14	2258	116	24.28
INT					
JPL	30	2	508	51	18.14
NAT.W	3	1	17	9*	–
B & H	9	1	130	53	16.25

LAST SEASON: BOWLING

	O.	M.	R.	W.	AV.
TEST					
OTHER FIRST CLASS					
INT					
JPL					
NAT.W					
B & H					

CAREER: BOWLING

	O.	M.	R.	W.	AV.
TEST					
OTHER FIRST CLASS	393.4	97	1242	19	65.37
INT					
JPL	37	2	182	8	22.75
NAT.W	2	0	6	0	–
B & H	14	1	77	3	25.67

FRASER, A.R.C.   Middlesex

Full Name: Angus Robert Charles Fraser.
Role: Right-hand bat, right-arm fast-medium bowler, fine leg third-man fielder.
Born: 8 August 1965, Billinge, Lancashire.
Height: 6′ 5″ **Weight:** 15st. 8lbs.
Nickname: Gus, Gnat, Jacques Cousteau ("due to a bad round of golf in La Manga").
County debut: 1984.
Parents: Don and Irene Fraser.
Marital status: Single.
Family links with cricket: Father keen follower of cricket; brother Alastair joined Middlesex staff this year.
Education: Gayton High School, Harrow; Orange Hill Senior High School.
Qualifications: 6 O-levels, coaching certificate.
Jobs outside cricket: Worked at Makro in North Acton last winter.
Off-season 1985–86: Playing for Porirua in Wellington, New Zealand.
Overseas tours: Toured Barbados with Thames Valley Gentlemen in

February 1985, La Manga with Middlesex in April 1985.

Cricketers particularly learnt from: Don Bennett, Don Wilson, Ross Chiese.

Cricketers particularly admired: Dennis Lillee, Richard Hadlee, Clive Radley.

Other sports: Rugby (for Harrow 'Cocks'), golf, snooker, football. Follows Liverpool F.C., rugby internationals, golf, darts.

Relaxations: "Having a pint down the pub with mates, a round of golf, driving."

Extras: Took 3 wickets in 4 balls v Glamorgan last year.

Opinions on cricket: "16 x 4-day championship matches. Politics and sport should not cross, and England should play South Africa and not be told what to do by other cricket-playing nations. It is too easy to qualify to play for England."

Best batting performance: 1 Middlesex v Cambridge University, Cambridge 1985.

Best bowling performance: 4-48 Middlesex v Cambridge University, Cambridge 1985.

LAST SEASON: BATTING

	I.	N.O.	R.	H.S.	AV.
TEST					
OTHER FIRST CLASS	1	0	1	1	–
INT					
JPL	3	0	8	7	2.67
NAT.W					
B & H	2	0	2	2	1.00

CAREER: BATTING

	I.	N.O.	R.	H.S.	AV.
TEST					
OTHER FIRST CLASS	1	0	1	1	–
INT					
JPL	3	0	8	7	2.67
NAT.W					
B & H	2	0	2	2	1.00

LAST SEASON: BOWLING

	O.	M.	R.	W.	AV.
TEST					
OTHER FIRST CLASS	43.1	5	119	8	14.88
INT					
JPL	51	3	213	7	30.42
NAT.W					
B & H	38	3	133	2	66.50

CAREER: BOWLING

	O.	M.	R.	W.	AV.
TEST					
OTHER FIRST CLASS	77.1	12	243	9	27.00
INT					
JPL	51	3	213	7	30.42
NAT.W					
B & H	38	3	133	2	66.50

63. Which equally famous author took part in a 50 stand at Lord's with Sir Arthur Conan Doyle, creator of Sherlock Holmes?

64. Which Australian Test player bowls in dark glasses?

FRASER-DARLING, D. Nottinghamshire

Full Name: David Fraser-Darling.
Role: Right-hand bat, right-arm medium bowler.
Born: 30 September 1963, Sheffield.
Height: 6' 5" **Weight:** 15st.
Nickname: Meat.
County debut: 1984.
1st-Class catches 1985: 4 (career: 5).
Parents: Alasdair and Mary.
Marital status: Single.
Education: Edinburgh University.
Qualifications: 7 O-levels, 2 A-levels.
Cricketing superstitions: Left sock, shoe, pad, etc. on first.
Cricketers particularly learnt from: David Stanley, Tony Dyer and all at Notts.
Cricketers particularly admired: Mike Hendrick.
Other sports: Football; used to play rugby. Watches any sport.
Relaxations: Music, films, drinking.
Extras: Played rugby for Scotland U-19 v England, Wales and Ireland 1981.
Best batting performance: 23* Nottinghamshire v Warwickshire, Wincanton 1985.
Best bowling performance: 2-14 Nottinghamshire v Cambridge University, Trent Bridge 1984.

LAST SEASON: BATTING

	I.	N.O.	R.	H.S.	AV.
TEST					
OTHER FIRST CLASS	4	1	33	23*	11.00
INT					
JPL	1	0	7	7	–
NAT.W					
B & H					

CAREER: BATTING

	I.	N.O.	R.	H.S.	AV.
TEST					
OTHER FIRST CLASS	4	1	33	23*	11.00
INT					
JPL	1	0	7	7	–
NAT.W					
B & H					

LAST SEASON: BOWLING

	O.	M.	R.	W.	AV.
TEST					
OTHER FIRST CLASS	19	3	88	0	–
INT					
JPL	10	0	69	2	34.50
NAT.W					
B & H					

CAREER: BOWLING

	O.	M.	R.	W.	AV.
TEST					
OTHER FIRST CLASS	48	12	143	3	47.67
INT					
JPL	10	0	69	2	34.50
NAT.W					
B & H					

FRENCH, B.N.   Nottinghamshire

Full Name: Bruce Nicholas French.
Role: Right-hand bat, wicket-keeper.
Born: 13 August 1959, Warsop, Notts.
Height: 5′ 8″ **Weight:** 10st.
Nickname: Frog.
County debut: 1976, age 16 yrs 10 mths (youngest Notts player).
County cap: 1980.
No. of One-Day Internationals. 3.
1st-Class 50s scored: 14.
Place in batting averages: 211 average: 16.89; (1984: 146 average: 26.81).
Parents: Maurice and Betty French.
Wife and date of marriage: Ellen Rose, 9 March 1978.
Children: Charles Daniel, 31 August 1978; Catherine Ellen, 28 December 1980.
Education: Meden School, Warsop.
Qualifications: O-level and C.S.E.
Jobs outside cricket: Warehouseman, window cleaner, bricklayer's labourer.

LAST SEASON: BATTING

	I.	N.O.	R.	H.S.	AV.
TEST					
OTHER FIRST CLASS	34	8	439	52*	16.89
INT					
JPL	12	5	178	37	25.42
NAT.W	4	2	81	49	40.50
B & H	3	1	15	8	7.50

CAREER: BATTING

	I.	N.O.	R.	H.S.	AV.
TEST					
OTHER FIRST CLASS	260	52	3805	98	18.29
INT	2	0	11	7	5.50
JPL	54	18	512	37	14.22
NAT.W	11	4	189	49	27.00
B & H	21	4	198	48*	11.65

LAST SEASON: BOWLING

	O.	M.	R.	W.	AV.
TEST					
OTHER FIRST CLASS					
INT					
JPL					
NAT.W					
B & H					

CAREER: BOWLING

	O.	M.	R.	W.	AV.
TEST					
OTHER FIRST CLASS	1	0	22	0	–
INT					
JPL					
NAT.W					
B & H					

LAST SEASON: WICKET KEEPING

	C.	ST.			
TEST					
OTHER FIRST CLASS	65	6			
INT					
JPL	9	–			
NAT.W	3	1			
B & H	2	–			

CAREER: WICKET KEEPING

	C.	ST.			
TEST					
OTHER FIRST CLASS					
INT	3	1			
JPL	59	10			
NAT.W	17	2			
B & H	34	8			

Off-season 1985–86: On tour with England to West Indies.
Family links with cricket: Brothers, Neil, David, Charlie, Joe, play for Welbeck C.C. Father, Treasurer Welbeck C.C.
Cricketers particularly learnt from: Bob Taylor, Clive Rice.
Cricket superstitions: Right pad on before left when keeping wicket.
Other sports: Rock climbing, fell walking and all aspects of mountaineering.
Relaxations: Reading, pipe smoking and drinking Theakston's Ale.
Extras: Equalled Notts. record for dismissals in match with 10 (7ct. 3 st.), and dismissals in innings with 6 catches. New Notts. record for dismissals in a season with 87 (75 ct. 12 st.). Wicket-Keeper of the Year 1984.
Best batting performance: 98 Nottinghamshire v Lancashire, Trent Bridge 1984.

GARD, T. Somerset

Full Name: Trevor Gard.
Role: Right-hand bat, wicket-keeper.
Born: 2 June 1957, West Lambrook.
Height: 5″ 7″ **Weight:** 10st. 7lbs.
Nickname: Gardy.
County debut: 1976.
County cap: 1983.
1st-Class 50s scored: 3.
Place in batting averages: 228 average: 13.36; (1984: 265 average: 11.00).
Parents: David and Brenda Gard.
Wife and date of marriage: Amanda Kay, 29 September 1979.
Education: Huish Episcopi Comprehensive School.
Qualifications: 0-levels in English and Technical Drawing. Aircraft Engineer Turner.

Jobs outside cricket: Engineering; farm worker.
Overseas tours: Antigua 1981 with Somerset.
Cricketers particularly learnt from: Derek Taylor, Bob Taylor.
Cricketing superstitions: "Never keep wicket without wearing county cap."
Other sports: Field sports, snooker. Watches soccer.
Relaxations: Field sports (hunting, shooting and fishing), rearing pheasants.
Extras: Made debut for Somerset 2nd XI at 15.
Best batting performance: 51* Somerset v Indians, Taunton 1979; 51 Somerset v Glamorgan, Swansea 1983.

	I.	N.O.	R.	H.S.	AV.
TEST					
OTHER FIRST CLASS	26	4	294	47	13.36
INT					
JPL	3	2	17	11*	–
NAT.W	2	1	7	7	–
B & H	2	2	1	1*	–

LAST SEASON: WICKET KEEPING

	C.	ST.			
TEST					
OTHER FIRST CLASS	31	7			
INT					
JPL	2	2			
NAT.W	3	–			
B & H	4	–			

CAREER: BATTING

	I.	N.O.	R.	H.S.	AV.
TEST					
OTHER FIRST CLASS	99	19	1121	51*	14.01
INT					
JPL	11	5	64	14*	10.66
NAT.W	4	2	24	17	12.00
B & H	8	4	46	19	11.50

CAREER: WICKET KEEPING

	C.	ST.			
TEST					
OTHER FIRST CLASS	146	33			
INT					
JPL	22	6			
NAT.W	9	3			
B & H	14	2			

GARNER, J.   Somerset

Full Name: Joel Garner.
Role: Right-hand bat, right-arm fast bowler.
Born: 16 December 1952, Barbados.
Height: 6′ 8″ **Weight:** 17st.
Nickname: Big Bird.
County debut: 1977.
County cap: 1979.
Test debut: 1976–77.
No. of Tests: 51.
No. of One-Day Internationals: 76.
50 wickets in a season: 2.
1st-Class 50s scored: 4.
1st-Class 100s scored: 1.
1st-Class 5 w. in innings: 42.
1st-Class 10 w. in match: 7.
One-day 50s: 1.
Place in batting averages: 246 average: 11.50.
Place in bowling averages: 15 average: 23.84; (1984: 2 average: 16.00).
1st-Class catches 1985: 4 (career: 102).
Marital status: Single.
Education: Boys' Foundation School, Christchurch, Barbados.
Jobs outside cricket: Telegraph operator.
Off-season 1985–86: Playing in West Indies.
Overseas tours: Toured with West Indies in Australia 1979–80, Pakistan 1980–81, Australia 1981-82, India 1982-83, England 1980 and 1984.

Overseas teams played for: Made debut for Barbados in Shell Shield Competition in 1975–76.

Other sports: Football for Cable & Wireless team in Barbados, as goalkeeper.

Relaxations: Sea-bathing, bird-watching, soul music, jazz. Manchester United.

Extras: Has played as professional for Littleborough in Central Lancashire League. Takes size 16 in boots which are custom-built. Awarded MBE 1985.

Injuries 1985: Tore ligaments in left knee. Withdrew from plans to play for South Australia as a result.

Best batting performance: 104 West Indies v Gloucestershire, Bristol 1980.

Best bowling performance: 8-31 Somerset v Glamorgan, Cardiff 1977.

LAST SEASON: BATTING

	I.	N.O.	R.	H.S.	AV.
TEST					
OTHER FIRST CLASS	11	3	92	22	11.50
INT					
JPL	7	2	105	30	21.00
NAT.W	1	0	0	0	–
B & H					

CAREER: BATTING

	I.	N.O.	R.	H.S.	AV.
TEST	60	13	609	60	12.95
OTHER FIRST CLASS	127	35	1766	104	19.20
INT	31	13	195	37	10.83
JPL	44	16	431	59*	15.39
NAT.W	12	4	113	38*	14.13
B & H	7	3	50	17	12.50

LAST SEASON: BOWLING

	O.	M.	R.	W.	AV.
TEST					
OTHER FIRST CLASS	295.1	77	739	31	23.84
INT					
JPL	67	9	229	13	17.61
NAT.W	32.4	5	102	5	20.40
B & H					

CAREER: BOWLING

	O.	M.	R.	W.	AV.
TEST	1961.4	528	4792	220	21.78
OTHER FIRST CLASS	3630.5	1057	8716	511	17.06
INT	697.2	110	2102	116	18.12
JPL	486.1	70	1556	87	17.88
NAT.W	257.3	72	624	59	10.58
B & H	167.4	40	404	36	11.22

65. What was so special about the first ball to Ian Botham in the Fifth Test v Australia at Edgbaston in August 1985?

66. True or false? Graham Gooch has never scored a century against Australia.

67. What does superstitious Test umpire David Shepherd do when the score is 111 or 222 or 333 etc.?

GARNHAM, M.A.   Leicestershire

Full Name: Michael Anthony Garnham.
Role: Right-hand bat, wicket-keeper.
Born: 20 August 1960, Johannesburg, South Africa.
Height: 5' 10" **Weight:** 11st.
Nickname: Fred.
County debut: 1979 (Gloucestershire), 1980 (Leicestershire).
1st-Class 50s scored: 11.
1st-Class 100s scored: 1.
One-day 50s: 2.
Place in batting averages: 151 average: 24.64; (1984: 129 average: 28.96).
Parents: Pauline Anne and Robert Arthur Garnham (divorced).
Wife and date of marriage: Lorraine, 15 September 1984.
Education: Camberwell Grammar, Melbourne, Australia; Scotch College, Perth, Australia; Park School, Barnstaple, North Devon; North Devon College; University of East Anglia (for one year).
Qualifications: 10 O-levels, 2 A-levels.
Family links with cricket: Father was a club cricketer in Essex. He lost the sight of an eye keeping wicket.
Overseas tours: England Schools tour of India 1977–78; Young England tour of Australia 1979.
Overseas teams played for: Melbourne University & North Sydney 1979–80 (as prize for Young Keeper of the Year award, 1979); Glenelg, South Australia, 1980–81.

LAST SEASON: BATTING

	I.	N.O.	R.	H.S.	AV.
TEST					
OTHER FIRST CLASS	26	4	542	100	24.64
INT					
JPL	9	2	179	41	25.57
NAT.W	2	2	36	29*	–
B & H	4	2	44	34*	22.00

LAST SEASON: WICKET KEEPING

	C.	ST.		
TEST				
OTHER FIRST CLASS	53	7		
INT				
JPL	13	1		
NAT.W	3	–		
B & H	10	–		

CAREER: BATTING

	I.	N.O.	R.	H.S.	AV.
TEST					
OTHER FIRST CLASS	104	18	2083	100	24.22
INT					
JPL	63	13	893	79*	17.86
NAT.W	9	3	129	29*	21.50
B & H	18	6	289	55	24.08

CAREER: WICKET KEEPING

	C.	ST.		
TEST				
OTHER FIRST CLASS	160	23		
INT				
JPL	77	10		
NAT.W	8	1		
B & H	25	–		

Cricketers particularly learnt from: Brian Roe (ex-Somerset), Alan Knott and Bob Taylor.
Other sports: Squash. Follows athletics.
Relaxations: Carpentry, D.I.Y., music, reading.
Extras: Moved to England in 1975 after living in Australia for 10 years and in South Africa for four years. Played for Devon in 1976, 1977 (possibly youngest ever) before joining Gloucs. Summer Staff in 1978. Signed for Leicestershire 1980 season and was banned by the registration committee from competitive first team cricket for a month for breach of registration regulations. Played for Gloucestershire 2nd XI since 1976, making John Player League debut in 1978 v Warwickshire at Birmingham and Championship debut in 1979. Retired at end of 1985.
Best batting performance: 100 Leicestershire v Oxford University, Oxford 1985.

GATTING, M.W.   Middlesex

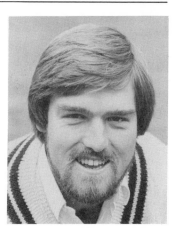

Full Name: Michael William Gatting.
Role: Right-hand bat, right-arm medium bowler. Captain of Middlesex 1983–.
Born: 6 June 1957, Kingsbury, Middlesex.
Height: 5' 10'' **Weight:** 13st. 8lbs.
Nickname: Gatt.
County debut: 1975.
County cap: 1977.
Test debut: 1977–78.
No. of Tests: 41.
No. of One-Day Internationals: 42.
1000 runs in a season: 7.
1st-Class 50s scored: 83.
1st-Class 100s scored: 33.
1st-Class 200s scored: 3.
1st-Class 5 w. in innings: 2.
One-day 50s 34.
One-day 100s: 4.
Place in batting averages: 11 average: 56.89; (1984: 4 average: 68.39).
Place in bowling averages: 27 average: 26.63.
1st-Class catches 1985: 20 (career: 237).
Parents: Bill and Vera Gatting.
Wife and date of marriage: Elaine, September 1980.
Children: One son (Andrew).
Education: Wykeham Primary School; John Kelly Boys' High School.

Jobs outside cricket: "Running my sports shop in Radlett."
Off-season 1985–86: With England in West Indies; golf and holiday.
Family links with cricket: Father used to play club cricket.
Overseas tours: Toured West Indies with England Young Cricketers 1979–80; with England in West Indies 1981, India 1981–82, New Zealand and Pakistan 1983–84.
Overseas teams played for: Club cricket in Sydney, Australia, off-season 1979–80.
Other sports: Football, table-tennis, tennis, swimming, golf, offered soccer trials but turned them down in favour of cricket. Supports Spurs.
Relaxations: Reading (expert on the books of Tolkien), crosswords, cinema.
Extras: Played for England Young Cricketers 1974. Topped Middlesex first-class batting averages, 1981, 1982, 1983, and 1984 and bowling averages in 1982. Scored fastest first-class century in 1984—79 minutes v Kent.
Best batting performance: 258 Middlesex v Somerset, Bath 1984.
Best bowling performance: 5-34 Middlesex v Glamorgan, Swansea 1982.

LAST SEASON: BATTING

	I.	N.O.	R.	H.S.	AV.
TEST	9	3	527	160	87.83
OTHER FIRST CLASS	25	2	1123	114	48.83
INT	2	1	38	31*	–
JPL	7	2	245	69*	49.00
NAT.W	2	0	33	17	16.50
B & H	6	3	269	143*	89.67

CAREER: BATTING

	I.	N.O.	R.	H.S.	AV.
TEST	70	10	2246	207	37.43
OTHER FIRST CLASS	328	56	13366	258	49.14
INT	39	10	902	115*	31.10
JPL	112	12	2921	109	29.21
NAT.W	32	7	884	95*	35.36
B & H	41	12	1333	143*	45.97

LAST SEASON: BOWLING

	O.	M.	R.	W.	AV.
TEST	5	0	16	0	–
OTHER FIRST CLASS	88.5	17	277	11	25.18
INT	–	–	–	–	–
JPL	12	1	68	3	22.67
NAT.W	7.3	3	7	1	–
B & H					

CAREER: BOWLING

	O.	M.	R.	W.	AV.
TEST	54	12	167	2	83.50
OTHER FIRST CLASS	1036.2	239	2858	113	25.29
INT	41.2	14	212	6	35.33
JPL	373.1	12	1819	69	26.36
NAT.W	131.3	20	488	16	30.50
B & H	161.4	12	621	33	18.81

68. Who was the first Test victim of Les Taylor of Leicestershire and England?

69. What was special about Graham Gooch's dismissal by Jeff Thomson in the Fifth Test at Edgbaston in 1985?

GIFFORD, N.   Warwickshire

Full Name: Norman Gifford.
Role: Left-hand bat, slow left-arm bowler.
Born: 30 March 1940, Ulverston, Cumbria.
Height: 5' 10" **Weight:** 13st. 7lbs.
Nickname: Giff.
County debut: 1960 (Worcestershire), 1983 (Warwickshire).
County cap: 1983.
Benefit: 1974 (£11,047).
Testimonial: 1981 (with Worcestershire).
Test debut: 1964.
No. of Tests: 15.
50 wickets in a season: 21.
1st-Class 50s scored: 3.
1st-Class 5 w. in innings: 89.
1st-Class 10 w. in match: 14.
Place in batting averages: — average: —; (1984: 269 average: 10.43).
Place in bowling averages: 71 average: 33.50; (1984: 60 average: 29.52).
1st-Class catches 1985: 9 (career: 311).
Cricketers particularly learnt from: Charles Hallows (Worcs. coach).
Qualifications: City & Guilds.
Jobs outside cricket: Estimator, industrial decorating.
Family links with cricket: Father played amateur cricket and football, and was also cricket umpire.
Off-season 1985–86: On tour, as assistant manager for England B.
Overseas tours: Rest of World to Australia 1971–72; India, Pakistan and Sri Lanka 1972–73; Sharjah 1985 as captain.

LAST SEASON: BATTING

	I.	N.O.	R.	H.S.	AV.
TEST					
OTHER FIRST CLASS	25	8	132	26	7.77
INT					
JPL	7	4	44	16	14.67
NAT.W	1	0	2	2	–
B & H	1	1	0	0*	–

CAREER: BATTING

	I.	N.O.	R.	H.S.	AV.
TEST	20	9	179	25*	16.27
OTHER FIRST CLASS	720	225	6602	89	13.34
INT	1	0	0	0	–
JPL	134	59	941	32*	12.54
NAT.W	32	7	221	38	8.84
B & H	39	13	297	33	11.42

LAST SEASON: BOWLING

	O.	M.	R.	W.	AV.
TEST					
OTHER FIRST CLASS	611.5	188	1541	46	33.50
INT					
JPL	98	4	475	26	18.26
NAT.W	17	2	56	2	28.00
B & H	44	3	138	2	69.00

CAREER: BOWLING

	O.	M.	R.	W.	AV.
TEST	514	173	1026	33	31.09
OTHER FIRST CLASS	146.4 19192.5	14 6539	44071	1902	23.17
INT	20	1	50	4	12.50
JPL	1488.1	91	6707	255	26.30
NAT.W	443	96	1299	52	24.98
B & H	635.3	94	2163	81	26.70

Other sports: Football, golf.
Relaxations: Horse-racing.
Extras: Was awarded M.B.E. in 1979. Played in one match for Rest of World v Australia 1972. Suffers badly from the sun on overseas tours. Took 100 wickets in a season four times. Uncle, Harry Gifford, played rugby union for England. Released by Worcs. at end of 1982 season. Debut 1960, cap 1961, captain 1971–80. England selector, and assistant manager of England side on tour. Appointed Warwickshire Captain 1985.
Best batting performance: 89 Worcestershire v Oxford University, Oxford 1963.
Best bowling performance: 8-28 Worcestershire v Yorkshire, Sheffield 1968.

GLADWIN, C. Essex

Full Name: Christopher Gladwin.
Role: Left-hand bat, right-arm medium bowler.
Born: 10 May 1962, East Ham.
Nickname: Gladders.
County debut: 1981.
County cap: 1984.
1000 runs in a season: 1.
1st-Class 50s scored: 14.
1st-Class 100s scored: 1.
One-day 50s: 3.
Place in batting averages: 144 average: 25.00; (1984: 94 average: 33.24).
1st-Class catches 1985: 4 (career: 21).
Education: Langdon Comprehensive, Newham.
Overseas tours: Toured West Indies with Young England team, 1980.

Injuries 1985: Season restricted by a back injury.
Best batting performance: 162 Essex v Cambridge University, Cambridge 1984.

LAST SEASON: BATTING

	I.	N.O.	R.	H.S.	AV.
TEST					
OTHER FIRST CLASS	22	2	500	92*	25.00
INT					
JPL	1	1	21	21*	–
NAT.W	1	0	15	15	–
B & H	2	0	43	29	21.50

CAREER: BATTING

	I.	N.O.	R.	H.S.	AV.
TEST					
OTHER FIRST CLASS	82	5	2419	162	31.42
INT					
JPL	24	1	474	75	20.60
NAT.W	3	0	16	15	5.33
B & H	7	0	178	41	25.43

LAST SEASON: BOWLING

	O.	M.	R.	W.	AV.
TEST					
OTHER FIRST CLASS	3	0	12	0	–
INT					
JPL					
NAT.W					
B & H					

CAREER: BOWLING

	O.	M.	R.	W.	AV.
TEST					
OTHER FIRST CLASS	21	1	71	0	–
INT					
JPL					
NAT.W					
B & H					

GOLDIE, C.F.E.   Hampshire

Full Name: Christopher Frederick Evelyn Goldie.
Role: Right-hand bat, wicket-keeper.
Born: 2 November 1960, Johannesburg.
Height: 5′ 6″ **Weight:** 9st. 7lbs.
Nicknames: Stumpy, Pygmy, Manders "and many others which are unprintable".
County debut: 1983.
1st-Class 50s scored: 1.
Parents: Thomas Hugh Evelyn and Eva Johanna (Janet) Goldie.
Marital status: Single.
Family links with cricket: Father played for Somerset II before war, for Oxfordshire and premier league in Jo'burg for Old Johannians. Uncle played for Devon and still plays aged 73; and brother is a keen club cricketer. Both father and brother play for Richmond C.C.
Education: St. Paul's School, Barnes; Pembroke College, Cambridge.
Qualifications: 8 O-levels, 3 A-levels, B.A. Hons (Cantab), "studied Arabic for two years (very badly) and history for one year (a little better)."
Jobs outside cricket: Spent winter 1982–83 working as an insurance broker for Willis Faber & Dumas, who also employ Mike Griffiths (ex-Sussex) and the present chairman of selectors.

Overseas tours: M.C.C. tour to U.S.A., September 1982; Vic Lewis Allstars tours to Finland, August 1981 and Holland, August 1982; Gordon Greenidge Benefit tour to Paris, September 1983.

Overseas teams played for: Grosvenor-Fynnland C.C., Durban, 1983–84; Durban Harlequins C.C. 1984–85.

Cricketers particularly learnt from: Ted Whitfield (ex-Northants. and Surrey) and Gwyn Hughes (ex-Cambridge and Glamorgan) whilst at school. Brian 'Tonker' Taylor at Cambridge and latterly Peter Sainsbury. "Above all, all credit or blame must go to my father."

Cricketers particularly admired: Bob Taylor, Malcolm Marshall.

Other sports: Golf, squash — "both badly". Knee injury forced early retirement from soccer. Watches rugby — supporter of Cambridge Univ. and Rosslyn Park F.C., soccer and American football.

Relaxations: Reading, films, good T.V., good company, Everton F.C. and fruit machines that pay out lots of money.

Extras: Spent two years on Middlesex staff but never came anywhere near to a first team game. Cambridge blue 1981 and 1982, scoring 77 as nightwatchman in 1981, set a latter-day record for dismissals by a Cambridge keeper in 1982–83.

Best batting performance: 77 Cambridge University v Oxford University, Lord's 1981.

LAST SEASON: BATTING

	I.	N.O.	R.	H.S.	AV.
TEST					
OTHER FIRST CLASS	—	—	—	—	—
INT					
JPL					
NAT.W					
B & H					

LAST SEASON: WICKET KEEPING

	C.	ST.			
TEST					
OTHER FIRST CLASS	1	1			
INT					
JPL					
NAT.W					
B & H					

CAREER: BATTING

	I.	N.O.	R.	H.S.	AV.
TEST					
OTHER FIRST CLASS	24	3	302	77	14.38
INT					
JPL					
NAT.W					
B & H	4	1	6	3*	2.00

CAREER: WICKET KEEPING

	C.	ST.			
TEST					
OTHER FIRST CLASS	35	9			
INT					
JPL					
NAT.W					
B & H	–	–			

70. What is the Primary Club?

71. What is special about the Primary Club tie?

GOOCH, G.A.   Essex

Full Name: Graham Alan Gooch.
Role: Right-hand bat, right-arm
medium bowler.
Born: 23 July 1953, Leytonstone.
Height: 6′ 0″ **Weight:** 13st.
Nickname: Zap, Goochie.
County debut: 1973.
County cap: 1975.
Benefit: 1985.
Test debut: 1975.
No. of Tests: 48.
No. of One-Day Internationals: 40.
1000 runs in a season: 9.
1st-Class 50s scored: 104.
1st-Class 100s scored: 50.
1st-Class 200s scored: 4.
1st-Class 5 w. in innings: 3.
One-day 50s: 60.
One-day 100s: 17.

Place in batting averages: 3 average: 71.22; (1984: 6 average: 67.34).
Place in bowling averages: 28 average: 26.65; (1984: 15 average: 22.37).
1st-Class catches 1985: 25 (career: 297).
Parents: Alfred and Rose Gooch.
Wife and date of marriage: Brenda, 23 October 1976.
Children: Hannah.
Education: Norlington Junior High School, Leytonstone.
Qualifications: Four-year apprenticeship in toolmaking.
Jobs outside cricket: Toolmaker.
Family links with cricket: Father played local cricket for East Ham
Corinthians. Second cousin, Graham Saville, played for Essex C.C.C. and is
now N.C.A. coach for Eastern England.
Overseas tours: West Indies with England Young Cricketers 1972; England
to Australia 1978–79 and 1979–80, West Indies 1981, India 1981–82.
Overseas teams played for: Perth C.C., W. Australia; W. Province, South
Africa.
Cricketers particularly admired: Bob Taylor, a model sportsman; Mike
Procter for his enthusiasm; Barry Richards for his ability.
Other sports: Squash, soccer, golf.
Relaxations: "Relaxing at home."
Extras: Published book (Pelham Books) entitled *Batting* in 1980. Wrote a
diary of 1981 cricket year, published in April 1982 by Stanley Paul. *Out of the
Wilderness* published by Collins in 1985. Trains with West Ham. Hit a
century before lunch v Leicester, 28 June 1981. Kept wicket for England v
India in 2nd innings at Madras, 1982. Captained English rebel team in
South Africa, 1982 and was banned from Test cricket for three years. Holds
record one-day innings of 198 n.o. v Sussex, May 1982. Hit a hole in one at

Tollygunge Golf Club during England's tour in India, 1981–82. First bowler to bowl both right and left handed in a Test match (v India at Calcutta, imitating Dilip Doshi). Shared in second wicket record partnership for county, 321 with K.S. McEwan v Northants. at Ilford in 1978. Holds record (jointly) for Essex for catches in match (6) and innings (5) v Gloucestershire, 1982. Essex captain 1986.

Best batting performance: 227 Essex v Derbyshire, Chesterfield 1984.
Best bowling performance: 7-14 Essex v Worcestershire, Ilford 1982.

LAST SEASON: BATTING

	I.	N.O.	R.	H.S.	AV.
TEST	9	0	487	196	54.11
OTHER FIRST CLASS	24	2	1721	202	78.23
INT	3	1	289	117*	144.50
JPL	9	1	415	171	51.87
NAT.W	5	1	298	93*	74.50
B & H	7	1	430	89	71.67

CAREER: BATTING

	I.	N.O.	R.	H.S.	AV.
TEST	84	4	3027	196	37.84
OTHER FIRST CLASS	442	41	18144	227	45.25
INT	39	2	1335	117*	36.08
JPL	155	13	4277	176	30.11
NAT.W	28	1	1134	133	42.00
B & H	60	4	2743	198*	48.98

LAST SEASON: BOWLING

	O.	M.	R.	W.	AV.
TEST	41.2	10	102	2	51.00
OTHER FIRST CLASS	243	56	671	27	24.85
INT	15	0	70	2	35.00
JPL	47.4	0	230	9	25.55
NAT.W	58	8	154	4	38.50
B & H	47	7	158	7	22.57

CAREER: BOWLING

	O.	M.	R.	W.	AV.
TEST	6 189.3	1 52	450	10	45.00
OTHER FIRST CLASS	20 1776	1 443	4872	159	30.64
INT	1 146.5	0 7	682	18	37.89
JPL	546.1	31	2448	89	27.50
NAT.W	166.1	23	509	14	36.36
B & H	316.5	31	1030	36	28.61

GOULD, I.J. — Sussex

Full Name: Ian James Gould.
Role: Left-hand bat, wicket-keeper.
Born: 19 August 1957, Taplow, Bucks.
Height: 5' 8'' **Weight:** 11st. 10lbs.
Nickname: Gunner.
County debut: 1975 (Middlesex), 1981 (Sussex).
County cap: 1977 (Middlesex), 1981 (Sussex).
No. of One-Day Internationals: 18.
1st-Class 50s scored: 23.
1st-Class 100s scored: 2.
One-day 50s: 8.
Place in batting averages: 64 average: 36.24; (1984: 178 average: 23.00).
Parents: Doreen and George Gould.
Wife: Jo.

158

Children: Gemma Louise, 30 June 1984.
Education: Westgate School.
Jobs outside cricket: Barman.
Cricketing superstitions: "Turning up late."
Overseas tours: Toured West Indies with England Young Cricketers 1976; with England in Australia and New Zealand 1982–83.
Overseas teams played for: Auckland, 1980.
Cricketers particularly learnt from: Derek Pringle. Admires David Gower "because he's England captain".
Other sports: Amateur footballer for Slough Town F.C. at full-back; golf, swimming.
Relaxations: Spending time with the family.
Injuries 1985: Back injury.
Extras: Made debut for Middlesex in 1975, gaining cap in 1977. Was offered contract for 1981 by Middlesex but chose to join Sussex. Vice-captain in 1985.
Best batting performance: 128 Middlesex v Worcestershire, Worcester 1978.

LAST SEASON: BATTING

	I.	N.O.	R.	H.S.	AV.
TEST					
OTHER FIRST CLASS	25	8	616	101	36.24
INT					
JPL	10	4	131	34	21.83
NAT.W	1	1	23	23*	–
B & H	4	3	36	18*	–

CAREER: BATTING

	I.	N.O.	R.	H.S.	AV.
TEST					
OTHER FIRST CLASS	270	42	5398	128	23.68
INT	14	2	155	42	12.91
JPL	107	17	1507	69*	16.74
NAT.W	17	1	274	58	17.13
B & H	34	6	487	72	17.39

LAST SEASON: BOWLING

	O.	M.	R.	W.	AV.
TEST					
OTHER FIRST CLASS	4	0	75	0	–
INT					
JPL					
NAT.W					
B & H					

CAREER: BOWLING

	O.	M.	R.	W.	AV.
TEST					
OTHER FIRST CLASS	16.3	2	110	0	–
INT					
JPL					
NAT.W					
B & H					

LAST SEASON: WICKET KEEPING

	C.	ST.		
TEST				
OTHER FIRST CLASS	35	4		
INT				
JPL	11	1		
NAT.W	–	–		
B & H	5	1		

CAREER: WICKET KEEPING

	C.	ST.		
TEST				
OTHER FIRST CLASS	417	66		
INT	15	3		
JPL	102	21		
NAT.W	15	6		
B & H	40	3		

GOWER, D.I.   Leicestershire

Full Name: David Ivon Gower.
Role: Left-hand bat, off-break
bowler. Vice-captain of Leics.
1982–83, Captain 1984–.
Born: 1 April 1957, Tunbridge
Wells, Kent.
Height: "5' 11" and a bit more."
Weight: 11st. 11lbs.
Nickname: Stoat, Lubo, Lu.
County debut: 1975.
County cap: 1977.
Test debut: 1978.
No. of Tests: 76.
No. of One-Day Internationals: 77.
1000 runs in a season: 6.
1st-Class 50s scored: 83.
1st-Class 100s scored: 32.
1st-Class 200s scored: 2.
One-day 50s: 33.
One-day 100s: 17.
Place in batting averages: 14 average: 54.70; (1984: 73 average: 35.67).
1st-Class catches 1985: 10 (career: 159).
Parents: Richard Hallam and Sylvia Mary Gower.
Marital status: Single.
Education: Marlborough House School; King's School, Canterbury;
University College, London (did not complete law course).
Qualifications: 8 O-levels, 3 A-levels.
Jobs outside cricket: Worked at Bostik Ltd.
Family links with cricket: Father was club cricketer.
Cricketing superstitions: "They change every time they go wrong."
Overseas tours: Toured South Africa with English Schools XI 1974–75 and
West Indies with England Young Cricketers 1976; Derrick Robins XI to
Canada 1976 and to Far East 1977; with England to Australia 1978–79 and
1979–80, to West Indies 1980–81, India 1981–82, Australia and New Zealand
1982–83, New Zealand 1983–84, India and Australia 1984–85.
Overseas teams played for: Claremont-Cottesloe, Perth, Australia,
1977–78.
Cricketers particularly learnt from: "Ray Illingworth and Jack Birkenshaw,
amongst many others whose advice has come my way."
Cricketers particularly admired: Graeme Pollock and many others.
Off-season 1985–86: England tour of West Indies.
Other sports: Golf, squash, water and snow skiing.
Relaxations: Music, photographs, beaches, vintage port and crosswords.
Extras: Played for King's Canterbury 1st XI for three years. Has written
Anyone for Cricket jointly with Bob Taylor about the 1978–79 Australian tour.
Also *With Time to Spare*, an autobiography published in 1980. Published

Heroes and Contemporaries (Collins) 1983. Writes regular column for Wisden Cricket Monthly. Appointed England captain 1984.
Best batting performance: 215 England v Australia, Edgbaston 1985.
Best bowling performance: 3-47 Leicestershire v Essex, Leicester 1977.

LAST SEASON: BATTING

	I.	N.O.	R.	H.S.	AV.
TEST	9	0	732	215	81.33
OTHER FIRST CLASS	20	2	745	135	41.39
INT	3	0	105	102	35.00
JPL	9	2	274	114*	39.14
NAT.W	2	0	53	41	26.50
B & H	7	1	166	43	27.67

CAREER: BATTING

	I.	N.O.	R.	H.S.	AV.
TEST	129	11	5385	215	45.64
OTHER FIRST CLASS	293	27	10205	187	38.37
INT	74	7	2427	158	36.22
JPL	102	16	3421	135*	39.77
NAT.W	22	3	916	156	48.21
B & H	37	4	931	114*	28.21

LAST SEASON: BOWLING

	O.	M.	R.	W.	AV.
TEST					
OTHER FIRST CLASS	2.1	0	16	0	–
INT					
JPL					
NAT.W	1	0	8	0	–
B & H					

CAREER: BOWLING

	O.	M.	R.	W.	AV.
TEST	5	1	15	1	–
OTHER FIRST CLASS	36.1	4	194	3	64.67
INT	0.3	0	5	0	–
JPL					
NAT.W	1	0	8	0	–
B & H					

GRAVENEY, D.A.   Gloucestershire

Full Name: David Anthony Graveney.
Role: Right-hand bat, slow left-arm bowler.
Born: 2 January 1953, Bristol.
Height: 6' 4'' **Weight:** 14st.
Nickname: Gravity, Grav.
County debut: 1972.
County cap: 1976.
50 wickets in a season: 4.
1st-Class 50s scored: 15.
1st-Class 100s scored: 2.
1st-Class 5 w. in innings: 28.
1st-Class 10 w. in match: 4.
One-day 50s: 1.
Place in batting averages: 194 average: 19.00; (1984: 231 average: 15.93).
Place in bowling averages: 18 average: 24.71; (1984: 59 average: 29.41).
1st-Class catches 1985: 17 (career: 151).
Parents: Ken Graveney and Jeanne (deceased).

Wife and date of marriage: Julie, 23 September 1978.

Children: Adam 13 October 1982.

Education: Millfield School, Somerset.

Jobs outside cricket: Company director. Accountant.

Family links with cricket: Son of J.K. Graveney, Captain of Gloucestershire, who took 10 wickets for 66 runs v Derbyshire at Chesterfield in 1949, and nephew of Tom Graveney of Gloucestershire, Worcestershire and England. Brother, John, selected for English Public Schools v English Schools at Lord's.

Other sports: Golf, soccer, squash.

Relaxations: "Playing sport, TV and cinema. Relaxing at a good pub."

Extras: Treasurer of the County Cricketers' Association.

Best batting performance: 119 Gloucestershire v Oxford University, Oxford 1980.

Best bowling performance: 8-85 Gloucestershire v Nottinghamshire, Cheltenham 1974.

LAST SEASON: BATTING

	I.	N.O.	R.	H.S.	AV.
TEST					
OTHER FIRST CLASS	25	11	266	53*	19.00
INT					
JPL	7	5	103	56*	51.50
NAT.W	2	0	16	12	8.00
B & H	2	0	3	3	1.50

CAREER: BATTING

	I.	N.O.	R.	H.S.	AV.
TEST					
OTHER FIRST CLASS	390	106	5353	119	18.85
INT					
JPL	112	39	1136	56*	15.56
NAT.W	21	6	254	44	16.80
B & H	33	7	319	49*	12.27

LAST SEASON: BOWLING

	O.	M.	R.	W.	AV.
TEST					
OTHER FIRST CLASS	410.5	133	1013	41	24.71
INT					
JPL	59.3	1	294	9	32.66
NAT.W	24	3	104	4	26.00
B & H	40	4	117	4	29.25

CAREER: BOWLING

	O.	M.	R.	W.	AV.
TEST					
OTHER FIRST CLASS	6959.4	2078	18159	635	28.60
INT					
JPL	799.1	47	3687	117	31.51
NAT.W	233.5	35	809	30	26.97
B & H	329.5	34	1204	43	28.00

72. For which state in Australia does Test fast bowler Craig McDermott play?

73. In 1985 Geoffrey Boycott scored his hundredth first-class 100 for Yorkshire. Who is the only Yorkshireman to have scored more hundreds?

GRAY, A.H.   Surrey

Full Name: Anthony Hollis Gray.

Role: Right-hand bat, right-hand fast bowler.

Born: 23 May 1963, Belmont, Port of Spain, Trinidad.

Height: 6′ 6″ **Weight:** 15st.

Nickname: Big Man.

County debut: 1985.

County cap: 1985.

50 wickets in a season: 1.

1st-Class 5 w. in innings: 9.

1st-Class 10 w. in match: 2.

Place in bowling averages: 13 average: 22.99.

1st-Class catches in 1985: 17 (career: 17).

Parents: Anthony and Merle Gray.

Education: Marlick Ser. Comprehensive, St. Augustine, Ser. Comprehensive.

Qualifications: 3 O-Levels, 1 CXC.

Off-season 1985-86: Training.

Cricketing superstitions: Always bats with cap on.

Cricketers particularly learnt from: Alf Gover.

Cricketers particularly admired: Viv Richards, Mike Holding.

Other sports: Football, basketball, table-tennis. Watches football.

Relaxations: Watching sports, watching movies, music, going the the parks.

Extras: The only son in a family of five. Trinidad and Tobago Player of the Year 1985. Surrey C.C. Supporters' Association Player of the Year 1985. Hat-trick v Yorkshire 1985.

LAST SEASON: BATTING

	I.	N.O.	R.	H.S.	AV.
TEST					
OTHER FIRST CLASS	10	1	48	20	5.33
INT					
JPL	3	2	4	2*	–
NAT.W	–	–	–	–	–
B & H					

CAREER: BATTING

	I.	N.O.	R.	H.S.	AV.
TEST					
OTHER FIRST CLASS	29	4	292	41*	11.68
INT					
JPL	3	2	4	2*	–
NAT.W	–	–	–	–	–
B & H					

LAST SEASON: BOWLING

	O.	M.	R.	W.	AV.
TEST					
OTHER FIRST CLASS	524	99	1816	79	22.99
INT					
JPL	70	1	302	15	20.13
NAT.W	11	0	66	2	33.00
B & H					

CAREER: BOWLING

	O.	M.	R.	W.	AV.
TEST					
OTHER FIRST CLASS	860.2	147	2993	125	23.94
INT					
JPL	70	1	302	15	20.13
NAT.W	11	0	66	2	33.00
B & H					

Best batting performance: 41* Trinidad v Australia, Pointe-à-Pierre 1983–84.
Best bowling performance: 8–40 Surrey v Yorkshire, Sheffield 1985.

GREEN, A.M. Sussex

Full Name: Allan Michael Green.
Role: Right-hand bat, off-break bowler, short-leg fielder.
Born: 28 May 1960, Pulborough, Sussex.
Height: 5′ 11″ **Weight:** 11st.
Nickname: Gilbert.
County debut: 1980.
County cap: 1985.
1000 runs in a season: 2.
1st-Class 50s scored: 24.
1st-Class 100s scored: 3.
One-day 50s: 3.
Place in batting averages: 38 average: 42.21; (1984: 150 average: 26.47).
1st-Class catches 1985: 16 Career: 46).
Parents: Michael and Sheila Green.
Marital status: Single.
Education: Knoll School, Hove; Brighton Sixth Form College.
Qualifications: 5 O-levels.
Jobs outside cricket: Sports shop assistant, labourer.
Off-season 1985-86: Playing and coaching in O.F.S., South Africa.
Cricketing superstitions: "Strap left pad on first and like to bat in same clothes, smell permitting."

LAST SEASON: BATTING

	I.	N.O.	R.	H.S.	AV.
TEST					
OTHER FIRST CLASS	43	4	1646	133	42.21
INT					
JPL	11	0	322	70	29.27
NAT.W	2	0	7	6	3.50
B & H	4	0	59	38	14.75

CAREER: BATTING

	I.	N.O.	R.	H.S.	AV.
TEST					
OTHER FIRST CLASS	156	9	4431	133	30.14
INT					
JPL	22	3	637	83	33.52
NAT.W	5	0	133	74	26.60
B & H	8	0	140	38	17.50

LAST SEASON: BOWLING

	O.	M.	R.	W.	AV.
TEST					
OTHER FIRST CLASS	53.3	10	153	3	51.00
INT					
JPL					
NAT.W					
B & H	3	1	22	0	–

CAREER: BOWLING

	O.	M.	R.	W.	AV.
TEST					
OTHER FIRST CLASS	232.1	34	808	19	42.53
INT					
JPL					
NAT.W	1	0	7	0	–
B & H	6	2	26	1	–

Family links with cricket: Father played for Findon C.C. "as a fielder".
Other sports: Snooker, football. Follows horse-racing.
Injuries 1985: "Being hit on the body at short-leg to the captain's bowling (numerous occasions)."
Cricketers particularly learnt from: Ian Thomson, Chris Waller, Roger Marshall, Tony Buss, Alvin Kallicharran.
Relaxations: "Sleeping, going to concerts, eating, drinking and listening to music."
Opinions on cricket: Should play 16 4-day championship matches.
Best batting performance: 133 Sussex v Surrey, The Oval 1985.
Best bowling performance: 2–30 Sussex v Worcestershire, Hove 1983.

GREENIDGE, C.G.   Hampshire

Full Name: Cuthbert Gordon Greenidge.
Role: Right-hand bat, right-arm medium bowler.
Born: 1 May 1951, St Peter, Barbados.
County debut: 1970.
County cap: 1972.
Benefit: 1983 (£28,648).
Test debut: 1972–73.
No. of Tests: 66.
No. of One-Day Internationals: 68.
1000 runs in a season: 14.
1st-Class 50s scored: 135.
1st-Class 100s scored: 56.
1st-Class 200s scored: 9.
1st-Class 5 w. in innings: 1.
One-day 50s: 66.
One-day 100s: 23.
Place in batting averages: 40 average: 41.20; (1984: 1 average: 82.83).
1st-Class catches 1985: 16 (career: 402).
Wife and date of marriage: Anita, September 1977.
Children: Carl, born 1978.
Education: Black Bess School; St Peter's Boys' School; Sutton Secondary School, Reading, Berkshire.
Qualifications: Studied accountancy and book-keeping.
Jobs outside cricket: Working for Sutton's Seeds, Reading; Dimplex, Southampton.
Family links with cricket: Wife is cousin of West Indian and Leicestershire fast bowler Andy Roberts.
Overseas tours: Toured with West Indies to India, Sri Lanka and Pakistan

1974–75; Australia 1975–76; England 1976, 1980 and 1984; Australia 1979–80; Pakistan 1980; Australia 1981–82; India 1983; Australia 1984–85.

Overseas teams played for: Barbados.

Other sports: "Played some soccer but particularly I enjoyed rugby." Golf.

Extras: Could have played for either England or West Indies. Persuaded to join Hampshire by John Arlott after playing for Berkshire U-19s. Scored two centuries in one match (134 and 101) for West Indies v England at Manchester 1976, and v Kent at Bournemouth (136 and 120) in 1978. Shared in partnership of 285 for second wicket with D.R. Turner v Minor Counties South at Amersham in 1973, being the record partnership for all one-day competitions. Awarded MBE in 1985.

Best batting performance: 273* D.H. Robins' XI v Pakistan, Eastbourne 1974.

Best bowling performance: 5–49 Hampshire v. Surrey, Southampton 1971.

LAST SEASON: BATTING

	I.	N.O.	R.	H.S.	AV.
TEST					
OTHER FIRST CLASS	32	2	1236	204	41.20
INT					
JPL	9	3	490	124*	81.66
NAT.W	4	0	176	89	44.00
B & H	4	0	245	123	61.25

CAREER: BATTING

	I.	N.O.	R.	H.S.	AV.
TEST	111	13	4816	223	49.14
OTHER FIRST CLASS	584	46	23645	273*	43.95
INT	68	7	2912	115	47.74
JPL	162	11	5556	163*	36.79
NAT.W	30	1	1244	177	42.90
B & H	49	2	1767	173*	37.60

LAST SEASON: BOWLING

	O.	M.	R.	W.	AV.
TEST					
OTHER FIRST CLASS	4	1	16	0	–
INT					
JPL					
NAT.W	1	0	1	0	–
B & H					

CAREER: BOWLING

	O.	M.	R.	W.	AV.
TEST	1.3	1.2	4	0	–
OTHER FIRST CLASS	155.5	37	468	17	27.53
INT	10	0	45	1	–
JPL	18	0	89	1	–
NAT.W	1.5	0	5	0	–
B & H	12.1	1	57	0	–

74. Who is the only Surrey cricketer to have scored 100 first-class hundreds for his county?

75. Who is the only Hampshire cricketer to have scored 100 first-class hundreds for his county?

GREIG, I.A.   Sussex

Full Name: Ian Alexander Greig.
Role: Right-hand bat, right-arm
medium bowler, slip fielder.
Born: 8 December 1955, Queens-
town, South Africa.
Height: 5' 11" **Weight:** 12st. 7lbs.
Nickname: Washies, Greigy.
County debut: 1980.
County cap: 1981.
Test debut: 1982.
No. of Tests: 2.
50 wickets in a season: 3.
1st-Class 50s scored: 17.
1st-Class 100s scored: 4.
1st-Class 5 w. in innings: 8.
1st-Class 10 w. in match: 2.
One-day 50s: 2.
Place in batting averages: 175
average: 22.00; (1984: 142
average: 27.10).
Place in bowling averages: 92 average: 37.24; (1984: 70 average: 30.85).
1st-Class catches 1985: 13 (career: 88).
Parents: Joyce and Sandy Greig.
Wife and date of marriage: Cheryl, 8 January 1982.
Education: Queen's College, Queenstown, South Africa; Downing College,
Cambridge.
Qualifications: B.A. (Cantab) in Law.
Family links with cricket: Brother of A.W. Greig, former Captain of Sussex
and England. Brother-in-law of R.P. Hodson (Cambridge University and
Yorkshire).
Overseas tours: Captain of Combined Universities tour to Australia
1979–80.
Overseas teams played for: Debut for Border 1974; also played for
Griqualand West while doing national service in South Africa; Waverley
C.C., Sydney.
Cricketers particularly learnt from: "Coaches at school in South Africa,
Colin Milburn, Fred Rumsey, Dennis Amiss, Ian Thompson and Tony
Greig. Have learnt a lot from G.G. Arnold."
Jobs outside cricket: Marketing trainee.
Other sports: Rugby.
Relaxations: "Sleeping—pop music—general outdoor life."
Extras: Three cricket blues at Cambridge University and Captain in 1979;
two rugby blues. Released at end of 1985 season "for economic reasons".
Best batting performance: 147* Sussex v Oxford University, Oxford 1983.
Best bowling performance: 7–43 Sussex v Cambridge University, Cambridge
1981.

LAST SEASON: BATTING

	I.	N.O.	R.	H.S.	AV.
TEST					
OTHER FIRST CLASS	16	4	264	43	22.00
INT					
JPL	9	2	88	39	12.57
NAT.W	2	0	9	8	4.50
B & H	4	0	32	31	8.00

CAREER: BATTING

	I.	N.O.	R.	H.S.	AV.
TEST	4	0	26	14	6.50
OTHER FIRST CLASS	178	23	3977	147*	25.66
INT					
JPL	59	13	984	48	21.39
NAT.W	9	0	184	82	20.44
B & H	33	3	482	51	16.08

LAST SEASON: BOWLING

	O.	M.	R.	W.	AV.
TEST					
OTHER FIRST CLASS	283	58	931	25	37.24
INT					
JPL	54.5	2	280	7	40.00
NAT.W	9	1	30	0	–
B & H	34.3	4	129	6	21.50

CAREER: BOWLING

	O.	M.	R.	W.	AV.
TEST	31.2	6	114	4	28.50
OTHER FIRST CLASS	2767.2	578	8629	297	29.05
INT					
JPL	407.1	15	2040	62	32.90
NAT.W	85.5	11	287	12	23.92
B & H	288.5	28	1000	38	26.32

GRIFFITHS, B.J.   Northamptonshire

Full Name: Brian James Griffiths.
Role: Right-hand bat, right-arm medium bowler.
Born: 13 June 1949, Wellingborough.
Height: 6' 1'' **Weight:** 14st. 6lbs.
Nickname: Jim.
County debut: 1974.
County cap: 1978.
50 wickets in a season: 5.
1st-Class 5 w. in innings: 13.
Place in bowling averages: 45 average: 28.69; (1984: 73 average: 30.98).
1st-Class catches 1985: 2 (career: 34).
Parents: James and Muriel Griffiths.
Wife and date of marriage: Paula, 30 September 1972.
Children: Rachel, 26 June 1973; Leighton, 6 November 1975.
Education: Irthlingborough Secondary School.
Jobs outside cricket: Has worked for a haulage firm, and as a bank porter.
Family links with cricket: Uncle played occasionally for Northamptonshire.
Other sports: Football, darts.
Relaxations: Reading, quizzes and crosswords.

Best batting performance: 16 Northamptonshire v Gloucestershire, Bristol 1982.
Best bowling performance: 8-50 Northamptonshire v Glamorgan, Northampton 1981.

LAST SEASON: BATTING

	I.	N.O.	R.	H.S.	AV.
TEST					
OTHER FIRST CLASS	8	4	17	12	4.25
INT					
JPL	1	0	1	1	–
NAT.W					
B & H	–	–	–	–	–

CAREER: BATTING

	I.	N.O.	R.	H.S.	AV.
TEST					
OTHER FIRST CLASS	131	48	272	16	3.28
INT					
JPL	27	14	61	11*	4.69
NAT.W	4	2	2	1*	1.00
B & H	9	3	15	6	2.50

LAST SEASON: BOWLING

	O.	M.	R.	W.	AV.
TEST					
OTHER FIRST CLASS	313.4	72	918	32	28.69
INT					
JPL	22	2	99	1	–
NAT.W					
B & H	18	4	37	1	–

CAREER: BOWLING

	O.	M.	R.	W.	AV.
TEST					
OTHER FIRST CLASS	4284.2	1017	12158	423	28.74
INT					
JPL	782.4	63	3188	115	27.72
NAT.W	180	22	703	27	26.04
B & H	301.2	41	1046	40	26.15

HADLEE, R.J.   Nottinghamshire

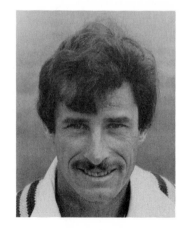

Full Name: Richard John Hadlee.
Role: Left-hand bat, right-arm fast bowler.
Born: 3 July 1951, Christchurch, New Zealand.
Height: 6′ 1″ **Weight:** 11st. 9lbs.
Nickname: Paddles.
County debut: 1978.
County cap: 1978.
Benefit: 1986.
Test debut: 1972–73.
No. of Tests: 50.
No. of One-Day Internationals: 76.
1000 runs in a season: 1.
50 wickets in a season: 7.
1st-Class 50s scored: 43.
1st Class 100s scored: 8.
1st-Class 200s scored: 1.
1st-Class 5 w. in innings: 61.
1st-Class 10 w. in match: 8.
One-day 50s: 9.
One-day 100s: 1.
Place in batting averages: 86 average: 32.89; (1984: 17 average: 51.26).

Place in bowling averages: 2 average: 17.39; (1984: 1 average: 14.06).
1st-Class catches 1985: 17 (career: 153).
Parents: Walter Arnold and Lillius Agnes Hadlee.
Wife and date of marriage: Karen Ann, 24 August 1973.
Children: Nicholas John and Daniel.
Education: Heaton Intermediate, Christchurch Boys' High School.
Qualifications: School certificate and university entrance.
Jobs outside cricket: Employed by New Zealand C.C.; managed by International Management Group; contracted to Leopard Breweries and Armoured Security Services.
Family links with cricket: Father played for New Zealand 1937–49, captaining New Zealand on tour of U.K. 1949. Brother, Dayle, played for New Zealand 1969–78. Brother Barry played for Canterbury. His father, Walter, succeeded Gordon Burgess as president of the New Zealand council.
Overseas tours: With New Zealand to England 1973, 1978, 1983; Australia 1973–74, 1980–81; India, Pakistan 1976; World Cup in U.K. 1975, 1979, 1983.
Overseas teams played for: Canterbury, New Zealand, 1971–; Tasmania 1979–80; World XI v Australia 1979, World Series Cricket.
Cricketers particularly learnt from: "My brother Dayle, Dennis Lillee—I admire his approach to the game— competitive, inspires his team, great bowler."
Cricketers particularly admired: Viv Richards, Gary Sobers, Greg Chappell, Abdul Qadir.
Other sports: Golf. Played goalkeeper for Rangers and for Woolston in New Zealand Southern League, "but I never took it seriously." Follows soccer, rugby, tennis, golf, snooker, etc.
Relaxations: "Watching movies, music, writing weekly newspaper columns."
Extras: Awarded M.B.E. 1980. Hat-trick v Central Districts 1972 at Nelson. Only bowler to take 100 wickets, in 1981 season. Top of English bowling averages 1980, 1981, 1982 and 1984. New Zealand Personality of the Year 1978 and nominated in final six on five occasions. New Zealand Bowler of the Year 1978–84 inc. Has written autobiography *Hadlee*. Author of *Hadlee on Cricket*, *Hadlee's Humour* and *Hadlee Hits Out*. New Zealand records: (1) Most wickets

LAST SEASON: BATTING

	I.	N.O.	R.	H.S.	AV.
TEST					
OTHER FIRST CLASS	29	11	592	73*	32.89
INT					
JPL	13	3	270	42	27.00
NAT.W	5	0	118	56	23.60
B & H	2	1	68	39	–

CAREER: BATTING

	I.	N.O.	R.	H.S.	AV.
TEST	96	12	2088	103	24.85
OTHER FIRST CLASS	272	56	6649	210*	30.78
INT	62	7	952	79	17.31
JPL	64	17	1310	100*	27.87
NAT.W	10	2	214	56	26.75
B & H	30	8	762	70	34.64

LAST SEASON: BOWLING

	O.	M.	R.	W.	AV.
TEST					
OTHER FIRST CLASS	473.5	136	1026	59	17.39
INT					
JPL	92	7	393	19	20.68
NAT.W	49	11	160	5	32.00
B & H	12	1	29	2	14.50

CAREER: BOWLING

	O.	M.	R.	W.	AV.
TEST	577.2 1613.2	68 428	6341	266	23.83
OTHER FIRST CLASS	1009 4701.1	163 1415	14085	826	17.05
INT	277.1 307	57 76	2162	101	21.41
JPL	512.2	60	1885	104	18.12
NAT.W	119.3	30	315	16	19.69
B & H	332.3	70	897	63	14.24

in Test cricket. (2) Most number of 5 wickets in a Test innings. (3) Most wickets in a Test innings, and in a Test match, 11 for 58. (4) Best bowling in a Test match, 7 for 23 v India 1976. (5) Most number of 10 wickets in a Test match, three times. (6) First New Zealand player to take Test double of 100 wickets and 1000 runs. In 1984 did "double" of 1000 runs and 100 wickets in first-class cricket—first time achieved since F.J. Titmus in 1967.
Best batting performance: 210* Nottinghamshire v Middlesex, Lord's 1984.
Best bowling performance: 8-14 Nottinghamshire v Lincolnshire, Trent Bridge, 1985.

HARDEN, R.J.   Somerset

Full Name: Richard John Harden.
Role: Right-hand bat, left-arm medium bowler.
Born: 16 August 1965, Bridgwater.
Height: 6′ 0″ **Weight:** 13st. 3lbs.
Nickname: Rich.
County debut: 1985.
1st-Class 50s scored: 1.
1st-Class 100s scored: 1.
Place in batting averages: 109 average: 30.50.
1st-Class catches 1985: 9 (career: 9).
Parents: Chris and Ann Harden.
Marital status: Single.
Family links with cricket: Grandfather played club cricket for Bridgwater.
Education: Kings College, Taunton.
Qualifications: 8 O-levels, 2 A-levels.

LAST SEASON: BATTING

	I.	N.O.	R.	H.S.	AV.
TEST					
OTHER FIRST CLASS	17	5	366	107	30.50
INT					
JPL	3	0	21	20	7.00
NAT.W					
B & H	3	0	31	13	10.33

CAREER: BATTING

	I.	N.O.	R.	H.S.	AV.
TEST					
OTHER FIRST CLASS	17	5	366	107	30.52
INT					
JPL	3	0	21	20	7.00
NAT.W					
B & H	3	0	31	13	10.33

LAST SEASON: BOWLING

	O.	M.	R.	W.	AV.
TEST					
OTHER FIRST CLASS	12.3	5	33	2	16.50
INT					
JPL					
NAT.W					
B & H					

CAREER: BOWLING

	O.	M.	R.	W.	AV.
TEST					
OTHER FIRST CLASS	12.3	5	33	2	16.50
INT					
JPL					
NAT.W					
B & H					

Jobs outside cricket: Insurance clerk, winter 1983.
Off-season 1985–86: Playing and coaching in New Zealand.
Cricketers particularly learnt from: Roy Marshall.
Cricketers particularly admired: I.V.A. Richards, D. Gower.
Other sports: Squash, hockey.
Relaxations: Listening to music, eating good food and playing snooker or pool.
Best batting performance: 107 Somerset v Cambridge University, Taunton 1985.

HARDIE, B.R. Essex

Full Name: Brian Ross Hardie.
Role: Right-hand bat, right-arm medium bowler, bat/pad fielder.
Born: 14 January 1950, Stenhousemuir.
Height: 5′ 10″ **Weight:** 12st.
Nickname: Lager.
County debut: 1973.
County cap: 1974.
Benefit: 1983 (£48,486).
1000 runs in a season: 10.
1st-Class 50s scored: 69.
1st-Class 100s scored: 18.
One-day 50s: 27.
One-day 100s: 3.
Place in batting averages: 66 average: 36.16; (1984: 80 average: 34.74).
1st-Class catches 1985: 22 (career: 263).

Parents: James Millar and Elspet Hardie.
Wife and date of marriage: Fiona, 28 October 1977.
Education: Stenhousemuir Primary School, Larbert High School.
Qualifications: 7 O-levels, 3 H-levels, N.C.A. Advanced cricket coach.
Jobs outside cricket: Computer operator, bank clerk, shipping clerk.
Off-season 1985–86: Working with Essex C.C.C. on promotions and sponsorships.
Family links with cricket: Father and brother, Keith, played for Scotland.
Overseas teams played for: Two seasons in New Zealand club cricket 1980–81 and 1981–82.
Cricketers particularly learnt from: "Everyone has something to offer."
Other sports: Football, golf.
Relaxations: Sport.
Extras: Played for Stenhousemuir in East of Scotland League. Debut for Scotland 1970. Scored two centuries for Scotland v M.C.C. at Aberdeen in

1971, but not then regarded as first-class match. Man of the match in 1985 NatWest Final.

Best batting performance: 162 Essex v Warwickshire, Edgbaston 1975.

LAST SEASON: BATTING

	I.	N.O.	R.	H.S.	AV.
TEST					
OTHER FIRST CLASS	45	7	1374	162	36.16
INT					
JPL	13	0	312	73	24.00
NAT.W	5	0	239	110	47.80
B & H	6	2	226	113	56.50

CAREER: BATTING

	I.	N.O.	R.	H.S.	AV.
TEST					
OTHER FIRST CLASS	466	58	13953	162	34.20
INT					
JPL	154	13	3390	108*	24.04
NAT.W	27	0	928	110	34.37
B & H	54	13	1168	113	28.49

LAST SEASON: BOWLING

	O.	M.	R.	W.	AV.
TEST					
OTHER FIRST CLASS	6	1	35	1	–
INT					
JPL					
NAT.W					
B & H					

CAREER: BOWLING

	O.	M.	R.	W.	AV.
TEST					
OTHER FIRST CLASS	21	2	115	3	38.33
INT					
JPL	4.5	0	24	1	–
NAT.W	8	1	16	1	–
B & H					

HARDY, J.J.E. Somerset

Full Name: Jonathan James Ean Hardy.
Role: Left-hand bat.
Born: 2 October 1960, Nakuru, Kenya.
Height: 6' 3" **Weight:** 14st.
Nickname: Greigy, J.J.
County debut: 1984 (Hampshire).
1st-Class 50s scored: 7.
1st-Class 100s scored: 1.
One-day 50s: 1.
Place in batting averages: 70 average: 35.33; (1984: 68 average: 36.64).
1st-Class catches 1985: 5 (career: 14).
Parents: Ray and Petasue Hardy.
Marital status: Single.
Family links with cricket: Father played for Yorkshire Schools; related to Nottinghamshire Gunn's.
Education: Pembroke House, Gilgil, Kenya; Canford School, Dorset.
Qualifications: 10 O-levels, 3 A-levels (English, Economics, Geography).
Off-season 1985–86: Paarl C.C., South Africa.
Overseas teams played for: Pirates, Durban 1981–85.

Cricketers particularly admired: Graeme Pollock, Greg Chappell, Malcolm Marshall.
Other sports: Hockey (capt. Dorset U-19), rugby, squash.
Relaxations: Photography, walking.
Extras: Suffered from Bilharzia, a tropical parasitic disease from January 1981 to July 1983. Scored 94* on debut championship innings while Hampshire followed on. Left Hampshire at end of the 1985 season and joined Somerset.
Best batting performance: 107* Hampshire v Essex, Southampton 1985.

LAST SEASON: BATTING

	I.	N.O.	R.	H.S.	AV.
TEST					
OTHER FIRST CLASS	26	5	742	107*	35.33
INT					
JPL	3	1	46	36	23.00
NAT.W	2	1	2	1*	–
B & H	1	0	4	4	–

CAREER: BATTING

	I.	N.O.	R.	H.S.	AV.
TEST					
OTHER FIRST CLASS	46	11	1255	107*	35.86
INT					
JPL	12	3	186	58	20.66
NAT.W	2	1	2	1*	–
B & H	1	0	4	4	–

LAST SEASON: BOWLING

	O.	M.	R.	W.	AV.
TEST					
OTHER FIRST CLASS					
INT					
JPL					
NAT.W					
B & H					

CAREER: BOWLING

	O.	M.	R.	W.	AV.
TEST					
OTHER FIRST CLASS	1	0	3	0	–
INT					
JPL					
NAT.W					
B & H					

HARPER, R.A. Northamptonshire

Full Name: Roger Andrew Harper.
Role: Off-break bowler, right-hand bat.
Born: 19 March 1963, Georgetown, Guyana.
Height: 6′ 5″ **Weight:** 14st. 8 lbs.
Nickname: Juice (as in orange!).
County debut: 1985.
Test debut: 1983–84.
No. of Tests: 14.
No. of One-Day Internationals: 18.
50 wickets in a season: 1.
1st-Class 50s scored: 6.
1st-Class 100s scored: 1.
1st-Class 5 w. in innings: 12.
1st-Class 10 w. in match: 11.
Place in batting averages: 62 average: 37.85.
Place in bowling averages: 85 average: 36.53; (1984: — average —).

174

1st-Class catches: 22 (career 87).
Parents: Henry and Lynette Harper.
Marital status: Single.
Family links with cricket: Brother plays for Guyana.
Education: Queen's College High School.
Qualifications: 7 O-levels.
Off-season 1985–86: No off-season; playing in the West Indies.
Overseas tours: West Indies to India 1983, Australia 1984, England 1984, Australia 1984–85.
Overseas teams played for: Guyana 1980–.
Cricketers particularly learnt from: Brother Mark, Clive Lloyd.
Cricketers particularly admired: Clive Lloyd, Lance Gibbs, Gary Sobers.
Other sports: Plays table-tennis, follows tennis and athletics.
Injuries 1985: Abductor strain.
Relaxations: Movies, music, good novels.
Extras: Captain West Indies Youths on tour of England in 1982.
Opinions on cricket: "County Championship games should be four days. Number of overs should be reduced to 100 per day. I think those two points would improve the quality of cricket. You would be able to think about it a bit more and not rush around like a robot."
Best batting performance: 127 Northamptonshire v Kent, Maidstone 1985.
Best bowling performance: 6-57 West Indies v England, Old Trafford 1984.

LAST SEASON: BATTING

	I.	N.O.	R.	H.S.	AV.
TEST					
OTHER FIRST CLASS	28	8	757	127	37.85
INT					
JPL	9	1	72	18	9.00
NAT.W	1	0	0	0	–
B & H	–	–	–	–	–

CAREER: BATTING

	I.	N.O.	R.	H.S.	AV.
TEST	17	2	203	39*	13.53
OTHER FIRST CLASS	83	11	1757	127	24.40
INT	4	2	71	45*	35.50
JPL	9	1	72	18	9.00
NAT.W	1	0	0	0	–
B & H	–	–	–	–	–

LAST SEASON: BOWLING

	O.	M.	R.	W.	AV.
TEST					
OTHER FIRST CLASS	775.3	187	2107	58	36.33
INT					
JPL	84	5	375	9	41.66
NAT.W	9	4	13	0	–
B & H	22	1	85	3	28.33

CAREER: BOWLING

	O.	M.	R.	W.	AV.
TEST	424.4	124	966	34	28.41
OTHER FIRST CLASS	2276.3	552	5737	200	28.68
INT	154	10	602	24	25.08
JPL	84	5	375	9	41.66
NAT.W	9	4	13	0	–
B & H	22	1	85	3	28.33

76. Who is the only Kent cricketer to have scored 100 first-class hundreds for his county?

HARTLEY, P.J.   Yorkshire

Full Name: Peter John Hartley.
Role: Right-hand bat, right-arm
medium bowler.
Born: 18 April 1960, Keighley.
Height: 6′ 0″ **Weight:** 13st.
County debut: 1982 (Warwickshire),
1985 (Yorkshire).
1st-Class 5 w. in innings: 2.
Place in batting averages: 186
average: 19.98; (1984: — average: —).
Place in bowling averages: 93
average: 37.90.

1st-Class catches 1985: 1 (career: 1).
Parents: Thomas and Molly Hartley.
Marital status: Single.
Education: Greenhead Grammar
School; Bradford College.
Qualifications: City & Guilds in
Textiles, Textile Supervisor.
Jobs outside cricket: Textiles.
Off-season 1985-86: Playing club
cricket in Adelaide, Australia.
Overseas teams played for: Hamilton, Melville, New Zealand, 1983–84.
Cricketers particularly learnt from: Phil Carrick, Steve Oldham, Mike Page.
Cricketers particularly admired: Dennis Lillee, Barry Richards.
Other sports: Golf, tennis, football.
Injuries 1985: Torn rib muscles.
Relaxations: Any sport, music.
Best batting performance: 35 Yorkshire v Warwickshire, Edgbaston 1985.
Best bowling performance: 5-75 Yorkshire v Nottinghamshire, Scarborough
1985.

LAST SEASON: BATTING

	I.	N.O.	R.	H.S.	AV.
TEST					
OTHER FIRST CLASS	11	3	159	35	19.88
INT					
JPL	2	0	2	2	1.00
NAT.W					
B & H					

	I.	N.O.	R.	H.S.	AV.
TEST					
OTHER FIRST CLASS	15	4	190	35	17.27
INT					
JPL	2	0	2	2	1.00
NAT.W					
B & H					

LAST SEASON: BOWLING

	O.	M.	R.	W.	AV.
TEST					
OTHER FIRST CLASS	315.5	40	1175	31	37.90
INT					
JPL	11	1	36	1	–
NAT.W					
B & H					

CAREER: BOWLING

	O.	M.	R.	W.	AV.
TEST					
OTHER FIRST CLASS	372.5	51	1390	33	42.12
INT					
JPL	15	2	55	1	–
NAT.W					
B & H					

HARTLEY, S.N.   Yorkshire

Full Name: Stuart Neil Hartley.
Role: Right-hand bat, right-arm
medium bowler, outfielder.
Born: 18 March 1956, Shipley,
West Yorkshire.
Height: 5′ 11½″ **Weight:** 12st. 3lbs.
Nickname: Tommy.
County debut: 1978.
County cap: 1981.
1st-Class 50s scored: 19.
1st-Class 100s scored: 4.
One-day 50s: 11.
Place in batting averages: 105
average: 30.78; (1984: 154
average: 25.70).
1st-Class catches 1985: 7 (career: 44).
Parents: Marjorie and Horace Hartley.
Marital status: Divorced.
Education: Beckfoot Grammar

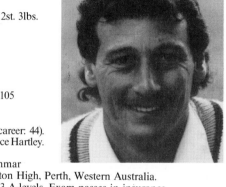

School, Bingley; Cannington High, Perth, Western Australia.
Qualifications: 8 O-levels, 3 A-levels. Exam passes in insurance.
Jobs outside cricket: Trained insurance underwriter.
Family links with cricket: Father played league cricket.
Overseas tours: Captained North of England N.C.A. team in Holland in 1975;
Gibraltar 1981.
Overseas teams played for: Orange Free State, 1981–82.
Cricketers particularly learnt from: Doug Padgett and Mike Fearnley—
Yorkshire County Cricket Club coaching staff.
Cricketers particularly admired: Imran Khan, Clive Rice.
Off season 1985–86: Coaching in Durban.

LAST SEASON: BATTING

	I.	N.O.	R.	H.S.	AV.
TEST					
OTHER FIRST CLASS	20	2	554	108*	30.78
INT					
JPL	12	1	276	72	25.09
NAT.W	1	0	69	69	–
B & H	2	1	20	16	–

CAREER: BATTING

	I.	N.O.	R.	H.S.	AV.
TEST					
OTHER FIRST CLASS	164	23	3524	114	24.99
INT					
JPL	75	14	1311	73	21.49
NAT.W	8	0	215	69	26.88
B & H	16	5	360	65*	32.73

LAST SEASON: BOWLING

	O.	M.	R.	W.	AV.
TEST					
OTHER FIRST CLASS	96.3	16	349	9	38.28
INT					
JPL	11.2	0	81	2	40.50
NAT.W	2	0	21	0	–
B & H					

CAREER: BOWLING

	O.	M.	R.	W.	AV.
TEST					
OTHER FIRST CLASS	531.2	97	1901	42	45.26
INT					
JPL	182.3	3	1073	35	30.65
NAT.W	26	2	102	1	–
B & H	73	3	281	11	25.55

Other sports: Golf.
Injuries 1985: Operation in April on lower spine, disc removed and cracked vertebra repaired.
Extras: "Started to play cricket in Perth, Western Australia, where I lived for 2½ years, 1967–69. I would like to live in Perth in the future." Amateur football with Bradford City 1970–75. Rugby Union with Bingley R.U.F.C. Has been acting captain of Yorkshire.
Best batting performance: 114 Yorkshire v Gloucestershire, Bradford 1982.
Best bowling performance: 4-51 Yorkshire v Surrey, The Oval 1985.

HASSAN, S.B.   Nottinghamshire

Full Name: Sheikh Basharat Hassan.
Role: Right-hand bat, right-arm medium bowler, occasional wicket-keeper.
Born: 24 March 1944, Nairobi, Kenya.
Height: 5′ 11″ **Weight:** 10st. 10lbs.
Nickname: Basher.
County debut: 1966.
County cap: 1970.
Benefit: 1978 (£20,000).
No. of Tests: 0 (unofficial Tests: 18 for Kenya and 6 for East Africa).
1000 runs in a season: 5.
1st-Class 50s scored: 80.
1st-Class 100s scored: 15.
One-day 50s: 36.
One-day 100s 4.
Place in batting averages: —
average: —; (1984: 187 average: 21.70).
1st-Class catches 1985: 4 (career: 308).
Parents: Haji Sarwar Hussain (father) and Sairan Sheikh (mother).
Wife: Dorothy Ann.
Children: Jamil, 22 October 1980; Sarah, 30 June 1982.
Education: City High School, Nairobi.
Qualifications: Advanced coaching certificate.
Jobs outside cricket: Sales representative, printing, cars.
Family links with cricket: Father and brothers all play.
Overseas teams played for: Kenya, 1960–65; East Africa, 1962–63.
Overseas tours: West Indies, Dubai.
Cricket superstitions: "Never take off my 'necklace' which was given to me by my father."
Cricketers particularly learnt from: M.J.K. Smith, Sir Garfield Sobers, Tom Graveney.
Cricketers particularly admired: Viv Richards, Richard Hadlee.

Other sports: Hockey, football, athletics.
Relaxations: Watching Notts. County and Nottingham Forest football clubs, golf, athletics, gardening.
Extras: Played first Test for Kenya at age of 15½, the youngest in the country. Made debut for East Africa Invitation XI v M.C.C. 1963–64. Played for Kenya against touring sides. Scored a century with the aid of a runner v Kent at Canterbury in 1977. Best sprinter at Notts. Short-listed Kenyan Olympic team in 1960. Announced retirement in 1985 while fielding substitute for England in Trent Bridge Test v Australia.
Best batting performance: 182* Nottinghamshire v Gloucestershire, Trent Bridge 1977.
Best bowling performance: 3-33, Nottinghamshire v Lancashire, Old Trafford 1976.

LAST SEASON: BATTING

	I.	N.O.	R.	H.S.	AV.
TEST					
OTHER FIRST CLASS	5	1	109	34	27.25
INT					
JPL	2	0	19	15	9.50
NAT.W	1	0	17	17	–
B & H					

CAREER: BATTING

	I.	N.O.	R.	H.S.	AV.
TEST					
OTHER FIRST CLASS	549	54	14394	182*	29.08
INT					
JPL	196	31	5168	120*	29.53
NAT.W	27	1	568	79	21.85
B & H	48	7	1070	99*	26.10

LAST SEASON: BOWLING

	O.	M.	R.	W.	AV.
TEST					
OTHER FIRST CLASS					
INT					
JPL					
NAT.W					
B & H					

CAREER: BOWLING

	O.	M.	R.	W.	AV.
TEST					
OTHER FIRST CLASS	141.2	35	407	6	67.83
INT					
JPL	16.3	0	131	2	65.50
NAT.W	7.1	2	20	3	6.67
B & H					

77. Who is the only Middlesex cricketer to have scored 100 first-class hundreds for his county?

78. Who is the only Gloucestershire cricketer to have scored 100 first-class hundreds for his county?

HAYES, K.A.   Lancashire

Full Name: Kevin Anthony Hayes.
Role: Right-hand bat; right-arm medium bowler.
Born: 26 September 1962, Mexborough, Yorkshire.
Height: 5' 7'' **Weight:** 11st. 7lbs.
Nickname: Viking, Two-heads, Hazell, Crazy.
County debut: 1980.
1st-Class 50s scored: 7.
1st-Class 100s scored: 2.
1st-Class 5 w. in innings: 1.
One-day 50s: 1.
Place in batting averages: —
average: —; (1984: 254 average: 13.93).
1st-Class catches 1985: 3 (career 15).
Parents: Edward and Pam Hayes.
Marital status: Single.
Education: Queen Elizabeth's School, Blackburn; Merton College, Oxford.
Qualifications: B.A.(Hons) Chemistry.
Off-season 1985–86: Working at home.
Overseas teams: City District C.C., Canberra, 1984–85.
Family links with cricket: Brother, David, played for Lancashire U-13 and U-15, and captained U-15 Schools.
Cricketing superstitions: 111.
Other sports: "Any."
Cricketers particularly admired: Richard Hadlee, Viv Richards.
Relaxations: "Listening to most types of music, crosswords."
Extras: Oxford Blue—captain of University in 1984.
Best batting performance: 152 Oxford University v Warwickshire, Oxford 1982.

LAST SEASON: BATTING

	I.	N.O.	R.	H.S.	AV.
TEST					
OTHER FIRST CLASS	7	0	310	117	44.29
INT					
JPL	2	1	5	3	–
NAT.W					
B & H	1	0	0	0	–

CAREER: BATTING

	I.	N.O.	R.	H.S.	AV.
TEST					
OTHER FIRST CLASS	70	4	1578	152	23.91
INT					
JPL	5	2	64	53	21.33
NAT.W					
B & H	11	0	174	67	15.82

LAST SEASON: BOWLING

	O.	M.	R.	W.	AV.
TEST					
OTHER FIRST CLASS					
INT					
JPL					
NAT.W					
B & H					

CAREER: BOWLING

	O.	M.	R.	W.	AV.
TEST					
OTHER FIRST CLASS	160.1	40	537	17	31.59
INT					
JPL	1	0	5	0	–
NAT.W					
B & H	39	9	119	4	29.75

Best bowling performance: 6-58 Oxford University v Warwickshire, Edgbaston 1983.

HAYHURST, A.N. Lancashire

Full Name: Andrew Neil Hayhurst.
Role: Right-hand bat, right-arm medium bowler.
Born: 23 November 1962, Davyhulme, Manchester.
Height: 6' 0'' **Weight:** 12st. 12lbs.
Nickname: Barney.
County debut: 1985.
Parents: William and Margaret Hayhurst.
Marital status: Single.
Family links with cricket: Father played club cricket.
Education: St. Mark's Primary School; Worsley Wardley High; Eccles College; Carnegie College, Leeds.
Qualifications: 8 O-levels, 3 A-levels, B.A. (Hons) Human Movement.
Off-season 1985–86: Lecturer at Worsley Further Education College.
Cricketers particularly learnt from: Father and Geoff Ogden (Worsley C.C.).
Cricketers particularly admired: Geoff Boycott, Ian Botham, Viv Richards.
Other sports: Football, golf—all sports.
Relaxations: Watching all sports. Good food.

CAREER: BATTING

	I.	N.O.	R.	H.S.	AV.
TEST					
OTHER FIRST CLASS	1	0	17	17	–
INT					
JPL	1	1	12	12*	–
NAT.W	1	0	7	7	–
B & H					

LAST SEASON: BATTING

	I.	N.O.	R.	H.S.	AV.
TEST					
OTHER FIRST CLASS	1	0	17	17	–
INT					
JPL	1	1	12	12*	–
NAT.W	1	0	7	7	–
B & H					

CAREER: BOWLING

	O.	M.	R.	W.	AV.
TEST					
OTHER FIRST CLASS	13	4	37	3	12.33
INT					
JPL	5	0	31	0	–
NAT.W	5	0	30	0	–
B & H					

LAST SEASON: BOWLING

	O.	M.	R.	W.	AV.
TEST					
OTHER FIRST CLASS	13	4	37	3	12.33
INT					
JPL	5	0	31	0	–
NAT.W	5	0	30	0	–
B & H					

Extras: Scored a record 197 runs whilst playing for North of England v South, Southampton 1982. Represented N.A.Y.C. v M.C.C., 1982. Holds record number of runs for Lancashire Cricket Fed. U-19 (av: 105.00), 1982. Holds record number of runs in Manchester & District Cricket Association League, whilst playing for Worsley C.C. in 1984: 1193 runs (av: 70-17). Represented Greater Manchester U-19 County at football 1981–82.

Opinions on cricket: "2nd XI cricket should be played on better pitches if that cricket is to be a successful grounding for future 1st XI players."

Best batting performance: 17 Lancashire v Leicestershire, Old Trafford 1985.

Best bowling performance: 3-37 Lancashire v Leicestershire, Old Trafford 1985.

HAYWARD, R.E. Somerset

Full Name: Richard Edward Hayward.

Role: Left-hand bat, left-arm medium bowler.

Born: 15 February 1954, Hillingdon, Middlesex.

Height: 6′ 1″ **Weight:** 12st. 7lbs.

Nickname: Shots.

County debut: 1981 (Hampshire), 1985 (Somerset).

1st-Class 50s scored: 7.

1st-Class 100s scored: 3.

One-day 50s: 2.

Place in batting averages: 104 average: 30.89.

1st-Class catches: 3 (career: 22).

Parents: Alec Henry Francis and Sylvia Hayward.

Marital status: Single.

Family links with cricket: Father is chairman of Ickenham C.C. Uncle, Sir Richard Hayward, is President of Civil Service cricket and President of the Kent Association of Cricket Clubs.

Education: Latymer Upper Grammar School, Hammersmith.

Qualifications: 7 O-levels, 2 A-levels, N.C.A. Advanced Coaching Certificate.

Jobs outside cricket: Spent six years as an executive officer in Civil Service after leaving school.

Cricketing superstitions: Always puts right pad on first.

Overseas tours: Toured New Zealand, Australia, Singapore and Hong Kong with Club Cricket Conference.

Overseas teams played for: Nelson Cricket Association, 1981–82, Central Districts 1982–85. First overseas player to captain a provincial side.

Cricketers particularly learnt from or admired: Sir Gary Sobers, John Rice, Paul Terry and Mike Bailey of Hampshire C.C.C.

Other sports: Soccer, squash, golf.
Relaxation: Watching films.
Extras: England Schools 1970; Minor Counties Representative XI v India 1979. Played for Buckinghamshire 1978–79 and 1983–84, Hampshire 1981–82, scoring century on debut. Also appeared for Middlesex II.
Best batting performance: 102 Central Districts v Wellington, Palmerston North 1983–84.

LAST SEASON: BATTING

	I.	N.O.	R.	H.S.	AV.
TEST					
OTHER FIRST CLASS	12	3	278	100*	30.89
INT					
JPL	6	3	69	38*	23.00
NAT.W	1	1	8	8*	–
B & H					

CAREER: BATTING

	I.	N.O.	R.	H.S.	AV.
TEST					
OTHER FIRST CLASS	66	13	1423	102	26.85
INT					
JPL	12	6	128	38*	21.33
NAT.W	5	2	126	44*	42.00
B & H	10	3	251	78*	35.86

LAST SEASON: BOWLING

	O.	M.	R.	W.	AV.
TEST					
OTHER FIRST CLASS					
INT					
JPL					
NAT.W					
B & H					

CAREER: BOWLING

	O.	M.	R.	W.	AV.
TEST					
OTHER FIRST CLASS	20	7	55	0	–
INT					
JPL					
NAT.W					
B & H	17	2	65	2	32.50

HEMMINGS, E.E.   Nottinghamshire

Full Name: Edward Ernest Hemmings.
Role: Right-hand bat, off-break bowler.
Born: 20 February 1949, Leamington Spa, Warwickshire.
Height: 5′ 10″ **Weight:** 13st.
Nickname: Eddie.
County debut: 1966 (Warwickshire), 1979 (Nottinghamshire).
County cap: 1974 (Warwickshire), 1980 (Nottinghamshire).
Test debut: 1982.
No. of Tests: 5.
No. of One-Day Internationals: 5.
50 wickets in a season: 10.
1st-Class 50s scored: 17.
1st-Class 100s scored: 1.
1st-Class 5 w. in innings: 47.
1st-Class 10 w. in match: 11.

One-day 50s: 1.
Place in batting averages: 203 average: 17.47; (1984: 244 average: 14.59).
Place in bowling averages: 95 average: 38.24; (1984: 22 average: 23.62).
1st-Class catches 1985: 7 (career: 157).
Parents: Edward and Dorothy Phyliss Hemmings.
Wife and date of marriage: Christine Mary, 23 October 1971.
Children: Thomas Edward, 26 July 1977; James Oliver, 9 September 1979.
Education: Campion School, Leamington Spa.
Family links with cricket: Father and father's father played Minor Counties and League cricket.
Overseas tours: Derrick Robins XI tour to South Africa 1975; tour to Pakistan 1981 with International XI; Australia and New Zealand 1982–83.
Cricketers particularly learnt from: J.A. Jameson.
Cricketers particularly admired: R.T. Robinson.
Other sports: Golf.
Relaxations: "Watching football at any level—especially junior. Dining out with my wife."
Extras: Debut for Warwickshire 1966, cap 1974. No longer wears glasses, plays in contact lenses. Started his career as a medium-pacer, and was thought of as a successor to Tom Cartwright. "I was even known as 'Tommy's Ghost' around Edgbaston." Suffers from asthma. Took a hat-trick for Warwickshire in 1977 but had to wait four years to receive the inscribed match ball, when he had moved to Nottinghamshire. Hit first century — 127* v Yorkshire at Worksop, July 1982 — after 16 years in first-class game.
Best batting performance: 127* Nottinghamshire v Yorkshire, Worksop 1982.
Best bowling performance: 10-175 International XI v West Indies XI, Kingston 1982–83.

LAST SEASON: BATTING

	I.	N.O.	R.	H.S.	AV.
TEST					
OTHER FIRST CLASS	22	5	297	56*	17.47
INT					
JPL	10	4	76	35	12.66
NAT.W	3	2	38	31*	–
B & H	2	0	33	31	16.50

CAREER: BATTING

	I.	N.O.	R.	H.S.	AV.
TEST	10	1	198	95	22.00
OTHER FIRST CLASS	448	99	6947	127*	19.91
INT	2	0	4	3	2.00
JPL	135	37	1346	44*	13.73
NAT.W	20	4	200	31*	12.50
B & H	44	9	357	61*	10.81

LAST SEASON: BOWLING

	O.	M.	R.	W.	AV.
TEST					
OTHER FIRST CLASS	716.3	171	2103	55	38.24
INT					
JPL	55	3	268	8	33.50
NAT.W	54	9	196	5	39.20
B & H	32.4	4	108	4	27.00

CAREER: BOWLING

	O.	M.	R.	W.	AV.
TEST	244.4	71	558	12	46.50
OTHER FIRST CLASS	10471.5	2912	28180	975	28.91
INT	41.5	4	175	5	35.00
JPL	1274	87	5869	208	28.21
NAT.W	295.1	48	990	26	38.08
B & H	561.4	70	1738	54	32.19

HENDERSON, S.P.   Glamorgan

Full Name: Stephen Peter
Henderson.
Role: Left-hand bat, right-arm
medium bowler, slip fielder.
Born: 24 September 1958, Oxford.
Height: 6′ 2″ **Weight:** 14st.
Nickname: Hendo.
County debut: 1977 (Worcester-
shire), 1983 (Glamorgan).
1st-Class 50s scored: 12.
1st-Class 100s scored: 3.
1st-Class 200s scored: 1.
One-day 50s: 3.
Place in batting averages: 34
average: 38.25; (1984: 118
average: 30.44).
1st-Class catches 1985: 3 (career: 46).
Parents: Derek and Ann.
Marital status: Single.
Family links with cricket: Father
Oxford Blue 1950.
Education: Downside School; Durham University; Magdalene College,
Cambridge.
Qualifications: B.A. (Durham); B.A. (Cantab).
Jobs outside cricket: Chartered Surveyor, spot welder, barman.
Cricketing superstitions: "Getting out in the 60s."
Overseas tours: Barbados 1980 with Worcester C.C.C.; U.S.A. 1981 with
M.C.C.; Africa 1983 with McAlpines.
Cricketers particularly learnt from: Gordon Wilcock, Basil D'Oliveira.
Other sports: Rugby, squash, hockey, tennis, golf.
Relaxations: Photography, television, reading, conservation of hedgehogs.

LAST SEASON: BATTING

	I.	N.O.	R.	H.S.	AV.
TEST					
OTHER FIRST CLASS	12	4	306	111	38.25
INT					
JPL	5	1	57	23	14.25
NAT.W					
B & H	3	1	19	16	9.50

CAREER: BATTING

	I.	N.O.	R.	H.S.	AV.
TEST					
OTHER FIRST CLASS	116	17	2611	209*	26.37
INT					
JPL	32	7	485	65*	19.40
NAT.W	2	0	50	33	25.00
B & H	14	2	146	82	12.17

LAST SEASON: BOWLING

	O.	M.	R.	W.	AV.
TEST					
OTHER FIRST CLASS	8	2	31	0	–
INT					
JPL					
NAT.W					
B & H					

CAREER: BOWLING

	O.	M.	R.	W.	AV.
TEST					
OTHER FIRST CLASS	44.4	8	216	3	72.00
INT					
JPL	1.4	0	17	0	–
NAT.W					
B & H	12	1	69	4	17.25

Extras: Captained Cambridge University 1983. Blues 1982 & 83. Made debut for Worcestershire in 1977, but left staff in 1981. Left Glamorgan in 1985.
Best batting performance: 209* Cambridge University v Middlesex, Cambridge 1982.
Best bowling performance: 2-48 Glamorgan v Surrey, Glamorgan 1983.

HENRIKSEN, S. Lancashire

Full Name: Søren Henriksen.
Role: Right-hand bat, right-arm fast-medium bowler.
Born: 1 December 1964, Denmark.
Height: 6' 3" **Weight:** 14st. 8 lbs.
Nickname: Herbie.
County debut: 1985.
1st-Class catches 1985: 1 (career: 1).
Parents: Annie and Bendt.
Marital status: Single.
Family links with cricket: Father played for Svanholm C.C., Denmark.
Education: Trade School, Copenhagen.
Qualifications: Trade exams.
Jobs outside cricket: Office job in City Hall.
Overseas tours: Sweden 1979 with

Svanholm CC; England 1981, 82, 84 with Danish Schools Teams; Kenya 1983

LAST SEASON: BATTING

	I.	N.O.	R.	H.S.	AV.
TEST					
OTHER FIRST CLASS	2	2	10	10*	–
INT					
JPL	1	0	1	1	–
NAT.W	1	1	1	1*	–
B & H	–	–	–	–	–

CAREER: BATTING

	I.	N.O.	R.	H.S.	AV.
TEST					
OTHER FIRST CLASS	2	2	10	10*	–
INT					
JPL	1	0	1	1	–
NAT.W	1	1	1	1*	–
B & H	–	–	–	–	–

LAST SEASON: BOWLING

	O.	M.	R.	W.	AV.
TEST					
OTHER FIRST CLASS	12	1	44	1	–
INT					
JPL	50	0	239	4	59.75
NAT.W	10	1	51	2	25.50
B & H	7	0	32	0	–

CAREER: BOWLING

	O.	M.	R.	W.	AV.
TEST					
OTHER FIRST CLASS	12	1	44	1	–
INT					
JPL	50	0	239	4	59.75
NAT.W	10	1	51	2	25.50
B & H	7	0	32	0	–

with Danish Sports Academic Club; Holland 1983 with Young Denmark.
Cricketers particularly learnt from: Ole Mortensen.
Other sports: Plays badminton, table-tennis, handball; follows football, cricket, speedway, Formula 1, boxing.
Injuries 1985: Shoulder and side — not serious.
Relaxations: Music, T.V., videos, swimming.
Best batting performance: 10* Lancashire v Surrey, The Oval 1985.

HICK, G.A. Worcestershire

Full Name: Graeme Ashley Hick.
Role: Right-hand bat, off-break bowler, slips and gully fielder.
Born: 23 May 1966, Harare, Zimbabwe.
County debut: 1984.
1st-Class 50s scored: 7.
1st-Class 100s scored: 3.
1st-Class 200s scored: 1.
One-day 50s: 2.
Place in batting averages: 19 average: 52.71.
1st-Class catches 1985: 14 (career: 15).
Parents: John and Eva Hick.
Marital status: Single.
Family links with cricket: Father connected with cricket administration since 1972 and in 1984 elected to Zimbabwe Cricket Union Board of Control.
Education: Banket Primary; Prince Edward Boys' High School, Zimbabwe.
Qualifications: 4 O-levels, N.C.A. coaching award.
Jobs outside cricket: Zimbabwe Cricket Union coach.
Off-season 1985–86: In Zimbabwe playing cricket.
Cricketing superstitions: Left pad always put on first.
Overseas tours: Zimbabwe XI 1983 World Cup; Zimbabwe v Sri Lanka in Sri Lanka; Zimbabwe U-23 Triangular Tournament, Zambia; Zimbabwe to U.K. 1985.
Overseas teams played for: Old Harrarians, Zimbabwe, since 1982.
Cricketers particularly learnt from: David Houghton, Basil D'Oliveira, father.
Cricketers particularly admired: Duncan Fletcher (Zimbabwe captain) for approach and understanding of the game.
Relaxations: Watching movies, television, listening to music.
Extras: Youngest player participating in 1983 Prudential World Cup (aged

17); youngest player to represent Zimbabwe. Scored 1234 runs in 1984 Birmingham League season; scored 964 runs in 1984 2nd XI for Worcestershire; scored 185 in Birmingham League — highest score since the war; scored 11 centuries (six in a row) in both above competitions.

Opinions on cricket: "Politics should not be involved in cricket."

Best batting performance: 230 Zimbabwe v Oxford University, Oxford 1985.

Best bowling performance: 3-39 Zimbabwe v Sri Lanka Board Presidents XI, Moratuwa 1983–84.

LAST SEASON: BATTING

	I.	N.O.	R.	H.S.	AV.
TEST					
OTHER FIRST CLASS	25	1	1265	230	52.71
INT					
JPL	8	1	205	90	29.28
NAT.W					
B & H					

CAREER: BATTING

	I.	N.O.	R.	H.S.	AV.
TEST					
OTHER FIRST CLASS	49	5	1926	230	43.77
INT					
JPL	8	1	205	90	29.28
NAT.W					
B & H					

LAST SEASON: BOWLING

	O.	M.	R.	W.	AV.
TEST					
OTHER FIRST CLASS	146	26	501	8	62.63
INT					
JPL	10	0	66	3	22.00
NAT.W					
B & H					

CAREER: BOWLING

	O.	M.	R.	W.	AV.
TEST					
OTHER FIRST CLASS	299	56	1009	18	56.06
INT					
JPL	10	0	66	3	22.00
NAT.W					
B & H					

HILL, A.   Derbyshire

Full Name: Alan Hill.
Role: Right-hand bat, off-break bowler.
Born: 29 June 1950, Buxworth, Derbyshire.
Height: 6' 0" **Weight:** 12st. 4lbs.
Nickname: Bud.
County debut: 1972.
County cap: 1976.
Benefit: 1986.
1000 runs in a season: 4.
1st-Class 50s scored: 62.
1st-Class 100s scored: 15.
One-day 50s: 13.
One-day 100s: 2.
Place in batting averages: 111 average: 30.27; (1984: 96 average: 32.98).
1st-Class catches 1985: 3 (career: 88).
Parents: Hilda and Jack.

Wife and date of marriage: Linda, 18 March 1978.

Children: Elizabeth Anne, Eleanor Jane, Laura Louise.

Education: Buxworth Primary School; New Mills Grammar School; Chester College of Education.

Qualifications: B.Ed. Physical Education teacher. Advanced Cricket Coaching Award.

Jobs outside cricket: Teaching posts, clerical work, promotional assistant.

Off-season 1985–86: Organising benefit.

Family links with cricket: Father and brother both played local league cricket. Brother, Bernard, played for Derbyshire 2nd XI.

Cricketers particularly admired: Sir Garfield Sobers.

Overseas teams played for: Orange Free State in 1976–77 Currie Cup Competition.

Relaxations: Other sports, particularly football; music, reading.

Other sports: Soccer, rugby.

Injuries 1985: Cracked bone in leg, broken finger.

Extras: England Schoolboy cricketer 1968; also represented National Association of Young Cricketers.

Opinions on cricket: "In favour of (a) reduction in amount of cricket played with one 3- or 4-day game per week and 1-day games on Saturday and Sunday, leaving one day off; (b) more specialised coaching required at all levels, including county. Video equipment a necessity at professional level; (c) would like to see the abolition of the current benefit system in favour of a fairer system whereby all professional cricketers would receive a sum at the end of their careers, that sum being dependent upon their length of service."

Best batting performance: 160* Derbyshire v Warwickshire, Coventry 1976.

Best bowling performance: 3-5 Orange Free State v N. Transvaal, Pretoria 1976–77.

LAST SEASON: BATTING

	I.	N.O.	R.	H.S.	AV.
TEST					
OTHER FIRST CLASS	14	3	333	120	30.27
INT					
JPL	2	0	51	26	25.50
NAT.W					
B & H	3	1	138	107*	69.00

CAREER: BATTING

	I.	N.O.	R.	H.S.	AV.
TEST					
OTHER FIRST CLASS	407	41	10918	160*	29.83
INT					
JPL	78	4	1628	120	22.00
NAT.W	15	1	306	72	21.86
B & H	26	2	886	107*	36.08

LAST SEASON: BOWLING

	O.	M.	R.	W.	AV.
TEST					
OTHER FIRST CLASS					
INT					
JPL					
NAT.W					
B & H					

CAREER: BOWLING

	O.	M.	R.	W.	AV.
TEST					
OTHER FIRST CLASS	83.2	16	343	8	42.88
INT					
JPL	8	0	32	3	10.67
NAT.W					
B & H					

HINKS, S.G.   Kent

Full Name: Simon Graham Hinks.
Role: Left-hand bat, bat/pad fielder "but only to Deadly".
Born: 12 October 1960, Northfleet, Kent.
Height: 6' 2" **Weight:** 13st. 4lbs.
Nickname: Hinksy.
County debut: 1982.
County cap: 1985.
1000 runs in a season: 1.
1st-Class 50s scored: 11.
1st-Class 100s scored: 1.
One-day 50s: 2.
Place in batting averages: 77 average: 34.13; (1984: 261 average: 11.57).
1st-Class catches 1985: 23 (career: 29).
Parents: Mary and Graham Hinks.
Marital status: Single.
Education: Dover Road Infant and Junior Schools, Northfleet; St. George's C. of E. School, Gravesend.
Qualifications: 5 O-levels, 1 A-level.
Jobs outside cricket: Menswear manager, By One, Gravesend; sheepskin and leatherwear sales representative; gardener.
Off-season 1985–86: Coaching in Tasmania.
Family links with cricket: Father captained Gravesend C.C. and is now chairman. Brother Jonathan plays for Gravesend and Kent U-19s.
Cricket superstitions: "Put gear on in set order."
Overseas teams played for: Pirates, Johannesburg, 1981–82; University of

LAST SEASON: BATTING

	I.	N.O.	R.	H.S.	AV.
TEST					
OTHER FIRST CLASS	48	3	1536	117	34.13
INT					
JPL	14	0	214	32	15.28
NAT.W	3	0	144	95	48.00
B & H	5	0	94	49	18.80

CAREER: BATTING

	I.	N.O.	R.	H.S.	AV.
TEST					
OTHER FIRST CLASS	76	4	1986	117	27.58
INT					
JPL	21	2	336	52*	17.68
NAT.W	3	0	144	95	48.00
B & H	5	0	94	49	18.80

LAST SEASON: BOWLING

	O.	M.	R.	W.	AV.
TEST					
OTHER FIRST CLASS	33	1	120	1	–
INT					
JPL	1	0	3	1	–
NAT.W	12	0	59	1	–
B & H					

CAREER: BOWLING

	O.	M.	R.	W.	AV.
TEST					
OTHER FIRST CLASS	50.4	5	178	3	59.33
INT					
JPL	9	1	39	2	19.50
NAT.W	12	0	59	1	–
B & H					

Tasmania, 1983–84, 1984–85, 1985–86.
Cricketers particularly learnt from: "Learnt from my father and members of local club, Gravesend. Admire Clive Lloyd's style and power and anyone who has proved themselves over a long period."
Other sports: Most ball games.
Relaxations: T.V., music, sleep.
Injuries 1985: "Major transplant to remove county cap after last game of the season!"
Best batting performance: 117 Kent v Surrey, Canterbury 1985.

HOFFMAN, D.S. Warwickshire

Full Name: Dean Stuart Hoffman.
Role: Right-hand bat, right-arm seam bowler.
Born: 13 January 1966, Birmingham.
Height: 6′ 2″ **Weight:** 13st.
Nicknames: Tootsie or Deano.
County debut: 1985.
Place in bowling averages: 102 average 40.00.
1st-Class catches: 3 (career 3).
Parents: Pauline and Ken.
Marital status: Single.
Family links with cricket: Father and brother play for Walmley C.C.
Education: Moor End Lane School.
Qualifications: Cricket coach.
Jobs outside cricket: Sales person for Argos.
Off-season 1985–86: Tour to Barbados, coaching in South Africa.

LAST SEASON: BATTING

	I.	N.O.	R.	H.S.	AV.
TEST					
OTHER FIRST CLASS	15	4	39	13*	3.55
INT					
JPL	3	2	3	2	–
NAT.W	1	0	3	3	–
B & H					

CAREER: BATTING

	I.	N.O.	R.	H.S.	AV.
TEST					
OTHER FIRST CLASS	15	4	39	13*	3.55
INT					
JPL	3	2	3	2	–
NAT.W	1	0	3	3	–
B & H					

LAST SEASON: BOWLING

	O.	M.	R.	W.	AV.
TEST					
OTHER FIRST CLASS	326.4	55	1160	29	40.00
INT					
JPL	57	2	252	5	50.40
NAT.W	22	1	100	2	50.00
B & H					

CAREER: BOWLING

	O.	M.	R.	W.	AV.
TEST					
OTHER FIRST CLASS	326.4	55	1160	29	40.00
INT					
JPL	57	2	252	5	50.40
NAT.W	22	1	100	2	50.00
B & H					

Overseas tours: Young England tour to the West Indies, 1985.
Cricketers particularly learnt from: David Brown and Bob Willis.
Cricketers particularly admired: Bob Willis, Graham Gooch.
Other sports: Plays golf, snooker; follows football, tennis.
Relaxations: Listening to music, playing golf.
Best batting performance: 13* Warwickshire v Worcestershire, Nuneaton 1985.
Best bowling performance: 4-100 Warwickshire v Nottinghamshire, Nuneaton 1985.

HOLDING, M.A. — Derbyshire

Full Name: Michael Anthony Holding.
Role: Right-hand bat, right-arm fast bowler.
Born: 16 February 1954, Kingston, Jamaica.
County debut: 1981 (Lancashire), 1983 (Derbyshire).
Test debut: 1975.
No. of Tests: 55.
No. of One-Day Internationals: 86.
50 wickets in a season: 1.
1st-Class 50s scored: 1.
1st-Class 5 w. in innings: 29.
1st-Class 10 w. in match: 4.
Place in batting averages: 167 average: 22.94.
Place in bowling averages: 9 average: 22.48.

LAST SEASON: BATTING

	I.	N.O.	R.	H.S.	AV.
TEST					
OTHER FIRST CLASS	19	1	413	80	22.94
INT					
JPL	10	2	219	58	27.37
NAT.W	1	0	27	27	–
B & H	3	1	60	38	30.00

LAST SEASON: BOWLING

	O.	M.	R.	W.	AV.
TEST					
OTHER FIRST CLASS	354.5	67	1124	50	22.48
INT					
JPL	96	11	394	15	26.26
NAT.W	12	2	36	1	–
B & H	23	2	85	1	–

CAREER: BATTING

	I.	N.O.	R.	H.S.	AV.
TEST	71	10	786	69	12.89
OTHER FIRST CLASS	110	16	1580	80	16.81
INT	35	9	215	64	8.22
JPL	13	2	238	58	21.63
NAT.W	3	1	39	27	19.50
B & H	4	1	61	38	20.33

CAREER: BOWLING

	O.	M.	R.	W.	AV.
TEST	140.5 1786.1	15	5414	233	23.24
OTHER FIRST CLASS	56	5	6924	284	24.38
INT	789	89	2613	122	21.42
JPL	144.4	18	563	26	21.65
NAT.W	48	6	157	6	26.17
B & H	45	8	134	4	33.50

Overseas tours: With West Indies to Australia 1975–76, 1981–82; to England 1976, 1980–84; to India 1983–84. International team to Pakistan 1981–82.
Overseas teams played for: Jamaica, Tasmania.
Extras: Played for Lancashire in 1981.
Best batting performance: 80 Derbyshire v Yorkshire, Chesterfield 1985.
Best bowling performance: 8-91 West Indies v England, The Oval 1976.

HOLMES, G.C. Glamorgan

Full Name: Geoffrey Clark Holmes.
Role: Right-hand bat, right-arm medium bowler, cover fielder.
Born: 16 September 1958, Newcastle-on-Tyne.
Height: 5′ 10″ **Weight:** 10st. 10lbs.
County debut: 1978.
County cap: 1985.
1000 runs in a season: 2.
1st-Class 50s scored: 16.
1st-Class 100s scored: 3.
1st-Class 5 w. in innings: 1.
One-day 50s: 5.
Place in batting averages: 107 average: 30.51; (1984: 123 average: 29.68).
Place in bowling averages: 99 average: 38.56.
1st-Class catches 1985: 10 (career: 39).

LAST SEASON: BATTING

	I.	N.O.	R.	H.S.	AV.
TEST					
OTHER FIRST CLASS	40 2368.1	3 596	1129	112	30.51
INT					
JPL	12	2	226	45	22.60
NAT.W	3	0	24	20	8.00
B & H	4	1	163	70	54.33

CAREER: BATTING

	I.	N.O.	R.	H.S.	AV.
TEST					
OTHER FIRST CLASS	162	27	3564	112	26.40
INT					
JPL	55	11	904	73	20.54
NAT.W	5	0	48	20	9.60
B & H	10	2	225	70	28.13

LAST SEASON: BOWLING

	O.	M.	R.	W.	AV.
TEST					
OTHER FIRST CLASS	346.3	86	1041	27	38.56
INT					
JPL	74	1	392	19	20.63
NAT.W	30	6	63	6	10.50
B & H	38.2	6	148	7	21.15

CAREER: BOWLING

	O.	M.	R.	W.	AV.
TEST					
OTHER FIRST CLASS	685.4	145	2329	56	41.39
INT					
JPL	243.3	10	1198	49	24.44
NAT.W	38	7	96	6	16.00
B & H	77.2	11	292	13	22.46

Parents: George and Rita Holmes.
Wife: Christine.
Education: West Denton High School.
Qualifications: 6 O-levels, A-levels in Maths and Chemistry. Advanced cricket coach.
Jobs outside cricket: Trainee estimator, has worked as milkman.
Overseas teams played for: Villa C.C., Antigua, 1980–81; Bathurst R.U.C.C., New South Wales, 1983–84; Fish Hoek, South Africa, 1984–85.
Cricketers particularly learnt from: Javed Miandad.
Off-season 1985–86: Playing and coaching abroad.
Family links with cricket: Father played in the Northumberland League.
Other sports: Soccer, snooker.
Relaxations: Reading, especially cricket books, T.V., sport.
Best batting performance: 112 Glamorgan v Leicestershire, Leicester 1985.
Best bowling performance: 5-86 Glamorgan v Surrey, The Oval 1980.

HOPKINS, J.A. Glamorgan

Full Name: John Anthony Hopkins.
Role: Right-hand bat, occasional wicket-keeper.
Born: 16 June 1953, Maesteg.
Nickname: Ponty.
County debut: 1970.
County cap: 1977.
1000 runs in a season: 7.
1st-Class 50s scored: 53.
1st-Class 100s scored: 16.
1st-Class 200s scored: 1.
One-day 50s: 23.
One-day 100s: 2.
Place in batting averages: 148 average: 24.81; (1984: 93 average: 33.33).
1st-Class catches 1985: 8 (career: 181).
Education: Trinity College of Education, Carmarthen.
Qualifications: Trained as a teacher.
Jobs outside cricket: Teacher.
Family links with cricket: Younger brother of J.D. Hopkins who appeared for Middlesex C.C.C. and formerly on Glamorgan staff.
Extras: Known as fine baritone singer and raconteur in the Glamorgan "cabaret" act.
Best batting performance: 230 Glamorgan v Worcestershire, Worcester 1977.

LAST SEASON: BATTING

	I.	N.O.	R.	H.S.	AV.
TEST					
OTHER FIRST CLASS	34	2	794	114*	24.81
INT					
JPL	10	2	229	72*	28.62
NAT.W	2	0	27	15	13.50
B & H	4	0	35	18	8.75

CAREER: BATTING

	I.	N.O.	R.	H.S.	AV.
TEST					
OTHER FIRST CLASS	460	29	12099	230	28.07
INT					
JPL	142	13	2819	130*	21.85
NAT.W	16	0	309	63	19.31
B & H	36	2	961	103*	28.26

LAST SEASON: BOWLING

	O.	M.	R.	W.	AV.
TEST					
OTHER FIRST CLASS	6	1	22	0	–
INT					
JPL					
NAT.W					
B & H					

CAREER: BOWLING

	O.	M.	R.	W.	AV.
TEST					
OTHER FIRST CLASS	19.2	2	90	0	–
INT					
JPL					
NAT.W					
B & H					

HOWARTH, G.P. Surrey

Full Name: Geoffrey Philip Howarth.
Role: Right-hand bat, off-break bowler, slip fielder
Born: 29 March 1951, Auckland, New Zealand.
Height: 5′ 10½″ **Weight:** 12st.
Nickname: Kiwi, Bones.
County debut: 1971.
County cap: 1974.
Test debut: 1974–75.
No. of Tests: 47.
No. of One-Day Internationals: 70.
1000 runs in a season: 4.
1st-Class 50s scored: 87.
1st-Class 100s scored: 32.
1st-Class 5 w. in innings: 1.
One-day 50s: 18.
One-day 100s: 2.

Place in batting averages: — average: —; (1984: 162 average: 24.50).
1st-Class catches 1985: 0 (career: 226).
Parents: George and Anne.
Marital status: Separated.
Education: Auckland Grammar School.
Qualifications: New Zealand School Certificate.
Off-season 1985–86: Playing in New Zealand.
Family links with cricket: Younger brother of H.J. Howarth, New Zealand Test cricketer.

Overseas tours: Toured with New Zealand to Pakistan and India 1976–77, England 1978 and 1983, Australia 1980–81 and 1982–83; Far East, Sri Lanka and South Africa with D.H. Robins' XI.

Overseas teams played for: New Zealand U-23s XI v Auckland at Auckland 1968–69; Auckland.

Other sports: "Golf, tennis, squash etc. Enjoy watching most sports on T.V."

Relaxations: Music, T.V., reading.

Extras: Joined Surrey staff 1969. Scored two centuries in a match (122 and 102) for New Zealand v England at Auckland 1977–78. Stayed with Bob Willis's parents during early days with Surrey. Was awarded M.B.E. in 1981, O.B.E. 1984. Captain of New Zealand 1980. Captain of Surrey 1984. Left staff after 1985 when regulations relating to overseas players severely restricted appearances.

Best batting performance: 183 Surrey v Hampshire, The Oval 1979.

Best bowling performance: 5-32 Auckland v Central Districts, Auckland 1973–74.

LAST SEASON: BATTING

	I.	N.O.	R.	H.S.	AV.
TEST					
OTHER FIRST CLASS	4	1	58	53	19.33
INT					
JPL					
NAT.W					
B & H					

CAREER: BATTING

	I.	N.O.	R.	H.S.	AV.
TEST	83	5	2531	147	32.44
OTHER FIRST CLASS	492	37	14595	183	32.08
INT	64	5	1378	76	23.35
JPL	100	1	2245	122	22.67
NAT.W	17	0	300	34	17.65
B & H	43	3	1220	80	30.50

LAST SEASON: BOWLING

	O.	M.	R.	W.	AV.
TEST					
OTHER FIRST CLASS					
INT					
JPL					
NAT.W					
B & H					

CAREER: BOWLING

	O.	M.	R.	W.	AV.
TEST	40 49	4 16	271	3	90.33
OTHER FIRST CLASS	565.6 603.1	127 166	3322	109	30.48
INT	15	0	68	3	22.67
JPL	18.2	0	85	5	17.00
NAT.W	2.1	0	25	2	12.50
B & H					

79. What former England Test cricketer is now team manager of Kent and played for them in 1985 after retiring nine years before?

80. Who is the current secretary of the M.C.C.?

HUGHES, D.P.   Lancashire

Full Name: David Paul Hughes.
Role: Right-hand bat, slow left-arm bowler.
Born: 13 May 1947, Newton-le-Willows.
Height: 5′ 11″ **Weight:** 12st.
Nickname: Yozzer.
County debut: 1967.
County cap: 1970.
Testimonial: 1981.
1000 runs in a season: 2.
50 wickets in a season: 2.
1st-Class 50s scored: 38.
1st-Class 100s scored: 8.
1st-Class 5 w. in innings: 20.
1st-Class 10 w. in match: 2.
One-day 50s: 9.
Place in batting averages: 116 average: 29.36; (1984: 181 average:2.77).
1st-Class catches 1985: 9 (career: 242).
Parents: Both deceased.
Wife and date of marriage: Christine, March 1973.
Children: James, July 1975.
Education: Newton-le-Willows Grammar School.
Qualifications: N.C.A. coaching certificate.
Family links with cricket: Father, Lloyd, a professional with Bolton League Club, Walkden, before and after Second World War.
Overseas tours: With Derrick Robins to South Africa 1972–73; England Counties side to West Indies 1974–75.
Overseas teams played for: Played for Tasmania while coaching there in 1975–76 and 1976–77.
Cricketers particularly learnt from: "At the start of my career I spoke to all the leading left-arm spin bowlers in the game for help."
Relaxations: Golf, member of Warrington Golf Club.
Extras: Coached in South Africa 1977–78; coached in Tasmania 1978–79 and 1979–80. Gillette Cup "specialist". Hit 24 runs off John Mortimer v Gloucestershire in penultimate over in Gillette semi-final in 1972. Hit 26 runs off last over of innings v Northamptonshire in Gillette Final at Lord's, 1976. Bowled 13 consecutive maiden overs v Gloucestershire at Bristol, 1980. John Player League 9th wicket partnership of 86 with P. Lever v Essex (Leyton) 1973.
Best batting performance: 153 Lancashire v Glamorgan, Old Trafford 1983.
Best bowling performance: 7-24 Lancashire v Oxford University, Oxford 1970.

LAST SEASON: BATTING

	I.	N.O.	R.	H.S.	AV.
TEST					
OTHER FIRST CLASS	16	2	.411	75*	29.36
INT					
JPL	9	1	154	28	19.25
NAT.W	1	0	31	31	–
B & H					

LAST SEASON: BOWLING

	O.	M.	R.	W.	AV.
TEST					
OTHER FIRST CLASS	21	12	26	1	–
INT					
JPL					
NAT.W	1	0	5	0	–
B & H					

CAREER: BATTING

	I.	N.O.	R.	H.S.	AV.
TEST					
OTHER FIRST CLASS	463	84	8612	153	22.72
INT					
JPL	179	42	2539	92	18.53
NAT.W	34	15	759	71	39.95
B & H	45	13	854	52	26.69

CAREER: BOWLING

	O.	M.	R.	W.	AV.
TEST					
OTHER FIRST CLASS	6701.1	2080	18254	610	29.93
INT					
JPL	786.1	62	3387	161	21.03
NAT.W	300.2	29	1166	44	26.50
B & H	218.2	39	702	28	25.07

HUGHES, S.P.   Middlesex

Full Name: Simon Peter Hughes.
Role: Right-hand bat, right-arm fast-medium bowler.
Born: 20 December 1959, Kingston, Surrey.
Height: 5′ 10″ **Weight:** 11st. 7lbs.
Nickname: Yozzer, Heinz (57 varieties), Spam.
County debut: 1980.
County cap: 1981.
1st-Class 5 w. in innings: 6.
Place in batting averages: 197 average: 18.80; (1984: 248 average 14.40).
Place in bowling averages: 101 average: 38.83; (1984: 67 average: 30.03).
1st-Class catches 1985: 6 (career: 22).
Parents: Peter and Erica Hughes.
Marital status: Single.
Education: Latymer Upper School, Hammersmith; Durham University.
Qualifications: 10 O-levels, 4 A-levels, B.A. Geography and Anthropology.
Jobs outside cricket: Writes regular sports column in local weekly paper, and monthly for the *Cricketer*.

Off-season 1985–86: "International Ambassadors" Tour to India, then playing for Fremantle C.C., Perth.

Family links with cricket: Father very keen coach and player who owned indoor cricket school. "Uncle once hit a ball over the school pavilion!"

Overseas tours: Personal overseas spell playing in Sri Lanka 1979; Middlesex C.C.C. tour to Zimbabwe winter 1980; with Overseas XI (captained by J.M. Brearley), to Calcutta (v Indian XI) 1980–81.

Overseas teams played for: Colts C.C., Colombo, Sri Lanka, and Sri Lanka Board President's XI; Northern Transvaal 1982–83; Grosvenor-Fynaland 1983–84; Auckland University 1984–85.

Cricketers particularly learnt from: Father, Jack Robertson, Mike Brearley, Mike Selvey and G.O. Allen.

Cricketers particularly admired: John Emburey, Clive Radley, Malcolm Marshall, Richard Hadlee.

Other sports: Soccer (for university), tennis, golf.

Relaxations: "Travelling, particularly by train; old comedy films (e.g. Laurel and Hardy); music — play organ and piano; writing; addicted to curry; cycling."

Extras: Took 4-82 v Kent on Championship debut, plus played in County Championship and Gillette Cup winning sides (Lord's Final) in 1980 in first season. Selected for England U-25 XI v Sri Lanka (Trent Bridge) July 1981. Awarded cap after only 20 matches.

Opinions on cricket: "Time for uncovered wickets to provide more variety."

Best batting performance: 41* Middlesex v Gloucestershire, Uxbridge, 1984.

Best bowling performance: 6-32 Middlesex v Gloucestershire, Bristol 1983.

LAST SEASON: BATTING

	I.	N.O.	R.	H.S.	AV.
TEST					
OTHER FIRST CLASS	11	6	94	30*	18.80
INT					
JPL	6	4	66	22*	33.00
NAT.W					
B & H					

CAREER: BATTING

	I.	N.O.	R.	H.S.	AV.
TEST					
OTHER FIRST CLASS	75	35	366	41*	9.15
INT					
JPL	10	6	77	22*	19.25
NAT.W	4	2	9	6	4.50
B & H	3	1	12	8*	6.00

LAST SEASON: BOWLING

	O.	M.	R.	W.	AV.
TEST					
OTHER FIRST CLASS	266.2	43	932	24	38.83
INT					
JPL	54	0	245	10	24.50
NAT.W					
B & H					

CAREER: BOWLING

	O.	M.	R.	W.	AV.
TEST					
OTHER FIRST CLASS	1783	329	5921	208	28.47
INT					
JPL	176.1	4	871	29	30.03
NAT.W	93.2	15	354	14	25.29
B & H	31	4	109	2	54.50

HUMPAGE, G.W.　　　　　Warwickshire

Full Name: Geoffrey William
Humpage.
Role: Right-hand bat, wicket-keeper;
can also bowl right-arm medium.
Born: 24 April 1954, Birmingham.
Height: 5′ 9″ **Weight:** 12st. 7lbs.
Nickname: Farsley.
County debut: 1974.
County cap: 1976.
No. of One-Day Internationals: 3.
1000 runs in a season: 8.
1st-Class 50s scored: 65.
1st-Class 100s scored: 21.
1st-Class 200s scored: 2.
One-day 50s: 28.
One-day 100s 3.
Place in batting averages: 58
average: 37.80; (1984: 23
average: 48.49).
Parents: Ernest and Mabel Humpage.
Wife and date of marriage: Valerie Anne, 14 September 1983 (2nd
marriage).

LAST SEASON: BATTING

	I.	N.O.	R.	H.S.	AV.
TEST					
OTHER FIRST CLASS	42	6	1361	159	37.80
INT					
JPL	14	2	412	62	34.33
NAT.W	2	0	25	14	12.50
B & H	4	1	131	62	43.67

CAREER: BATTING

	I.	N.O.	R.	H.S.	AV.
TEST					
OTHER FIRST CLASS	409	51	13239	254	36.98
INT	2	0	11	6	5.50
JPL	134	20	2943	109*	25.81
NAT.W	23	4	521	77	27.42
B & H	44	7	1158	100*	31.30

LAST SEASON: BOWLING

	O.	M.	R.	W.	AV.
TEST					
OTHER FIRST CLASS					
INT					
JPL					
NAT.W					
B & H					

CAREER: BOWLING

	O.	M.	R.	W.	AV.
TEST					
OTHER FIRST CLASS	130.1	17	444	10	44.40
INT					
JPL	94.5	2	527	15	35.13
NAT.W					
B & H	27	2	123	3	41.00

LAST SEASON: WICKET KEEPING

	C.	ST.			
TEST					
OTHER FIRST CLASS	76	4			
INT					
JPL	6	7			
NAT.W	3	–			
B & H	3	–			

CAREER: WICKET KEEPING

	C.	ST.			
TEST					
OTHER FIRST CLASS	472	56			
INT	2	–			
JPL	91	19			
NAT.W	24	5			
B & H	51	2			

Children: Philip Andrew Guy, 16 November 1977.
Education: Golden Hillock Comprehensive School, Birmingham.
Jobs outside cricket: Former police cadet, then police constable, Birmingham City Police; Coach, Scarborough C.C., Western Australia, 1978–79; sports executive for Pace Insurance Consultants, Birmingham.
Other sports: Soccer, squash, tennis, swimming, golf, snooker, table-tennis.
Relaxations: Reading, listening to E.L.O.
Extras: Good impressionist, particularly Frankie Howerd. Took part in record Warwickshire, and English first-class 4th wicket partnership of 470 v Lancs. at Southport, July 1982, with Kallicharran making 230 n.o. Humpage made 254 n.o. including 13 sixes. Previous 4th wicket record was 448 for Surrey at The Oval v Yorks, in 1899, by R. Abel and T.W. Hayward. Joined England "Rebels" in South Africa in 1982.
Best batting performance: 254 Warwickshire v Lancashire, Southport 1982.
Best bowling performance: 13 Warwickshire v Gloucestershire, Edgbaston 1980.

HUMPHRIES, D.J.   Worcestershire

Full Name: David John Humphries.
Role: Left-hand bat, wicket-keeper.
Born: 6 August 1953, Alveley, Shropshire.
Height: 5' 8" **Weight:** 13st.
Nickname: Humpty.
County debut: 1974 (Leicestershire), 1977 (Worcestershire).
County cap: 1978 (Worcestershire).
1st-Class 50s scored: 25.
1st-Class 100s scored: 4.
One-day 50s: 2.
Place in batting averages: —
average: —; (1984: 135
average: 28.00).
Parents: Dennis John and Olive Mary Humphries.
Wife and date of marriage: Lorraine Mary, 7 September 1974.
Children: Rebecca Louise, 10 October 1978.
Education: Bridgnorth Secondary Modern; Wulfrun College, Wolverhampton.
Qualifications: 6 O-levels, 8 C.S.E.s, 1 A-level, O.N.C. Engineering Part 1.
Jobs outside cricket: Has been marketing assistant, Kay & Co. Ltd., Worcester. Lottery manager, Worcestershire C.C.C.

Family links with cricket: Father Club Captain of Cannock C.C. and still plays. Brother plays Birmingham League and ex-Staffordshire Schools.
Other sports: Football, golf.
Relaxations: Skittles, darts.
Extras: Played for Shropshire 1971–73, debut for Leicestershire 1974, left county after 1976 season. Released by Worcestershire at end of 1985.
Best batting performance: 133* Worcestershire v Derbyshire, Worcester 1984.

LAST SEASON: BATTING

	I.	N.O.	R.	H.S.	AV.
TEST					
OTHER FIRST CLASS	1	1	62	62*	–
INT					
JPL					
NAT.W					
B & H					

CAREER: BATTING

	I.	N.O.	R.	H.S.	AV.
TEST					
OTHER FIRST CLASS	252	46	5116	133*	24.84
INT					
JPL	94	12	1144	62	13.95
NAT.W	10	1	178	58	19.78
B & H	28	4	317	41	13.21

LAST SEASON: WICKET KEEPING

	C.	ST.			
TEST					
OTHER FIRST CLASS	–	–			
INT					
JPL					
NAT.W					
B & H					

CAREER: WICKET KEEPING

	C.	ST.			
TEST					
OTHER FIRST CLASS	292	60			
INT					
JPL	93	23			
NAT.W	8	2			
B & H	37	8			

HUSSAIN, M.   Worcestershire

Full Name: Mehriyar Hussain.
Role: Right-hand bat, off-break bowler.
Born: 17 October 1963, South Shields.
Nickname: Mel.
Height: 6'1".
County debut: 1985.
Extras: Played with Hampshire 2nd XI, 1982–84.

LAST SEASON: BATTING

	I.	N.O.	R.	H.S.	AV.
TEST					
OTHER FIRST CLASS	1	0	4	4	–
INT					
JPL					
NAT.W					
B & H					

CAREER: BATTING

	I.	N.O.	R.	H.S.	AV.
TEST					
OTHER FIRST CLASS	1	0	4	4	–
INT					
JPL					
NAT.W					
B & H					

ILLINGWORTH, R.K.　　　Worcestershire

Full name: Richard Keith Illingworth.
Role: Right-hand bat, slow left-arm bowler.
Born: 1963, Bradford, Yorkshire.
Height: 5′ 11½″ **Weight:** 11st. 10lbs.
Nickname: Illy, Lucifer.
County debut: 1982.
50 wickets in a season: 1.
1st-Class 50s scored: 1.
1st-Class 5 w. in innings: 5.
1st-Class 10 w. in match: 1.
Place in batting averages: 226 average: 13.75; (1984: 148 average: 26.62).
Place in bowling averages: 42 average: 28.27; (1984: 85 average: 32.84).
1st-Class catches 1985: 8 (career: 29).
Parents: Keith and Margaret Illingworth.

LAST SEASON: BATTING

	I.	N.O.	R.	H.S.	AV.
TEST					
OTHER FIRST CLASS	20	8	165	39*	13.75
INT					
JPL	4	4	12	8*	–
NAT.W	–	–	–	–	–
B & H	2	1	9	9*	–

CAREER: BATTING

	I.	N.O.	R.	H.S.	AV.
TEST					
OTHER FIRST CLASS	91	25	975	55	14.77
INT					
JPL	21	11	78	21	7.80
NAT.W	2	0	30	22	15.00
B & H	5	2	30	11*	10.00

LAST SEASON: BOWLING

	O.	M.	R.	W.	AV.
TEST					
OTHER FIRST CLASS	406.5	113	1046	37	28.27
INT					
JPL	29	2	149	8	18.62
NAT.W	32	2	117	1	–
B & H	34	3	146	6	24.33

CAREER: BOWLING

	O.	M.	R.	W.	AV.
TEST					
OTHER FIRST CLASS	2076.2	564	5559	160	34.74
INT					
JPL	178	9	797	41	19.43
NAT.W	55.1	8	167	3	55.67
B & H	85	12	324	13	24.92

Wife and date of marriage: Anne, 2 September 1985.
Education: Wrose Brow Middle and Salts Grammar School.
Qualifications: 6 0-levels. Qualified coach.
Off-season 1985–86: Playing and coaching.
Family links with cricket: Father plays Bradford League cricket. Mother secretary Yorkshire C.A. Centre of Excellence nets.
Overseas tours: Denmark Youth Tournament N.A.Y.C. 1981; Whitbread scholarship playing for Colts C.C., Brisbane, 1982–83; Wisden Cricket XI, Barbados 1983.
Cricketers particularly learnt from: Father, Keith Illingworth.
Other sports: Any ball game, follows Leeds United.
Relaxations: Listening to music (Dire Straits). Dining out and relaxing at home.
Injuries 1985: Chest infection.
Best batting performance: 55 Worcestershire v Leicestershire, Hereford 1983.
Best bowling performance: 5-26 Worcestershire v Gloucestershire, Worcester 1983.

IMRAN KHAN   Sussex

Full Name: Ahmad Khan Niazi Imran.
Role: Right-hand bat, right-arm fast bowler.
Born: 25 November 1952, Lahore, Pakistan.
Height: 6′ 0″ **Weight:** 12st. 2lbs.
Nickname: Immie.
County debut: 1971 (Worcester-shire), 1977 (Sussex).
County cap: 1976 (Worcestershire), 1978 (Sussex).
Test debut: 1971.
No. of Tests: 51.
No. of One-Day Internationals: 55.
1000 runs in a season: 5.
50 wickets in a season: 6.
1st-Class 50s scored: 72.
1st-Class 100s scored: 23.
1st-Class 5 w. in innings: 59.
1st-Class 10 w. in match: 11.
One-day 50s: 37.
One-day 100s: 3.
Place in batting averages: 5 average: 68.46.
Place in bowling averages: 6 average: 20.39.
1st-Class catches 1985: 0 (career: 97).

Marital status: Single.
Education: Aitchison College; Cathedral School, Lahore; Worcester Royal Grammar School; Keble College, Oxford University.
Qualifications: B.A. Hons. in politics and economics.
Jobs outside cricket: "I play cricket all the year round."
Family links with cricket: Cousin of Pakistan cricketers, Majid Khan and Javed Burki.
Overseas tours: Toured with Pakistan to England in 1971, 1974, 1982 and 1983 World Cup; Australia and West Indies 1976–77; India 1979–80. Australia, 1981–82, 1983–84.
Overseas teams played for: Various Lahore teams, and N.S.W. 1984–85.
Cricketers particularly learnt from: John Snow, Basil D'Oliveira, Majid Khan.
Other sports: Squash, swimming, hockey.
Relaxations: Shooting, listening to music (Western and Eastern).
Extras: Debut for Lahore A 1969–70. Debut for Worcestershire 1971, cap 1976. Left Worcestershire in 1977. Oxford cricket blue 1973–74–75. Captain in 1974. Scored two centuries in a match, 117 n.o. and 106, Oxford University v Notts. at Oxford in 1974. Had a match double of 111 n.o. and 13 for 99 v Lancashire at Worcester in 1976. Played World Series Cricket. Has bad scar on left arm resulting from falling off a slide in Lahore, and cannot fully extend his arm. Drinks no alcohol. Does not smoke. Captain of Pakistan 1982–83.
Best batting performance: 170 Oxford University v Northamptonshire, Oxford 1974.
Best bowling performance: 8-58 Pakistan v Sri Lanka, Faisalabad 1981–82.

LAST SEASON: BATTING

	I.	N.O.	R.	H.S.	AV.
TEST					
OTHER FIRST CLASS	21	8	890	117*	68.46
INT					
JPL	12	3	615	104*	68.33
NAT.W	2	0	66	38	33.00
B & H	3	1	106	82*	53.00

CAREER: BATTING

	I.	N.O.	R.	H.S.	AV.
TEST	77	12	2023	123	31.12
OTHER FIRST CLASS	406	67	11551	170	36.70
INT	45	14	1023	102*	33.00
JPL	106	17	2873	104*	32.28
NAT.W	24	5	604	114*	31.79
B & H	39	7	1158	82*	36.19

LAST SEASON: BOWLING

	O.	M.	R.	W.	AV.
TEST					
OTHER FIRST CLASS	422.1	114	1040	51	20.39
INT					
JPL	92.2	11	320	20	16.00
NAT.W	20	5	34	2	17.00
B & H	33	8	88	4	22.00

CAREER: BOWLING

	O.	M.	R.	W.	AV.
TEST	410 1546.1	68 371	5316	232	22.91
OTHER FIRST CLASS	713.4 5951.5	129 2201	18259	842	21.69
INT	353.3	51	1152	56	20.57
JPL	785.4	67	2893	154	18.78
NAT.W	229.3	43	696	27	25.78
B & H	387.3	83	1082	56	19.32

INCHMORE, J.D.   Worcestershire

Full Name: John Darling Inchmore.
Role: Right-hand bat, right-arm
fast-medium bowler.
Born: 22 February 1949, Ashington,
Northumberland.
Nickname: Inchers.
County debut: 1973.
County cap: 1976.
Benefit: 1985.
50 wickets in a season: 2.
1st-Class 50s scored: 7.
1st-Class 100s scored: 1.
1st-Class 5 w. in innings: 18.
1st-Class 10 w. in match: 1.
Place in batting averages: 220
average: 14.29; (1984: 210
average: 18.44).
Place in bowling averages: 21
average: 25.58; (1984: 74
average: 31.00).

1st-Class catches 1985: 4 (career: 68).
Education: Ashington Grammar School; St. Peter's College, Saltley,
Birmingham.
Qualifications: B.Ed. (physical education).
Overseas teams played for: Northern Transvaal in 1976–77 Currie Cup
Competition.
Jobs outside cricket: Represents Allied Dunbar Allowance.
Cricketers learnt from: Vanburn Holder.
Extras: Played for Northumberland 1970. Played for both Worcestershire
and Warwickshire 2nd XIs in 1972 and for Stourbridge in the Birmingham
League. Sponsored by Severn House Publishers Ltd. for use of a car.

LAST SEASON: BATTING

	I.	N.O.	R.	H.S.	AV.
TEST					
OTHER FIRST CLASS	9	2	100	24	14.29
INT					
JPL	7	4	53	20*	17.66
NAT.W	1	1	0	0*	–
B & H	4	2	22	16*	11.00

CAREER: BATTING

	I.	N.O.	R.	H.S.	AV.
TEST					
OTHER FIRST CLASS	238	51	3082	113	16.48
INT					
JPL	90	26	976	45	15.25
NAT.W	15	4	118	32*	10.73
B & H	35	10	321	49*	12.84

LAST SEASON: BOWLING

	O.	M.	R.	W.	AV.
TEST					
OTHER FIRST CLASS	338.5	72	844	33	25.58
INT					
JPL	79	1	378	15	25.20
NAT.W	35.5	5	116	8	14.50
B & H	38	4	158	2	79.00

CAREER: BOWLING

	O.	M.	R.	W.	AV.
TEST					
OTHER FIRST CLASS	4809.5	944	14215	497	28.60
INT					
JPL	916.3	61	3859	160	24.11
NAT.W	213.2	34	756	34	22.24
B & H	470.4	60	1626	63	25.81

Best batting performance: 113 Worcestershire v Essex, Worcester 1974.
Best bowling performance: 8-58 Worcestershire v Yorkshire, Worcester 1977.

JAMES, K.D. Hampshire

Full Name: Kevan David James.
Role: Left-hand bat, left-arm fast-medium bowler.
Born: 18 March 1961, Lambeth, South London.
Height: 6' 0½" **Weight:** 11st. 7lbs.
Nickname: Jambo, Jaimo.
County debut: 1980 (Middlesex), 1985 (Hampshire).
1st-Class 100s scored: 1.
1st-Class 5 w. in innings: 2.
Place in batting averages: 54 average: 38.29.
Place in bowling averages: 113 average: 42.33.
1st-Class catches 1985: 6 (career: 9).
Parents: David and Helen James.
Marital status: Single.
Education: Edmonton County High School.

Qualifications: 5 O-levels; qualified coach.
Off-season 1985–86: Mapping out a long-term career.
Family links with cricket: Father and brother play club cricket in North London.
Overseas tours: Young England tour of Australia, 1978–79; Young England tour of West Indies, 1979–80.

LAST SEASON: BATTING

	I.	N.O.	R.	H.S.	AV.
TEST					
OTHER FIRST CLASS	11	4	268	124	38.29
INT					
JPL	3	2	55	34	–
NAT.W	–	–	–	–	–
B & H	4	0	49	27	12.25

CAREER: BATTING

	I.	N.O.	R.	H.S.	AV.
TEST					
OTHER FIRST CLASS	33	10	605	124	26.30
INT					
JPL	9	5	121	34	30.25
NAT.W	–	–	–	–	–
B & H	6	0	66	27	11.00

LAST SEASON: BOWLING

	O.	M.	R.	W.	AV.
TEST					
OTHER FIRST CLASS	177.4	43	635	15	42.33
INT					
JPL	70.5	4	296	5	59.20
NAT.W	12	0	31	0	–
B & H	45	8	148	5	29.60

CAREER: BOWLING

	O.	M.	R.	W.	AV.
TEST					
OTHER FIRST CLASS	533.4	140	1585	51	31.08
INT					
JPL	155.1	8	680	14	48.57
NAT.W	12	0	31	0	–
B & H	77	11	261	9	29.00

Overseas teams played for: Canterbury Province U-23, New Zealand, 1980; Sydenham C.C., Christchurch, New Zealand, 1980–81; Wellington, New Zealand, 1982–83, 1984–85.
Other sports: Soccer. Watches American football.
Cricketers particularly learnt from: Don Bennett, Middlesex coach.
Relaxations: "Watching Spurs; anything that does not involve cricket."
Injuries 1985: Broken wrist.
Extras: Released by Middlesex at end of 1984 season and joined Hampshire.
Best batting performance: 124 Hampshire v Somerset, Taunton 1985.
Best bowling performance: 5-28 Middlesex v Cambridge University, Cambridge 1983.

JAMES, S.P.   Glamorgan

Full Name: Stephen Peter James.
Role: Right-hand opening bat.
Born: 7 September 1967, Lydney.
Height: 5' 11" **Weight:** 12st.
Nickname: Pedro.
County debut: 1985.
Parents: Peter and Margaret James.
Marital status: Single.
Family links with cricket: Father played for Gloucestershire 2nd XI.
Education: Monmouth School, starting at Swansea University in October 1985.
Qualifications: 10 O-levels, 3 A-levels.
Jobs outside cricket: Student, taking Classics.
Off-season 1985–86: At University.
Overseas tours: Welsh Schools U-17 tour to Barbados 1984 (as captain); Monmouth School tour to Sri Lanka, 1985 (as captain).
Cricketers particularly learnt from: "'Sonny' Avery, Graham 'Budgie' Burgess, and latterly Alan Jones. 'Budgie' has helped me throughout my school career."
Other sports: Rugby.
Relaxations: Listening to music.
Extras: Did not get onto the field on debut because of rain.

JARVIS, K.B.S.   Kent

Full Name: Kevin Bertram Sidney Jarvis.
Role: Right-hand bat, right-arm fast-medium bowler.
Born: 23 April 1953, Dartford, Kent.
Height: 6' 3" **Weight:** 13st.
Nickname: Jarvo.
County debut: 1975.
County cap: 1977.
50 wickets in a season: 7.
1st-Class 5 w. in innings: 18.
1st-Class 10 w. in match: 3.
Place in bowling averages: 51 average: 32.82; (1984: 27 average: 24.83).
1st-Class catches 1985: 5 (career: 55).
Parents: Herbert John and Margaret Elsie Jarvis.
Wife and date of marriage: Margaret Anne, 16 September 1978.
Children: Simon Martin, 16 April 1985.
Education: Springhead School, Northfleet, Kent; Thames Polytechnic.
Qualifications: 6 O-levels, 3 A-levels, N.C.A. coach. I.S.M.A., M.A.M.S.A.
Jobs outside cricket: Accountancy.
Overseas tours: Derrick Robins' XI to Far East 1977; Jamaica 1982.
Overseas teams played for: Played and coached for South Melbourne, Australia.
Off-season 1985–86: "Reminiscing 1985 season and preparing for 1986 season."
Other sports: Squash, golf, badminton, tennis.
Relaxations: Reading, music.

LAST SEASON: BATTING

	I.	N.O.	R.	H.S.	AV.
TEST					
OTHER FIRST CLASS	18	5	41	7	3.15
INT					
JPL	3	2	1	1*	–
NAT.W	1	1	2	2*	–
B & H	2	1	0	0*	–

CAREER: BATTING

	I.	N.O.	R.	H.S.	AV.
TEST					
OTHER FIRST CLASS	168	70	316	19	3.22
INT					
JPL	40	23	54	8*	3.17
NAT.W	11	5	16	5*	2.67
B & H	23	15	16	4*	2.00

LAST SEASON: BOWLING

	O.	M.	R.	W.	AV.
TEST					
OTHER FIRST CLASS	530.4	115	1674	51	32.82
INT					
JPL	80	3	319	18	17.72
NAT.W	30	2	151	2	75.50
B & H	43.1	7	197	9	21.89

CAREER: BOWLING

	O.	M.	R.	W.	AV.
TEST					
OTHER FIRST CLASS	5529.4	1219	17392	594	29.28
INT					
JPL	886.1	77	3637	166	21.90
NAT.W	227.5	28	847	36	23.53
B & H	504.2	78	1776	82	21.66

Injuries 1985: Damage to knee ligaments.
Best batting performance: 19 Kent v Derbyshire, Maidstone 1984.
Best bowling performance: 8-97 Kent v Worcestershire, Worcester 1978.

JARVIS, P.W. Yorkshire

Full Name: Paul William Jarvis.
Role: Right-hand bat, right-arm fast-medium bowler.
Born: 29 June 1965, Redcar, North Yorkshire.
Height: 5′ 11½″ **Weight:** 12st. 4lbs.
Nickname: Gnasher, Jarve, Jarvo, Beaver ("and many more unprintable").
County debut: 1981.
1st-Class 5 w. in innings: 5.
Place in batting averages: 251 average: 10.79; (1984: 235 average: 15.70).
Place in bowling averages: 52 average: 30.23; (1984: 98 average 34.84).

1st-Class catches 1985: 6 (career: 13).
Parents: Malcolm and Marjorie Jarvis.
Marital status: Single.
Family links with cricket: Father has played league cricket for 30 years with Marske C.C.; brother, Andrew, played for English Schools U-15s, and also had trials for Northamptonshire and Derbyshire.
Education: Bydales Comprehensive School, Marske.
Qualifications: 4 O-levels.
Jobs outside cricket: Trainee groundsman, Marske Cricket Club.
Off-season 1985–86: Playing and coaching for Averdale C.C. in Cape Town.
Cricketing superstitions: "The number 111."
Cricketers particularly learnt from: "Learnt a lot from Maurice Hill and Albert Padmore; admire Dennis Lillee."
Overseas teams played for: Mosman Middle Harbour C.C.,, Sydney, 1984–85.
Other sports: Football, running and fitness, golf, tennis. Follows most sports.
Injuries 1985: Torn muscle above left hip. Lower back strain.
Relaxations: Watching television, films, listening to music.
Extras: Youngest player ever to play for Yorkshire 1st XI in John Player League and County Championships (16 years, 2 months, 1 day in John Player League, 16 years, 2 months, 13 days for County Championship). Hat-

trick in J.P.S.L. v Derbyshire (Derby) 27.6.82. Played for Young England v West Indies 1982 and Australia 1983. Hat-trick in championship v Derbyshire (Chesterfield) — youngest ever player to achieve feat.

Best batting performance: 37 Yorkshire v Surrey, The Oval 1984.

Best bowling performance: 6-61 Yorkshire v Lancashire, Old Trafford 1984.

LAST SEASON: BATTING

	I.	N.O.	R.	H.S.	AV.
TEST					
OTHER FIRST CLASS	16	2	151	28	10.79
INT					
JPL	3	1	8	6*	4.00
NAT.W	1	0	16	16	–
B & H	2	0	23	20	11.50

CAREER: BATTING

	I.	N.O.	R.	H.S.	AV.
TEST					
OTHER FIRST CLASS	38	11	337	37	12.48
INT					
JPL	13	7	42	9*	7.00
NAT.W	1	0	16	16	–
B & H	2	0	23	20	11.50

LAST SEASON: BOWLING

	O.	M.	R.	W.	AV.
TEST					
OTHER FIRST CLASS	371.5	54	1330	44	30.23
INT					
JPL	40	3	151	10	15.10
NAT.W	22	2	97	3	32.33
B & H	37	4	150	11	13.64

CAREER: BOWLING

	O.	M.	R.	W.	AV.
TEST					
OTHER FIRST CLASS	869.5	142	3108	87	35.72
INT					
JPL	179	7	784	47	16.68
NAT.W	34	2	177	3	59.00
B & H	37	4	150	11	13.64

81. In 1985 Ian Botham set a new record of first-class sixes in a season. What was the previous record, set by whom and when?

82. When was the first Oxford v Cambridge match and who won?

83. In what year was W.G. Grace born?

84. When was the first Yorkshire v Lancashire match?

85. Who was the first bowler to exceed 300 Test wickets and when?

JAVED MIANDAD — Glamorgan

Full Name: Miandad Khan Javed.
Role: Right-hand bat, leg-break and googly bowler.
Born: 12 June 1957, Karachi.
Height: 5' 9" **Weight:** 11st. 7lbs.
Nickname: J.J., Mum 'n Dad.
County debut: 1976 (Sussex), 1980 (Glamorgan).
County cap: 1977 (Sussex), 1980 (Glamorgan).
Test debut: 1976–77.
No. of Tests: 68.
No. of One-Day Internationals: 75.
1000 runs in a season: 5.
1st-Class 50s scored: 105.
1st-Class 100s scored: 56.
1st-Class 200s scored: 7.
1st-Class 5 w. in innings: 6.
1st-Class 10 w. in match: 1.
One-day 50s: 50.
One-day 100s: 3.
Place in batting averages: 7 average: 62.61; (1984: 7 average: 64.00).
1st-Class catches 1985: 13 (career: 276).
Marital status: Married.
Education: C.M.S. Secondary School, Karachi.
Jobs outside cricket: Assistant Vice-President in Habib Bank of Pakistan.
Family links with cricket: Father played in India. Two brothers play for a bank in Pakistan.
Overseas tours: Toured with Pakistan to Australia and West Indies 1976–77; England 1978 and 1982; New Zealand and Australia 1978–79; India 1979–80 and 1983–84; Australia 1981–82 (captain), 1982–83 and 1983–84.
Overseas teams played for: Karachi Whites; Karachi; Sind; Habib Banks.
Other sports: Hockey, soccer, swimming.
Relaxations: Reading sports books, spending time with family, watching television.
Extras: Was Vice-captain of Pakistan U-19 team in England in 1974 and was Captain of U-19 side in Sri Lanka 1974–75. Made debut for Sussex in 1976, gaining his cap in 1977. Left Sussex for Glamorgan at end of 1980 season. Scored a century on debut for Glamorgan, and was immediately awarded his cap. Captain of Glamorgan for that part of 1982 when he was not playing for Pakistan. Youngest-ever double century maker in Test cricket at age of 19 years 4 months. (Scored 163 for Pakistan v New Zealand on Test debut, Lahore, 1966–67, and 206 v New Zealand at Karachi in third Test.) Pakistan captain 1980–81. Second Pakistani to top 4000 runs in Test cricket.
Best batting performance: 311 Karachi Whites v Nat. Bank, Karachi 1974–75.
Best bowling performance: 7-39 Habib Bank v I.D.B.P., Lahore 1980–81.

LAST SEASON: BATTING

	I.	N.O.	R.	H.S.	AV.
TEST					
OTHER FIRST CLASS	29	6	1441	200*	62.61
INT					
JPL	11	2	573	95*	63.66
NAT.W	2	1	50	29	–
B & H	3	0	128	57	42.67

CAREER: BATTING

	I.	N.O.	R.	H.S.	AV.
TEST	108	16	5044	280*	54.83
OTHER FIRST CLASS	397	66	17490	311	52.84
INT	72	14	2155	119*	37.16
JPL	93	16	3137	107*	40.74
NAT.W	11	2	378	75	42.00
B & H	21	2	828	95	43.58

LAST SEASON: BOWLING

	O.	M.	R.	W.	AV.
TEST					
OTHER FIRST CLASS	27.3	2	120	3	40.00
INT					
JPL					
NAT.W					
B & H					

CAREER: BOWLING

	O.	M.	R.	W.	AV.
TEST	130.6 66.4	20 10	672	17	39.53
OTHER FIRST CLASS			5691	174	32.71
INT	58	3	209	5	41.80
JPL	13.5	0	68	2	34.00
NAT.W	2	0	12	1	–
B & H	2	0	14	0	–

JEFFERIES, S.T.   Lancashire

Full Name: Stephen Thomas Jefferies.
Role: Left-hand bat, left-arm fast-medium bowler.
Born: 8 December 1959, Cape Town, South Africa.
County debut: 1982 (Derbyshire), 1983 (Lancashire).
1st-Class 50s scored: 11.
1st-Class 5 w. in innings: 10.
1st-Class 10 w. in match: 2.
Place in batting averages: —
average: —; (1984: 156 average: 25.32).
Place in bowling averages: —
average: —; (1984: 82 average: 32.37).
1st-Class catches 1985: 6 (career: 23).
Education: Plumstead High School.
Jobs outside cricket: Physical training instructor with South African Navy.
Overseas teams played for: Western Province, South Africa.
Extras: Professional with Crompton in Central Lancashire League. Played for South African Schools XI in 1978. With Derbyshire in 1982. Left Lancashire staff 1985.
Best batting performance: 93 Lancashire v Sussex, Old Trafford 1985.
Best bowling performance: 8-46 Lancashire v Nottinghamshire, Trent Bridge 1983.

LAST SEASON: BATTING

	I.	N.O.	R.	H.S.	AV.
TEST					
OTHER FIRST CLASS	7	0	274	93	39.14
INT					
JPL	1	0	35	35	–
NAT.W					
B & H	1	0	32	32	–

CAREER: BATTING

	I.	N.O.	R.	H.S.	AV.
TEST					
OTHER FIRST CLASS	112	19	2491	93	26.79
INT					
JPL	14	3	338	37*	30.72
NAT.W	2	1	23	23*	–
B & H	3	0	73	39	24.33

LAST SEASON: BOWLING

	O.	M.	R.	W.	AV.
TEST					
OTHER FIRST CLASS	116.1	13	379	12	31.58
INT					
JPL	6	0	45	1	–
NAT.W					
B & H	7	0	45	1	–

CAREER: BOWLING

	O.	M.	R.	W.	AV.
TEST					
OTHER FIRST CLASS	2694.3	590	7696	283	27.19
INT					
JPL	123.1	10	542	18	30.11
NAT.W	21.5	1	88	3	29.33
B & H	82.4	17	265	12	22.08

JESTY, T.E.   Surrey

Full Name: Trevor Edward Jesty.
Role: Right-hand bat, right-arm medium bowler.
Born: 2 June 1948, Gosport, Hampshire.
Height: 5' 9'' **Weight:** 11st. 10lbs.
Nickname: Jets.
County debut: 1966 (Hampshire), 1985 (Surrey).
County cap: 1971 (Hampshire), 1985 (Surrey).
Benefit: 1982 (Hampshire).
No. of One-Day Internationals: 10.
1000 runs in a season: 8.
50 wickets in a season: 2.
1st-Class 50s scored: 83.
1st-Class 100s scored: 30.
1st-Class 200s scored: 1.
1st-Class 5 w. in innings: 18.
One-day 50s: 35.
One-day 100s: 6.
Place in batting averages: 35 average: 43.43; (1984: 47 average: 40.62).
Place in bowling averages: 88 average: 36.93; (1984: 99 average: 35.16).
1st-Class catches 1985: 19 (career: 232).
Parents: Aubrey Edward and Sophia Jesty.
Wife and date of marriage: Jacqueline, 12 September 1970.
Children: Graeme Barry, 27 September 1972; Lorna Samantha, 7 November 1976.

Education: Privet County Secondary Modern, Gosport.

Jobs outside cricket: Cricket coach in South Africa and New Zealand. Representative for wine company.

Family links with cricket: Brother, Aubrey Jesty, wicket-keeper and left-hand bat. Could have joined Hampshire staff, but decided to continue with his apprenticeship.

Overseas teams played for: Border in 1973–74, and Griqualand West in 1974–75 and 1975–76 in the Currie Cup Competition, South Africa.

Cricketers particularly learnt from: Barry Richards.

Other sports: Soccer, golf.

Relaxations: Watching soccer, and gardening.

Extras: Took him 10 years to score maiden first-class century. Missed most of 1980 season through injury. Made Vice-captain of Hampshire in 1981. Considered to be most unlucky not to be chosen for England tour of Australia 1982–83 after brilliant 1982 season, then was called in as a replacement. Left Hampshire at end of 1984 when not appointed captain. Took over captaincy of Surrey in 1985.

Best batting performance: 248 Hampshire v Cambridge University, Cambridge 1984.

Best bowling performance: 7-75 Hampshire v Worcestershire, Southampton 1976.

LAST SEASON: BATTING

	I.	N.O.	R.	H.S.	AV.
TEST					
OTHER FIRST CLASS	36	8	1216	141*	43.43
INT.					
JPL	11	2	129	32	14.33
NAT.W	1	0	1	1	–
B & H	3	1	157	69*	78.50

CAREER: BATTING

	I.	N.O.	R.	H.S.	AV.
TEST					
OTHER FIRST CLASS	620	83	18186	248	33.87
INT	10	4	127	52*	21.17
JPL	216	30	4758	166*	25.58
NAT.W	27	2	745	118	29.80
B & H	57	5	1643	105	31.60

LAST SEASON: BOWLING

	O.	M.	R.	W.	AV.
TEST					
OTHER FIRST CLASS	144.2	28	517	14	36.93
INT					
JPL	71.2	1	400	9	44.44
NAT.W	7	2	17	0	–
B & H	27	1	77	6	12.83

CAREER: BOWLING

	O.	M.	R.	W.	AV.
TEST					
OTHER FIRST CLASS	5968.3	1590	15582	569	27.39
INT	18	0	93	1	–
JPL	1274.3	76	5962	246	24.23
NAT.W	299	50	984	38	25.89
B & H	459.4	60	1570	65	24.15

86. Which Test team and where, in 1985 scored almost 700 runs but was still defeated by 9 wickets?

JOHNSON, G.W. Kent

Full Name: Graham William Johnson.
Role: Right-hand bat, off-break bowler.
Born: 8 November 1946, Beckenham, Kent.
Height: 6' 1".
Nickname: Johno, Coat-hanger, Prat.
County debut: 1965.
County cap: 1970.
Benefit: 1983.
1000 runs in a season: 3.
50 wickets in a season: 3.
1st-Class 50s scored: 53.
1st-Class 100s scored: 11.
1st-Class 5 w. in innings: 22.
1st-Class 10 w. in match: 3.
One-day 50s: 25.
One-day 100s: 1.
Place in batting averages: 190 average: 19.75; (1984: 190 average: 21.35).
Place in bowling averages: 124 average: 45.55; (1984: 75 average: 31.28).
1st-Class catches 1985: 6 (career: 311).
Parents: Bill and Mamie Johnson.
Education: Malcolm Primary, Penge; Beckenham & Penge Grammar School; Shooter's Hill Grammar School; London School of Economics, London University.
Qualifications: 11 O-levels, 3 A-levels, B.Sc. Economics. Qualified coach.
Jobs outside cricket: Investment analyst with Selection Trust Ltd (mining finance company), Bradstock, Blunt and Barney (insurance brokers) and currently with Barclays Bank/Transvaal Cricket Council.
Family links with cricket: "Father played club cricket in Essex and S.E. London and has umpired 2nd XI county cricket. Brother with Brentwood C.C. and Lloyds Insurance, brother-in-law once removed (G. Dilley) has played a bit."
Overseas tours: Derrick Robins' XI to South Africa and West Indies; John Player League Champions to West Indies; Kent to West Indies, Canada, Holland and Jersey.
Overseas teams played for: Koh-i-noor Crescents in Premier League in Johannesburg, South Africa, for five years.
Cricketers particularly learnt from: Coached by father; Claude Lewis, George Pope, Colin Page and Les Ames—"learnt bits and pieces from most Kent players over last 20 years and by watching other county and Test players."
Other sports: Rugby, football, squash, golf, water-skiing and wind-surfing. Watches most sports except wrestling and horse-racing.
Relaxations: Music, real ale, meeting interesting people, travel, current affairs, ecology.

Extras: "Suffer from hay fever, bad memory for names, tend to get chirpy after taking wickets." Released by Kent during 1985 season and took job in insurance.

Best batting performance: 168 Kent v Surrey, The Oval 1976.

Best bowling performance: 7-76 Kent v Northamptonshire, Canterbury 1983.

LAST SEASON: BATTING

	I.	N.O.	R.	H.S.	AV.
TEST					
OTHER FIRST CLASS	16	4	237	30*	19.75
INT					
JPL	6	5	65	36*	–
NAT.W	–	–	–	–	–
B & H	3	3	29	14*	–

CAREER: BATTING

	I.	N.O.	R.	H.S.	AV.
TEST					
OTHER FIRST CLASS	605	78	12922	168	24.52
INT					
JPL	183	30	3671	89	23.99
NAT.W	31	5	745	120*	28.65
B & H	59	8	1209	85*	23.71

LAST SEASON: BOWLING

	O.	M.	R.	W.	AV.
TEST					
OTHER FIRST CLASS	156.3	24	501	11	45.55
INT					
JPL	24.4	3	95	3	31.67
NAT.W	6	1	23	0	–
B & H	31	7	87	3	29.00

CAREER: BOWLING

	O.	M.	R.	W.	AV.
TEST					
OTHER FIRST CLASS	6865.3	1942	17601	567	31.04
INT					
JPL	362	23	1606	80	20.07
NAT.W	77.3	3	300	5	60.00
B & H	146	22	494	19	26.00

JOHNSON, P.   Nottinghamshire

Full Name: Paul Johnson.

Role: Right-hand bat, right-arm occasional bowler, outfielder.

Born: 24 April 1965, Newark.

Height: 5' 8'' **Weight:** 11st. 5lbs.

Nickname: Johno, Dwarf.

County debut: 1982.

1st-Class 50s scored: 13.

1st-Class 100s scored: 4.

One-day 50s: 1.

One-day 100s: 1.

Place in batting averages: 100 average: 31.10; (1984: 20 average: 49.78).

1st-Class catches 1985: 13 (career: 29).

Parents: Donald and Joyce Johnson.

Marital status: Single.

Family links with cricket: Father played local cricket and is a qualified coach.

Education: Grove Comprehensive School, Newark.

Qualifications: 9 C.S.E.s, senior coaching certificate.
Off-season 1985–86: Driver for engineering company.
Cricketing superstitions: Always wears some kind of head wear, left pad on first.
Cricketers particularly learnt from: "Too many to mention."
Other sports: Football referee, golf (14 handicap), watches ice-hockey (Nottingham Panthers), football (Forest and County).
Relaxations: Good films and music.
Extras: Played for English Schools cricket in 1980–81 season. Youngest member ever to join the Nottinghamshire C.C.C. staff. Hit 16 sixes in School County Cup game v Joseph Whittaker, 195 n.o. Played for Young England U-19, 1982 and 1983. Made 235 for Notts. 2nd XI, July 1982, aged 17. Won man of match award in first NatWest game (101 n.o. v Staffs).
Injuries 1985: Appendicitis operation (missed last six weeks of season).
Opinions on cricket: "Counties should make more effort to play 2nd XI games on first-class wickets."
Best batting performance: 133 Nottinghamshire v Kent, Folkestone 1984.

LAST SEASON: BATTING

	I.	N.O.	R.	H.S.	AV.
TEST					
OTHER FIRST CLASS	34	4	933	118	31.10
INT					
JPL	12	0	229	63	19.08
NAT.W	4	1	146	101*	48.67
B & H	3	0	20	16	6.67

CAREER: BATTING

	I.	N.O.	R.	H.S.	AV.
TEST					
OTHER FIRST CLASS	83	8	2282	133	30.43
INT					
JPL	30	4	465	63	17.88
NAT.W	4	1	146	101*	48.67
B & H	5	0	30	16	6.00

LAST SEASON: BOWLING

	O.	M.	R.	W.	AV.
TEST					
OTHER FIRST CLASS	26	4	152	1	–
INT					
JPL					
NAT.W	1	0	5	0	–
B & H					

CAREER: BOWLING

	O.	M.	R.	W.	AV.
TEST					
OTHER FIRST CLASS	30	4	175	3	58.33
INT					
JPL					
NAT.W	1	0	5	0	–
B & H					

87. How many English cricketers were banned from Test cricket for three years ending in 1985, for playing unofficial Tests in South Africa?

88. Which two members of the England touring party to India in 1984–85 flew home before the Australian leg of the tour?

JONES, A.L.   Glamorgan

Full Name: Alan Lewis Jones.
Role: Left-hand opening bat.
Born: 1 June 1957, Alltwen, near Swansea.
Height: 5′ 8½″ **Weight:** 10st. 4lbs.
Nickname: Jonah, occasionally Posh.
County debut: 1973, at age of 16 years 99 days. Youngest player for Glamorgan.
County cap: 1983.
1000 runs in a season: 2.
1st-Class 50s scored: 35.
1st-Class 100s scored: 5.
One-day 50s: 8.
Place in batting averages: 140 average: 25.44; (1984: 66 average: 36.96).
1st-Class catches 1985: 11 (career: 97).
Parents: Ieuan and Marion Jones.
Wife and date of marriage: Diane, 27 September 1980.
Education: Ystalyfera Grammar School; Cwmtawe Comprehensive School; Cardiff College of Education.
Qualifications: 8 O-levels. Teacher training certificate. Qualified advanced coach.
Jobs outside cricket: Working in chartered accountant's office training to be certified accountant. Has worked as life assurance salesman.
Off-season 1985–86: Schoolteacher.
Overseas tours: West Indies with England Young Cricketers 1976; Australasia with Derrick Robins' XI in 1980.
Overseas teams played for: Played with Hamilton-Wickham in Newcastle, Australia, in 1978–79; Papatoetoe, Auckland, 1984–85.
Cricketers particularly learnt from: Alan Jones.
Cricketers particularly admired: Alan Jones, Gordon Greenidge, Andy Roberts.
Cricketing superstitions: "Put pads, gloves etc., on in a particular order. Don't like Nelson (111) and 13."
Other sports: Rugby.
Relaxations: Keeps up-to-date with previous biology studies; keep-fit enthusiast.
Injuries 1985: Dislocated right shoulder twice.
Extras: Made debut for Glamorgan 2nd XI in 1972, aged 15. Played for Briton Ferry Town in 1979 in South Wales League.
Opinions on cricket: "Would like to see a two-year trial period for 16 4-day matches, with an improvement of pace and bounce of first-class pitches."
Best batting performance: 132 Glamorgan v Hampshire, Cardiff 1984.

CAREER: BATTING

	I.	N.O.	R.	H.S.	AV.
TEST					
OTHER FIRST CLASS	257	20	6119	132	25.82
INT					
JPL	78	3	1642	82	21.89
NAT.W	8	1	167	60*	23.86
B & H	14	0	188	36	13.43

CAREER: BOWLING

	O.	M.	R.	W.	AV.
TEST					
OTHER FIRST CLASS	15.5	0	152	1	–
INT					
JPL	0.4	0	5	0	–
NAT.W					
B & H					

LAST SEASON: BATTING

	I.	N.O.	R.	H.S.	AV.
TEST					
OTHER FIRST CLASS	27	2	636	80	25.44
INT					
JPL	7	0	117	53	16.71
NAT.W	3	1	87	60*	43.50
B & H	1	0	4	4	–

LAST SEASON: BOWLING

	O.	M.	R.	W.	AV.
TEST					
OTHER FIRST CLASS	1	0	24	0	–
INT					
JPL					
NAT.W					
B & H					

JONES, A.N.   Sussex

Full Name: Adrian Nicholas Jones.
Role: Left-hand bat, right-arm fast bowler.
Born: 22 July 1961, Woking.
Height: 6′ 2″ **Weight:** 14st.
Nickname: Quincy, Jonah.
County debut: 1981.
1st-Class 5 w. in innings: 2.
Place in batting averages: 181 average: 20.75.
Place in bowling averages: 114 average: 42.40; (1984: 28 average 25.44).
1st-Class catches 1985: 1 (career: 5).
Parents: William Albert and Emily Doris Jones.
Family links with cricket: Father and brother, Glynne, both fine club cricketers.
Education: Forest Grange Preparatory School; Seaford College.
Qualifications: 8 O-levels, 2 A-levels. N.C.A. coaching qualification.
Jobs outside cricket: Working in a warehouse, sales representative.
Off-season 1985–86: Selling life insurance.
Cricketing superstitions: "Drink lots of tea. Always fold a sweater up before handing to the umpire when bowling."
Overseas teams played for: Old Selbournians and Bohemians, South Africa, 1981–82; Border 1981–82; Red and White C.C., Haarlem, Holland, 1980.
Cricketers particularly learnt from: Geoff Arnold, Imran Khan, Garth Le Roux.

Cricketers particularly admired: John Snow.
Other sports: Rugby, hockey, golf. Watching indoor hockey.
Relaxations: "Listening to UB40 all day. Watching Laurel and Hardy films. Driving."
Extras: Played for Young England in 1981.
Opinions on cricket: "There should be an alternative system for the awarding of a benefit than the present haphazard method. Perhaps an endowment scheme taken out when the player is capped."
Best batting performance: 35 Sussex v Middlesex, Hove 1984.
Best bowling performance: 5-29 Sussex v Gloucestershire, Hove 1984.

LAST SEASON: BATTING

	I.	N.O.	R.	H.S.	AV.
TEST					
OTHER FIRST CLASS	9	5	83	26	20.75
INT					
JPL	1	1	1	1*	–
NAT.W					
B & H	1	0	4	4	–

CAREER: BATTING

	I.	N.O.	R.	H.S.	AV.
TEST					
OTHER FIRST CLASS	36	17	229	35	12.05
INT					
JPL	1	1	1	1*	–
NAT.W	1	1	3	3*	–
B & H	2	0	6	4	3.00

LAST SEASON: BOWLING

	O.	M.	R.	W.	AV.
TEST					
OTHER FIRST CLASS	246	37	848	20	42.40
INT					
JPL	35.2	2	155	10	15.50
NAT.W					
B & H	3.2	0	22	0	–

CAREER: BOWLING

	O.	M.	R.	W.	AV.
TEST					
OTHER FIRST CLASS	669.2	110	2333	74	31.53
INT					
JPL	79.2	5	373	21	17.76
NAT.W	10	1	49	1	–
B & H	3.2	0	22	0	–

JONES, A.P. Somerset

Full Name: Andrew Paul Jones.
Role: Right-hand bat, right-arm medium bowler.
Born: 22 September 1964, Southampton.
Height: 6′ 2″.
County debut: 1985.
1st-Class catches 1985: 1 (career: 1).
Education: Toynbee Secondary School, Eastleigh; Barton Peverill College, Eastleigh.
Other Sports: Golf (Hampshire and Somerset), basketball (Somerset).
Extras: Played for Hampshire 2nd XI 1983 and Somerset 2nd XI 1984.

LAST SEASON: BATTING

	I.	N.O.	R.	H.S.	AV.
TEST					
OTHER FIRST CLASS	4	2	3	1*	1.50
INT					
JPL					
NAT.W					
B & H					

CAREER: BATTING

	I.	N.O.	R.	H.S.	AV.
TEST					
OTHER FIRST CLASS	4	2	3	1*	1.50
INT					
JPL					
NAT.W					
B & H					

LAST SEASON: BOWLING

	O.	M.	R.	W.	AV.
TEST					
OTHER FIRST CLASS	37	4	142	3	47.33
INT					
JPL					
NAT.W					
B & H					

CAREER: BOWLING

	O.	M.	R.	W.	AV.
TEST					
OTHER FIRST CLASS	37	4	142	3	47.33
INT					
JPL					
NAT.W					
B & H					

89. Which famous poet played in the first Eton v Harrow match, for which side, when was it and how many runs did he score?

90. Where, when and against whom was Sunil Gavaskar's last match as captain of India, and what was special about it?

91. Which England Test cricketer published his autobiography under the title *The Sun Has Got His Hat On?*

92. Who was the first batsman to score a century in each of his first three Tests?

JOSEPH, R.F.   Northamptonshire

Full Name: Ray Fitzpatrick Joseph.
Role: Right-hand bat, right-arm
fast-medium bowler.
Born: 12 February 1961, Guyana.
County debut: 1985.
1st-Class catches 1985: 0 (career: 4).
Extras: Made debut for Guyana in
Shell Shield in 1979–80 season, the
same year that he made his first-class
debut for Berbice. Left Northampton-
shire staff at end of 1985 season.
Best batting performance: 26*
Northamptonshire v Hampshire,
Northampton 1985.
Best bowling performance: 6-114
Guyana v Jamaica, Kingston
1983–84.

LAST SEASON: BATTING

	I.	N.O.	R.	H.S.	AV.
TEST					
OTHER FIRST CLASS	1	1	26	26*	–
INT					
JPL	–	–	–	–	–
NAT.W	1	0	6	6	–
B & H	–	–	–	–	–

CAREER: BATTING

	I.	N.O.	R.	H.S.	AV.
TEST					
OTHER FIRST CLASS	36	21	128	26*	8.53
INT					
JPL	–	–	–	–	–
NAT.W	1	0	6	6	–
B & H	–	–	–	–	–

LAST SEASON: BOWLING

	O.	M.	R.	W.	AV.
TEST					
OTHER FIRST CLASS	38	5	143	4	35.75
INT					
JPL	4	0	21	0	–
NAT.W	8	0	47	0	–
B & H	11	2	32	0	–

CAREER: BOWLING

	O.	M.	R.	W.	AV.
TEST					
OTHER FIRST CLASS	534.2	75	2070	44	47.05
INT					
JPL	4	0	21	0	–
NAT.W	8	0	47	0	–
B & H	11	2	32	0	–

---

93. Who was the first captain of England in a Test Match?

94. Which England Test cricketer refused to take part in a
B.B.C. programme on the centenary of W.G. Grace's birth,
on the grounds that "Grace overbowled me and ruined my
health before I was 25" and still lived to be 80?

KALLICHARRAN, A.I.   Warwickshire

Full Name: Alvin Isaac Kallicharran.
Role: Left-hand bat, off-cutter.
Born: 21 March 1949, Guyana.
Height: 5' 4".
Nickname: Kalli.
County debut: 1971.
County cap: 1972.
Benefit: 1983 (£34,094).
Test debut: 1971–72.
No. of Tests: 66.
No. of One-Day Internationals: 31.
1000 runs in a season: 11.
1st-Class 50s scored: 111.
1st-Class 100s scored: 72.
1st-Class 200s scored: 6.
1st-Class 5 w. in innings: 1.
One-day 50s: 47.
One-day 100s: 8.
Place in batting averages: 90
average: 31.85; (1984: 15 average: 52.29).
1st-Class catches 1985: 6 (career: 286).
Marital status: Married.
Children: One son, Rohan.
Family links with cricket: Brother, Derek Isaac, played for Guyana.
Off-season 1985–86: Playing cricket and coaching in South Africa. Kallicharran has been told he can never again play for the West Indies after two years with Transvaal. Now with Orange Free State.
Overseas tours: With West Indies to New Zealand 1971; England in 1973 and 1976; India, Sri Lanka and Pakistan, 1974–75; Australia 1975–76 and 1979–80; India and Sri Lanka, 1978–79 as Captain; Pakistan, 1980.

LAST SEASON: BATTING

	I.	N.O.	R.	H.S.	AV.
TEST					
OTHER FIRST CLASS	35	2	1051	151*	31.85
INT					
JPL	14	0	445	97	31.78
NAT.W	2	0	93	66	46.50
B & H	4	0	249	104	62.25

CAREER: BATTING

	I.	N.O.	R.	H.S.	AV.
TEST	109	10	4399	187	44.43
OTHER FIRST CLASS	630	67	25371	243*	45.06
INT	28	4	826	78	34.41
JPL	146	16	3825	102*	29.42
NAT.W	23	2	1031	206	49.10
B & H	51	6	1882	122*	41.82

LAST SEASON: BOWLING

	O.	M.	R.	W.	AV.
TEST					
OTHER FIRST CLASS	11.4	0	56	0	–
INT					
JPL	10	0	50	3	16.67
NAT.W	12	0	41	3	13.67
B & H	6	0	44	0	–

CAREER: BOWLING

	O.	M.	R.	W.	AV.
TEST	3.1 63.3	1 13	158	4	39.50
OTHER FIRST CLASS	13.3 909.1	0 132	3285	71	46.27
INT	17	3	64	3	21.33
JPL	161.1	5	880	14	62.85
NAT.W	80.4	9	277	14	19.78
B & H	34	0	153	0	–

Overseas teams played for: Guyana 1966–67 in Shell Shield Competition; Queensland in 1977–78 Sheffield Shield Competition.
Extras: Scored 100 n.o. and 101 in first two innings in Test matches, v New Zealand in 1971. Signed for World Series Cricket but resigned before playing. He made his home in England. With Geoff Humpage took part in record — for Warwickshire and for all English counties — 4th wicket stand of 470 v Lancashire at Southport in July 1982. Kallicharran made 230 n.o., Humpage 254 n.o. Previous record was 448 by Abel and Hayward for Surrey v Yorkshire at the Oval in 1899. Top of Warwickshire batting averages in 1982 and 1983.
Best batting performance: 243* Warwickshire v Glamorgan, Edgbaston 1983.
Best bowling performance: 5-45 Transvaal v Western Province, Cape Town 1982–83.

KAPIL DEV Worcestershire

Full Name: Kapil Dev.
Role: Right-hand bat, right-arm fast bowler.
Born: 6 January 1959, Haryana, India.
Height: 6′ 3″.
Nickname: Haryana Hurricane.
County debut: 1981 (Northampton-shire). 1984 (Worcestershire).
Test debut: 1978–79.
No. of Tests: 68.
No. of One-Day Internationals: 61.
1st-Class 50s scored: 34.
1st-Class 100s scored: 9.
1st-Class 5 w. in innings: 29.
1st-Class 10 w. in match: 3.
One-day 50s: 8.
One-day 100s: 1.

Place in batting averages: 33 average: 43.95; (1984: 40 average: 42.67).
Place in bowling averages: 28 average: 21.76; (1984: 21 average: 23.40).
1st-Class catches 1985: 11 (career: 19).
Education: Punjab University.
Marital status: Married.
Cricketers particularly learnt from: Coach, Desh Prem Azad.
Overseas tours: Australia 1980–81 and 1985–86; England 1979; World Cup 1983 in England.
Relaxations: Hunting, riding, dancing.
Extras: Played for Nelson in Lancashire League for part of 1981 season. Does not smoke or drink. Started as a spin bowler. Youngest player to take 100 Test

wickets at 21 years 25 days, and score 1000 Test runs at 21 years, 27 days. Captain of India, and led them to the 1983 World Cup victory. Played for Northamptonshire 1981–83. "The first Test Match I ever saw was the first I played in."
Best batting performance: 193 Haryana v Punjab, Chandigarh 1979–80.
Best bowling performance: 8-38 Haryana v Services, Rohtak 1977–78.

LAST SEASON: BATTING

	I.	N.O.	R.	H.S.	AV.
TEST					
OTHER FIRST CLASS	21	2	816	100	42.95
INT					
JPL	7	0	111	36	15.85
NAT.W	3	1	46	38*	23.00
B & H	4	0	54	32	13.50

CAREER: BATTING

	I.	N.O.	R.	H.S.	AV.
TEST	101	9	2788	126*	30.30
OTHER FIRST CLASS	149	17	4145	193	31.40
INT	57	8	1336	175*	27.26
JPL	25	0	474	75	18.96
NAT.W	7	1	69	38*	11.50
B & H	6	1	121	49	24.20

LAST SEASON: BOWLING

	O.	M.	R.	W.	AV.
TEST					
OTHER FIRST CLASS	304.5	83	805	37	21.76
INT					
JPL	45.1	0	272	3	90.67
NAT.W	33	1	116	7	16.57
B & H	40	9	139	3	46.33

CAREER: BOWLING

	O.	M.	R.	W.	AV.
TEST	2420.3	482	7406	258	28.71
OTHER FIRST CLASS	2265.1	513	7327	294	24.92
INT	536.2	80	1929	79	24.41
JPL	171.5	12	756	26	29.07
NAT.W	95.1	18	254	13	19.54
B & H	74.3	18	233	7	33.29

KIMBER, S.J.S.   Worcestershire

Full Name: Simon Julian Spencer Kimber.
Role: Right-hand bat, right-arm medium bowler.
Born: 6 October 1963, Ormskirk.
Height: 6' 2" **Weight:** 13st.
Nickname: Woody, Pirate.
County debut: 1985.
1st-Class catches 1985: 1 (career: 1).
Parents: Ron and Joan Kimber.
Marital status: Single.
Family links with cricket: Father played good standard of league cricket in England and Jamaica.
Education: Durban, South Africa.
Qualifications: Matric certificate. Studying for insurance exams.
Jobs outside cricket: Insurance broker.
Off-season 1985–86: Playing in Durban, South Africa.
Overseas teams played for: Pinetown 1982–83, Durban Collegians 1983–84 and 1984–85 in Natal, South Africa.

226

Cricketers particularly learnt from: Father, P. Perry.
Cricketers particularly admired: R. Hadlee.
Other sports: Plays squash, tennis, football, golf; follows football, athletics.
Relaxations: Music, reading.
Extras: Left staff after 1985 season.
Best bowling performance: 3-40 Worcestershire v Cambridge University, Cambridge 1985.

LAST SEASON: BATTING

	I.	N.O.	R.	H.S.	AV.
TEST					
OTHER FIRST CLASS	1	1	14	14*	–
INT					
JPL					
NAT.W					
B & H					

CAREER: BATTING

	I.	N.O.	R.	H.S.	AV.
TEST					
OTHER FIRST CLASS	1	1	14	14*	–
INT					
JPL					
NAT.W					
B & H					

LAST SEASON: BOWLING

	O.	M.	R.	W.	AV.
TEST					
OTHER FIRST CLASS	20	2	72	3	24.00
INT					
JPL					
NAT.W					
B & H					

CAREER: BOWLING

	O.	M.	R.	W.	AV.
TEST					
OTHER FIRST CLASS	20	2	72	3	24.00
INT					
JPL					
NAT.W					
B & H					

KING, C.L.   Worcestershire

Full Name: Collis Llewellyn King.
Role: Right-hand bat, right-arm medium bowler.
Born: 11 June 1951, Barbados.
County debut: 1977 (Glamorgan), 1983 (Worcestershire).
Test debut: 1976.
No. of Tests: 9.
No. of One-Day Internationals: 18.
1st-Class 50s scored: 24.
1st-Class 100s scored: 13.
1st-Class 5 w. in innings: 1.
One-day 50s: 6.
One-day 100s: 2.
1st-Class catches 1985: 8 (career: 97).
Extras: Played for Glamorgan in 1977, and further experience in England in Lancashire League.
Appeared for Worcestershire in 1983 when League commitment allowed, and registration held for 1984. Played for West Indies in 1979 Prudential World

Cup Final, scoring 86. Went to South Africa with West Indian 'Rebels' and now appears with Natal.

Best batting performance: 163 West Indians v Northamptonshire, Northampton 1976.
Best bowling performance: 5-91 Barbados v Jamaica, Bridgetown 1975–76.

LAST SEASON: BATTING

	I.	N.O.	R.	H.S.	AV.
TEST					
OTHER FIRST CLASS					
INT					
JPL					
NAT.W	1	0	11	11	–
B & H					

LAST SEASON: BOWLING

	O.	M.	R.	W.	AV.
TEST					
OTHER FIRST CLASS					
INT					
JPL					
NAT.W	8	0	36	1	–
B & H					

CAREER: BATTING

	I.	N.O.	R.	H.S.	AV.
TEST	16	3	418	100*	32.15
OTHER FIRST CLASS	167	21	5779	163	39.05
INT	14	2	280	86	23.33
JPL	20	1	586	127	30.84
NAT.W	5	0	104	55	20.80
B & H	7	0	167	61	23.86

CAREER: BOWLING

	O.	M.	R.	W.	AV.
TEST	97	24	282	3	94.00
OTHER FIRST CLASS	1305.4	300	3819	119	32.09
INT	124	7	529	11	48.09
JPL	103	5	502	12	41.83
NAT.W	42.2	7	153	6	25.50
B & H	43	9	145	1	–

KNOTT, A.P.E. Kent

Full Name: Alan Philip Eric Knott.
Role: Right-hand bat, wicket-keeper, can bowl off-breaks.
Born: 9 April 1946, Belvedere, Kent.
Height: 5′ 8″ **Weight:** 10st. 10lbs.
Nickname: Knotty, Flea.
County debut: 1964.
County cap: 1965.
Benefit: 1976 (£27,037).
Test debut: 1967.
No. of Tests: 95.
No. of One-Day Internationals: 20.
1000 runs in a season: 2.
1st-Class 50s scored: 81.
1st-Class 100s scored: 17.
One-day 50s: 6.
Place in batting averages: 187 average: 19.95; (1984: 142 average: 14.75).
Parents: Eric and Margaret Knott.

Wife and date of marriage: Jan Linda, 21 March 1969.
Education: Northumberland Heath Secondary Modern School, Erith, Kent.

Qualifications: Advanced cricket coach.

Jobs outside cricket: Proprietor of sports shop and gymnasium in Herne Bay.

Family links with cricket: "My father, uncle, brother, cousin and myself have all played for the same club in club cricket, Belvedere C.C. My father was a fine club wicket-keeper who kept me out of the side as keeper. I used to bowl off-spinners while he kept. He taught me cricket from the age of four."

Overseas tours: International Cavaliers 1965; M.C.C. U-25 tour to Pakistan 1967; West Indies 1967–68 and 1973–74; Ceylon and Pakistan 1968–69; Australia and New Zealand 1970–71, 1974–75; India, Sri Lanka and Pakistan 1972–73; India, Sri Lanka and Australia 1976–77.

Cricketers particularly learnt from: Father, Claude Lewis (Kent coach and ex-player) and Godfrey Evans.

Other sports: Most sports, especially soccer and table-tennis, badminton, squash. Played football for Tooting and Mitcham reserves.

Relaxations: Listening to music, watching movies either on T.V. or at the cinema, watching soccer, family.

Extras: Played for World Series cricket and in six "Supertests". Set record for more runs in Test cricket than any other wicket-keeper. Dismissed seven batsmen, seven caught, in Test debut v Pakistan, Nottingham 1967. Retired at end of 1985 season.

Best batting performance: 156 M.C.C. v South Zone, Bangalore 1972–73.

LAST SEASON: BATTING

	I.	N.O.	R.	H.S.	AV.
TEST					
OTHER FIRST CLASS	24	5	379	87*	19.95
INT					
JPL	9	1	61	18	7.62
NAT.W	2	0	40	24	20.00
B & H	5	1	47	23	11.75

CAREER: BATTING

	I.	N.O.	R.	H.S.	AV.
TEST	149	15	4389	135	32.75
OTHER FIRST CLASS	596	119	13716	156	28.76
INT	14	4	200	50	20.00
JPL	127	27	1628	60	16.28
NAT.W	36	5	455	46	14.68
B & H	58	7	888	65	17.41

LAST SEASON: BOWLING

	O.	M.	R.	W.	AV.
TEST					
OTHER FIRST CLASS					
INT					
JPL					
NAT.W					
B & H					

CAREER: BOWLING

	O.	M.	R.	W.	AV.
TEST					
OTHER FIRST CLASS	6.2 8	0 0	87	2	43.50
INT					
JPL					
NAT.W					
B & H					

LAST SEASON: WICKET KEEPING

	C.	ST.
TEST		
OTHER FIRST CLASS	53	1
INT		
JPL	8	1
NAT.W	5	–
B & H	3	1

CAREER: WICKET KEEPING

	C.	ST.
TEST	250	19
OTHER FIRST CLASS	961	114
INT	15	1
JPL	183	35
NAT.W	56	6
B & H	78	10

LAMB, A.J.   Northamptonshire

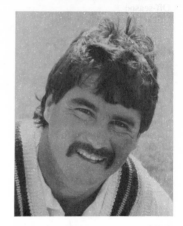

Full Name: Allan Joseph Lamb.
Role: Right-hand bat.
Born: 20 June 1954, Langebaanweg, Cape Province, South Africa.
Height: 5' 8" **Weight:** 12st. 12lbs.
Nickname: Lambie, Legger.
County debut: 1978.
County cap: 1978.
Test debut: 1982.
No. of Tests: 38.
No. of One-Day Internationals: 43.
1000 runs in a season: 6.
1st-Class 50s scored: 91.
1st-Class 100s scored: 41.
One-day 50s: 38.
One-day 100s: 9.
Place in batting averages: 41
average: 41.04; (1984: 49
average: 40.30).
1st-Class catches 1985: 14 (career: 183).
Parents: Michael and Joan Lamb.
Wife and date of marriage: Lindsay St Leger, 8 December 1979.
Education: Wynberg Boys' High School; Abbotts College.
Qualifications: Matriculation.
Jobs outside cricket: Timber representative. Promotions and selling.
Family links with cricket: Father played in the Boland League; brother played for Western Province "B". Brother-in-law, Tony Bucknall, won 10 caps for England at rugger.
Overseas tours: With England to Australia and New Zealand 1982–83; New Zealand and Pakistan 1983–84; India and Australia 1984–85.

LAST SEASON: BATTING

	I.	N.O.	R.	H.S.	AV.
TEST	8	1	256	67	36.57
OTHER FIRST CLASS	18	3	647	122*	43.13
INT	3	1	34	25	17.00
JPL	7	4	463	132*	154.30
NAT.W	2	0	49	42	24.50
B & H	4	1	30	20	10.00

CAREER: BATTING

	I.	N.O.	R.	H.S.	AV.
TEST	64	6	2211	137*	38.12
OTHER FIRST CLASS	350	64	14191	178	49.62
INT	42	8	1569	118	46.15
JPL	89	16	2959	132*	40.53
NAT.W	21	1	678	101	33.90
B & H	31	5	1118	106*	43.00

LAST SEASON: BOWLING

	O.	M.	R.	W.	AV.
TEST	1	0	10	0	–
OTHER FIRST CLASS	3	1	7	0	–
INT					
JPL					
NAT.W	0.2	0	4	1	–
B & H					

CAREER: BOWLING

	O.	M.	R.	W.	AV.
TEST	4	1	22	1	–
OTHER FIRST CLASS	29.2	7	99	4	24.75
INT					
JPL					
NAT.W	1.2	0	12	1	–
B & H					

Overseas teams played for: Western Province in Currie Cup Competition, 1972–81.
Off-season 1985–86: Playing for England in West Indies.
Cricketing superstitions: "I try to use the same batting shirt which I have scored runs in."
Cricketers particularly learnt from: "Everyone."
Other sports: Squash, golf. Follows most sports.
Relaxations: Shooting, fishing.
Extras: Made first-class debut for Western Province in 1972–73 Currie Cup. Applied to be registered as English in 1980 but application deferred. Was top of batting averages 1980. Was primarily a bowler when first played schoolboy cricket in South Africa. Missed two years of first-class cricket because of military training. Qualified to play for England 1982.
Best batting performance: 178 Northamptonshire v Leicestershire, Leicester 1979.

LAMPITT, S.R.   Worcestershire

Full Name: Stuart Richard Lampitt.
Role: Right-hand bat, right-arm fast-medium bowler.
Born: 29 July 1966, Wolverhampton.
Height: 5′ 11″.
County debut: 1985.
Education: Kingswinford School; Dudley College of Technology.
Other sports: Played football for West Midlands Schools.

LAST SEASON: BATTING

	I.	N.O.	R.	H.S.	AV.
TEST					
OTHER FIRST CLASS	1	0	0	0	–
INT					
JPL					
NAT.W					
B & H					

CAREER: BATTING

	I.	N.O.	R.	H.S.	AV.
TEST					
OTHER FIRST CLASS	1	0	0	0	–
INT					
JPL					
NAT.W					
B & H					

LAST SEASON: BOWLING

	O.	M.	R.	W.	AV.
TEST					
OTHER FIRST CLASS	1	0	1	0	–
INT					
JPL					
NAT.W					
B & H					

CAREER: BOWLING

	O.	M.	R.	W.	AV.
TEST					
OTHER FIRST CLASS	1	0	1	0	–
INT					
JPL					
NAT.W					
B & H					

LARKINS, W.   Northamptonshire

Full Name: Wayne Larkins.
Role: Right-hand bat, right-arm
medium bowler.
Born: 22 November 1953.
Height: 5' 11" **Weight:** 12st.
Nickname: Ned.
County debut: 1972.
County cap: 1976.
Benefit: 1986.
Test debut: 1979–80.
No. of Tests: 6.
No. of One-Day Internationals: 6.
1000 runs in a season: 8.
1st-Class 50s scored: 62.
1st-Class 100s scored: 35.
1st-Class 200s scored: 2.
1st-Class 5 w. in innings: 1.
One-day 50s: 36.
One-day 100s: 10.
Place in batting averages: 61 average: 36.88; (1984: 70 average: 36.00).
1st-Class catches 1985: 19 (career: 147).
Parents: Mavis Larkins (father deceased).
Wife and date of marriage: Jane Elaine, 22 March 1975.
Children: Philippa Jane, 30 May 1981.
Education: Bushmead, Eaton Socon, Huntingdon.
Family links with cricket: Father was umpire. Brother, Melvin, "played for
Bedford Town for many years."
Overseas tours: England tour to Australia and India 1979–80.
Cricketers particularly learnt from: Mushtaq Mohammad.
Other sports: Golf, football (currently with Buckingham and was on Notts. Co.
books), squash.
Jobs outside cricket: Farming.
Off-season 1985–86: Organising benefit year.
Relaxations: Gardening.
Injuries 1985: Missed start of season after gashing knee while playing
football.
Extras: Northants. considered releasing him in 1974. With Peter Willey,
received 2016 pints of beer (seven barrels) from a Northampton brewery as a
reward for their efforts in Australia in 1979–80. Hat-trick for Northants. v
Cambridge and Oxford, Benson & Hedges, 1980. Banned from English Test
Cricket for three years for joining rebel tour of South Africa in 1982.
Best batting performance: 252 Northamptonshire v Glamorgan, Cardiff 1983.
Best bowling performance: 5-59 Northamptonshire v Worcestershire,
Worcester 1984.

LAST SEASON: BATTING

	I.	N.O.	R.	H.S.	AV.
TEST					
OTHER FIRST CLASS	42	0	1549	163	36.88
INT					
JPL	13	2	535	126	48.63
NAT.W	2	0	109	75	54.50
B & H	5	0	215	105	43.00

CAREER: BATTING

	I.	N.O.	R.	H.S.	AV.
TEST	11	0	176	34	16.00
OTHER FIRST CLASS	483	27	16038	252	35.17
INT	6	0	84	34	14.00
JPL	166	12	4215	172*	27.37
NAT.W	27	2	896	92*	35.84
B & H	48	3	1571	132	34.91

LAST SEASON: BOWLING

	O.	M.	R.	W.	AV.
TEST					
OTHER FIRST CLASS	83	16	284	1	–
INT					
JPL	60	2	284	7	40.57
NAT.W	12	3	38	2	19.00
B & H					

CAREER: BOWLING

	O.	M.	R.	W.	AV.
TEST					
OTHER FIRST CLASS	487.5	95	1644	39	42.15
INT	2	0	21	0	–
JPL	305.5	9	1505	54	27.87
NAT.W	73.5	9	249	4	62.25
B & H	105.3	14	413	16	25.81

95. Which batsman has scored most runs in the John Player League?

96. What happened of cricketing importance at 1.00 p.m. on 15 March 1877 in Melbourne?

97. Who won the first Test Match between England v Australia and by how much?

LAWRENCE, D.V.　　　　Gloucestershire

Full Name: David Valentine Lawrence.
Role: Right-hand bat, right-arm fast bowler, slip fielder.
Born: 28 January 1964, Gloucester.
Height: 6′ 3″ **Weight:** 15st.
Nickname: Syd, Bruno.
County debut: 1981.
County cap: 1985.
50 wickets in a season: 1.
1st-Class 5 w. in innings: 8.
Place in batting averages: 237 average: 12.33.
Place in bowling averages: 16 average: 24.62; (1984: 107 average: 37.34).
1st-Class catches 1985: 3 (career: 14).
Parents: Joseph and Joyce Lawrence.
Education: Linden School, Gloucester.
Off-season 1985–86: Playing for three months in Tasmania, then England B tour.
Overseas teams played for: Scarborough C.C., Perth, Western Australia.
Cricketers particularly learnt from: Michael Holding, Richard Hadlee, Dennis Lillee.
Cricketers particularly admired: Viv Richards.
Other sports: Rugby football. "Was offered terms to play professional rugby league winter 1985–86, but turned down.".
Relaxations: "Like listening to jazz, funk and dancing."
Opinions on cricket: "The over-rate fines should not have been applied to one-day cricket."

LAST SEASON: BATTING

	I.	N.O.	R.	H.S.	AV.
TEST					
OTHER FIRST CLASS	26	5	259	41	12.33
INT					
JPL	1	1	3	3*	–
NAT.W	3	2	2	1*	–
B & H	2	2	22	22*	–

CAREER: BATTING

	I.	N.O.	R.	H.S.	AV.
TEST					
OTHER FIRST CLASS	60	13	416	41	8.85
INT					
JPL	4	3	31	17	–
NAT.W	4	2	2	1*	1.00
B & H	3	3	23	22*	–

LAST SEASON: BOWLING

	O.	M.	R.	W.	AV.
TEST					
OTHER FIRST CLASS	524.2	66	2093	85	24.62
INT					
JPL	52.2	0	311	6	51.83
NAT.W	21.3	1	112	4	28.00
B & H	39	2	139	4	34.75

CAREER: BOWLING

	O.	M.	R.	W.	AV.
TEST					
OTHER FIRST CLASS	1178.3	174	4397	135	32.57
INT					
JPL	168	1	939	37	25.37
NAT.W	72.2	8	335	10	35.50
B & H	61	2	239	10	23.90

Best batting performance: 41 Gloucestershire v Nottinghamshire, Trent Bridge 1985.
Best bowling performance: 7-48 Gloucestershire v Sussex, Hove 1985.

LENHAM, N.J.   Sussex

Full Name: Neil John Lenham.
Role: Right-hand bat, right-arm medium bowler.
Born: 17 December 1965, Worthing.
Height: 5′ 11″ **Weight:** 10st. 12lbs.
Nickname: Spelvin, Nellie, Archie, Little Treasure.
County debut: 1984.
1st-Class 50s scored: 3.
Place in batting averages: 81 average: 33.79.
1st-Class catches 1985: 4 (career: 5).
Parents: Leslie John and Valerie Anne Lenham.
Marital status: Single.
Family links with cricket: Father, ex-Sussex county cricketer and N.C.A. National Coach.
Education: Broadwater Manor House Prep. School; Brighton College.
Qualifications: 5 O-levels, 2 A-levels.
Cricketing superstitions: Adjusting all equipment to obtain comfort.
Overseas tours: 1981 tour to Barbados with Sussex U-16; 1982 tour to Barbados with Sussex Young Cricketers; 1985 England Young Cricketers tour to West Indies (as captain).
Cricketers particularly learnt from: Les Lenham, John Spencer.
Cricketers particularly admired: Ken McEwan, Barry Richards.
Other sports: Hockey, squash, golf, wind-surfing; follows golf and snooker.
Relaxations: Music, listening to Van Morrison, Neil Diamond and Janis Joplin; reading.
Extras: Made debut for Young England 1983. Scored double century for Brighton College v Hurstpierpoint 1984. Broke record for number of runs scored in season at a public school in 1984 (1534 average 80.74).
Best batting performance: 89 Sussex v Kent, Canterbury 1985.

LAST SEASON: BATTING

	I.	N.O.	R.	H.S.	AV.
TEST					
OTHER FIRST CLASS	16	2	473	89	33.79
INT					
JPL	1	1	1	1*	–
NAT.W					
B & H					

CAREER: BATTING

	I.	N.O.	R.	H.S.	AV.
TEST					
OTHER FIRST CLASS	17	2	504	89	33.60
INT					
JPL	1	1	1	1*	–
NAT.W					
B & H					

LE ROUX, G.S.   Sussex

Full Name: Garth Sterling Le Roux.
Role: Right-hand bat, right-arm
fast bowler.
Born: 4 September 1955, Cape
Town, South Africa.
Height: 6′ 3″ **Weight:** 15st.
Nickname: Rocky.
County debut: 1978.
County cap: 1981.
50 wickets in a season: 3.
1st-Class 50s scored: 19.
1st-Class 5 w. in innings: 31.
1st-Class 10 w. in match: 3.
One-day 50s: 4.
Place in batting averages: 73
average: 35.08; (1984: 219
average: 17.83).
Place in bowling averages: 43
average: 28.30; (1984: 9
average: 21.12).
1st-Class catches 1985: 1 (career: 61).
Parents: Pierre and Audrey Le Roux.
Marital status: Single.
Education: Wynberg Boys' High School; Stellenbosch University.
Qualifications: B.A. Physical Education.
Overseas tours: World XI in World Series Cricket Tour.
Overseas teams played for: Western Province.
Other sports: Golf, squash.
Relaxations: Horse-riding, listening to music.
Extras: Played for Packer's World Series cricket.

LAST SEASON: BATTING

	I.	N.O.	R.	H.S.	AV.
TEST					
OTHER FIRST CLASS	16	4	421	61	35.08
INT					
JPL	6	2	142	54	35.50
NAT.W	2	1	0	0*	–
B & H	3	0	26	21	8.67

CAREER: BATTING

	I.	N.O.	R.	H.S.	AV.
TEST					
OTHER FIRST CLASS	218	61	3932	83	25.05
INT					
JPL	49	11	978	88	25.73
NAT.W	10	2	80	22	10.00
B & H	19	6	360	50	27.70

LAST SEASON: BOWLING

	O.	M.	R.	W.	AV.
TEST					
OTHER FIRST CLASS	402.2	72	1132	40	28.30
INT					
JPL	76.3	5	340	12	28.33
NAT.W	17.5	4	45	6	7.50
B & H	41	5	140	9	15.56

CAREER: BOWLING

	O.	M.	R.	W.	AV.
TEST					
OTHER FIRST CLASS	5235.1	1168	13632	654	20.84
INT					
JPL	452.5	23	1945	94	20.69
NAT.W	114.2	22	300	24	12.50
B & H	216.4	24	848	37	22.11

Best batting performance: 83 Sussex v Surrey, Hove 1982.
Best bowling performance: 8-107 Sussex v Somerset, Taunton 1981.

LETHBRIDGE, C.　　　　Warwickshire

Full Name: Christopher Lethbridge.
Role: Right-hand bat, right-arm
medium bowler.
Born: 23 June 1961,
Castleford, Yorkshire.
Height: 5′ 10″ **Weight:** 13st. 6lbs.
Nickname: Arthur.
County debut: 1981.
1st-Class 50s scored: 3.
1st-Class 5 w. in innings: 1.
One-day 50s: 1.
Place in batting averages: —
average: —; (1984: 176 average: 23.14).
Place in bowling averages: —
average: —; (1984: 86 average: 32.90).
1st-Class catches 1985: 0 (career: 16).
Parents: Chris and Margaret
Lethbridge.

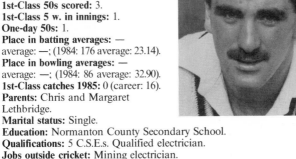

Marital status: Single.
Education: Normanton County Secondary School.
Qualifications: 5 C.S.E.s. Qualified electrician.
Jobs outside cricket: Mining electrician.
Cricketers particularly learnt from: David Brown, Don Wilson and Clive
Jackson (Junior Coach with Leeds United and Wakefield Trinity).
Cricketers particularly admired: Geoff Boycott.

LAST SEASON: BATTING

	I.	N.O.	R.	H.S.	AV.
TEST					
OTHER FIRST CLASS	3	1	84	47	42.00
INT					
JPL	1	1	2	2*	—
NAT.W	1	0	4	4	—
B & H	1	0	0	0	—

CAREER: BATTING

	I.	N.O.	R.	H.S.	AV.
TEST					
OTHER FIRST CLASS	58	13	1033	87*	22.96
INT					
JPL	20	12	210	57*	26.25
NAT.W	3	0	27	19	9.00
B & H	6	2	34	13*	8.50

LAST SEASON: BOWLING

	O.	M.	R.	W.	AV.
TEST					
OTHER FIRST CLASS	65	7	263	5	52.60
INT					
JPL	6	0	43	1	—
NAT.W	12	2	39	1	—
B & H	19	1	108	0	—

CAREER: BOWLING

	O.	M.	R.	W.	AV.
TEST					
OTHER FIRST CLASS	832.3	141	2996	77	38.91
INT					
JPL	241.3	8	1250	39	32.05
NAT.W	88	10	316	8	39.50
B & H	93	7	343	11	31.18

Other sports: Football.
Relaxations: "Having a drink and a good disco. Watching sport."
Extras: "Dismissed Geoff Boycott with my first ball in first-class cricket and also scored 69." Left staff after 1985 season.
Best batting performance: 87* Warwickshire v Somerset, Taunton 1982.
Best bowling performance: 5-68 Warwickshire v Glamorgan, Cardiff 1982.

LEVER, J.K. Essex

Full Name: John Kenneth Lever.
Role: Right-hand bat, left-arm fast-medium bowler.
Born: 24 February 1949, Stepney.
Height: 6′ 0″ **Weight:** 13st.
Nickname: Jake, J.K. Stanley.
County debut: 1967.
County cap: 1970.
Test debut: 1976–77.
No. of Tests: 20.
No. of One-Day Internationals: 22.
Benefit: 1980 (£66,250).
50 wickets in a season: 15.
1st-Class 50s scored: 2.
1st-Class 5 w. in innings: 79.
1st-Class 10 w. in match: 12.
Place in batting averages: 124 average: 13.79; (1984: 258 average: 12.13).
Place in bowling averages: 23 average: 25.91; (1984: 12 average: 21.98).
1st-Class catches 1985: 8 (career: 177).
Parents: Ken and Doris Lever.
Wife and date of marriage: Chris, 30 July 1983.
Children: Jocelyn Jennifer, 9 January 1985.
Education: Highlands Junior; Dane County Secondary School.
Qualifications: 3 O-levels, 3 R.S.A.s.
Jobs outside cricket: Clerk with Access Social Club; Byron Shipping; Dominion Insurance.
Off-season 1985–86: Manager, Natal cricket.
Cricketing superstitions: "Too many to mention."
Overseas tours: India, Sri Lanka and Australia, 1976–77; Pakistan and New Zealand, 1977–78; Australia, 1978–79 and 1979–80.
Cricketers particularly learnt from: "A little from a lot."
Cricketers particularly admired: Sir Gary Sobers.
Other sports: "All sports." Football, squash, badminton, tennis, golf.
Relaxations: Music, cooking.
Extras: Took 10 wickets in his Test debut in 1976 v India at Delhi. Took 106 wickets at an average of 15.80 in 1978, and 106 wickets at an average of 17.30 in

1979, and 106 wickets at an average of 16.28 in 1983. President of Blythswood C.C. Member of Ilford C.C. since the age of 14. Another of the renowned Essex comedians. Has reputation of "not breaking down". On the executive of the Cricketers' Association. Banned from Test Cricket for three years for joining rebel tour of South Africa in 1982.

Opinions on cricket: "To see over-rate fines disappear from one-day cricket in 1986, and hope once again that we shall be allowed to finish championship games at 6.30 p.m."

Best batting performance: 91 Essex v Glamorgan, Cardiff 1970.

Best bowling performance: 8-37 Essex v Gloucestershire, Bristol 1984.

LAST SEASON: BATTING

	I.	N.O.	R.	H.S.	AV.
TEST					
OTHER FIRST CLASS	23	9	193	24*	13.79
INT					
JPL	3	0	15	14	5.00
NAT.W	1	1	1	1*	–
B & H	–	–	–	–	–

CAREER: BATTING

	I.	N.O.	R.	H.S.	AV.
TEST	29	4	306	53	12.24
OTHER FIRST CLASS	453	179	3004	91	10.96
INT	11	4	56	27*	8.00
JPL	97	58	376	23	9.64
NAT.W	22	15	82	15*	11.72
B & H	23	15	92	13	11.50

LAST SEASON: BOWLING

	O.	M.	R.	W.	AV.
TEST					
OTHER FIRST CLASS	720.3	188	1995	77	25.91
INT					
JPL	92.2	5	408	19	21.47
NAT.W	53	17	137	5	27.40
B & H	50.5	4	164	9	18.22

CAREER: BOWLING

	O.	M.	R.	W.	AV.
TEST	166.7 463.2	27 104	1785	67	26.64
OTHER FIRST CLASS	210.4 12517.3	40 2782	35042	1482	23.65
INT	33 148	5 15	713	24	29.71
JPL	1658.5	193	5956	329	18.10
NAT.W	386.3	89	992	62	16.00
B & H	706.4	139	2104	122	17.25

98. Who was the only President of the United States known to have watched a Test Match, when and where?

99. In what year was the County Championship officially begun?

LILLEY, A.W.   Essex

Full Name: Alan William Lilley.
Role: Right-hand bat, wicket-keeper.
Born: 8 May 1959, Ilford, Essex.
Height: 5' 11" **Weight:** 13st. 4lbs.
Nickname: Lil.
County debut: 1978.
1st-Class 50s scored: 7.
1st-Class 100s scored: 1.
One-day 50s: 5.
One-day 100s: 1.
Place in batting averages: 76
average: 21.50.
1st-Class catches 1985: 7 (career: 23).
Parents: Min and Ron Lilley.
Wife and date of marriage: Helen,
6 October 1984.
Education: Caterham High School,
Ilford.
Family links with cricket: Father
played for Osborne C.C. as a bowler for 18 years.
Off-season 1985–86: Coaching at Indoor Cricket School.
Overseas teams played for: Perth C.C., Western Australia, 1979–80.
Cricketers particularly learnt from: Stuart Turner (his coach in early days).
Other sports: Badminton, swimming.
Extras: Was on M.C.C. Young Pro. staff at Lord's one season after leaving
school. Scored century in second innings of debut v Notts. Plays for
Ilford.
Best batting performance: 100* Essex v Nottinghamshire, Trent Bridge
1978.
Best bowling performance: 2-11 Essex v Surrey, Chelmsford 1984.

LAST SEASON: BATTING

	I.	N.O.	R.	H.S.	AV.
TEST					
OTHER FIRST CLASS	26	2	516	68*	21.50
INT					
JPL	10	2	193	49	24.12
NAT.W	3	1	47	26	23.50
B & H	5	1	41	12	10.25

CAREER: BATTING

	I.	N.O.	R.	H.S.	AV.
TEST					
OTHER FIRST CLASS	74	4	1691	100*	24.16
INT					
JPL	70	5	1004	60	15.44
NAT.W	8	2	190	59*	31.67
B & H	20	2	408	119	22.67

LAST SEASON: BOWLING

	O.	M.	R.	W.	AV.
TEST					
OTHER FIRST CLASS	29.4	0	184	3	61.33
INT					
JPL					
NAT.W					
B & H	1	0	4	1	–

CAREER: BOWLING

	O.	M.	R.	W.	AV.
TEST					
OTHER FIRST CLASS	38	2	205	5	41.00
INT					
JPL	2.3	0	19	3	6.33
NAT.W	8	3	33	2	16.50
B & H	1	0	4	1	–

LLOYD, C.H.   Lancashire

Full Name: Clive Hubert Lloyd.
Role: Left-hand bat, right-arm medium bowler.
Born: 31 August 1944, Georgetown, Guyana.
Height: 6′ 4½″ **Weight:** 14st.
Nickname: Big C, Hubert.
County debut: 1968.
County cap: 1969.
Testimonial: 1977 (£27,199).
Test debut: 1966–67.
No. of Tests: 110.
No. of One-Day Internationals: 87.
1000 runs in a season: 10.
1st-Class 50s scored: 129.
1st-Class 100s scored: 73.
1st-Class 200s scored: 5.
One-day 50s: 58.
One-day 100s: 11.
Place in batting averages: 16 average: 52.00; (1984: 16 average: 52.80).
1st-Class catches 1985: 13 (career: 379)
Parents: Arthur Christopher and Sylvia Thelma Lloyd.
Wife and date of marriage: Waveney, 11 September 1971.
Children: Melissa Monica Simone, 22 February 1974; Samantha Louise, 26 January 1976; Clive Jason Christopher, 15 June 1981.
Education: Fountain A.M.E. School and Chatham High School, Georgetown, Guyana.
Qualifications: Cricket coaching certificate. Honorary degrees from Universities of Manchester and Hull.
Jobs outside cricket: Civil servant, Guyana Ministry of Health.
Family links with cricket: Cousin of Lance Gibbs of Warwickshire C.C.C. and West Indies. "My parents had no interest in sport."
Overseas tours: India and Ceylon 1966–67; Australia and New Zealand 1968–69; England 1969, 1973, 1976, 1980 and 1984; Australia 1979–80 and 1984–85; Pakistan 1980–81; India 1983–84.
Off-season 1985–86: Coaching and T.V. commentary in Australia; manager Guyana Shell Shield.
Other sports: Tennis, table-tennis, squash, soccer, basketball. Was a schoolboy athletics champion.
Relaxations: Coaching, charity work, T.V., music.
Injuries 1985: Torn hamstring.
Extras: Offered terms by Warwickshire before signing for Lancashire. Played for Haslingden in Lancashire League in 1967. Played for Rest of the World XI in 1967, 1968, five matches in 1970 and two in 1971 and 1972. Has written articles for *Lancashire Evening Post* and *Bolton Express.* Has had knee injury problems since 1976. Was strong supporter of World Series Cricket. Published (by Stanley Paul) *Living for Cricket* in 1980. Eye-sight deteriorated after he tried

to separate two boys fighting, at age 12, and received a blow in the eye, and has worn spectacles ever since. Has scored 6 centuries v Yorkshire, a Lancashire record. Scored 201 n.o. in 120 minutes for West Indies v Glamorgan at Swansea, 1976, to equal record for fastest double century in first-class cricket. Captain of West Indies 1974–85. Captain of Lancashire 1981–83 and resumed in 1985. Resigned from Test cricket and the West Indies captaincy in 1985.
Best batting performance: 242* West Indies v India, Bombay 1974–75.
Best bowling performance: 4-48 Lancashire v Leicestershire, Old Trafford 1970.

LAST SEASON: BATTING

	I.	N.O.	R.	H.S.	AV.
TEST					
OTHER FIRST CLASS	7	1	288	131	48.00
INT					
JPL	11	1	387	108	38.70
NAT.W	2	0	121	91	60.50
B & H	2	1	51	43*	—

CAREER: BATTING

	I.	N.O.	R.	H.S.	AV.
TEST	175	14	7515	242*	46.67
OTHER FIRST CLASS	547	81	23370	217*	50.15
INT	69	19	1977	102	39.54
JPL	156	38	4697	134*	39.86
NAT.W	36	5	1756	126	56.65
B & H	43	6	1170	124	31.62

LAST SEASON: BOWLING

	O.	M.	R.	W.	AV.
TEST					
OTHER FIRST CLASS					
INT					
JPL					
NAT.W					
B & H					

CAREER: BOWLING

	O.	M.	R.	W.	AV.
TEST	39 234	6 69	622	10	62.20
OTHER FIRST CLASS	34 1263	7 302	3482	104	33.48
INT	3 55.4	0 7	210	8	26.25
JPL	221	16	935	36	25.97
NAT.W	92.3	16	320	12	26.67
B & H	83.3	18	302	12	25.17

LLOYD, T.A.　　　　　　Warwickshire

Full Name: Timothy Andrew Lloyd.
Role: Left-hand bat, off-break bowler.
Born: 5 November 1956, Oswestry.
Height: 5′ 10″ **Weight:** 11st. 10lbs.
Nickname: Teflon, Towser.
County debut: 1977.
County cap: 1980.
Test debut: 1984.
No. of Tests: 1.
No. of One-Day Internationals: 3.
1000 runs in a season: 5.
1st-Class 50s scored: 43.
1st-Class 100s scored: 14.
1st-Class 200s scored: 1.
One-day 50s: 31.
One-day 100s: 1.
Place in batting averages: 53
average: 38.44; (1984: 21
average: 49.16).

1st-Class catches 1985: 5 (career: 92).
Marital status: Single.
Education: Oswestry Boys' High School; Dorset College of Higher Education.
Qualifications: O-levels, A-levels, H.N.D. Tourism. N.C.A. Advanced coach.
Jobs outside cricket: Agent for Italian colour printer, book publishing, lorry driver.
Overseas tours: Derrick Robins' tour to South America 1979; Warwickshire C.C.C. tour to Zambia 1977; Kingfishers to South Africa 1978; Warwickshire Wanderers to Barbados 1978.
Overseas teams played for: Orange Free State, Zingari C.C.
Cricketers particularly learnt from: Dennis Amiss. Greatly admired Gary Sobers.
Other sports: Soccer, golf, table-tennis, squash, American football, horse-racing.
Relaxations: Greyhound racing, eating good food, (trying to cook it), theatre.
Injuries 1985: Thumb broken and dislocated — missed three weeks.
Extras: Scores 202 n.o. for Shropshire Schools v Worcestershire. Played for Oswestry C.C. at age 17. Played for Shropshire and Warwickshire 2nd XI, both in 1975. Played in one John Player League match in 1976 v Yorkshire at Leeds. "Half my first-class wickets are international players."
Best batting performance: 208* Warwickshire v Gloucestershire, Edgbaston 1983.

LAST SEASON: BATTING

	I.	N.O.	R.	H.S.	AV.
TEST					
OTHER FIRST CLASS	34	2	1230	160	38.44
INT					
JPL	10	0	230	69	23.00
NAT.W	2	1	9	9	—
B & H	4	1	181	137*	60.33

CAREER: BATTING

	I.	N.O.	R.	H.S.	AV.
TEST	1	1	10	10*	—
OTHER FIRST CLASS	293	31	9642	208*	36.80
INT	3	0	101	49	33.67
JPL	89	11	2437	90	31.34
NAT.W	16	3	525	81	40.38
B & H	25	3	792	137*	36.00

LAST SEASON: BOWLING

	O.	M.	R.	W.	AV.
TEST					
OTHER FIRST CLASS	31	1	127	4	31.75
INT					
JPL					
NAT.W	3	1	4	1	—
B & H					

CAREER: BOWLING

	O.	M.	R.	W.	AV.
TEST					
OTHER FIRST CLASS	216	41	867	13	66.69
INT					
JPL	22.1	0	139	1	—
NAT.W	3	1	4	1	—
B & H	13	1	56	0	—

100. Which of the Bedser twins, Alec and Eric, was born first?

101. Who in 1984, became the youngest bowler ever to take a hat-trick for Yorkshire?

LLOYDS, J.W.   Gloucestershire

Full Name: Jeremy William Lloyds.
Role: Left-hand bat, off-break bowler, close fielder.
Born: 17 November 1954, Penang, Malaya.
Height: 5' 11½" **Weight:** 11st. 7lbs.
Nickname: Jo'burg, J.J. or Jerry.
County debut: 1979 (Somerset), 1985 (Gloucestershire).
County cap: 1982 (Somerset), 1985 (Gloucestershire).
1st-Class 50s scored: 26.
1st-Class 100s scored: 6.
1st-Class 5 w. in innings: 7.
1st-Class 10 w. in match: 1.
One-day 50s: 1.
Place in batting averages: 109 average: 30.30; (1984: 48 average: 40.60).

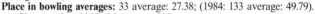

Place in bowling averages: 33 average: 27.38; (1984: 133 average: 49.79).
1st-Class catches 1985: 25 (career: 110).
Parents: Edwin William and Grace Cicely Lloyds.
Marital status: Single.
Education: St Dunstan's Prep. School; Blundell's School.
Qualifications: 10 O-levels, N.C.A. advanced coach.
Jobs outside cricket: Lloyds Bank, Taunton, for 1½ years. M.C.C. Young Professionals at Lord's 1975 for four years.
Family links with cricket: Father played Blundell's 1st XI 1932–35, selected for Public Schools Rest v Lord's Schools at Lord's 1935, Inter-State cricket in Malaya and Singapore 1950–55. Brother, Christopher Edwin Lloyds, played for Blundell's 1st XI 1964–66 and Somerset 2nd XI in 1966.
Overseas tours: With Somerset in Antigua, 1981; with Gloucestershire to Barbados, 1985.
Overseas teams played for: St Stithian's Old Boys, Johannesburg, 1978–79, 79–80; Toombul D.C.C., Brisbane, 1980–81, 1981–82; North Sydney District 1982–83; Orange Free State 1983–84.
Cricketers particularly learnt from: Don Wilson, Derek Taylor and Brian Davison.
Cricketers particularly admired: John Hampshire and Graeme Pollock.
Off-season 1985–86: Having a complete break from cricket!
Other sports: Rugby, soccer, golf, tennis, swimming, squash. Watches motor-racing.
Relaxations: Music, cinema, driving, reading.
Extras: Scored 132 n.o. and 102 n.o. for Somerset in same Championship match, June 1982. Took 30 catches in 1982 season for Somerset. Moved to Gloucestershire for 1985 season.
Opinions on cricket: "B & H competition to start in June and County

Championship to start earlier to allow more cricket to be played before start of the B & H. Weather plays too great a part in zonal games."

Best batting performance: 132* Somerset v Northamptonshire, Northampton 1982.

Best bowling performance: 7-88 Somerset v Essex, Chelmsford 1982.

LAST SEASON: BATTING

	I.	N.O.	R.	H.S.	AV.
TEST					
OTHER FIRST CLASS	33	6	818	101	30.30
INT					
JPL	6	0	28	9	4.67
NAT.W	2	0	60	40	30.00
B & H	—	—	—	—	—

CAREER: BATTING

	I.	N.O.	R.	H.S.	AV.
TEST					
OTHER FIRST CLASS	196	27	4868	132*	28.81
INT					
JPL	41	9	382	33	11.93
NAT.W	8	2	145	40*	24.17
B & H	11	0	153	51	13.91

LAST SEASON: BOWLING

	O.	M.	R.	W.	AV.
TEST					
OTHER FIRST CLASS	180.1	42	575	21	27.38
INT					
JPL					
NAT.W					
B & H					

CAREER: BOWLING

	O.	M.	R.	W.	AV.
TEST					
OTHER FIRST CLASS	1678.2	399	5242	156	33.60
INT					
JPL	28.5	3	134	3	44.67
NAT.W	9	1	18	0	—
B & H	2	0	6	0	—

LORD, G.J. Warwickshire

Full Name: Gordon John Lord.
Role: Left-hand bat, slow left-arm bowler.
Born: Birmingham.
Height: 5′ 10″ **Weight:** 11st. 10lbs.
Nickname: Plod.
County debut: 1983.
1st-Class 50s scored: 2.
1st-Class 100s scored: 1.
One-day 50s: 1.
One-day 100s: 1.
Place in batting averages: 130 average: 27.10.
1st-Class catches 1985: 0 (career: 4).
Parents: Michael David and Christine Frances Lord.
Marital status: Single.
Education: Warwick School; Durham University.
Qualifications: 7 O-Levels, 4 A-Levels and B.A. Gen.
Overseas tours: England U-19 tour Australia 1978–79 and West Indies 1979–80.

Cricketers particularly learnt from: Allan Wilkins (school coach), R.N. Abberley (2nd XI coach), Norman Graham (University coach).
Other sports: Squash, tennis, swimming, running. Watches rugby, athletics, boxing.
Relaxations: All forms of music, particularly church organ music; astronomy, reading, people.
Best batting performance: 199 Warwickshire v Yorkshire, Edgbaston 1985.

LAST SEASON: BATTING

	I.	N.O.	R.	H.S.	AV.
TEST					
OTHER FIRST CLASS	11	1	271	199	27.10
INT					
JPL	5	0	170	103	34.00
NAT.W					
B & H					

CAREER: BATTING

	I.	N.O.	R.	H.S.	AV.
TEST					
OTHER FIRST CLASS	20	1	445	199	23.42
INT					
JPL	9	0	233	103	25.88
NAT.W					
B & H					

LAST SEASON: BOWLING

	O.	M.	R.	W.	AV.
TEST					
OTHER FIRST CLASS	5	0	19	0	—
INT					
JPL					
NAT.W					
B & H					

CAREER: BOWLING

	O.	M.	R.	W.	AV.
TEST					
OTHER FIRST CLASS	13	3	31	0	—
INT					
JPL					
NAT.W					
B & H					

LOVE, J.D.   Yorkshire

Full Name: James Derek Love.
Role: Right-hand bat.
Born: 22 April 1955, Leeds.
Height: 6' 2'' **Weight:** 14st.
Nickname: Jim.
County debut: 1975.
County cap: 1980.
No. of One-Day Internationals: 3.
1000 runs in a season: 2.
1st-Class 50s scored: 41.
1st-Class 100s scored: 12.
One-day 50s: 13.
One-day 100s: 2.
Place in batting averages: 42
average: 40.74; (1984: 143
average: 27.05).
1st-Class catches 1985: 8 (career: 93).
Parents: Derek Oliver and Betty
Love.

Marital status: Divorced.
Education: Brudenell County Secondary, Leeds.
Jobs outside cricket: Civil servant for three years until left to become professional cricketer.
Family links with cricket: Father played local cricket; brother Robert plays for Castleford C.C. in Yorkshire League.
Overseas teams played for: Whitbread Scholarship to Mosman Middle Harbour and District C.C. in 1977–78; Scarborough C.C., Perth, Western Australia, 1978–79; Mosman Middle Harbour and District C.C. 1982–83, 1984–85.
Off-season 1985–86: Trying to find employment.
Cricketers particularly learnt from: Doug Padgett, county coach.
Other sports: Local football, golf.
Relaxations: Shooting.
Injuries 1985: Badly gashed knee.
Opinions on cricket: "I wish employment could be found for more cricketers when the season ends."
Best batting performance: 170* Yorkshire v Worcestershire, Worcester 1979.

LAST SEASON: BATTING

	I.	N.O.	R.	H.S.	AV.
TEST					
OTHER FIRST CLASS	28	5	937	106	40.74
INT					
JPL	12	1	231	100*	21.00
NAT.W	—	—	—	—	—
B & H	4	2	126	90*	63.00

CAREER: BATTING

	I.	N.O.	R.	H.S.	AV.
TEST					
OTHER FIRST CLASS	287	43	7806	170*	31.99
INT	3	0	61	43	20.33
JPL	101	12	1913	100*	21.49
NAT.W	11	2	94	61*	10.44
B & H	25	6	742	118*	39.05

LAST SEASON: BOWLING

	O.	M.	R.	W.	AV.
TEST					
OTHER FIRST CLASS	1	0	8	1	—
INT					
JPL					
NAT.W					
B & H					

CAREER: BOWLING

	O.	M.	R.	W.	AV.
TEST					
OTHER FIRST CLASS	65	15	241	2	120.5
INT					
JPL	3	0	7	1	—
NAT.W					
B & H					

102. Who is the youngest player ever to play Test cricket, at what age and for what county?

103. Who was the youngest player to play Test cricket for the West Indies?

LYNCH, M.A. Surrey

Full Name: Monte Allan Lynch.
Role: Right-hand bat, right-arm medium and off-break bowler.
Born: 21 May 1958, Georgetown, Guyana.
Weight: 12st.
Nickname: Mont.
County debut: 1977.
County cap: 1982.
1000 runs in a season: 4.
1st-Class 50s scored: 37.
1st-Class 100s scored: 21.
One-day 50s: 38.
One-day 100s: 7.
Place in batting averages: 17 average: 53.56; (1984: 57 average: 38.65).
1st-Class catches 1985: 36 (career: 136).

Parents: Lawrence and Doreen Austin Lynch.
Marital status: Single.
Education: Ryden's School, Walton-on-Thames.
Family links with cricket: "Father and most of family played at some time or another."
Other sports: Football, table-tennis.
Extras: Hitting 141 n.o. for Surrey v Glamorgan at Guildford in August 1982, off 78 balls in 88 minutes, one six hit his captain's, Roger Knight's, car, denting it. Repeated trick in 1983 v Worcestershire in John Player Special League. Joined West Indies "rebels" in South Africa 1983–84.
Best batting performance: 145 Surrey v Warwickshire, The Oval 1984.
Best bowling performance: 3-6 Surrey v Glamorgan, Swansea 1981.

LAST SEASON: BATTING

	I.	N.O.	R.	H.S.	AV.
TEST					
OTHER FIRST CLASS	39	7	1714	145	53.56
INT					
JPL	11	0	420	136	38.18
NAT.W	1	0	31	31	—
B & H	4	0	33	11	8.25

CAREER: BATTING

	I.	N.O.	R.	H.S.	AV.
TEST					
OTHER FIRST CLASS	278	32	8603	145	34.97
INT					
JPL	96	13	2422	136	29.18
NAT.W	14	3	312	129	28.36
B & H	25	0	533	85	21.32

LAST SEASON: BOWLING

	O.	M.	R.	W.	AV.
TEST					
OTHER FIRST CLASS	6	1	46	0	—
INT					
JPL					
NAT.W					
B & H					

CAREER: BOWLING

	O.	M.	R.	W.	AV.
TEST					
OTHER FIRST CLASS	179.4	31	709	15	47.27
INT					
JPL	4.3	0	41	0	—
NAT.W	11	5	26	1	—
B & H					

MAHER, B.J.M.   Derbyshire

Full Name: Bernard Joseph Michael Maher.
Role: Right-hand bat, wicket-keeper.
Born: 11 February 1958, Hillingdon.
Height: 5' 10" **Weight:** 11st. 6lbs.
Nickname: "Tends to vary. 'Sewer Rat' or 'Rodders' most popular at present."
County debut: 1981.
1st-Class 50s scored: 2.
Place in batting averages: 236 average: 12.50; (1984: 230 average: 16.22).
Parents: Francis J. and Mary Ann Maher.
Marital status: Single.
Family links with cricket: Brother kept wicket for school; father follows Derbyshire C.C.C. quite closely.
Education: Abbotsfield Comprehensive; Bishopsmalt Grammar; Harrow College; Loughborough University.
Qualifications: 10 O-levels, 3 A-levels, B.Sc. Hons in Economics and Accountancy. Nearly qualified accountant. N.C.A. coaching award 1982.
Jobs outside cricket: "While playing and coaching abroad 1982–83 and 1983–84 my contract entailed working as an accountant five mornings a week."
Overseas tours: With the Middlesex Cricket League touring team to Trinidad and Tobago, 1978; Amsterdam with Loughborough University 1981.
Cricketers particularly learned from: "Bob Taylor, John Hampshire, Phil Russell, the Derbyshire coach, Alan Knott, George Barton (Hillingdon C.C.) who taught me how to keep, Grayson Heath (Natal manager)."

LAST SEASON: BATTING

	I.	N.O.	R.	H.S.	AV.
TEST					
OTHER FIRST CLASS	18	6	150	46	12.50
INT					
JPL	5	1	37	14*	9.25
NAT.W	1	0	0	0	–
B & H	2	1	2	2	–

CAREER: BATTING

	I.	N.O.	R.	H.S.	AV.
TEST					
OTHER FIRST CLASS	55	16	501	66	12.85
INT					
JPL	15	3	70	14*	5.83
NAT.W	1	0	0	0	–
B & H	2	1	2	2	–

LAST SEASON: WICKET KEEPING

	C.	ST.			
TEST					
OTHER FIRST CLASS	19	2			
INT					
JPL	–	–			
NAT.W	–	–			
B & H	3	1			

CAREER: WICKET KEEPING

	C.	ST.			
TEST					
OTHER FIRST CLASS	68	7			
INT					
JPL	11	6			
NAT.W	–	–			
B & H	3	1			

Other sports: Tennis, squash, badminton, windsurfing, skiing, riding, rugby union.
Relaxations: Reading cricketers' autobiographies, golf, "not too well", hiking (especially around the Lake District and Snowdonia); listening to music.
Extras: Caught five catches in innings on debut v Gloucestershire 2nd XI. Cap in August 1982.
Best batting performance: 66 Derbyshire v Essex, Chesterfield 1984.

MAKINSON, D.J.   Lancashire

Full Name: David John Makinson.
Role: Right-hand bat, left-arm medium bowler.
Born: 12 January 1961, Eccleston, Lancashire.
Height: 6' 3'' **Weight:** 12st. 7lbs.
Nickname: Maki, Chimp.
County debut: 1984.
1st-Class 50s scored: 1.
Place in batting averages: 101 average: 31.00.
Place in bowling averages: 74 average: 33.72.
Parents: Thomas Andrew and Rhoda.
Wife and date of marriage: Susan, 9 April 1983.
Education: St. Mary's High School; Leyland Mts. Technical College; Bolton Institute of Technology.
Qualifications: 4 O-levels, O.N.C. in Mechanical Engineering, H.N.C. in Automobile Engineering. Qualified Engineering Technician.
Jobs outside cricket: Draughtsman (Leyland Trucks).
Overseas tours: New York 1985 with Lancashire.
Overseas teams played for: Maroochydore, Queensland, 1984–85.
Off-season 1985–86: Working in engineering.
Cricketers particularly learnt from: "Watching most top-class players."
Cricketers particularly admired: Ian Botham, Tony Greig, Clive Lloyd.
Other sports: Football, running and exercising, swimming. Watches most sports on television except horse-racing.
Relaxations: Sunbathing, watching television, listening to records, visiting the occasional pub.
Extras: "Went in to save hat-trick six times in 1985 season. Neal Redford came closest to getting me when I was dropped at 3rd slip."
Opinions on cricket: "English wickets should be prepared to encourage bowlers to try and bowl quicker (i.e. more pace and bounce). Too much cricket

is played; a reduction would mean more time for players to work out problems in nets. 4-day games would produce more results obtained on merit rather than manufactured by declarations."

Best batting performance: 58* Lancashire v Nottinghamshire, Trent Bridge 1985.

Best bowling performance: 5-60 Lancashire v Derbyshire, Old Trafford 1985.

LAST SEASON: BATTING

	I.	N.O.	R.	H.S.	AV.
TEST					
OTHER FIRST CLASS	21	9	372	58*	31.00
INT					
JPL	4	2	29	13	14.50
NAT.W	1	0	17	17	–
B & H	2	1	5	5	–

CAREER: BATTING

	I.	N.O.	R.	H.S.	AV.
TEST					
OTHER FIRST CLASS	26	11	390	58*	26.00
INT					
JPL	8	4	33	13	8.25
NAT.W	1	0	17	17	–
B & H	2	1	5	5	–

LAST SEASON: BOWLING

	O.	M.	R.	W.	AV.
TEST					
OTHER FIRST CLASS	366	68	1079	32	33.72
INT					
JPL	71.5	5	315	12	26.25
NAT.W	17	3	86	1	–
B & H	27	0	128	4	32.00

CAREER: BOWLING

	O.	M.	R.	W.	AV.
TEST					
OTHER FIRST CLASS	459	85	1392	39	35.69
INT					
JPL	148.1	6	661	28	23.60
NAT.W	17	3	86	1	–
B & H	27	0	128	4	32.00

MALCOLM, D.E.   Derbyshire

Full Name: Devon Eugene Malcolm.
Role: Right-hand bat, right-arm bowler.
Born: 22 February 1963, Kingston, Jamaica.
Height: 6′ 2″ **Weight:** 14st.
County debut: 1984.
Place in bowling averages: —
average: —; (1984: 122
average: 42.13).
1st-Class catches 1985: 0 (career: 4).
Parents: Albert Malcolm and Brendale Malcolm (deceased).
Marital status: Single.
Education: St. Elizabeth Technical High School; Richmond College.
Qualifications: College certificates.
Off-season 1985–86: Playing cricket in New Zealand.
Cricketers particularly admired: Michael Holding, Richard Hadlee.

Other sports: Football, table-tennis.
Relaxations: Reggae, funk and soul music.
Best batting performance: 23 Derbyshire v Nottinghamshire, Trent Bridge 1984.
Best bowling performance: 3-78 Derbyshire v Kent, Maidstone 1984.

LAST SEASON: BATTING

	I.	N.O.	R.	H.S.	AV.
TEST					
OTHER FIRST CLASS	1	0	0	0	–
INT					
JPL					
NAT.W					
B & H					

CAREER: BATTING

	I.	N.O.	R.	H.S.	AV.
TEST					
OTHER FIRST CLASS	9	1	40	23	5.00
INT					
JPL					
NAT.W					
B & H					

LAST SEASON: BOWLING

	O.	M.	R.	W.	AV.
TEST					
OTHER FIRST CLASS	17	2	82	3	27.33
INT					
JPL					
NAT.W					
B & H					

CAREER: BOWLING

	O.	M.	R.	W.	AV.
TEST					
OTHER FIRST CLASS	173.2	26	756	19	39.79
INT					
JPL					
NAT.W					
B & H					

MALLENDER, N.A. Northamptonshire

Full Name: Neil Alan Mallender.
Role: Right-hand bat; right-arm fast-medium bowler.
Born: 13 August 1961, Kirk Sandall, Nr. Doncaster.
Height: 6′ 0″ **Weight:** 13st.
Nickname: Ghostie.
County debut: 1980.
County cap: 1984.
50 wickets in a season: 2.
1st-Class 50s scored: 2.
1st-Class 5 w. in innings: 8.
1st-Class 10 w. in match: 1.
Place in batting averages: 175 average: 15.71; (1984: 268 average: 10.44).
Place in bowling averages: 59 average: 31.29; (1984: 83 average: 32.62).
1st-Class catches 1985: 6 (career: 28).
Parents: Ron and Jean Mallender.
Wife and date of marriage: Caroline, 1 October 1983.

Education: Beverley Grammar School, East Yorkshire.
Qualifications: 7 O-levels.
Family links with cricket: Brother, Graham, used to play good representative cricket before joining the R.A.F.
Off season 1985–86: Playing and coaching in New Zealand.
Cricket superstitions: Left boot on first.
Overseas tours: Young England tour to West Indies, 1980.
Overseas teams played for: Belmont D.C.C., N.S.W., 1980–81; Bathurst, N.S.W., 1982–83; Otago and Kaikorai C.C., New Zealand, 1983–84.
Cricketers particularly learnt from: Peter Willey, Warren Lees.
Other sports: Golf. Watching rugby league (especially Hull F.C.).
Relaxations: Playing golf. Modern music.
Best batting performance: 71* Northamptonshire v Oxford University, Oxford 1983.
Best bowling performance: 7-23 Otago v Auckland, Auckland 1984–85.

LAST SEASON: BATTING

	I.	N.O.	R.	H.S.	AV.
TEST					
OTHER FIRST CLASS	25	8	267	52*	15.71
INT					
JPL	4	3	20	12*	–
NAT.W	1	1	8	8*	–
B & H	–	–	–	–	–

CAREER: BATTING

	I.	N.O.	R.	H.S.	AV.
TEST					
OTHER FIRST CLASS	146	43	1380	88	13.40
INT					
JPL	27	13	146	22	10.42
NAT.W	7	3	39	11*	9.75
B & H	6	2	19	7	4.75

LAST SEASON: BOWLING

	O.	M.	R.	W.	AV.
TEST					
OTHER FIRST CLASS	521.4	98	1533	49	31.29
INT					
JPL	95	7	391	16	24.43
NAT.W	11	2	23	2	11.50
B & H	32	1	155	6	25.83

CAREER: BOWLING

	O.	M.	R.	W.	AV.
TEST					
OTHER FIRST CLASS	3066.2	675	9285	318	29.20
INT					
JPL	443	27	2112	84	25.14
NAT.W	152.4	26	428	25	17.12
B & H	158.2	18	589	19	31.00

104. Who was the youngest player to play Test cricket for Australia?

MALONE, S.J.   Glamorgan

Full Name: Steven John Malone.
Role: Right-hand bat, right-arm
fast-medium bowler, outfielder.
Born: 19 October 1953, Chelmsford.
Height: 6' 1" **Weight:** 12st.
Nickname: Piggy, Beaker.
County debut: 1975 (Essex), 1980
(Hampshire), 1985 (Glamorgan).
1st-Class 5 w. in innings: 3.
1st-Class 10 w. in match: 1.
Place in bowling averages: 128
average: 50.31; (1984: — average: —).
1st-Class catches 1985: 2 (career: 13).
Parents: John and Norma Malone.
Wife and date of marriage: Elizabeth,
14 March 1981.
Education: St Edmund's Preparatory
School, Ipswich; King's School, Ely.
Qualifications: H.N.C. building construction.
Jobs outside cricket: Salesman, interior designer and coach.
Off season 1985–86: Playing cricket in Pinetown, Natal, South Africa.
Overseas teams played for: Collegians in Durban, South Africa, 1981–82;
Pinetown, Natal, 1982–83, 1983–84, 1984–85, 1985–86. '
Cricketers particularly learnt from: John Lever, Malcolm Marshall.
Cricketers particularly admired: "John Lever for his non-stop trying."
Other sports: Plays football, squash, swimming, golf; follows football, golf,
tennis.
Injuries 1985: Heel injury.
Relaxations: Watching television, listening to music, reading.
Extras: Joined Essex staff for 1978 and 1979 seasons after having played a
number of 2nd XI games since 1974. Made 1st XI debut for Essex in 1975 v

LAST SEASON: BATTING

	I.	N.O.	R.	H.S.	AV.
TEST					
OTHER FIRST CLASS	6	1	2	2	0.40
INT					
JPL	–	–	–	–	–
NAT.W					
B & H					

CAREER: BATTING

	I.	N.O.	R.	H.S.	AV.
TEST					
OTHER FIRST CLASS	46	15	180	23	5.81
INT					
JPL	11	5	16	8*	2.66
NAT.W	3	3	11	7*	–
B & H	8	4	19	16	4.75

LAST SEASON: BOWLING

	O.	M.	R.	W.	AV.
TEST					
OTHER FIRST CLASS	174.1	23	654	13	50.31
INT					
JPL	4	0	32	0	–
NAT.W					
B & H					

CAREER: BOWLING

	O.	M.	R.	W.	AV.
TEST					
OTHER FIRST CLASS	1265.2	259	4236	118	35.90
INT					
JPL	316.5	15	1639	64	25.60
NAT.W	77.4	23	219	14	15.64
B & H	111	20	359	21	17.09

Cambridge University. Played also in 1978, again v Cambridge University. Released end of 1979 season and joined Hampshire for 1980 season. Equalled Derek Shackleton's record for Hants. by taking 10 wickets in a day v Oxford University, 13 May 1982. Released by Hampshire at end of 1984 season. Joined Glamorgan 1985; left staff at end of season.

Opinions on cricket: "Over-rate fines are too high, which makes captains bowl more spinners and encourages fast bowlers into the game."

Best batting performance: 23 Hampshire v Kent, Bournemouth 1981.

Best bowling performance: 7-55 Hampshire v Oxford University, Oxford 1982.

MARKS, V.J. Somerset

Full Name: Victor James Marks.
Role: Right-hand bat, off-break bowler.
Born: 25 June 1955, Middle Chinnock, Somerset.
Height: 5' 9" **Weight:** 11st. 8lbs.
Nickname: Vic.
County debut: 1975.
County cap: 1979.
Test debut: 1982.
No. of Tests: 6.
No. of One-Day Internationals: 33.
1000 runs in a season: 1.
50 wickets in a season: 5.
1st-Class 50s scored: 55.
1st-Class 100s scored: 4.
1st-Class 5 w. in innings: 28.
1st-Class 10 w. in match: 3.
One-day 50s: 9.
Place in batting averages: 106 average: 30.52; (1984: 14 average: 52.58).
Place in bowling averages: 73 average: 33.63; (1984: 35 average: 25.97).
1st-Class catches 1985: 8 (career: 103).
Parents: Harold and Joan Marks.
Wife and date of marriage: Anna, 9 September 1978.
Children: Amy, 27 November 1979.
Education: Blundell's School; Oxford University.
Qualifications: M.A. Classics.
Jobs outside cricket: Teaching — but not since March 1981.
Family links with cricket: "Father a dangerous village cricketer."
Cricketers particularly learnt from: Tom Cartwright, Arthur Milton.
Cricketers particularly admired: Colin Dredge.
Overseas tours: Derrick Robins' tour of Canada 1977; England in Australia and New Zealand 1982-83, New Zealand and Pakistan 1983-84, India and Australia 1984-85.

Overseas teams played for: Grade cricket with Bayswater Morley C.C. in Perth, Western Australia, 1981–82.

Other sports: Squash, golf.

Extras: Half-blue for rugby fives at Oxford University. Debut for Oxford University C.C. 1975, Blue 1975–76–77–78, Captain 1976–77. Somerset Vice-captain 1984. Author: *Somerset County Cricket Scrapbook* (1984); *Marks Out of XI* (1985).

Best batting performance: 134 Somerset v Worcestershire, Weston-super-Mare 1984.

Best bowling performance: 8-17 Somerset v Lancashire, Bath 1984.

LAST SEASON: BATTING

	I.	N.O.	R.	H.S.	AV.
TEST					
OTHER FIRST CLASS	34	5	885	82	30.52
INT					
JPL	11	2	188	39	20.88
NAT.W	2	0	30	26	15.00
B & H	3	0	36	29	12.00

CAREER: BATTING

	I.	N.O.	R.	H.S.	AV.
TEST	10	1	249	83	27.66
OTHER FIRST CLASS	350	55	8567	134	29.04
INT	24	3	285	44	13.57
JPL	87	23	1400	72	21.87
NAT.W	19	6	384	55	29.54
B & H	34	8	689	81*	26.50

LAST SEASON: BOWLING

	O.	M.	R.	W.	AV.
TEST					
OTHER FIRST CLASS	804.2	201	2421	72	33.63
INT					
JPL	83	5	330	10	33.00
NAT.W	27	5	82	4	20.50
B & H	32	5	113	1	–

CAREER: BOWLING

	O.	M.	R.	W.	AV.
TEST	180.2	54	484	11	44.00
OTHER FIRST CLASS	6672.1	1835	18410	566	32.53
INT	295.2	28	1077	44	24.48
JPL	585	39	2229	93	23.96
NAT.W	166.1	23	545	18	30.28
B & H	367.5	68	1061	37	28.68

105. Which county cricketer was born in South Africa of English parents and brought up partly in Australia and was qualified to play for all three countries?

MARPLES, C.   Derbyshire

Full Name: Christopher Marples.
Role: Right-hand bat, wicket-keeper.
Born: 3 August 1964, Chesterfield.
Height: 6′ 0″ **Weight:** 12st. 4lbs.
Nickname: Jed.
County debut: 1985.
Place in batting averages: 248
average: 11.40.
Parents: Terence John and Patricia
Ann.
Marital status: Single.
Family links with cricket: Father
played a good standard of local cricket.
Education: Tupton Hall
Comprehensive.
Qualifications: O-levels and C.S.E.s.,
City and Guilds Roadworks.
Jobs outside cricket: Plays
professional football for Chesterfield,
worked for Derbyshire County Council for four years.
Off-season 1985–86: Playing football.
Overseas tours: Chesterfield to Barbados, 1981.
Cricketers particularly learnt from: Bob Taylor.
Cricketers particularly admired: Bob Taylor and Alan Knott.
Other sports: Plays football; follows all sports.
Relaxations: Listening to music, Prince and T. Rex.
Extras: The first goalkeeper and wicket-keeper to play both sports at
professional level.
Best batting performance: 34 Derbyshire v Somerset, Derby 1985.

LAST SEASON: BATTING

	I.	N.O.	R.	H.S.	AV.
TEST					
OTHER FIRST CLASS	15	5	114	34	11.40
INT					
JPL	4	2	42	20*	21.00
NAT.W					
B & H					

CAREER: BATTING

	I.	N.O.	R.	H.S.	AV.
TEST					
OTHER FIRST CLASS	15	5	114	34	11.40
INT					
JPL	4	2	42	20*	21.00
NAT.W					
B & H					

LAST SEASON: WICKET KEEPING

	C.	ST.			
TEST					
OTHER FIRST CLASS	23	1			
INT					
JPL	7	–			
NAT.W					
B & H					

CAREER: WICKET KEEPING

	C.	ST.			
TEST					
OTHER FIRST CLASS	23	1			
INT					
JPL	7	–			
NAT.W					
B & H					

MARSH, S.A.   Kent

Full Name: Steven Andrew Marsh.
Role: Right-hand bat, wicket-keeper.
Born: 27 January 1961, Westminster.
Height: 5' 11" **Weight:** 11st. 9lbs.
Nickname: Marshy, Swampy.
Parents: Mel Graham and Valerie
Ann Marsh.
Marital status: "Single — but only
just."
Education: Walderslade Secondary
School for Boys; Mid-Kent College
of Higher and Further Education,
Maidstone.
Qualifications: 6 O-levels,
2 A-levels, O.N.D. in Business Studies.
Cricketing superstitions: "When
batting, getting into double figures."
Jobs outside cricket: Office clerk:
cricket coach.
Off-season 1985–86: Playing in Cape Town.
Family links with cricket: Father played local cricket for Lordswood.
Overseas tours: Barbados, 1979 with Lordswood C.C., Kent.
Cricketers particularly learnt from: "Alan Igglesden — I have learnt to keep to
leg-side bowling."
Cricketers particularly admired: Gary Sobers.
Other sports: Football, golf, snooker, horse-racing.
Relaxations: Watching T.V.
Extras: Won 2nd XI cap 1983.
Best batting performance: 48 Kent v Nottinghamshire, Folkestone 1984.

LAST SEASON: BATTING

	I.	N.O.	R.	H.S.	AV.
TEST					
OTHER FIRST CLASS	4	1	59	31*	19.67
INT					
JPL	1	0	2	2	–
NAT.W					
B & H					

CAREER: BATTING

	I.	N.O.	R.	H.S.	AV.
TEST					
OTHER FIRST CLASS	14	3	180	48*	16.36
INT					
JPL	2	1	3	2	–
NAT.W					
B & H					

LAST SEASON: WICKET KEEPING

	C.	ST.
TEST		
OTHER FIRST CLASS	9	3
INT		
JPL	2	–
NAT.W		
B & H		

CAREER: WICKET KEEPING

	C.	ST.
TEST		
OTHER FIRST CLASS	26	3
INT		
JPL	3	–
NAT.W		
B & H		

MARSHALL, M.D.   Hampshire

Full Name: Malcolm Denzil Marshall.
Role: Right-hand bat, right-arm fast bowler.
Born: 18 April 1958, Barbados.
Height: 5' 11'' **Weight:** 12st.
Nickname: Denz, Maco, Marshie.
County debut: 1979.
County cap: 1981.
Test debut: 1978–79.
No. of Tests: 40.
No. of One-Day Internationals: 60.
50 wickets in a season: 5.
1st-Class 50s scored: 20.
1st-Class 100s scored: 4.
1st-Class 5 w. in innings: 56.
1st-Class 10 w. in match: 10.
One-day 50s: 1.
Place in batting averages: 149 average: 24.77; (1984: 262 average: 11.44).
Place in bowling averages: 3 average: 17.68; (1984: 3 average: 16.15).
1st-Class catches 1985: 10 (career: 79).
Parents: Mrs Eleanor Inniss.
Marital status: Single.
Education: Parkinson Comprehensive School, Barbados.
Jobs outside cricket: Promoter of banks products.
Family links with cricket: Cousin plays for Texaco as a fast bowler.
Overseas tours: With West Indies to India and Sri Lanka 1978–79; Australia 1979–80, 1984–85; Pakistan 1980–81; India 1983–84; England 1980 and 1984; Zimbabwe 1981.
Overseas teams played for: Barbados debut 1977–78.

LAST SEASON: BATTING

	I.	N.O.	R.	H.S.	AV.
TEST					
OTHER FIRST CLASS	33	2	768	66*	24.77
INT					
JPL	6	0	63	33	10.50
NAT.W	3	1	32	29	16.00
B & H	3	0	37	25	12.33

CAREER: BATTING

	I.	N.O.	R.	H.S.	AV.
TEST	48	3	800	92	17.77
OTHER FIRST CLASS	205	25	4275	116*	23.75
INT	32	12	339	56*	16.95
JPL	42	11	549	46	17.70
NAT.W	10	6	96	29*	24.00
B & H	16	1	172	25	11.47

LAST SEASON: BOWLING

	O.	M.	R.	W.	AV.
TEST					
OTHER FIRST CLASS	688.1	193	1680	95	17.68
INT					
JPL	83.5	6	343	14	24.50
NAT.W	36	5	104	3	34.67
B & H	34	5	98	6	16.33

CAREER: BOWLING

	O.	M.	R.	W.	AV.
TEST	1478.2	313	4157	188	22.11
OTHER FIRST CLASS	4604.1	1351	11674	679	17.19
INT	542	60	1783	70	25.47
JPL	499.5	61	1667	73	22.83
NAT.W	149.4	28	392	14	28.00
B & H	195	41	534	29	18.41

Cricketers particularly learnt from: "The West Indies team."
Other sports: Tennis, basketball, darts, softball cricket.
Relaxations: Soul-music, reggae.
Extras: Took nine wickets in debut match v Glamorgan in May 1979. Scored his first first-class century (109) in Zimbabwe, October 1981, for the West Indies against Zimbabwe. Most wickets in the Shell Shield Competition (25) by a Barbadian. Broke record of number of wickets taken in 22 match season (i.e. since 1969) with 133.
Best batting performance: 116* Hampshire v Lancashire, Southampton 1982.
Best bowling performance: 8-71 West Indies v England, Leeds 1984.

MARTINDALE, D.J.R.   Nottinghamshire

Full Name: Duncan John Richardson Martindale.
Role: Right-hand bat, cover fielder.
Born: 13 December, 1963.
Height: 5′ 11½″ **Weight:** 12st.
Nickname: Bloers.
County debut: 1985.
1st-Class 50s scored: 1.
1st-Class 100s scored: 1.
Place in batting averages: 121 average: 28.81.
1st-Class catches 1985: 6 (career: 6).
Parents: Don and Isabel.
Marital status: Single.
Family links with cricket: Father and grandfather played club cricket in Nottingham; great uncle played for Nottinghamshire 2nd XI.
Education: Lymm Grammar School; Trent Polytechnic.
Qualifications: 9 O-levels, 2 A-levels, H.N.D. Business Studies, N.C.A. Coaching Award.
Off-season 1985–86: Three weeks in India; four months in Adelaide.
Cricketers particularly learnt from: Everybody at Trent Bridge.
Cricketers particularly admired: "Geoff Boycott, Viv Richards, Richard Hadlee, to name three of many."
Other sports: All sports, particularly long-distance running and squash.
Relaxations: Reading, listening to all types of music, watching T.V.
Extras: Scored century (104 n.o.) in fifth first-class innings.
Opinions on cricket: "Commercial involvement should be maintained and developed but should not interfere with the *nature* of the game. Too much cricket played — first-class cricket should be limited to 16 games, 4-day cricket.

County cricket clubs should liaise with schools so that there is a nationwide system of development of cricket education for children from 10-16 years."
Best batting performance: 104* Nottinghamshire v Lancashire, Old Trafford 1985.

LAST SEASON: BATTING

	I.	N.O.	R.	H.S.	AV.
TEST					
OTHER FIRST CLASS	14	3	317	104*	28.82
INT					
JPL	2	0	40	33	20.00
NAT.W	1	1	20	20*	–
B & H					

CAREER: BATTING

	I.	N.O.	R.	H.S.	AV.
TEST					
OTHER FIRST CLASS	14	3	317	104*	28.82
INT					
JPL	2	0	40	33	20.00
NAT.W	1	1	20	20*	–
B & H					

LAST SEASON: BOWLING

	O.	M.	R.	W.	AV.
TEST					
OTHER FIRST CLASS	2	0	8	0	–
INT					
JPL					
NAT.W					
B & H					

CAREER: BOWLING

	O.	M.	R.	W.	AV.
TEST					
OTHER FIRST CLASS	2	0	8	0	–
INT					
JPL					
NAT.W					
B & H					

MARU, R.G.   Hampshire

Full Name: Rajesh J. Govind Maru.
Role: Right-hand bat, slow left-arm bowler, close fielder.
Born: 28 October 1962, Nairobi.
Height: 5′ 6″ **Weight:** 10st. 7lbs.
Nickname: Raj.
County debut: 1980 (Middlesex), 1984 (Hampshire).
50 wickets in a season: 1.
1st-Class 50s scored: 1.
1st-Class 5 w. in innings: 2.
Place in batting averages: 169 average: 22.70; (1984: 239 average: 15.38).
Place in bowling averages: 25 average: 26.34; (1984: 100 average: 35.40).
1st-Class catches 1985: 15 (career: 51).
Parents: Jamnadass and Prabhavati Maru.
Family links with cricket: Brother has played for Middlesex 2nd XI.
Qualifications: Cricket coach.
Jobs outside cricket: Cricket coach.

Off-season 1985–86: Blenheim C.C. in New Zealand.
Cricketing superstitions: Nelsons. 111, 222 and 333.
Overseas tours: Young England tour of West Indies 1980; N.C.A. tour of Canada; Barbican International XI to Dubai; Middlesex to Zimbabwe 1980–81.
Cricketers particularly learnt from: Jack Robertson, Derek Underwood, David Graveney, Malcolm Marshall.
Other sports: Plays badminton, table-tennis, squash, swimming. Follows football and rugby union.
Relaxations: Music and wine bars.
Extras: Played for Middlesex 1980–83.
Best batting performance: 62 Hampshire v Sussex, Portsmouth 1985.
Best bowling performance: 7-79 Hampshire v Middlesex, Bournemouth 1984.

LAST SEASON: BATTING

	I.	N.O.	R.	H.S.	AV.
TEST					
OTHER FIRST CLASS	19	9	227	62	22.70
INT					
JPL	–	–	–	–	–
NAT.W					
B & H					

CAREER: BATTING

	I.	N.O.	R.	H.S.	AV.
TEST					
OTHER FIRST CLASS	55	16	620	62	15.90
INT					
JPL	1	1	3	3*	–
NAT.W					
B & H					

LAST SEASON: BOWLING

	O.	M.	R.	W.	AV.
TEST					
OTHER FIRST CLASS	704.5	197	1923	73	26.34
INT					
JPL	7	0	45	0	–
NAT.W					
B & H					

CAREER: BOWLING

	O.	M.	R.	W.	AV.
TEST					
OTHER FIRST CLASS	1533.3	407	4353	143	30.44
INT					
JPL	15	0	86	2	43.00
NAT.W					
B & H					

106. Which England batsman bats left-handed, bowls right, deals cards left, hammers a nail right and brushes his teeth with either hand?

107. When did Paul Downton make his first first-class century and against whom?

MAYNARD, C.   Lancashire

Full Name: Christopher Maynard.
Role: Right-hand bat, wicket-keeper,
occasional right-arm medium bowler.
Born: 8 April 1958, Haslemere,
Surrey.
Height: 5′ 11½″ **Weight:** 11st. 7lbs.
Nickname: Tosh.
County debut: 1978 (Warwickshire),
1982 (Lancashire).
1st-Class 50s scored: 7.
One-Day 50s: 1.
Place in batting averages: 241
average: 12.09; (1984: 157
average: 25.13).
Parents: John and Joan Maynard.
Marital status: Single.
Family links with cricket: Father
and brother, Steve, used to play for
Sutton Coldfield C.C. Now in South
Africa.

Education: Bishop Vesey's Grammar School, Sutton Coldfield.
Qualifications: 10 O-levels, 1 A-level.

LAST SEASON: BATTING

	I.	N.O.	R.	H.S.	AV.
TEST					
OTHER FIRST CLASS	27	5	266	43	12.09
INT					
JPL	6	2	53	19*	13.25
NAT.W	2	1	0	0*	–
B & H	3	1	64	41	32.00

CAREER: BATTING

	I.	N.O.	R.	H.S.	AV.
TEST					
OTHER FIRST CLASS	124	22	1879	85	18.42
INT					
JPL	51	10	616	46	15.02
NAT.W	6	2	22	16	5.50
B & H	14	5	216	60	24.00

LAST SEASON: BOWLING

	O.	M.	R.	W.	AV.
TEST					
OTHER FIRST CLASS					
INT					
JPL					
NAT.W					
B & H					

CAREER: BOWLING

	O.	M.	R.	W.	AV.
TEST					
OTHER FIRST CLASS	2	0	8	0	–
INT					
JPL					
NAT.W					
B & H					

LAST SEASON: WICKET KEEPING

	C.	ST.		
TEST				
OTHER FIRST CLASS	43	8		
INT				
JPL	4	2		
NAT.W	1	–		
B & H	3	–		

CAREER: WICKET KEEPING

	C.	ST.		
TEST				
OTHER FIRST CLASS	158	25		
INT				
JPL	55	9		
NAT.W	3	2		
B & H	23	1		

Jobs outside cricket: Has been salesman and has worked for jewellery firm.
Overseas tours: Australia with Derrick Robins' U-23 XI in 1979–80.
Overseas teams played for: West Rand, Johannesburg, 1981–82.
Other sports: Anything — mainly hockey in the winter.
Relaxations: Reading, taking it easy.
Extras: Was on Warwickshire staff for six years (only played 26 matches), making debut in 1979. Also played for Lancashire in 1982.
Best batting performance: 85 Warwickshire v Kent, Edgbaston 1979.

MAYNARD, M.P. Glamorgan

Full Name: Matthew Peter Maynard.
Role: Right-hand bat.
Born: Oldham, Lancashire.
Height: 5′ 11″ **Weight:** 12st.
Nickname: Walter.
County debut: 1984.
1st-Class 50s scored: 1.
1st-Class 100s scored: 1.
1st-Class catches 1985: 1 (career: 1).
Parents: Pat Maynard, Ken Maynard (deceased).
Marital status: Single.
Family links with cricket: Father pro'd for Duckinfield.
Education: Ysgol David Hughes, Anglesey.
Jobs outside cricket: "In the 3 million club!"
Off-season 1985–86: Labouring on brick site.

Cricketing superstitions: Putting equipment on in a certain order.
Overseas tours: Barbados with North Wales, 1982.
Cricketers particularly learnt from: Colin Page, Alan Jones, Bill Clutterbuck.
Cricketers particularly admired: Barry Richards, Richard Hadlee, Javed Miandad.
Other sports: Plays football, rugby, golf; follows rugby and American football.
Relaxations: Music, watching films.
Extras: Scored century on debut v Yorkshire at Swansea. Also youngest centurion for Glamorgan.
Best batting performance: 102 Glamorgan v Yorkshire, Swansea 1985.

LAST SEASON: BATTING

	I.	N.O.	R.	H.S.	AV.
TEST					
OTHER FIRST CLASS	3	0	198	102	66.00
INT					
JPL	3	0	31	18	10.33
NAT.W					
B & H					

CAREER: BATTING

	I.	N.O.	R.	H.S.	AV.
TEST					
OTHER FIRST CLASS	3	0	198	102	66.00
INT					
JPL	3	0	31	18	10.33
NAT.W					
B & H					

LAST SEASON: BOWLING

	O.	M.	R.	W.	AV.
TEST					
OTHER FIRST CLASS	0.1	0	4	0	–
INT					
JPL					
NAT.W					
B & H					

CAREER: BOWLING

	O.	M.	R.	W.	AV.
TEST					
OTHER FIRST CLASS	0.1	0	4	0	–
INT					
JPL					
NAT.W					
B & H					

McEWAN, K.S. Essex

Full Name: Kenneth Scott McEwan.
Role: Right-hand bat, off-break bowler and occasional wicket-keeper.
Born: 16 July 1952, Bedford, Cape Province, South Africa.
Height: 5′ 9″ **Weight:** 11st. 11lbs.
Nickname: Kenny.
County debut: 1974.
County cap: 1974.
Benefit: 1984.
1000 runs in a season: 12.
1st-Class 50s scored: 106.
1st-Class 100s scored: 59.
1st-Class 200s scored: 2.
One-day 50s: 46.
One-day 100s: 13.
Place in batting averages: 79 average: 34.03; (1984: 29 average: 46.18).
1st-Class catches 1985: 17 (career: 335).
Education: Queen's College, Queenstown, South Africa.
Overseas teams played for: Eastern Province and Western Province, South Africa; Western Australia.
Other sports: Tennis, rugby, golf and watches most sports.
Extras: Debut for Eastern Province in 1972–73 Currie Cup Competition. Played for T.N. Pearce's XI v West Indies at Scarborough in 1973. Was

originally recommended to Sussex C.C.C. by Tony Greig, who coached him at school. (i) Has played in team winning domestic competitions in three different countries — County Championships with Essex 1979, 1983 and 1984; Sheffield Shield with Western Australia 1980–81; Currie Cup with Western Province 1981–82; (ii) scored four consecutive centuries in 1977; (iii) has made century against every county; (iv) only wicket-keeper to score 100 in same John Player League game (v Worcester in 1980). Voted Players' Player of the Year 1983. Retired at end of 1985 season to go farming in South Africa.
Best batting performance: 218 Essex v Sussex, Chelmsford 1977.

LAST SEASON: BATTING

	I.	N.O.	R.	H.S.	AV.
TEST					
OTHER FIRST CLASS	42	4	1293	121	34.03
INT					
JPL	15	4	583	118	53.00
NAT.W	5	1	148	66	37.00
B & H	7	2	176	100*	35.20

CAREER: BATTING

	I.	N.O.	R.	H.S.	AV.
TEST					
OTHER FIRST CLASS	631	56	23135	218	40.24
INT					
JPL	178	19	5531	162*	34.78
NAT.W	27	3	842	119	35.08
B & H	60	6	1925	133	35.65

LAST SEASON: BOWLING

	O.	M.	R.	W.	AV.
TEST					
OTHER FIRST CLASS					
INT					
JPL					
NAT.W					
B & H					

CAREER: BOWLING

	O.	M.	R.	W.	AV.
TEST					
OTHER FIRST CLASS	39.4	3	281	3	93.67
INT					
JPL	2	0	7	0	–
NAT.W	1	0	5	0	–
B & H					

108. What is the connection between the Reverend Stirling Cookesley Voules and Ian Botham?

109. True or false? Ian Botham holds the record for the fastest century for Somerset.

110. Which batsman has scored the most first-class runs in one day in England and how many?

McEWAN, S.M.　　　Worcestershire

Full Name: Steven Michael McEwan.
Role: Right-hand bat, right-arm fast-medium bowler.
Born: 5 May 1962, Worcester.
Height: 6' 1" **Weight:** 12st. 6 lbs.
Nickname: Mac.
County debut: 1985.
Place in bowling averages: 102 average: 39.69.
1st-Class catches in 1985: 1 (career: 1).
Parents: Michael James and Valerie Jeanette McEwan.
Marital status: Single.
Family links with cricket: Father and uncle played club cricket.
Education: Worcester Royal Grammar School.
Education: 6 O-levels, 3 A-levels.
Qualifications: Technician's certificate in building.
Jobs outside cricket: Assistant buyer, Spicers (Builders) Ltd.
Off-season 1985–86: Playing cricket in New Zealand.
Cricketers particularly learnt from: Everyone at Worcestershire.
Cricketers particularly admired: Richard Hadlee, Malcolm Marshall.
Other sports: Plays soccer, skittles; follows American football, snooker and golf.
Relaxations: Watching movies, reading, music.
Extras: Took 10 wickets for 13 runs in an innings in 1983 for Worcester Nomads against Moreton-in-Marsh. Also broke school bowling record, 60

LAST SEASON: BATTING

	I.	N.O.	R.	H.S.	AV.
TEST					
OTHER FIRST CLASS	8	5	25	13*	8.33
INT					
JPL	1	0	0	0	–
NAT.W					
B & H					

CAREER: BATTING

	I.	N.O.	R.	H.S.	AV.
TEST					
OTHER FIRST CLASS	8	5	25	13*	8.33
INT					
JPL	1	0	0	0	–
NAT.W					
B & H					

LAST SEASON: BOWLING

	O.	M.	R.	W.	AV.
TEST					
OTHER FIRST CLASS	177	29	635	16	39.69
INT					
JPL	32	0	176	5	35.20
NAT.W					
B & H					

CAREER: BOWLING

	O.	M.	R.	W.	AV.
TEST					
OTHER FIRST CLASS	177	29	635	16	39.69
INT					
JPL	32	0	176	5	35.20
NAT.W					
B & H					

wickets, at W.R.G.S., 1982. During 1985, wages sponsored by Worcestershire Supporters' Association.

Best batting performance: 13* Worcestershire v Oxford University, Oxford 1985.

Best bowling performance: 3-47 Worcestershire v Leicestershire, Leicester 1985.

McFARLANE, L.L. Glamorgan

Full Name: Leslie Leopold McFarlane.
Role: Right-hand bat, right-arm fast-medium bowler.
Born: 19 August 1952, Jamaica.
Nickname: Les.
County debut: 1982 (Lancashire), 1985 (Glamorgan).
1st-Class 5 w. in innings: 1.
Place in bowling averages: 137 average: 63.00; (1984: 50 average: 28.22).
1st-Class catches 1985: 4 (career: 13).
Extras: Played in Northampton Town League. Made debut for Northamptonshire in 1979, but left at end of season. Played for Bedfordshire. Lancashire 1982–84. Left Glamorgan at end of 1985 season.

Best batting performance: 15* Lancashire v Northamptonshire, Southport 1984.

Best bowling performance: 6-59 Lancashire v Warwickshire, Southport 1982.

LAST SEASON: BATTING

	I.	N.O.	R.	H.S.	AV.
TEST					
OTHER FIRST CLASS	6	2	14	8	3.50
INT					
JPL	3	3	1	1*	–
NAT.W	1	1	1	1*	–
B & H					

CAREER: BATTING

	I.	N.O.	R.	H.S.	AV.
TEST					
OTHER FIRST CLASS	42	20	129	15*	5.86
INT					
JPL	10	5	17	6*	3.40
NAT.W	1	1	1	1*	–
B & H	–	–	–	–	–

LAST SEASON: BOWLING

	O.	M.	R.	W.	AV.
TEST					
OTHER FIRST CLASS	259	42	1008	16	63.00
INT					
JPL	23.3	2	111	4	27.75
NAT.W	33	5	120	2	60.00
B & H					

CAREER: BOWLING

	O.	M.	R.	W.	AV.
TEST					
OTHER FIRST CLASS	1153.2	203	4140	102	40.59
INT					
JPL	160.3	8	709	27	26.25
NAT.W	45	9	138	3	46.00
B & H	15	0	68	0	–

MEDLYCOTT, K.T.   Surrey

Full Name: Keith Thomas Medlycott.
Role: Right-hand bat, slow left-
arm bowler.
Born: 12 May 1965, Whitechapel,
London.
Height: 5′ 10″ **Weight:** 12st. 2lbs.
Nickname: Medders.
County debut: 1984.
1st-Class 100s scored: 1.
Parents: Thomas Alfred and June
Elizabeth.
Marital status: Single.
Education: Parmiters Grammar
School; Wandsworth Comprehensive.
Qualifications: 2 O-levels.
Cricketers particularly learnt from:
G.G. Arnold.
Other sports: Football.
Relaxations: "Sleeping!"
Extras: Scored 100 on debut (117 n.o.).
Best batting performance: 117* Surrey v Cambridge University, Banstead
1984.
Best bowling performance: 2-15 Surrey v Kent, The Oval 1984.

LAST SEASON: BATTING

	I.	N.O.	R.	H.S.	AV.
TEST					
OTHER FIRST CLASS	3	1	11	5	5.50
INT					
JPL	–	–	–	–	–
NAT.W					
B & H					

CAREER: BATTING

	I.	N.O.	R.	H.S.	AV.
TEST					
OTHER FIRST CLASS	9	6	139	117*	46.33
INT					
JPL	–	–	–	–	–
NAT.W					
B & H					

LAST SEASON: BOWLING

	O.	M.	R.	W.	AV.
TEST					
OTHER FIRST CLASS	24	12	39	1	–
INT					
JPL					
NAT.W					
B & H					

CAREER: BOWLING

	O.	M.	R.	W.	AV.
TEST					
OTHER FIRST CLASS	122	46	225	8	28.13
INT					
JPL					
B & H					

MENDIS, G.D.   Lancashire

Full Name: Gehan Dixon Mendis.
Role: Right-hand opening bat.
Born: 24 April 1955, Colombo, Sri
Lanka.
Height: 5' 8'' **Weight:** 10st. 7lbs.
Nickname: Mendo, Dick, Cho.
County debut: 1974.
County cap: 1980 (Sussex).
1000 runs in a season: 6.
1st-Class 50s scored: 54.
1st-Class 100s scored: 21.
1st-Class 200s scored: 2.
One-day 50s: 22.
One-day 100s: 6.
Place in batting averages: 23
average: 47.46; (1984: 90
average: 35.56).
1st-Class catches 1985: 8 (career: 91).
Parents: Sam Dixon Charles and
Sonia Marcelle Mendis.

Wife and date of marriage: Angela, 12 June 1976.
Children: Hayley, 11 December 1982.
Education: St Thomas College, Mount Lavinia, Sri Lanka; Brighton, Hove &
Sussex Grammar School; Bede College, Durham University.
Qualifications: B.Ed. Mathematics, Durham; N.C.A. coaching certificate.
Jobs outside cricket: Teacher at Rosemead School, Littlehampton, Sussex;
Richard Ellis, Perth, Western Australia.
Off-season 1985–86: In England seeking future career.
Overseas teams played for: Maharaja Organisation XI in Sri Lanka 1980–81;
Colombo C.C.: Sebastianites C.C., and Mount Lawley C.C., Western
Australia; Nedlands C.C., Perth.
Overseas tours: Maharaja Organisation XI to India 1980; Rohan Kanhai's
Invitation XI to Pakistan 1981; numerous international teams to West
Indies.
Cricketers particularly admired: Barry Richards.
Other sports: Played table-tennis for Sussex at junior level. "Follow most,
depending on what part of the world I'm in."
Relaxations: Music and wine bars.
Extras: Played for Sussex 2nd XI since 1971. Played Sussex Schools U-15.
Played in one John Player League match 1973. Played for T.C.C.B. XI in 1981.
Top of J.P.L. batting averages in 1981 for all counties. Plays in yellow helmet.
Has twice turned down invitations to play for Sri Lanka in order to be free to
be chosen for England. "Took my first 1st-Class wicket in 1985 — batsmen
beware!" Left Sussex at the end of the 1985 season and joined Lancashire.
Opinions on cricket: "Cricket authorities should look after players' interests
and well-being during the off-season."
Best batting performance: 209* Sussex v Somerset, Hove 1984.

LAST SEASON: BATTING

	I.	N.O.	R.	H.S.	AV.
TEST					
OTHER FIRST CLASS	43	6	1756	143*	47.46
INT					
JPL	14	2	360	78*	30.00
NAT.W	2	0	31	28	15.50
B & H	4	0	71	42	17.75

CAREER: BATTING

	I.	N.O.	R.	H.S.	AV.
TEST					
OTHER FIRST CLASS	363	33	11621	209*	35.22
INT					
JPL	109	12	2902	125*	29.91
NAT.W	22	2	755	141*	37.75
B & H	37	1	988	109	27.44

LAST SEASON: BOWLING

	O.	M.	R.	W.	AV.
TEST					
OTHER FIRST CLASS	4	0	65	1	–
INT					
JPL					
NAT.W					
B & H					

CAREER: BOWLING

	O.	M.	R.	W.	AV.
TEST					
OTHER FIRST CLASS	8.3	0	97	1	–
INT					
JPL					
NAT.W					
B & H					

METCALFE, A.A.   Yorkshire

Full Name: Ashley Anthony Metcalfe.
Role: Right-hand bat, off-break bowler.
Born: 25 December 1963, Horsforth, Leeds.
Height: 5′ 9″ **Weight:** 11st. 7lbs.
County debut: 1983.
1st-Class 50s scored: 3.
1st-Class 100s scored: 2.
One-day 50s: 1.
One-day 100s: 1.
Place in batting averages: 177 average: 21.42; (1984: 228 average: 16.62).
1st-Class catches 1985: 1 (career: 7).
Marital status: Single (engaged to Ray Illingworth's daughter, Diane).
Parents: Tony and Ann.
Family links with cricket: Father played in local league.
Education: Ladderbanks Middle School; Bradford Grammar School; University College, London.
Qualifications: 9 0-levels, 3 A-levels, coaching certificate 1983.
Jobs outside cricket: Worked for Grattan Mail Order Co., Paul Madeley's D.I.Y.
Off-season 1985–86: Club cricket in Melbourne.
Overseas tours: N.C.A. tour of Denmark 1981.

Cricketers particularly learnt from: Doug Padgett, Ray Illingworth, Don Wilson.
Cricketers particularly admired: Viv Richards, Alan Border, Len Hutton.
Other sports: Squash, rugby, golf. Follows most.
Relaxations: Watching films or T.V., music, holidays.
Extras: "I made 122 on my debut for Yorkshire against Nottinghamshire at Park Avenue in 1983. I was the youngest ever player to do so and it was the highest ever score on a debut."
Injuries 1985: Pulled ligaments in ankle, missed first six weeks of season.
Opinions on cricket: "Politics should not interfere with sport — South Africa should be eligible for Test Cricket."
Best batting performance: 122 Yorkshire v Nottinghamshire, Scarborough 1983.

LAST SEASON: BATTING

	I.	N.O.	R.	H.S.	AV.
TEST					
OTHER FIRST CLASS	12	0	257	109	21.42
INT					
JPL	8	0	91	28	11.37
NAT.W	1	0	33	33	–
B & H					

CAREER: BATTING

	I.	N.O.	R.	H.S.	AV.
TEST					
OTHER FIRST CLASS	27	0	602	122	22.30
INT					
JPL	19	1	448	115*	24.88
NAT.W	2	0	33	33	16.50
B & H					

LAST SEASON: BOWLING

	O.	M.	R.	W.	AV.
TEST					
OTHER FIRST CLASS	3	0	4	0	–
INT					
JPL					
NAT.W					
B & H					

CAREER: BOWLING

	O.	M.	R.	W.	AV.
TEST					
OTHER FIRST CLASS	5	0	10	0	–
INT					
JPL					
NAT.W					
B & H					

111. Who were the finalists in the 1985 Benson & Hedges Cup? And who won?

112. Which current English cricketer has the nickname Syd?

METSON, C.P.   Middlesex

Full Name: Colin Peter Metson.
Role: Right-hand bat, wicket-keeper.
Born: 2 July 1963, Cuffley, Hertfordshire.
Height: 5′ 7″ **Weight:** 10st. 8lbs.
Nickname: Dempster, Meto, Reggie.
County debut: 1981.
1st-Class 50s scored: 2.
Place in batting averages: —
average: —; (1984: 158
average: 25.00).
Parents: Denis Alwyn Metson and
Jean Mary.
Marital status: Single.
Family links with cricket: Father
played good club cricket and for
M.C.C.; brother plays club cricket.
Education: Stanborough School,
Welwyn Garden City; Enfield Grammar School; Durham University.
Qualifications: 10 O-levels, 5 A-levels, B.A. Hons Economic History, N.C.A.
Preliminary Coaching Award.
Jobs outside cricket: Trainee accounts clerk.
Off-season 1985–86: Working in London.
Cricketing superstitions: "Always put right pad on before left; try to use the same equipment right through the season if possible, especially wicketkeeping gloves."
Cricketers particularly learnt from: "Jack Robertson, Bob Taylor, my father."
Cricketers particularly admired: Bob Taylor, Rod Marsh, Mike Brearley, Wayne Daniel.

LAST SEASON: BATTING

	I.	N.O.	R.	H.S.	AV.
TEST					
OTHER FIRST CLASS	9	3	59	14*	9.83
INT					
JPL	4	2	27	14*	13.50
NAT.W					
B & H					

CAREER: BATTING

	I.	N.O.	R.	H.S.	AV.
TEST					
OTHER FIRST CLASS	27	9	397	96	22.06
INT					
JPL	7	4	49	15*	16.33
NAT.W					
B & H					

LAST SEASON: WICKET KEEPING

	C.	ST.			
TEST					
OTHER FIRST CLASS	18	–			
INT					
JPL	3	–			
NAT.W					
B & H					

CAREER: WICKET KEEPING

	C.	ST.			
TEST					
OTHER FIRST CLASS	47	2			
INT					
JPL	9	2			
NAT.W					
B & H					

Other sports: Football, hockey, tennis, squash, golf. Follows American football, football.
Injuries 1985: Mainly bruised fingers.
Relaxations: Computers, sleeping.
Extras: Young Wicketkeeper of the Year 1981; three Young England Tests v India 1981. Captain Durham University 1984, losing finalists in UAU competition. Beat Cambridge University twice. Middlesex 2nd XI Player of the Year 1984.
Opinions on cricket: "Look to play 4-day cricket as long as the pitches can be prepared to last . Play J.P.L. on Saturdays and have Sundays off. No fines for slow over-rates in cup competitions."
Best batting performance: 96 Middlesex v Gloucestershire, Lord's 1984.

MILLER, A.J.T. Middlesex

Full Name: Andrew John Trevor Miller.
Role: Left-hand opening bat.
Born: 30 May 1963, Chesham.
Height: 5′ 11″ **Weight:** 12st.
Nickname: Dusty, Wino.
County debut: 1983.
1000 runs in a season: 1.
1st-Class 50s scored: 10.
1st-Class 100s scored: 2.
One-day 50s: 2.
One-day 100s: 1.
Place in batting averages: 93 average: 31.63; (1984: 216 average: 18.07).
1st-Class catches 1985: 3 (career: 6).
Parents: John Innes and Sheila Mary Miller.
Marital status: Single.
Education: Belmont School; Haileybury; Oxford University.
Qualifications: 10 O-levels, 3 A-levels; B.A. Hons Biochemistry.
Jobs outside cricket: Clerk for travel agents between school and university.
Off season 1985–86: Playing in Australia.
Overseas tours: Australia with Oxford and Cambridge Combined Universities 1985.
Cricketing superstitions: "Always put left pad on first and like to use same kit twice if I've got a few first innings."
Cricketers particularly learnt from: Opening partners Richard Ellis (Oxford) and Graham Barlow (Middlesex).
Cricketers particularly admired: The majority of international players.

Other sports: Rugby, squash and golf.

Injuries 1985: Badly bruised thumb — unable to bat for three weeks.

Relaxations: "I love playing and watching rugby, playing squash, music, having a drink with team-mates and friends."

Extras: "First Oxonian since 1975 to score a century in the Varsity Match. First century by Combined Universities batsman in Benson and Hedges competition. Got maiden first-class wicket in maiden over (4th ball) — unlikely ever to bowl again! (I'm that bad)." Captain of Oxford University 1985. Scored 231 v Combined Services 1984.

Opinions on cricket: "1) First team county players are expected to play too much cricket — perhaps 4-day championship matches would be the answer. 2) Surely a fairer championship would ensue if counties played each other once and once only."

Best batting performance: 128* Oxford University v Cambridge University, Lord's 1984.

LAST SEASON: BATTING

	I.	N.O.	R.	H.S.	AV.
TEST					
OTHER FIRST CLASS	20	4	506	78	31.63
INT					
JPL					
NAT.W					
B & H	4	0	102	57	25.50

CAREER: BATTING

	I.	N.O.	R.	H.S.	AV.
TEST					
OTHER FIRST CLASS	63	8	1781	128*	32.38
INT					
JPL					
NAT.W	1	0	0	0	–
B & H	8	0	338	101	42.25

LAST SEASON: BOWLING

	O.	M.	R.	W.	AV.
TEST					
OTHER FIRST CLASS					
INT					
JPL					
NAT.W					
B & H	7	1	30	1	–

CAREER: BOWLING

	O.	M.	R.	W.	AV.
TEST					
OTHER FIRST CLASS	1	0	4	1	–
INT					
JPL					
NAT.W					
B & H	7	1	30	1	–

113. Which cricketer first said that his idea of heaven was to be batting against his own bowling?

MILLER, G.   Derbyshire

Full Name: Geoffrey Miller.
Role: Right-hand bat, off-break bowler.
Born: 8 September 1952, Chesterfield.
Height: 6′ 2″ **Weight:** 11st. 6lbs.
Nickname: Dusty.
County debut: 1973.
County cap: 1976.
Benefit: 1985.
Test debut: 1976.
No. of Tests: 34.
No. of One-Day Internationals: 25.
50 wickets in a season: 4.
1st-Class 50s scored: 45.
1st-Class 100s scored: 2.
1st-Class 5 w. in innings: 34.
1st-Class 10 w. in match: 6.
One-day 50s: 16.
Place in batting averages: 123 average: 28.62; (1984: 107 average: 32.17).
Place in bowling averages: 115 average: 43.00; (1984: 32 average: 25.70).
1st-Class catches 1985: 27 (career: 231).
Parents: Gwen and Keith Miller.
Wife: Carol.
Children: Helen Jane; Anna Louise; James Daniel.
Education: Chesterfield Grammar School.
Family links with cricket: Father played local cricket in Chesterfield. Brother plays for Chesterfield C.C.

LAST SEASON: BATTING

	I.	N.O.	R.	H.S.	AV.
TEST					
OTHER FIRST CLASS	31	5	744	105	28.62
INT					
JPL	7	0	99	38	14.14
NAT.W	1	0	0	0	–
B & H	3	1	34	26	17.00

LAST SEASON: BOWLING

	O.	M.	R.	W.	AV.
TEST					
OTHER FIRST CLASS	385.2	78	1204	28	43.00
INT					
JPL	32	0	164	4	41.00
NAT.W	9	4	15	0	–
B & H	27	5	54	5	10.80

CAREER: BATTING

	I.	N.O.	R.	H.S.	AV.
TEST	51	4	1213	98*	25.80
OTHER FIRST CLASS	391	68	9175	130	28.40
INT	18	2	136	46	8.50
JPL	127	25	2055	84	20.14
NAT.W	15	3	273	59*	22.75
B & H	44	8	892	88*	24.78

CAREER: BOWLING

	O.	M.	R.	W.	AV.
TEST	280.1 484.4	79 140	1859	60	30.98
OTHER FIRST CLASS	256.2 6570.3	48 1877	17645	679	25.99
INT	13 194	1 19	813	25	32.52
JPL	731.1	52	3119	112	27.84
NAT.W	182	45	477	16	29.81
B & H	426	84	1188	48	24.75

Overseas tours: With England Young Cricketers to India 1970–71 and West Indies 1972; toured with England to India, Sri Lanka, Australia 1976–77; Pakistan and New Zealand 1977–78, Australia 1978–79 and 1979–80 but had to return December 1979 through injury, West Indies 1981, Australia and New Zealand 1982–83.

Cricketers particularly learnt from: E.J. Barlow, R. Illingworth, F. Titmus.

Other sports: Golf, table-tennis, football.

Relaxations: Crosswords, reading, television, family life. Watching Chesterfield F.C. particularly, and all sports in general.

Extras: Became Captain of Derbyshire half-way through 1979 season, but relinquished it half-way though 1981 season in favour of Barry Wood. Declined to sign for Derbyshire for 1982 season, and was released. Negotiated with several other counties, but signed again.

Best batting performance: 130 Derbyshire v Lancashire, Old Trafford 1984.

Best bowling performance: 8-70 Derbyshire v Leicestershire, Coalville 1982.

MOIR, D.G. Derbyshire

Full Name: Dallas Gordon Moir.

Role: Right-hand bat, slow left-arm bowler.

Born: 13 April 1957, Imtarfa, Malta ("am Scottish however").

Height: 6′ 8″ **Weight:** 16st.

Nickname: "Usual nicknames for a Scotsman in England."

County debut: 1981.

50 wickets in a season: 2.

1st-Class 50s scored: 3.

1st-Class 100s scored: 1.

1st-Class 5 w. in innings: 9.

1st-Class 10 w. in match: 1.

One-day 50s: 1.

Place in batting averages: 189 average: 19.78; (1984: 168 average: 24.27).

Place in bowling averages: — average: —; (1984: 106 average: 37.22).

1st-Class catches 1985: 7 (career: 64).

Parents: Douglas Lennox and Anthea Gillian Moir.

Marital status: Single.

Family links with cricket: Father and brother play league cricket in Aberdeen.

Education: Aberdeen Grammar School; Aberdeen College of Commerce.

Jobs outside cricket: Computer operator.
Cricketing superstitions: Puts right pad on first.
Other sports: Rugby, basketball, golf.
Relaxations: Girl friend, music, crosswords.
Extras: Played for Scottish U-21 XI for five years (1974–78). Played for Scotland in their first year in Benson & Hedges Cup (1980). Played for Scotland in 1980 against Holland, Ireland, Worcestershire and West Indies. Top wicket taker for Derbyshire in 1982 with 76 wickets. Declined offer of new contract for "personal" (non-cricketing) reasons at end of 1982 season, but then changed mind and was a regular member of the side. Left staff after 1985 season.
Best batting performance: 107 Derbyshire v Warwickshire, Chesterfield 1984.
Best bowling performance: 6-60 Derbyshire v Nottinghamshire, Trent Bridge 1984.

LAST SEASON: BATTING

	I.	N.O.	R.	H.S.	AV.
TEST					
OTHER FIRST CLASS	9	0	178	46	19.78
INT					
JPL	4	0	26	13	6.50
NAT.W					
B & H	1	0	2	2	–

CAREER: BATTING

	I.	N.O.	R.	H.S.	AV.
TEST					
OTHER FIRST CLASS	86	11	1168	107	15.57
INT					
JPL	16	0	182	79	11.37
NAT.W	1	0	23	23	–
B & H	7	1	83	44	13.83

LAST SEASON: BOWLING

	O.	M.	R.	W.	AV.
TEST					
OTHER FIRST CLASS	186	48	517	12	43.08
INT					
JPL	22	0	88	0	–
NAT.W					
B & H	11	3	43	2	21.50

CAREER: BOWLING

	O.	M.	R.	W.	AV.
TEST					
OTHER FIRST CLASS	2379.5	626	6678	199	33.56
INT					
JPL	141	8	629	12	52.41
NAT.W	24	6	58	3	19.33
B & H	54	7	217	2	108.5

114. Before Ian Botham captured the record, which English bowler had taken the most wickets in Tests, and what was that record?

MONKHOUSE, G.   Surrey

Full Name: Graham Monkhouse.
Role: Right-hand bat, right-arm
medium bowler, slip fielder.
Born: 26 April 1955, Carlisle,
Cumbria.
Height: 6′ 1″ **Weight** 13st. 8lbs.
Nickname: Farmer.
County debut: 1981.
County cap: 1984.
50 wickets in a season: 1.
1st-Class 50s scored: 2.
1st-Class 100s scored: 1.
1st-Class 5 w. in innings: 2.
Place in batting averages: 80
average: 33.83; (1984: 213
average: 18.22).
Place in bowling averages: 29
average: 26.70; (1984: 30
average: 25.46).

1st-Class catches 1985: 8 (career: 29).
Parents: James Chris and Nancy Monkhouse.
Marital status: Single.
Family links with cricket: Father is chairman and ex-captain of Edenhall
C.C., Cumberland Senior League, Division I.
Education: Penrith Queen Elizabeth Grammar School; Nottinghamshire
College of Agriculture.
Qualifications: "Various O-levels, O.N.C. Business Studies, H.N.D. Agri-
culture." N.C.A. Advanced cricket coach.
Jobs outside cricket: Ex-professional footballer, representative for J. Bibby
Agriculture 1976, farm manager 1976–79.
Off-season 1985–86: Farming.
Cricketing habits: "Falling asleep when listening to 'Teddy' Thomas talking
cricket."
Overseas teams played for: Oostelikes C.C., South Africa, 1979–80, 1981–82;
Harlequins C.C. 1982–83.
Overseas Tours: McAlpine Tour to South Africa 1984; English Counties tour
to Zimbabwe 1985.
Cricketers particularly learnt from: Surrey Cricket Manager, M.J. Stewart,
Roy Miles.
Other sports: Played professional football with Workington A.F.C. 4th
Division. Other clubs: Carlisle United, Netherfield, Penrith A.F.C. Played
county junior tennis, badminton at U-16 level, and when allowed plays
football for Dennis Waterman "Showbiz XI" in charity games in and
around London. Plays club cricket for Wimbledon C.C. in the Surrey
Championship League when not required by Surrey.

Relaxations: Photography, reading.

Injuries 1985: Broken left arm in June while batting v Middlesex.

Extras: Youngest player to be capped by Cumberland in the Minor Counties; Surrey member of Cricketers' Association.

Opinions on cricket: 1) Cricketers and cricket teams should be allowed to play anywhere in the world of their choosing. 2) Four-day county championship; one-day cricket at weekends. 3)With football, continuing and deserving in many cases, to receive very bad press, the authorities in cricket must make every effort to promote and encourage new sponsors and sponsorship deals. The 1985 Test series and one-day finals have surely created new interest in cricket, as a vehicle for promoting companies' products.

Best batting performance: 100* Surrey v Kent, The Oval 1985.

Best bowling performance: 7-51 Surrey v Nottinghamshire, The Oval 1985.

LAST SEASON: BATTING

	I.	N.O.	R.	H.S.	AV.
TEST					
OTHER FIRST CLASS	14	8	203	47	33.83
INT					
JPL	3	0	10	5	3.33
NAT.W					
B & H	2	1	29	24*	–

CAREER: BATTING

	I.	N.O.	R.	H.S.	AV.
TEST					
OTHER FIRST CLASS	74	29	996	100*	22.13
INT					
JPL	23	11	151	37	12.58
NAT.W	3	0	15	8	5.00
B & H	8	4	55	24*	13.75

LAST SEASON: BOWLING

	O.	M.	R.	W.	AV.
TEST					
OTHER FIRST CLASS	383.4	78	1068	40	26.70
INT					
JPL	54.2	1	287	9	31.88
NAT.W					
B & H	35.2	1	150	6	25.00

CAREER: BOWLING

	O.	M.	R.	W.	AV.
TEST					
OTHER FIRST CLASS	1455.3	343	4093	159	25.74
INT					
JPL	333.2	18	1457	48	30.35
NAT.W	101.3	9	351	13	27.00
B & H	109.2	9	435	17	25.59

115. Who, when and where, was the batsman whose wicket gave Ian Botham the record number of Test victims?

Full Name: Steven Monkhouse.
Role: Right-hand bat, left-arm fast-medium bowler.
Born: 24 November 1962, Bury, Lancashire.
Height: 6′ 3″.
County debut: 1985.
Education: Derby Technical Grammar School; Peel College, Bury.
Extras: Plays for Ramsbottom in Lancashire League. Appeared for Lancashire 2nd XI 1984.
Best batting performance: 5 Warwickshire v Surrey, The Oval 1985.

LAST SEASON: BATTING

	I.	N.O.	R.	H.S.	AV.
TEST					
OTHER FIRST CLASS	2	1	7	5	–
INT					
JPL					
NAT.W					
B & H					

CAREER: BATTING

	I.	N.O.	R.	H.S.	AV.
TEST					
OTHER FIRST CLASS	2	1	7	5	–
INT					
JPL					
NAT.W					
B & H					

LAST SEASON: BOWLING

	O.	M.	R.	W.	AV.
TEST					
OTHER FIRST CLASS	17	2	61	1	–
INT					
JPL					
NAT.W					
B & H					

CAREER: BOWLING

	O.	M.	R.	W.	AV.
TEST					
OTHER FIRST CLASS	17	2	61	1	–
INT					
JPL					
NAT.W					
B & H					

116. Which former Labour M.P. and Minister wrote in his autobiography, published in 1985, "I would rather have scored a century against Australia at Lord's than anything else I have done in my life."?

MOORES, P. — Sussex

Full Name: Peter Moores.
Role: Right-hand bat, wicket-keeper.
Born: 18 December 1962,
Macclesfield, Cheshire.
Height: 6′ **Weight:** 12st. 4lbs.
Nickname: Action Man.
County debut: 1983 (Worcestershire),
1985 (Sussex).
Parents: Bernard and Winifred
Moores.
Marital status: Single.
Education: The King Edward VI
School, Macclesfield.
Qualifications: 7 O-levels, 3 A-levels,
Senior Coach.
Jobs outside cricket: Assistant
recreational supervisor.
Cricketing superstitions: Always
wear same hat when keeping.
Cricketers particularly learnt from: Basil D'Oliveira, Don Wilson.
Cricketers particularly admired: Alan Knott, Bob Taylor and Clive Lloyd.
Other sports: Football, squash, badminton, table-tennis, general fitness.
Watches football.
Relaxations: Listening to music, reading sporting autobiographies.
Extras: "Played for H.M.C. Schools, M.C.C. Schools, England Schools and for
the National Cricket Association of Young Cricketers. Joined Worcestershire
staff from the M.C.C. Young Pros staff which I joined at the beginning of the
1982 season." Released at end of 1984 by Worcestershire.
Best batting performance: 45 Worcestershire v Somerset, Weston 1984.

LAST SEASON: BATTING

	I.	N.O.	R.	H.S.	AV.
TEST					
OTHER FIRST CLASS	–	–	–	–	–
INT					
JPL	–	–	–	–	–
NAT.W	–	–	–	–	–
B & H					

CAREER: BATTING

	I.	N.O.	R.	H.S.	AV.
TEST					
OTHER FIRST CLASS	15	3	215	45	17.92
INT					
JPL	3	3	24	14*	–
NAT.W	–	–	–	–	–
B & H					

LAST SEASON: WICKET KEEPING

	C.	ST.		
TEST				
OTHER FIRST CLASS	1	–		
INT				
JPL	3	–		
NAT.W	1	–		
B & H				

CAREER: WICKET KEEPING

	C.	ST.		
TEST				
OTHER FIRST CLASS	19	6		
INT				
JPL	5	2		
NAT.W	1	–		
B & H				

MORRIS, H.   Glamorgan

Full Name: Hugh Morris.
Role: Left-hand bat, cover fielder.
Born: 5 October 1963, Cardiff.
Height: 5′ 8″ **Weight:** 12st. 4lbs.
Nickname:"H", Huge, Banacek.
County debut: 1981.
1st-class 50s scored: 7.
1st-Class 100s scored: 1.
One-day 50s: 4.
Place in batting averages: 38
average: 26.79; (1984: 88
average: 33.87).
1st-Class catches 1985: 4 (career: 14).
Parents: Roger and Anne Morris.
Marital status: Single.
Education: Blundell's School,
South Glamorgan Institute.
Qualifications: 9 O-levels, 3 A-levels,

1 AO level, B.A. Physical Education, N.C.A. Coaching Award.
Family links with cricket: Brother played for Wales U-16, and Glamorgan U-19.
Father played club cricket.
Off-season 1985–86: Playing with C.B.C. Old Boys, Pretoria.
Cricketing superstitions: "Getting off '0' and '111'. Put right pad on first."
Overseas tours: With English Public Schoolboy tour to West Indies, 1980–81;
to Sri Lanka 1982–83; to USA (Los Angeles) with Haverfordwest C.C.,
1984.
Cricketers particularly learnt from or admired: Javed Miandad, Alan Jones,
Tom Cartwright, Ian Botham, Kevin Lyons.
Other sports: Rugby, squash, tennis, golf, soccer, snooker.

LAST SEASON: BATTING

	I.	N.O.	R.	H.S.	AV.
TEST					
OTHER FIRST CLASS	18	4	375	62	26.79
INT					
JPL	7	1	224	91	37.33
NAT.W	3	0	117	75	39.00
B & H					

CAREER: BATTING

	I.	N.O.	R.	H.S.	AV.
TEST					
OTHER FIRST CLASS	60	14	1379	114*	29.98
INT					
JPL	14	2	367	91	30.58
NAT.W	3	0	117	75	39.00
B & H	1	0	10	10	–

LAST SEASON: BOWLING

	O.	M.	R.	W.	AV.
TEST					
OTHER FIRST CLASS	3	0	32	0	–
INT					
JPL					
NAT.W					
B & H					

CAREER: BOWLING

	O.	M.	R.	W.	AV.
TEST					
OTHER FIRST CLASS	15.5	1	100	1	–
INT					
JPL					
NAT.W					
B & H					

Relaxations: Watching rugby, listening to music, travelling and having a few drinks.

Extras: Highest schoolboy cricket average in 1979 of 89.71 and highest in 1981 of 184.6 and highest in 1982 of 149.2. Captain of England U-19 Schoolboys in 1981 and 1982. Played for Young England v Young West Indies 1982, and captained Young England v Australians. Won Gray-Nicholls "Most Promising Schoolboy" Award 1981, and Young Cricketer of 1982. Played first-class rugby for Aberavon 1984–85 and South Glamorgan Institute scoring over 150 points.

Best batting performance: 114* Glamorgan v Yorkshire, Cardiff 1984.

MORRIS, J.E. Derbyshire

Full Name: John Edward Morris.
Role: Right-hand bat,
right-arm medium bowler.
Born: 1 April 1964, Crewe, Cheshire.
Height: 5′ 10″ **Weight:** 11st. 8lbs.
Nickname: Animal.
County debut: 1982.
1st-Class 50s scored: 7.
1st-Class 100s scored: 4.
One-day 50s: 5.
One-day 100s: 1.
Place in batting averages: 125
average: 27.77; (1984: 78
average: 35.11).
1st-Class catches 1985: 5 (career: 13).
Parents: George (Eddie) and Jean
Morris.
Marital status: Single.
Education: Shavington Comprehensive
School; Dane Bank College of Further Education.
Qualifications: O-levels.
Jobs outside cricket: Worked as a carpet fitter.
Overseas tours: Umbilo C.C., Durban, S. Africa, 1982–83, 1983–84.
Family links with cricket: "Father played for Crewe C.C. for many years as an opening bowler."
Cricketers particularly learnt from: "Tony Borrington, Phil Russell and my father."
Other sports: Football, basketball, snooker. Watching athletics and motor-racing.
Injuries 1985: Pre-season knee operation.
Relaxations: Movies, music, good food.

Opinions on cricket: "There are too many overseas players qualifying to play for England. The rules should be tightened up."
Best batting performance: 135 Derbyshire v Leicestershire, Leicester 1984.

LAST SEASON: BATTING

	I.	N.O.	R.	H.S.	AV.
TEST					
OTHER FIRST CLASS	27	1	722	109*	27.77
INT					
JPL	12	2	214	52	21.40
NAT.W	1	0	12	12	–
B & H	4	0	18	9	4.50

CAREER: BATTING

	I.	N.O.	R.	H.S.	AV.
TEST					
OTHER FIRST CLASS	77	3	2049	135	27.69
INT					
JPL	32	3	762	104	26.27
NAT.W	3	0	27	12	9.00
B & H	7	0	98	51	14.00

LAST SEASON: BOWLING

	O.	M.	R.	W.	AV.
TEST					
OTHER FIRST CLASS	5.1	0	55	0	–
INT					
JPL					
NAT.W					
B & H					

CAREER: BOWLING

	O.	M.	R.	W.	AV.
TEST					
OTHER FIRST CLASS	18.1	2	128	1	–
INT					
JPL					
NAT.W					·
B & H					

MORTENSEN, O.H.   Derbyshire

Full Name: Ole Henrik Mortensen.
Role: Right-hand bat, right-arm fast-medium bowler.
Born: 29 January 1958, Vejle, Denmark.
Height: 6′ 4″ **Weight:** 14st. 2lbs.
Nickname: Stan (coined by Bob Taylor after England footballer Stan Mortensen), Blood Axe.
County debut: 1983.
50 wickets in a season: 1.
1st-Class 5 w. in innings: 4.
1st-Class 10 w. in match: 1.
Place in batting averages: —
average: —; (1984: 233 average: 15.75).
Place in bowling averages: 56 average: 31.09; (1984: 78 average: 31.67).
1st-Class catches 1985: 4 (career: 13).
Parents: Willy Ernst and Inge Wicka Mortensen.
Wife and date of marriage: Jette Jepmond.
Children: Julie Jepmond Mortensen, 30 August 1982.

Family links with cricket: "My small brother, Michael, used to play cricket. He is now a professional tennis player, and has played in Davis Cup for Denmark."

Education: Brondbyoster School; Avedore School.

Jobs outside cricket: Worked as a tax assistant in Denmark.

Off-season 1985–86: Playing and coaching Brighton C.C., Melbourne.

Overseas tours: Touring East Africa in 1976 with the Danish national side, and Scotland, Wales, Ireland and Holland.

Overseas teams played for: Ellerslie in Auckland, New Zealand, 1983–84 and Svanholm C.C., Denmark.

Cricketers particularly learnt from: Torben Jensen, Jorgen Janson, Peter Hargreaves and many others.

Cricketers particularly admired: Dennis Lillee, Bob Taylor.

Other sports: Tennis, golf, football.

Relaxations: Music, books, movies.

Injuries 1985: Problems with left knee.

Extras: *Derbyshire's Dane* by Peter Hargreaves, published 1984. Has played for Denmark.

Opinions on cricket: "Play 4-day matches with one day off every week. Overs reduced from 112 to 100 a day."

Best batting performance: 40* Derbyshire v Glamorgan, Derby 1984.

Best bowling performance: 6-27 Derbyshire v Yorkshire, Sheffield 1983.

LAST SEASON: BATTING

	I.	N.O.	R.	H.S.	AV.
TEST					
OTHER FIRST CLASS	15	7	39	16*	4.88
INT					
JPL	5	4	0	0*	–
NAT.W	1	1	4	4*	–
B & H	1	0	2	2	–

CAREER: BATTING

	I.	N.O.	R.	H.S.	AV.
TEST					
OTHER FIRST CLASS	46	26	178	40*	8.90
INT					
JPL	11	8	12	5	4.00
NAT.W	2	2	6	4*	–
B & H	1	0	2	2	–

LAST SEASON: BOWLING

	O.	M.	R.	W.	AV.
TEST					
OTHER FIRST CLASS	340	75	1026	33	31.09
INT					
JPL	95.5	10	387	14	27.64
NAT.W	10.4	2	37	1	–
B & H	30.2	1	99	5	19.80

CAREER: BOWLING

	O.	M.	R.	W.	AV.
TEST					
OTHER FIRST CLASS	1071	238	3201	117	27.36
INT					
JPL	226.4	19	929	38	24.44
NAT.W	34.4	9	103	5	20.60
B & H	41.2	3	129	8	16.13

117. Who captained the unofficial Australian tour to South Africa in 1985–86?

MORTON, W. Warwickshire

Full Name: William Morton.
Role: Left-hand bat, slow left-arm bowler, gully fielder.
Born: 21 April 1961, Stirling.
Height: 6' 2'' **Weight:** 13st. 5 lbs.
Nickname: Morts, Angus.
County debut: 1984.
Place in bowling averages: —
average: —; (1984: 112
average: 39.21).
1st-Class catches 1985: 3 (career: 9).
Parents: Donald and Jane Morton (both deceased).
Wife and date of marriage: Donna, 19 January 1985.
Family links with cricket: Brother, Donald, plays Scottish Counties cricket.
Education: Wallace High School.
Qualifications: 4 O-levels.
Jobs outside cricket: Gravedigger for six years before turning professional.
Off-season 1985–86: Sydney, Australia.
Cricketers particularly learnt from: Raymond Bond (Stirling Co. Coach), Dave Wilson (Scottish Coach) and the coaching staff at Edgbaston (N. Abberley and Alan Oakman) and Norman Gifford.
Cricketers particularly admired: Norman Gifford and Phil Edmonds.
Other sports: Follows Hearts in the Scottish Premier League.
Relaxations: Watching sport on T.V. and having a beer and a game of darts with team-mate Steve Wall.

LAST SEASON: BATTING

	I.	N.O.	R.	H.S.	AV.
TEST					
OTHER FIRST CLASS	1	0	3	3	–
INT.					
JPL					
NAT.W					
B & H					

CAREER: BATTING

	I.	N.O.	R.	H.S.	AV.
TEST					
OTHER FIRST CLASS	11	2	50	13*	5.55
INT					
JPL	1	0	10	10	–
NAT.W	1	1	11	11*	–
B & H	3	1	16	11*	8.00

LAST SEASON: BOWLING

	O.	M.	R.	W.	AV.
TEST					
OTHER FIRST CLASS	46	7	159	2	79.50
INT					
JPL					
NAT.W					
B & H					

CAREER: BOWLING

	O.	M.	R.	W.	AV.
TEST					
OTHER FIRST CLASS	302.5	75	924	25	36.96
INT					
JPL	4	0	25	0	–
NAT.W	12	1	47	4	11.75
B & H	33	10	90	6	15.00

Extras: "In first-class debut against Surrey, May 1984, I injured my back while batting and was out for six weeks."
Best batting performance: 13* Warwickshire v Surrey, Edgbaston 1984.
Best bowling performance: 4-40 Scotland v Ireland, Downpatrick 1984.

MOXON, M.D. Yorkshire

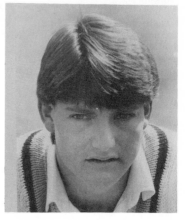

Full Name: Martin Douglas Moxon.
Role: Right-hand bat, right-arm medium bowler.
Born: 4 May 1960, Barnsley, Yorkshire.
Height: 6' 0" **Weight:** 13st. 7lbs.
Nickname: Froggy.
County debut: 1981.
County cap: 1984.
No. of One-Day Internationals: 5.
1000 runs in a season: 2.
1st-Class 50s scored: 22.
1st-Class 100s scored: 11.
One-day 50s: 11.
Place in batting averages: 39 average: 41.34; (1984: 74 average 36.57).
1st-Class catches 1985: 11 (career: 48).
Parents: Audrey and Derek Moxon.
Marital status: Single.
Education: Holgate Grammar School, Barnsley.
Qualifications: 8 O-levels, 3 A-levels, H.N.C. in Business Studies, N.C.A. Coaching Award.
Family links with cricket: Father and grandfather played local league cricket. Father was coach to Wombwell Cricket Lovers' Society.
Jobs outside cricket: Bank clerk with Barclays Bank for two years before turning full-time professional.
Cricketing superstitions: "When getting ready to bat I always follow the same routine."
Overseas tours: Captain of North of England U-19 Tour of Canada, 1979; with England to India and Australia 1984–85.
Overseas teams played for: Griqualand West in South Africa 1982–83 and 1983–84.
Injuries 1985: Finger injury — out one month.
Cricketers particularly learnt from: Doug Padgett, Ray Illingworth, Phil Carrick.
Cricketers particularly admired: Viv Richards.

288

Other sports: Plays football in the local league in the winter and "am a keen supporter of Barnsley F.C."

Relaxations: Watching Barnsley F.C., listening to most types of music, having a drink with friends.

Extras: Captained Yorkshire Schools U-15s and North of England U-15s. Played for Yorkshire Cricket Federation U-19s. Captained Yorkshire Senior Schools. Like Yorkshire colleagues, G. Stevenson and A. Sidebottom, he played for Wombwell Cricket Lovers' Society U-18 side which competes in the Joe Lumb U-18 Competition. Made the highest score by a player on his Yorkshire debut — 116 v Essex. First Yorkshire player to make centuries on his first two championship games in Yorkshire: 116 v Essex at Headingly; 111 v Derbyshire at Sheffield. Changed spectacles to contact lenses in 1981. Scored 153 in first "Roses" innings. Picked for Lord's Test of 1984 and West Indies, but had to withdraw through injury.

Best batting performance: 168 Yorkshire v Worcestershire, Worcester 1985.

Best bowling performance: 3-60 D.B. Close's XI v Sri Lankans, Scarborough 1984.

LAST SEASON: BATTING

	I.	N.O.	R.	H.S.	AV.
TEST					
OTHER FIRST CLASS	36	1	1447	168	41.34
INT					
JPL	10	1	322	86	35.77
NAT.W	1	1	82	82*	–
B & H	4	0	110	43	27.50

CAREER: BATTING

	I.	N.O.	R.	H.S.	AV.
TEST					
OTHER FIRST CLASS	136	5	4813	168	36.74
INT	5	0	132	70	26.40
JPL	30	4	767	86	29.50
NAT.W	5	2	177	82*	59.00
B & H	11	0	362	79	32.91

LAST SEASON: BOWLING

	O.	M.	R.	W.	AV.
TEST					
OTHER FIRST CLASS	40	5	166	5	33.20
INT					
JPL					
NAT.W					
B & H					

CAREER: BOWLING

	O.	M.	R.	W.	AV.
TEST					
OTHER FIRST CLASS	223	31	825	15	55.00
INT					
JPL	31	0	197	3	65.66
NAT.W	4	0	17	1	–
B & H	25	0	111	2	55.50

118. What is the name of the famous Australian cricket commentator who captained New South Wales, first commentated in 1934 and who made his 10th and final tour of England in 1985?

MUNTON, T.A.   Warwickshire

Full Name: Timothy Alan Munton.
Role: Right-hand bat, right-arm
fast-medium bowler.
Born: 30 July 1965, Melton
Mowbray.
Height: 6' 5''.
County debut: 1985.
Education: Sarson High School,
King Edward VII Upper School.
Extras: Appeared for Leicestershire
2nd XI 1982–84.

LAST SEASON: BATTING

	I.	N.O.	R.	H.S.	AV.
TEST					
OTHER FIRST CLASS	–	–	–	–	–
INT					
JPL					
NAT.W					
B & H					

CAREER: BATTING

	I.	N.O.	R.	H.S.	AV.
TEST					
OTHER FIRST CLASS	–	–	–	–	–
INT					
JPL					
NAT.W					
B & H					

LAST SEASON: BOWLING

	O.	M.	R.	W.	AV.
TEST					
OTHER FIRST CLASS	9	0	35	0	–
INT					
JPL					
NAT.W					
B & H					

CAREER: BOWLING

	O.	M.	R.	W.	AV.
TEST					
OTHER FIRST CLASS	9	0	35	0	–
INT					
JPL					
NAT.W					
B & H					

119. What former England Test all-rounder now runs a group
of cricket schools in Australia?

MURPHY, A.J.   Lancashire

Full Name: Anthony John Murphy
Role: Right-hand bat,
right-arm medium bowler.
Born: 6 August 1962, Manchester.
Height: 6' 0'' **Weight:** 13st.
Nickname: Audi, Ed.
County debut: 1985.
Parents: John Desmond and
Elizabeth Catherine.
Marital status: Single.
Education: Xaverian College,
Manchester; Swansea University.
Qualifications: 9 O-levels, 4 A-levels.
Jobs outside cricket: Computer
operator for Barclays Bank.
Off-season 1985–86: Playing in Perth.
Cricketers particularly learnt from:
"Anyone who has anything relevant
to say about my game."

Cricketers particularly admired: Michael Holding, Clive Lloyd.
Other sports: Plays hockey, volleyball, football, squash. Follows Manchester
City F.C. and Miami Dolphins.
Relaxations: "Music and a quiet pint with friends at my local."
Best batting performance: 2* Lancashire v Leicestershire, Leicester 1985.
Best bowling performance: 3-84 Lancashire v Worcestershire, Worcester
1985.

LAST SEASON: BATTING

	I.	N.O.	R.	H.S.	AV.
TEST					
OTHER FIRST CLASS	3	1	3	2*	1.50
INT					
JPL					
NAT.W					
B & H					

CAREER: BATTING

	I.	N.O.	R.	H.S.	AV.
TEST					
OTHER FIRST CLASS	3	1	3	2*	1.50
INT					
JPL					
NAT.W					
B & H					

LAST SEASON: BOWLING

	O.	M.	R.	W.	AV.
TEST					
OTHER FIRST CLASS	56.5	15	207	6	34.50
INT					
JPL					
NAT.W					
B & H					

CAREER: BOWLING

	O.	M.	R.	W.	AV.
TEST					
OTHER FIRST CLASS	56.5	15	207	6	34.50
INT					
JPL					
NAT.W					
B & H					

NEALE, P.A.
Worcestershire

Full Name: Phillip Anthony Neale.
Role: Right-hand bat, right-arm medium bowler.
Born: 5 June 1954, Scunthorpe.
Height: 5' 11" **Weight:** 11st.
Nickname: Phil.
County debut: 1975.
County cap: 1978.
1000 runs in a season: 7.
1st-Class 50s scored: 63.
1st-Class 100s scored: 19.
One-day 50s: 21.
One-day 100s: 2.
Place in batting averages: 32
average: 44.09; (1984: 26
average: 47.39).
1st-Class catches 1985: 5 (career: 85).
Parents: Geoff and Elsie Neale.
Wife and date of marriage: Christine, 26 September 1976.
Children: Kelly Joanne, 9 November 1979; Craig Andrew, 11 February 1982.
Education: Frederick Gough Grammar School, Scunthorpe; John Leggot Sixth Form College, Scunthorpe; Leeds University.
Qualifications: 10 O-levels, 2 A-levels, B.A. Hons. Russian. Preliminary football and cricket coaching awards.
Off-season 1985–86: Playing and coaching in New Zealand.
Cricketing superstitions: Always puts left pad on first.
Cricketers particularly learnt from: "All the senior players at Worcester."

LAST SEASON: BATTING

	I.	N.O.	R.	H.S.	AV.
TEST					
OTHER FIRST CLASS	42	10	1411	152*	44.09
INT					
JPL	13	1	275	83	22.91
NAT.W	4	0	178	81	44.50
B & H	5	2	205	94*	68.33

CAREER: BATTING

	I.	N.O.	R.	H.S.	AV.
TEST					
OTHER FIRST CLASS	383	51	11925	183*	35.92
INT					
JPL	133	26	3193	102	29.84
NAT.W	16	0	481	81	30.06
B & H	38	6	1002	128	31.31

LAST SEASON: BOWLING

	O.	M.	R.	W.	AV.
TEST					
OTHER FIRST CLASS					
INT					
JPL					
NAT.W					
B & H					

CAREER: BOWLING

	O.	M.	R.	W.	AV.
TEST					
OTHER FIRST CLASS	42.4	3	201	1	–
INT					
JPL	8.2	0	50	2	25.00
NAT.W					
B & H					

Other sports: Football; enjoys watching all sports and occasionally plays pool, snooker and squash.

Relaxations: Reading, watching television, "playing with my children".

Extras: Played for Lincolnshire 1973–74. Scored 100 runs before lunch v Warwickshire at Worcester, 1979. Captain 1983–. Testimonial season with Lincoln City 1984–85. Now retired from football.

Best batting performance: 183* Worcestershire v Nottinghamshire. Worcester 1977.

NEEDHAM, A. Surrey

Full Name: Andrew Needham.
Role: Right-hand bat, off-break bowler.
Born: 23 March 1957, Calow, Derbyshire.
Height: 5' 10'' **Weight:** 10st. 8lbs.
Nickname: Needers.
County debut: 1977.
1000 runs in a season: 1.
1st-Class 50s scored: 9.
1st-Class 100s scored: 4.
1st-Class 5 w. in innings: 5.
One-day 50s: 3.
Place in batting averages: 55 average: 37.63; (1984: 184 average: 22.21).
Place in bowling averages: 119 average: 44.22; (1984: 102 average: 36.10).
1st-Class catches 1985: 13 (career: 37).
Marital status: Single.
Family links with cricket: Father played in Bassetlaw League.
Education: Ecclesbourne Grammar School, Derbyshire; Paisley Grammar School, Scotland; Watford Grammar School.
Qualifications: 6 O-levels.
Cricketing superstitions: Always puts left pad on first.
Overseas tours: With M.C.C. to Bangladesh 1980–81; with Surrey C.C.C. to Hong Kong, Singapore and Bangkok 1980; with Surrey Y.C. to Antigua.
Cricketers particularly learnt from: Fred Titmus.
Other sports: Watches Chesterfield (football).
Relaxations: "Losing money on horses and cards."
Best batting performance: 138* Surrey v Warwickshire, The Oval 1985.
Best bowling performance: 6-30 Surrey v Oxford University, Oxford 1983.

LAST SEASON: BATTING

	I.	N.O.	R.	H.S.	AV.
TEST					
OTHER FIRST CLASS	37	5	1223	138	38.21
INT					
JPL	9	2	216	52*	30.85
NAT.W	1	0	26	26	–
B & H	1	1	8	8*	–

LAST SEASON: BOWLING

	O.	M.	R.	W.	AV.
TEST					
OTHER FIRST CLASS	351.4	76	1017	23	44.22
INT					
JPL	11	0	104	2	52.00
NAT.W	11	0	55	2	27.50
B & H					

CAREER: BATTING

	I.	N.O.	R.	H.S.	AV.
TEST					
OTHER FIRST CLASS	115	15	2364	138	23.64
INT					
JPL	32	7	483	55	19.32
NAT.W	1	0	26	26	–
B & H	5	1	98	30	24.50

CAREER: BOWLING

	O.	M.	R.	W.	AV.
TEST					
OTHER FIRST CLASS	1388.3	335	4202	103	40.80
INT					
JPL	75.3	4	429	11	39.00
NAT.W	11	0	55	2	27.50
B & H	9	0	40	0	–

NEWELL, M.   Nottinghamshire

Full Name: Michael Newell.
Role: Right-hand opening bat, occasional wicket-keeper.
Born: 25 February 1965, Blackburn.
Height: 5' 8" **Weight:** 11st. 3lbs.
Nickname: Sam, Judas, Mule or Dot.
County debut: 1984.
1st-Class 50s scored: 4.
Place in batting averages: 160 average: 23.77.
1st-Class catches 1985: 4 (career: 10).
Parents: Barry and Janet Newell.
Marital status: Single.
Family links with cricket: "Father chairman of local club for which my brother Paul plays."
Education: West Bridgford Comprehensive.
Qualifications: 8 O-levels, 3 A-levels. Qualified coach.
Jobs outside cricket: Part-time barman; has worked in childrens' home; packer at Gunn and Moore.
Off-season 1985–86: Playing for Nedland C.C. in Perth.
Cricketing superstitions: Always puts right pad on first; always bats in short sweater and long-sleeved shirt.
Overseas tours: N.C.A. U-19 tour to Holland 1983.
Cricketers particularly learnt from: All the batsmen at Nottinghamshire, Mike Bore and Bob White.

Cricketers particularly admired: Richard Hadlee and Graham Gooch.
Other sports: Football ("of a low standard"); watches rugby union and football.
Relaxations: Good films, music and drinking.
Opinions on cricket: "2nd XI championship needs to be organised better so that every county plays every other county once. This would be fairer than the present system of averages."
Best batting performance: 76 Nottinghamshire v Cambridge University, Trent Bridge 1984.

LAST SEASON: BATTING

	I.	N.O.	R.	H.S.	AV.
TEST					
OTHER FIRST CLASS	13	0	309	74	23.77
INT					
JPL					
NAT.W					
B & H					

CAREER: BATTING

	I.	N.O.	R.	H.S.	AV.
TEST					
OTHER FIRST CLASS	20	1	418	76	22.00
INT					
JPL					
NAT.W					
B & H					

LAST SEASON: BOWLING

	O.	M.	R.	W.	AV.
TEST					
OTHER FIRST CLASS	12	2	62	1	–
INT					
JPL					
NAT.W					
B & H					

CAREER: BOWLING

	O.	M.	R.	W.	AV.
TEST					
OTHER FIRST CLASS	16	2	76	1	–
INT					
JPL					
NAT.W					
B & H					

120. Which famous British author who created perhaps the most widely known fictional character in the last 100 years, played for the M.C.C., scored a century in his first match at Lord's, and once clean bowled W.G. Grace?

NEWMAN, P.G.   Derbyshire

Full Name: Paul Geoffrey Newman.
Role: Right-hand bat, right-arm
fast-medium bowler.
Born: 10 January 1959,
Leicester.
Height: 6′ 2½″ **Weight:** 13st. 7lbs.
Nickname: Judge.
County debut: 1980.
50 wickets in a season: 1.
1st-Class 50s scored: 3.
1st-Class 100s scored: 1.
1st-Class 5 w. in innings: 2.
One-day 50s: 1.
Place in batting averages: 163
average: 23.23; (1984: 251
average: 14.16).
Place in bowling averages: 60
average: 31.31; (1984: 96
average: 34.34).

1st-Class catches 1985: 2 (career: 18).
Marital status: Single.
Education: Alderman Newton's Grammar School, Leicester.
Qualifications: 6 O-levels.
Jobs outside cricket: Various temporary jobs.
Off-season 1985–86: Pietermaritzburg, South Africa.
Overseas tours: English Counties XI to Zimbabwe 1985.
Overseas teams played for: Queensland Cricket Assn. Colts XI, 1981–82; Old
Collegians and Pietermaritzburg, South Africa, 1983–84.
Other sports: Golf, football, snooker, pool.

LAST SEASON: BATTING

	I.	N.O.	R.	H.S.	AV.
TEST					
OTHER FIRST CLASS	29	3	604	115	23.23
INT					
JPL	10	3	114	46	16.28
NAT.W	1	0	19	19	–
B & H	4	1	76	56*	25.33

CAREER: BATTING

	I.	N.O.	R.	H.S.	AV.
TEST					
OTHER FIRST CLASS	98	16	1253	115	15.28
INT					
JPL	27	7	230	46	11.50
NAT.W	4	1	69	35	23.00
B & H	11	6	138	56*	27.60

LAST SEASON: BOWLING

	O.	M.	R.	W.	AV.
TEST					
OTHER FIRST CLASS	400	79	1315	42	31.31
INT					
JPL	84.4	5	403	9	44.77
NAT.W	12	1	25	0	–
B & H	21	4	82	1	–

CAREER: BOWLING

	O.	M.	R.	W.	AV.
TEST					
OTHER FIRST CLASS	1879.5	335	6481	196	33.07
INT					
JPL	378	22	1662	60	27.70
NAT.W	75.4	7	245	8	30.63
B & H	150.5	21	592	20	29.60

Relaxations: Crosswords, Barry Manilow's music, T.V., watching Leicester F.C., keeping up scrapbooks and eating.

Cricketing superstitions: Always wears wrist bands to bowl. Puts left pad on first.

Extras: Played for Leicestershire 2nd XI in 1978 and 1979, but was released. As a schoolboy, was a wicket-keeper. Took 50 wickets in his first season with Derbyshire. Won Commercial Union U-23 Bowling Award for 1981. Won Whitbread Scholarship to Brisbane, Australia 1981–82.

Best batting performance: 115 Derbyshire v Leicestershire, Chesterfield 1985.

Best bowling performance: 7-104 Derbyshire v Surrey, The Oval 1984.

NEWPORT, P.J.   Worcestershire

Full Name: Philip John Newport.
Role: Right-hand bat, right-arm fast-medium bowler.
Born: 11 October 1962, High Wycombe.
Height: 6' 2" **Weight:** 13st. 7lbs.
Nickname: Newps, Pagnell.
County debut: 1982.
1st-Class 5 w. in innings: 1.
Place in batting averages: 179 average: 21.13; (1984: 114 average: 31.17).
Place in bowling averages: 26 average: 26.39; (1984: 84 average: 32.81).
1st-Class catches 1985: 2 (career: 5).
Parents: John and Sheila Diana.
Marital status: Single.
Education: Royal Grammar School, High Wycombe; Portsmouth Polytechnic.
Qualifications: 8 O-levels, 3 A-levels, B.A.(Hons) Geography, basic coaching qualification.
Jobs outside cricket: Schoolmaster.
Off-season 1985–86: Teaching at Worcester R.G.S.
Superstitions: "Always put a 10p. in left pocket when batting."
Family links with cricket: "Father is a good club cricketer, my younger brother Stewart plays with High Wycombe C.C."
Overseas tours: With N.C.A. to Denmark 1981.
Cricketers particularly learnt from: "I have been helped by numerous people rather than one specific individual."
Other sports: Plays soccer, badminton, rugby union, and fan of American football, especially Chicago Bears.

Relaxations: Listening to music, reading, Trivial Pursuits, backgammon.
Injuries 1985: Lower pelvic injury.
Extras: Had trial as schoolboy for Southampton F.C. Played cricket for N.A.Y.C. England Schoolboys 1981. Also for Buckinghamshire in Minor Counties in 1981, Minor Counties final 1982. Wears contact lens in left eye only.
Opinions on cricket: "J.P.L. cricket can only be described as detrimental to a cricketer's development into a better player. It encourages negative bowling and unnecessary unorthodoxy in batting."
Best batting performance: 41* Worcestershire v Warwickshire, Edgbaston 1983.
Best bowling performance: 5-18 Worcestershire v Gloucestershire, Gloucester 1985.

LAST SEASON: BATTING

	I.	N.O.	R.	H.S.	AV.
TEST					
OTHER FIRST CLASS	26	10	338	36	21.13
INT					
JPL	3	3	30	18*	–
NAT.W	1	1	4	4*	–
B & H					

CAREER: BATTING

	I.	N.O.	R.	H.S.	AV.
TEST					
OTHER FIRST CLASS	46	17	635	41*	21.90
INT					
JPL	8	4	82	24	20.50
NAT.W	2	1	29	25	–
B & H					

LAST SEASON: BOWLING

	O.	M.	R.	W.	AV.
TEST					
OTHER FIRST CLASS	362.2	57	1214	46	26.39
INT					
JPL	50	0	295	5	59.00
NAT.W	21.2	2	86	1	–
B & H					

CAREER: BOWLING

	O.	M.	R.	W.	AV.
TEST					
OTHER FIRST CLASS	655	97	2259	76	29.72
INT					
JPL	93	1	436	14	31.14
NAT.W	27.2	2	113	1	–
B & H					

121. Hampshire's 60-year-old record for an 8th wicket stand of 178 was broken in their game against Somerset in May 1984. Which two batsmen created the new record and what is it?

NICHOLAS, M.C.J.   Hampshire

Full Name: Mark Charles Jefford
Nicholas.
Role: Right-hand bat, right-arm
fast-medium bowler.
Born: 29 September 1957, London.
Height: 5′ 11½″ **Weight:** 12st. 7lbs.
Nickname: Albert, Busby, M.C.J.
County debut: 1978.
County cap: 1982.
1000 runs in a season: 4.
1st-Class 50s scored: 34.
1st-Class 100s scored: 15.
1st-Class 200s scored: 1.
1st-Class 5 w. in innings: 1.
One-day 50s: 12.
One-day 100s: 1.
Place in batting averages: 50

average: 39.42; (1984: 87
average: 33.89).
1st-Class catches 1985: 20 (career: 98).
Parents: Anne Nicholas.
Marital status: Single.
Education: Fernden Prep. School; Bradfield College.
Qualifications: 8 O-levels, 3 A-levels.
Jobs outside cricket: Worked in Classified Advertising for the *Observer*; sales
for agencies; writing for papers and magazines; P.R.; publishing.
Family links with cricket: Grandfather played for Essex as batsman and
wicket-keeper and toured with M.C.C.
Overseas tours: Toured South Africa with Dragons (Public Schools team)
1976–77 as Captain; with M.C.C. to Bangladesh February 1981; and to East
and Central Africa October 1981; Dubai with *Cricketer* International XI,
November 1981; Dubai and Bahrain with "England XI", March 1981.
Overseas teams played for: Captain of Southern Lakes in Australia 1978–79
and Grosvenor/Fynnland, Durban, 1982–83, 1983–84.
Cricketing superstitions: "Kit and clothing must fit."
Cricketers particularly learnt from: Barry Richards, Mike Brearley, Graham
Gooch.
Off-season 1985–86: Captain England B tour to Bangladesh, Sri Lanka and
Zimbabwe. Also travelling around America.
Other sports: Regular football with Old Bradfieldians (Arthurian League).
Relaxations: Bruce Springsteen concerts.
Injuries 1985: Missed one game with broken finger.
Extras: Scored 155 n.o. before lunch in 2nd XI match v Hampshire Cricket
League at the start of the 1980 season. Appointed captain 1984.
Opinions on cricket: "Our problems are self-inflicted. Banning of 'rebels', 40-

overs cricket ruins technique. We play too much, so too mediocre."
Best batting performance: 206* Hampshire v Oxford University, Oxford 1982.
Best bowling performance: 5-45 Hampshire v Worcestershire, Southampton 1983.

LAST SEASON: BATTING

	I.	N.O.	R.	H.S.	AV.
TEST					
OTHER FIRST CLASS	41	5	1419	146	39.42
INT					
JPL	10	2	214	61*	26.75
NAT.W	4	0	65	39	16.25
B & H	5	0	184	74	36.80

CAREER: BATTING

	I.	N.O.	R.	H.S.	AV.
TEST					
OTHER FIRST CLASS	253	30	7561	206*	33.91
INT					
JPL	71	10	1632	108	26.75
NAT.W	17	1	345	63	21.56
B & H	24	1	533	74	23.17

LAST SEASON: BOWLING

	O.	M.	R.	W.	AV.
TEST					
OTHER FIRST CLASS	129	25	464	8	58.00
INT					
JPL	65.3	1	358	13	27.53
NAT.W	45	2	160	7	22.86
B & H	23	3	78	6	13.00

CAREER: BOWLING

	O.	M.	R.	W.	AV.
TEST					
OTHER FIRST CLASS	558.4	122	1770	44	40.23
INT					
JPL	205	2	1100	39	28.20
NAT.W	69.2	7	251	9	27.89
B & H	97	7	388	16	24.25

NORTH, P.D.   Glamorgan

Full Name: Philip David North.
Role: Right-hand bat, slow left-arm bowler, slip fielder.
Born: 16 May 1965, Newport, Gwent.
Height: 5' 5'' **Weight:** 9st.
Nickname: Philge, Dilip.
County debut: 1985.
Parents: Arthur and Audrey North.
Marital status: Single.
Family links with cricket: Father played club cricket.
Education: St. Julian's Comprehensive; Nash College of Further Education.
Qualifications: 5 O-levels, T.E.C. Mechanical Engineering, qualified toolmaker.
Jobs outside cricket: Toolmaker with brake manufacturer.
Off-season 1985–86: Playing in Brisbane.

Cricketing superstitions: "Change every time I take wickets or score runs."
Overseas teams played for: Southport C.C., Brisbane, 1985–86.
Cricketers particularly learnt from: John Steele, Alan Jones.
Cricketers particularly admired: Phil Edmonds, Dilip Doshi.
Other sports: Plays golf (11 handicap); follows soccer (Newport County).
Injuries 1985: Knock on elbow when batting — out one week.
Relaxations: "Music (world authority on 'Level 42'), white wine, watching films and 'Brookside')."
Extras: "Batted with Matthew Maynard on our debuts when he scored his hundred, 11th wicket partnership of 52, I was 0 n.o. at the end. Nothing to do with cricket but, when I was an apprentice with Lucas Girling I machined three of the four disc brakes that were on Richard Noble's 'Thrust II' world land speed record-breaking car."
Opinions on cricket: "Go back to uncovered wickets."

LAST SEASON: BATTING

	I.	N.O.	R.	H.S.	AV.
TEST					
OTHER FIRST CLASS	1	1	0	0*	–
INT					
JPL					
NAT.W					
B & H					

CAREER: BATTING

	I.	N.O.	R.	H.S.	AV.
TEST					
OTHER FIRST CLASS	1	1	0	0*	–
INT					
JPL					
NAT.W					
B & H					

LAST SEASON: BOWLING

	O.	M.	R.	W.	AV.
TEST					
OTHER FIRST CLASS	27	7	60	1	–
INT					
JPL					
NAT.W					
B & H					

CAREER: BOWLING

	O.	M.	R.	W.	AV.
TEST					
OTHER FIRST CLASS	27	7	60	1	–
INT					
JPL					
NAT.W					
B & H					

122. Which current county player is nicknamed "Judge"?

123. Which current county player is nicknamed "Benny"?

OLD, C.M.   Warwickshire

Full Name: Christopher Middleton Old.
Role: Left-hand bat, right-arm fast-medium bowler.
Born: 22 December 1948, Middlesbrough, Yorkshire.
Height: 6′ 3″ **Weight:** 14st. 7lbs.
Nickname: Chilly.
County debut: 1966 (Yorkshire), 1983 (Warwickshire).
County cap: 1966 (Yorkshire), 1984 (Warwickshire).
Test debut: 1972–73.
No. of Tests: 46.
No. of One-Day Internationals: 32.
Benefit: 1979 (£32,916).
50 wickets in a season: 9.
1st-Class 50s scored: 27.
1st-Class 100s scored: 6.
1st-Class 5 w. in innings: 39.
1st-Class 10 w. in match: 2.
One-day 50s: 13.
Place in batting averages: — average: —; (1984: 177 average: 23.12).
Place in bowling averages: 91 average: 35.85; (1984: 56 average: 29.02).
1st-Class catches 1985: 1 (career: 214).
Parents: Christopher Middleton Old (deceased) and Phyllis Old.
Wife: Alison.
Children: Juliette Louise, 28 June 1973; Simon Christopher and Paul Edward, 5 November 1975.
Education: Acklam Hall Secondary Grammar School, Middlesbrough.
Jobs outside cricket: Started as a bank clerk.
Off-season 1985–86: Working for Sportshost.
Family links with cricket: Father played local league cricket in Middlesbrough. Brother, Alan, played cricket for Durham, rugby union for England. On 2 February 1974, Chris played cricket in a Test v West Indies, while Alan played rugby for England v Ireland.
Overseas tours: India, Pakistan, Sri Lanka 1972–73; West Indies 1973–74; Australia and New Zealand 1974–75; India, Sri Lanka and Australia 1976–77; Pakistan and New Zealand 1977–78; Australia 1978–79; West Indies 1981.
Other sports: Golf, rugby union, squash.
Relaxations: Gardening.
Injuries 1985: Operation on shoulder tendons in June.
Extras: Took 4 wickets in 5 balls England v Pakistan, Birmingham 1978. Plagued by injuries: both knees were operated on in 1970 and 1971. Released

by Yorkshire at end of 1982 season. Was captain of Yorkshire from 1981–82 having made debut in 1966, and awarded cap in 1969. Banned from Test cricket for three years for playing for England rebel team in South Africa in 1982. Scored century in 37 minutes v Warwickshire at Birmingham in 1977, the second fastest century in first-class cricket at the time.

Best batting performance: 116 Yorkshire v Indians, Bradford 1974.
Best bowling performance: 7-20 Yorkshire v Gloucestershire, Middlesbrough 1969.

LAST SEASON: BATTING

	I.	N.O.	R.	H.S.	AV.
TEST					
OTHER FIRST CLASS	7	2	122	41	24.40
INT					
JPL	1	0	31	31	–
NAT.W					
B & H	1	1		17	17*	–

CAREER: BATTING

	I.	N.O.	R.	H.S.	AV.
TEST	66	9	845	65	14.83
OTHER FIRST CLASS	596	82	6911	116	13.45
INT	25	7	338	51*	18.77
JPL	126	30	1994	82*	20.77
NAT.W	26	2	348	55*	14.50
B & H	38	9	724	78*	24.97

LAST SEASON: BOWLING

	O.	M.	R.	W.	AV.
TEST					
OTHER FIRST CLASS	153.2	38	466	13	35.85
INT					
JPL	5	0	30	0	–
NAT.W					
B & H	10	1	41	0	–

CAREER: BOWLING

	O.	M.	R.	W.	AV.
TEST	210.3 1195.5	42 268	4020	143	28.11
OTHER FIRST CLASS	361.5 7670.3	69 2008	21061	928	22.70
INT	39.2 240.1	2 40	999	45	22.20
JPL	1203.5	125	4593	212	21.66
NAT.W	352.2	69	1030	49	21.02
B & H	585.5	124	1601	84	19.06

OLDHAM, S. Yorkshire

Full Name: Stephen Oldham.
Role: Right-hand bat, right-arm fast-medium bowler ("up hill").
Born: 26 July 1948, High Green, Sheffield.
Height: 6′ 1″ **Weight:** 14st. (summer), 15st. (winter).
Nickname: Esso.
County debut: 1980 (Derbyshire), 1974 and 1984 (Yorkshire).
County cap: 1980 (Derbyshire).
50 wickets in a season: 1.
1st-Class 50s scored: 1.
1st-Class 5 w. in innings: 4.
Place in bowling averages: — average: —; (1984: 111 average: 39.06).
1st-Class catches 1985: 1 (career: 38).
Parents: Robert and Kathleen Oldham.

Wife: Linda.
Children: Sally and Katherine.
Education: Crossfield High Green School.
Qualifications: 6 O-levels, 2 A-levels.
Jobs outside cricket: Qualified engineer. Assistant works manager.
Cricket superstitions: "Always play back to fast bowling."
Cricketers particularly learnt from: Chris Old, Mike Hendrick.
Cricketers particularly admired: Geoff Boycott.
Other sports: Football, golf.
Relaxations: "Helping to run my local football club. Drinking Tetley's."
Extras: Best man at Graham Stevenson's wedding. Debut for Yorkshire 1974 and left after 1979 season. Returned to Yorkshire 1984.
Best batting performance: 50 Yorkshire v Sussex, Hove 1979.
Best bowling performance: 7-78 Derbyshire v Warwickshire, Edgbaston 1982.

LAST SEASON: BATTING

	I.	N.O.	R.	H.S.	AV.
TEST					
OTHER FIRST CLASS	2	1	8	6	–
INT					
JPL	6	6	45	28*	–
NAT.W	1	1	0	0*	–
B & H					

CAREER: BATTING

	I.	N.O.	R.	H.S.	AV.
TEST					
OTHER FIRST CLASS	98	41	648	50-	11.37
INT					
JPL	41	22	210	38*	11.05
NAT.W	7	3	42	19	10.50
B & H	12	4	18	4*	2.25

LAST SEASON: BOWLING

	O.	M.	R.	W.	AV.
TEST					
OTHER FIRST CLASS	39	10	102	4	25.50
INT					
JPL	39.5	0	163	11	14.81
NAT.W	10	0	45	1	–
B & H					

CAREER: BOWLING

	O.	M.	R.	W.	AV.
TEST					
OTHER FIRST CLASS	3021	646	8919	273	32.67
INT					
JPL	858.5	52	3695	153	24.15
NAT.W	150.5	16	561	25	22.44
B & H	337.4	54	1087	57	18.98

124. Which English county captain was awarded the O.B.E. in the 1985 New Year's Honours list?

OLLIS, R.L.   Somerset

Full Name: Richard Leslie Ollis.
Role: Left-hand bat.
Born: 14 January 1961, Bristol.
Height: 6′ 1″ **Weight:** 13st.
Nickname: 'Aulage.
County debut: 1981.
1st-Class 50s scored: 4.
Place in batting averages: 206
average: 17.11: (1984: 271
average: 10.18).
1st-Class catches 1985: 6 (career: 19).
Parents: Richard Frederick and
Barbara Ann Ollis.
Marital status: Single.
Family links with cricket: Father
plays cricket for local club in
Keynsham.
Education: Castle County Primary;
Wellsway Comprehensive,
Keynsham.
Jobs outside cricket: Assistant Distribution Manager in family transport
company.
Cricketing superstitions: Always puts right pad on first.
Overseas tours: Somerset tour to Antigua, October 1981.
Cricketers particularly learnt from: "My father and Jim King of Keynsham
C.C."
Other sports: Football, squash, golf, follows most sports.
Extras: Left staff after 1985 season.
Best batting performance: 99* Somerset v Gloucestershire, Bristol 1983.

LAST SEASON: BATTING

	I.	N.O.	R.	H.S.	AV.
TEST					
OTHER FIRST CLASS	20	1	325	55	17.11
INT					
JPL	3	0	67	46	22.33
NAT.W					
B & H	4	1	39	24	13.00

CAREER: BATTING

	I.	N.O.	R.	H.S.	AV.
TEST					
OTHER FIRST CLASS	60	4	1016	99*	18.14
INT					
JPL	6	0	75	46	12.50
NAT.W					
B & H	4	1	39	24	13.00

LAST SEASON: BOWLING

	O.	M.	R.	W.	AV.
TEST					
OTHER FIRST CLASS	4	1	8	0	—
INT					
JPL					
NAT.W					
B & H					

CAREER: BOWLING

	O.	M.	R.	W.	AV.
TEST					
OTHER FIRST CLASS	5	1	10	0	—
INT					
JPL					
NAT.W					
B & H					

ONTONG, R.C.   Glamorgan

Full Name: Rodney Craig Ontong.
Role: Right-hand bat, right-arm bowler.
Born: 9 September 1955, Johannesburg, South Africa.
County debut: 1975.
County cap: 1979.
1000 runs in a season: 5.
50 wickets in a season: 4.
1st-Class 50s scored: 61.
1st-Class 100s scored: 17.
1st-Class 200s scored: 1.
1st-Class 5 w. in innings: 26.
1st-Class 10 w. in match: 3.
One-day 50s: 11.
One-day 100s: 1.
Place in batting averages: 21 average: 48.74; (1984: 72 average: 35.67).
Place in bowling averages: 37 average: 27.77; (1984: 57 average: 29.12).
1st-Class catches 1985: 11 (career: 131).
Education: Selbourne College, East London, South Africa.
Overseas teams played for: Made debut in 1972–73 for Border in Currie Cup Competition. Transferred to Transvaal for 1976–77 season, before returning to Border.
Extras: Took over Glamorgan captaincy during 1984.
Best batting performance: 204* Glamorgan v Middlesex, Swansea 1984.
Best bowling performance: 8-67 Glamorgan v Nottinghamshire, Trent Bridge 1985.

LAST SEASON: BATTING

	I.	N.O.	R.	H.S.	AV.
TEST					
OTHER FIRST CLASS	30	7	1121	130	48.74
INT					
JPL	10	1	171	40	19.00
NAT.W	2	1	85	55	—
B & H	3	0	92	58	30.67

LAST SEASON: BOWLING

	O.	M.	R.	W.	AV.
TEST					
OTHER FIRST CLASS	585.5	145	1777	64	27.77
INT					
JPL	92.2	8	335	12	27.91
NAT.W	23	3	74	0	—
B & H	33	4	105	7	15.00

CAREER: BATTING

	I.	N.O.	R.	H.S.	AV.
TEST					
OTHER FIRST CLASS	455	54	11896	204*	29.67
INT					
JPL	106	12	2200	100	23.40
NAT.W	13	2	394	64	35.82
B & H	27	3	474	81	19.75

CAREER: BOWLING

	O.	M.	R.	W.	AV.
TEST					
OTHER FIRST CLASS	6450.3	1497	18812	632	29.77
INT					
JPL	676	36	3147	102	30.85
NAT.W	121	21	454	9	50.44
B & H	251.4	47	764	41	18.63

ORMROD, J.A. — Lancashire

Full Name: Joseph Alan Ormrod.
Role: Right-hand bat, off-break
bowler.
Born: 22 December 1942,
Ramsbottom, Lancashire.
County debut: 1962 (Worcester-
shire), 1984 (Lancashire).
County cap: 1966 (Worcestershire),
1984 (Lancashire).
Benefit: 1977 (£19,000) with
Worcestershire.
1000 runs in a season: 13.
1st-Class 50s scored: 111.
1st-Class 100s scored: 30.
1st-Class 200s scored: 2.
1st-Class 5 w. in innings: 1.
One-day 50s: 34.
One-day 100s: 1.
Place in batting averages: —
average: —; (1984: 103
average: 32.41).
1st-Class catches 1985: 3 (career: 399).
Education: Kirkcaldy High School.
Jobs outside cricket: Runs his own contract flooring business, specialising in gymnasiums.
Overseas tours: Pakistan 1966–67.
Extras: Reached 20,000 runs in first-class cricket, but "I have never been a man for statistics. The spirit and flavour of the game has always meant much more to me than plain figures." Record J.P.L. partnership for any

LAST SEASON: BATTING

	I.	N.O.	R.	H.S.	AV.
TEST					
OTHER FIRST CLASS	7	0	54	23	7.72
INT					
JPL					
NAT.W					
B & H	1	0	0	0	–

CAREER: BATTING

	I.	N.O.	R.	H.S.	AV.
TEST					
OTHER FIRST CLASS	846	95	23205	204*	30.90
INT					
JPL	184	17	4074	110*	24.39
NAT.W	34	2	697	59	21.78
B & H	59	6	1625	124*	30.66

LAST SEASON: BOWLING

	O.	M.	R.	W.	AV.
TEST					
OTHER FIRST CLASS					
INT					
JPL					
NAT.W					
B & H					

CAREER: BOWLING

	O.	M.	R.	W.	AV.
TEST					
OTHER FIRST CLASS	299	53	1094	25	43.76
INT					
JPL	19	0	105	3	35.00
NAT.W					
B & H	6.3	0	29	1	–

wicket, with Dipak Patel, of 224 v Hampshire at Southampton, August 1982. Worcestershire 1962–83 (cap 1966). Left Lancashire after 1985 season.
Best batting performance: 204* Worcestershire v Kent, Dartford 1973.
Best bowling performance: 5-27 Worcestershire v Gloucestershire, Bristol 1972.

O'SHAUGHNESSY, S.J. Lancashire

Full Name: Steven Joseph O'Shaughnessy.
Role: Right-hand bat, right-arm medium bowler.
Born: 9 September 1961, Bury, Lancashire.
Height: 5' 10½''.
County debut: 1980.
County cap: 1985.
1000 runs in a season: 1.
1st-Class 50s scored: 13.
1st-Class 100s scored: 5.
One-day 50s: 7.
One-day 100s: 1.
Place in batting averages: 230 average: 13.09; (1984: 83 average: 34.32).
Place in bowling averages: 77 average: 34.73; (1984: 113 average: 39.63).
1st-Class catches 1985: 10 (career: 32).

LAST SEASON: BATTING

	I.	N.O.	R.	H.S.	AV.
TEST					
OTHER FIRST CLASS	23	2	275	63	13.09
INT					
JPL	13	0	305	60	23.46
NAT.W	2	0	36	22	18.00
B & H	4	0	215	90	53.75

CAREER: BATTING

	I.	N.O.	R.	H.S.	AV.
TEST					
OTHER FIRST CLASS	131	20	3001	159*	27.04
INT					
JPL	54	11	957	101*	22.25
NAT.W	10	3	144	49*	20.57
B & H	17	0	446	90	26.24

LAST SEASON: BOWLING

	O.	M.	R.	W.	AV.
TEST					
OTHER FIRST CLASS	142	21	521	15	34.73
INT					
JPL	61.1	0	332	5	66.49
NAT.W	21	3	68	3	22.67
B & H	34	5	135	9	15.00

CAREER: BOWLING

	O.	M.	R.	W.	AV.
TEST					
OTHER FIRST CLASS	933.3	164	3229	98	32.95
INT					
JPL	327.1	11	1564	40	39.10
NAT.W	89	10	335	10	33.50
B & H	141	28	453	24	18.88

Education: Harper Green Secondary School, Farnworth, Lancashire.
Overseas tours: Canada 1979 with N.C.A. U-19 XI; West Indies 1980 with England Young Cricketers.
Relaxations: Snooker.
Extras: Scored 100 in 35 minutes v Leicestershire, 11 September 1983 to equal the fastest first-class century scored by Percy Fender in 1920 (the bowling to O'Shaughnessy was not of the highest standard).
Best batting performance: 159* Lancashire v Somerset, Bath 1984.
Best bowling performance: 4-66 Lancashire v Nottinghamshire, Trent Bridge 1982.

PALMER, G.V. Somerset

Full Name: Gary Vincent Palmer.
Role: Right-hand bat, right-arm fast-medium bowler.
Born: 1 November 1965, Taunton, Somerset.
Height: 6′ 1″ **Weight:** 11st. 7lbs.
Nickname: Pedlar.
County debut: 1982.
1st-Class 50s scored: 2.
1st-Class 5 w. in innings: 1.
Place in batting averages: 184.
average: 20.50; (1984: 227 average: 16.61).
Place in bowling averages: —
average: —; (1984: 116 average: 41.03).
1st-Class catches 1985: 2 (career: 25).
Parents: Kenneth Ernest and Joy Valerie Palmer.

Marital status: Single.
Education: North Town Junior School; Queen's College, Junior and Senior.
Qualifications: S.R.A. Part 1 Squash Coaching Certificate, N.C.A. Cricket Coaching Award. G.C.E.s.
Jobs outside cricket: Squash coaching.
Off-season 1985–86: Coaching and playing squash.
Family links with cricket: Father, K.E. Palmer, played for Somerset and England. Toured Pakistan with Commonwealth team, 1963. Test Umpire. Coach at Somerset C.C.C. in winter. Grandfather did the double for 13 consecutive seasons in club cricket, and scored 25 centuries for Devizes C.C.
Overseas tours: English Schools U-19 Zimbabwe 1982–83; England Young Cricketers to West Indies 1984—85.

Cricketers particularly learnt from: "Learnt from my father from an early age. I admire Viv Richards, Joel Garner, Ian Botham."
Other sports: Squash.
Relaxations: "Listening to music — the up-to-date variety."
Extras: Somerset U-19 Squash champion. Youngest professional ever: had summer contract with Somerset at 14. Captain of England U-15. English Schools U-16 Cricketer of the Year. Possibly youngest cricketer to play for England U-19. Made debut for Somerset 1st XI at 16. Opened his first-class career v Leicestershire by bowling two maidens.
Best batting performance: 78 Somerset v Gloucestershire, Bristol 1983.
Best bowling performance: 5-38 Somerset v Warwickshire, Taunton 1983.

LAST SEASON: BATTING

	I.	N.O.	R.	H.S.	AV.
TEST					
OTHER FIRST CLASS	11	3	164	45*	20.50
INT					
JPL	3	1	32	21	16.00
NAT.W					
B & H	3	1	20	15*	10.00

CAREER: BATTING

	I.	N.O.	R.	H.S.	AV.
TEST					
OTHER FIRST CLASS	46	7	615	78	15.77
INT					
JPL	14	7	137	38*	19.57
NAT.W	–	–	–	–	–
B & H	4	1	24	15*	8.00

LAST SEASON: BOWLING

	O.	M.	R.	W.	AV.
TEST					
OTHER FIRST CLASS	167	19	683	7	97.56
INT					
JPL	26.5	0	128	9	14.22
NAT.W					
B & H	33	1	161	4	40.25

CAREER: BOWLING

	O.	M.	R.	W.	AV.
TEST					
OTHER FIRST CLASS	713	117	2601	57	45.63
INT					
JPL	141.1	1	745	21	35.47
NAT.W	20	0	102	1	–
B & H	51	3	240	5	48.00

125. Which two current West Indian Test players were awarded the M.B.E. in the 1985 New Year's Honours list?

PARKER, P.W.G.　　　　　　　Sussex

Full Name: Paul William Giles Parker.
Role: Right-hand bat, leg-break bowler.
Born: 15 January 1956, Bulawayo, Rhodesia.
Height: 5' 10½" **Weight:** 12st.
Nickname: Porky, Polly.
County debut: 1976.
County cap: 1979.
Test debut: 1981.
No. of Tests: 1.
1000 runs in a season: 6.
1st-Class 50s scored: 54.
1st-Class 100s scored: 24.
1st-Class 200s scored: 1.
One-day 50s: 25.
One-day 100s: 4.
Place in batting averages: 78
average: 34.08; (1984: 28 average: 47.00).
1st-Class catches 1985: 14 (career: 146).
Parents: Anthony John and Margaret Edna Parker.
Wife and date of marriage: Teresa, 25 January 1980.
Children: James William Ralph, 6 November 1980; Jocelyn Elizabeth, 10 September 1984.
Education: Collyer's Grammar School; St Catharine's College, Cambridge.
Qualifications: M.A. (Cantab.).
Family links with cricket: Father played with Essex II. Uncle, David Green, played for Northamptonshire and Worcestershire. Two brothers, Guy and Rupert, "very keen and active cricketers". Father wrote *The Village Cricket Match* and was sports editor of I.T.N.
Overseas tours: Combined Oxford & Cambridge XI tour of Australia 1979–80.
Overseas teams played for: Sturt C.C. in Adelaide, Australia, 1979–80; Natal, South Africa, 1980–81.
Jobs outside cricket: Winter employment with Messrs. Laing & Cruikshank (Stockbrokers), London.
Cricketers particularly learnt from: J. Denman, Sussex C.C.C.
Other sports: Most ball games.
Relaxations: Reading, crosswords, bridge, music.
Extras: Was selected for Cambridge against Oxford rugby match in 1977 but had to withdraw through injury. Was first reserve for England in Australia tour 1979–80. Vice-captain of Sussex, 1981–83.
Opinions on cricket: Advocates 4-day cricket and the continuance of covered wickets.

Best batting performance: 215 Cambridge University v Essex, Cambridge 1976.
Best bowling performance: 2-21 Sussex v Surrey, Guildford 1984.

LAST SEASON: BATTING

	I.	N.O.	R.	H.S.	AV.
TEST					
OTHER FIRST CLASS	28	4	818	105	34.08
INT					
JPL	11	2	308	85	34.22
NAT.W	2	0	116	109	58.00
B & H	4	0	100	48	25.00

CAREER: BATTING

	I.	N.O.	R.	H.S.	AV.
TEST	2	0	13	13	6.50
OTHER FIRST CLASS	369	52	11056	215	34.88
INT					
JPL	116	19	2624	121*	37.05
NAT.W	24	3	749	109	35.67
B & H	40	4	992	77	27.56

LAST SEASON: BOWLING

	O.	M.	R.	W.	AV.
TEST					
OTHER FIRST CLASS	1	0	12	0	–
INT					
JPL					
NAT.W					
B & H					

CAREER: BOWLING

	O.	M.	R.	W.	AV.
TEST					
OTHER FIRST CLASS	137.3	23	553	10	55.30
INT					
JPL	5	0	20	2	10.00
NAT.W	2	0	17	1	–
B & H					

PARKS, R.J. Hampshire

Full Name: Robert James Parks.
Role: Right-hand bat, wicket-keeper.
Born: 15 June 1959, Cuckfield, Sussex.
Height: 5′ 7½″ **Weight:** 10st.
Nickname: Bobby.
County debut: 1980.
County cap: 1982.
1st-Class 50s scored: 7.
Place in batting averages: 143 average: 25.13; (1984: 221 average: 17.76).
Education: Eastbourne Grammar School; Southampton Institute of Technology.
Qualifications: 9 O-levels, 1 A-level, O.N.D. and H.N.D. in Business Studies.
Family links with cricket: Father, Jim Parks, played for Sussex and England, as did his grandfather, J.H. Parks. Uncle, H.W. Parks, also played for Sussex.
Jobs outside cricket: Training in accountancy, working for Jardine Air Cargo.

Cricketing superstitions: Left pad on first.
Cricketers particularly learnt from: A. Knott, J. Rice.
Cricketers particularly admired: R. Taylor, N. Pocock.
Other sports: Squash, football.
Relaxations: Backgammon and reading.
Extras: Broke the Hampshire record for the number of dismissals in a match, against Derbyshire in 1982 (10 catches).
Opinions on cricket: "An effort should be made to liaise with the Football Association in order to curtail the increased overlapping of their season into ours."
Best batting performance: 89 Hampshire v Cambridge University, Cambridge 1984.

LAST SEASON: BATTING

	I.	N.O.	R.	H.S.	AV.
TEST					
OTHER FIRST CLASS	24	9	377	53*	25.13
INT					
JPL	2	1	8	5	–
NAT.W	1	1	6	6*	–
B & H	4	3	25	11*	–

CAREER: BATTING

	I.	N.O.	R.	H.S.	AV.
TEST					
OTHER FIRST CLASS	147	36	1922	89	17.32
INT					
JPL	29	15	276	36*	19.71
NAT.W	7	3	61	25	15.25
B & H	17	6	93	11*	8.45

LAST SEASON: WICKET KEEPING

	C.	ST.			
TEST					
OTHER FIRST CLASS	58	4			
INT					
JPL	12	3			
NAT.W	3	2			
B & H	12	1			

CAREER: WICKET KEEPING

	C.	ST.			
TEST					
OTHER FIRST CLASS	309	39			
INT					
JPL	86	18			
NAT.W	18	3			
B & H	31	4			

126. Which Middlesex wicket-keeper played soccer for the first time for England at the age of 38?

PARSONS, G.J.   Warwickshire

Full Name: Gordon James Parsons.
Role: Left-hand bat, right-arm
medium bowler, outfielder.
Born: 17 October 1959, Slough.
Height: 6' 1" **Weight:** 13st. 6lbs.
("Give or take a lb. or two").
Nickname: Bullhead, Triangle.
County debut: 1978 (Leicestershire).
County cap: 1984.
50 wickets in a season: 2.
1st-Class 50s scored: 11.
1st-Class 5 w. in innings: 7.
1st-Class 10 w. in match: 1.
Place in batting averages: 221
average: 14.17; (1984: 126
average: 29.41).
Place in bowling averages: 116
average: 43.91; (1984: 81
average: 32.30).

1st-Class catches 1985: 0 (career: 40).
Parents: Dave and Evelyn Parsons.
Marital status: Single.
Education: Woodside County Secondary School, Slough.
Qualifications: 5 O-levels.
Jobs outside cricket: Worked as clerk at T.L. Bennett, Ratby, Leicester.
Family links with cricket: Father played club cricket.
Off-season 1985--86: Coaching in South Africa.
Overseas tours: Australasia with Derrick Robins' U-23 XI in 1979–80;
E.S.C.A. tour to India 1977–78; Zimbabwe with Leicestershire in 1981.
Overseas teams played for: Maharaja's in Sri Lanka, 1979, 1981–82, 1982–83;
Boland, South Africa, 1983–84.
Cricketers particularly learnt from: "Alf Gover, Ken Higgs, Roger Tolchard
and Andy Roberts have given me plenty of good advice. Plus too many to
mention—particularly in the team."
Cricketers particularly admired: Jonathan Agnew, Mike Garnham, David
Allett.
Other sports: Golf.
Injuries 1985: Twisted left ankle (out for two weeks).
Extras: Played for Leicester 2nd XI since 1976 and also for Buckingham-
shire in 1977. Left Leicestershire after 1985 season and joined Warwickshire.
Opinions on cricket: "112 overs a day would be a good idea, without over-rate
fines. Would like to try 16 4-day games in the championship."
Best batting performance: 197 Worcestershire v Cambridge University,
Worcester 1984.
Best bowling performance: 7-46 Worcestershire v Lancashire, Worcester
1982.

LAST SEASON: BATTING

	I.	N.O.	R.	H.S.	AV.
TEST					
OTHER FIRST CLASS	16	4	170	32	14.17
INT					
JPL	9	2	85	24*	12.14
NAT.W	–	–	–	–	–
B & H	3	2	41	25*	–

CAREER: BATTING

	I.	N.O.	R.	H.S.	AV.
TEST					
OTHER FIRST CLASS	167	38	2442	76	18.93
INT					
JPL	40	11	273	24*	9.41
NAT.W	5	0	54	23	10.80
B & H	11	6	128	29*	25.60

LAST SEASON: BOWLING

	O.	M.	R.	W.	AV.
TEST					
OTHER FIRST CLASS	356.2	76	1010	23	43.91
INT					
JPL	89	2	407	14	29.07
NAT.W	11.1	3	31	1	–
B & H	71	6	285	9	31.67

CAREER: BOWLING

	O.	M.	R.	W.	AV.
TEST					
OTHER FIRST CLASS	2941.5	627	9438	314	30.06
INT					
JPL	514.2	26	2277	76	29.96
NAT.W	104.5	12	433	10	43.30
B & H	234.5	28	813	31	26.23

PATEL, D.N.　　　　Worcestershire

Full Name: Dipak Narshi Patel.
Role: Right-hand bat, off-break bowler.
Born: 25 October 1958, Nairobi, Kenya.
Height: 5′ 11½″ **Weight:** 10st. 9lbs.
Nickname: Dip.
County debut: 1976.
County cap: 1979.
1000 runs in a season: 5.
50 wickets in a season: 2.
1st-Class 50s scored: 39.
1st-Class 100s scored: 14.
1st-Class 5 w. in innings: 12.
One-day 50s: 10.
One-day 100s: 1.
Place in batting averages: 133 average: 26.72; (1984: 89 average: 33.70).
Place in bowling averages: 86 average: 36.59; (1984: 92 average: 33.82).
1st-Class catches 1985: 17 (career: 129).
Parents: Narshibhai and Laxmiben Patel.
Wife and date of marriage: Vina, 27 February 1983.
Education: George Salter Comprehensive School, West Bromwich, West Midlands.
Qualifications: 3 O-levels.
Off-season 1985–86: Manager/coach for Auckland Cricket Association.
Jobs outside cricket: Sales assistant, Oakfield Tile Co. Ltd., Worcester.

Family links with cricket: Three uncles played for Kenya XI. Cousin, Harshad, was on Worcester staff.

Overseas tours: Zambia 1977 with Warwickshire; South America 1979 with Derrick Robins' XI; Australia with U-23 XI 1979–80; Trinidad and Tobago 1984 with World Invitation XI.

Overseas teams played for: Hawthorn C.C., Melbourne, on Whitbread Scholarship 1979–80; Birkenhead City C.C., Auckland, 1980–85.

Other sports: Golf, squash, snooker, football. Follows W.B.A.

Cricketers particularly learnt from: Norman Gifford, Glenn Turner, Kapil Dev, Basil D'Oliveira.

Relaxations: T.V.

Cricketing superstitions: Left pad on first.

Extras: Has lived in U.K. since 1967. Discovered by Basil D'Oliveira. Shared record J.P.L. partnership of 224 with Alan Ormrod v Hampshire at Southampton, August 1982. Shared in first-class 6th wicket partnership record for county, 227 with E.J.O. Hemsley, v Oxford University at Oxford, 1976. Vice-captain 1985.

Best batting performance: 197 Worcestershire v Cambridge University, Worcester 1984.

Best bowling performance: 7-46 Worcestershire v Lancashire, Worcester 1982.

LAST SEASON: BATTING

	I.	N.O.	R.	H.S.	AV.
TEST					
OTHER FIRST CLASS	42	3	1042	88	26.72
INT					
JPL	15	0	390	76	26.00
NAT.W	4	0	97	54	24.25
B & H	5	0	36	16	7.20

CAREER: BATTING

	I.	N.O.	R.	H.S.	AV.
TEST					
OTHER FIRST CLASS	337	22	8905	197	28.27
INT					
JPL	117	9	2208	125	20.44
NAT.W	13	1	252	54	21.00
B & H	32	4	642	90*	22.93

LAST SEASON: BOWLING

	O.	M.	R.	W.	AV.
TEST					
OTHER FIRST CLASS	442	117	1244	34	36.59
INT					
JPL	56.2	3	337	8	42.12
NAT.W	39	2	140	4	35.00
B & H	32.4	0	142	5	28.40

CAREER: BOWLING

	O.	M.	R.	W.	AV.
TEST					
OTHER FIRST CLASS	4255.4	1106	12011	334	35.96
INT					
JPL	511.4	17	2471	82	30.13
NAT.W	94.1	10	336	10	33.60
B & H	210.4	21	766	25	30.64

127. Which cricketer scored more first-class centuries after the age of 40 than he did before?

PATEL, H.V.   Worcestershire

Full Name: Harshad Vallabh Patel.
Role: Right-hand opening bat, right-arm slow bowler ("occasionally").
Born: 29 January 1964, Nairobi, Kenya.
Height: 5′ 9″ **Weight:** 10st. 2lbs.
Nickname: Indian or "H".
County debut: 1985.
Parents: Vallabhbhai Parbubhai and Shanta V. Patel.
Marital status: Single.
Family links with cricket: Father played for East Africa and Dipak Patel (cousin) W.C.C.C.
Education: George Salter High School, Rowley Regis College.
Qualifications: 7 O-levels, qualified cricket coach,
Jobs outside cricket: Recreation assistant, also warehouse assistant.
Off-season 1985–86: Playing cricket in New Zealand.
Cricketing superstitions: Not to shave in the morning,
Cricketers particularly learnt from: Mainly from father, David Steele, Basil D'Oliveira.
Cricketers particularly admired: Viv Richards, Geoff Boycott.
Other sports: "Mainly ball sports. Follow football (West Bromwich Albion) although I support Liverpool."
Relaxations: Music, T.V.

LAST SEASON: BATTING

	I.	N.O.	R.	H.S.	AV.
TEST					
OTHER FIRST CLASS	1	0	39	39	–
INT					
JPL					
NAT.W					
B & H					

CAREER: BATTING

	I.	N.O.	R.	H.S.	AV.
TEST					
OTHER FIRST CLASS	1	0	39	39	–
INT					
JPL					
NAT.W					
B & H					

PATTERSON, B.P.   Lancashire

Full Name: Balfour Patrick
Patterson.
Role: Right-hand bat, right-arm
fast bowler, outfielder.
Born: 15 September 1961, Portland,
Jamaica.
Height: 6' 2½'' **Weight:** 14st.
Nickname: Balf, Pato.
County debut: 1984.
1st-Class 5 w. in innings: 4.
1st-Class 10 w. in match: 1.
Place in bowling averages: 38
average: 27.90.
1st-Class catches 1985: 4 (career: 6).
Parents: Maurice and Emelda
Patterson.
Marital status: Single.
Family links with cricket: Father

and grandfather played for parish in
Jamaica.
Education: Happy Grove High School; Wolmers High School for Boys.
Qualifications: Jamaica School Certificates, O-levels.
Jobs outside cricket: Accounts clerk.
Off-season 1985–86: Playing for Jamaica in Shell Shield.
Overseas teams played for: Tasmania 1984–85.
Cricketers particularly learnt from: Anderson Roberts.
Cricketers particularly admired: Present West Indian team; Dennis Lillee.
Other sports: Basketball, football, squash, table-tennis, for fitness and
pleasure. Watches football.
Relaxations: Swimming, listening to music, watching television.

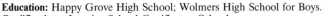

LAST SEASON: BATTING

	I.	N.O.	R.	H.S.	AV.
TEST					
OTHER FIRST CLASS	15	5	38	22	3.80
INT					
JPL	1	1	3	3*	–
NAT.W					
B & H	1	1	15	15*	–

CAREER: BATTING

	I.	N.O.	R.	H.S.	AV.
TEST					
OTHER FIRST CLASS	29	7	81	22	3.68
INT					
JPL	1	1	3	3*	–
NAT.W					
B & H	1	1	15	15*	–

LAST SEASON: BOWLING

	O.	M.	R.	W.	AV.
TEST					
OTHER FIRST CLASS	364.3	59	1144	41	27.90
INT					
JPL	1.2	0	6	0	–
NAT.W					
B & H	11	1	34	1	–

CAREER: BOWLING

	O.	M.	R.	W.	AV.
TEST					
OTHER FIRST CLASS	799.3	118	2683	82	32.72
INT					
JPL	1.2	0	6	0	–
NAT.W					
B & H	11	1	34	1	–

Injuries 1985: Strained groin mid-season.
Best batting performance: 22 Lancashire v Northamptonshire, Lytham 1985.
Best bowling performance: 7-49 Lancashire v Oxford University, Oxford 1985.

PAULINE, D.B. Surrey

Full Name: Duncan Brian Pauline.
Role: Right-hand bat, right-arm bowler.
Born: 15 December 1960, Aberdeen.
Height: 5′ 10″ **Weight:** 12st. 7lbs.
Nickname: The Colonel.
County debut: 1979.
1st-Class 50s scored: 13.
1st-Class 100s scored: 1.
1st-Class 5 w. in innings: 1.
One-day 50s: 4.
Place in batting averages: 57
average: 24.50; (1984: 164
average: 24.47).
Place in bowling averages: 90
average: 35.44.
1st-Class catches 1985: 4 (career: 18).
Parents: Brian and Vivienne Pauline.

Marital status: Single.
Family links with cricket: Father and uncle both played in Aberdeen.
Education: Ashley Road School, Aberdeen; Bishop Fox, East Molesey.
Jobs outside cricket: Pop-corn maker.
Off-season 1985–86: In Sydney.
Overseas tours: Australia with Young England XI in 1978; Surrey C.C.C. Far East Tour 1979; Barbados 1985.
Overseas teams played for: Glenwood Old Boys, Durban; Waverley, Sydney.
Other sports: Golf, squash, snooker and pool.
Injuries 1985: Out for two weeks with back trouble.
Extras: Played for Surrey Schools U-12 and U-15. Played for South-East England U-15. England U-19 v West Indies and v Australia. Opening bat for one of England's oldest clubs, East Molesey, founded 1730. Name is pronounced with the 'ine' to rhyme with 'keen' (Scottish).
Opinions on cricket: "I think there would be more interesting games if 3-day cricket was to be changed to 4-day."
Best batting performance: 115 Surrey v Sussex, The Oval 1983.
Best bowling performance: 5-52 Surrey v Derbyshire, Derby 1985.

PAYNE, I.R. Gloucestershire

Full Name: Ian Roger Payne.
Role: Right-hand bat, right-arm medium bowler.
Born: 9 May 1958, Kennington.
Height: 5′ 10″ **Weight:** 13st.
Nickname: Clouseau, Freda, Inspector.
County debut: 1977 (Surrey), 1985 (Gloucestershire).
1st-Class 5 w. in innings: 1.
One-day 50s: 2.
1st-Class catches 1985: 4 (career: 34).
Parents: Richard John and Agnes Ross Payne.
Wife and date of marriage: Julie, 22 September 1979.
Children: Nicola Mary, 17 August 1984.
Education: Emanuel School, Wandsworth.
Qualifications: 5 O-levels. Advanced Cricket Coach.
Jobs outside cricket: Many varied jobs.
Off-season 1985–86: "Hopefully working."
Cricketing superstitions: "Always changing them as they fail, which is very often."
Overseas tours: Antigua 1978 with Surrey Young Cricketers; Far East 1979 with Surrey; Barbados 1985 with Gloucestershire.

320

Overseas teams played for: Nedlands C.C., Perth, 1980–81, 1982–83.

Cricketers particularly learnt from: Craig Sarjeant, D.K. Lillee, B.D. Richards.

Other sports: Soccer, golf, squash. Follows all except horse-racing.

Relaxations: Reading, music, travelling, T.V. and films; watching fifth repeat of "Star Trek".

Injuries 1985: "Missed returning to play for Gloucestershire v Surrey after contracting chickenpox from the Surrey membership secretary (my wife). I think I was sabotaged!"

Extras: Released at end of 1984 by Surrey after making debut in 1977. "If I become a County Captain I shall write a diary of the season and call it 'Captain's Log, Star date . . .'"

Best batting performance: 43 Surrey v Essex, The Oval 1983.

Best bowling performance: 5-13 Surrey v Gloucestershire, The Oval 1983.

LAST SEASON: BATTING

	I.	N.O.	R.	H.S.	AV.
TEST					
OTHER FIRST CLASS	6	1	106	37	21.20
INT					
JPL	6	4	73	37	36.50
NAT.W	3	2	103	53	–
B & H	1	0	2	2	–

CAREER: BATTING

	I.	N.O.	R.	H.S.	AV.
TEST					
OTHER FIRST CLASS	43	6	444	43	12.00
INT					
JPL	32	14	312	37	17.33
NAT.W	6	3	163	56*	54.33
B & H	3	0	6	2	2.00

LAST SEASON: BOWLING

	O.	M.	R.	W.	AV.
TEST					
OTHER FIRST CLASS	64	13	214	4	53.50
INT					
JPL	68	4	329	7	47.00
NAT.W	31	4	99	1	–
B & H	5	0	25	2	12.50

CAREER: BOWLING

	O.	M.	R.	W.	AV.
TEST					
OTHER FIRST CLASS	424.4	· 107	1341	30	44.70
INT					
JPL	266	10	1361	44	30.93
NAT.W	55	8	183	8	22.88
B & H	38	6	131	8	16.38

128. Which current county cricketer's nickname is "Gadge"?

129. What famous Australian Test cricketer wrote a classic book, recently republished, on the Bodyline series of 1932–33, entitled *Cricket Crisis*?

PENN, C.   Kent

Full Name: Christopher Penn.
Role: Left-hand bat, right-arm
medium bowler.
Born: 19 June 1963, Dover.
Height: 6′ 1″. **Weight:** 14st.
Nickname: Penny, Cliff.
County debut: 1982.
County cap: 1982.
1st-Class 50s scored: 2.
1st-Class 100s scored: 1.
Place in batting averages: —
average: —; (1984: 167
average: 24.38).
Place in bowling averages: 69
average: 33.29.
1st-Class catches 1985: 1 (career: 14).
Parents: Reg and Brenda Penn.
Wife and date of marriage: Ann,
22 March 1986.
Education: Dover Grammar School.
Qualifications: 8 O-levels, 2 A-levels.
Jobs outside cricket: Farm worker, car cleaner for hire company.
Off-season 1985–86: First English winter for four years.
Family links with cricket: Father played club cricket for Dover C.C.
Overseas tours: N.C.A. tour of Denmark 1981; Whitbread Scholarship to
Australia 1982–83.
Overseas teams played for: Koohinore Crescents, Johannesburg, 1981–82 and
1983–84; West Perth 1982–83; Johannesburg Municipals 1983–84, Wits
University 1984–85.

LAST SEASON: BATTING

	I.	N.O.	R.	H.S.	AV.
TEST					
OTHER FIRST CLASS	7	2	102	50	20.40
INT					
JPL	1	0	20	20	–
NAT.W					
B & H					

CAREER: BATTING

	I.	N.O.	R.	H.S.	AV.
TEST					
OTHER FIRST CLASS	31	8	497	115	21.61
INT					
JPL	15	4	112	40	10.18
NAT.W	1	0	5	5	–
B & H	5	2	36	17	12.00

LAST SEASON: BOWLING

	O.	M.	R.	W.	AV.
TEST					
OTHER FIRST CLASS	124.4	17	466	14	33.29
INT					
JPL	8	0	41	1	–
NAT.W					
B & H					

CAREER: BOWLING

	O.	M.	R.	W.	AV.
TEST					
OTHER FIRST CLASS	410.2	67	1400	31	45.16
INT					
JPL	144	6	739	24	30.79
NAT.W	12	1	34	1	–
B & H	35	2	124	4	31.00

Cricketers particularly learnt from: "My father, Colin Page, Brian Luckhurst, Graham Johnson, Barney Lock, the present Kent team."
Cricketers particularly admired: Alan Knott, Dennis Lillee.
Other sports: Rugby, football, golf, squash. Follows all sports.
Relaxations: Music, swimming, art and art history, Indian food.
Extras: Played for Young England v Young West Indies, August 1982.
Opinions on cricket: "Possibly too much car travel and risk of bad road accident."
Best batting performance: 115 Kent v Lancashire, Old Trafford 1984.
Best bowling performance: 4-63 Kent v Middlesex, Lord's 1985.

PHILLIP, N. Essex

Full Name: Norbert Phillip.
Role: Right-hand bat, right-arm fast-medium bowler.
Born: 12 June 1948, Bioche, Dominica, West Indies.
Height: 6' 0" **Weight:** 12st. 4lbs.
Nickname: Nobbie in England and Zidi in Dominica.
County debut: 1978.
County cap: 1978.
Test debut: 1977–78.
No. of Tests: 9.
No. of One-Day Internationals: 1.
1000 runs in a season: 1.
50 wickets in a season: 5.
1st-Class 50s scored: 21.
1st-Class 100s scored: 1.
1st-Class 5 w. in innings: 30
1st-Class 10 w. in match: 2.
One-day 50s: 6.

Place in batting averages: — average: —; (1984: 204 average: 19.53).
Place in bowling averages: — average: —; (1984: 40 average: 26.79).
1st-Class catches 1985: 3 (career: 75).
Parents: Philbert and Irene Phillip.
Wife and date of marriage: Elizabeth, 31 October 1975.
Children: Twin boys, Frank and Franklyn, 28 February 1972.
Education: Dominica Grammar School.
Qualifications: O-level History. National Cricket Association coaching certificate.
Jobs outside cricket: Sports officer with Government of Dominica.
Overseas tours: India and Sri Lanka with West Indies, 1978–79.
Overseas teams played for: Windward Islands; Combined Islands.

Other sports: Football, athletics.

Relaxations: Reading and listening to music, "especially reggae, soul and calypso".

Extras: "I acted as Assistant-Secretary of the Dominica Cricket Association, and Chairman of the Association's Youth Sub-Committee. I am involved in cricket coaching as a Sports Officer to the Government of Dominica." Captain of Windward Islands. Left at end of 1985 season.

Best batting performance: 134 Essex v Gloucestershire, Gloucester 1978.

Best bowling performance: 7-33 Windwards v Leewards, Roseau 1981–82.

LAST SEASON: BATTING

	I.	N.O.	R.	H.S.	AV.
TEST					
OTHER FIRST CLASS	7	0	129	50	18.43
INT					
JPL	7	1	89	23	14.83
NAT.W					
B & H	1	0	3	3	–

CAREER: BATTING

	I.	N.O.	R.	H.S.	AV.
TEST	15	5	297	47	29.70
OTHER FIRST CLASS	319	32	6716	134	23.40
INT	1	0	0	0	–
JPL	98	19	1515	95	19.17
NAT.W	15	2	201	45	15.46
B & H	20	7	232	33*	17.85

LAST SEASON: BOWLING

	O.	M.	R.	W.	AV.
TEST					
OTHER FIRST CLASS	75.3	14	242	6	40.33
INT					
JPL	54.3	0	252	6	42.00
NAT.W					
B & H	15	2	69	2	34.50

CAREER: BOWLING

	O.	M.	R.	W.	AV.
TEST	303.2	46	1041	28	37.17
OTHER FIRST CLASS	5248.2	1029	15991	660	24.23
INT	7	0	22	1	–
JPL	719	44	2879	134	21.48
NAT.W	129	16	473	21	22.52
B & H	306.4	37	1113	44	25.30

---

130. Who were the three county cricketers about whom David Foot wrote, *Cricket's Unholy Trinity* published last year?

131. Which England Test captain once ate 210 oysters in Brisbane?

PHILLIPSON, C.P.   Sussex

Full Name: Christopher Paul
Phillipson.
Role: Right-hand bat, right-arm
medium bowler, slip fielder.
Born: 10 February 1952, Vrindaban,
India.
Height: 6'2" **Weight:** 13st. 5lbs.
Nickname: Phillipo, Log.
County debut: 1970.
County cap: 1980.
Benefit: 1985.
1st-Class 50s scored: 12.
1st-Class 5 w. in innings: 4.
One-day 50s: 6.
1st-Class catches 1985: 0
(career: 135).
Parents: Rev. Christopher Quentin
and Muriel Regina Phillipson.
Wife and date of marriage: Adell,
24 March 1979.
Children: Kirstin Jane, 3 March 1981; Christopher Ross, 14 September
1983.
Education: Prebendal School, Chichester; Ardingly College; Loughborough
College.
Qualifications: Teacher's certificate (P.E. and geography), 2 A-levels. N.C.A.
coaching certificate.
Family links with cricket: "My wife's mother's family (Dell) achieved fame in
the Eastern Cape in 1908 when they formed a cricket team in Bathurst made
up solely of their own family and played as such for several years."
Off-season 1985-86: Playing and coaching in Cape Town.

LAST SEASON: BATTING

	I.	N.O.	R.	H.S.	AV.
TEST					
OTHER FIRST CLASS					
INT					
JPL	2	2	20	15*	–
NAT.W					
B & H					

CAREER: BATTING

	I.	N.O.	R.	H.S.	AV.
TEST					
OTHER FIRST CLASS	225	61	3046	87	18.57
INT					
JPL	103	39	1348	71	21.06
NAT.W	19	7	301	70*	25.08
B & H	29	13	390	66*	24.38

LAST SEASON: BOWLING

	O.	M.	R.	W.	AV.
TEST					
OTHER FIRST CLASS					
INT					
JPL					
NAT.W					
B & H					

CAREER: BOWLING

	O.	M.	R.	W.	AV.
TEST					
OTHER FIRST CLASS	1787	387	5213	153	34.07
INT					
JPL	458.4	29	2141	77	27.80
NAT.W	64.4	6	261	9	29.00
B & H	122.3	7	532	15	35.47

Other sports: General fitness training, running, squash and swimming in the off-season.
Relaxations: Listening to contemporary music.
Extras: "Acting as 2nd XI captain/coach while maintaining playing contract and playing a certain amount of limited overs cricket in the county side."
Best batting performance: 87 Sussex v Hampshire, Hove 1980.
Best bowling performance: 6-56 Sussex v Nottinghamshire, Hove 1972.

PICK, R.A. Nottinghamshire

Full Name: Robert Andrew Pick.
Role: Left-hand bat, right-arm fast-medium bowler.
Born: 19 November 1963, Nottingham.
Height: 5' 10" **Weight:** 12st. 7lbs.
Nickname: Picky, Toothy, Dad.
County debut: 1983.
1st-Class 50s scored: 1.
1st-Class 5 w. in innings: 2.
1st-Class 10 w. in match: 1.
Place in batting averages: 145 average: 25.00; (1984: 205 average: 19.20).
Place in bowling averages: 111 average: 42.15; (1984: 72 average: 30.92).
1st-Class catches 1985: 3 (career: 6).
Parents: Bob and Lillian.
Marital status: Single.

LAST SEASON: BATTING

	I.	N.O.	R.	H.S.	AV.
TEST					
OTHER FIRST CLASS	15	5	250	63	25.00
INT					
JPL	4	3	30	11	–
NAT.W	1	1	6	6*	–
B & H	1	1	3	3*	–

CAREER: BATTING

	I.	N.O.	R.	H.S.	AV.
TEST					
OTHER FIRST CLASS	33	12	430	63	20.48
INT					
JPL	7	4	35	11	11.67
NAT.W	3	3	41	34*	–
B & H	1	1	3	3*	–

LAST SEASON: BOWLING

	O.	M.	R.	W.	AV.
TEST					
OTHER FIRST CLASS	290	52	1096	26	42.15
INT					
JPL	40.4	3	245	7	35.00
NAT.W	44	5	172	5	34.40
B & H	11	0	54	0	–

CAREER: BOWLING

	O.	M.	R.	W.	AV.
TEST					
OTHER FIRST CLASS	668.3	120	2369	58	40.85
INT					
JPL	149.4	4	792	21	37.71
NAT.W	80	8	335	9	37.22
B & H	11	0	54	0	–

Family links with cricket: Father, uncles and cousins all play local cricket.
Education: Alderman Derbyshire Comprehensive, High Pavement College.
Qualifications: 6 O-levels, 1 A-level.
Jobs outside cricket: Labourer.
Cricketers particularly admired: Bob White, Mike Hendrick, Mike Harris.
Other sports: Football, basketball and fishing.
Relaxations: Good food and music.
Extras: Played three Tests for Young England against Young Australia 1983.
Best batting performance: 63 Nottinghamshire v Warwickshire, Nuneaton 1985.
Best bowling performance: 5-25 Nottinghamshire v Oxford University, Oxford 1984.

PICKLES, C.S. Yorkshire

Full Name: Christopher Stephen Pickles.
Role: Right-hand bat, right-arm medium bowler.
Born: 30 January 1966, Cleckheaton.
Height: 6' 1" **Weight:** 13st. 7lbs.
Nickname: Pick, Piccolo.
County debut: 1985.
1st-Class catches 1985: 3 (career: 3).
Parents: Ronald Albert and Christine Mary Pickles.
Marital status: Single.
Family links with cricket: Father and brother both play local league cricket.
Education: Whitcliffe Mount School.
Qualifications: Qualified cricket coach.
Jobs outside cricket: Work in textiles.
Off-season 1985-86: Learning to drive a car.
Overseas tours: Bermuda in 1985 with N.C.A. U-19 team.
Cricketers particularly learnt from: Ian Steen, Doug Padgett, my father.
Cricketers particularly admired: Geoff Boycott, Michael Holding.
Other sports: Plays rugby union, follows local rugby club.
Relaxations: Playing sport, listening to music and watching television.
Best batting performance: 31* Yorkshire v Leicestershire, Bradford 1985.
Best bowling performance: 2-31 Yorkshire v Kent, Scarborough 1985.

LAST SEASON: BATTING

	I.	N.O.	R.	H.S.	AV.
TEST					
OTHER FIRST CLASS	3	1	52	31*	26.00
INT					
JPL	6	3	32	13*	10.67
NAT.W					
B & H					

CAREER: BATTING

	I.	N.O.	R.	H.S.	AV.
TEST					
OTHER FIRST CLASS	3	1	52	31*	26.00
INT					
JPL	6	3	32	13*	10.67
NAT.W					
B & H					

LAST SEASON: BOWLING

	O.	M.	R.	W.	AV.
TEST					
OTHER FIRST CLASS	126.3	30	385	6	64.17
INT					
JPL	64	4	288	7	41.14
NAT.W					
B & H					

CAREER: BOWLING

	O.	M.	R.	W.	AV.
TEST					
OTHER FIRST CLASS	126.3	30	385	6	64.17
INT					
JPL	64	4	288	7	41.14
NAT.W					
B & H					

PIERSON, A.R.K.　　　Warwickshire

Full Name: Adrian Roger Kirshaw Pierson.
Role: Right-hand bat, off-break bowler.
Born: 21 July 1963, Enfield, Middlesex.
Height: 6' 4'' **Weight:** 12 st.
Nickname: Skirlog, Stick.
County debut: 1985.
1st-Class catches 1985: 3 (career: 3).
Place in batting averages: 234; average: 12.86.
Parents: Patrick Blake Kirshaw and Patricia Margaret Pierson.
Marital status: Single.
Education: Lochinver House Primary; Kent College, Canterbury; Hatfield Polytechnic.
Qualifications: 2 A-levels, Advanced Coaching Certificate.
Jobs outside cricket: Worked on light aircraft at Elstree Aerodrome, 1982.
Off-season 1985-86: Coaching cricket.
Cricketing superstitions: Always puts left pad on first.
Cricketers particularly learnt from: Don Wilson, Norman Gifford, Neal Abberley.
Cricketers particularly admired: John Emburey, Phil Edmonds, Tony Greig.

Other sports: Hockey, golf. Follows all sport.

Relaxations: Music, driving.

Opinions on cricket: "All Benson and Hedges and NatWest games should be played on Saturdays, instead of midweek. Perhaps it would be even more interesting if coloured clothing and a white ball were used for one-day games, as in night cricket."

Best batting performance: 17* Warwickshire v Kent, Canterbury 1985.

Best bowling performance: 3-92 Warwickshire v Oxford University, Oxford 1985.

LAST SEASON: BATTING

	I.	N.O.	R.	H.S.	AV.
TEST					
OTHER FIRST CLASS	14	7	90	17*	12.86
INT					
JPL	3	0	7	4	2.33
NAT.W	1	1	1	1*	–
B & H					

CAREER: BATTING

	I.	N.O.	R.	H.S.	AV.
TEST					
OTHER FIRST CLASS	14	7	90	17*	12.86
INT					
JPL	3	0	7	4	2.33
NAT.W	1	1	1	1*	–
B & H					

LAST SEASON: BOWLING

	O.	M.	R.	W.	AV.
TEST					
OTHER FIRST CLASS	155	30	587	8	73.37
INT					
JPL	35	2	154	1	–
NAT.W	12	2	32	0	–
B & H					

CAREER: BOWLING

	O.	M.	R.	W.	AV.
TEST					
OTHER FIRST CLASS	155	30	587	8	73.37
INT					
JPL	35	2	154	1	–
NAT.W	12	2	32	0	–
B & H					

132. For which counties did the first-class umpire, David Constant, play?

PIGOTT, A.C.S. Sussex

Full Name: Anthony Charles Shackleton Pigott.
Role: Right-hand bat, right-arm fast bowler.
Born: 4 June 1958, London.
Height: 6' 1" **Weight:** 12st. 7lbs.
Nickname: Lester.
County debut: 1978.
County cap: 1982.
Test debut: 1983–84.
No. of Tests: 1.
50 wickets in a season: 2.
1st-Class 50s scored: 2.
1st-Class 5 w. in innings: 10.
1st-Class 10 w. in match: 1.
Place in bowling averages: 70
average: 33.32.
1st-Class catches 1985: 7
(career: 47).
Parents: Tom and Juliet Pigott.
Wife and date of marriage: Nikki, 26 February 1984.
Children: Elliott, 15 March 1983.
Education: Harrow School.
Qualifications: 5 O-levels. Junior coaching certificate.
Jobs outside cricket: Sportsmaster at Claremont Prep. School, Hastings.
Family links with cricket: Father captained club side.
Overseas tours: With Derrick Robins' XI to Australasia 1980; part of England tour to New Zealand 1983–84.
Overseas teams played for: Waverley C.C., Sydney, Australia, 1976–77, 1977–78,

LAST SEASON: BATTING

	I.	N.O.	R.	H.S.	AV.
TEST					
OTHER FIRST CLASS	3	2	10	10*	–
INT					
JPL	–	–	–	–	–
NAT.W	1	0	0	0	–
B & H					

CAREER: BATTING

	I.	N.O.	R.	H.S.	AV.
TEST	2	1	12	8*	–
OTHER FIRST CLASS	104	22	1226	63	14.95
INT					
JPL	25	9	188	49	11.75
NAT.W	4	0	70	30	17.50
B & H	10	4	25	6*	4.17

LAST SEASON: BOWLING

	O.	M.	R.	W.	AV.
TEST					
OTHER FIRST CLASS	184.4	39	633	19	33.32
INT					
JPL	54.5	1	331	15	22.06
NAT.W	17.4	3	41	5	8.20
B & H					

CAREER: BOWLING

	O.	M.	R.	W.	AV.
TEST	17	7	75	2	37.50
OTHER FIRST CLASS	2063.5	383	6921	247	28.02
INT					
JPL	369.4	13	1766	81	21.80
NAT.W	61.4	7	198	9	22.00
B & H	129	12	560	19	29.47

1979–80; Whitbread Scholarship 1979–80; Wellington, New Zealand, 1982–83 and 1983–84.

Cricketers particularly admired: G.G. Arnold, J.A. Snow and I.T. Botham.

Other sports: Squash, raquets, football, tennis, rugger.

Relaxations: "My son and family and decorating home."

Extras: Public School Raquets Champion 1975. Had operation on back, April 1981, missing most of season, and was told by a specialist he would never play cricket again. First three wickets in first-class cricket were a hat-trick. Postponed wedding to make Test debut when called into England party on tour of New Zealand. Originally going to Somerset for 1984 season, but then remained with Sussex.

Best batting performance: 63 Sussex v Nottinghamshire, Hove 1983.

Best bowling performance: 7-74 Sussex v Northamptonshire, Eastbourne 1982.

POCOCK, P.I.   Surrey

Full Name: Patrick Ian Pocock.

Role: Right-hand bat, off-break bowler.

Born: 24 September 1946, Bangor, Caernarvonshire.

Height: 6′ 1½″ **Weight:** 13st.

Nickname: Percy.

County debut: 1964.

County cap: 1967.

Test debut: 1967–68.

No. of Tests: 20.

No. of One-Day Internationals: 1.

Benefit: 1977 (£18,500).

50 wickets in a season: 16.

1st-Class 50s scored: 1.

1st-Class 5 w. in innings: 60.

1st-Class 10 w. in match: 7.

Place in batting averages: 77 average: 15.25.

Place in bowling averages: 75 average: 34.00; (1984: 33 average: 25.73).

1st-Class catches 1985: 2 (career: 179).

Parents: James Reginald and Cecelia Frances Pocock.

Wife and date of marriage: Diane, 8 March 1966.

Children: Samantha, 8 March 1971; Toby, 18 May 1973.

Education: Merton C. of E. Secondary Boys' School; Wimbledon Technical School.

Qualifications: M.C.C. Advanced Coach.

Jobs outside cricket: Various posts in sales and marketing. Has own company, Pat Pocock Sports Promotions Ltd.

Family links with cricket: Brothers, Nigel and Tim, are very active members of Merton Cricket Club. "W.G. Grace's mother was a Pocock, a relative of mine."

Overseas tours: Toured Pakistan in 1966–67; West Indies 1967–68 and 1973–74; Sri Lanka and Pakistan 1968–69; India, Pakistan and Sri Lanka 1972–73; India 1984–85.

Overseas teams played for: Northern Transvaal in 1971–72 Currie Cup Competition.

Other sports: Squash and golf.

Relaxations: "Holidays."

Extras: Organised the Chubb World Double Wicket Championship at Wembley in April 1979, the first time a cricket competition has been televised indoors. Took four wickets in four balls, five in six, six in nine and seven in eleven v Sussex at Eastbourne in 1972. Responsible for the La Manga cricket development in Spain. Recalled to England side during 1984 after eight-year absence.

Best batting performance: 75* Surrey v Nottinghamshire, The Oval 1968.

Best bowling performance: 9-57 Surrey v Glamorgan, Cardiff 1979.

LAST SEASON: BATTING

	I.	N.O.	R.	H.S.	AV.
TEST					
OTHER FIRST CLASS	18	6	183	41	15.25
INT					
JPL	4	2	12	6*	6.00
NAT.W	–	–	–	–	–
B & H	2	0	14	14	7.00

CAREER: BATTING

	I.	N.O.	R.	H.S.	AV.
TEST	37	4	206	33	6.24
OTHER FIRST CLASS	528	143	4568	75*	11.87
INT	1	0	4	4	–
JPL	101	35	488	22	7.39
NAT.W	17	5	64	14	5.33
B & H	32	16	124	19	7.75

LAST SEASON: BOWLING

	O.	M.	R.	W.	AV.
TEST					
OTHER FIRST CLASS	576.2	131	1632	48	34.00
INT					
JPL	82.2	1	466	12	38.83
NAT.W	8	0	35	0	–
B & H	37	6	102	4	25.50

CAREER: BOWLING

	O.	M.	R.	W.	AV.
TEST	1108.2	279	2976	67	44.42
OTHER FIRST CLASS	15267.2	4446	38577	1510	25.55
INT	10	1	20	0	–
JPL	1372	129	5570	206	27.03
NAT.W	311	66	849	31	27.39
B & H	656.4	119	2045	72	28.40

133. True or false? Graham Gooch scored a century the first day of 1985 English first-class batting season for Essex v Kent.

PONT, I.L.
Essex

Full Name: Ian Leslie Pont.
Role: Right-hand bat, right-arm
fast-medium bowler, outfielder.
Born: 28 August 1961, Brentwood.
Height: 6' 3" **Weight:** 14 st.
Nickname: Pud, Puck, Pike, Ponty.
County debut: 1985.
1st-Class 5 w. in innings: 1.
Parents: Duncan and Eileen Pont.
Marital status: Single.
Family links with cricket: Brother
Keith at Essex.
Education: Brentwood School,
Essex.
Qualifications: 7 O-levels, 3
A-levels, N.C.A. Cricket Coach.
Off-season 1985-86: Playing in
Durban.
Overseas tours: Public Schools to
India 1978-79 and Australia 1979-80; N.C.A. Young Cricketers to Canada
1980.
Cricketers particularly learnt from: Richard Hadlee, Bob White, John
Lever.
Cricketers particularly admired: Richard Hadlee.
Other sports: Hockey, darts, javelin, baseball. Watches soccer, golf.
Injuries 1985: Torn tricep muscle in bowling arm.
Relaxations: Reading psychology books.
Extras: Spent time on Nottinghamshire staff before joining Essex. Also
appeared for Buckinghamshire. Took hat-trick in 2nd XI match v Gloucester-
shire, 1985.

LAST SEASON: BATTING

	I.	N.O.	R.	H.S.	AV.
TEST					
OTHER FIRST CLASS	5	2	48	12	16.00
INT					
JPL	–	–	–	–	–
NAT.W	–	–	–	–	–
B & H					

CAREER: BATTING

	I.	N.O.	R.	H.S.	AV.
TEST					
OTHER FIRST CLASS	12	3	80	16	8.89
INT					
JPL	–	–	–	–	–
NAT.W	–	–	–	–	–
B & H					

LAST SEASON: BOWLING

	O.	M.	R.	W.	AV.
TEST					
OTHER FIRST CLASS	115.5	15	485	19	25.53
INT					
JPL	23	0	111	5	22.20
NAT.W	12	0	54	1	–
B & H					

CAREER: BOWLING

	O.	M.	R.	W.	AV.
TEST					
OTHER FIRST CLASS	194.4	28	787	22	35.77
INT					
JPL	49	0	222	7	31.72
NAT.W	12	0	54	1	–
B & H					

Best batting performance: 16 Nottinghamshire v Middlesex, Lord's 1982.
Best bowling performance: 5-103 Essex v Somerset, Taunton 1985.

PONT, K.R. Essex

Full Name: Keith Rupert Pont.
Role: Right-hand bat, right-arm medium bowler.
Born: 16 January 1953, Wanstead.
Height: 6' 2'' **Weight:** 13st.
Nickname: Monty, Plod, Ponty, Rodney Port, Vintage.
County debut: 1970.
County cap: 1976.
Benefit: 1986.
1st-Class 50s scored: 35.
1st-Class 100s scored: 7.
1st-Class 5 w. in innings: 2.
One-day 50s: 5.
Place in batting averages: 153 average: 24.50.
1st-Class catches 1985: 4 (career: 91).
Wife: Veronica.
Education: Secondary school.
Jobs outside cricket: Has been furniture representative, insurance clerk and in road haulage management.
Family links with cricket: Younger brother Ian, played for England U-19, and Notts. and now plays for Essex. Elder brother, Kelvin, was on M.C.C. staff.
Cricketing superstitions: "None really, touch wood."

LAST SEASON: BATTING

	I.	N.O.	R.	H.S.	AV.
TEST					
OTHER FIRST CLASS	15	3	294	62*	24.50
INT					
JPL	3	1	29	13	14.50
NAT.W					
B & H					

CAREER: BATTING

	I.	N.O.	R.	H.S.	AV.
TEST					
OTHER FIRST CLASS	292	43	6416	125*	25.77
INT					
JPL	137	29	1867	55*	17.28
NAT.W	20	2	245	39	13.61
B & H	40	10	624	60*	20.80

LAST SEASON: BOWLING

	O.	M.	R.	W.	AV.
TEST					
OTHER FIRST CLASS	115	23	398	9	44.22
INT					
JPL	17	1	79	2	39.50
NAT.W					
B & H					

CAREER: BOWLING

	O.	M.	R.	W.	AV.
TEST					
OTHER FIRST CLASS	1051.5	206	3087	92	33.55
INT					
JPL	514.4	37	2356	90	26.17
NAT.W	76.5	9	283	12	23.57
B & H	226.2	19	878	33	26.60

Other sports: Scuba-diving, golf. Watches skiing.
Extras: The first person to pedal on a bicycle from third man to third man whilst a first-class match is in progress, while playing for Essex.
Best batting performance: 125* Essex v Glamorgan, Southend 1983.
Best bowling performance: 5-17 Essex v Glamorgan, Cardiff 1982.

POPPLEWELL, N.F.M.   Somerset

Full Name: Nigel Francis Mark Popplewell.
Role: Right-hand bat, right-arm medium bowler.
Born: 8 August 1957, Farnborough, Kent.
Height: 5' 10" **Weight:** 12st. 7lbs.
Nickname: Pops.
County debut: 1979.
County cap: 1983.
1000 runs in a season: 2.
1st-Class 50s scored: 22.
1st-Class 100s scored: 4.
1st-Class 5 w. in innings: 1.
One-day 50s: 6
Place in batting averages: 57 average: 38.00; (1984: 99 average 32.82).
1st-Class catches in 1985: 10 (career: 110).

Parents: Oliver and Margaret Popplewell.
Wife: Ingrid.
Education: Radley College; Selwyn College, Cambridge University.
Qualifications: B.A. Hons. in Natural Science, M.A. (Cantab).
Jobs outside cricket: Teacher.
Family links with cricket: Father played for Cambridge University for three years, 1949–51. Younger brother has played for Cambridge 2nd XI.
Overseas tours: Australia with Combined Oxford and Cambridge XI.
Cricketers particularly learnt from: Peter Roebuck, Trevor Gard.
Other sports: Rugby, squash, boxing, hockey. Played rugby and squash for College. Boxed in a single bout for Cambridge at Middleweight. "Athletics in a very amateur and incompetent manner."
Relaxations: Gardening, brewing.
Extras: Cambridge cricket Blue. Played for Hampshire 2nd XI. Retired from first-class cricket at end of 1985.
Best batting performance: 172 Somerset v Essex, Southend 1985.
Best bowling performance: 5-33 Somerset v Northamptonshire, Lord's 1983.

	I.	N.O.	R.	H.S.	AV.
TEST					
OTHER FIRST CLASS	30	2	1064	172	38.00
INT					
JPL	11	1	287	74*	28.70
NAT.W	3	0	29	18	9.67
B & H	4	0	103	39	25.75

CAREER: BATTING

	I.	N.O.	R.	H.S.	AV.
TEST					
OTHER FIRST CLASS	214	27	5070	172	27.11
INT					
JPL	65	10	1360	84	24.72
NAT.W	13	2	297	68*	27.00
B & H	25	3	420	67	19.09

LAST SEASON: BOWLING

	O.	M.	R.	W.	AV.
TEST					
OTHER FIRST CLASS	27.5	2	157	0	–
INT					
JPL					
NAT.W					
B & H					

CAREER: BOWLING

	O.	M.	R.	W.	AV.
TEST					
OTHER FIRST CLASS	1381.5	306	4441	103	43.12
INT					
JPL	201.1	13	985	34	28.97
NAT.W	36.2	8	127	4	31.75
B & H	111.1	10	457	10	45.70

POTTER, L. Leicestershire

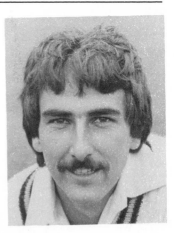

Full Name: Laurie Potter.
Role: Right-hand bat, slow left-arm and medium pace bowler, slip fielder.
Born: 7 November 1962, Bexleyheath, Kent.
Height: 6′ 1″ **Weight:** 14st.
Nickname: Potts, Liz, Lounge.
County debut: 1981 (Kent).
1st-Class 50s scored: 11.
1st-Class 100s scored: 4.
Place in batting averages: 196 average: 18.85; (1984: 169 average: 23.92).
Place in bowling averages: 87 average: 36.76.
1st-Class catches 1985: 10 (career: 32).
Parents: Ronald Henry Ernest and Audrey Megan Potter.
Wife and date of marriage: Diana Frances, 28 September 1985.
Education: Kelmscott Senior High School, Perth, Western Australia.
Qualifications: Australian leaving exams.
Off-season 1985–86: Playing and coaching in South Africa.
Overseas tours: With Australian U-19 team to Pakistan 1981.
Overseas teams played for: Australia U-19 team, West Perth C.C., 1977–82; Griqualand West, 1984-85.
Cricketers particularly learnt from: Norm O'Neill, Alan Beukas (Griqualand West), majority of senior players at Kent.

Cricketers particularly admired: Derek Underwood, Alan Knott.
Other sports: Australian rules football, soccer, squash.
Relaxations: Music, watching movies (cinema), reading, following sports.
Extras: Captained Australia U-19 team to Pakistan 1981. Played for Young England v Young India 1981. Parents emigrated to Australia when he was 4. His mother wrote to Kent in 1978 asking for trial for him. Captained Young Australia as well as Young England. Decided to leave Kent after 1985 season.
Best batting performance: 165 Griqualand West v Border, East London 1984-85.
Best bowling performance: 4-63 Griqualand West v Boland, Stellenbosch 1984-85.

LAST SEASON: BATTING

	I.	N.O.	R.	H.S.	AV.
TEST					
OTHER FIRST CLASS	15	2	245	58	18.85
INT					
JPL	5	0	116	52	23.20
NAT.W					
B & H					

CAREER: BATTING

	I.	N.O.	R.	H.S.	AV.
TEST					
OTHER FIRST CLASS	90	8	2413	165*	29.43
INT					
JPL	30	1	577	52	19.89
NAT.W	2	0	86	45	43.00
B & H	3	0	84	49	28.00

LAST SEASON: BOWLING

	O.	M.	R.	W.	AV.
TEST					
OTHER FIRST CLASS	258.4	66	772	21	36.76
INT					
JPL	26	1	96	6	16.00
NAT.W					
B & H					

CAREER: BOWLING

	O.	M.	R.	W.	AV.
TEST					
OTHER FIRST CLASS	532.1	130	1531	43	35.61
INT					
JPL	60	3	245	15	16.33
NAT.W					
B & H					

134. Who scored the first double-century of the English first-class season?

135. Who was the last man to play for England at both cricket and soccer?

136. When did David Gower play his first Test, where, against whom, and what did he do to his first ball?

PRICE, M.R. Glamorgan

Full Name: Mark Richard Price.
Role: Right-hand bat, slow left-
arm bowler, slip fielder.
Born: 20 April 1960, Liverpool.
Height: 6′ 2″ **Weight:** 13st.
Nickname: Grimbo, Dale.
County debut: 1984.
Place in batting averages: 191
average: 19.43.
Place in bowling averages: 108
average: 41.00.
1st-Class catches 1985: 2 (career: 2).
Parents: Alan and Nellie.
Wife and date of marriage: Caroline,
March 1984.
Family links with cricket: Father
played Lancashire League for
Ramsbottom.
Education: Harper Green High,
Farnworth, Bolton.

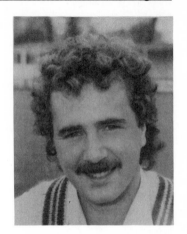

Qualifications: 7 C.S.E.s. Engineer.
Jobs outside cricket: Engineering; building sites.
Cricketers particularly admired: Ian Botham, Bishan Bedi.
Other sports: Football, snooker, table-tennis, boxing.
Best batting performance: 36 Glamorgan v Nottinghamshire, Swansea
1985.
Best bowling performance: 4-97 Glamorgan v Leicestershire, Swansea 1985.

LAST SEASON: BATTING

	I.	N.O.	R.	H.S.	AV.
TEST					
OTHER FIRST CLASS	11	4	136	36	19.43
INT					
JPL	5	0	53	22	10.60
NAT.W	1	0	6	6	–
B & H					

CAREER: BATTING

	I.	N.O.	R.	H.S.	AV.
TEST					
OTHER FIRST CLASS	13	4	144	36	16.00
INT					
JPL	5	0	53	22	10.60
NAT.W	1	0	6	6	–
B & H					

LAST SEASON: BOWLING

	O.	M.	R.	W.	AV.
TEST					
OTHER FIRST CLASS	258.4	59	697	17	41.00
INT					
JPL	31.4	0	147	2	73.50
NAT.W	15	2	43	3	14.33
B & H					

CAREER: BOWLING

	O.	M.	R.	W.	AV.
TEST					
OTHER FIRST CLASS	289.4	63	806	19	42.42
INT					
JPL	31.4	0	147	2	73.50
NAT.W	15	2	43	3	14.33
B & H					

PRICHARD, P.J.   Essex

Full Name: Paul John Prichard.
Role: Right-hand bat, cover/mid-wicket fielder.
Born: 7 January 1965, Brentwood.
Height: 5′ 10″ **Weight:** 11st. 7lbs.
Nickname: Digger, Pablo.
County debut: 1984.
1st-Class 50s scored: 11.
1st-Class 100s scored: 1.
One-day 50s: 1.
Place in batting averages: 135
average: 25.97; (1984: 98
average: 32.89).
1st-Class catches 1985: 14
(career: 24).
Parents: Margaret and John.
Marital status: Single.
Family links with cricket: Father
played club cricket in Essex.
Education: Brentwood County High School.
Qualifications: N.C.A. Senior Coaching Award.
Off-season 1985–86: Promotional work for Dewey Warren Insurance Brokers
and playing for Sutherland C.C., Sydney.
Cricketing superstitions: "None touch wood!"
Overseas tours: Kingfishers tour of South Africa, January 1981.
Overseas teams played for: V.O.B. Cavaliers, Cape Town, 1981–82.
Cricketers particularly learnt from: All at Essex.
Cricketers particularly admired: "Too many to mention."
Other sports: Football, golf. Follows American football.
Relaxations: "Sailing my boat, listening to music."
Injuries 1985: Broken and dislocated finger.
Best batting performance: 100 Essex v Lancashire, Old Trafford 1984.

LAST SEASON: BATTING

	I.	N.O.	R.	H.S.	AV.
TEST					
OTHER FIRST CLASS	34	4	779	95	25.97
INT					
JPL	6	0	101	33	16.83
NAT.W	4	0	161	94	40.25
B & H	4	1	99	32	33.00

CAREER: BATTING

	I.	N.O.	R.	H.S.	AV.
TEST					
OTHER FIRST CLASS	63	6	1667	100	29.25
INT					
JPL	6	0	101	33	16.83
NAT.W	4	0	161	94	40.25
B & H	4	1	99	32	33.00

PRIDGEON, A.P.   Worcestershire

Full Name: Alan Paul Pridgeon.
Role: Right-hand bat, right-arm
medium bowler.
Born: 22 February 1954, Wall
Heath, Staffordshire.
Height: 6′ 3″ **Weight:** 13st. 2lbs.
Nickname: Pridge.
County debut: 1972.
County cap: 1980.
50 wickets in a season: 5.
1st-Class 50s scored: 1.
1st-Class 5 w. in innings: 8.
1st-Class 10 w. in match: 1.
Place in batting averages: —
average: —; (1984: 61
average: 29.53).
Place in bowling averages: —
average: —; (1984: 61
average: 29.53).
1st-Class catches 1985: 0 (career: 62).
Parents: Albert Ernest and Sybil Ruby Pridgeon.
Wife and date of marriage: Jane, 7 October 1978.
Children: Laura, 8 August 1983.
Education: Summerhill Secondary Modern, Kingswinford, West Midlands.
Qualifications: 6 C.S.E.s, Qualified F.A. coach and qualified N.C.A. coach.
Jobs outside cricket: Semi-professional footballer, F.A. coach (not full badge);
salesman and has worked for Manpower Commission.
Overseas tours: Worcestershire Club tour to Barbados 1980.
Overseas teams played for: Howick and Pakuranga, New Zealand, 1983–84.

LAST SEASON: BATTING

	I.	N.O.	R.	H.S.	AV.
TEST					
OTHER FIRST CLASS	–	–	–	–	–
INT					
JPL					
NAT.W					
B & H					

CAREER: BATTING

	I.	N.O.	R.	H.S.	AV.
TEST					
OTHER FIRST CLASS	185	75	1032	67	9.38
INT					
JPL	48	26	143	17	6.50
NAT.W	8	5	34	13*	11.33
B & H	16	8	70	13*	8.75

LAST SEASON: BOWLING

	O.	M.	R.	W.	AV.
TEST					
OTHER FIRST CLASS	9	2	14	1	–
INT					
JPL					
NAT.W					
B & H					

CAREER: BOWLING

	O.	M.	R.	W.	AV.
TEST					
OTHER FIRST CLASS	4808	962	14240	418	34.07
INT					
JPL	791.3	40	3642	111	32.81
NAT.W	105.1	19	347	8	43.38
B & H	305.2	32	1215	23	52.83

Cricketers particularly learnt from: I.V.A. Richards, Dennis Lillee, Norman Gifford.
Cricketers particularly admired: Steve Perryman ("fire man").
Other sports: Semi-professional footballer for Dudley Town F.C., West Midlands League; golf, snooker, tennis. Follows horse-racing.
Cricketing superstitions: "Hate batting while Sylvester Clarke is bowling."
Relaxations: Horse-racing, taking dog (Muffin) for walks.
Best batting performance: 67 Worcestershire v Warwickshire, Worcester 1984.
Best bowling performance: 7-35 Worcestershire v Oxford University, Oxford 1976.

PRINGLE, D.R. Essex

Full Name: Derek Raymond Pringle.
Role: Right-hand bat, right-arm fast-medium bowler, 1st slip fielder.
Born: 18 September 1958, Nairobi, Kenya.
Height: 6' 4½" **Weight:** 14st. 7lbs.
Nickname: Pring.
County debut: 1978.
County cap: 1982.
Test debut: 1982.
No. of Tests: 10.
No. of One-Day Internationals: 9.
50 wickets in a season: 2.
1st-Class 50s scored: 22.
1st-Class 100s scored: 7.
1st-Class 5 w. in innings: 9.
1st-Class 10 w. in match: 1.
One-day 50s: 14.
Place in batting averages: 158 average: 24.22; (1984: 174 average: 23.50).
Place in bowling averages: 46 average: 29.36; (1984: 48 average: 27.87).
1st-Class catches 1985: 18 (career: 76).
Parents: Donald James (deceased) and Doris May Pringle.
Marital status: Single.
Education: St Mary's School, Nairobi; Felsted School, Essex; Cambridge.
Qualifications: 8 O-levels, 3 A-levels, B.A. (Hons.) Cantab.
Family links with cricket: Father represented Kenya and East Africa (played in World Cup 1975).
Overseas tours: With England Schools to India 1978–79; Oxbridge tour of Australia 1979–80; England to Australia and New Zealand 1982–83.
Cricketers particularly learnt from: "Main influence was my father, and also Gordon Barker (ex-Essex), the coach at Felsted."

Cricketers particularly admired: "None from close quarters, many from afar."
Cricket superstitions: "Ignore the popular press."
Other sports: Squash, golf. Watches Manchester United and rugby union.
Relaxations: Reading novels, especially by V.S. Naipaul and Günter Grass; photography.
Extras: "Took all ten wickets for Nairobi Schools U-13½ v Up Country Schools U-13½. Captain of Cambridge 1982 season. Narrowly missed an Oscar for best ad-libbing extra in 'Chariots of Fire'."
Best batting performance: 127* Cambridge University v Worcestershire, Cambridge 1981.
Best bowling performance: 7-32 Essex v Middlesex, Chelmsford 1983.

LAST SEASON: BATTING

	I.	N.O.	R.	H.S.	AV.
TEST					
OTHER FIRST CLASS	31	4	654	121*	24.22
INT					
JPL	13	3	372	81*	37.20
NAT.W	5	2	129	55	43.00
B & H	6	0	30	10	5.00

CAREER: BATTING

	I.	N.O.	R.	H.S.	AV.
TEST	17	3	247	47*	17.64
OTHER FIRST CLASS	182	36	4372	127*	29.95
INT	7	2	78	34*	15.60
JPL	42	11	1014	81*	32.70
NAT.W	13	3	203	55	20.30
B & H	31	5	718	68	27.62

LAST SEASON: BOWLING

	O.	M.	R.	W.	AV.
TEST					
OTHER FIRST CLASS	604.1	146	1556	53	29.36
INT					
JPL	98.3	5	484	19	25.47
NAT.W	57	12	198	11	17.09
B & H	56.2	4	203	8	25.38

CAREER: BOWLING

	O.	M.	R.	W.	AV.
TEST	253.2	53	752	16	47.00
OTHER FIRST CLASS	2934.1	702	8116	297	27.33
INT	82	5	401	12	33.42
JPL	391.2	19	1844	61	30.22
NAT.W	144.4	33	411	19	21.63
B & H	305.3	39	1057	46	22.98

137. When did David Gower play his first Test, where, and against whom, and what did he do to his first ball?

138. Which Test and county captain could not command a regular place in his English county side?

RADFORD, N.V.   Worcestershire

Full Name: Neal Victor Radford.
Role: Right-hand bat, right-arm fast-medium bowler, gully fielder.
Born: 7 June 1957, Luanshya, Zambia.
Height: 5′ 11″ **Weight:** 12st. 6lbs.
Nickname: Radiz.
County debut: 1980 (Lancashire), 1985 (Worcestershire).
County cap: 1985.
50 wickets in a season: 1.
1st-Class 50s scored: 3.
1st-Class 5 w. in innings: 11.
1st-Class 10 w. in match: 1.
Place in batting averages: 210 average: 17.00.
Place in bowling averages: 17 average: 24.68.
1st-Class catches 1985: 4 (career: 40).
Parents: Edith Joyce and Victor Reginald Radford.
Wife: Lynne.
Family links with cricket: Brother Wayne pro for Gowerton (S.W.C.A.) and Glamorgan 2nd XI. Also Orange Free State in Currie Cup.
Education: Athlone Boys High School, Johannesburg.
Qualifications: Matriculation and university entrance. N.C.A. Advanced Coach.
Jobs outside cricket: Auditor.
Overseas teams played for: Transvaal 1979–83; South African Schools XI; South African Army.
Other sports: "Golf, squash, (have a bash at most). Follow all sport."

LAST SEASON: BATTING

	I.	N.O.	R.	H.S.	AV.
TEST					
OTHER FIRST CLASS	25	7	306	57*	17.00
INT					
JPL	10	5	125	30*	25.00
NAT.W	2	1	16	16	–
B & H	3	1	17	13*	8.50

CAREER: BATTING

	I.	N.O.	R.	H.S.	AV.
TEST					
OTHER FIRST CLASS	111	27	1507	76*	17.94
INT					
JPL	26	12	258	48*	18.42
NAT.W	5	2	45	16	15.00
B & H	5	1	32	14	8.00

LAST SEASON: BOWLING

	O.	M.	R.	W.	AV.
TEST					
OTHER FIRST CLASS	778.4	130	2493	101	24.68
INT					
JPL	83.3	3	434	19	22.84
NAT.W	44	8	140	6	23.33
B & H	38	5	147	3	49.00

CAREER: BOWLING

	O.	M.	R.	W.	AV.
TEST					
OTHER FIRST CLASS	2691.5	531	8676	308	28.17
INT					
JPL	252.5	15	1120	52	21.53
NAT.W	78.3	14	245	12	20.42
B & H	63.2	10	230	5	46.00

Relaxations: Music, T.V., films.
Extras: Only bowler to take 100 first-class wickets in 1985.
Opinions on cricket: "Demands of acquiring certain over-rates are too taxing and not conducive to good cricket."
Best batting performance: 76* Lancashire v Derbyshire, Blackpool 1981.
Best bowling performance: 6-41 Transvaal B v Griqualand West, Kimberley 1980–81.

RADLEY, C.T. Middlesex

Full Name: Clive Thornton Radley.
Role: Right-hand bat, leg-break bowler.
Born: 13 May 1944, Hertford.
Height: 5′ 10″ **Weight:** 12st.
Nickname: Radders.
County debut: 1964.
County cap: 1967.
Benefit: 1977 (£26,000).
Test debut: 1977–78.
No. of Tests: 8.
No. of One-Day Internationals: 4.
1000 runs in a season: 16.
1st-Class 50s scored: 129.
1st-Class 100s scored: 43.
1st-Class 200s scored: 1.
One-day 50s: 51.
One-day 100s: 7.
Place in batting averages: 18
average: 52.89; (1984: 82 average: 34.58).

LAST SEASON: BATTING

	I.	N.O.	R.	H.S.	AV.
TEST					
OTHER FIRST CLASS	38	12	1375	200	52.89
INT					
JPL	11	2	108	37	12.00
NAT.W	2	0	45	27	22.50
B & H	4	0	64	40	16.00

CAREER: BATTING

	I.	N.O.	R.	H.S.	AV.
TEST	10	0	481	158	48.10
OTHER FIRST CLASS	824	125	24768	200	35.43
INT	4	1	250	117*	83.33
JPL	234	23	6171	133*	29.24
NAT.W	52	6	1418	105*	30.83
B & H	61	11	1536	121*	30.72

LAST SEASON: BOWLING

	O.	M.	R.	W.	AV.
TEST					
OTHER FIRST CLASS	13	3	43	2	21.50
INT					
JPL					
NAT.W					
B & H					

CAREER: BOWLING

	O.	M.	R.	W.	AV.
TEST					
OTHER FIRST CLASS	44	10	160	8	20.00
INT					
JPL	3.4	1	17	1	–
NAT.W					
B & H					

1st-Class catches 1985: 12 (career: 497).
Parents: Laura Radley and late Arthur Radley.
Wife and date of marriage: Linda, 22 September 1973.
Children: Louise, 18 September 1978; Paul Craig Thornton, 26 July 1980.
Education: King Edward VI Grammar School, Norwich.
Jobs outside cricket: Has coached in South Africa and Australia.
Family links with cricket: Father played club cricket.
Overseas tours: Pakistan and New Zealand 1977–78; Australia 1978–79.
Cricketers particularly learnt from: Ken Barrington.
Cricketers particularly admired: Bob Willis.
Other sports: Squash, golf.
Extras: Played for Norfolk under former Middlesex and England player W.J. Edrich, who eased his way to Middlesex. Shared in the 6th wicket partnership record for Middlesex, 227 with F. Titmus v South Africa at Lord's in 1965. First fielder to hold 50 catches in J.P.L. Gold Award winner in 1983 Benson and Hedges Final.
Best batting performance: 200 Middlesex v Northamptonshire, Lord's 1985.

RANDALL, D.W.   Nottinghamshire

Full Name: Derek William Randall.
Role: Right-hand bat.
Born: 24 February 1951, Retford, Nottinghamshire.
Height: 5′ 8½″ **Weight:** 11st.
Nickname: Arkle, Rags.
County debut: 1972.
County cap: 1973.
Benefit: 1983 (£42,000).
Test debut: 1976–77.
No. of Tests: 47.
No. of One-Day Internationals: 49.
1000 runs in a season: 10.
1st-Class 50s scored: 121.
1st-Class 100s scored: 35.
1st-Class 200s scored: 2.
One-day 50s: 39.
One-day 100s: 4.
Place in batting averages: 16
average: 53.78; (1984: 46 average: 41.29).
1st-Class catches 1985: 24 (career: 254).
Parents: Frederick and Mavis Randall.
Wife and date of marriage: Elizabeth, September 1973.
Children: Simon, June 1977.
Education: Sir Frederick Milner Secondary Modern School, Retford.

Qualifications: O.N.C. Mechanical engineering. Mechanical draughtsman.

Jobs outside cricket: Coaching.

Family links with cricket: Father played local cricket, "tried to bowl fast off a long run and off the wrong foot too!"

Overseas tours: India, Sri Lanka and Australia 1976–77; Pakistan and New Zealand 1977–78; Australia 1978–79, Australia and India 1979–80. Toured Australia and New Zealand with England 1982–83; New Zealand and Pakistan 1983–84.

Overseas teams played for: North Perth, Australia.

Cricketers particularly learnt from: Sir Gary Sobers. Tom Graveney was boyhood idol. Reg Simpson.

Other sports: Football, squash, golf.

Relaxations: Listening to varied selection of tapes. Family man.

Extras: Played in one John Player League match in 1971 for Nottinghamshire. Before joining Notts. staff, played for Retford Cricket Club in the Bassetlaw League, and helped in Championship wins of 1968 and 1969. One of the finest fielders in cricket. Scored 174 in Centenary Test v Australia 1977.

Best batting performance: 209 Nottinghamshire v Middlesex, Trent Bridge 1979.

Best bowling performance: 3-15 Nottinghamshire v M.C.C., Lord's 1982.

LAST SEASON: BATTING

	I.	N.O.	R.	H.S.	AV.
TEST					
OTHER FIRST CLASS	47	7	2151	117	53.78
INT					
JPL	14	1	214	65	16.46
NAT.W	5	0	108	66	21.60
B & H	4	0	152	62	38.00

CAREER: BATTING

	I.	N.O.	R.	H.S.	AV.
TEST	79	5	2470	175	33.37
OTHER FIRST CLASS	517	50	18129	209	38.82
INT	45	5	1067	88	26.68
JPL	160	19	4122	107*	29.23
NAT.W	26	1	592	75	23.68
B & H	60	9	1723	103*	33.78

LAST SEASON: BOWLING

	O.	M.	R.	W.	AV.
TEST					
OTHER FIRST CLASS	28	2	174	5	34.80
INT					
JPL	0.2	0	3	0	–
NAT.W	1	0	3	0	–
B & H					

CAREER: BOWLING

	O.	M.	R.	W.	AV.
TEST	2 –	0 –	3	0	–
OTHER FIRST CLASS	66.1	5	356	11	32.36
INT	0.2	0	2	1	–
JPL	0.5	0	9	0	–
NAT.W	1	0	3	0	–
B & H	2.5	0	5	0	–

139. Which club was formed first, Yorkshire or Lancashire?

Full Name: Dermot Alexander Reeve.
Role: Right-hand bat, right-arm fast-medium bowler, "occasional member of 'wall of putty' (slips)".
Born: 2 April 1963, Hong Kong.
Height: 6' 0" **Weight:** 11st. 8lbs.
Nickname: Ears.
County debut: 1983.
50 wickets in a season: 1.
1st-Class 50s scored: 4.
1st-Class 100s scored: 1.
1st-Class 5 w. in innings: 3.
Place in batting averages: 209 average: 17.00; (1984: 144 average: 27.00).
Place in bowling averages: 50 average: 29.67; (1984: 34 average: 25.82).
1st-Class catches 1985: 6 (career: 27).
Parents: Monica and Alexander James Reeve.
Marital status: Single.
Education: King George V School, Kowloon, Hong Kong.
Qualifications: 7 O-levels.
Off-season 1985–86: Playing cricket in Perth, Western Australia.
Overseas tours: Hong Kong tour to Malaysia and Singapore 1980; Hong Kong British Forces tour to Malaysia 1982; M.C.C. tour to Holland and Denmark 1983.
Overseas teams played for: Claremont-Cottesloe C.C., Western Australia, 1982–83; Mount Lawley C.C., Perth, 1985–86.

LAST SEASON: BATTING

	I.	N.O.	R.	H.S.	AV.
TEST					
OTHER FIRST CLASS	15	5	170	56	17.00
INT					
JPL	2	1	19	19	–
NAT.W					
B & H	2	0	3	3	1.50

CAREER: BATTING

	I.	N.O.	R.	H.S.	AV.
TEST					
OTHER FIRST CLASS	57	14	848	119	19.72
INT					
JPL	12	7	83	19	16.60
NAT.W	4	3	35	16*	–
B & H	5	0	38	16	7.60

LAST SEASON: BOWLING

	O.	M.	R.	W.	AV.
TEST					
OTHER FIRST CLASS	475.5	107	1424	48	29.67
INT					
JPL	62.4	1	262	14	18.71
NAT.W					
B & H	27	5	122	0	–

CAREER: BOWLING

	O.	M.	R.	W.	AV.
TEST					
OTHER FIRST CLASS	1520.4	413	4077	145	28.12
INT					
JPL	222.5	8	985	46	21.41
NAT.W	55.5	11	154	7	22.00
B & H	74.4	8	335	7	47.86

Cricketers particularly learnt from: Don Wilson, Andy Wagner and most of the Sussex senior players.
Cricketers particularly admired: Derek Randall.
Other sports: Tennis. Follows soccer (Manchester United).
Injuries 1985: "Lots of head colds."
Relaxations: "Music, movies."
Extras: Formerly on Lord's groundstaff. Represented Hong Kong in the I.C.C. Trophy competition June 1982. Hong Kong Cricketer of the Year 1980–81. Hong Kong's Cricket Sports Personality of the Year 1981.
Opinions on cricket: "Advocate 16 4-day games as opposed to current system. Fining system for over-rates should be reviewed."
Best batting performance: 119 Sussex v Surrey, The Oval 1984.
Best bowling performance: 5-22 Sussex v Cambridge University, Cambridge 1984.

RHODES, S.J. Worcestershire

Full Name: Steven John Rhodes.
Role: Right-hand bat, wicket-keeper.
Born: 17 June 1964, Bradford.
Height: 5' 8" **Weight:** 11st. 9lbs.
Nickname: Wilf, Bumpy.
County debut: 1981 (Yorkshire), 1985 (Worcestershire).
1st-Class 50s scored: 1.
Place in batting averages: 138 average: 25.62.
Parents: Bill and Norma Rhodes.
Marital status: Single.
Family links with cricket: Father played for Nottinghamshire 1961-64.
Education: Bradford Moor Junior School; Lapage St Middle; Carlton-Bolling Comprehensive.
Qualifications: 4 O-levels, cricket coaching certificate.
Jobs outside cricket: Trainee manager in sports retailer in winters of 1980–81 and 1981–82.
Cricketing superstitions: "I like to make sure I am not last out of the changing room when fielding."
Overseas teams played for: Past Brothers Cricket Club, Bundaberg, Queensland, Australia, 1982–83 and 1983–84, and Bundaberg Cricket Association.
Cricketers particularly learnt from: "Phil Carrick, Doug Padgett, Kapil Dev and my father."
Cricketers particularly admired: Alan Knott ("seems to have lots of time with his keeping".).

Other sports: Golf, follows rugby league (Bradford Northern).

Extras: Played for Young England against Young Australia in 1983. Youngest wicket-keeper to play for Yorkshire. Holds record for most victims in an innings for Young England. Played for England Schools U-15s. Released by Yorkshire to join Worcestershire at end of 1984 season.

Opinions on cricket: "County Cricket should be played over four days to stop manufacturing of a game on the last day. Too many games are made by declarations rather than bowling sides out twice."

Best batting performance: 58* Worcester v Yorkshire, Worcester 1985.

LAST SEASON: BATTING

	I.	N.O.	R.	H.S.	AV.
TEST					
OTHER FIRST CLASS	34	13	538	58*	25.62
INT					
JPL	12	3	208	45*	23.11
NAT.W	3	2	21	9*	–
B & H	4	2	57	27*	28.50

CAREER: BATTING

	I.	N.O.	R.	H.S.	AV.
TEST					
OTHER FIRST CLASS	36	14	579	58*	26.32
INT					
JPL	13	3	214	45*	21.40
NAT.W	3	2	21	9*	–
B & H	4	2	57	27*	28.50

LAST SEASON: WICKET KEEPING

	C.	ST.			
TEST					
OTHER FIRST CLASS	54	3			
INT					
JPL	10	1			
NAT.W	5	1			
B & H	7	1			

CAREER: WICKET KEEPING

	C.	ST.			
TEST					
OTHER FIRST CLASS	57	3			
INT					
JPL	13	1			
NAT.W	5	1			
B & H	7	1			

RICE, C.E.B.   Nottinghamshire

Full Name: Clive Edward Butler Rice.

Role: Right-hand bat, right-arm fast-medium bowler.

Born: 23 July 1949, Johannesburg, South Africa.

Height: 6' 0" **Weight:** 13st. 3lbs.

Nickname: Ricey.

County debut: 1975.

County cap: 1975.

Benefit: 1982 (South Africa), 1985 (England).

1000 runs in a season: 11.

50 wickets in a season: 4.

1st-Class 50s scored: 109.

1st-Class 100s scored: 37.

1st-Class 200s scored: 3.

1st-Class 5 w. in innings: 20.

1st-Class 10 w. in match: 1.

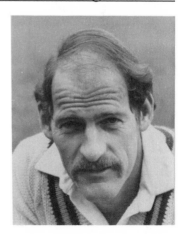

One-day 50s: 49.
One-day 100s: 7.
Place in batting averages: 13 average: 55.76; (1984: 22 average: 48.53).
Place in bowling averages: 57 average: 31.16; (1984: 65 average: 29.95).
1st-Class catches 1985: 21 (career: 301).
Parents: Patrick and Angela Rice.
Wife and date of marriage: Susan Elizabeth, 28 February 1975.
Children: Jackie Elizabeth, 27 June 1981; Mark Richard, 11 August 1983.
Education: St John's College and Damelin College, Johannesburg; Natal University, Pietermaritzburg.
Jobs outside cricket: Director of companies.
Family links with cricket: Grandfather, Phillip Syndercombe Bower, played for Repton and Oxford University. Brother, Richard Patrick Butler Rice, selected for Transvaal B but unavailable because of university exams. Brother, John Cromwell Rice, Captain of school 1st XI.
Overseas tours: World Team in World Series Cricket, Australia 1978–79.
Overseas teams played for: World Series Cricket; Transvaal; Bedfordview C.C., Johannesburg.
Cricketers particularly learnt from: Don Mackay-Coghill and Ali Bacher, Graeme Pollock.
Cricketers particularly admired: Mike Procter, Graeme Pollock, Richard Hadlee, Dennis Lillee.
Cricket superstitions: "111, 222 or 333 on scoreboard."
Off-season 1985–86: Playing in South Africa for Transvaal.
Other sports: Follows English football, rugby, motor-racing.
Relaxations: Reading, listening to music, studying stock markets.
Extras: Writes for local South African newspapers. Captain of Bedfordview C.C., Johannesburg. Made debut for Transvaal in 1969. Professional for Ramsbottom in Lancashire League, 1973. Originally appointed Captain of Nottinghamshire in 1978 but was at first relieved of his appointment after signing for World Series Cricket. Reappointed for 1979. Played three "Supertests" for W.S.C. Was sponsored at 5 rands (£2.77) a run, 50 rands (£27) a

LAST SEASON: BATTING

	I.	N.O.	R.	H.S.	AV.
TEST					
OTHER FIRST CLASS	33	8	1394	171*	55.76
INT					
JPL	13	0	296	67	22.76
NAT.W	4	0	72	35	18.00
B & H	4	1	145	73*	48.33

CAREER: BATTING

	I.	N.O.	R.	H.S.	AV.
TEST					
OTHER FIRST CLASS	607	94	21122	246	41.17
INT					
JPL	154	25	5365	120*	41.58
NAT.W	21	1	420	71	21.00
B & H	48	6	1484	130*	35.33

LAST SEASON: BOWLING

	O.	M.	R.	W.	AV.
TEST					
OTHER FIRST CLASS	284	82	779	25	31.16
INT					
JPL	77.4	2	438	7	62.57
NAT.W	30	0	170	1	–
B & H	27	3	99	3	33.00

CAREER: BOWLING

	O.	M.	R.	W.	AV.
TEST					
OTHER FIRST CLASS	6235.2	1647	16460	742	22.18
INT					
JPL	752.2	47	3325	136	24.44
NAT.W	150	19	537	25	21.48
B & H	365	57	1179	65	18.14

wicket, and 100 rands (£55) a catch in the 1980–81 Currie Cup competition in South Africa. Wisden Cricketer of the Year 1981. Most runs in John Player League in a season: 814 in 1977. Highest score for Transvaal in Datsun Shield, 169 v Griqualand West. Highest score for Nottinghamshire in John Player League, 120 against Glamorgan. 1984 and 1985 winner of Silk Cut Challenge all-rounders competition.

Opinions on cricket: "To improve the game we need to play less cricket in England. Quality not quantity. Give the players a chance to prepare for each game. We also have to make matches more of a spectacle than an every day occurence."

Injuries 1985: Broken middle finger on right hand.

Best batting performance: 246 Nottinghamshire v Sussex, Hove 1976.

Best bowling performance: 7–62 Transvaal v Western Province, Johannesburg 1975–76.

RICHARDS, C.J.   Surrey

Full Name: Clifton James Richards.
Role: Right-hand bat, wicket-keeper.
Born: 10 August 1958, Penzance.
Height: 5′ 11″ **Weight:** 11st. 8lbs.
Nickname: Jack.
County debut: 1976.
County cap: 1978.
No. of One-Day Internationals. 3.
1st-Class 50s scored: 20.
1st-Class 100s scored: 3.
One-day 50s: 1.
One-day 100s: 1.
Place in batting averages: 31 average: 44.33; (1984: 120 average: 30.27).
Parents: Clifton and Elizabeth June Richards.
Wife: Birgitta, 27 September 1980.
Education: Humphrey Davy Grammar School, Penzance.
Qualifications: 7 O-Levels.
Jobs outside cricket: Trainee electrical engineer, apprentice draughtsman.
Family links with cricket: Father a member of Penzance C.C. and Surrey C.C.C.
Overseas tours: Australia with Derrick Robins' U-23 XI in 1979–80; Far East with Surrey C.C.C. in 1978–79; England to India 1981–82.
Overseas teams played for: Klaas Vervelde XI, 1981.
Cricketing superstitions: Always last out of the dressing room when fielding.

Other sports: Tennis, golf, rugby, skiing, ice-skating, sailing. Follows most sports, especially American and other foreign sports.
Relaxations: Reading, television, driving.
Best batting performance: 117* Surrey v Nottinghamshire, The Oval 1982.

LAST SEASON: BATTING

	I.	N.O.	R.	H.S.	AV.
TEST					
OTHER FIRST CLASS	27	12	665	75*	44.33
INT					
JPL	9	4	113	21	22.60
NAT.W	1	1	9	9*	–
B & H	2	0	4	3	2.00

CAREER: BATTING

	I.	N.O.	R.	H.S.	AV.
TEST					
OTHER FIRST CLASS	269	66	5029	117*	24.77
INT	2	0	3	3	1.50
JPL	77	20	740	52	12.98
NAT.W	12	3	213	105*	23.67
B & H	25	7	218	32	12.11

LAST SEASON: WICKET KEEPING

	C.	ST.
TEST		
OTHER FIRST CLASS	41	7
INT		
JPL	4	3
NAT.W	1	–
B & H	8	–

CAREER: WICKET KEEPING

	C.	ST.
TEST		
OTHER FIRST CLASS	401	57
INT	1	–
JPL	65	28
NAT.W	24	4
B & H	36	5

RICHARDS, I.V.A.   Somerset

Full Name: Isaac Vivian Alexander Richards.
Role: Right-hand bat, off-break bowler.
Born: 7 March 1952, St John's, Antigua.
Height: 5' 11" **Weight:** 13st. 7lbs.
Nickname: Smokey, Viv, Vivvy.
County debut: 1974.
County cap: 1974.
Benefit: 1982 (£56,440).
Test debut: 1974–75.
No. of Tests: 77.
No. of One-Day Internationals: 98.
1000 runs in a season: 11.
1st-Class 50s scored: 97.
1st-Class 100s scored: 77.
1st-Class 200s scored: 9.
1st-Class 5 w. in innings: 1.
One-day 50s: 69.
One-day 100s: 19.
Place in batting averages: 1 average: 76.50; (1984: 31 average: 44.64).

1st-Class catches 1985: 19 (career: 329).
Parents: Malcolm and Gratel Richards.
Wife and date of marriage: Miriam, 24 March 1981.
Children: Daughter, Matara and son born on eve of 1983 NatWest final.
Education: St John's Boys School, Antigua Grammar School.
Jobs outside cricket: Worked as a waiter at D'Arcy's Bar and Restaurant, in St John's, Antigua. Apprentice mechanic. Assistant groundsman.
Family links with cricket: Father played cricket for Antigua as fast-bowler and all-rounder. He also played soccer for Antigua. Half-brother Donald opened bowling for Antigua, and also played for Leeward Islands. Brother Mervyn has played both cricket and soccer for Antigua.
Overseas tours: With West Indies to India, Sri Lanka and Pakistan 1974–75; Australia 1975–76, 1979–80, 1980-81, 1984-85; England 1976, 1980 and 1984; Pakistan 1980–81; India 1983–84.
Overseas teams played for: Leeward Islands 1971–72; Queensland in 1976– 77 Sheffield Shield Competition.
Cricketers particularly learnt from: Father; Pat Evanson; Shandy Perera.
Cricket superstitions: "I'm not a superstitious cricketer".
Other sports: Captained school soccer team as centre-half. Invited to go for a trial with Bath City F.C., the Southern League club, but no offer of terms followed. Played basketball for The Knickerbockers in Antigua. Squash.
Relaxations: Music. "I sit for hours listening to my stereo." Has large collection of L.P.s.
Extras: Made debut 1971–72 for Leeward Islands. Has written autobiography with David Foot, entitled *Viv Richards*. Helps to sponsor young cricketers, footballers and basketball players in Antigua. Brother Mervyn appointed national soccer coach in Antigua. Attended Alf Gover's cricket school in 1972. Shared in 4th wicket partnership record for Somerset of 251 with P.M. Roebuck v Surrey at Weston-Super-Mare in 1977. Record for most sixes hit in John Player League in one season, 26 in 1977. Took hat-trick v Essex in J.P.L. at Chelmsford, 1982.

LAST SEASON: BATTING

	I.	N.O.	R.	H.S.	AV.
TEST					
OTHER FIRST CLASS	24	0	1836	322	76.50
INT					
JPL	10	1	384	86	42.66
NAT.W	3	1	107	87*	53.50
B & H					

CAREER: BATTING

	I.	N.O.	R.	H.S.	AV.
TEST	116	7	5889	291	54.02
OTHER FIRST CLASS	456	31	20952	322	49.30
INT	89	11	4071	189*	52.19
JPL	125	15	4363	126*	39.66
NAT.W	29	2	1153	139*	42.70
B & H	35	6	1310	132*	45.17

LAST SEASON: BOWLING

	O.	M.	R.	W.	AV.
TEST					
OTHER FIRST CLASS	183	48	494	7	70.57
INT					
JPL	48.5	2	231	8	28.87
NAT.W	23	0	92	3	30.67
B & H					

CAREER: BOWLING

	O.	M.	R.	W.	AV.
TEST	17.1 445.5	2 125	1023	19	53.84
OTHER FIRST CLASS	26.3 1989.2	2 512	5896	142	41.52
INT	2 524	0 16	2345	62	37.82
JPL	318.5	12	1417	61	23.22
NAT.W	109.1	12	416	13	32.00
B & H	50.4	10	178	7	25.43

Opinions on cricket: "I have never contemplated wearing a helmet. My personal view is that a helmet with a visor takes a little of the batsman's vision — and just a little of the challenge out of the game."
Best batting performance: 322 Somerset v Warwickshire, Taunton 1985.
Best bowling performance: 5-88 West Indies v Queensland, Brisbane 1981–82.

RIPLEY, D. Northamptonshire

Full Name: David Ripley.
Role: Right-hand bat, wicket-keeper.
Born: 13 September 1966, Leeds.
Height: 5′ 10″ **Weight:** 11st.
Nickname: Rippers, Gripper, Puppy.
County debut: 1984.
1st-Class 50s scored: 1.
Place in batting averages: —
average: —; (1984: 236
average: 15.61).
Parents: Arthur and Brenda Ripley.
Marital status: Single.
Education: Woodlesford Primary and Royds High, both Leeds.
Qualifications: 5 O-levels.
Cricketing superstitions: "If having a good run will not have my hair cut; left pad first."
Overseas tours: To West Indies with England Young Cricketers 1984-85.

LAST SEASON: BATTING

	I.	N.O.	R.	H.S.	AV.
TEST					
OTHER FIRST CLASS	14	4	83	27	8.30
INT					
JPL	5	1	35	16	8.75
NAT.W	1	0	5	5	—
B & H					

CAREER: BATTING

	I.	N.O.	R.	H.S.	AV.
TEST					
OTHER FIRST CLASS	35	7	364	61	13.00
INT					
JPL	11	4	86	24	12.28
NAT.W	3	1	40	27*	20.00
B & H					

LAST SEASON: WICKET KEEPING

	C.	ST.
TEST		
OTHER FIRST CLASS	21	4
INT		
JPL	4	2
NAT.W	4	1
B & H		

CAREER: WICKET KEEPING

	C.	ST.
TEST		
OTHER FIRST CLASS	47	16
INT		
JPL	10	4
NAT.W	8	1
B & H		

Cricketers particularly learnt from: Brian Reynolds, Jim Yardley, Ian Stein, Billy Rhodes, Roy Wills.
Cricketers particularly admired: Alan Knott, Bob Taylor.
Other sports: Soccer, golf, pool. Follows soccer (Leeds United) and rugby league (Castleford).
Relaxations: Driving, listening to records.
Best batting performance: 61 Northamptonshire v Surrey, Northampton 1984.

ROBERTS, B. Derbyshire

Full Name: Bruce Roberts.
Role: Right-hand bat, right-arm medium bowler, slip fielder.
Born: 30 May 1962, Lusaka, Zambia.
Height: 6' 1" **Weight:** 14st.
County debut: 1983.
1000 runs in a season: 1.
1st-Class 50s scored: 12.
1st-Class 100s scored: 2.
One-day 50s: 4.
Place in batting averages: 113 average: 29.68; (1984: 151 average 26.38).
Place in bowling averages: — average: —; (1984: 130 average: 47.45).
1st-Class catches 1985: 22 (career: 51).
Parents: Arthur William and Sara Ann Roberts.
Marital status: Single.
Family links with cricket: Father played for Orange Free State.
Education: Ruzawi, Peterhouse, Prince Edward, Rhodesia.
Qualifications: O-levels.
Off-season 1985–86: In Johannesburg playing and coaching.
Overseas teams played for: Transvaal B 1982–83, 1983–84, 1984–85.
Cricketers particularly learnt from: "My father and Ali Bacher".
Cricketers particularly admired: Imran Khan, Michael Holding.
Other sports: Follows rugby.
Relaxations: Family.
Opinions on cricket: "Should play 4-day cricket rather than 3-day as would get better standard of cricket and more positive results."
Best batting performance: 100* Derbyshire v Gloucestershire, Derby 1985.
Best bowling performance: 4-32 Transvaal B v Orange Free State, Johannesburg 1982–83.

	I.	N.O.	R.	H.S.	AV.
TEST					
OTHER FIRST CLASS	42	4	1128	100*	29.68
INT					
JPL	13	1	400	77*	33.33
NAT.W	1	0	13	13	–
B & H	4	0	130	56	32.50

CAREER: BATTING

	I.	N.O.	R.	H.S.	AV.
TEST					
OTHER FIRST CLASS	100	11	2652	100*	29.80
INT					
JPL	22	3	569	77*	29.94
NAT.W	2	0	16	13	8.00
B & H	7	1	143	56	23.83

LAST SEASON: BOWLING

	O.	M.	R.	W.	AV.
TEST					
OTHER FIRST CLASS	20	1	106	0	–
INT					
JPL	4	0	28	1	–
NAT.W					
B & H					

CAREER: BOWLING

	O.	M.	R.	W.	AV.
TEST					
OTHER FIRST CLASS	521	89	1966	54	36.41
INT					
JPL	71.4	1	463	21	22.04
NAT.W					
B & H	30	2	151	4	37.75

ROBERTS, M.L.   Glamorgan

Full Name: Martin Leonard Roberts.
Role: Right-hand bat, wicket-keeper.
Born: 12 April 1966, Mullion.
Height: 6′ 1″ **Weight:** 12 st.
Nickname: Mert.
County debut: 1985.
Parents: Len and Marian Roberts.
Marital status: Single.
Education: Helston Comprehensive School.
Qualifications: 4 O-Levels.
Jobs outside cricket: Working at W.H. Smiths and helping out P.E. staff at Helston Comprehensive School.
Off-season 1985-86: Working at W.H. Smiths and coaching youngsters.
Cricketing superstitions: Always puts left batting pad on first.
Overseas tours: Holland with Young England amateur side, 1983.
Cricketers particularly learnt from: Ex-Cornwall wicket-keeper, Jessy Lowry, Graham Wiltshire and Bob Cottam, N.C.A. coaches.
Cricketers particularly admire: Bob Taylor, Alan Knott.
Other sports: Football, volleyball, golf. Follows snooker.
Injuries 1985: Twisted knee, missed one match.
Relaxations: Listening to music, watching films, going out occasionally.

LAST SEASON: BATTING

	I.	N.O.	R.	H.S.	AV.
TEST					
OTHER FIRST CLASS	1	0	0	0	–
INT					
JPL					
NAT.W					
B & H					

CAREER: BATTING

	I.	N.O.	R.	H.S.	AV.
TEST					
OTHER FIRST CLASS	1	0	0	0	–
INT					
JPL					
NAT.W					
B & H					

ROBINSON, P.E.   Yorkshire

Full Name: Phillip Edward Robinson.
Role: Right-hand bat, cover fielder.
Born: 3 August 1963, Keighley.
Height: 5' 10'' **Weight:** 13st. 7lbs.
Nickname: Red Robbo, Wimpey.
County debut: 1984.
1st-Class 50s scored: 9.
One-day 50s: 2.
Place in batting averages: 111
average: 30.00; (1984: 51
average: 39.79).
1st-Class catches 1985: 2 (career: 9).
Parents: Keith and Margaret Lesley
Robinson.
Marital status: Engaged.
Education: Hartington Middle,
Greenhead Comprehensive.
Qualifications: 2 O-levels.
Jobs outside cricket: Outworker supervisor (Swegmark Nelson Ltd).

LAST SEASON: BATTING

	I.	N.O.	R.	H.S.	AV.
TEST					
OTHER FIRST CLASS	16	1	450	79	30.00
INT					
JPL	7	1	191	78*	31.83
NAT.W	1	0	0	0	–
B & H	2	0	55	42	27.50

CAREER: BATTING

	I.	N.O.	R.	H.S.	AV.
TEST					
OTHER FIRST CLASS	40	6	1206	92	35.47
INT					
JPL	18	1	382	78*	22.47
NAT.W	1	0	0	0	–
B & H	3	0	59	42	19.67

LAST SEASON: BOWLING

	O.	M.	R.	W.	AV.
TEST					
OTHER FIRST CLASS					
INT					
JPL					
NAT.W					
B & H					

CAREER: BOWLING

	O.	M.	R.	W.	AV.
TEST					
OTHER FIRST CLASS	2	0	12	0	–
INT					
JPL					
NAT.W					
B & H					

Cricketing superstitions: "Always put my left boot on first."
Cricketers particularly learnt from: "I learn from all cricketers."
Cricketers particularly admired: Gary Sobers— "the best player I've seen."
Other sports: Football, badminton, swimming. Follows Manchester United.
Relaxations: Watching films, going out with friends.
Extras: Scored the highest score by a Yorkshire 2nd XI player of 233 in 1983 v Kent at Canterbury.
Injuries 1985: Torn ligaments in left ankle — out for four weeks.
Opinions on cricket: "I would like to see more English-born quick bowlers. There are too many foreign ones."
Best batting performance: 92 Yorkshire v Glamorgan, Bradford 1984.

ROBINSON, R.T.   Nottinghamshire

Full Name: Robert Timothy Robinson.
Role: Right-hand opening bat.
Born: 21 November 1958, Sutton-in-Ashfield, Nottinghamshire.
Height: 5′ 11½″ **Weight:** 12st. 3lbs.
Nickname: Robbo, Chop.
County debut: 1978.
County cap: 1983.
Test debut: 1984–85.
No. of Tests: 11.
No. of One-Day Internationals: 7.
1000 runs in a season: 3.
1st-Class 50s scored: 45.
1st-Class 100s scored: 10.
1st-Class 200s scored: 1.
One-day 50s: 15.
One-day 100s: 2.
Place in batting averages: 8
average: 59.96; (1984: 18 average: 50.80).
1st-Class catches 1985: 13 (career: 69).
Parents: Eddy and Christine Robinson.
Marital status: Single.
Education: Dunstable Grammar School; High Pavement College, Nottingham; Sheffield University.
Qualifications: Honours degree in Accounting and Financial Management.
Family links with cricket: Father, uncle, cousin and brother played local cricket. Brother played for Nottinghamshire Schoolboys.
Jobs outside cricket: Trainee accountant.
Off-season 1985–86: On tour to West Indies with England.
Cricketing superstitions: Always puts left pad on first.

Overseas tours: N.C.A. U-19 tour 1976; India and Australia 1984–85 with England.
Overseas teams played for: Durban Collegians, South Africa, 1980–81.
Cricketers particularly learnt from: Clive Rice, Eddie Hemmings.
Cricketers particularly admired: Geoff Boycott.
Other sports: Soccer, golf, badminton. Follows rugby.
Relaxations: Driving, listening to all music, films, doing nothing.
Extras: Played for Northants 2nd XI in 1974–75 and for Nottinghamshire 2nd XI in 1977. Had soccer trials with Portsmouth, Chelsea and Q.P.R.
Best batting performance: 207 Nottinghamshire v Warwickshire, Trent Bridge 1983.

LAST SEASON: BATTING

	I.	N.O.	R.	H.S.	AV.
TEST	9	1	490	175	61.25
OTHER FIRST CLASS	22	3	1129	130*	59.42
INT	2	0	33	26	16.50
JPL	10	1	273	77	30.33
NAT.W	5	1	417	139	104.25
B & H	4	0	247	120	61.75

CAREER: BATTING

	I.	N.O.	R.	H.S.	AV.
TEST	18	3	934	175	62.27
OTHER FIRST CLASS	220	28	7663	207	39.91
INT	7	0	97	37	13.86
JPL	71	8	1858	97*	29.49
NAT.W	13	2	636	139	57.82
B & H	25	2	644	120	28.00

LAST SEASON: BOWLING

	O.	M.	R.	W.	AV.
TEST					
OTHER FIRST CLASS					
INT					
JPL					
NAT.W					
B & H					

CAREER: BOWLING

	O.	M.	R.	W.	AV.
TEST	1	1	0	0	–
OTHER FIRST CLASS	15	0	94	2	47.00
INT					
JPL					
NAT.W					
B & H					

140. Which recent Test cricketer was elected a Member of Parliament in 1985?

141. Who was the last Yorkshire player to be capped for the first time for England before Arnie Sidebottom in 1985?

ROEBUCK, P.M.   Somerset

Full Name: Peter Michael Roebuck.
Role: Right-hand bat, leg-break bowler, slip fielder.
Born: 6 March 1956, Oxford.
Height: 6' 0" **Weight:** 13st. 5lbs.
Nickname: Rupert, The Oracle.
County debut: 1974.
County cap: 1978.
1000 runs in a season: 5.
1st-Class 50s scored: 68.
1st-Class 100s scored: 15.
1st-Class 5 w. in innings: 1.
One-day 50s: 18.
One-day 100s: 1.
Place in batting averages: 30 average: 44.82; (1984: 27 average: 47.28).
1st-Class catches 1985: 10 (career: 110).
Parents: James and Elizabeth Roebuck.
Marital status: Single.
Education: Park School, Bath; Millfield School; Emmanuel College, Cambridge University.
Qualifications: 1st Class Hons degree in law.
Jobs outside cricket: Teaching and occasional journalism in Australia.
Family links with cricket: Mother and sister both played for Oxford University Ladies. Young brother, Paul, played for E.S.C.A. U-15 and now Gloucestershire.
Overseas tours: Toured in Australia with Combined Oxford & Cambridge XI 1979–80. "Christians in Sport" Tour to India 1985.
Overseas teams played for: Played in Perth, Australia, 1979–80; also in Corfu, Sydney and Fiji.
Cricketers particularly learnt from: Viv Richards, Martin Crowe.
Cricketers particularly admired: R.J.O. Meyer, Viv Richards, Leary Constantine, Ken Barrington.
Cricket superstitions: "I'm trying to get rid of all these, but I have lots when I'm doing badly."
Other sports: "Vague efforts at golf, football, tennis and surfing."
Injuries 1985: Broken finger, missed four weeks.
Relaxations: "Reading, wining and dining, arguing, music."
Extras: Cambridge blue 1975–76–77. Plays in spectacles. Youngest Minor County cricketer, playing for Somerset 2nd XI at age of 13. Shared in 4th wicket partnership record for county of 251 with I.V.A. Richards v Surrey at Weston-Super-Mare in 1977. Books: *Slice of Cricket*; *It Never Rains*. Articles in *Sunday Independent*, *Guardian*, "and anyone else who asks". Founder member of campaign for fair play. Appointed captain for 1986.
Opinions on cricket: "Most of these will have to wait until I write my

autobiography, but I'll mention one. I deplore sporting links with South Africa because a nation which includes many coloured people and regards them as equals cannot decently play against one which regards the black man as inferior. I wish people would stop pretending, however regrettable it might be, that sport and politics are not as mixed as whisky and water."

Best batting performance: 159 Somerset v Northamptonshire, Northampton 1984.

Best bowling performance: 6-50 Cambridge University v Kent, Canterbury 1977.

LAST SEASON: BATTING

	I.	N.O.	R.	H.S.	AV.
TEST					
OTHER FIRST CLASS	33	5	1255	132*	44.82
INT					
JPL	8	1	219	74*	31.28
NAT.W	3	0	61	39	20.33
B & H	4	0	39	36	9.75

CAREER: BATTING

	I.	N.O.	R.	H.S.	AV.
TEST					
OTHER FIRST CLASS	375	54	11245	159	35.03
INT					
JPL	106	21	2556	105	30.07
NAT.W	26	2	693	98	28.88
B & H	40	5	822	53*	23.48

LAST SEASON: BOWLING

	O.	M.	R.	W.	AV.
TEST					
OTHER FIRST CLASS	16	3	47	0	–
INT					
JPL					
NAT.W					
B & H					

CAREER: BOWLING

	O.	M.	R.	W.	AV.
TEST					
OTHER FIRST CLASS	748.3	197	2069	42	49.26
INT					
JPL	12.3	0	65	2	32.50
NAT.W					
B & H	8.2	1	23	2	11.50

142. In the Fourth Test v Australia in 1985 three bowlers born in the same county spearheaded England's attack: who were they and what was the county?

143. Who was "The Little Wonder"?

ROMAINES, P.W.   Gloucestershire

Full Name: Paul William Romaines.
Role: Right-hand opening batsman.
Born: 25 December 1955, Bishop
Auckland, Co. Durham.
Height: 6′ 0″ **Weight:** 12st. 8lbs.
Nickname: Canny, Human.
County debut: 1975 (Northampton-
shire), 1982 (Gloucestershire).
County cap: 1983.
1000 runs in a season: 2.
1st-Class 50s scored: 22.
1st-Class 100s scored: 10.
One-day 50s: 16.
One-day 100s: 2.
Place in batting averages: 173
average: 22.23; (1984: 77
average: 35.46).
1st-Class catches 1985: 10
(career: 38).

Parents: George and Freda Romaines.
Wife and date of marriage: Julie Anne, 1979.
Education: Leeholme School, Bishop Auckland.
Qualifications: 8 0-levels. N.C.A. Qualified Coach.
Jobs outside cricket: Sales representative for L'Oreal.
Family links with cricket: Father played local cricket and is still an avid
watcher. Grandfather, W.R. Romaines, represented Durham in Minor Counties
cricket, and played v Australia in 1926.
Cricket superstitions: "Put left pad on first but during 1985 tried everything
which offered the slightest hint of success!"

LAST SEASON: BATTING

	I.	N.O.	R.	H.S.	AV.
TEST					
OTHER FIRST CLASS	34	4	667	114*	22.23
INT					
JPL	13	0	611	105	47.00
NAT.W	2	0	31	26	15.50
B & H	4	0	170	125	42.50

CAREER: BATTING

	I.	N.O.	R.	H.S.	AV.
TEST					
OTHER FIRST CLASS	172	12	4924	186	30.78
INT					
JPL	49	3	1505	105	32.71
NAT.W	12	1	324	82	29.45
B & H	9	1	349	125	43.63

LAST SEASON: BOWLING

	O.	M.	R.	W.	AV.
TEST					
OTHER FIRST CLASS	10	0	42	3	14.00
INT					
JPL					
NAT.W					
B & H					

CAREER: BOWLING

	O.	M.	R.	W.	AV.
TEST					
OTHER FIRST CLASS	15.3	2	59	3	19.67
INT					
JPL					
NAT.W					
B & H					

Cricketers particularly learnt from or admired: P. Willey, Zaheer Abbas, Barry Duddleston, Graham Gooch, Clive Radley, Ian Botham, Richard Hadlee, Malcolm Marshall.
Other sports: Squash, golf, soccer, follows athletics.
Relaxations: "Listening to music, having a good pint, antiques, people."
Extras: Joined Northants. in 1973, played until 1976 when was not retained. Debut for Northants. 1975. Minor county cricket with Durham County C.C. between 1977–1981.
Opinions on cricket: "Would like to see cricket played on uncovered pitches."
Best batting performance: 186 Gloucestershire v Warwickshire, Nuneaton 1982.

ROSE, B.C. Somerset

Full Name: Brian Charles Rose.
Role: Left-hand bat.
Born: 4 June 1950, Dartford, Kent.
Height: 6′ 1″ **Weight:** 13st. 8lbs.
Nickname: Harry.
County debut: 1969.
County cap: 1975.
Benefit: 1983 (£71,863).
Test debut: 1977–78.
No. of Tests: 9.
No. of One-Day Internationals: 2.
1000 runs in a season: 8.
1st-Class 50s scored: 50.
1st-Class 100s scored: 21.
1st-Class 200s scored: 2.
One-day 50s: 27.
One-day 100s: 3.
Place in batting averages: 54
average: 24.50; (1984: 124
average: 29.32).

1st-Class catches 1985: 2 (career: 120).
Parents: Jean and Charles Rose.
Wife and date of marriage: Stevie, 16 March 1978.
Children: Stuart Charles, 19 March 1979; Jamie Joseph, 14 December 1981.
Education: Weston-Super-Mare Grammar School; Borough Road College, Isleworth.
Jobs outside cricket: Teacher.
Off-season 1985–86: Golfing.
Injuries 1985: Broken arm.
Overseas tours: Pakistan, New Zealand 1977–78; West Indies 1981.
Overseas teams played for: Claremont-Cottesloe in Western Australia, 1979-80.

Other sports: Golf, squash.
Relaxations: Gardening.
Opinions on cricket: "There should be a 16-match championship."
Extras: Played for English Schools Cricket Association at Lord's in 1968.
Plays in spectacles. Captain 1978–83.
Best batting performance: 205 Somerset v Northamptonshire, Weston 1977.
Best bowling performance: 3-9 Somerset v Gloucestershire, Taunton 1975.

LAST SEASON: BATTING

	I.	N.O.	R.	H.S.	AV.
TEST					
OTHER FIRST CLASS	9	1	196	81*	24.50
INT					
JPL	4	1	93	53	31.00
NAT.W	1	0	1	1	–
B & H	1	1	18	18*	–

CAREER: BATTING

	I.	N.O.	R.	H.S.	AV.
TEST	16	2	358	70	25.57
OTHER FIRST CLASS	405	43	12034	205	33.24
INT	2	0	99	54	49.50
JPL	150	21	3367	112*	26.10
NAT.W	24	4	714	128	35.70
B & H	49	7	1293	137*	30.79

LAST SEASON: BOWLING

	O.	M.	R.	W.	AV.
TEST					
OTHER FIRST CLASS	1	0	8	0	–
INT					
JPL					
NAT.W					
B & H					

CAREER: BOWLING

	O.	M.	R.	W.	AV.
TEST					
OTHER FIRST CLASS	59.1	6	232	6	38.67
INT					
JPL	34	0	152	7	21.72
NAT.W					
B & H					

ROSE, G.D.   Middlesex

Full Name: Graham David Rose.
Role: Right-hand bat, right-arm
fast-medium bowler. "Field anywhere
the captain can hide me."
Born: 12 April 1964, Tottenham.
Height: 6' 3".
Nickname: Rosie.
County debut: 1983.
1st-Class 5 w. in innings: 1.
Parents: William and Edna Rose.
Marital status: Single.
Family links with cricket: Father
played club cricket.
Qualifications: 6 O-levels,
4 A-levels.
Off-season 1985-86: Playing in
Sydney.
Overseas tours: E.S.C.A. U-19 to
Zimbabwe.

Cricketers particularly learnt from: Jack Robertson, Ted Jackson.
Other sports: Golf, squash, pool. "Follow just about any sport."
Relaxations: Listening to most types of music, T.V., a little reading.
Injuries 1985: Back problem which now results in bowling in a girdle.
Opinions on cricket: Would like to see introduction of 4-day matches with 1-day competitions played at weekends.
Extras: Played for Young England v Young Australia 1983.
Best batting performance: 15 Middlesex v Somerset, Lord's 1985.
Best bowling performance: 6-41 Middlesex v Worcestershire, Worcester 1985

LAST SEASON: BATTING

	I.	N.O.	R.	H.S.	AV.
TEST					
OTHER FIRST CLASS	2	0	19	15	9.50
INT					
JPL	2	0	35	30	17.50
NAT.W					
B & H					

CAREER: BATTING

	I.	N.O.	R.	H.S.	AV.
TEST					
OTHER FIRST CLASS	2	0	19	15	9.50
INT					
JPL	3	0	68	33	22.66
NAT.W					
B & H					

LAST SEASON: BOWLING

	O.	M.	R.	W.	AV.
TEST					
OTHER FIRST CLASS	45.1	8	142	9	15.78
INT					
JPL	23	0	131	2	65.50
NAT.W					
B & H					

CAREER: BOWLING

	O.	M.	R.	W.	AV.
TEST					
OTHER FIRST CLASS	45.1	8	142	9	15.78
INT					
JPL	39	0	198	3	66.00
NAT.W					
B & H					

ROSEBERRY, M.A.   Middlesex

Full Name: Michael Anthony Roseberry.
Role: Right-hand bat, right-arm slow-medium bowler, slip and silly point fielder.
Born: 28 November 1966, Sunderland, Tyne and Wear.
Height: 6' 0'' **Weight:** 14st.
Nickname: Zorro.
County debut: 1985.
Parents: Matthew and Jean Roseberry.
Marital status: Single.
Family links with cricket: Uncle, Peter Wyness, played for Royal Navy.
Education: Durham School.
Qualifications: 5 0-levels, 1 A-level.
Off-season 1985-86: Coaching

cricket, playing rugby; Minor Counties U-25 tour of Kenya.

Cricketing superstitions: "Tend to put my front batting pad on first."

Overseas tours: Young England to West Indies, 1985; Durham School 1st XI to Barbados, 1983.

Cricketers particularly learnt from: Alec Coxon (ex-England and Yorkshire bowler), Don Wilson and Gordon Jenkins, M.C.C. Indoor School.

Cricketers particularly admired: Ian Botham, Geoff Boycott.

Other sports: "Rugby, squash, snooker and whatever takes my fancy. Follow rugby basketball, football."

Relaxations: Snooker, music, watching movies.

Extras: Won Lord's Taverners/M.C.C. Cricketer of the Year 1983. Won Sunday Sun/Dixon Sport Cricketer of the Year 1983. Won Cricket Societies' Wetherall award 1983, 1984. Won Cricket Societies' award for best Young Cricketer of Year 1984, also Frank Morris memorial award 1984.

LAST SEASON: BATTING

	I.	N.O.	R.	H.S.	AV.
TEST					
OTHER FIRST CLASS					
INT					
JPL	1	0	15	15	–
NAT.W					
B & H					

CAREER: BATTING

	I.	N.O.	R.	H.S.	AV.
TEST					
OTHER FIRST CLASS					
INT					
JPL	1	0	15	15	–
NAT.W					
B & H					

RUSSELL, P.E.   Derbyshire

Full Name: Philip Edgar Russell.

Role: Right-hand bat, right-arm medium and off-break bowler.

Born: 9 May 1944, Ilkeston.

County debut: 1965.

County cap: 1975.

50 wickets in a season: 3.

1st-Class 5 w. in innings: 5.

1st-Class catches 1985: 0 (career 124).

Education: Ilkeston Grammar School.

Jobs outside cricket: Works full-time for Derbyshire C.C.C. as county coach.

Extras: Not re-engaged after 1972 season but rejoined county in 1974. Retired from first-class cricket but re-appeared in 1985.

Best batting performance: 72 Derbyshire v Glamorgan, Swansea 1970.

Best bowling performance: 7-46 Derbyshire v Yorkshire, Sheffield 1976.

LAST SEASON: BATTING

	I.	N.O.	R.	H.S.	AV.
TEST					
OTHER FIRST CLASS	3	2	5	2*	–
INT					
JPL	2	2	3	3*	–
NAT.W					
B & H					

CAREER: BATTING

	I.	N.O.	R.	H.S.	AV.
TEST					
OTHER FIRST CLASS	210	46	2020	72	12.32
INT					
JPL	74	30	540	47*	12.27
NAT.W	7	1	53	27*	8.83
B & H	19	8	74	22*	6.73

LAST SEASON: BOWLING

	O.	M.	R.	W.	AV.
TEST					
OTHER FIRST CLASS	89.5	22	243	4	60.75
INT					
JPL	24	4	76	5	15.20
NAT.W					
B & H					

CAREER: BOWLING

	O.	M.	R.	W.	AV.
TEST					
OTHER FIRST CLASS	4082.5	1227	10351	339	30.53
INT					
JPL	763.3	78	3167	154	20.56
NAT.W	129.5	26	390	10	39.00
B & H	309.1	56	866	31	27.93

RUSSELL, R.C.　　　　　Gloucestershire

Full Name: Robert Charles Russell.
Role: Left-hand bat, wicket-keeper.
Born: 15 August 1963, Stroud.
Height: 5' 8½'' **Weight:** 9st. 8lbs.
Nickname: Jack.
County debut: 1981.
County cap: 1985.
1st-Class 50s scored: 4.
Place in batting averages: 227
average: 13.32; (1984: 166
average: 24.43).
Parents: Derek John and Jenifer
Mary Anne Russell.
Wife and date of marriage: Aileen
Ann, 6 March 1985.
Family links with cricket: Younger
brother plays for Stroud C.C.,
Gloucestershire Young Cricketers
and Gloucestershire 2nd XI.
Education: Archway Comprehensive School.
Qualifications: 7 O-levels, 2 A-levels.
Off-season 1985–86: "Waiting for the 1986 season."
Cricketing superstitions: "The numbers 37 and 87. Used only two different shirts during the 1985 season. I guard my wicket-keeping gloves, pads and white hat very closely, never leaving them in the dressing room overnight."
Overseas tours: Denmark with N.C.A. Young Cricketers 1981; with Gloucestershire to Barbados 1985; Mendip Acorns Pacific tour 1984.
Overseas teams played for: Takapuna C.C., New Zealand, 1983–84, 1984–85.

Cricketers particularly learnt from or admired: "Many that I have spoken to, Alan Knott and Bob Taylor in particular, with tremendous help and encouragement from Andy Brassington."

Other sports: Football, squash. Loves snooker.

Relaxations: "Playing and watching snooker. I usually spend my days off watching cricket videos. Going to the Prince Albert pub (Stroud). Also enjoy oil painting and writing."

Extras: Record for most dismissals in a match for first-class debut: eight (7 caught, 1 stumped) for Gloucestershire v Sri Lanka at Bristol, 1981. Youngest wicket-keeper for Gloucestershire (17 years 307 days). Represented Young England against Young West Indies in the Agatha Christie "Test Match" series, 1982. Gordon's Gin Wicket-keeper of the Month, July 1984. Played for Duchess of Norfolk's XI against West Indies at Arundel in 1984.

Injuries 1985: Fractured right thumb, missed three matches.

Opinions on cricket: "Too many overs have to be bowled in a day. 110 would be plenty. The season is long and hard enough as it is without having to play until gone 8 every evening. Nobody finds it harder than a first-class umpire!"

Best batting performance: 64* Gloucestershire v Worcestershire, Bristol 1983.

LAST SEASON: BATTING

	I.	N.O.	R.	H.S.	AV.
TEST					
OTHER FIRST CLASS	23	4	253	34	13.32
INT					
JPL	3	2	18	14	–
NAT.W	1	1	14	14*	–
B & H	2	0	0	0	0.00

CAREER: BATTING

	I.	N.O.	R.	H.S.	AV.
TEST					
OTHER FIRST CLASS	89	21	1355	64*	19.93
INT					
JPL	18	10	141	43	17.62
NAT.W	6	2	59	16	14.75
B & H	7	2	68	36*	13.60

LAST SEASON: WICKET KEEPING

	C.	ST.
TEST		
OTHER FIRST CLASS	59	5
INT		
JPL	6	1
NAT.W	5	1
B & H	5	–

CAREER: WICKET KEEPING

	C.	ST.
TEST		
OTHER FIRST CLASS	142	34
INT		
JPL	23	5
NAT.W	7	2
B & H	12	6

144. What was unusual about Alan Border's dismissal in the Fourth Test in England in 1985?

SAINSBURY, G.E.   Gloucestershire

Full Name: Gary Edward Sainsbury.
Role: Right-hand bat, left-arm medium bowler.
Born: 17 January 1958, Wanstead, London.
Height: 6′ 3″ **Weight:** 12st.
Nickname: Sains, Noddy.
County debut: 1979 (Essex), 1983 (Gloucestershire).
50 wickets in a season: 1.
1st-Class 5 w. in innings: 7.
Place in bowling averages: 4 average: 17.82; (1984: 88 average: 33.25).
1st-Class catches 1985: 2 (career: 11).
Parents: Gordon and Muriel Sainsbury.
Wife and date of marriage: Karen Frances, 24 December 1985.
Education: Beal Grammar School, Bath University.
Qualifications: 11 O-levels, 3 A-levels, BSc (Hons) Statistics. First stage of the N.C.A. Coaching Award.
Jobs outside cricket: Computer programmer, C.E. Heath & Co. Ltd., Assistant in Finance Section of Tower Hamlets Council's Social Services Department, Assistant in Research Department for Bristol and West Building Society.
Off-season 1985–86: Resume with Bristol and West Building Society.
Overseas teams played for: Hamilton-Wickham C.C., Newcastle, N.S.W., 1981–82.
Cricketers particularly learnt from: Bill Morris (Ilford Cricket School), John

LAST SEASON: BATTING

	I.	N.O.	R.	H.S.	AV.
TEST					
OTHER FIRST CLASS	5	3	11	8*	5.50
INT					
JPL	–	–	–	–	–
NAT.W					
B & H					

CAREER: BATTING

	I.	N.O.	R.	H.S.	AV.
TEST					
OTHER FIRST CLASS	50	28	123	13	5.59
INT					
JPL	8	4	20	6*	5.00
NAT.W	2	1	5	3*	–
B & H	3	2	2	1*	–

LAST SEASON: BOWLING

	O.	M.	R.	W.	AV.
TEST					
OTHER FIRST CLASS	178	59	481	27	17.82
INT					
JPL	49.3	2	200	8	25.00
NAT.W					
B & H					

CAREER: BOWLING

	O.	M.	R.	W.	AV.
TEST					
OTHER FIRST CLASS	1450	362	4282	141	30.37
INT					
JPL	242.5	18	1107	30	36.90
NAT.W	54	14	180	6	30.00
B & H	71.4	11	223	11	20.27

Gray (Wanstead C.C.), Mike Denness, John Lever.
Other sports: Squash, badminton, football, golf.
Relaxations: T.V., reading, listening to music.
Extras: "Played for Essex C.C.C. 1977–1982. First-class appearances limited to three matches. In my last season with them I was named Young Player of the Year."
Best batting performance: 13 Gloucestershire v Glamorgan, Cheltenham 1983.
Best bowling performance: 7-38 Gloucestershire v Northamptonshire, Northampton 1985.

SAXELBY, K.   Nottinghamshire

Full Name: Kevin Saxelby.
Role: Right-hand bat; right arm medium bowler.
Born: 23 February 1959.
Height: 6′ 2″ **Weight:** 14st.
Nickname: Sax.
County debut: 1978.
County cap: 1984.
50 wickets in a season: 1.
1st-Class 50s scored: 1.
1st-Class 5 w. in innings: 5.
1st-Class 10 w. in match: 1.
Place in batting averages: —
average: —; (1984: 220
average: 17.82).
Place in bowling averages: 98
average: 38.47; (1984: 93
average: 33.87).
1st-Class catches 1985: 1 (career: 11).
Parents: George Kenneth and Hilda Margaret Saxelby.
Wife: Peta Jean Wendy.
Children: Craig Robert, 6 June 1985.
Education: Magnus Grammar School, Newark.
Qualifications: 10 O-levels, 4 A-levels.
Overseas teams played for: North Perth, Australia, 1979–80; Durban Collegians, South Africa, 1980–81; Alma-Marist, Cape Town, 1982-83.
Off-season 1985–86: Farming.
Injuries 1985: Shoulder injury.
Other sports: Rugby union.
Relaxations: Gardening.
Best batting performance: 59* Nottinghamshire v Derbyshire, Chesterfield 1982.

Best bowling performance: 6-64 Nottinghamshire v Kent, Tunbridge Wells 1985.

LAST SEASON: BATTING

	I.	N.O.	R.	H.S.	AV.
TEST					
OTHER FIRST CLASS	13	4	78	29*	8.67
INT					
JPL	4	4	20	12*	-
NAT.W	1	1	6	6*	-
B & H	2	2	14	12*	-

CAREER: BATTING

	I.	N.O.	R.	H.S.	AV.
TEST					
OTHER FIRST CLASS	84	23	749	59*	12.28
INT					
JPL	23	14	110	23*	12.22
NAT.W	3	2	25	12	-
B & H	10	7	51	13*	17.00

LAST SEASON: BOWLING

	O.	M.	R.	W.	AV.
TEST					
OTHER FIRST CLASS	429	103	1385	36	38.47
INT					
JPL	65	4	283	15	18.86
NAT.W	44	7	140	6	23.33
B & H	33	6	134	4	33.50

CAREER: BOWLING

	O.	M.	R.	W.	AV.
TEST					
OTHER FIRST CLASS	1796.5	433	5608	184	30.84
INT					
JPL	380	11	1878	69	27.21
NAT.W	89.5	16	282	15	18.80
B & H	203.2	25	742	28	26.50

SCOTHERN, M. — Worcestershire

Full Name: Mark Scothern.
Role: Right-hand bat, right-arm fast-medium bowler.
Born: 9 March 1961, Skipton.
Height: 5′ 9½″.
County debut: 1985.

Best bowling performance: 1-42 Worcestershire v Cambridge University, Cambridge 1985.

LAST SEASON: BATTING

	I.	N.O.	R.	H.S.	AV.
TEST					
OTHER FIRST CLASS	-	-	-	-	-
INT					
JPL					
NAT.W					
B & H					

CAREER: BATTING

	I.	N.O.	R.	H.S.	AV.
TEST					
OTHER FIRST CLASS	-	-	-	-	-
INT					
JPL					
NAT.W					
B & H					

LAST SEASON: BOWLING

	O.	M.	R.	W.	AV.
TEST					
OTHER FIRST CLASS	16	6	42	1	-
INT					
JPL					
NAT.W					
B & H					

CAREER: BOWLING

	O.	M.	R.	W.	AV.
TEST					
OTHER FIRST CLASS	16	6	42	1	-
INT					
JPL					
NAT.W					
B & H					

SCOTT, C.W.　　　　Nottinghamshire

Full Name: Christopher Wilmot
Scott.
Role: Right-hand bat, wicket-keeper.
Born: 23 January 1964, Lincoln.
Height: 5′ 9″ **Weight:** 11st.
Nickname: George.
County debut: 1981.
1st-Class 50s scored: 1.
Parents: Kenneth and Kathleen Scott.
Marital status: Single.
Family links with cricket: Father
and elder brother play for
Collingham C.C. Younger brother
for Lincolnshire U-19s.
Education: Robert Pattinson
Comprehensive School.
Qualifications: 4 0-levels. 2 C.S.E.s.
Cricket coach.
Jobs outside cricket: Farming.
Overseas teams played for: Poverty Bay C.C., New Zealand, 1983–84.
Cricketers particularly learnt from: Everyone at Notts.
Other sports: Rugby Union, soccer.
Relaxations: Watching films, listening to records.
Extras: One of the youngest players to play for Nottinghamshire in
County Championship team — made debut at 17 years 157 days.
Best batting performance: 78 Nottinghamshire v Cambridge University,
Cambridge 1983.

LAST SEASON: BATTING

	I.	N.O.	R.	H.S.	AV.
TEST					
OTHER FIRST CLASS	1	1	39	39*	–
INT					
JPL					
NAT.W					
B & H					

CAREER: BATTING

	I.	N.O.	R.	H.S.	AV.
TEST					
OTHER FIRST CLASS	10	3	190	78	27.14
INT					
JPL	1	0	9	9	–
NAT.W					
B & H					

LAST SEASON: WICKET KEEPING

	C.	ST.
TEST		
OTHER FIRST CLASS	5	–
INT		
JPL		
NAT.W		
B & H		

CAREER: WICKET KEEPING

	C.	ST.
TEST		
OTHER FIRST CLASS	18	2
INT		
JPL	2	–
NAT.W		
B & H		

SHARMA, R.   Derbyshire

Full Name: Rajesh Sharma.
Role: Right-hand bat, off-break bowler, slip fielder.
Born: 27 June 1962. Kenya.
Height: 6′ 3″ **Weight:** 12st. 7lbs.
Nickname: Reg.
County debut: 1985.
1st-Class catches 1985: 6 (career 6).
Parents: M.R. and R.D. Sharma.
Marital status: Single.
Family links with cricket: Younger brother also has played, 2nd XI cricket.
Education: Parkland School for Boys.
Qualifications: C.S.E.s and O-levels.
Jobs outside cricket: Family business.
Off-season 1985–86: Working in family business.

Overseas teams played for: Mudgreeba, Queensland, 1982–83 and 1983–84.
Cricketers particularly learnt from: Ron Harland (played for local club).
Cricketers particularly admired: Viv Richards.
Other sports: Most sports, especially weight-lifting. Follows football and snooker.
Injuries 1985: Groin injury.
Relaxations: "Listening to music but most of all spending time with my pet dogs, Simba, Sable and Bruno."
Opinions on cricket: "I believe that overseas players have improved the standard of county cricket and their experience has helped younger players. However, I fail to understand the fairness of one county being allowed to have more overseas players than others. When each county is allowed an equal number of overseas players the standards will improve even more."
Best batting performance: 41* Derbyshire v Yorkshire, Chesterfield 1985.

LAST SEASON: BATTING

	I.	N.O.	R.	H.S.	AV.
TEST					
OTHER FIRST CLASS	12	2	209	41*	20.90
INT					
JPL	1	0	8	8	–
NAT.W					
B & H					

CAREER: BATTING

	I.	N.O.	R.	H.S.	AV.
TEST					
OTHER FIRST CLASS	12	2	209	41*	20.90
INT					
JPL	1	0	8	8	–
NAT.W					
B & H					

SHARP, G.   Northamptonshire

Full Name: George Sharp.
Role: Right-hand bat, wicket-keeper,
slow left-arm bowler.
Born: 12 March 1950, Hartlepool,
County Durham.
Height: 6′ 0″ **Weight:** 14st.
Nickname: Sharpie, Blunt or Chicken
George.
County debut: 1968.
County cap: 1973.
Benefit: 1982 (£25,000).
1st-Class 50s scored: 21.
One-day 50s: 1.
Place in batting averages: —
average: —; (1984: 253
average: 14.00).
Parents: George and Grace Sharp.
Wife and date of marriage: Audrey,
14 September 1974.

Education: Elwick Road Secondary Modern, Hartlepool.
Qualifications: N.C.A. Coaching Certificate.
Cricketers particularly learnt from or admired: K.V. Andrew, B. Taylor, A. Knott.
Jobs outside cricket: Peter Bennie Ltd.
Other sports: Football, squash.
Relaxations: Gardening.
Extras: Bowled for only the second time in his 12-year career v Yorkshire, 1980
and took Richard Lumb's wicket. Vice-captain of Northamptonshire. Retired
at end of 1985 season.
Best batting performance: 98 Northamptonshire v Yorkshire, Northampton
1983.

LAST SEASON: BATTING

	I.	N.O.	R.	H.S.	AV.
TEST					
OTHER FIRST CLASS	13	1	111	25	9.25
INT					
JPL	1	0	4	4	–
NAT.W					
B & H	2	2	7	6*	–

CAREER: BATTING

	I.	N.O.	R.	H.S.	AV.
TEST					
OTHER FIRST CLASS	396	81	6254	98	19.85
INT					
JPL	147	38	1650	51*	15.13
NAT.W	18	4	280	41*	20.00
B & H	38	10	447	43	15.96

LAST SEASON: WICKET KEEPING

	C.	ST.
TEST		
OTHER FIRST CLASS	16	3
INT		
JPL	2	2
NAT.W		
B & H	4	–

CAREER: WICKET KEEPING

	C.	ST.
TEST		
OTHER FIRST CLASS	564	90
INT		
JPL	163	38
NAT.W	28	5
B & H	51	7

SHARP, K.   Yorkshire

Full Name: Kevin Sharp.
Role: Left-hand bat, off-break
bowler.
Born: 6 April 1959, Leeds.
Height: 5′ 10″ **Weight:** 12st. 9lbs.
Nickname: Lambsy, Poodle.
County debut: 1976.
County cap: 1982.
1000 runs in a season: 1.
1st-Class 50s scored: 29.
1st-Class 100s scored: 11.
One-day 50s: 13.
One-day 100s: 2.
Place in batting averages: 146
average: 25.00; (1984: 55
average: 39.05).
1st-Class catches 1985: 15
(career: 72).
Parents: Joyce and Gordon Sharp.
Wife and date of marriage: Karen, 1 October 1983.
Education: Abbey Grange C. of E. High School, Leeds.
Qualifications: C.S.E. Grade I Religious Education. Coaching award.
Jobs outside cricket: Plasterer's labourer, warehouseman, driver for film
company.
Off-season 1985–86: Occasional coaching.
Family links with cricket: Father played with Woodhouse in Leeds League for
many years. Young brother, David, now playing local cricket.
Overseas tours: Derrick Robins' XI to Australasia 1980.
Overseas teams played for: Subiaco Floreat C.C., Perth, Australia; De Beers
C.C., Griqualand West, 1981–82.

LAST SEASON: BATTING

	I.	N.O.	R.	H.S.	AV.
TEST					
OTHER FIRST CLASS	34	4	750	96	25.00
INT					
JPL	11	3	546	114	68.25
NAT.W	1	0	5	5	–
B & H	4	0	82	45	20.50

CAREER: BATTING

	I.	N.O.	R.	H.S.	AV.
TEST					
OTHER FIRST CLASS	245	19	6995	173	30.95
INT					
JPL	87	9	1916	114	24.56
NAT.W	7	1	94	25	15.67
B & H	28	1	732	87*	27.11

LAST SEASON: BOWLING

	O.	M.	R.	W.	AV.
TEST					
OTHER FIRST CLASS	35	11	89	1	–
INT					
JPL					
NAT.W					
B & H					

CAREER: BOWLING

	O.	M.	R.	W.	AV.
TEST					
OTHER FIRST CLASS	129.1	33	410	8	51.25
INT					
JPL	0.1	0	1	0	–
NAT.W	1	0	7	0	–
B & H					

Cricketers particularly learnt from: Doug Padgett, Yorkshire coach; Mike Fearnley, former assistant Yorkshire coach.
Cricketers particularly admired: Richard Hadlee.
Other sports: Golf, soccer, swimming. Watching Leeds United F.C. and athletics.
Relaxations: Crosswords, listening to music, keeping my cricket gear clean.
Extras: 260 n.o. v Young West Indies 1977. Rested during latter part of 1980 season, on medical advice. Captain of England U-19 v West Indies U-19 1978 at Worcester. Winston Churchill Travelling Fellowship to Australia for two months, 1978. "I took the first wicket of my career in 1984 — a feat I never thought possible."
Best batting performance: 173 Yorkshire v Derbyshire, Chesterfield 1984.
Best bowling performance: 2-13 Yorkshire v Glamorgan, Bradford 1984.

---

145. Who was the legendary Yorkshire and England left-arm spinner who died in 1985 at the age of 62?

146. What Test commentator published a highly acclaimed biography of Geoff Boycott in 1985?

147. Which England captain played first-class cricket at the age of 56?

148. When David East of Essex took eight catches in one innings of a first-class match (v Somerset in August 1985) he equalled whose record?

SHAW, C. Yorkshire

Full Name: Christopher Shaw.
Role: Right-hand bat, right-arm
fast-medium bowler.
Born: 17 February 1964, Hemsworth,
West Yorkshire.
Height: 6' 0" **Weight:** 12st. 5lbs.
Nickname: Sandy.
County debut: 1984.
1st-Class 5 w. in innings: 1.
Place in bowling averages: 103
average: 40.19.
1st-Class catches 1985: 5 (career 5).
Parents: Brian and Betty Shaw.
Marital status: Single.
Family links with cricket: Father
good local league cricketer.
Education: Crofton High School.
Qualifications: 5 C.S.E.s; qualified
cricket coach.

Jobs outside cricket: Apprentice electrician (National Coal Board).
Off-season 1985–86: Playing and coaching in Wellington, New Zealand.
Overseas tours: Holland with N.C.A. U-19s North of England 1983; Barbados
with Yorkshire Cricket Association April 1984.
Cricketers particularly learnt from: Father, D. Padgett, S. Oldham and J.
Lawrence at his cricket school in Rothwell.
Cricketers particularly admired: D. Lillee, M. Holding.
Other sports: Likes watching all sports (favourite sport: rugby league); keen
supporter of Featherstone Rovers R.L.F.C.
Relaxations: Playing golf, listening to music, driving.

LAST SEASON: BATTING

	I.	N.O.	R.	H.S.	AV.
TEST					
OTHER FIRST CLASS	13	5	57	12	7.12
INT					
JPL	4	1	23	10*	7.66
NAT.W	1	1	6	6*	–
B & H					

CAREER: BATTING

	I.	N.O.	R.	H.S.	AV.
TEST					
OTHER FIRST CLASS	18	7	89	17	8.09
INT					
JPL	10	3	81	26	11.57
NAT.W	1	1	6	6*	–
B & H					

LAST SEASON: BOWLING

	O.	M.	R.	W.	AV.
TEST					
OTHER FIRST CLASS	417	95	1286	32	40.19
INT					
JPL	53	1	314	13	24.15
NAT.W	10.1	3	14	1	–
B & H					

CAREER: BOWLING

	O.	M.	R.	W.	AV.
TEST					
OTHER FIRST CLASS	470.4	100	1463	37	39.54
INT					
JPL	86.5	2	492	21	23.42
NAT.W	10.1	3	14	1	–
B & H					

Extras: "On debut at Lord's took 4-68 v Middlesex. Took 5-41 in my second J.P.S.L. match v Hampshire at Bournemouth."
Best batting performance: 17 Yorkshire v Worcestershire, Scarborough 1984.
Best bowling performance: 5-76 Yorkshire v Kent, Scarborough 1985.

SHEPHERD, J.N.   Gloucestershire

Full Name: John Neil Shepherd.
Role: Right-hand bat, right-arm medium bowler.
Born: 9 November 1943, St Andrew, Barbados.
Height: 5′ 10½″ **Weight:** 12st. 11lbs.
Nickname: Shep, Walter.
County debut: 1966 (Kent), 1982 (Gloucestershire).
County cap: 1967 (Kent), 1983 (Gloucestershire).
Test debut: 1969.
No. of Tests: 5.
Benefit: 1979 (£58,537).
1000 runs in a season: 2.
50 wickets in a season: 11.
1st-Class 50s scored: 66.
1st-Class 100s scored: 10.
1st-Class 5 w. in innings: 54.
1st-Class 10 w. in match: 2.
One-day 50s: 13.
One-day 100s: 1.
Place in batting averages: — average: —; (1984: 140 average: 27.66).
Place in bowling averages: — average: —; (1984: 71 average: 30.90).
1st-Class catches 1985: 0 (career: 290).
Parents: Ollie and Kathleen Shepherd.
Wife and date of marriage: Terri, 14 December 1968.
Children: Caroline, 31 May 1976; Jacqueline, 21 September 1978; David, 19 January 1982.
Education: Alleyn's School, Barbados.
Family links with cricket: Grandfather and two younger brothers all played.
Off-season 1985–86: Coaching at Gloucestershire C.C.C.
Overseas tours: South Africa in 1973 with Derrick Robins' XI, being first black cricketer to tour there.
Overseas teams played for: Debut 1964–65 in one match for Barbados. Played for Rhodesia in 1975–76 Currie Cup Competition. Five Tests for the West

Indies 1969 and 1970–71 but never played again for them after playing in Rhodesia.

Cricketers particularly learnt from: Charlie Griffith, Everton Weekes, Colin Cowdrey, John Snow.

Cricketers particularly admired: Seymour Nurse, Colin Cowdrey, Gary Sobers, Alan Knott, Derek Underwood, Ian Chappell, Clive Lloyd, Viv Richards.

Relaxations: Music, golf, squash.

Extras: Introduced to Kent by Colin Cowdrey. Released by Kent at end of 1981 season.

Cricketing superstitions: "Always clean my boots and pads before batting. When fielding try to be last one on field. Never like being on 22 or 33 or facing last over of any interval."

Injuries 1985: Back strain.

Best batting performance: 170 Kent v Northamptonshire, Folkestone 1968.

Best bowling performance: 8-40 West Indies v Gloucestershire, Bristol 1969.

LAST SEASON: BATTING

	I.	N.O.	R.	H.S.	AV.
TEST					
OTHER FIRST CLASS	–	–	–	–	–
INT					
JPL	4	2	18	11*	9.00
NAT.W					
B & H	2	0	10	9	5.00

CAREER: BATTING

	I.	N.O.	R.	H.S.	AV.
TEST	8	0	77	32	9.62
OTHER FIRST CLASS	603	106	13277	170	26.71
INT					
JPL	173	48	2952	94	23.61
NAT.W	32	3	517	101	17.83
B & H	52	7	761	96	16.91

LAST SEASON: BOWLING

	O.	M.	R.	W.	AV.
TEST					
OTHER FIRST CLASS	14	3	41	0	–
INT					
JPL	38	0	236	4	59.00
NAT.W					
B & H	44	4	155	6	25.83

CAREER: BOWLING

	O.	M.	R.	W.	AV.
TEST	240.5	70	479	19	25.21
OTHER FIRST CLASS	12275.5	3660	31497	1136	27.73
INT					
JPL	1432.1	107	5672	265	21.40
NAT.W	443.4	80	1388	60	23.13
B & H	629.1	88	2116	102	20.74

149. Which former Lancashire player is now manager of the county?

150. Which current county player has the nickname "Paddles"?

151. Which current county player has the nickname "Farsley"?

SIDEBOTTOM, A.   Yorkshire

Full Name: Arnold Sidebottom.
Role: Right-hand bat, right-arm
fast-medium bowler, outfielder.
Born: 1 April 1954, Barnsley.
Height: 6′ 2″ **Weight:** 13st. 10lbs.
Nickname: Woofer, Red Setter,
Arnie.
County debut: 1973.
County cap: 1980.
Test debut: 1985.
No. of Tests: 1.
50 wickets in a season: 2.
1st-Class 50s scored: 10.
1st-Class 100s scored: 1.
1st-Class 5 w. in innings: 14.
1st-Class 10 w. in match: 2.
One-day 50s: 1.
Place in batting averages: 56
average: 24.50; (1984: 108
average: 31.94).
Place in bowling averages: 80 average: 35.23; (1984: 8 average: 20.51).
1st-Class catches 1985: 2 (career: 38).
Parents: Jack and Florence Sidebottom.
Wife and date of marriage: Gillian, 17 June 1977.
Children: Ryan Jay, 1978; Dale, 1980.
Education: Barnsley Broadway Grammar School.
Jobs outside cricket: Professional footballer Manchester United, five years;
Huddersfield Town, two years; Halifax Town.
Family links with cricket: "Father good cricketer."

LAST SEASON: BATTING

	I.	N.O.	R.	H.S.	AV.
TEST	1	0	2	2	–
OTHER FIRST CLASS	10	3	194	55	27.72
INT					
JPL	4	1	16	14*	5.33
NAT.W	–	–	–	–	–
B & H	3	0	49	21	16.33

CAREER: BATTING

	I.	N.O.	R.	H.S.	AV.
TEST	1	0	2	2	–
OTHER FIRST CLASS	177	43	3181	124	23.74
INT					
JPL	53	18	593	52*	16.94
NAT.W	10	4	171	45	28.50
B & H	19	6	201	32	15.46

LAST SEASON: BOWLING

	O.	M.	R.	W.	AV.
TEST	18.4	3	65	1	–
OTHER FIRST CLASS	250	35	851	25	34.04
INT					
JPL	39.3	4	185	4	46.25
NAT.W	12	0	42	2	21.00
B & H	40	6	110	9	12.22

CAREER: BOWLING

	O.	M.	R.	W.	AV.
TEST	18.4	3	65	1	–
OTHER FIRST CLASS	3234	722	9395	389	24.15
INT					
JPL	653.2	29	2840	96	29.58
NAT.W	149.2	18	446	25	17.84
B & H	305	43	997	44	22.66

Cricketers particularly learnt from: Father, Doug Padgett, G. Boycott.
Cricketers particularly admired: S. Oldham, D. Bairstow, G. Stevenson.
Overseas tours: Rebel England team in South Africa in 1982.
Other sports: Professional football, tennis, table-tennis, badminton. Most sports.
Relaxations: Watching television, horse-racing, playing with sons.
Extras: Banned from Test cricket for three years for joining rebel team to South Africa in 1982. Injured toe during Test debut.
Best batting performance: 124 Yorkshire v Glamorgan, Cardiff 1977.
Best bowling performance: 7-18 Yorkshire v Oxford University, Oxford 1980.

SIMMONS, J. Lancashire

Full Name: Jack Simmons.
Role: Right-hand bat, off-break bowler, slip fielder.
Born: 28 March 1941, Clayton-le-Moors, near Accrington.
Height: 6′ 1″ **Weight:** 14st. 7lbs.
Nickname: Simmo, Flat Jack.
County debut: 1968.
County cap: 1971.
Benefit: 1980 (£128,000).
50 wickets in a season: 7.
1st-Class 50s scored: 33.
1st-Class 100s scored: 6.
1st-Class 5 w. in innings: 33.
1st-Class 10 w. in match: 4.
One-day 50s: 6.
Place in batting averages: 199 average: 18.65; (1984: 152 average: 25.79).

Place in bowling averages: 100 average: 38.57; (1984: 36 average: 26.10).
1st-Class catches 1985: 18 (career: 302).
Parents: Ada and Robert Simmons.
Wife and date of marriage: Jacqueline, 23 March 1963.
Children: Kelly Louise, 28 January 1979.
Education: Accrington Technical School, Blackburn Technical College.
Qualifications: 5 O-levels; O.N.C., City & Guilds in Quantities.
Jobs outside cricket: Draughtsman with Accrington Brick & Tile Co. Ltd., and Lancashire County Surveyors' Department. Partnership with Clive Lloyd as agents for cricketers, also partnership with Pat Pocock in managing cricket matches for club cricketers at La Manga in Spain.
Off-season 1985–86: With Lancastria Leisure working on opening a sports

centre called "Bowlers", opening April 1986. 6 indoor cricket courts, 14 flat bowling lanes, 16 snooker tables, restaurant and four bars. Total price £1.7m.

Cricketing superstitions: "I always like to be last on the field. To do the same things again if successful once, i.e. clothes or eating habits."

Family links with cricket: Father, Robert, played with Enfield, Lancashire League. Grandfather, Robert, also played for Enfield since 1887, "giving 92 years' association with the same club."

Overseas tours: Rhodesia and South Africa with Whitbread Wanderers 1975. Mike Brearley Invitation XI to Calcutta 1981. New York 1985 with C. Lloyd Lancashire XI.

Overseas teams played for: Played for Tasmania from 1972–73 to 1978–79 — where he is "a bit of a folk hero". Captained Tasmania to Gillette Cup for first time in 1979, and when they first entered Sheffield Shield (1978).

Cricketers particularly learnt from: "Coached by Clyde Walcott when I was a youngster. Learnt from Clive Lloyd with Lancashire. Jack Bond, Ray Illingworth, plus many more off-spinners."

Cricketers particularly admired: "Clive Lloyd (team man always), Viv Richards, Chappell brothers and great bowlers Dennis Lillee and Michael Holding."

Relaxations: Soccer, golf, horse-racing, "plus eating, playing cards, watching television and going on holiday."

Extras: "I didn't play for a couple of years because I broke my leg three times in ten months and the previous year broke my arm quite badly, all playing soccer — except one broken leg, which was broken going down to the football ground just after I had it out of plaster for the first time." Made debut for 2nd XI in 1959. Hat-trick v Nottinghamshire (Liverpool) 1977. Director of Burnley F.C.

Opinions on cricket: "Cricket fines too distracting and become a farce when trying to improve rate half way through and at end of the season."

Best batting performance: 112 Lancashire v Sussex, Hove 1970.

Best bowling performance: 7-59 Tasmania v Queensland, Brisbane 1978–79.

LAST SEASON: BATTING

	I.	N.O.	R.	H.S.	AV.
TEST					
OTHER FIRST CLASS	30	4	485	101	18.65
INT					
JPL	11	4	122	39	17.42
NAT.W	1	0	13	13	–
B & H	3	1	36	33	18.00

LAST SEASON: BOWLING

	O.	M.	R.	W.	AV.
TEST					
OTHER FIRST CLASS	543.1	154	1427	37	38.57
INT					
JPL	78	3	392	9	43.55
NAT.W	24	9	51	1	~
B & H	38	11	107	2	53.50

CAREER: BATTING

	I.	N.O.	R.	H.S.	AV.
TEST					
OTHER FIRST CLASS	484	121	8438	112	23.25
INT					
JPL	164	49	1847	65	16.06
NAT.W	31	13	427	54*	23.72
B & H	43	15	562	64	20.07

CAREER: BOWLING

	O.	M.	R.	W.	AV.
TEST					
OTHER FIRST CLASS	8885.2 466.2	2636 94	23909	859	27.83
INT					
JPL	1564.1	125	6343	245	25.88
NAT.W	519.5	92	1545	68	22.72
B & H	567.2	117	1558	65	23.97

SLACK, W.N. Middlesex

Full Name: Wilfred Norris Slack.
Role: Left-hand bat, right-arm medium bowler, short-leg fielder.
Born: 12 December 1954, Troumaca, St. Vincent, West Indies.
Height: 6' 0'' **Weight:** 13st. 5lbs.
Nickname: Slacky.
County debut: 1977.
County cap: 1981.
1000 runs in a season: 5.
1st-Class 50s scored: 46.
1st-Class 100s scored: 13.
1st-Class 200s scored: 3.
One-day 50s: 19.
Place in batting averages: 15 average 54.29; (1984: 38 average: 42.92).
1st-Class catches 1985: 27 (career: 122).
Parents: Grafton and Doreen Slack.
Wife and date of marriage: Rita, 20 June 1984.
Education: Wellesbourne Secondary, High Wycombe, Bucks.
Qualifications: City & Guilds: Radio and T.V. mechanics. Qualified N.C.A. Advanced Coach.
Jobs outside cricket: Digital electronics test engineer.
Overseas tours: To Pakistan with Rohan Kanhai's World XI in September 1981.
Overseas teams played for: Played in Auckland, New Zealand, in 1979–80; World XI in Pakistan 1981.
Cricketers particularly learnt from: Don Bennett, Clive Radley.
Other sports: Plays basketball for Bucks and Wycombe Pirates; tennis, squash, badminton, football.
Relaxations: Building electronic projects. Relaxing in a sauna and swimming pool. "Lying in bed."
Opinions on cricket: I think there is far too much first-class cricket being played. Sundays should be a rest day so that players could appear with local clubs and so people could watch local cricket. Saturdays should be for 1-day games of 55 overs (60 too long, 40 too short). Championship to be played over four days (Mon. to Thurs.) with no over-rate fines.
Extras: Played for Buckinghamshire in 1976. At 16 played for Wycombe Colts. Played for Freith in Haig Village Cricket Competition. Then joined High Wycombe; then Buckinghamshire in 1976; then Middlesex in 1977. Qualified to play both for West Indies and England.
Best batting performance: 248* Middlesex v Worcestershire, Lord's 1981.
Best bowling performance: 3-17 Middlesex v Leicestershire, Uxbridge 1982.

LAST SEASON: BATTING					
	I.	N.O.	R.	H.S.	AV.
TEST					
OTHER FIRST CLASS	43	8	1900	201*	54.29
INT					
JPL	11	1	350	74	35.00
NAT.W	2	0	130	98	65.00
B & H	6	2	170	60	42.50

CAREER: BATTING					
	I.	N.O.	R.	H.S.	AV.
TEST					
OTHER FIRST CLASS	262	31	9113	248*	39.45
INT					
JPL	65	8	1533	77	26.89
NAT.W	17	1	635	98	39.69
B & H	21	3	458	60*	25.44

LAST SEASON: BOWLING					
	O.	M.	R.	W.	AV.
TEST					
OTHER FIRST CLASS	9	1	29	0	–
INT					
JPL	10	0	65	1	–
NAT.W					
B & H					

CAREER: BOWLING					
	O.	M.	R.	W.	AV.
TEST					
OTHER FIRST CLASS	174.5	30	491	18	27.28
INT					
JPL	146.4	1	729	30	24.30
NAT.W	79	6	276	8	34.50
B & H	7	0	34	0	–

SMALL, G.C.   Warwickshire

Full Name: Gladstone Cleopthas Small.
Role: Right-hand bat, right-arm fast-medium bowler.
Born: 18 October 1961, St George, Barbados.
Height: 5′ 11″.
Nickname: Gladys.
County debut: 1980.
County cap: 1982.
50 wickets in a season: 3.
1st-Class 50s scored: 1.
1st-Class 5 w. in innings: 4.
1st-Class 10 w. in match: 1.
Place in batting averages: 219 average: 15.00; (1984: 214 average: 18.18).
Place in bowling averages: 31 average: 26.81; (1984: 52 average: 28.55).

1st-Class catches 1985: 7 (career: 32).
Parents: Chelston and Gladys Small.
Marital status: Single.
Education: Mosely School; Hall Green Technical College, Birmingham.
Overseas tours: With Young England to New Zealand 1979–80; Derrick Robins' XI tour of Australia, Tasmania, New Zealand 1980; Rohan Kanhai International XI tour of Pakistan 1981.
Cricketers particularly learnt from or admired: "I admire Dennis Lillee and

have learnt a lot from my manager David Brown."

Extras: In 1980, became youngest bowler to take five J.P.L. wickets in one innings. Was called up for England Test squad v Pakistan at Edgbaston, July 1982, but did not play. Bowled 18-ball over v Middlesex in August 1982, with 11 no balls.

Best batting performance: 57* Warwickshire v Oxfordshire, Oxford 1982.

Best bowling performance: 7-68 Warwickshire v Yorkshire, Edgbaston 1982.

LAST SEASON: BATTING

	I.	N.O.	R.	H.S.	AV.
TEST					
OTHER FIRST CLASS	27	8	285	31*	15.00
INT					
JPL	8	2	37	17	6.17
NAT.W	2	1	24	18	–
B & H	1	0	4	4	–

CAREER: BATTING

	I.	N.O.	R.	H.S.	AV.
TEST					
OTHER FIRST CLASS	139	34	1369	57*	13.04
INT					
JPL	34	13	180	40*	8.57
NAT.W	8	3	96	33	19.20
B & H	13	4	67	19*	7.44

LAST SEASON: BOWLING

	O.	M.	R.	W.	AV.
TEST					
OTHER FIRST CLASS	592.3	113	1850	69	26.81
INT					
JPL	92.1	2	430	21	20.47
NAT.W	20	3	64	1	–
B & H	41	10	122	6	20.33

CAREER: BOWLING

	O.	M.	R.	W.	AV.
TEST					
OTHER FIRST CLASS	2634.4	483	8816	283	31.15
INT					
JPL	494.3	31	2374	107	22.18
NAT.W	142.1	28	484	19	25.47
B & H	211.3	41	785	28	28.04

SMITH, C.L. Hampshire

Full Name: Christopher Lyall Smith.
Role: Right-hand bat.
Born: 15 October 1958, Durban, South Africa.
Height: 5′ 11″ **Weight:** 13st. 7lbs.
Nickname: Kippy.
County debut: 1979 (Glamorgan), 1980 (Hampshire).
County cap: 1981.
Test debut: 1983.
No. of Tests: 7.
No. of One-Day Internationals: 4.
1000 runs in a season: 4.
1st-Class 50s scored: 39.
1st-Class 100s scored: 25.
One-day 50s: 20.
One-day 100s: 1.
Place in batting averages: 9 average: 57.14; (1984: 133 average 28.21).

1st-Class catches 1985: 12 (career: 81).
Parents: John Arnold and Elaine Jessie Smith.
Marital status: Single.
Education: Northlands High School, Durban, South Africa.
Qualifications: Matriculation (2 A-level equivalents).
Jobs outside cricket: Chris Smith Promotions, sports marketing and promotions business.
Family links with cricket: Grandfather, Vernon Lyall Shearer, played for Natal; brother, Robin, also plays for Hampshire.
Overseas tours: Toured U.K. with Kingsmead Mynahs (Natal under-25s under another name) 1976; with England to New Zealand and Pakistan 1983–84.
Overseas teams played for: Kingsmead Mynahs; Natal Schools 1975; South African Schools 1976; Natal B debut 1978.
Off-season 1985–86: "Running my own business and studying business management on part-time basis."
Cricketers particularly admired: Barry Richards, Grayson Heath (my coach in South Africa).
Other sports: League squash, golf (handicap 15). Watches football (Southampton F.C.).
Relaxations: Walking in the countryside or lying on the beach. In winter, pheasant or partridge shooting at a friend's on Lulworth Estate.
Extras: Made debut for Glamorgan in 1979, leaving to join Gorseinon at end of season. Played for Gorseinon in South Wales League in 1979. Made Hampshire debut 1980. Became eligible to play for England in 1983. Captained Hampshire 2nd XI in 1981.
Opinions on cricket: "I feel that the counties should play each other once and that the games should be played over four days, Monday to Thursday with Friday off — Saturday either a Benson and Hedges game or NatWest fixture, and Sunday should remain John Player. Also feel that the game is not marketed properly. It could probably learn from some of the South African or Australian marketing men who promote games in those countries. I feel that each county should have a highly motivated sales personnel (apart from

LAST SEASON: BATTING

	I.	N.O.	R.	H.S.	AV.
TEST					
OTHER FIRST CLASS	39	4	2000	142*	57.14
INT					
JPL	8	3	221	63*	44.20
NAT.W	4	0	51	26	12.75
B & H	2	0	33	25	16.50

CAREER: BATTING

	I.	N.O.	R.	H.S.	AV.
TEST	12	1	358	91	32.54
OTHER FIRST CLASS	232	24	8566	193	41.18
INT	4	0	109	70	27.25
JPL	52	7	1813	95	40.28
NAT.W	12	2	282	101*	28.20
B & H	13	2	328	82*	29.82

LAST SEASON: BOWLING

	O.	M.	R.	W.	AV.
TEST					
OTHER FIRST CLASS	66	6	297	4	74.25
INT					
JPL					
NAT.W	12	3	32	3	10.67
B & H					

CAREER: BOWLING

	O.	M.	R.	W.	AV.
TEST	17	4	39	3	13.00
OTHER FIRST CLASS	504	92	1919	32	59.97
INT	6	0	28	2	14.00
JPL	3.3	1	10	2	5.00
NAT.W	12	3	32	3	10.67
B & H					

secretaries) to sell the game. So much money could be made and so many companies exploited to make money for the county game but it is not being done. Players should be able and allowed to sell themselves, i.e. by wearing advertising when playing. I do agree that it should only be allowed to be a certain size. Counties should be allowed to play two overseas players. It will raise the general standard of play by having other Test players involved and will therefore raise the standard of the English players. Also there are too many arm-chair critics on the game — particularly in South Africa. I find that sort of person unbearable."

Best batting performance: 193 Hampshire v Derbyshire, Derby 1983.
Best bowling performance: 3-35 Hampshire v Glamorgan, Southampton 1983.

SMITH, D.M. Worcestershire

Full Name: David Mark Smith.
Role: Left-hand bat, right-arm fast-medium bowler.
Born: 9 January 1956, Balham.
Height: 6' 4'' **Weight:** 15st.
Nickname: Smudger, Tom.
County debut: 1973 (Surrey), 1984 (Worcestershire).
County cap: 1980 (Surrey), 1984 (Worcestershire).
1000 runs in a season: 3.
1st-Class 50s scored: 35.
1st-Class 100s scored: 13.
One-day 50s: 14.
One-day 100s: 3.
Place in batting averages: 28 average: 46.38; (1984: 42 average: 42.04).
1st-Class catches 1985: 11 (career: 119).
Parents: Dennis Henry and Tina Smith.
Wife and date of marriage: Jacqui, 7 January 1977.
Children: Sarah Jane Louise, 4 April 1982.
Education: Battersea Grammar School.
Qualifications: 3 O-levels.
Jobs outside cricket: Two years with insurance company, one year with Harrods, one year spent in Rhodesia, two years with building firm. Contracts Manager, painting and decorating firm.
Family links with cricket: Father plays cricket for the B.B.C.
Overseas teams played for: Sydney University, Australia, 1980–81, 1982–83.
Off-season 1985–86: England tour to West Indies.
Cricketers particularly learnt from: Mickey Stewart and Graham Roope.

Cricketers particularly admired: Graham Gooch, Malcolm Marshall, Ian Botham.
Cricketing superstitions: "No room for them all."
Other sports: Football, motor-racing.
Relaxations: "I own my own racing car."
Injuries 1985: Broken thumb and disc trouble.
Extras: Played for Surrey 2nd XI in 1972. Was not retained after 1977 but was re-instated in 1978. Top of Surrey first-class batting averages in 1982. "Has a cocker spaniel called Winston." Sacked by Surrey during 1983 season.
Best batting performance: 189* Worcestershire v Kent, Worcester 1984.
Best bowling performance: 3-40 Surrey v Sussex, The Oval 1976.

LAST SEASON: BATTING

	I.	N.O.	R.	H.S.	AV.
TEST					
OTHER FIRST CLASS	28	4	1113	112	46.38
INT					
JPL	10	3	222	36	31.71
NAT.W	3	0	263	109	87.67
B & H	5	0	325	126	65.00

CAREER: BATTING

	I.	N.O.	R.	H.S.	AV.
TEST					
OTHER FIRST CLASS	274	57	7426	189*	34.22
INT					
JPL	98	23	1882	87*	25.09
NAT.W	19	5	841	109	60.07
B & H	35	5	918	126	30.60

LAST SEASON: BOWLING

	O.	M.	R.	W.	AV.
TEST					
OTHER FIRST CLASS					
INT					
JPL					
NAT.W					
B & H					

CAREER: BOWLING

	O.	M.	R.	W.	AV.
TEST					
OTHER FIRST CLASS	445	93	1485	28	53.04
INT					
JPL	124.5	6	606	12	50.50
NAT.W	29	5	113	3	37.67
B & H	56	4	266	8	33.25

152. Which current county player has the nickname "Bonk"?

153. Which current county player has the nickname "Fred"?

154. Which current county player has the nickname "Ponty"? (Not the Pont brothers.)

155. Which current county player has the nickname "Percy"?

SMITH, I.   Glamorgan

Full Name: Ian Smith.
Role: Right-hand bat, right-arm
medium bowler.
Born: 11 March 1967, Durham.
Education: Ryton Comprehensive
School.
Qualifications: 2 O-levels, 5 C.S.E.s.
Took N.C.A. Coaching Award
course 1985.
Parents: James and Mary Smith.
Family links with cricket: Father
N.C.A. Advanced Coach.
Overseas tours: West Indies with
Young England 1984–85.
Off-season 1985–86: Coaching at
Houghton-le-Spring Cricket Centre.
Cricketers particularly learnt from:
Alan Jones, Tom Cartwright.
Other sports: Represented county

at football, offered terms by Southampton, York City, Carlisle United. Now
plays for Blyth Spartans.

LAST SEASON: BATTING

	I.	N.O.	R.	H.S.	AV.
TEST					
OTHER FIRST CLASS	5	0	27	12	5.40
INT					
JPL	2	0	5	3	2.50
NAT.W					
B & H					

CAREER: BATTING

	I.	N.O.	R.	H.S.	AV.
TEST					
OTHER FIRST CLASS	5	0	27	12	5.40
INT					
JPL	2	0	5	3	2.50
NAT.W		1			
B & H					

LAST SEASON: BOWLING

	O.	M.	R.	W.	AV.
TEST					
OTHER FIRST CLASS	44.4	11	154	1	–
INT					
JPL					
NAT.W					
B & H					

CAREER: BOWLING

	O.	M.	R.	W.	AV.
TEST					
OTHER FIRST CLASS	44.4	11	154	1	–
INT					
JPL					
NAT.W					
B & H					

SMITH, K.D.   Warwickshire

Full Name: Kenneth David Smith.
Role: Right-hand bat.
Born: 9 July 1956, Newcastle-on-Tyne.
Height: 6′ 2″ **Weight:** 14st.
Nickname: Smithy, K.D.
County debut: 1973.
County cap: 1978.
1000 runs in a season: 4.
1st-Class 50s scored: 55.
1st-Class 100s scored: 9.
One-day 50s: 20.
One-day 100s: 2.
Place in batting averages: 218 average: 15.00; (1984: 222 average: 17.74).
1st-Class catches 1985: 1 (career: 70).
Parents: Kenneth Desmond and Joy Smith.
Wife and date of marriage: Sally Louise, 9 January 1982.
Education: Heaton Grammar School, Newcastle.
Qualifications: O-levels, N.C.A. cricket coaching award.
Jobs outside cricket: Coaching in Cape Town, South Africa and playing in New Zealand.
Family links with cricket: Father played first-class cricket for Leicestershire, 1950–51. Very good minor county cricketer for Northumberland. Brother Paul plays for Warwickshire.
Overseas tours: Derrick Robins' tour to South America 1979.

LAST SEASON: BATTING

	I.	N.O.	R.	H.S.	AV.
TEST					
OTHER FIRST CLASS	9	1	120	42	15.00
INT					
JPL					
NAT.W					
B & H					

CAREER: BATTING

	I.	N.O.	R.	H.S.	AV.
TEST					
OTHER FIRST CLASS	346	29	8734	140	27.55
INT					
JPL	57	3	1136	73	21.03
NAT.W	16	1	609	113	40.60
B & H	29	2	1020	84	37.78

LAST SEASON: BOWLING

	O.	M.	R.	W.	AV.
TEST					
OTHER FIRST CLASS					
INT					
JPL					
NAT.W					
B & H					

CAREER: BOWLING

	O.	M.	R.	W.	AV.
TEST					
OTHER FIRST CLASS	2	0	3	0	–
INT					
JPL					
NAT.W					
B & H					

Overseas teams played for: Milnerton C.C., Cape Town, 1977–78, 1979–80; Waverley C.C., Melbourne, 1980; Papatoetoe D.C.C. 1982–83.
Cricketers particularly learnt from: "My father and a bit from most people I have played with or against."
Other sports: Squash and watching football (Newcastle United).
Relaxations: "Listening to music, gardening, travelling abroad."
Extras: Left staff after 1985 season.
Best batting performance: 140 Warwickshire v Worcestershire, Worcester 1980.

SMITH, L.K. Worcestershire

Full Name: Lawrence Kilner Smith.
Role: Right-hand opening bat, occasional wicket-keeper.
Born: 6 January 1964, Mirfield, Spen Valley, Yorkshire.
Height: 5' 8" Weight: 9st.
Nickname: Smithy, Smudge.
County debut: 1985.
Parents: David Henry Kilner and Christine Sonia Smith.
Marital status: Single.
Family links with cricket: Father played for Derbyshire and Orange Free State.
Education: Stancliffe Hall, Derbyshire; C.B.C. and St. Andrew's, Welkom, South Africa; K.E.S. Johannesburg; Beachwood, Durban.
Jobs outside cricket: Worked as a video electrician for a company operating video games.
Off-season 1985–86: A winter at home in England for the first time in five years.
Overseas teams played for: Lived and played in South Africa for seven years. Played in Durban, Natal for Durban Collegians winning batting trophy in 1984–85 season.
Cricketers particularly learnt from: "My father particularly and since coming to Worcester, Basil D'Oliveira."
Cricketers particularly admired: Geoff Boycott for his tremendous dedication. David Gower, sheer class.
Other sports: "Squash, golf to relax though it doesn't always turn out that way. Follow motor sport and golf."
Relaxations: Music, movies.

Extras: Broke batting record, most runs in a season Stancliffe Hall 1977. First ever honours for cricket at St. Andrew's Welkom. O.F.S. schools side.

LAST SEASON: BATTING

	I.	N.O.	R.	H.S.	AV.
TEST					
OTHER FIRST CLASS	1	0	28	28	–
INT					
JPL	1	0	3	3	–
NAT.W					
B & H					

CAREER: BATTING

	I.	N.O.	R.	H.S.	AV.
TEST					
OTHER FIRST CLASS	1	0	28	28	–
INT					
JPL	1	0	3	3	–
NAT.W					
B & H					

SMITH, P.A.   Warwickshire

Full Name: Paul Andrew Smith.
Role: Right-hand bat; right-arm fast-medium bowler.
Born: 15 April 1964.
Height: 6' 2" **Weight:** 12st.
Nickname: Moonman, Smithy.
County debut: 1982.
1000 runs in a season: 1.
1st-Class 50s scored: 18.
1st-Class 100s scored: 1.
One-day 50s: 2.
Place in batting averages: 157 average: 23.97; (1984: 134 average: 28.11).
Place in bowling averages: 117 average: 43.96; (1984: 120 average: 41.95).
1st-Class catches 1985: 9 (career: 27).
Parents: Kenneth and Joy Smith.
Marital status: Single.
Education: Heaton Grammar School.
Qualifications: 5 O-levels.
Off-season 1985–86: Finding work (resting).
Family links with cricket: Father played for Leicestershire and Northumberland. Both brothers played for Warwickshire.
Cricket superstitions: "None any more."
Overseas teams played for: Florida, Johannesburg, 1982–83; South America 1983–84; Carlton, Melbourne, 1984–85.
Cricketers particularly learnt from: D. Amiss, D.J. Brown, R.G.D. Willis.
Relaxations: Listening to music.

Best batting performance: 114 Warwickshire v Oxford University, Edgbaston 1983.
Best bowling performance: 4-25 Warwickshire v Lancashire, Edgbaston 1985.

LAST SEASON: BATTING

	I.	N.O.	R.	H.S.	AV.
TEST					
OTHER FIRST CLASS	37	3	815	93	23.97
INT.					
JPL	13	4	224	50*	24.88
NAT.W	2	1	53	51*	–
B & H	4	1	58	25	19.33

CAREER: BATTING

	I.	N.O.	R.	H.S.	AV.
TEST					
OTHER FIRST CLASS	111	11	2696	114	26.96
INT.					
JPL	40	14	659	50*	25.34
NAT.W	6	2	111	51*	27.75
B & H	10	3	122	37	17.43

LAST SEASON: BOWLING

	O.	M.	R.	W.	AV.
TEST					
OTHER FIRST CLASS	237.2	24	1143	26	43.96
INT.					
JPL	68.3	0	360	11	32.72
NAT.W	10	0	60	1	–
B & H	14	0	75	2	37.50

CAREER: BOWLING

	O.	M.	R.	W.	AV.
TEST					
OTHER FIRST CLASS	786	99	3362	77	43.66
INT.					
JPL	173.1	4	975	29	33.62
NAT.W	26.4	0	132	5	26.40
B & H	38.1	1	184	5	36.80

SMITH, R.A.   Hampshire

Full Name: Robin Arnold Smith.
Role: Right-hand bat.
Born: 13 September 1963, Durban, South Africa.
Height: 5′ 11½″ **Weight:** 15st.
Nickname: Judge.
County debut: 1982.
County cap: 1985.
1000 runs in a season: 1.
1st-Class 50s scored: 18.
1st-Class 100s scored: 8.
One-day 50s: 5.
One-day 100s: 3.
Place in batting averages: 37 average: 42.58; (1984: 25 average: 48.30).
1st-Class catches 1985: 19 (career: 33).
Parents: John Arnold and Elaine Jessie Smith.
Marital status: Single.
Education: Northlands Boys High, Durban.
Qualifications: "Highly qualified with regard to my educational studies."

Jobs outside cricket: Horse-racing company.
Off-season 1985–86: Playing club cricket in Perth.
Family links with cricket: Grandfather played for Natal in Currie Cup. Brother Chris plays for Hampshire, Natal and England.
Cricket superstitions: "Always have a big night out before a game.'
Overseas teams played for: Natal B, 1980–81; Natal A, 1981–82.
Cricketers particularly admired: Barry Richards, Viv Richards, Graeme Pollock.
Other sports: Rugby, squash, golf. Follows soccer, athletics.
Relaxations: Backgammon, fishing, music and "siestas".
Extras: Played rugby for Natal Schools, 1980. South Africa Schools Cricket, 1979–80. Still holds South African shot-putt and hurdles U-19 records.
Opinions on cricket: "I would like to see the 4-day game introduced into English county cricket."
Best batting performance: 140 Hampshire v Derbyshire, Basingstoke 1985.

LAST SEASON: BATTING

	I.	N.O.	R.	H.S.	AV.
TEST					
OTHER FIRST CLASS	43	7	1533	140*	42.58
INT					
JPL	11	3	396	104	49.50
NAT.W	4	1	195	110	65.00
B & H	5	1	250	81	62.50

CAREER: BATTING

	I.	N.O.	R.	H.S.	AV.
TEST					
OTHER FIRST CLASS	122	18	3871	140*	37.22
INT					
JPL	19	4	612	104	40.80
NAT.W	4	1	195	110	65.00
B & H	6	1	259	81	51.80

LAST SEASON: BOWLING

	O.	M.	R.	W.	AV.
TEST					
OTHER FIRST CLASS	27.4	8	76	4	19.00
INT					
JPL					
NAT.W	2.5	0	13	2	6.50
B & H					

CAREER: BOWLING

	O.	M.	R.	W.	AV.
TEST					
OTHER FIRST CLASS	33.4	8	123	4	30.75
INT					
JPL					
NAT.W	2.5	0	13	2	6.50
B & H					

156. Which current county player has the nickname "Froggy"?

157. Which current county player has the nickname "Wilf"?

158. Which current county player has the nickname "Ghostie"?

159. Which current county player has the nickname "Dougall"?

STANDING, D.K.   Sussex

Full Name: David Kevin Standing.
Role: Right-hand bat, off-break
bowler, short-leg fielder.
Born: 21 October 1963, Brighton,
Sussex.
Height: 5' 7'' **Weight:** 11st.
Nickname: Uppers.
County debut: 1983.
1st-Class 50s scored: 2.
1st-Class catches 1985: 0 (career: 3).
Parents: David Eric and Valerie
Mavis Standing.
Marital status: Single.
Education: Tideway School,
Newhaven. Brighton and Hove
VI Form.
Qualifications: 8 O-levels, 1 A-level.
Family links with cricket: Father
local cricketer.
Off-season 1985–86: Working for our sponsors: T.S.B. Trustcard.
Overseas tours: West Indies with Sussex Young Cricketers as captain.
Cricketers particularly learnt from: Most Sussex senior players.
Cricketers particularly admired: Greg Chappell, Paul Parker.
Other sports: Football, golf, squash, snooker and others.
Relaxations: Reading, music.
Extras: Captained England Schools U-15. Played England Schools U-19.
Best batting performance: 60 Sussex v Worcestershire, Worcester 1983.

LAST SEASON: BATTING

	I.	N.O.	R.	H.S.	AV.
TEST					
OTHER FIRST CLASS	2	0	10	7	5.00
INT					
JPL					
NAT.W					
B & H					

CAREER: BATTING

	I.	N.O.	R.	H.S.	AV.
TEST					
OTHER FIRST CLASS	12	4	262	60	32.75
INT					
JPL					
NAT.W					
B & H					

LAST SEASON: BOWLING

	O.	M.	R.	W.	AV.
TEST					
OTHER FIRST CLASS					
INT					
JPL					
NAT.W					
B & H					

CAREER: BOWLING

	O.	M.	R.	W.	AV.
TEST					
OTHER FIRST CLASS	4.3	0	32	0	–
INT					
JPL					
NAT.W					
B & H					

STANWORTH, J.   Lancashire

Full Name: John Stanworth.
Role: Right-hand bat, wicket-keeper.
Born: 30 September 1960, Oldham, Lancs.
Height: 5' 10'' **Weight:** 10st. 7lbs.
Nickname: Stanny, Stick.
County debut: 1983.
1st-Class 50s scored: 1.
Parents: Robert and Freda Stanworth.
Marital status: Single.
Education: Chadderton Grammar School; North Cheshire College, Warrington.
Qualifications: 8 O-levels, 1 A-level, B.Ed. Physical Education.
Jobs outside cricket: Health and fitness programmer, P.E. teacher.
Off-season 1985–86: Teaching P.E.
Overseas tours: Australia 1978, playing and coaching in Grade cricket; West Indies 1981 with British Colleges Sports Association.
Cricketers particularly learnt from: "Bob Blair (ex-New Zealand and Wellington) gave me a kick up the pants in my formative years."
Cricketers particularly admired: Alan Knott, for his dedication. Bob Taylor for his "ease" behind the wicket.
Other sports: Rugby.
Relaxations: Car mechanics, T.V. music and films.
Extras: Instigated pre-season training for the squad.

LAST SEASON: BATTING

	I.	N.O.	R.	H.S.	AV.
TEST					
OTHER FIRST CLASS	10	2	70	50*	8.75
INT					
JPL	1	0	2	2	–
NAT.W					
B & H	1	1	8	8*	–

CAREER: BATTING

	I.	N.O.	R.	H.S.	AV.
TEST					
OTHER FIRST CLASS	26	7	178	50*	9.37
INT					
JPL	2	0	2	2	1.00
NAT.W	–	–	–	–	–
B & H	1	1	8	8*	–

LAST SEASON: WICKET KEEPING

	C.	ST.			
TEST					
OTHER FIRST CLASS	6	3			
INT					
JPL	–	–			
NAT.W					
B & H	1	–			

CAREER: WICKET KEEPING

	C.	ST.			
TEST					
OTHER FIRST CLASS	24	4			
INT					
JPL	8	–			
NAT.W	2	–			
B & H	1	–			

Opinions on cricket: "The view of the county cricketer should be given more importance in the making of decisions which directly affect his job."
Best batting performance: 50* Lancashire v Gloucestershire, Bristol 1985.

STEELE, J.F.   Glamorgan

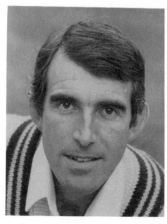

Full Name: John Frederick Steele.
Role: Right-hand bat, slow left-arm bowler.
Born: 23 July 1946, Stafford.
Height: 5′ 10½″ **Weight:** 11st. 7lbs.
Nickname: Steeley, Rustless.
County debut: 1970 (Leicestershire), 1984 (Glamorgan).
County cap: 1971 (Leicestershire), 1984 (Glamorgan).
Benefit: With Leicestershire in 1983 (£33,470).
1000 runs in a season: 6.
50 wickets in a season: 2.
1st-Class 50s scored: 69.
1st-Class 100s scored: 21.
1st-Class 5 w. in innings: 16.
One-day 50s: 14.
One-day 100s: 1.
Place in batting averages: 96 average: 31.44; (1984: 132 average: 28.28).
Place in bowling averages: 133 average: 52.82; (1984: 44 average: 27.46).
1st-Class catches 1985: 6 (career: 399).
Parents: Alfred and Grace Steele.
Wife and date of marriage: Susan, 16 April 1977.
Education: Endon Secondary Modern, Staffordshire.
Jobs outside cricket: Work study officer; Junior fireman. Staffordshire Fire Brigade.
Family links with cricket: Younger brother of David Steele of Derbyshire and England, and cousin of former Northants player B.S. Crump. Uncle, Stan Crump, played as professional in Lancashire League.
Overseas teams played for: Natal in 1973–74 and 1977–78 Currie Cup Competitions; Pinetown Cricket Club, Natal, S. Africa.
Other sports: Golf.
Relaxations: Music, reading.
Extras: Was 12th man for England v Rest of the World at Lord's in 1970, only a month after making debut. Played for Leicestershire 1970–1983.
Best batting performance: 195 Leicestershire v Derbyshire, Leicester 1971.
Best bowling performance: 7-29 Natal B v Griqualand West, Umzinto 1973–74; 7-29 Leicestershire v Gloucestershire, Leicester 1980.

LAST SEASON: BATTING

	I.	N.O.	R.	H.S.	AV.
TEST					
OTHER FIRST CLASS	12	3	283	100	31.44
INT					
JPL	4	2	18	9*	9.00
NAT.W					
B & H	3	0	8	8	2.67

CAREER: BATTING

	I.	N.O.	R.	H.S.	AV.
TEST					
OTHER FIRST CLASS	588	80	14772	195	29.08
INT					
JPL	135	36	1856	92	18.74
NAT.W	21	4	452	106*	26.59
B & H	52	6	1130	91	24.57

LAST SEASON: BOWLING

	O.	M.	R.	W.	AV.
TEST					
OTHER FIRST CLASS	215.1	60	581	11	52.82
INT					
JPL	32	0	148	7	21.14
NAT.W					
B & H	26	3	106	2	53.00

CAREER: BOWLING

	O.	M.	R.	W.	AV.
TEST					
OTHER FIRST CLASS	6391	2017	15210	575	26.45
INT					
JPL	1149.2	95	4557	191	23.85
NAT.W	217	44	647	22	29.41
B & H	569	92	1730	63	27.46

STEPHENSON, J.P.   Essex

Full Name: John Patrick Stephenson.
Role: Right-hand opening bat.
Born: 14 March 1965.
Height: 6' 1'' **Weight:** 11st. 7 lbs.
Nickname: Stanley.
County debut: 1985.
Parents: Patrick and Eve Stephenson.
Marital status: Single.
Education: Felstead Preparatory
School; Felstead Senior School;
Durham University.
Qualifications: 7 O-levels,
3 A-levels.
Off-season 1985–86: Doing second
year of degree course at university.
Overseas tours: Zimbabwe 1982–83
with ESCA U-19s.
Overseas teams played for:
Fitzroy C.C., Melbourne, 1983–84.
Cricketers particularly learnt from: Gordon Barker, Ray East.
Cricketers particularly admired: Richard Hadlee, Graham Gooch, Keith
Fletcher.
Other sports: Squash, football, hockey, snooker.
Injuries 1985: "Hit in the right eye by a ball which put me out for three weeks.
Recurring problem with right ankle."
Relaxations: Music, keep fit, health food, running, squash, snooker, singing.
Extras: Awarded 2nd XI cap in 1984 when he was leading run-scorer with

Essex 2nd XI. Young player of the year 1985 for Essex C.C.C. Captain of Durham University Cricket 1986.
Opinions on cricket: Talent in university cricket outside Oxford and Cambridge should be recognised.
Best batting performance: 10 Essex v Gloucestershire, Bristol 1985.

LAST SEASON: BATTING

	I.	N.O.	R.	H.S.	AV.
TEST					
OTHER FIRST CLASS	2	0	14	10	7.00
INT					
JPL					
NAT.W					
B & H					

CAREER: BATTING

	I.	N.O.	R.	H.S.	AV.
TEST					
OTHER FIRST CLASS	2	0	14	10	7.00
INT					
JPL					
NAT.W					
B & H					

STEVENSON, G.B. Yorkshire

Full Name: Graham Barry Stevenson.
Role: Right-hand bat, right-arm fast-medium bowler.
Born: 16 December 1955, Hemsworth, Yorkshire.
Height: 6′ 0″ **Weight:** 13st.
Nickname: "Several—unprintable!" Moonbeam.
County debut: 1973.
County cap: 1978.
Test debut: 1979–80.
No. of Tests: 2.
No. of One-Day Internationals: 4.
50 wickets in a season: 5.
1st-Class 50s scored: 15.
1st-Class 100s scored: 2.
1st-Class 5 w. in innings: 18.
1st-Class 10 w. in match: 2.
One-day 50s: 2.

Place in batting averages: — average: —; (1984: 259 average: 12.00).
Place in bowling averages: — average: —; (1984: 129 average: 46.95).
1st-Class catches 1985: 1 (career: 73).
Wife and date of marriage: Angela, 29 October 1977.
Children: Christopher George, 9 January 1982.
Education: Minsthorpe High School, where they did not play cricket.
Jobs outside cricket: Clerk at Foster Wheeler Power Products Ltd., Snaith, near Goole.

Family links with cricket: Two uncles, Keith and Jack Stevenson, both played local league cricket.

Overseas tours: Australia 1979–80; West Indies 1981.

Cricketers particularly learnt from: Geoff Boycott: "Boycott has been the biggest help to my career in all ways. He virtually opened my way into county cricket by arranging with Yorkshire for me to attend pre-season nets."

Other sports: Member of local club snooker team. Golf.

Relaxations: Watching Sheffield Wednesday F.C.

Extras: Toured Australia with England 1979–80, being called in after return to England through injury of Mike Hendrick. Vice-President Townville C.C. Steve Oldham was his best man. Batting No. 11 made 115 n.o. in a record stand of 149 for Yorkshire v Warwickshire, May 1982, with Geoff Boycott, beating previous Yorkshire record for last wicket by one run, set by Lord Hawke and David Hunter in 1898.

Best batting performance: 115* Yorkshire v Warwickshire, Edgbaston 1982.

Best bowling performance: 8-57 Yorkshire v Northamptonshire, Leeds 1980.

LAST SEASON: BATTING

	I.	N.O.	R.	H.S.	AV.
TEST					
OTHER FIRST CLASS	6	2	99	35*	24.75
INT					
JPL	3	0	24	13	8.00
NAT.W	–	–	–	–	–
B & H	2	0	5	3	2.50

CAREER BATTING

	I.	N.O.	R.	H.S.	AV.
TEST	2	1	28	27*	–
OTHER FIRST CLASS	224	32	3877	115*	20.19
INT	4	3	43	28*	–
JPL	113	14	1249	81*	12.61
NAT.W	13	1	190	34	15.83
B & H	25	5	176	36	8.80

LAST SEASON: BOWLING

	O.	M.	R.	W.	AV.
TEST					
OTHER FIRST CLASS	72.4	10	252	6	42.00
INT					
JPL	24	0	140	4	35.00
NAT.W	12	4	17	2	8.50
B & H	32	1	160	9	17.78

CAREER BOWLING

	O.	M.	R.	W.	AV.
TEST	52	7	183	5	36.60
OTHER FIRST CLASS	4346.3	970	13750	479	28.71
INT	32	3	125	7	17.86
JPL	1007.1	75	4564	184	24.80
NAT.W	193.3	36	612	30	20.40
B & H	377.3	53	1419	67	21.18

160. Which current Test commentator used to be a violinist with the National Youth Orchestra, as well as winning Cricket and Rugby blues at Cambridge, captaining both his county and England, winning the county championship, and scoring 2198 first-class runs in one season?

STEWART, A.J.   Surrey

Full Name: Alec James Stewart.
Role: Right-hand bat, wicket-keeper.
Born: 8 April 1963, Wimbledon.
Nickname: Stewie.
Height: 5' 11'' **Weight:** 12st.
County debut: 1981.
1000 runs in a season: 1.
1st-Class 50s scored: 11.
1st-Class 100s scored: 2.
One-day 50s: 3.
Place in batting averages: 95
average: 31.53; (1984: 111
average: 31.67).
1st-Class catches 1985: 29
(career: 66).
Parents: Michael James and Sheila
Marie Macdonald Stewart.
Marital status: Single.
Family links with cricket: Father

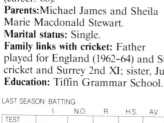

played for England (1962–64) and Surrey (1954–72). Brother Neil plays club
cricket and Surrey 2nd XI; sister, Judy, Malden Wanderers Ladies XI.
Education: Tiffin Grammar School.

LAST SEASON: BATTING

	I.	N.O.	R.	H.S.	AV.
TEST					
OTHER FIRST CLASS	36	4	1009	158	31.53
INT					
JPL	9	2	234	86	33.42
NAT.W	1	0	37	37	–
B & H	3	0	29	16	9.67

CAREER: BATTING

	I.	N.O.	R.	H.S.	AV.
TEST					
OTHER FIRST CLASS	78	11	2139	158	31.93
INT					
JPL	30	6	563	86	23.45
NAT.W	1	0	37	37	–
B & H	6	0	51	16	8.50

LAST SEASON: BOWLING

	O.	M.	R.	W.	AV.
TEST					
OTHER FIRST CLASS	6	0	43	0	–
INT					
JPL					
NAT.W					
B & H					

CAREER: BOWLING

	O.	M.	R.	W.	AV.
TEST					
OTHER FIRST CLASS	6	0	43	0	–
INT					
JPL	0.3	0	4	0	–
NAT.W					
B & H					

LAST SEASON: WICKET KEEPING

	C.	ST.
TEST		
OTHER FIRST CLASS	–	1
INT		
JPL	1	1
NAT.W		
B & H		

CAREER: WICKET KEEPING

	C.	ST.
TEST		
OTHER FIRST CLASS	–	1
INT		
JPL	1	1
NAT.W		
B & H		

Qualifications: 4 O-levels.

Overseas tours: 1980–81 tour of Australia with Surrey U-19.

Off-season 1985–86: Cricket in Perth, Western Australia, with Midland-Guildford.

Cricketers particularly learnt from: Geoff Arnold and Mickey Stewart.

Cricketers particularly admired: Alan Knott, Geoff Boycott, Tony Mann.

Other sports: "Football. Watch all sports. Enjoy horse-riding and caddying for my Uncle Bill at golf."

Relaxations: "Music (Cars and Aussie Crawl), Perth beaches, eating out, listening to girl-friend!"

Injuries 1985: Bad hip injury incurred during NatWest 1st round, missed two weeks.

Extras: "My Uncle Bill has had a big influence on my career to date."

Opinions on cricket: "That all, or at least as many 2nd XI games as possible should be played on first-class grounds rather than club pitches which are a lot lower standard and slower than most county pitches. That all championship matches be played over four days, therefore meaning more 'results', and also it would prepare the players better for a 5-day Test Match."

Best batting performance: 158 Surrey v Kent, Canterbury 1985.

STORIE, A.C.   Northamptonshire

Full Name: Alastair Caled Storie.

Role: Right-hand bat, right-arm medium bowler.

Born: 25 July 1965, Glasgow.

Height: 5′ 8″ **Weight:** 9st. 11lbs.

Nickname: Ally, Wolf.

County debut: 1985.

1st-Class 50s scored: 3.

1st-Class 100s scored: 1.

Place in batting averages: 49 average: 40.70.

1st-Class catches 1985: 3 (career 3).

Parents: Hank and Jenny Storie.

Marital status: Single.

Family links with cricket: Father played club cricket in Glasgow and Johannesburg.

Education: St Stithians College, Johannesburg; UNISA Correspondence University.

Qualifications: J.M.B. Matriculation.

Off-season 1985–86: Playing and coaching in Johannesburg.

Cricketing superstitions: Always puts left pad on first.

Overseas teams played for: Transvaal Schools 1978, 1980, 1981, 1982, 1983; Transvaal B 1985.
Cricketers particularly learnt from: Willie Watson, Peter Stringer.
Cricketers particularly admired: Clive Rice, Barry Richards.
Other sports: Represented South Africa U-19 hockey team 1982–83. Follows football, rugby union.
Relaxations: Music, reading.
Extras: First Northamptonshire batsman to score a 100 on first-class debut.
Best batting performance: 106 Northamptonshire v Hampshire, Northampton 1985.

LAST SEASON: BATTING

	I.	N.O.	R.	H.S.	AV.
TEST					
OTHER FIRST CLASS	12	2	407	106	40.70
INT					
JPL					
NAT.W					
B & H					

CAREER: BATTING

	I.	N.O.	R.	H.S.	AV.
TEST					
OTHER FIRST CLASS	12	2	407	104	40.70
INT					
JPL					
NAT.W					
B & H					

LAST SEASON: BOWLING

	O.	M.	R.	W.	AV.
TEST					
OTHER FIRST CLASS	18	6	51	0	–
INT					
JPL					
NAT.W					
B & H					

CAREER: BOWLING

	O.	M.	R.	W.	AV.
TEST					
OTHER FIRST CLASS	18	6	51	0	–
INT					
JPL					
NAT.W					
B & H					

161. Which cricket commentator played for England, once took eight catches in an innings, scored 1000 runs in a season 11 times, and scored 1347 runs and took 101 wickets in one season?

STOVOLD, A.W. Gloucestershire

Full Name: Andrew Willis Stovold.
Role: Right-hand bat, wicket-keeper.
Born: 19 March 1953, Bristol.
Height: 5′ 7″ **Weight:** 12st. 4lbs.
Nickname: Stumper, Squeak, Stov,
Stovers.
County debut: 1973.
County cap: 1976.
1000 runs in a season: 6.
1st-Class 50s scored: 78.
1st-Class 100s scored: 16.
1st-Class 200s scored: 1.
One-day 50s: 29.
One-day 100s: 2.
Place in batting averages: 188
average: 19.83; (1984: 110
average: 31.75).
1st-Class catches 1985: 20
(career: 303).

Parents: Lancelot Walter and Dorothy Patricia Willis-Stovold.
Wife and date of marriage: Kay Elizabeth, 30 September 1978.
Children: Nicholas, 18 June 1981; Neil, 24th February 1983.

LAST SEASON: BATTING

	I.	N.O.	R.	H.S.	AV.
TEST					
OTHER FIRST CLASS	37	2	694	112	19.83
INT					
JPL	6	2	104	47*	26.00
NAT.W	2	0	92	71	46.00
B & H	4	0	108	60	27.00

CAREER: BATTING

	I.	N.O.	R.	H.S.	AV.
TEST					
OTHER FIRST CLASS	487	26	13986	212*	30.34
INT					
JPL	152	20	3199	98*	24.23
NAT.W	23	2	639	82	30.43
B & H	45	5	1567	123	39.18

LAST SEASON: BOWLING

	O.	M.	R.	W.	AV.
TEST					
OTHER FIRST CLASS					
INT					
JPL					
NAT.W					
B & H					

CAREER: BOWLING

	O.	M.	R.	W.	AV.
TEST					
OTHER FIRST CLASS	25.3	6	86	2	43.00
INT					
JPL					
NAT.W					
B & H					

LAST SEASON: WICKET KEEPING

	C.	ST.			
TEST					
OTHER FIRST CLASS					
INT					
JPL	1	–			
NAT.W					
B & H					

CAREER: WICKET KEEPING

	C.	ST.			
TEST					
OTHER FIRST CLASS	303	45			
INT					
JPL	80	13			
NAT.W					
B & H					

Education: Filton High School; Loughborough College of Education.
Qualifications: Certificate of Education.
Jobs outside cricket: Teacher at Tockington Manor Prep. School.
Cricketing superstitions: "Keeping the same routine until I have a bad run, then trying something else. Always prepare for batting in the same order."
Family links with cricket: Father played local club cricket for Old Down C.C. Brother, Martin, also played county cricket for Gloucestershire.
Cricketers particularly admired: M.J. Proctor, B.A. Richards, R.J. Hadlee.
Overseas tours: England Schools to India, 1970–71; England Young Cricketers to West Indies 1972.
Overseas teams played for: Orange Free State, 1974–75, 1975–76.
Off season 1985–86: Teaching.
Other sports: Football, golf, squash. Follows Rugby Union, hunting, horse-racing.
Relaxations: Gardening, walking.
Best batting performance: 212* Gloucestershire v Northamptonshire, North-ampton 1982.

SUCH, P.M. Nottinghamshire

Full Name: Peter Mark Such.
Role: Right-hand bat, off-break bowler.
Born:12 June 1964, Helensburgh, Scotland.
Height: 6′ 1″ **Weight:** 11st. 7lbs.
Nickname: Suchy.
County debut: 1982.
1st-Class 5 w. in innings: 5.
Place in bowling averages: 83 average: 36.00; (1984: 14 average: 22.31).
1st-Class catches 1985: 7 (career: 26).
Parents: John and Margaret Such.
Marital status: Single.
Education: Harry Carlton Comprehensive.

Qualifications: 9 0-levels, 3 A-levels. Qualified cricket coach (senior).
Jobs outside cricket: Van driver.
Off-season 1985–86: Playing for Bathurst C.C., N.S.W.
Family links with cricket: Father and brother village cricketers.
Cricketers particularly admired: Bob White, Eddie Hemmings.
Overseas teams played for: Kempton Park C.C., South Africa, 1982–83.

Other sports: Follows football and American football.
Relaxations: Music, T.V., films.
Extras: Played for Young England v Young Australia in three "Tests" in 1983.
Best batting performance: 16 Nottinghamshire v Middlesex, Lord's 1984.
Best bowling performance: 6-123 Nottinghamshire v Kent, Trent Bridge 1983.

LAST SEASON: BATTING

	I.	N.O.	R.	H.S.	AV.
TEST					
OTHER FIRST CLASS	12	5	18	8	2.57
INT					
JPL	–	–	–	–	–
NAT.W					
B & H	–	–	–	–	–

CAREER: BATTING

	I.	N.O.	R.	H.S.	AV.
TEST					
OTHER FIRST CLASS	46	17	63	16	2.17
INT					
JPL	1	1	0	0*	–
NAT.W					
B & H	–	–	–	–	–

LAST SEASON: BOWLING

	O.	M.	R.	W.	AV.
TEST					
OTHER FIRST CLASS	405.1	105	1152	32	36.00
INT					
JPL	8	0	50	2	25.00
NAT.W					
B & H	11	1	50	3	16.67

CAREER: BOWLING

	O.	M.	R.	W.	AV.
TEST					
OTHER FIRST CLASS	1238.1	322	3593	119	30.19
INT					
JPL	15	0	116	2	58.00
NAT.W					
B & H	11	1	50	3	16.67

SWALLOW, I.G.   Yorkshire

Full Name: Ian Geoffrey Swallow.
Role: Right-hand bat, off-break bowler, cover fielder.
Born: 18 December 1962, Barnsley.
Height: 5' 7" **Weight:** 9st. 7lbs.
Nickname: Chicken George or Zola.
County debut: 1983.
Place in batting averages: 249 average: 11.22; (1984: 182 average: 22.67).
Place in bowling averages: 135 average: 55.83; (1984: 117 average: 41.33).
1st-Class catches 1985: 4 (career: 14).
Parents: Joyce and Geoffrey Swallow.
Marital status: Single.
Family links with cricket: Father and brother both played for Elsecar village C.C., where he also started his career at the age of 10 years.

Education: Hayland Kirk, Balk, Comprehensive School; Barnsley Technical College.
Qualifications: 3 O-levels.
Jobs outside cricket: Stores clerk.
Cricketing superstitions: "Always put left pad on first."
Cricketers particularly learnt from: Yorkshire C.C.C. coach (D.E.V. Padgett), P. Carrick, G. Boycott.
Cricketers particularly admired: G. Boycott, I.V.A. Richards, J. Emburey.
Other sports: Football and most sports for fun. Follows Barnsley F.C.
Relaxations: Sports in general, pop music.
Extras: Took hat-trick v Warwickshire 2nd XI 1984. Figures: 4-3-2-4.
Best batting performance: 34* Yorkshire v Somerset, Middlesbrough 1984.
Best bowling performance: 4-52 Yorkshire v Kent, Tunbridge Wells 1984.

LAST SEASON: BATTING

	I.	N.O.	R.	H.S.	AV.
TEST					
OTHER FIRST CLASS	11	2	101	25*	11.22
INT					
JPL					
NAT.W					
B & H	1	1	10	10*	–

CAREER: BATTING

	I.	N.O.	R.	H.S.	AV.
TEST					
OTHER FIRST CLASS	23	7	256	34*	16.00
INT					
JPL	1	0	2	2	–
NAT.W					
B & H	3	2	18	10*	–

LAST SEASON: BOWLING

	O.	M.	R.	W.	AV.
TEST					
OTHER FIRST CLASS	225	46	670	12	55.83
INT					
JPL					
NAT.W					
B & H	11	1	42	0	–

CAREER: BOWLING

	O.	M.	R.	W.	AV.
TEST					
OTHER FIRST CLASS	484.5	116	1372	29	47.31
INT					
JPL	4	0	31	0	–
NAT.W					
B & H	36	4	151	2	75.50

162. Why did Fred Trueman give Neil Hawke a bottle of champagne in September 1984?

163. What was unusual about Kim Hughes's contribution to Australia in the Centenary Test v England at Lord's in 1980?

SYKES, J.F.   Middlesex

Full Name: James Frederick Sykes.
Role: Right-hand bat, off-break
bowler, slips or gully fielder.
Born: 30 December 1965,
Shoreditch.
Height: 6′ 2″ **Weight:** 13st. 7lbs.
Nickname: Eric, Sykesy.
County debut: 1983.
1st-Class 50s scored: 1.
1st-Class 100s scored: 1.
Place in batting averages: 127
average: 27.50.
Place in bowling averages: 120
average: 44.23.
1st-Class catches in 1985: 10
(career 10).
Parents: James and Kathleen Sykes.
Education: Bow Comprehensive.
Qualifications: 1 O-Level.
Off-season 1985–86: Coaching in Durban, South Africa.
Overseas tours: England U-19 to West Indies, 1984–85.
Cricketers particularly learnt from: John Emburey, Don Bennett.
Cricketers particularly admired: Clive Radley.
Other sports: Squash, golf. Follows most sports.
Relaxations: Girls, soul music.
Best batting performance: 126 Middlesex v Cambridge University, Cambridge
1985.
Best bowling performance: 3-58 Middlesex v Nottinghamshire, Lord's 1985.

LAST SEASON: BATTING

	I.	N.O.	R.	H.S.	AV.
TEST					
OTHER FIRST CLASS	13	3	275	126	27.50
INT					
JPL	4	0	41	25	10.25
NAT.W					
B & H					

CAREER: BATTING

	I.	N.O.	R.	H.S.	AV.
TEST					
OTHER FIRST CLASS	14	3	279	126	25.36
INT					
JPL	5	1	43	25	10.75
NAT.W					
B & H					

LAST SEASON: BOWLING

	O.	M.	R.	W.	AV.
TEST					
OTHER FIRST CLASS	191.5	42	575	13	44.23
INT					
JPL	24	0	74	2	37.00
NAT.W					
B & H					

CAREER: BOWLING

	O.	M.	R.	W.	AV.
TEST					
OTHER FIRST CLASS	212.5	48	629	14	44.93
INT					
JPL	26	0	85	2	42.50
NAT.W					
B & H					

TAVARÉ, C.J.   Kent

Full Name: Christopher James
Tavaré.
Role: Right-hand bat, right-arm
bowler, slip fielder.
Born: 27 October 1954, Orpington,
Kent.
Height: 6′ 1½″ **Weight:** 12st. 8lbs.
Nickname: Tav, Rowdy.
County debut: 1974.
County cap: 1978.
Test debut: 1980.
No. of Tests: 30.
No. of One-Day Internationals: 29.
1000 runs in a season: 9.
1st-Class 50s scored: 85.
1st-Class 100s scored: 28.
One-day 50s: 31.
One-day 100s: 8.
Place in batting averages: 69
average: 36.03; (1984: 127 average: 29.21).
1st-Class catches 1985: 20 (career: 247).
Parents: Andrew and June Tavaré.
Wife and date of marriage: Vanessa, 22 March 1980.
Education: Sevenoaks School; Oxford University.
Qualifications: Studied zoology.
Family links with cricket: Father, uncle Jack Tavaré, and uncle, Derrick
Attwood, all played school and club cricket, father and Uncle Jack at
Chatham House, father and Uncle Derrick at Bickley Park C.C. Elder brother,
Stephen, and younger brother, Jeremy, both play cricket.

LAST SEASON: BATTING

	I.	N.O.	R.	H.S.	AV.
TEST					
OTHER FIRST CLASS	40	6	1225	150*	36.03
INT					
JPL	14	3	583	101	53.00
NAT.W	3	1	80	62*	40.00
B & H	5	0	180	143	36.00

CAREER: BATTING

	I.	N.O.	R.	H.S.	AV.
TEST	55	2	1753	149	33.07
OTHER FIRST CLASS	377	44	12932	168*	38.84
INT	28	2	720	83*	27.69
JPL	116	7	3236	136*	32.68
NAT.W	22	2	823	118*	41.15
B & H	53	2	1408	143	27.61

LAST SEASON: BOWLING

	O.	M.	R.	W.	AV.
TEST					
OTHER FIRST CLASS					
INT					
JPL					
NAT.W					
B & H					

CAREER: BOWLING

	O.	M.	R.	W.	AV.
TEST	6	3	11	0	–
OTHER FIRST CLASS	45.4	4	282	2	141.0
INT					
JPL	2	0	3	0	–
NAT.W					
B & H					

Overseas teams played for: University of Western Australia, Perth, 1977–78; West Perth C.C. for half a season 1978–79.

Other sports: "Take an interest in most sports, especially American football in winter."

Relaxations: Music, zoology, playing scrabble, seeing films, gardening, and woodwork.

Extras: Played for England Schools v All-India Schools at Birmingham in 1973, scoring 124 n.o. Oxford University cricket blue 1975–76–77. Whitbread Scholarship to Perth, Australia, 1978–79. Suffers from asthma and hay-fever. Was top-scorer with 82 n.o., and Man of the Match, on debut for England in 55-over match v West Indies at Headingley, May 1980. Captain 1983–84.

Best batting performance: 168* Kent v Essex, Chelmsford 1982.

TAYLOR, L.B. Leicestershire

Full Name: Leslie Brian Taylor.
Role: Right-hand bat, right-arm fast-medium bowler.
Born: 25 October 1953, Earl Shilton, Leicestershire.
Height: 6′ 3½″ **Weight:** 14st. 7lbs.
Nickname: Les.
County debut: 1977.
County cap: 1981.
Test debut: 1985.
No. of Tests: 2.
50 wickets in a season: 4.
1st-Class 5 w. in innings: 15.
1st-Class 10 w. in match: 1.
Place in bowling averages: 11 average: 22.93; (1984: 105 average: 36.90).
1st-Class catches 1985: 6 (career: 38).

Parents: Peggy and Cyril Taylor.
Wife and date of marriage: Susan, 12 July 1973.
Children: Jamie, 24 June 1976; Donna, 10 November 1978; Suzy, 3 June 1981.
Education: Heathfield High School, Earl Shilton.
Qualifications: Qualified carpenter and joiner.
Off-season 1985–86: England tour of West Indies
Family links with cricket: Relation of the late Sam Coe, holder of highest individual score for Leicestershire, 252 not out v Northants. at Leicester in 1914.
Overseas tours: South America with Derrick Robins' XI in 1978–79.

Overseas teams played for: Natal 1982–84.
Other sports: Swimming and football.
Injuries 1985: Groin strain (missed most of B. & H. zonal matches).
Relaxations: Game-shooting and fox-hunting with the Atherstone Hunt.
Opinions on cricket: Should not be subjected to over-rate fines in one-day cricket.
Extras: Was banned from Test cricket for three years for joining rebel England tour of South Africa in 1982.
Best batting performance: 47 Leicestershire v Derbyshire, Derby 1983.
Best bowling performance: 7-28 Leicestershire v Derbyshire, Leicester 1981.

LAST SEASON: BATTING

	I.	N.O.	R.	H.S.	AV.
TEST	1	1	1	1*	–
OTHER FIRST CLASS	17	8	88	20*	9.78
INT					
JPL	2	2	7	6*	–
NAT.W	1	1	0	0*	–
B & H	–	–	–	–	–

CAREER: BATTING

	I.	N.O.	R.	H.S.	AV.
TEST	1	1	1	1*	–
OTHER FIRST CLASS	134	59	761	47	10.15
INT					
JPL	21	17	75	15*	18.75
NAT.W	5	4	12	5*	–
B & H	7	3	11	5	2.75

LAST SEASON: BOWLING

	O.	M.	R.	W.	AV.
TEST	63.3	11	178	4	44.50
OTHER FIRST CLASS	503.2	130	1198	56	21.39
INT					
JPL	53.5	6	173	12	14.41
NAT.W	22	4	66	5	13.20
B & H	30.5	5	85	8	10.63

CAREER: BOWLING

	O.	M.	R.	W.	AV.
TEST	63.3	11	178	4	44.50
OTHER FIRST CLASS	4051	999	10985	457	24.04
INT					
JPL	607.3	55	2513	138	18.21
NAT.W	115.1	19	389	25	15.56
B & H	237.2	50	791	39	20.28

164. What size does Derek Pringle of Essex and England take in cricket boots?

165. At what approximate speed does the fastest woman fast bowler bowl: 80 mph, 70 mph or 50 mph?

TAYLOR, N.R.   Kent

Full Name: Neil Royston Taylor.
Role: Right-hand bat, off-break bowler, bat/pad fielder.
Born: 21 July 1959, Farnborough, Kent.
Height: 6' 1" **Weight:** 13st. 8lbs.
Nickname: Map.
County debut: 1979.
County cap: 1982.
1000 runs in a season: 3.
1st-Class 50s scored: 22.
1st-Class 100s scored: 14.
One-day 50s: 6.
One-day 100s: 3.
Place in batting averages: 26 average: 46.83; (1984: 106 average: 32.29).
1st-Class catches 1985: 6 (career: 60).
Parents: Leonard and Audrey Taylor.
Wife: Jane Claire, 25 September 1982.
Education: Cray Valley Technical High School.
Qualifications: 8 O-levels, 2 A-levels.
Jobs outside cricket: Insurance broker, and working in Civil Service.
Off-season 1985–86: Coaching abroad.
Family links with cricket: Brother Colin played for Kent U-19s.
Overseas tours: With England Schools Team to India 1977–78; Kent to Vancouver 1979.
Overseas teams played for: Randburg in Johannesburg, South Africa, 1980–85;

LAST SEASON: BATTING

	I.	N.O.	R.	H.S.	AV.
TEST					
OTHER FIRST CLASS	25	7	843	120*	46.83
INT					
JPL	5	0	59	21	11.80
NAT.W	1	0	51	51	–
B & H	–	–	–	–	–

CAREER: BATTING

	I.	N.O.	R.	H.S.	AV.
TEST					
OTHER FIRST CLASS	184	28	5458	155*	34.99
INT					
JPL	39	2	892	74	24.10
NAT.W	8	0	186	51	23.25
B & H	13	0	563	121	43.31

LAST SEASON: BOWLING

	O.	M.	R.	W.	AV.
TEST					
OTHER FIRST CLASS	64	9	220	6	36.67
INT					
JPL					
NAT.W					
B & H					

CAREER: BOWLING

	O.	M.	R.	W.	AV.
TEST					
OTHER FIRST CLASS	144	28	508	11	46.18
INT					
JPL					
NAT.W					
B & H					

(Coach at St Stithians College 1981–85).
Cricketers particularly learnt from: Bob Woolmer, Mark Benson.
Cricketing superstitions: Always puts batting gear on in same order.
Other sports: Rugby—played for Kent U-21 XV—golf, squash.
Relaxations: Listening to records, reading.
Extras: Made 110 on debut match for Kent C.C.C. v Sri Lanka, 1979. Won four Man of the Match awards in first five matches. Scored highest score by Kent player in Benson and Hedges cricket: 121 v Sussex and Somerset.
Best batting performance: 155* Kent v Glamorgan, Cardiff 1983.
Best bowling performance: 2-20 Kent v Somerset, Canterbury 1985.

TAYLOR, N.S.   Surrey

Full Name: Nicholas Simon Taylor.
Role: Right-hand bat, right-arm fast-medium bowler, outfielder.
Born: 2 June 1963, Holmfirth, Yorkshire.
Height: 6′ 3″ **Weight:** 14st.
Nickname: Bond, Harry, Don.
County debut: 1981 (Yorkshire), 1984 (Surrey).
1st-Class 5 w. in innings: 1.
Place in batting averages: 247 average: 11.40.
Place in bowling averages: 66 average: 32.17.
1st-Class catches 1985: 1 (career: 5).
Parents: Kenneth and Avril Taylor.
Marital status: Single.
Education: Gresham's School, Holt, Norfolk.
Qualifications: 7 O-levels, 3 A-levels.
Jobs outside cricket: Squash coach, builder, gym instructor.
Overseas teams played for: Hawthorn, Melbourne, 1982–83; Wangari, New Zealand, 1983–84; Springs, South Africa, 1984–84.
Off-season 1985–86: Playing cricket in Australia (St Mary's C.C.).
Family links with cricket: Father, Ken, played for Yorkshire and England.
Cricketers particularly learnt from: Dennis Lillee, Geoff Arnold and father.
Cricketing superstitions: "Always hold the ball in left hand when starting to run in to bowl."
Other sports: Squash (played in British Open U-19s), swimming, tennis, gym, pool.

Relaxations: Fly fishing, shooting, books, making money, going abroad.

Extras: Released by Yorkshire 1983 and joined Surrey for 1984. Released at end of 1985.

Opinions on cricket: "A person should be judged on playing ability, not personality. Coaches should have more say in selection and the committee less."

Best batting performance: 21* Surrey v Kent, Canterbury 1985.

Best bowling performance: 7-44 Surrey v Cambridge University, Cambridge 1985.

LAST SEASON: BATTING

	I.	N.O.	R.	H.S.	AV.
TEST					
OTHER FIRST CLASS	8	3	57	21*	11.40
INT					
JPL	–	–	–	–	–
NAT.W					
B & H	2	0	2	2	1.00

CAREER: BATTING

	I.	N.O.	R.	H.S.	AV.
TEST					
OTHER FIRST CLASS	15	5	73	21*	7.30
INT					
JPL	1	1	9	9*	–
NAT.W					
B & H	2	0	2	2	1.00

LAST SEASON: BOWLING

	O.	M.	R.	W.	AV.
TEST					
OTHER FIRST CLASS	149	22	579	18	32.17
INT					
JPL	8	0	47	1	–
NAT.W					
B & H	18.4	3	84	1	–

CAREER: BOWLING

	O.	M.	R.	W.	AV.
TEST					
OTHER FIRST CLASS	424.2	81	1553	50	31.06
INT					
JPL	12	0	64	1	–
NAT.W					
B & H	18.4	3	84	1	–

---

166. What was unusual about Neil Harvey's 167 for Australia v England at Melbourne in 1958–59?

167. Which bowler in his Test debut took 8 for 84 in the first innings and 8 for 53 in the second?

168. Who never keeps wicket without wearing his county cap?

TEDSTONE, G.A.   Warwickshire

Full Name: Geoffrey Alan Tedstone.
Role: Right-hand bat, wicket-keeper.
Born: 19 January 1961, Southport, Lancs.
Height: 5' 7'' **Weight:** 10st. 6lbs.
Nickname: Ted.
County debut: 1982.
1st-Class 50s scored: 1.
Parents: Ken and Win Tedstone.
Marital status: Single.
Education: Warwick School; St. Paul's College, Cheltenham.
Qualifications: 6 O-levels, 4 A-levels; B.Ed. Degree. Qualified P.E. Teacher.
Jobs outside cricket: Coach, teacher.
Family links with cricket: Father was a keen club cricketer. Sister, Janet, plays for England Ladies.
Brother, Roger, plays for Leamington C.C.
Overseas tours: England Young Cricketers to West Indies 1980; British Colleges to West Indies 1981.
Cricketers particularly admired: Neal Abberley, Geoff Humpage, Bob Taylor.
Other sports: Hockey for Warwickshire, squash, soccer. Watches Rugby union and Wolverhampton Wanderers F.C.
Relaxations: Records, films, pubs.
Extras: "Can also bowl vicious in-swingers!"
Best batting performance: 67* Warwickshire v Cambridge University 1983.

LAST SEASON: BATTING

	I.	N.O.	R.	H.S.	AV.
TEST					
OTHER FIRST CLASS	1	0	22	22	–
INT					
JPL					
NAT.W					
B & H					

CAREER: BATTING

	I.	N.O.	R.	H.S.	AV.
TEST					
OTHER FIRST CLASS	22	5	310	67*	17.22
INT					
JPL	2	0	25	13	12.50
NAT.W					
B & H					

LAST SEASON: WICKET KEEPING

	C.	ST.			
TEST					
OTHER FIRST CLASS	1	1			
INT					
JPL					
NAT.W					
B & H					

CAREER: WICKET KEEPING

	C.	ST.			
TEST					
OTHER FIRST CLASS	29	7			
INT					
JPL	2	–			
NAT.W					
B & H					

TERRY, V.P. — Hampshire

Full Name: Vivian Paul Terry.
Role: Right-hand bat, right-arm medium bowler, slip or cover fielder.
Born: 14 January 1959, Osnabruck, West Germany.
Height: 6' 0'' **Weight:** 12st. 6lbs.
County debut: 1978.
County cap: 1983.
Test debut: 1984.
No. of Tests: 2.
1000 runs in a season: 3.
1st-Class 50s scored: 23.
1st-Class 100s scored: 11.
One-day 50s: 6.
One-day 100s: 4.
Place in batting averages: 85 average: 32.92; (1984: 24 average: 48.32).
1st-Class catches 1985: 34 (career: 77).
Parents: Michael and Patricia Terry.
Marital status: Single.
Education: Durlston Court, Barton-on-Sea, Hampshire; Millfield School, Somerset.
Qualifications: 8 O-levels, 1 A-level.
Off-season 1985–86: Searching for a job; plenty of golf and squash.
Overseas tours: E.S.C.A. tour to India 1977–78; Gordon Greenidge benefit tour to Paris and Isle of Wight; English Counties tour to Zimbabwe 1985.
Overseas teams played for: Sydney 1978–79; in New Zealand 1980–81.

LAST SEASON: BATTING

	I.	N.O.	R.	H.S.	AV.
TEST					
OTHER FIRST CLASS	41	2	1284	148*	32.92
INT					
JPL	13	1	412	82	34.33
NAT.W	4	1	340	165*	113.33
B & H	5	0	43	14	8.60

CAREER: BATTING

	I.	N.O.	R.	H.S.	AV.
TEST	3	0	16	8	5.33
OTHER FIRST CLASS	132	16	4218	175*	36.36
INT					
JPL	58	11	1376	110	29.27
NAT.W	11	1	431	165*	43.10
B & H	16	0	338	72	21.13

LAST SEASON: BOWLING

	O.	M.	R.	W.	AV.
TEST					
OTHER FIRST CLASS					
INT					
JPL					
NAT.W					
B & H					

CAREER: BOWLING

	O.	M.	R.	W.	AV.
TEST					
OTHER FIRST CLASS	13.5	4	39	0	–
INT					
JPL					
NAT.W					
B & H					

Cricketers particularly learnt from: Chris Smith.
Cricketers particularly admired: Robin Smith, Gordon Greenidge.
Other sports: Golf, squash, soccer.
Relaxations: Music, sleeping.
Best batting performance: 175* Hampshire v Gloucestershire, Bristol 1984.

THOMAS, D.J.   Surrey

Full Name: David James Thomas.
Role: Left-hand bat, left-arm medium bowler.
Born: 30 June 1959, Solihull, Warwickshire.
Height: 6' 0'' **Weight:** 12st. 7lbs.
Nickname: Teddy.
County debut: 1977.
County cap: 1982.
50 wickets in a season: 2.
1st-Class 50s scored: 7.
1st-Class 100s scored: 2.
1st-Class 5 w. in innings: 6.
1st-Class 10 w. in match: 1.
One-day 50s: 5.
Place in batting averages: 233 average: 12.89; (1984: 209 average: 18.48).
Place in bowling averages: 89 average: 37.06; (1984: 46 average: 27.57).
1st-Class catches 1985: 10 (career: 41).
Parents: Howard James and Heather Thomas.
Wife and date of marriage: Miranda, February 1982.
Education: Licensed Victuallers' School, Slough.
Jobs outside cricket: Salesman for Securicor Communications.
Family links with cricket: Father played for R.A.F. Brother, Howard, played for Bucks U-19.
Overseas tours: Surrey C.C.C. tour of the Far East, also Antigua; *Cricketer* International in Dubai; Whitbread Scholarship in Australia in 1982–83.
Overseas teams played for: Northern Transvaal 1980–81; Natal 1983–4.
Cricketers particularly learnt from or admired: Mike Procter, Robin Jackman.
Other sports: Golf, squash. Follows football, rugby, racing.
Extras: Played for England U-19 v West Indies U-19, and for Derrick Robins' XI v New Zealand U-25 XI.
Best batting performance: 119 Surrey v Nottinghamshire, The Oval 1983.
Best bowling performance: 6-36 Surrey v Somerset, The Oval 1984.

LAST SEASON: BATTING

	I.	N.O.	R.	H.S.	AV.
TEST					
OTHER FIRST CLASS	12	3	116	25*	12.89
INT					
JPL	5	0	132	34	26.40
NAT.W	1	0	5	5	–
B & H	3	1	17	7	8.50

CAREER: BATTING

	I.	N.O.	R.	H.S.	AV.
TEST					
OTHER FIRST CLASS	160	32	2502	119	19.55
INT					
JPL	60	12	927	72	19.31
NAT.W	14	5	202	53	22.44
B & H	11	1	75	19	7.50

LAST SEASON: BOWLING

	O.	M.	R.	W.	AV.
TEST					
OTHER FIRST CLASS	354.4	62	1186	32	37.06
INT					
JPL	52	1	259	9	28.77
NAT.W	10	0	56	0	–
B & H	39	8	113	2	56.50

CAREER: BOWLING

	O.	M.	R.	W.	AV.
TEST					
OTHER FIRST CLASS	2990.2	651	9423	284	33.18
INT					
JPL	547.2	32	2530	77	32.85
NAT.W	170.5	20	606	18	33.67
B & H	143.3	24	510	13	39.23

THOMAS, J.G.   Glamorgan

Full Name: John Gregory Thomas.
Role: Right-hand bat, right-arm fast bowler.
Born: 12 August 1960, Trebanos, Swansea.
Height: 6′ 3″ **Weight:** 14st.
County debut: 1979.
1st-Class 50s scored: 3.
1st-Class 5 w. in innings: 6.
1st-Class 10 w. in match: 1.
Place in batting averages: 193 average: 19.14; (1984: 241 average: 14.95).
Place in bowling averages: 63 average: 31.59; (1984: 89 average: 33.51).
1st-Class catches 1985: 6 (career: 32).
Parents: Illtyd and Margaret Thomas.
Marital status: Single.
Family links with cricket: Father played village cricket.
Education: Cwmtawe Comprehensive School; South Glamorgan Institute of Higher Education.
Qualifications: Qualified teacher, advanced cricket coach.
Off-season 1985–86: On tour with England to West Indies.
Cricketing superstitions: The number 111.
Overseas tours: To West Indies with British Colleges March–April 1982.

Overseas teams played for: Border Cricket Union, South Africa.
Other sports: Watches rugby.
Relaxations: Any sport, music.
Extras: Bowling award for 4 wickets or more most times in 1983, John Player Special League (three occasions).
Best batting performance: 84 Glamorgan v Surrey, Guildford 1982.
Best bowling performance: 5-56 Glamorgan v Somerset, Cardiff 1984.

LAST SEASON: BATTING

	I.	N.O.	R.	H.S.	AV.
TEST					
OTHER FIRST CLASS	16	2	268	60*	19.14
INT					
JPL	7	1	46	12	7.66
NAT.W	1	1	2	2*	–
B & H	3	0	14	9	4.67

CAREER: BATTING

	I.	N.O.	R.	H.S.	AV.
TEST					
OTHER FIRST CLASS	91	13	1177	84	15.09
INT					
JPL	33	8	362	37	14.48
NAT.W	3	1	41	24	20.50
B & H	6	0	37	17	6.17

LAST SEASON: BOWLING

	O.	M.	R.	W.	AV.
TEST					
OTHER FIRST CLASS	340.3	54	1232	39	31.59
INT					
JPL	60	2	326	10	32.60
NAT.W	7	2	17	5	3.40
B & H	32	5	108	10	10.80

CAREER: BOWLING

	O.	M.	R.	W.	AV.
TEST					
OTHER FIRST CLASS	1587	308	5622	191	29.44
INT					
JPL	239.1	13	1236	51	24.23
NAT.W	18	2	89	5	17.80
B & H	65.3	8	245	12	20.42

THORNE, D.A. Warwickshire

Full Name: David Anthony Thorne.
Role: Right-hand bat, left-arm medium bowler, "short-leg fielder if unlucky".
Born: 12 December 1964, Coventry.
Height: 6' 0" **Weight:** 11st. 10lbs.
Nickname: Spike, E.M.I., Greystoke.
County debut: 1983.
1st-Class 50s scored: 9.
1st-Class 100s scored: 1.
1st-Class 5 w. in innings: 1.
Place in batting averages: 20 average: 49.94; (1984: 173 average: 23.53).
Place in bowling averages: — average: —; (1984: 108 average: 37.67).
1st-Class catches 1985: 8 (career: 18).
Parents: Dennis and Barbara Thorne.
Marital status: Single.

Family links with cricket: Father is a qualified coach in Warwickshire area. Brothers, Robert and Philip, both played for Warwickshire Schools. Mother played for Hinckley Ladies.

Education: Bablake School, Coventry (Grammar School); Keble College, Oxford.

Qualifications: 10 O-levels, 3 A-levels.

Jobs outside cricket: Components packager for Quinton Hazell car components. Worked as a labourer on building site pre-season 1983. Student.

Off-season 1985–86: Studying at Keble College. Tour at Christmas.

Overseas tours: Oxbridge to Hong Kong and Australia 1985–86.

Cricketing superstitions: "Always left pad on first. If I get runs I try to wear the same trousers no matter how dirty until I fail again."

Cricketers particularly learnt from: "My dad, Neal Abberley and 'the coach' Alan Oakman."

Cricketers particularly admired: Dennis Amiss, Douglas Jardine (after "Bodyline" on T.V.).

Other sports: "Rugby, football and occasionally golf. Follow any sports except horse-racing and jumping which I cannot stand."

Relaxations: Listening to music, films, reading and eating and drinking well.

Injuries 1985: "Long-standing problem with back restricted bowling and frequent brain failure affected my batting."

Extras: "Was hit for 26 in my 3rd over in my first John Player League game by Trevor Jesty. Was out first ball for 0 in my first-class debut v Oxford University. Once took 7 for 7 in a school's first XI match including a hat-trick and all 7 bowled. Secretary O.U.C.C. 1985, captain 1986."

Opinions on cricket: "There is too much county cricket played and inevitably too much travelling involved. There are too many contrived finishes so perhaps we should return to uncovered wickets."

Best batting performance: 124 Oxford University v Zimbabwe, Oxford 1985.

Best bowling performance: 5-39 Oxford University v Cambridge University, Lord's 1984.

LAST SEASON: BATTING

	I.	N.O.	R.	H.S.	AV.
TEST					
OTHER FIRST CLASS	20	3	849	124	49.94
INT					
JPL	5	2	22	7	7.33
NAT.W					
B & H	4	0	64	28	16.00

CAREER: BATTING

	I.	N.O.	R.	H.S.	AV.
TEST					
OTHER FIRST CLASS	43	9	1217	124	35.79
INT					
JPL	13	3	134	42	13.40
NAT.W	1	0	8	8	–
B & H	8	1	104	28*	14.86

LAST SEASON: BOWLING

	O.	M.	R.	W.	AV.
TEST					
OTHER FIRST CLASS	174.1	30	600	9	66.67
INT					
JPL	14	0	94	3	31.33
NAT.W					
B & H	36	3	157	1	–

CAREER: BOWLING

	O.	M.	R.	W.	AV.
TEST					
OTHER FIRST CLASS	422.2	78	1354	26	52.08
INT					
JPL	77.5	1	482	10	48.20
NAT.W					
B & H					

TOMLINS. K.P.   Middlesex

Full Name: Keith Patrick Thomas.
Role: Right-hand bat.
Born: 23 October 1957, Kingston-upon-Thames.
Height: 5' 9" **Weight:** 11st. 10lbs.
Nickname: Tommo.
County debut: 1977.
County cap: 1983.
1st-Class 50s scored: 13.
1st-Class 100s scored: 4.
One-day 50s: 6.
Place in batting averages: 141
average: 25.29; (1984: 191 average: 21.35).
1st-Class catches 1985: 6 (career: 63).
Parents: Royston John and Joan
Muriel Tomlins.
Marital status: Single.
Education: St Benedict's School,
Ealing; College of St Hilda and St Bede,
Durham University.
Qualifications: 5 O-levels, 3 A-levels.
Family links with cricket: Father and eldest brother play for Wycombe House C.C. in Osterley, Middlesex.
Jobs outside cricket: Stage-hand at Richmond Theatre. Sports and music management with Williams Maloney Associates. Ship hand with B.P. on survey ship.
Off-season 1985–86: Parnell C.C., Auckland.
Overseas tours: South America with Derrick Robins' XI in 1979; West Indies with British Colleges 1978 and Easling C.C. 1980; Zimbabwe with Middlesex C.C.C. 1980.

LAST SEASON: BATTING

	I.	N.O.	R.	H.S.	AV.
TEST					
OTHER FIRST CLASS	15	1	354	58	25.29
INT					
JPL	2	0	37	36	18.50
NAT.W					
B & H	–	–	–	–	–

CAREER: BATTING

	I.	N.O.	R.	H.S.	AV.
TEST					
OTHER FIRST CLASS	123	14	2883	146	26.45
INT					
JPL	44	8	594	59	16.50
NAT.W	5	0	193	80	38.60
B & H	6	0	103	40	17.17

LAST SEASON: BOWLING

	O.	M.	R.	W.	AV.
TEST					
OTHER FIRST CLASS	2	0	9	0	–
INT					
JPL					
NAT.W					
B & H					

CAREER: BOWLING

	O.	M.	R.	W.	AV.
TEST					
OTHER FIRST CLASS	96.3	21	326	4	81.50
INT					
JPL	62	2	307	11	27.90
NAT.W					
B & H					

Overseas teams played for: Greenpoint C.C., Cape Town, 1979–80; Merewether D.C.C., Newcastle, New South Wales, 1980–81.
Other sports: Playing member of Richmond Rugby Club, golf.
Relaxations: Reading, music.
Extras: Left staff after 1985 season.
Best batting performance: 146 Middlesex v Oxford University, Oxford 1982.
Best bowling performance: 2–28 Middlesex v Kent, Lord's 1982.

TOPLEY, T.D. Essex

Full Name: Thomas Donald Topley.
Role: Right-hand bat, right-arm medium bowler.
Born: 25 February 1964, Canterbury.
Height: 6′ 3″ **Weight:** 13st. 8lbs.
Nickname: Toppers.
County debut: 1985.
1st-Class catches 1985: 2 (career 2).
Parents: Tom and Rhoda Topley.
Marital status: Single.
Family links with cricket: Brother, Peter, played for Kent.
Education: Royal Hospital School, Holbrook.
Qualifications: 6 O-levels. N.C.A. Coach.
Jobs outside cricket: Cricket coach; exporting to the Gulf States.

Off season 1985-86: Playing abroad or resting.
Cricketing superstitions: Pitching the ball up to all other opening bowlers.

LAST SEASON: BATTING

	I.	N.O.	R.	H.S.	AV.
TEST					
OTHER FIRST CLASS	4	2	15	9*	7.50
INT					
JPL	–	–	–	–	–
NAT.W					
B & H					

CAREER: BATTING

	I.	N.O.	R.	H.S.	AV.
TEST					
OTHER FIRST CLASS	4	2	15	9*	7.50
INT					
JPL	–	–	–	–	–
NAT.W					
B & H					

LAST SEASON: BOWLING

	O.	M.	R.	W.	AV.
TEST					
OTHER FIRST CLASS	161.1	37	464	17	27.29
INT					
JPL	8	1	26	2	13.00
NAT.W					
B & H					

CAREER: BOWLING

	O.	M.	R.	W.	AV.
TEST					
OTHER FIRST CLASS	161.1	37	464	17	27.29
INT					
JPL	8	1	26	2	13.00
NAT.W					
B & H					

Cricketers particularly learnt from: Don Wilson, Geoff Arnold.
Cricketers particularly admired: Anyone who gives 100 per cent.
Other sports: Rugby, football and all other ball sports.
Relaxations: Watching T.V., going out in the countryside.
Extras: Spent three years prior to joining Essex on the M.C.C. Young
Professionals at Lord's as 12th man — held famous Test match catch England
v West Indies at Lord's. Also appeared for Surrey during 1985.
Best batting performance: 9* Essex v Middlesex, Lord's 1985.
Best bowling performance: 4-57 Essex v Middlesex, Lord's 1985.

TREMLETT, T.M. Hampshire

Full Name: Timothy Maurice
Tremlett.
Role: Right-hand bat, right-arm
medium bowler, "third man".
Born: 26 July 1956,
Wellington, Somerset.
Height: 6' 2" **Weight:** 13st. 7lbs.
Nickname: Hurricane, Trooper, R2.
County debut: 1976.
County cap: 1983.
50 wickets in a season: 3.
1st-Class 50s scored: 15.
1st-Class 100s scored: 1.
1st-Class 5 w. in innings: 7.
Place in batting averages: 112
average: 30.00; (1984: 211
average: 18.25).
Place in bowling averages: 7
average: 21.60; (1984: 7
average: 20.34).
1st-Class catches 1985: 5 (career: 57).
Parents: Maurice Fletcher and Melina May Tremlett.
Wife and date of marriage: Carolyn Patricia, 28 September 1979.
Children: Christopher Timothy, 2 September 1981; Alastair Jonathan, 1
February 1983; Benjamin Paul, 2 May 1984.
Education: Bellemoor Secondary Modern; Richard Taunton Sixth-Form
College.
Qualifications: 5 O-levels, 1 A-level. Advanced coaching certificate.
Jobs outside cricket: "One winter spent labouring on building site for muscle-
building (did not seem to work)." Furrier.
Off-season 1985–86: England B tour to Bangladesh, Sri Lanka, Zimbabwe.
Family links with cricket: Father played for Somerset and England 1947–48
against West Indies in the West Indies. Captained Somerset 1958–60. Younger

brother plays in local club cricket for Deanery C.C.

Overseas tours: English Counties tour to Zimbabwe 1985.

Overseas teams played for: Oudtshoorn Teachers' Training College, Western Cape, South Africa, 1978–79.

Cricketers particularly learnt from: "My father, and in general watching and listening to other cricketers, first-class or club players."

Cricketers particularly admired: Vincent Van der Bijl, Mike Hendrick, Malcolm Marshall.

Cricket superstitions: "I always like to be the last to leave the dressing room when taking the field. However, due to a run of defeats in 1980, nobody seemed too keen on taking the field."

Other sports: Golf (handicap 7), table-tennis, squash, swimming and badminton.

Relaxations: Collecting cricket books, record collecting, gardening, cinema.

Injuries 1985: "A severe nervous twitch — the result of numerous close finishes in one-day cricket."

Extras: Member of local cricket club, Deanery. Batted in almost every position for Hants in batting order from 1 to 11 in 1979. Hampshire C.C.C. colleague, John Southern, was best man at his wedding. Captained both his school and sixth-form college at cricket.

Opinions on cricket: "I think it would be a good idea to give sides points, if they lose so many hours (through rain), during a county championship match. They might be awarded points:–

There are 19 hours cricket possible each match. For losing the full three days –4 points.
Example 1.
15 hours –1 point, 16 hours –2 points, etc.
Example 2.
10 or 11 hours –1 point, 12 or 13 hours –2 points, 14 or 15 hours –3 points, etc.

I realise the weather is all part of the game, but some counties, e.g. Gloucestershire 1981, lose a lot more time than others. Perhaps these extra

LAST SEASON: BATTING

	I.	N.O.	R.	H.S.	AV.
TEST					
OTHER FIRST CLASS	29	14	450	102*	30.00
INT					
JPL	3	2	25	17	–
NAT.W	1	1	8	8*	–
B & H	4	2	19	17*	9.50

LAST SEASON: BOWLING

	O.	M.	R.	W.	AV.
TEST					
OTHER FIRST CLASS	665.5	181	1620	75	21.60
INT					
JPL	99	4	534	23	23.21
NAT.W	40	9	117	6	19.50
B & H	42.5	6	166	9	18.44

CAREER: BATTING

	I.	N.O.	R.	H.S.	AV.
TEST					
OTHER FIRST CLASS	181	39	2988	102*	21.04
INT					
JPL	42	17	270	35	10.80
NAT.W	11	2	71	17	7.89
B & H	19	6	148	29	11.38

CAREER: BOWLING

	O.	M.	R.	W.	AV.
TEST					
OTHER FIRST CLASS	2882.2	857	6712	291	23.07
INT					
JPL	641.4	32	2985	109	27.38
NAT.W	171.2	33	510	21	24.28
B & H	239.5	40	764	34	22.47

points, just over one-fifth of the total in a match, would help to counter any unfavourable geographical position. Futhermore, is it not time for neutral umpires in Test matches?"

Best batting performance: 102* Hampshire v Somerset, Taunton 1985.
Best bowling performance: 6-82 Hampshire v Derbyshire, Portsmouth 1983.

TURNER, D.R. Hampshire

Full Name: David Roy Turner.
Role: Left-hand bat, right-arm medium bowler, cover fielder.
Born: 5 February 1949, Corsham, near Chippenham, Wiltshire.
Height: 5' 6" **Weight:** 11st. 8lbs.
Nickname: Birdy. Fossil.
County debut: 1966.
County cap: 1970.
Benefit: 1981 (£23,011).
1000 runs in a season: 7.
1st-Class 50s scored: 69.
1st-Class 100s scored: 24.
One-day 50s: 52.
One-day 100s: 3.
Place in batting averages: 120 average: 28.86; (1984: 45 average: 41.36).
1st-Class catches 1985: 2 (career: 174).
Parents: Robert Edward and Evelyn Peggy Turner.
Wife and date of marriage: Henriette, 18 February 1977.
Children: Nicola Marianna, 15 March 1984.
Education: Chippenham Boys' High School.
Qualifications: O-levels.
Jobs outside cricket: Player-coach for the Paarl Cricket Club, South Africa, 1972–80, 1982–85.
Overseas tours: With Derrick Robins' XI to South Africa 1972–73.
Overseas teams played for: Western Province in the winning 1977–78 Currie Cup Competition side.
Cricketers particularly learnt from: Roy Marshall.
Cricketers particularly admired: Mike Procter.
Cricket records: Shared in an unbeaten partnership of 283 with C.G. Greenidge, a record in any one-day competition, in Benson & Hedges Cup, Hampshire v Minor Counties South at Amersham in 1973.
Other sports: Golf, football.

Relaxations: Chess, gardening, reading, television, watching war films.
Injuries 1985: Split finger.
Extras: Played for Wiltshire in 1965. Took a hat-trick in a Lambert & Butler 7-a-side floodlit tournament at Ashton Gate (Bristol) on 17 September 1981 against Glamorgan. Captained his school at soccer, rugger and cricket.
Opinions on cricket: "I would like the cricket authorities to try for one season, 16 4-day Championship matches, coupled with a Saturday 60-overs limited cricket league, along with the usual Sunday John Player League. The 117 overs a day rule should be scrapped and there should be tighter controls on overseas players."
Best batting performance: 181* Hampshire v Surrey, The Oval 1969.
Best bowling performance: 2-7 Hampshire v Glamorgan, Bournemouth 1981.

LAST SEASON: BATTING

	I.	N.O.	R.	H.S.	AV.
TEST					
OTHER FIRST CLASS	9	2	202	49*	28.86
INT					
JPL	9	1	222	65	27.75
NAT.W	2	1	74	38*	–
B & H	4	2	164	63*	82.00

CAREER: BATTING

	I.	N.O.	R.	H.S.	AV.
TEST					
OTHER FIRST CLASS	590	55	15637	181*	29.23
INT					
JPL	206	19	5476	114	29.28
NAT.W	30	3	786	86	29.11
B & H	58	8	1766	123*	35.32

LAST SEASON: BOWLING

	O.	M.	R.	W.	AV.
TEST					
OTHER FIRST CLASS					
INT					
JPL					
NAT.W					
B & H					

CAREER: BOWLING

	O.	M.	R.	W.	AV.
TEST					
OTHER FIRST CLASS	96.4	26	332	9	36.88
INT					
JPL	1.3	0	11	0	–
NAT.W	1	0	4	0	–
B & H	0.2	0	4	0	–

169. What have Gary Sobers, Phil Mead, Hedley Verity and David Gower in common?

170. What have Clive Lloyd, Zaheer Abbas, Eddie Barlow and Bill Bowes in common?

171. What have Ian Botham, Trevor Bailey, Joel Garner, Fred Titmus and Imran Khan in common?

TURNER, M.S.   Somerset

Full Name: Murray Stewart Turner.
Role: Right-hand bat, right-arm
medium bowler, close fielder.
Born: 27 January 1964, Shaftesbury,
Dorset.
Height: 6' 5'' **Weight:** 13st. 7lbs.
Nickname: Ziggy.
County debut: 1984.
Place in batting averages: 83
average: 23.83.
Place in bowling averages: 127
average: 49.85.
1st-Class catches 1985: 2 (career 2).
Parents: John and Kathleen Turner.
Marital status: Single.
Education: Huish Grammar School,
Taunton, Somerset.
Qualifications: 3 O-levels.
Jobs outside cricket: Service
reception in a main Ford dealer.
Overseas tours: Barbados with Somerset 1985.
Off-season 1985–86: "Looking for another county."
Cricketers particularly admired: Dennis Lillee, Michael Holding, Joel Garner,
David Joseph (Taunton C.C.).
Other sports: Football, darts, snooker, pool, golf. Follows football (Crystal
Palace).
Injuries 1985: Split webbing on left hand (six stitches).
Cricketing superstitions: Wears a floppy white hat whenever possible.
Relaxations: Rock/pop concerts (especially David Bowie); good films.

LAST SEASON: BATTING

	I.	N.O.	R.	H.S.	AV.
TEST					
OTHER FIRST CLASS	12	6	143	24*	23.83
INT					
JPL	5	1	26	8*	6.50
NAT.W					
B & H	3	1	42	19	21.00

CAREER: BATTING

	I.	N.O.	R.	H.S.	AV.
TEST					
OTHER FIRST CLASS	14	6	144	24*	18.00
INT					
JPL	5	1	26	8*	6.50
NAT.W					
B & H	3	1	42	19	21.00

LAST SEASON: BOWLING

	O.	M.	R.	W.	AV.
TEST					
OTHER FIRST CLASS	185.5	30	648	13	49.85
INT					
JPL	45	2	245	6	40.83
NAT.W					
B & H	41.5	4	156	4	39.00

CAREER: BOWLING

	O.	M.	R.	W.	AV.
TEST					
OTHER FIRST CLASS	214.5	38	733	13	56.39
INT					
JPL	45	2	245	6	40.83
NAT.W					
B & H	41.5	4	156	4	39.00

Extras: "I can bowl right-arm seamers and also left-arm spin. Scored 101 not out and took 8-35 in same game in 1984 season." Left staff after 1985 season.

Opinions on cricket: "Too many people who run county cricket clubs from the position of committee member know too little about the game and the players on their staff."

Best batting performance: 24* Somerset v Warwickshire, Taunton 1985.

Best bowling performance: 4-74 Somerset v Warwickshire, Taunton 1985.

TURNER, S.   Essex

Full Name: Stuart Turner.
Role: Right-hand bat, right-arm fast-medium bowler.
Born: 18 July 1943, Chester.
Height: 6′ 0½″ **Weight:** 12st. 7lbs.
Nickname: Stu.
County debut: 1965.
County cap: 1970.
Benefit: 1979.
50 wickets in a season: 6.
1st-Class 50s scored: 41.
1st-Class 100s scored: 4.
1st-Class 5 w. in innings: 27.
1st-Class 10 w. in match: 1.
One-day 50s: 11.
Place in batting averages: —
average: —; (1984: 160
average: 24.63).
Place in bowling averages: —
average: —; (1984: 58 average: 29.38).
1st-Class catches 1985: 0 (career: 217).
Parents: Arthur Leonard and Alice Turner.
Wife and date of marriage: Jacqueline Linda, 9 April 1966.
Children: Jeremy Paul, 12 February 1968; Emma Louise, 21 January 1970.
Education: Epping Junior School; Epping Secondary Modern.
Qualifications: Advanced cricket coach.
Jobs outside cricket: Insurance claims broker. Coaching cricket both in South Africa and England.
Overseas tours: Toured West Indies 1974 with Derrick Robins' XI; South Africa 1975 with Derrick Robins' XI.
Overseas teams played for: Natal in Currie Cup and Gillette Cup Competitions 1976-77-78. Won both in 1976-77.
Cricketers particularly learnt from: "Learnt from so many—one never stops learning."

Cricketers particularly admired: "G. Sobers — a great privilege to play against him."

Cricket records: First player to take 200 wickets and score 2000 runs in the John Player League.

Other sports: Golf, squash, occasional football, enjoys as many sports as possible, watching and playing.

Relaxations: "Reading, playing records, watching television, driving, doing anything that takes my fancy and just enjoying life."

Extras: A century before lunch against Kent (108 mins.) 3 May 1979, Chelmsford. Hat-trick against Surrey at The Oval, 4 May 1971. Spent 1966 and 1967 out of the game, returning in 1968.

Best batting performance: 121 Essex v Somerset, Taunton 1970.

Best bowling performance: 6-26 Essex v Northamptonshire, Northampton 1977.

LAST SEASON: BATTING

	I.	N.O.	R.	H.S.	AV.
TEST					
OTHER FIRST CLASS	7	0	78	35	11.14
INT					
JPL	5	4	42	15*	–
NAT.W.	2	1	10	7*	–
B & H	3	1	11	7	5.50

CAREER: BATTING

	I.	N.O.	R.	H.S.	AV.
TEST					
OTHER FIRST CLASS	509	100	9339	122	22.83
INT					
JPL	204	44	3141	87	19.63
NAT.W	29	4	449	50*	17.96
B & H	53	17	608	55*	16.89

LAST SEASON: BOWLING

	O.	M.	R.	W.	AV.
TEST					
OTHER FIRST CLASS	121.5	26	321	11	29.18
INT					
JPL	88	6	433	11	39.36
NAT.W	46	3	154	8	19.25
B & H	59	10	156	8	19.50

CAREER: BOWLING

	O.	M.	R.	W.	AV.
TEST					
OTHER FIRST CLASS	8859	2266	21213	819	25.90
INT					
JPL	1733.5	168	7038	301	23.38
NAT.W	354.5	70	1027	50	20.54
B & H	697.2	123	2001	101	19.81

---

172. What have Bob Woolmer, Colin Cowdrey and Robin Jackman in common?

173. Which England Test captain was born in Australia?

174. What have Len Hutton, Fred Tate, Jim Parks, Colin Cowdrey, the Nawab of Pataudi and Walter Hadlee in common?

TURNER, S.J.   Somerset

Full Name: Simon Jonathan Turner.
Role: Left-hand bat, wicket-keeper.
Born: 28 April 1960, Cuckfield, Sussex.
Height: 6′ 1½″ **Weight:** 12st. 10lbs.
County debut: 1984.
1st-Class catches 1985: 2 (career 2).
Parents: Derek Edward and Doris Lilian Turner.
Marital status: Single.
Family links with cricket: Elder brother Richard captain of Weston-Super-Mare; younger brother Robert keeper for Millfield and Somerset U-19s. Father chairman of Weston-Super-Mare C.C.
Education: Broadoak Comprehensive; Broadoak Sixth Form; Weston Technical College and Bristol Polytechnic.
Qualifications: 6 O-levels, 6 C.S.E.s. Technical Apprenticeship; City and Guilds Mechanical Engineering Technicians Certificate; B.P.I.C.S. Certificate in Production and Inventory Control.
Overseas tours: Barbados 1985 with Somerset.
Jobs outside cricket: 1977 Apprenticeship at Westland Helicopters; 1981 Product Planner at Westlands and 1982 Computer Progammer at Westlands.
Off-season 1985–86: Computer programming at Westland Helicopters.
Cricketers particularly learnt from: Andy Brassington, Trevor Gard and Brian Mason (Weston C.C.).

LAST SEASON: BATTING

	I.	N.O.	R.	H.S.	AV.
TEST					
OTHER FIRST CLASS	1	1	9	9*	–
INT					
JPL	1	1	8	8*	–
NAT.W					
B & H					

CAREER: BATTING

	I.	N.O.	R.	H.S.	AV.
TEST					
OTHER FIRST CLASS	7	4	84	27*	28.00
INT					
JPL	3	2	16	8*	–
NAT.W	1	0	7	7	–
B & H					

LAST SEASON: WICKET KEEPING

	C.	ST.
TEST		
OTHER FIRST CLASS	2	2
INT		
JPL		
NAT.W		
B & H		

CAREER: WICKET KEEPING

	C.	ST.
TEST		
OTHER FIRST CLASS	14	5
INT		
JPL	–	1
NAT.W	1	1
B & H		

Cricketers particularly admired: Alan Knott, Rod Marsh, John Poole of Weston C.C.
Other sports: Squash, football, running and badminton. Follows Aston Villa F.C.
Relaxations: Woodwork, car maintenance and music — playing and listening.
Injuries 1985: Broken bone in right foot, damaged right thumb ligament.
Best batting performance: 27* Somerset v Glamorgan, Taunton 1984.

TWIZELL, P.H. — Gloucestershire

Full Name: Peter Henry Twizell.
Role: Right-hand bat, right-arm medium bowler.
Born: 18 June 1959, Rothbury, Northumberland.
Height: 6' 3" **Weight:** 15st. 7lbs.
Nickname: Big Hen, H.F.T.
County debut: 1985.
Parents: Sylvia Rose Daykin.
Marital status: Single.
Education: Ponteland High School.
Qualifications: 9 C.S.E.s.
Jobs outside cricket: Steel erector, welder.
Off-season 1985–86: Coaching and playing in New Zealand.
Overseas tours: Gloucestershire to Barbados 1985.
Cricketers particularly learnt from: Norman Graham.

LAST SEASON: BATTING

	I.	N.O.	R.	H.S.	AV.
TEST					
OTHER FIRST CLASS	–	–	–	–	–
INT					
JPL	–	–	–	–	–
NAT.W					
B & H					

CAREER: BATTING

	I.	N.O.	R.	H.S.	AV.
TEST					
OTHER FIRST CLASS	–	–	–	–	–
INT					
JPL	–	–	–	–	–
NAT.W	1	1	9	9*	–
B & H					

LAST SEASON: BOWLING

	O.	M.	R.	W.	AV.
TEST					
OTHER FIRST CLASS	28	6	98	2	49.00
INT					
JPL	2	0	23	1	–
NAT.W					
B & H					

CAREER: BOWLING

	O.	M.	R.	W.	AV.
TEST					
OTHER FIRST CLASS	28	6	98	2	49.00
INT					
JPL	2	0	23	1	–
NAT.W	12	1	45	1	–
B & H					

Cricketers particularly admired: Bill Athey, Brian Davison.
Other sports: "Squash (badly), football. Follow rugby, whippet racing."
Injuries 1985: Torn body muscles.
Relaxations: Watching T.V., drinking socially.

UNDERWOOD, D.L. Kent

Full Name: Derek Leslie Underwood.
Role: Right-hand bat, slow left-arm bowler.
Born: 8 June 1945, Bromley, Kent.
Height: 5' 11" **Weight:** 12st.
Nickname: Deadly, Unders.
County debut: 1962.
County cap: 1964.
Benefit: 1975 (£24,114), 2nd benefit 1986.
Test debut: 1966.
No. of Tests: 86.
No. of One-Day Internationals: 26.
50 wickets in a season: 21.
1st-Class 50s scored: 1.
1st-Class 100s scored: 1.
1st-Class 5 w. in innings: 151.
1st-Class 10 w. in match: 47.
Place in batting averages: — average: —; (1984: 196 average: 20.75).
Place in bowling averages: 32 average: 26.90; (1984: 6 average: 19.62).
1st-Class catches 1985: 7 (career: 255).
Parents: Leslie Underwood (deceased), and Evelyn Underwood.
Wife and date of marriage: Dawn, 6 October 1973.
Children: Heather, 7 February 1976; Fiona, 22 November 1977.
Education: Beckenham & Penge Grammar School.
Jobs outside cricket: Company representative, cricket coach, P.E. school-master. Director of company of Law Stationers.
Family links with cricket: "I played with my father and brother for a local village team, Farnborough. I played for Beckenham with my brother until I played for the Kent 1st XI. My brother now plays for Orpington C.C."
Overseas tours: Pakistan 1966–67; Sri Lanka and Pakistan 1968–69; Australia and New Zealand 1970–71 and 1974–75; India, Sri Lanka and Pakistan 1972–73; West Indies 1973–74; India, Sri Lanka and Australia 1976–77; Australia and India 1979–80.
Other sports: Occasional golf.
Relaxations: Photography, philately, coarse fishing, gardening.
Extras: Second youngest player to receive county cap. Played World Series

Cricket 1978–79. Youngest player ever to take 100 wickets in debut season. Banned from Test cricket for three years for joining rebel team from England to South Africa. Writes articles for *Cricketer International* magazine. Top of Kent first-class bowling averages in 1982, 1983 and 1984. Awarded M.B.E. Scored maiden century in 1984 in 618th innings.

Best batting performance: 111 Kent v Sussex, Hastings 1984.
Best bowling performance: 9-28 Kent v Sussex, Hastings 1964.

LAST SEASON: BATTING

	I.	N.O.	R.	H.S.	AV.
TEST					
OTHER FIRST CLASS	25	9	124	16*	7.75
INT					
JPL	6	4	13	5*	6.50
NAT.W	1	1	19	19*	–
B & H	2	0	5	3	2.50

CAREER: BATTING

	I.	N.O.	R.	H.S.	AV.
TEST	116	35	937	45*	11.56
OTHER FIRST CLASS	548	151	3817	111	9.62
INT	13	4	53	17	5.89
JPL	90	36	366	22	6.77
NAT.W	32	11	154	28	7.33
B & H	42	18	189	27	7.88

LAST SEASON: BOWLING

	O.	M.	R.	W.	AV.
TEST					
OTHER FIRST CLASS	807	290	1802	67	26.90
INT					
JPL	80	7	330	11	30.00
NAT.W	33	12	82	4	20.50
B & H	43	12	108	4	27.00

CAREER: BOWLING

	O.	M.	R.	W.	AV.
TEST	542.2 2920.4	142 1097	7674	297	25.84
OTHER FIRST CLASS	390.5 17949	85 7157	39653	2071	19.15
INT	6 205	0 26	734	32	22.93
JPL	1462.1	188	5388	326	16.52
NAT.W	540.3	143	1623	67	24.22
B & H	711.2	153	1928	90	21.42

VAREY, D.W. Lancashire

Full Name: David William Varey.
Role: Right-hand opening bat, occasional off-break bowler.
Born: 15 October 1961, Darlington.
Height: 6′ 2″ **Weight:** 13st.
Nickname: Wilbur, D-Dubs, Dubsy, Hoorah Henry.
County debut: 1984.
1st-Class catches 1985: 5 (career: 19).
Parents: Bill (deceased) and Monica Varey.
Marital status: Single.
Education: Birkenhead School; Pembroke College, Cambridge.
Qualifications: B.A. Hons French and German.
Family links with cricket: Brother, John, is an Oxford Blue.

Off-season 1985–86: With South Hobart C.C., Tasmania.

Overseas teams played for: South Hobart C.C., Tasmania, 1984–85.

Cricketers particularly learnt from: Peter Lever, Mick Bowyer, Mike Fell, Dave Ewing.

Cricketers particularly admired: Clive Lloyd, Viv Richards, Ian Botham.

Other sports: Rugby, snooker. Follows rugby, soccer (Everton).

Injuries 1985: Sprained left knee.

Relaxations: Disco dancing, body-popping, reading, watching T.V., music.

Opinions on cricket: Too many overs in a day in championship matches, fines in limited-over cricket too severe.

Extras: Played for Cheshire 1977, Lancashire 2nd XI debut 1980. Blues in 1982 and 1983. Secretary C.U.C.C. 1983.

Best batting performance: 151* Cambridge University v Northamptonshire, Cambridge 1982.

LAST SEASON: BATTING

	I.	N.O.	R.	H.S.	AV.
TEST					
OTHER FIRST CLASS	34	3	960	112	30.97
INT					
JPL					
NAT.W					
B & H	3	0	29	16	9.67

CAREER: BATTING

	I.	N.O.	R.	H.S.	AV.
TEST					
OTHER FIRST CLASS	90	9	2166	156*	26.74
INT					
JPL					
NAT.W					
B & H	5	0	58	27	11.60

LAST SEASON: BOWLING

	O.	M.	R.	W.	AV.
TEST					
OTHER FIRST CLASS					
INT					
JPL					
NAT.W					
B & H					

CAREER: BOWLING

	O.	M.	R.	W.	AV.
TEST					
OTHER FIRST CLASS	1	0	4	0	–
INT					
JPL					
NAT.W					
B & H					

175. What have Denis Compton, Greg Chappell, Alex Bedser, Hanif Mohammad, Richie Benaud and Richard Hadlee in common?

176. Who has scored the most runs in Test cricket, for any country, so far?

WALKER, A.   Northamptonshire

Full Name: Alan Walker.
Role: Left-hand bat, right-arm fast-medium bowler, outfielder.
Born: 7 July 1962, Emley, Nr. Huddersfield.
Height: 5′ 11″ **Weight:** 12st. 7lbs.
Nickname: Arthur Scargill.
County debut: 1983.
Place in batting averages: 223 average: 13.83.
Place in bowling averages: 76 average: 34.17; (1984: 118 average: 41.41).
1st-Class catches 1985: 6 (career: 13).
Parents: Malcolm and Enid Walker.
Wife and date of marriage: Janice, 17 September 1983.
Education: Emley Junior School, Kirkburton Middle School, Shelley High (Huddersfield) School.
Qualifications: 2 O-levels, 4 C.S.E.s.
Jobs outside cricket: Miner.
Off-season 1985–86: Coaching in South Africa.
Overseas tours: Denmark, with N.C.A. U-19s North of England 1980.
Overseas teams played for: Uitenhage, South Africa, 1984–85.
Cricketers particularly learnt from: David Steele.
Cricketers particularly admired: Dennis Lillee, Richard Hadlee.
Other sports: Football. Follows rugby league, any sport on T.V.
Injuries 1985: Back strain.

LAST SEASON: BATTING

	I.	N.O.	R.	H.S.	AV.
TEST					
OTHER FIRST CLASS	14	8	83	18*	13.83
INT					
JPL	4	2	12	6*	6.00
NAT.W					
B & H	–	–	–	–	–

CAREER: BATTING

	I.	N.O.	R.	H.S.	AV.
TEST					
OTHER FIRST CLASS	33	15	165	19	9.17
INT					
JPL	6	2	32	13	8.00
NAT.W	–	–	–	–	–
B & H	–	–	–	–	–

LAST SEASON: BOWLING

	O.	M.	R.	W.	AV.
TEST					
OTHER FIRST CLASS	251.4	51	786	23	34.17
INT					
JPL	82.2	6	345	17	20.79
NAT.W					
B & H	31.5	1	149	7	21.29

CAREER: BOWLING

	O.	M.	R.	W.	AV.
TEST					
OTHER FIRST CLASS	726.1	133	2482	72	34.47
INT					
JPL	186	11	789	35	22.54
NAT.W	37.5	4	145	5	29.00
B & H	31.5	1	149	7	21.29

Relaxations: "Watching T.V., listening to music, D.I.Y., having a pint."
Best batting performance: 19 Northamptonshire v Sussex, Horsham 1984.
Best bowling performance: 4-38 Northamptonshire v Kent, Northampton 1985.

WALL, S. Warwickshire

Full Name: Stephen Wall.
Role: Right-hand bat, right-arm
medium bowler.
Born: 10 December 1959, Ulverston,
Lancashire.
Height: 6′ **Weight:** 12st. 7lbs.
Nickname: Max, Wally.
County debut: 1984.
Place in batting averages: 244
average: 11.64.
Place in bowling averages: 78
average: 34.75.
1st-Class catches 1985: 5 (career: 6).
Parents: Marjorie and Peter Wall.
Wife and date of marriage: Alison,
20 June 1981.
Children: Rebecca Louise, 13
August 1984.
Education: Dowdales.
Qualifications: 6 C.S.E.s. Boilermaker.
Cricket superstitions: "Keeping my equipment in good condition."
Cricketers particularly learnt from: Chris Old, Anton Ferreira.
Cricketers particularly admired: Dennis Amiss, David Gower.

LAST SEASON: BATTING

	I.	N.O.	R.	H.S.	AV.
TEST					
OTHER FIRST CLASS	16	5	128	28	11.64
INT					
JPL	2	1	8	6*	–
NAT.W					
B & H	1	0	6	6	–

CAREER: BATTING

	I.	N.O.	R.	H.S.	AV.
TEST					
OTHER FIRST CLASS	25	9	175	28	10.94
INT					
JPL	2	1	8	6*	–
NAT.W					
B & H	1	0	6	6	–

LAST SEASON: BOWLING

	O.	M.	R.	W.	AV.
TEST					
OTHER FIRST CLASS	301.1	43	973	28	34.75
INT					
JPL	18	1	97	2	48.50
NAT.W					
B & H	39	5	141	3	47.00

CAREER: BOWLING

	O.	M.	R.	W.	AV.
TEST					
OTHER FIRST CLASS	441.5	72	1518	37	41.03
INT					
JPL	36	2	195	4	48.75
NAT.W					
B & H	39	5	141	3	47.00

Other sports: Golf, soccer, darts.
Injuries 1985: Torn thigh muscle.
Relaxations: "Playing golf on days off."
Extras: Played for Cumberland in 1983 and finished 8th in Minor Counties bowling averages.
Best batting performance: 28 Warwickshire v Lancashire, Old Trafford 1985.
Best bowling performance: 4-59 Warwickshire v Glamorgan, Edgbaston 1985.

WALLER, C.E. Sussex

Full Name: Christopher Edward Waller.
Role: Right-hand bat, slow left-arm bowler, gully fielder.
Born: 3 October 1948, Guildford.
Height: 5′ 10½″ **Weight:** 11st. 10lbs.
Nickname: Wal.
County debut: 1967 (Surrey), 1974 (Sussex).
County cap: 1976.
Benefit: 1984.
50 wickets in a season: 4.
1st-Class 50s scored: 2.
1st-Class 5 w. in innings: 22.
1st-Class 10 w. in match: 1.
Place in bowling averages: 118 average: 44.10; (1984: 29 average: 25.45).
1st-Class catches 1985: 2 (career: 133).
Parents: Frederick Edward and Iris Waller.
Wife and date of marriage: Lesley Deborah, 25 March 1972.
Children: Alexandra Lois, 21 August 1975; Stephanie Kate, 16 May 1977; Adrian Paul, 5 August 1979.
Education: St Bede's C. of E. Secondary School, Send, Woking, Surrey.
Qualifications: N.C.A. advanced coach and staff coach.
Jobs outside cricket: Coaching at Alf Gover's Cricket School, Wandsworth; Crystal Palace National Sports Centre; Sussex C.C.C. Indoor School.
Family links with cricket: Father played for Horsley C.C. for 47 years as an opening batsman and off-spin bowler. "I first played for Horsley C.C. at the age of 11."
Cricketers particularly learnt from: Norman Gifford and Mickey Stewart.
Cricketers particularly admired: Viv Richards.
Other sports: Squash, football, golf, snooker. Watches all sports.

Relaxations: Listening to records, watching T.V., drinking dark rum and Usher's beer, eating Indian cuisine.

Extras: Debut for Surrey in 1967, cap 1972. Left after 1973 season. Coached 1977–78 in New South Wales, Australia, for World Series Cricket. "I have to navigate as well as drive on our away trips as passenger Colin Wells hasn't a very good sense of direction."

Best batting performance: 51* Sussex v Cambridge University, Cambridge 1981.

Best bowling performance: 7-64 Surrey v Sussex, The Oval 1971.

LAST SEASON: BATTING

	I.	N.O.	R.	H.S.	AV.
TEST					
OTHER FIRST CLASS	9	3	37	8	6.17
INT					
JPL					
NAT.W	–	–	–	–	–
B & H	–	–	–	–	–

CAREER: BATTING

	I.	N.O.	R.	H.S.	AV.
TEST					
OTHER FIRST CLASS	266	111	1481	51*	9.56
INT					
JPL	38	17	169	18*	8.05
NAT.W	7	2	18	14*	3.60
B & H	13	8	42	11*	8.40

LAST SEASON: BOWLING

	O.	M.	R.	W.	AV.
TEST					
OTHER FIRST CLASS	381.4	119	882	20	44.10
INT					
JPL					
NAT.W	1	1	0	1	–
B & H	11	4	21	1	–

CAREER: BOWLING

	O.	M.	R.	W.	AV.
TEST					
OTHER FIRST CLASS	7180	2108	18312	630	29.07
INT					
JPL	566.5	40	2408	83	29.01
NAT.W	100.2	14	342	10	34.20
B & H	281.3	38	887	29	30.59

WALSH C.A.   Gloucestershire

Full Name: Courtney Andrew Walsh.

Role: Right-hand bat, right-arm fast bowler.

Born: 30 October 1962, Kingston, Jamaica.

Height: 6′ 5½″ **Weight:** 13st. 7lbs.

Nickname: Mask, Walshy.

County debut: 1984.

County cap: 1985.

Place in batting averages: 174 average: 15.75.

Place in bowling averages: 5 average: 20.07; (1984: 104 average: 36.84).

1st-Class catches 1985: 4 (career: 15).

Parents: Joan Wollaston and Erick Walsh.

Marital status: Single.

Education: Excelsior High School.
Qualifications: G.C.E. and C.X.L.
Overseas tours: To England 1984 and Australia 1984–85, with West Indies.
Overseas teams played for: West Indies, Jamaica.
Other sports: Football. Follows basketball and track and field events.
Relaxations: Music and watching T.V.
Extras: Took record 10-43 in Jamaican school cricket in 1979.
Best batting performace: 37 Gloucestershire v Hampshire, Bristol 1985.
Best bowling performance: 7-51 Gloucestershire v Warwickshire, Cheltenham 1985.

LAST SEASON: BATTING

	I.	N.O.	R.	H.S.	AV.
TEST					
OTHER FIRST CLASS	18	6	189	37	15.75
INT					
JPL	4	1	5	3	1.67
NAT.W	2	1	8	6*	–
B & H	–	–	–	–	–

CAREER: BATTING

	I.	N.O.	R.	H.S.	AV.
TEST	7	4	44	18*	14.67
OTHER FIRST CLASS	65	17	495	37	10.31
INT	–	–	–	–	–
JPL	6	1	28	14	5.60
NAT.W	4	1	31	14	10.33
B & H	–	–	–	–	–

LAST SEASON: BOWLING

	O.	M.	R.	W.	AV.
TEST					
OTHER FIRST CLASS	560.3	132	1706	85	20.07
INT					
JPL	71.4	3	318	11	28.90
NAT.W	28	4	107	3	35.67
B & H	21.3	3	62	4	15.50

CAREER: BOWLING

	O.	M.	R.	W.	AV.
TEST	171.2	34	507	16	31.68
OTHER FIRST CLASS	1626	344	5281	215	24.56
INT	40	2	198	4	49.50
JPL	93.2	8	390	13	30.00
NAT.W	28	4	107	3	35.67
B & H	21.3	3	62	4	15.50

WARD D.M. Surrey

Full Name: David Mark Ward.
Role: Right-hand bat, gully fielder.
Born: 10 February 1961, Croydon.
Height: 6′ 1″ **Weight:** 12st. 9lb.
Nickname: Cocker, Wardy, Jaws, Gnasher.
County debut: 1984.
1st-Class 100s scored: 1.
One-day 50s: 1.
Place in batting averages: 49 average: 39.86.
1st-Class catches 1985: 5 (career 6).
Parents: Dora Kathleen and Thomas Ward.
Marital status: Single.
Family links with cricket: "Grandad played for the Tamworth Arms."
Education: Haling Manor High

School; Croydon Technical College.
Qualifications: 2 O-levels, City and Guilds in Carpentry and Joinery.
Jobs outside cricket: Carpenter.
Off-season 1985–86: Playing in Australia.
Overseas tours: Barbados 1985 with Surrey.
Overseas teams played for: Caulfield C.C.; Allrounders Australia C.C.
Cricketing superstitions: Marks across corner of non-striking crease with bat.
Cricketers particularly learnt from: G.G. Arnold, G. Clinton, G. Howarth, M. Lynch.
Cricketers particularly admired: G. Gooch, Keith Ebdon and I.T. Botham.
Other sports: Football, snooker, table-tennis, bridge, jumping.
Injuries 1985: Toothache.
Relaxations: Eating out, George Benson, watching T.V., movies and biting sharks.
Opinions on cricket: "Avoid the politics and get on with the game!"
Best batting performance: 143 Surrey v Derbyshire, Derby 1985.

LAST SEASON: BATTING

	I.	N.O.	R.	H.S.	AV.
TEST					
OTHER FIRST CLASS	10	3	279	143	39.86
INT					
JPL	6	2	99	42*	24.75
NAT.W					
B & H					

CAREER: BATTING

	I.	N.O.	R.	H.S.	AV.
TEST					
OTHER FIRST CLASS	10	3	279	143	39.86
INT					
JPL	8	4	190	59*	47.50
NAT.W					
B & H					

177. Who has scored the most Test runs in England so far?

178. Who scored more Test runs for Australia, Don **Bradman** or Greg Chappell?

179. Who has scored most runs for South Africa?

WARING, I.C. — Sussex

Full Name: Ian Charles Waring.
Role: Left-hand bat, right-arm fast-medium bowler.
Born: 6 December 1963, Chesterfield.
Height: 6′ 1″ **Weight:** 13st. 10lbs.
Nickname: Eddie.
County debut: 1985.
Parents: Jack and Dorothy Waring.
Marital status: Single.
Education: Tupton Hall.
Qualifications: 7 O-levels, coaching certificate.
Off-season 1985–86: Coaching at Bishops School, Cape Town.
Overseas tours: Gibraltar 1980 with Sheffield Cricket Lovers.
Overseas teams played for: Pretoria High School Old Boys 1983–84; Alma Marist, Cape Town, 1984–85.

Cricketers particularly learnt from: Tony Pigott, Tony Borrington and Les Lenham.
Cricketers particularly admired: Barry Richards, Imran Khan, P. Kirsten.
Other sports: Football, swimming, basketball and anything outdoors. Follows all sports on T.V.
Relaxations: Listening to music, reading autobiographies and photography.
Extras: Took wicket with first ball at Lord's.
Opinions on cricket: "(a) Overseas players should play in fewer games, and (b) standards of dress should be maintained, i.e. blazers to games and behaviour on field."

LAST SEASON: BATTING

	I.	N.O.	R.	H.S.	AV.
TEST					
OTHER FIRST CLASS	–	–	–	–	–
INT					
JPL	–	–	–	–	–
NAT.W					
B & H					

CAREER: BATTING

	I.	N.O.	R.	H.S.	AV.
TEST					
OTHER FIRST CLASS	–	–	–	–	–
INT					
JPL	–	–	–	–	–
NAT.W					
B & H					

LAST SEASON: BOWLING

	O.	M.	R.	W.	AV.
TEST					
OTHER FIRST CLASS					
INT					
JPL	11	0	58	0	–
NAT.W					
B & H					

CAREER: BOWLING

	O.	M.	R.	W.	AV.
TEST					
OTHER FIRST CLASS					
INT					
JPL	11	0	58	0	–
NAT.W					
B & H					

WARNER, A.E. — Derbyshire

Full Name: Allan Esmond Warner.
Role: Right-hand bat, right-arm fast bowler, outfielder.
Born: 12 May 1959, Birmingham, England.
Height: 5′ 8″ **Weight:** 10st.
Nickname: Esis.
County debut: 1982 (Worcestershire), 1985 (Derbyshire).
1st-Class 50s scored: 2.
1st-Class 5 w. in innings: 2.
Place in batting averages: 204 average: 17.44.
Place in bowling averages: 112 average: 42.21; (1984: 123 average: 42.13).
1st-Class catches 1985: 2 (career: 12).
Parents: Edgar and Sarah Warner.
Children: Alvin, 6 September 1980.
Education: Tabernacle School, St. Kitts, West Indies.
Qualifications: C.S.E. Maths, Bricklaying.
Cricketers particularly learnt from: John Browny, Henry Benjamin.
Cricketers particularly admired: M. Marshall and M. Holding.
Other sports: Football, table-tennis. Follows football, boxing and athletics.
Relaxations: Watching movies; music (soul, reggae and calypso).
Extras: Released by Worcestershire (debut 1982) at end of 1984 and joined Derbyshire.
Opinions on cricket: "Too many overs bowled in a day. And, in the John Player

LAST SEASON: BATTING	I.	N.O.	R.	H.S.	AV.
TEST					
OTHER FIRST CLASS	20	2	314	60	17.44
INT					
JPL	6	2	47	17	11.75
NAT.W	1	0	17	17	–
B & H	4	1	17	13*	5.67

CAREER: BATTING	I.	N.O.	R.	H.S.	AV.
TEST					
OTHER FIRST CLASS	59	11	794	67	16.54
INT					
JPL	21	6	92	17	6.13
NAT.W	2	0	19	17	9.50
B & H	9	3	61	29*	10.17

LAST SEASON: BOWLING	O.	M.	R.	W.	AV.
TEST					
OTHER FIRST CLASS	267.3	40	1013	24	42.21
INT					
JPL	47.2	0	264	13	20.30
NAT.W	12	1	46	1	–
B & H	30	3	125	6	20.83

CAREER: BOWLING	O.	M.	R.	W.	AV.
TEST					
OTHER FIRST CLASS	865.1	146	2960	85	34.82
INT					
JPL	177.5	5	868	32	27.12
NAT.W	31.3	3	129	3	43.00
B & H	96.5	9	373	14	26.64

Special League, bowlers must come off a longer run."
Best batting performance: 67 Worcestershire v Warwickshire, Edgbaston 1982.
Best bowling performance: 5-27 Worcestershire v Glamorgan, Worcester 1984.

WATERMAN, P.A.   Surrey

Full Name: Peter Andrew Waterman.
Role: Right-hand bat, right-arm fast-medium bowler.
Born: 26 March 1961, Hendon, London.
Height: 6' 1½" **Weight:** 13st. 7lbs.
Nickname: Minder, Dennis, Del Boy.
County debut: 1983.
1st-Class catches 1985: 2 (career: 4).
Parents: Bernard Charles and Bernadette Catherine Waterman.
Marital status: Single.
Education: Rooks Heath High School, Pinner Sixth Form College.
Qualifications: 5 O-levels, Higher Technical Education Council Certificate in electronic and electrical engineering.
Jobs outside cricket: Systems analyst since September 1979 with Marconi Space and Defence Systems Ltd.
Overseas tours: Australasia, 1983, Club Cricket Conference.

LAST SEASON: BATTING

	I.	N.O.	R.	H.S.	AV.
TEST					
OTHER FIRST CLASS	2	1	1	1*	–
INT					
JPL	3	2	8	8	–
NAT.W					
B & H	–	–	–	–	–

CAREER: BATTING

	I.	N.O.	R.	H.S.	AV.
TEST					
OTHER FIRST CLASS	6	3	7	6*	2.33
INT					
JPL	3	2	8	8	–
NAT.W					
B & H	1	0	2	2	–

LAST SEASON: BOWLING

	O.	M.	R.	W.	AV.
TEST					
OTHER FIRST CLASS	115	25	382	12	31.83
INT					
JPL	34	1	196	1	–
NAT.W					
B & H	6	0	27	0	–

CAREER: BOWLING

	O.	M.	R.	W.	AV.
TEST					
OTHER FIRST CLASS	212.2	39	727	18	40.39
INT					
JPL	47	2	240	2	120.0
NAT.W					
B & H	16	0	87	0	–

Overseas teams played for: Manly-Warringah 1983–84.
Cricketers particularly admired: D.K. Lillee, M. Holding.
Other sports: Football, golf, tennis.
Relaxations: Live music, reading, travel, videos.
Extras: Hat-trick v Sussex 2nd XI 1983 and sprained ankle in subsequent celebration! Released at end of 1985 season.
Best batting performance: 6* Surrey v Sussex, The Oval 1983.
Best bowling performance: 3-22 Surrey v Cambridge University, Cambridge 1985.

WATERTON, S.N.V. Northamptonshire

Full Name: Stuart Nicholas Varney Waterton.
Role: Right-hand bat; wicket-keeper.
Born: 6 December 1960, Dartford.
Height: 5′ 11½″ **Weight:** 11st. 10lbs.
Nickname: Buck.
County debut: 1980 (Kent).
1st-Class 50s scored: 1.
Place in batting averages: —
average: —; (1984: 189
average: 21.44).
Parents: Barry and Olive Waterton (deceased).
Marital status: Single.
Family links with cricket: "Father was a magnificent back garden bowler and avid watcher."
Education: St George's Church of England School; Gravesend School for Boys; London School of Economics, London University.
Qualifications: 10 O-levels, 3 A-levels, N.C.A. Preliminary Coaching Award, B.Sc. Hons. Economics.
Off-season 1985–86: Training and preparing for 1986 season.
Jobs outside cricket: Civil servant, winter 1979–80.
Cricketers particularly learnt from: Alan Knott, Bob Taylor,George Baker.
Cricketers particularly admired: Bob Taylor, Alan Knott, Glenn Turner, Viv Richards.
Cricket superstitions: "I try to do everything the same following a particularly good day."
Overseas teams played for: Goudstad Onderwyskollege, Johannesburg, 1984–85; Florida C.C. 1985.
Other sports: Golf, road-running and cross-country. Follows most sports apart from soccer and horse-racing.
Relaxations: Music, T.V.

Extras: Second wicket-keeper from Gravesend School to play for Kent C.C.C.—David Nicolls being the other. England Young Wicket Keeper of the Year 1980. Record individual score for Kent Schools Player, 163 v Sussex Schools 1979. Record number of runs aggregated in a season for Gravesend School, 983 runs at average of 75 in 1979. England Young Wicket-keeper of the Year 1980. Played for U.A.U. 1981–83 (captain '83 but did not take the field due to bad weather). Made NatWest debut in 1984 final. Member (with Lauri Potter) of Ashford C.C. side which won the Courage Kent League in 1985. Batting average in 2nd XI of 59.86 in 1985. Left Kent after 1985 season to further career.

Opinions on cricket: (a) More should be done by county clubs to help young players to find employment during the winter. (b) It should be remembered with regard to over-rates that quality is preferable to quantity — and therefore the end of season scramble to bowl at ridiculously high rate so as to avoid being fined should be unneccessary. (c) It is important to consider the financial viability of County Championship cricket, since money is so vital, other possible means of bringing in crowds should be assessed.

Best batting performance: 50 Kent v Lancashire, Old Trafford 1984.

LAST SEASON: BATTING

	I.	N.O.	R.	H.S.	AV.
TEST					
OTHER FIRST CLASS	2	2	22	16*	–
INT					
JPL	1	1	10	10*	–
NAT.W					
B & H					

CAREER: BATTING

	I.	N.O.	R.	H.S.	AV.
TEST					
OTHER FIRST CLASS	28	5	386	50	16.78
INT					
JPL	3	2	31	15	–
NAT.W	1	1	4	4*	–
B & H					

LAST SEASON: WICKET KEEPING

	C.	ST.
TEST		
OTHER FIRST CLASS	5	2
INT		
JPL	3	–
NAT.W		
B & H		

CAREER: WICKET KEEPING

	C.	ST.
TEST		
OTHER FIRST CLASS	41	10
INT		
JPL	5	2
NAT.W	1	–
B & H		

180. Who has scored most runs for West Indies?

181. Who has scored the most Test runs for New Zealand?

182. Who has the highest Test batting average of all time and what is it?

WATKINSON, M. — Lancashire

Full Name: Michael Watkinson.
Role: Right-hand bat, right-arm medium bowler.
Born: 1 August 1961, Westhoughton.
Height: 6' 1½" **Weight:** 13st.
Nickname: Winkler, Herman.
County debut: 1982.
1st-Class 50s scored: 8.
1st-Class 100s scored: 1.
1st-Class 5 w. in innings: 4.
One-day 50s: 1.
Place in batting averages: 150 average: 24.71; (1984: 128 average: 29.04).
Place in bowling averages: 62 average: 31.49; (1984 124 average: 42.37).
1st-Class catches 1985: 6 (career: 15).

Parents: Albert and Marian Watkinson.
Marital status: Single.
Education: Rivington and Blackrod High School, Horwich.
Qualifications: 8 O-levels, H.T.C. Civil Engineering.
Jobs outside cricket: Draughtsman.
Off-season 1985–86: Playing and coaching in Canberra, Australia.
Overseas teams played for: Woder Valley C.C., Canberra, 1984–85.
Cricketers particularly learnt from: Paul Allott, Steve O'Shaughnessy.
Cricketers particularly admired: Clive Lloyd, Imran Khan.
Other sports: Football.

LAST SEASON: BATTING

	I.	N.O.	R.	H.S.	AV.
TEST					
OTHER FIRST CLASS	29	1	692	106	24.71
INT					
JPL	9	3	97	34*	16.16
NAT.W	2	0	87	56	43.50
B & H	4	0	37	34	9.25

CAREER: BATTING

	I.	N.O.	R.	H.S.	AV.
TEST					
OTHER FIRST CLASS	78	11	1528	106	22.81
INT					
JPL	25	11	253	34*	18.07
NAT.W	6	1	101	56	20.20
B & H	6	1	42	34	8.40

LAST SEASON: BOWLING

	O.	M.	R.	W.	AV.
TEST					
OTHER FIRST CLASS	420.1	94	1228	39	31.49
INT					
JPL	67	5	338	11	30.73
NAT.W	24	6	89	0	–
B & H	29.1	1	166	4	41.50

CAREER: BOWLING

	O.	M.	R.	W.	AV.
TEST					
OTHER FIRST CLASS	1111.4	240	3431	104	32.99
INT					
JPL	245	16	1148	43	26.69
NAT.W	76.3	11	276	4	69.00
B & H	126.1	12	523	24	21.79

Extras: Played with Cheshire C.C.C. in Minor Counties, and NatWest Trophy (v Middlesex) 1982 season.
Best batting performance: 106 Lancashire v Surrey, Southport 1985.
Best bowling performance: 6-39 Lancashire v Leicestershire, Leicester 1984.

WATSON, R.G. Lancashire

Full Name: Roger Graeme Watson.
Role: Left-hand bat, off-break bowler.
Born: 14 January 1964, Rawtenstall.
County debut: 1985.
Extras: Released by Lancashire at the end of the 1985 season.
Best batting performance: 18 Lancashire v Oxford University, Oxford 1985.

LAST SEASON: BATTING

	I.	N.O.	R.	H.S.	AV.
TEST					
OTHER FIRST CLASS	1	0	18	18	–
INT					
JPL					
NAT.W					
B & H					

CAREER: BATTING

	I.	N.O.	R.	H.S.	AV.
TEST					
OTHER FIRST CLASS	1	0	18	18	–
INT					
JPL					
NAT.W					
B & H					

183. Who has scored the second highest Test batting average of all time?

184. Of all England Test bowlers who has the best average and what is it?

WELLS, A.P.   Sussex

Full Name: Alan Peter Wells.
Role: Right-hand bat, right-arm
medium bowler, cover fielder.
Born: 2 October 1961.
Height: 6' 0'' **Weight:** 12st. 4lbs.
Nickname: Morph, Bomber.
County debut: 1981.
1000 runs in a season: 1.
1st-Class 50s scored: 15.
1st-Class 100s scored: 3.
One-day 50s: 6.
Place in batting averages: 165
average: 23.08; (1984: 101
average: 32.66).
1st-Class catches 1985: 12
(career: 36).
Parents: Ernest William Charles and
Eunice Mae Wells.

Marital status: Single.
Education: Tideway Comprehensive, Newhaven.
Qualifications: 5 O-levels, N.C.A. Coaching certificate.
Jobs outside cricket: Laboratory assistant. Coached in South Africa.
Family links with cricket: Father played for many years for local club. Eldest
brother, Ray, plays club cricket. Brother of C.M. Wells of Sussex.
Cricketing supersitions: "Have to put bat at junction of return and popping
crease at the end of each over. Never stand inside the return crease when
backing up. When repairing wicket count how many times I tap ground.
Double whirl of arms with bat when going in to bat. Plus many more."
Overseas tours: N.C.A. U-19 tour of Canada, 1979.
Cricketers particularly learnt from: Father, Chris Waller, Roger Marshall, Les
Lenham.

LAST SEASON: BATTING

	I.	N.O.	R.	H.S.	AV.
TEST					
OTHER FIRST CLASS	33	7	600	102	23.08
INT					
JPL	12	4	253	57*	31.62
NAT.W	2	1	10	6	–
B & H	4	0	170	62	42.50

CAREER: BATTING

	I.	N.O.	R.	H.S.	AV.
TEST					
OTHER FIRST CLASS	112	21	2621	127	28.80
INT					
JPL	44	9	893	71*	25.51
NAT.W	7	2	51	24	10.20
B & H	12	2	334	62	33.40

LAST SEASON: BOWLING

	O.	M.	R.	W.	AV.
TEST					
OTHER FIRST CLASS					
INT					
JPL	1	0	5	0	–
NAT.W					
B & H					

CAREER: BOWLING

	O.	M.	R.	W.	AV.
TEST					
OTHER FIRST CLASS	12	1	42	0	–
INT					
JPL	1	0	5	0	–
NAT.W	1	0	1	0	–
B & H	2.1	1	17	1	–

Other sports: Table-tennis, squash, darts, snooker, tennis.
Relaxations: Listening to music, eating out, drinking in country pubs.
Extras: Played for England Young Cricketers v India 1981.
Best batting performance: 127 Sussex v Northamptonshire, Northampton 1984.

WELLS, C.M. Sussex

Full Name: Colin Mark Wells.
Role: Right-hand bat, right-arm medium bowler.
Born: 3 March 1960, Newhaven, Sussex.
Height: 6′ 0″ **Weight:** 12st. 7lbs.
Nickname: Bomber.
County debut: 1979.
County cap: 1982
No. of One-Day Internationals: 2.
1000 runs in a season: 3.
50 wickets in a season: 1.
1st-Class 50s scored: 25.
1st-Class 100s scored: 10.
1st-Class 200s scored: 1.
1st-Class 5 w. in innings: 2.
One-day 50s: 12.
One-day 100s: 1.

Place in batting averages: 103 average: 30.97; (1984: 36 average: 43.41).
Place in bowling averages: 96 average: 38.34; (1984: 23 average: 23.66).
1st-Class catches 1985: 7 (career: 39).
Parents: Ernest William Charles and Eunice Mae Wells.
Marital status: Single.
Education: Tideway Comprehensive School, Newhaven.
Qualifications: 9 O-levels, two C.S.E.s. 1 A-level, M.C.C. Intermediate Coaching Certificate.
Jobs outside cricket: Laboratory assistant.
Family links with cricket: Father, Billy, had trials for Sussex and played for Sussex Cricket Association. Both brothers play cricket and youngest brother, Alan, played for England Schools and toured Canada with N.C.A. 1979, and plays for Sussex.
Cricket superstitions: Left boot and left pad put on first.
Overseas tours: With England to Sharjah 1985.
Other sports: Football, rugby, hockey, basketball, tennis, table-tennis.
Relaxations: Sea-angling, philately, listening to music.
Extras: Played in three John Player League matches in 1978. Was

recommended to Sussex by former Sussex player, Ian Thomson. Highest 4th wicket partnership for Sussex v Glamorgan with Imran Khan of 256.
Best batting performance: 203 Sussex v Hampshire, Hove 1984.
Best bowling performance: 5-25 Sussex v Kent, Hastings 1984.

LAST SEASON: BATTING

	I.	N.O.	R.	H.S.	AV.
TEST					
OTHER FIRST CLASS	37	6	960	100*	30.97
INT					
JPL	12	4	307	53	38.37
NAT.W	2	0	111	76	55.50
B & H	4	0	85	55	21.25

CAREER: BATTING

	I.	N.O.	R.	H.S.	AV.
TEST					
OTHER FIRST CLASS	221	33	6118	203	32.54
INT	2	0	22	17	11.00
JPL	80	12	1772	104*	26.05
NAT.W	13	0	252	76	19.38
B & H	25	1	586	80	24.42

LAST SEASON: BOWLING

	O.	M.	R.	W.	AV.
TEST					
OTHER FIRST CLASS	537.4	144	1457	38	38.34
INT					
JPL	107.4	8	375	12	31.25
NAT.W	10	2	21	1	–
B & H	33	7	98	3	32.67

CAREER: BOWLING

	O.	M.	R.	W.	AV.
TEST					
OTHER FIRST CLASS	1921.2	486	5478	166	33.00
INT					
JPL	423.4	33	1605	64	25.07
NAT.W	81.4	14	213	6	35.50
B & H	123	20	418	18	23.22

WESTON, M.J.   Worcestershire

Full Name: Martin John Weston.
Role: Right-hand bat, right-arm medium bowler.
Born: 8 April 1959, Worcester.
Height: 6' 1" **Weight:** 14st.
Nickname: Spaghetti, Wesso.
County debut: 1979.
County cap: 1985.
1000 runs in a season: 1.
1st-Class 50s scored: 18.
1st-Class 100s scored: 3.
One-day 50s: 6.
One-day 100s: 1.
Place in batting averages: 117 average: 29.14; (1984: 137 average: 27.92).
Place in bowling averages: 107 average: 40.90; (1984:-17 average: 22.50).
1st-Class catches 1985: 5 (career: 38).
Parents: John Franklyn and Sheila Margaret Weston.
Marital status: Single.

Education: St George's C. of E. Junior; Samuel Southall Secondary Modern.
Qualifications: City & Guilds and Advance Crafts in Bricklaying.
Overseas tours: 1980 tour to Barbados with Worcestershire C.C.C.
Cricketers particularly learnt from: Dipak Patel.
Other sports: Football, darts, dominoes, squash.
Relaxations: Horse-racing.
Best batting performance: 145* Worcestershire v Northamptonshire, Worcester 1984.
Best bowling performance: 4-44 Worcestershire v Northamptonshire, Wellingborough 1984.

LAST SEASON: BATTING

	I.	N.O.	R.	H.S.	AV.
TEST					
OTHER FIRST CLASS	30	1	845	132	29.14
INT					
JPL	13	2	147	32	13.36
NAT.W	3	1	49	35	24.50
B & H	5	0	60	46	12.00

LAST SEASON: BOWLING

	O.	M.	R.	W.	AV.
TEST					
OTHER FIRST CLASS	273.5	72	777	19	40.90
INT					
JPL	68	2	295	11	26.81
NAT.W	14.5	0	74	1	–
B & H	26	2	107	4	26.75

CAREER: BATTING

	I.	N.O.	R.	H.S.	AV.
TEST					
OTHER FIRST CLASS	150	7	3609	145*	25.24
INT					
JPL	51	4	935	109	19.89
NAT.W	7	1	104	35	17.33
B & H	15	0	321	56	21.40

CAREER: BOWLING

	O.	M.	R.	W.	AV.
TEST					
OTHER FIRST CLASS	524.4	121	1537	41	37.49
INT					
JPL	124.5	2	602	21	28.66
NAT.W	38.5	6	156	5	31.20
B & H	29	2	122	4	30.50

185. When did Ian Botham first play for England?

186. When did Imran Khan first play for Pakistan?

187. When did Richard Hadlee first play for New Zealand?

WHEELER, M.B.H.   Northamptonshire

Full Name: Matthew Benjamin
Harold Wheeler.
Role: Right-hand bat,
right-arm medium bowler.
Born: 14 August 1962, Windlesham,
Surrey.
Height: 6′ 2″ **Weight:** 13st.
Nickname: Rooney, Squealer.
County debut: 1985.
Parents: Michael and Hilary
Wheeler.
Marital status: Single.
Education: Winchester College;
Exeter University.
Qualifications: B.A. in English
Literature.
Jobs outside cricket: Taught English
at Cothill House, Abingdon 1984–85.
Off-season 1985–86: Abroad
playing and coaching.

Overseas teams played for: Coached at Geelong Grammar School, Melbourne,
1980–81.
Cricketers particularly learnt from: Bob Carter (Assistant coach Northampton-
shire). Vince Broderick (Northamptonshire), coach at Winchester.
Cricketers particularly admired: D.K. Lillee, A.M.E. Roberts, A.J. Lamb.
Other sports: Soccer, squash, tennis, skiing, golf — generally anything.
Follows soccer, golf and anything on "Grandstand" except racing.
Relaxations: "Ideal relaxation is two weeks skiing, but more accessibly reading
(a hangover from an English degree), writing (at the moment only for private
consumption), and playing golf."

LAST SEASON: BATTING

	I.	N.O.	R.	H.S.	AV.
TEST					
OTHER FIRST CLASS	–	–	–	–	–
INT					
JPL					
NAT.W					
B & H					

CAREER: BATTING

	I.	N.O.	R.	H.S.	AV.
TEST					
OTHER FIRST CLASS	–	–	–	–	–
INT					
JPL					
NAT.W					
B & H					

LAST SEASON: BOWLING

	O.	M.	R.	W.	AV.
TEST					
OTHER FIRST CLASS	34	3	117	1	–
INT					
JPL					
NAT.W					
B & H					

CAREER: BOWLING

	O.	M.	R.	W.	AV.
TEST					
OTHER FIRST CLASS	34	3	117	1	–
INT					
JPL					
NAT.W					
B & H					

Extras: Played for English Universities 1983–84. Left staff after 1985 season.

WHITAKER, J.J. Leicestershire

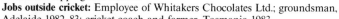

Full Name: John James Whitaker.
Role: Right-hand bat, off-break bowler.
Born: 5 May 1962, Skipton, Yorkshire.
Height: 6' 0'' **Weight:** 13st.
County debut: 1983.
1000 runs in a season: 2.
1st-Class 50s scored: 12.
1st-Class 100s scored: 5.
One-day 50s: 5.
One-day 100s: 3.
Place in batting averages: 71 average: 35.38; (1984: 69 average: 36.57).
1st-Class catches 1985: 6 (career: 30).
Parents: Rowland and Anne Whitaker.
Education: Uppingham School.
Jobs outside cricket: Employee of Whitakers Chocolates Ltd.; groundsman, Adelaide 1982–83; cricket coach and farmer, Tasmania 1983.
Family links with cricket: Father plays club cricket.
Overseas tours: Australia 1981–82 with Uppingham School.

LAST SEASON: BATTING

	I.	N.O.	R.	H.S.	AV.
TEST					
OTHER FIRST CLASS	34	3	1103	109	35.38
INT					
JPL	10	2	260	86*	32.50
NAT.W	2	0	72	46	36.00
B & H	6	2	113	73*	28.25

CAREER: BATTING

	I.	N.O.	R.	H.S.	AV.
TEST					
OTHER FIRST CLASS	82	9	2505	160	34.32
INT					
JPL	25	5	855	132	42.75
NAT.W	4	0	243	155	60.75
B & H	10	2	221	73*	27.63

LAST SEASON: BOWLING

	O.	M.	R.	W.	AV.
TEST					
OTHER FIRST CLASS					
INT					
JPL	0.2	0	4	0	–
NAT.W					
B & H					

CAREER: BOWLING

	O.	M.	R.	W.	AV.
TEST					
OTHER FIRST CLASS					
INT					
JPL	0.2	0	4	0	–
NAT.W					
B & H					

Overseas teams played for: Glenelg C.C., Adelaide, 1982–83; Old Scotch C.C., Tasmania, 1983–84; Somerset West, South Africa, 1984–85.
Cricketers particularly learnt from: Maurice Hallam (coach at Uppingham) and Brian Davison.
Cricketers particularly admire: Geoff Boycott, Dennis Amiss.
Cricketing superstitions: Pack gear in same way every game.
Other sports: Rugby, hockey, tennis, golf.
Relaxations: Discos, watching movies, eating out.
Extras: "I have learnt a great deal from playing in Australia where cricket is only at weekends and where it is played very hard."
Opinions on cricket: "I do not think 4-day cricket will improve anybody's standard, so we should keep 3-day cricket. People try to complicate cricket too much; it should be kept as simple as possible and played as simply as possible. I think both umpiring and wickets should be more consistent."
Best batting performance: 160 Leicestershire v Somerset, Leicester 1984.

WHITTICASE, P. Leicestershire

Full Name: Philip Whitticase.
Role: Right-hand bat, wicket-keeper.
Born: 15 March 1965, Birmingham.
Height: 5' 8" **Weight:** 10st.
Nickname: Jasper, Tracy.
County debut: 1984.
1st-Class 50s scored: 1.
Parents: Larry Gordon and Ann Whitticase.
Marital status: Single.
Family links with cricket: Grandfather and father club cricketers (both wicket-keepers).
Education: Buckpool Secondary; Crestwood Comprehensive.
Qualifications: 5 O-levels, 4 C.S.E.s.
Jobs outside cricket: Worked for Asda Superstores; Inland Revenue.

Off-season 1985–86: Playing in Australia.
Overseas teams played for: South Bunbury, Western Australia, 1983.
Cricketers particularly learnt from: D. Collins, Stourbridge Cricket Club.
Cricketers particularly admired: Bob Taylor, Alan Knott.
Other sports: Football, table-tennis, golf. Follows football (used to be on Schoolboy Forms with Birmingham City F.C.).
Relaxations: "Football, golf, listening to music. I find most sports interesting and relaxing. Also playing cards (learnt a lot of new games due to bad weather)."

Injuries 1985: Strained tendon below platella.

Opinions on cricket: "I think that sport in general should not be governed by political matters. Anybody ought to be able to play any sport, wherever they like, without being disciplined for their actions. This not only jeopardises the individual himself but also the spectator."

Extras: Played for M.C.C. v Scotland. Took two catches in P. Clift's hat-trick v Derby at Chesterfield 1985.

Best batting performance: 55* Leicestershire v Sussex, Hove 1985.

LAST SEASON: BATTING

	I.	N.O.	R.	H.S.	AV.
TEST					
OTHER FIRST CLASS	5	1	149	55*	37.25
INT					
JPL					
NAT.W					
B & H					

CAREER: BATTING

	I.	N.O.	R.	H.S.	AV.
TEST					
OTHER FIRST CLASS	14	3	184	55*	16.73
INT					
JPL	1	1	5	5*	–
NAT.W					
B & H					

LAST SEASON: WICKET KEEPING

	C.	ST.			
TEST					
OTHER FIRST CLASS	9	–			
INT					
JPL					
NAT.W					
B & H					

CAREER: WICKET KEEPING

	C.	ST.			
TEST					
OTHER FIRST CLASS	27	–			
INT					
JPL	1	–			
NAT.W					
B & H					

WILD, D.J.   Northamptonshire

Full Name: Duncan James Wild.
Role: Left-hand bat, right-arm medium bowler.
Born: 28 November 1962, Northampton.
Height: 6' 0" **Weight:** 12st. 7lbs.
Nickname: Oscar.
County debut: 1980.
1st-Class 50s scored: 4.
1st-Class 100s scored: 2.
One-day 50s: 2.
Place in batting averages: 117 average: 29.17; (1984: 86 average: 34.20).
Place in bowling averages: — average: —; (1984:-87 average: 32.90).
1st-Class catches 1985: 4 (career: 13).

Parents: John and Glenys Wild.
Marital status: Single.
Education: Cherry Orchard Middle; Northampton School for Boys.
Qualifications: 7 O-levels.
Jobs outside cricket: Law costs draughtsman.
Family links with cricket: Father played for Northamptonshire.
Overseas tours: England Young Cricketers to West Indies 1980.
Off-season 1985–86: Playing in New Zealand.
Extras: Played for England Young Cricketers v Young India in 3-Test series 1981. Also for Young England v Young West Indies, August 1982.
Best batting performance: 144 Northamptonshire v Lancashire, Southport 1984.
Best bowling performance: 3-15 Northamptonshire v Hampshire, Southampton 1984.

LAST SEASON: BATTING

	I.	N.O.	R.	H.S.	AV.
TEST					
OTHER FIRST CLASS	22	4	525	80	29.17
INT					
JPL	7	3	109	63*	27.25
NAT.W	1	0	1	1	–
B & H	2	2	17	15*	–

CAREER: BATTING

	I.	N.O.	R.	H.S.	AV.
TEST					
OTHER FIRST CLASS	77	11	1783	144	27.02
INT					
JPL	30	11	354	63*	18.63
NAT.W	5	0	23	11	4.60
B & H	6	3	82	48	27.33

LAST SEASON: BOWLING

	O.	M.	R.	W.	AV.
TEST					
OTHER FIRST CLASS	82.5	7	368	2	184.0
INT					
JPL	44	2	230	11	20.90
NAT.W	20	3	71	2	35.50
B & H					

CAREER: BOWLING

	O.	M.	R.	W.	AV.
TEST					
OTHER FIRST CLASS	343	57	1313	21	62.52
INT					
JPL	230	6	1085	39	27.82
NAT.W	67	9	240	9	26.78
B & H	8	1	41	0	–

188. Is it possible to compile a team of current first-class cricketers born in Yorkshire but playing for other counties who would beat the current Yorkshire team?

189. True or false? Keith Fletcher was playing first-class cricket before Neil Foster was born.

WILLEY, P.   Leicestershire

Full Name: Peter Willey.
Role: Right-hand bat, off-break bowler.
Born: 6 December 1949, Sedgefield, County Durham.
Height: 6′ 1″ **Weight:** 13st.
Nickname: Chin, Will.
County debut: 1966 (Northamptonshire), 1984 (Leicestershire).
County cap: 1971 (Northamptonshire), 1984 (Leicestershire).
Test debut: 1976.
No. of Tests: 21.
No. of One-Day Internationals: 22.
Benefit: 1981 (£31,400) with Northamptonshire.
1000 runs in a season: 6.
50 wickets in a season: 3.

1st-Class 50s scored: 73.
1st-Class 100s scored: 33.
1st-Class 200s scored: 1.
1st-Class 5 w. in innings: 25.
1st-Class 10 w. in match: 3.
One-day 50s: 54.
One-day 100s: 7.
Place in batting averages: 29 average: 46.14; (1984: 71 average: 35.90).
Place in bowling averages: 41 average: 28.25; (1984: 66 average: 30.02).
1st-Class catches 1985: 10 (career: 177).
Parents: Oswald and Maisie Willey.
Wife and date of marriage: Charmaine, 23 September 1971.
Education: Secondary School, Seaham, County Durham.
Jobs outside cricket: Has worked as a groundsman, labourer and in a shoe factory. Coached in South Africa 1978–79.
Family links with cricket: Father played local club cricket in County Durham.
Off-season 1985–86: On tour with England to West Indies.
Overseas tours: Toured Australia with England 1979–80; West Indies, 1981.
Overseas teams played for: Eastern Province, South Africa.
Other sports: Golf, shooting, follows all sports.
Relaxations: Reading, taking Irish Setter for long walks and shooting.
Extras: With Wayne Larkins, received 2016 pints of beer (seven barrels) from a brewery in Northampton as a reward for their efforts in Australia with England in 1978–79. Hit a six off his first ball v Middlesex in J.P.L., 26 July

1981. Shared in 4th wicket partnership record for county, 370 with R.T. Virgin v Somerset at Northampton in 1976. Youngest player ever to play for Northamptonshire C.C.C. at 16 years 180 days v Cambridge in 1966. Banned from Test cricket for three years for joining England rebel tour of South Africa in 1982. Left Northamptonshire at end of 1983 (debut 1966, cap 1971) and moved to Leicestershire as vice-captain.

Best batting performance: 227 Northamptonshire v Somerset, Northampton 1976.

Best bowling performance: 7-37 Northamptonshire v Oxford University, Oxford 1975.

LAST SEASON: BATTING

	I.	N.O.	R.	H.S.	AV.
TEST	2	1	39	36	–
OTHER FIRST CLASS	30	3	1253	147	46.41
INT	2	0	12	12	6.00
JPL	10	2	165	40	20.62
NAT.W	2	0	69	52	34.50
B & H	7	3	291	86*	72.75

CAREER: BATTING

	I.	N.O.	R.	H.S.	AV.
TEST	40	6	962	102*	28.29
OTHER FIRST CLASS	659	93	17409	227	30.76
INT	20	1	487	64	25.63
JPL	205	17	5364	107	28.53
NAT.W	35	4	943	89	30.42
B & H	53	9	1327	88*	30.16

LAST SEASON: BOWLING

	O.	M.	R.	W.	AV.
TEST					
OTHER FIRST CLASS	399.3	115	1017	36	28.25
INT	30	3	113	3	37.67
JPL	62	6	214	11	19.45
NAT.W	23	8	40	3	13.33
B & H	71	5	226	5	45.20

CAREER: BOWLING

	O.	M.	R.	W.	AV.
TEST	177.5	49	441	6	73.50
OTHER FIRST CLASS	7718.1	2144	18445	633	29.14
INT	156	9	594	12	49.50
JPL	1193.5	109	4761	183	26.01
NAT.W	333.3	51	1002	27	37.11
B & H	485.4	82	1316	34	38.71

190. Which England captain said to another England captain, when asked if he had just had a haircut before play began: 'No, it all fell out in the night."?

191. In 1985 Neil Fairbrother scored a century for Lancashire in both Roses matches. Who was the last player to achieve this feat, for whom and when?

WILLIAMS, N.F.   Middlesex

Full Name: Neil Fitzgerald Williams.
Role: Right-hand bat, right-arm fast-medium bowler.
Born: 2 July 1962, Hopewell, St. Vincent, West Indies.
Height: 5' 11" **Weight:** 11st. 7lbs.
Nickname: Joe.
County debut: 1982.
County cap: 1984.
50 wickets in a season: 2.
1st-Class 50s scored: 2.
1st-Class 5 w. in innings: 4.
1st-Class 10 w. in match: 1.
Place in batting averages: 170 average: 22.24; (1984: 232 average: 15.83).
Place in bowling averages: 54 average: 30.76; (1984: 91 average: 33.74).
1st-Class catches 1985: 3 (career: 24).
Parents: Alexander and Aldreta Williams.
Marital status: Single.
Education: Cane End Primary School, St. Vincent; Acland Burghley School.
Qualifications: School Leavers Certificate, 6 O-levels, 1 A-level.
Family links with cricket: "Uncle Joe was 12th man for St. Vincent."
Overseas tours: English Counties to Zimbabwe 1985.
Overseas teams played for: Windward Islands 1983; Tasmania 1983–84.

LAST SEASON: BATTING

	I.	N.O.	R.	H.S.	AV.
TEST					
OTHER FIRST CLASS	21	4	378	67	22.24
INT					
JPL	8	2	47	15	7.83
NAT.W	2	1	12	7*	–
B & H	3	1	36	29*	18.00

CAREER: BATTING

	I.	N.O.	R.	H.S.	AV.
TEST					
OTHER FIRST CLASS	98	24	1505	67	20.34
INT					
JPL	20	8	146	31*	12.16
NAT.W	6	2	28	10	7.00
B & H	8	3	104	29*	20.80

LAST SEASON: BOWLING

	O.	M.	R.	W.	AV.
TEST					
OTHER FIRST CLASS	490.2	69	1784	58	30.76
INT					
JPL	93	1	462	15	30.80
NAT.W	18	1	57	1	–
B & H	66	9	236	6	39.33

CAREER: BOWLING

	O.	M.	R.	W.	AV.
TEST					
OTHER FIRST CLASS	2129.4	414	7324	245	29.89
INT					
JPL	255.3	7	1172	43	27.25
NAT.W	77	11	277	11	25.18
B & H	151.3	19	577	19	30.37

Cricketers particularly learnt from: Wilf Slack, Roland Butcher.
Cricketers particularly admired: Viv Richards, Andy Roberts, Michael Holding, Dennis Lillee, Malcolm Marshall.
Other sports: Follows most.
Relaxations: Relax to sound of reggae. A big Soca fan, soul music too.
Extras: Was on stand-by for England in New Zealand and Pakistan 1983–84.
Best batting performance: 67 Middlesex v Cambridge University, Cambridge 1985.
Best bowling performance: 7-55 English Counties XI v Zimbabwe, Harare 1984–85.

WILLIAMS, R.G.   Northamptonshire

Full Name: Richard Grenville Williams.
Role: Right-hand bat, off-break bowler.
Born: 10 August 1957, Bangor, Caernarvonshire.
Height: 5′ 6″ **Weight:** 12st.
Nickname: Chippy.
County debut: 1974.
County cap: 1979.
1000 runs in a season: 6.
1st-Class 50s scored: 40.
1st-Class 100s scored: 15.
1st-Class 5 w. in innings: 7.
One-day 50s: 16.
Place in batting averages: 97 average: 31.43; (1984: 102 average: 32.49).
Place in bowling averages: 105 average: 40.79; (1984: 121 average: 42.13).
1st-Class catches 1985: 9 (career: 75).
Parents: Gordon and Rhianwen Williams.
Wife and date of marriage: Helen Laura, 24 April 1982.
Education: Ellesmere Port Grammar School.
Family links with cricket: Father played for Caernarvonshire.
Jobs outside cricket: Qualfied carpenter.
Off-season 1985–86: Coaching and playing in New Zealand.
Overseas tours: Australasia in February and March 1980 with Derrick Robins' U-23 XI; West Indies with England Young Cricketers 1976; Zimbabwe with English Counties 1985.

Overseas teams played for: Stockton C.C. and Belmont C.C. in Sydney, Australia, on Whitbread Scholarship. .

Relaxations: Fly fishing and shooting.

Injuries 1985: Broken finger (fielding).

Extras: Debut for 2nd XI in 1972 aged 14 years 11 months. Made maiden century in 1979 and then scored four centuries in five innings. Hat-trick v Gloucestershire, at Northampton, 1980. Was first player to score a century against the 1980 West Indies touring team. Was stand-by for England in India, 1981.

Best batting performance: 175* Northamptonshire v Leicestershire, Leicester 1980.

Best bowling performance: 7-73 Northamptonshire v Cambridge University, Cambridge 1980.

LAST SEASON: BATTING

	I.	N.O.	R.	H.S.	AV.
TEST					
OTHER FIRST CLASS	31	3	880	118	31.43
INT					
JPL	7	1	63	15	10.50
NAT.W	2	0	16	8	8.00
B & H	5	2	140	58	46.67

CAREER: BATTING

	I.	N.O.	R.	H.S.	AV.
TEST					
OTHER FIRST CLASS	331	40	8931	175*	30.69
INT					
JPL	105	18	2008	82	23.08
NAT.W	21	4	444	94	26.12
B & H	26	7	602	83	31.68

LAST SEASON: BOWLING

	O.	M.	R.	W.	AV.
TEST					
OTHER FIRST CLASS	312.2	75	979	24	40.79
INT					
JPL	48.5	2	244	7	34.85
NAT.W	22	3	82	4	20.50
B & H	33	6	88	1	–

CAREER: BOWLING

	O.	M.	R.	W.	AV.
TEST					
OTHER FIRST CLASS	3277.4	843	9295	270	34.43
INT					
JPL	355.4	25	1688	57	29.61
NAT.W	118	16	363	18	20.17
B & H	134	23	421	11	38.27

192. Which wicket-keeper has made the most Test dismissals?

193. Which non wicket-keeper has held most Test catches?

194. How heavy should a new, regulation cricket ball be?

195. Which great British military commander gave an order that in future every new barracks should have a cricket ground built next to it, and when?

WRIGHT, A.J.   Gloucestershire

Full Name: Anthony John Wright.
Role: Right-hand bat, right-arm medium bowler.
Born: 27 July 1962, Stevenage.
Height: 6' 0" **Weight:** 13st.
Nickname: Paul Getty, Billy.
County debut: 1982.
1st-Class 50s scored: 10.
1st-Class 100s scored: 1.
One-day 50s: 1.
Place in batting averages: 192 average: 19.15; (1984: 145 average: 26.97).
1st-Class catches 1985: 2 (career: 21).
Parents: Patricia and Michael Wright.
Marital status: Single.
Education: Alleyn's Grammar School, Stevenage.
Qualifications: 6 O-levels.
Jobs outside cricket: Plasterer's labourer.
Overseas tours: Barbados 1980 with Gloucestershire.
Overseas teams played for: Port Melbourne 1981–82, 1982–83.
Cricketers particularly learnt from: John Childs, Barry Duddleston.
Cricketers particularly admired: Zaheer Abbas, Vivian Richards.
Other sports: Rugby, golf, squash, snooker.
Extras: Played for 2nd XI since 1979. Played twice in John Player League in 1980. Did not play in 1981. Hit 65 in his first-class debut v Warwickshire.
Best batting performance: 139 Gloucestershire v Surrey, Cheltenham 1984.

LAST SEASON: BATTING

	I.	N.O.	R.	H.S.	AV.
TEST					
OTHER FIRST CLASS	16	3	249	47*	19.15
INT					
JPL	3	1	17	9	8.50
NAT.W					
B & H					

CAREER: BATTING

	I.	N.O.	R.	H.S.	AV.
TEST					
OTHER FIRST CLASS	91	10	1999	139	24.68
INT					
JPL	22	4	204	52	11.33
NAT.W	1	0	14	14	–
B & H	3	0	14	7	4.67

LAST SEASON: BOWLING

	O.	M.	R.	W.	AV.
TEST					
OTHER FIRST CLASS					
INT					
JPL					
NAT.W					
B & H					

CAREER: BOWLING

	O.	M.	R.	W.	AV.
TEST					
OTHER FIRST CLASS	1	0	3	0	–
INT					
JPL	4	0	18	0	–
NAT.W					
B & H					

WRIGHT, J.G. Derbyshire

Full Name: John Geoffrey Wright.
Role: Left-hand bat,
Born: 5 July 1954, Darfield,
New Zealand.
Height: 6′ 1″ **Weight:** 12st. 7lbs.
Nickname: Shake.
County debut: 1977.
County cap: 1977.
Test debut: 1977–78.
No. of Tests: 41.
No. of One-Day Internationals: 72.
1000 runs in a season: 6.
1st-Class 50s scored: 83.
1st-Class 100s scored: 40.
One-day 50s: 37.
One-day 100s: 4.
Place in batting averages: 10
average: 56.93; (1984: 10
average: 60.05).
1st-Class catches 1985: 6 (career: 150).
Parents: Geoff and Helen Wright.
Wife: Susan.
Education: Christ's College, Christchurch, New Zealand; University of Otago, Dunedin, New Zealand.
Qualifications: B.Sc. in Biochemistry.
Family links with cricket: "Father played first-class cricket."
Overseas tours: With New Zealand to England 1978; Australia 1980–81; Sri Lanka and Pakistan 1984–85; West Indies 1985.
Overseas teams played for: Northern Districts, Canterbury, New Zealand.
Cricketers particularly learnt from: Eddie Barlow, David Steele.

LAST SEASON: BATTING

	I.	N.O.	R.	H.S.	AV.
TEST					
OTHER FIRST CLASS	16	2	797	177*	56.93
INT					
JPL					
NAT.W					
B & H					

CAREER: BATTING

	I.	N.O.	R.	H.S.	AV.
TEST	71	2	2133	141	30.91
OTHER FIRST CLASS	363	28	14508	190	43.31
INT	70	1	1767	84	25.61
JPL	91	6	2710	108	31.88
NAT.W	12	2	555	87*	55.50
B & H	30	2	1005	102	35.89

LAST SEASON: BOWLING

	O.	M.	R.	W.	AV.
TEST					
OTHER FIRST CLASS	6	0	42	0	–
INT					
JPL					
NAT.W					
B & H					

CAREER: BOWLING

	O.	M.	R.	W.	AV.
TEST	5	1	5	0	–
OTHER FIRST CLASS	36.4	4	179	2	89.50
INT	4	1	8	0	–
JPL					
NAT.W					
B & H					

Cricketers particularly admired: "Cutter" Curtayne.
Cricket superstitions: "Ironed shirts are bad luck."
Other sports: Horse-racing, tennis, rugby.
Relaxations: Music.
Extras: Holds record of 7 centuries for Derbyshire in a season — beating record of 6 held by Peter Kirsten in previous season, after record of 5 had stood for 49 years. Vice-captain of New Zealand 1984.
Opinions on cricket: "If viable financially 4-day county matches might produce better first-class cricket."
Best batting performance: 190 Derbyshire v Yorkshire, Derby 1982.

WYATT, J.G. Somerset

Full Name: Julian George Wyatt.
Role: Right-hand bat, right-arm medium bowler.
Born: 19 June 1963, Paulton, Somerset.
Height: 5' 10'' **Weight:** 11st. 8lbs.
Nickname: Jules, Earp.
County debut: 1983.
1st-Class 50s scored: 8.
1st-Class 100s scored: 3.
Place in batting averages: 98 average: 31.38; (1984: 131 average: 23.79).
1st-Class catches 1985: 7 (career: 16).
Parents: Christopher Hedley and Dinah Ruby Wyatt.
Marital status: Single.
Education: Wells Cathedral School, Somerset.
Qualifications: 5 O-levels, N.C.A. Senior Coaching Certificate.
Jobs outside cricket: Brandon Tool Hire 1980–83.
Off-season 1985–86: Cricket in Melbourne and working for Brandon Tool Hire.
Overseas teams played for: Kew C.C., Melbourne, 1984–85.
Cricketers particularly admired: B. Rose, P. Denning, C. Dredge, T. Gard.
Other sports: Squash, football, golf; follows rugby.
Injuries 1985: Broken thumb, missed one month's cricket.
Relaxations: "Socialising at local pubs."
Opinions on cricket: "L.B.W. law and slip fielders should be abolished."
Best batting performance: 145 Somerset v Oxford University, Oxford 1985.

CAREER: BATTING

	I.	N.O.	R.	H.S.	AV.
TEST					
OTHER FIRST CLASS	66	2	1834	145	28.66
INT					
JPL	7	1	56	21	9.33
NAT.W	2	0	3	3	1.50
B & H	4	0	39	22	9.75

LAST SEASON: BATTING

	I.	N.O.	R.	H.S.	AV.
TEST					
OTHER FIRST CLASS	26	0	816	145	31.38
INT					
JPL	4	0	19	13	4.75
NAT.W	1	0	3	3	–
B & H	4	0	39	22	9.75

CAREER: BOWLING

	O.	M.	R.	W.	AV.
TEST					
OTHER FIRST CLASS	13	1	63	2	31.50
INT					
JPL					
NAT.W					
B & H					

LAST SEASON: BOWLING

	O.	M.	R.	W.	AV.
TEST					
OTHER FIRST CLASS	10	0	59	1	–
INT					
JPL					
NAT.W					
B & H					

YOUNIS AHMED   Glamorgan

Full Name: Mohammed Younis Ahmed.
Role: Left-hand bat, left-arm medium bowler.
Born: 20 October 1947, Lahore, Pakistan.
Height: 5′ 10″ **Weight:** 12st.
Nickname: Yoon.
County debut: 1965 (Surrey), 1979 (Worcestershire), 1985 (Glamorgan).
County cap: 1979 (Worcestershire), 1985 (Glamorgan).
Test debut: 1969–70.
No. of Tests: 2.
1000 runs in a season: 13.
1st-Class 50s scored: 117.
1st-Class 100s: 42.
1st-Class 200s scored: 1.
One-day 50s: 46.
One-day 100s: 5.

Place in batting averages: 6 average: 64.59; (1984: 33 average: 44.16).
1st-Class catches 1985: 3 (career: 235).
Parents: Father, Inaitullah Ahmed; mother, Shamin Ahmed.
Wife and date of marriage: Gloria Ahmed, 15 September 1972.
Children: Samir Ahmed, 2 January 1975; Yasmine Ahmed, 16 January 1979.
Education: Moslem High School, Lahore; Government College, Lahore.

Qualifications: Matriculation. B.A. degree.

Jobs outside cricket: Runs coaching clinics in Melbourne. Owns and runs own travel agency.

Family links with cricket: Younger brother of Saeed Ahmed who played for Pakistan.

Overseas tours: West Indies 1970; Commonwealth tour Pakistan–Kuwait, 1971; South Australia 1972–73; South Africa 1973–74; International XI to Rhodesia 1974–75.

Overseas teams played for: Pakistan Inter Board Schools; South Australia in 1972–73 Sheffield Shield; Universal Club, Rhodesia, 1974–75–76–77.

Cricketers particularly learnt from or admired: Saeed Ahmed (brother), Sir Gary Sobers, Sir Don Bradman.

Other sports: Squash, tennis.

Relaxations: Reading cricket books, theatre.

Extras: Debut in 1962 at age of 14 years 4 months for Pakistan School v South Zone (counts as first-class). Debut for Surrey in 1965, cap 1969. Is now eligible to play for England. Suffers from hay fever. Sacked by Worcestershire in 1983 season.

Best batting performance: 221* Worcestershire v Nottinghamshire, Trent Bridge 1979.

Best bowling performance: 4-10 Surrey v Cambridge University, Cambridge 1975.

LAST SEASON: BATTING

	I.	N.O.	R.	H.S.	AV.
TEST					
OTHER FIRST CLASS	30	8	1421	177	64.59
INT					
JPL	11	1	155	37	15.50
NAT.W	1	0	3	3	–
B & H	3	0	61	55	20.33

CAREER: BATTING

	I.	N.O.	R.	H.S.	AV.
TEST	4	0	89	62	22.25
OTHER FIRST CLASS	719	112	24454	221*	40.29
INT					
JPL	215	23	5776	113	30.08
NAT.W	26	2	735	87	30.63
B & H	57	7	1434	115	28.68

LAST SEASON: BOWLING

	O.	M.	R.	W.	AV.
TEST					
OTHER FIRST CLASS	74.4	22	178	2	89.00
INT					
JPL	8.3	0	27	3	9.00
NAT.W	12	2	24	0	–
B & H					

CAREER: BOWLING

	O.	M.	R.	W.	AV.
TEST					
OTHER FIRST CLASS	108.5 532.3	11 138	1817	41	44.32
INT					
JPL	132.3	0	635	17	37.35
NAT.W	46	4	149	4	37.25
B & H	51	2	208	9	23.11

196. Which England Test bowler asked to be buried 22 yards from which England Test batsman, so that "I can send him down a ball now and then."?

ZAHEER ABBAS Gloucestershire

Full Name: Syed Zaheer Abbas.
Role: Right-hand bat, off-break bowler.
Born: 24 July 1947, Sialkot, Pakistan.
Height: 5′ 11½″ **Weight:** 11st. 3lbs.
Nickname: Zed.
County debut: 1972.
County cap: 1975.
Benefit: 1983.
Test debut: 1969–70.
No. of Tests: 76.
No. of One-Day Internationals: 59.
1000 runs in a season: 11.
1st-Class 50s scored: 145.
1st-Class 100s scored: 99.
1st-Class 200s: 9.
1st-Class 5 w. in innings: 1.
One-day 50s: 59.
One-day 100s: 18.
Place in batting averages: — average: —; (1984: 115 average: 30.75).
1st-Class catches 1985: 1 (career: 262).
Parents: Syed Gaulam Shabbir and Kaneez Fatima.
Education: High School Jehangir Road; Islamia College, Karachi.
Wife and date of marriage: Najma, October 1972.
Children: Two daughters, Rudaba and Roshana.
Overseas tours: England 1971 and 1974; Australia and New Zealand 1972–73; Australia and West Indies, 1976–77; Australia and New Zealand, 1978–79, 1983–84.
Cricketers particularly admired: Hanif Mohammed, but "Rohan Kanhai was my greatest hero of all."
Overseas teams played for: Karachi Whites; Pakistan International Airways; Dawood Club.
Relaxations: Cinema, music.
Extras: Debut for Karachi Whites 1965–66. Was dismissed for hitting the ball twice for Pakistan International Airways v Karachi Blues at Karachi in 1969–70. Played for Rest of the World v Australia 1971–72. Scored two centuries in a match three times: twice in 1976 (216 n. o. and 156 n. o., v Surrey at The Oval; 230 n. o. and 104 n. o., v Kent at Canterbury) and once in 1977 (205 n. o. and 108 n. o., v Sussex at Cheltenham). Shared in 2nd wicket record partnership for Pakistan, 291 with Mushtaq Mohammed v England at Birmingham in 1971. Wears spectacles. In 1981, was the first man to score 1000 runs in a calendar month — June — for 22 years. Played World Series Cricket. Vice-captain of Pakistan 1981–. Scored century before lunch for Pakistan v Derby, 1982. Captained Pakistan for first time in 1983. Published *Zed* — autobiography. Left staff 1985.

Best batting performance: 274 Pakistan v England, Edgbaston 1971.
Best bowling performance: 5-15 Dawood Industries v Railways, Lahore 1975–76.

LAST SEASON: BATTING

	I.	N.O.	R.	H.S.	AV.
TEST					
OTHER FIRST CLASS	1	0	38	38	–
INT					
JPL					
NAT.W					
B & H					

CAREER: BATTING

	I.	N.O.	R.	H.S.	AV.
TEST	123	11	5058	274	45.16
OTHER FIRST CLASS	663	78	29227	230*	49.96
INT	57	6	2464	123	48.31
JPL	132	17	4663	129*	40.54
NAT.W	22	1	980	158	46.67
B & H	47	6	1455	98	35.49

LAST SEASON: BOWLING

	O.	M.	R.	W.	AV.
TEST	·				
OTHER FIRST CLASS					
INT					
JPL					
NAT.W					
B & H					

CAREER: BOWLING

	O.	M.	R.	W.	AV.
TEST	60.2	1 9	132	3	44.00
OTHER FIRST CLASS			927	25	37.08
INT	39.4	2	187	5	37.40
JPL	16	0	73	2	36.50
NAT.W	11.3	0	41	2	20.50
B & H					

197. True or false? During the Lord's Test v Pakistan in 1982, three England players, Gower, Lamb and Jackman went to dinner together. They ordered duck. The next day all three were out for ducks.

198. What is the highest first-class score ever made by any batsman, who was he and what was the match?

ANSWERS

Q. 1. M.C.C. v Hertfordshire, 22 June 1814.

Q. 2. 1914.

Q. 3. 1927. Essex v New Zealand.

Q. 4. Victorian Cricket Association celebrated the State of Victoria's 150th anniversary.

Q. 5. Nicknames: Buttons, Woolly, Jumper. Real names: Cardigan Adolphus.

Q. 6. They were all club beneficiaries in 1985.

Q. 7. Cecil Parkin.

Q. 8. Charlie Parker of Gloucestershire.

Q. 9. Kim Barnett of Derbyshire.

Q. 10. Hampshire: Greenidge, Marshall, C. Smith, R. Smith, Tremlett, Parks, C. Smith and R. Smith.

Q. 11. They were both born in West Germany.

Q. 12. Les Taylor of Leicestershire and England.

Q. 13. Keith Fletcher of Essex and England.

Q. 14. Don Mosey.

Q. 15. F.S. Trueman of Yorkshire and England.

Q. 16. T.E. Bailey of Essex and England.

Q. 17. Tony Lewis of Glamorgan and England.

Q. 18. Jack Fingleton of New South Wales and Australia, and opening bat for Australia in the Bodyline series of 1932–33.

Q. 19. Yorkshire and Leicestershire.

Q. 20. P.G. Wodehouse.

Q. 21. Dennis Lillee.

Q. 22. Queensland.

Q. 23. Somerset.

Q. 24. Ian.

Q. 25. F.R. Spofforth.

Q. 26. Haslingden in 1971.

Q. 27. Wicket-keeper Rodney Marsh.

Q. 28. Clive Lloyd after West Indies lost to Australia in Sydney in 1985.

Q. 29. Viv Richards.

Q. 30. Brockton Point Ground, Vancouver, Canada.

Q. 31. W.G. Grace.

Q. 32. 40 innings, 21 matches.

Q. 33. Andrew Hilditch.

Q. 34. Brian Close, 18 years, 149 days v New Zealand at Old Trafford in 1949.

Q. 35. True.

Q. 36. True.

Q. 37. True.

Q. 38. John Woodcock.

Q. 39. Cambridge University, Sussex and England.

Q. 40. Gloucestershire.

Q. 41. Derek Randall of Nottinghamshire and England.

Q. 42. Short leg.

Q. 43. 15: won 9, drawn 5, lost 1.

Q. 44. Raman Subba Row of Surrey and England.

Q. 45. They were all awarded their county caps in 1985.

Q. 46. Former Test player Hanif Mohammad.

Q. 47. P.G.H. Fender of Surrey and England, v Warwick Armstrong's Australians in 1921.

Q. 48. John Nyren.

Q. 49. Harlequin.

Q. 50. Azure blue.

Q. 51. By hitting the ball out of the ground — not just out of the field of play.

Q. 52. 1978.

Q. 53. 1744. 22 yards, then as now.

Q. 54. Western Australia, South Australia, Queensland, Victoria, Tasmania and New South Wales.

Q. 55. New South Wales.

Q. 56. South Australia.

Q. 57. Bill Athey of Gloucestershire, but he did not play.

Q. 58. Western Province, Eastern Province, Transvaal, Northern Transvaal and Natal.

Q. 59. 903 for 7 declared, by England, at The Oval in 1938.

Q. 60. True. He played once for England v South Africa in 1965.

Q. 61. Don Oslear.

Q. 62. Dennis Amiss.

Q. 63. P.G. Wodehouse. (Any reader who knows the actual occasion is invited to write to the Editor and tell him.)

Q. 64. Slow left-armer Murray Bennett.

Q. 65. He hit it for six.

Q. 66. False. But it took him till his 20th Test v Australia, at The Oval on 29 August 1985.

Q. 67. Stands on one leg.

Q. 68. Simon O'Donnell of Australia at Edgbaston on 16 August 1985.

Q. 69. It was Thomson's 200th wicket in Test cricket and 100th v England.

Q. 70. A club for anybody who has ever been out first ball in any level of cricket. Subscription of £5 buys the club tie and the money goes to help blind boys. Apply to Leslie Harris, 14 Shrewsbury Road, Beckenham, Kent.

Q. 71. All members have to wear it on Saturdays.

Q. 72. Queensland.

Q. 73. Herbert Sutcliffe.

Q. 74. Jack Hobbs.

Q. 75. Phil Mead.

Q. 76. Frank Woolley.

Q. 77. Patsy Hendren.

Q. 78. Walter Hammond.

Q. 79. Brian Luckhurst.

Q. 80. J.A. Bailey of Oxford University and Essex.

Q. 81. Arthur Wellard of Somerset, 66 in 1935.

Q. 82. 1827. Draw.

Q. 83. 1848.

Q. 84. 1849.

Q. 85. F.S. Trueman of Yorkshire and England in 1964.

Q. 86. India v England, Madras, January 1985, scored 272 and 412: England 652 for 7 declared and 35 for 1.

Q. 87. 15.

Q. 88. Bruce French of Nottinghamshire and Pat Pocock of Surrey.

Q. 89. Lord Byron, in 1805. He scored 11 __ 7, the second highest score for Harrow.

Q. 90. 10 March 1985 at Melbourne, against Pakistan. India won the (so-called) World Cricket Championship (50 overs) Final.

Q. 91. Derek Randall.

Q. 92. Mohammed Azharuddin for India v England 1984–85.

Q. 93. James Lillywhite of Sussex.

Q. 94. G.L. Jessop of Gloucestershire and England.

Q. 95. Dennis Amiss.

Q. 96. A. Shaw of England bowled the first ball in Test cricket to Mr. C. Bannerman of Australia.

Q. 97. Australia by 45 runs.

Q. 98. President Dwight Eisenhower, Pakistan v Australia, Karachi, 1959.

Q. 99. 1890.

Q. 100. Eric.

Q. 101. Paul Jarvis, aged 20 v Derbyshire on 24 July 1984.

Q. 102. Mushtaq Mohammad, 15, Pakistan.

Q. 103. Gary Sobers, 17.

Q. 104. Ian Craig, 17.

Q. 105. Mike Garnham of Leicestershire.

Q. 106. David Gower.

Q. 107. 1985. 104 for Middlesex v Northamptonshire.

Q. 108. Voules was the first captain of Somerset C.C.C. in 1891 and Botham the latest.

Q. 109. False. Nigel Popplewell scored a century v Gloucestershire in 41 minutes at Bath in 1983.

Q. 110. C.G. Macartney, 345, Australia v Nottinghamshire, 1921.

Q. 111. Essex and Leicestershire. Leicestershire won.

Q. 112. David Lawrence of Gloucestershire.

Q. 113. Lord Cobham of Worcestershire.

Q. 114. Bob Willis of Surrey, Warwickshire and England: 325.

Q. 115. Graeme Wood of Australia at Lord's, 1 July 1985.

Q. 116. Woodrow Wyatt, cousin of former England Test captain, R.E.S. Wyatt.

Q. 117. Kim Hughes.

Q. 118. Alan McGilvray.

Q. 119. Barry Knight of Essex, Leicestershire and England.

Q. 120. Sir Arthur Conan Doyle, creator of Sherlock Holmes.

Q. 121. Tim Tremlett (102 n.o.) and Kevan James (124). 227.

Q. 122. Robin Smith of Hampshire.

Q. 123. Mark Benson of Kent.

Q. 124. Keith Fletcher of Essex and England.

Q. 125. Joel Garner and Gordon Greenidge.

Q. 126. Les Compton, brother of Denis.

Q. 127. Sir Jack Hobbs.

Q. 128. Paul Romaines of Gloucestershire.

Q. 129. Jack Fingleton.

Q. 130. Gloucestershire's Charlie Parker, Lancashire's Cecil Parkin and Somerset's Jack MacBryan.

Q. 131. Percy Chapman (see his biography by David Lemmon).

Q. 132. Kent and Leicestershire.

Q. 133. False. He scored only 99.

Q. 134. Graham Gooch, 202 v Nottinghamshire on 3 May.

Q. 135. Arthur Milton of Gloucestershire and Arsenal.

Q. 136. June 1978, at Edgbaston, v Pakistan. He hooked his first ball for 4.

Q. 137. Martyn Moxon of Yorkshire.

Q. 138. G.P. Howarth of New Zealand.

Q. 139. Yorkshire in 1863, one year before Lancashire.

Q. 140. Pakistan's fast bowler Sarfraz Nawaz in the Punjab.

Q. 141. Bill Athey, now of Gloucestershire, the Centenary Test in 1980.

Q. 142. Cheshire, Botham, Allott and Agnew.

Q. 143. John Wisden of Sussex, Kent and Middlesex and founder of Wisden's Cricketers Almanack.

Q. 144. It was the first time a touring batsman had been stumped in a Test in England for five years.

Q. 145. Johnny Wardle.

Q. 146. Don Mosey.

Q. 147. R.E.S. Wyatt.

Q. 148. Australian Test player Wally Grout for Queensland v Western Australia in 1959–60.

Q. 149. Jack Bond.

Q. 150. Richard Hadlee of Nottinghamshire and New Zealand.

Q. 151. Geoff Humpage of Warwickshire.

Q. 152. John Birch of Nottinghamshire.

Q. 153. Mike Garnham of Leicestershire.

Q. 154. John Hopkins of Glamorgan.

Q. 155. Pat Pocock of Surrey and England.

Q. 156. Martyn Moxon of Yorkshire.

Q. 157. Steven Rhodes of Worcestershire.

Q. 158. Neil Mallender of Northamptonshire.

Q. 159. Nigel Cowley of Hampshire.

Q. 160. Tony Lewis of Cambridge University, Glamorgan and England.

Q. 161. Peter Walker of Glamorgan and England.

Q. 162. To mark the fact that Hawke was Trueman's 300th Test victim in the Fifth Test at The Oval in 1964. Hawke kept the bottle unopened.

Q. 163. Hughes batted on all five days, scoring 117 and 84.

Q. 164. Size 12.

Q. 165. 70 mph — according to Sarah Potter, England fast bowler.

Q. 166. It was the first century by an Australian against England for 11 Tests.

Q. 167. Bob Massie for Australia v England, Second Test at Lord's 1972.

Q. 168. Trevor Gard of Somerset.

Q. 169. They were/are all left-handers.

Q. 170. They all wore/wear spectacles while playing cricket.

Q. 171. They were all born in the star sign, Sagittarius.

Q. 172. They were all born in India.

Q. 173. G.O. Allen, in Sydney in 1902.

Q. 174. Their sons all followed them into first-class cricket.

Q. 175. Their brothers all played first-class cricket.

Q. 176. Sunil Gavaskar of India.

Q. 177. Geoff Boycott of Yorkshire; 8114.

Q. 178. Chappell, 7110, Bradman, 6996, but Bradman played 71 fewer innings.

Q. 179. Bruce Mitchell, 3471.

Q. 180. Garfield Sobers, 8032.

Q. 181. Bev Congdon, 3448.

Q. 182. Donald Bradman of Australia, 99.94.

Q. 183. Graeme Pollock of South Africa, 60.97.

Q. 184. S.F. Barnes, 16.43.

Q. 185. 1977.

Q. 186. 1971.

Q. 187. 1972.

Q. 188. Probably. Make up your own team. But such a Yorkshire-born-but-not-playing-for-Yorkshire team could be: Geoff Cook (captain, Northants.), Balderstone (Leics.), Athey (Gloucs.), Whitaker (Leics.), Boon (Leics.), Old (Warks.), Rhodes (Worcs. wicket-keeper), Mallender (Northants.), Illingworth (Worcs.), and Taylor (Surrey).

Q. 189. False by a couple of months. Fletcher first played on 25 July 1962 v Glamorgan; Foster was born in May 1962.

Q. 190. A youthful David Gower to Ray Illingworth when the latter was the disciplinarian captain of Leicestershire.

Q. 191. Barry Wood for Lancashire in 1970.

Q. 192. Rodney Marsh of Australia.

Q. 193. Greg Chappell; 122 in 87 Tests.

Q. 194. 5½ to 5¾ ounces (or 155.9 to 163 grammes)

Q. 195. Duke of Wellington in 1841.

Q. 196. Bowler: Alfred Shaw. Batsman: Arthur Shrewsbury. Both of Nottinghamshire and England.

Q. 197. True. (See David Gower's book *Heroes and Contemporaries*.)

Q. 198. 499. Hanif Mohammad. Karachi v Bahawalpur at Karachi 1958–59.